INSTITUTES

OF

NATURAL LAW;

BEING THE SUBSTANCE OF A

COURSE OF LECTURES

ON

GROTIUS DE JURE BELLI ET PACIS,

READ IN ST. JOHN'S COLLEGE, CAMBRIDGE.

BY T. RUTHERFORTH, D. D., F. R. S.,

ARCHDEACON OF ESSEX, AND CHAPLAIN TO HER ROYAL HIGHNESS, THE PRINCESS DOWAGER OF WALES.

SECOND AMERICAN EDITION,

CAREFULLY REVISED AND CORRECTED.

THE LAWBOOK EXCHANGE, LTD.
Clark, New Jersey

ISBN 978-1-58477-457-0

Lawbook Exchange edition 2004, 2016

The quality of this reprint is equivalent to the quality of the original work.

THE LAWBOOK EXCHANGE, LTD.
33 Terminal Avenue
Clark, New Jersey 07066-1321

Please see our website for a selection of our other publications and fine facsimile reprints of classic works of legal history:
www.lawbookexchange.com

Library of Congress Cataloging-in-Publication Data

Rutherforth, T. (Thomas), 1712-1771.
Institutes of natural law : being the substance of a course of lectures on Grotius De jure belli et pacis read in St. John's College, Cambridge / by T. Rutherforth.
p. cm.
Originally published: 2nd American ed., carefully rev. and corr. Baltimore: W. and J. Neal, 1832.
Includes bibliographical references.
ISBN 1-58477-457-6 (cloth: alk. paper)
1. Grotius, Hugo, 1583-1645. De jure belli et pacis. 2. International law—Sources. 3. War (International law)—Sources. 4. Natural law. 1. Title.

KZ2093.A3I572004
340'.112—dc22 2004041681

Printed in the United States of America on acid-free paper

INSTITUTES

OF

NATURAL LAW;

BEING THE SUBSTANCE OF A

COURSE OF LECTURES

ON

GROTIUS DE JURE BELLI ET PACIS,

READ IN ST. JOHN'S COLLEGE, CAMBRIDGE.

BY T. RUTHERFORTH, D. D., F. R. S.,

ARCHDEACON OF ESSEX, AND CHAPLAIN TO HER ROYAL HIGHNESS, THE PRINCESS DOWAGER OF WALES.

SECOND AMERICAN EDITION,

CAREFULLY REVISED AND CORRECTED.

BALTIMORE:
PUBLISHED BY WILLIAM AND JOSEPH NEAL.
JOHN D. TOY, PRINTER.

1832.

TABLE OF CONTENTS.

CHAPTER I.

OF LAW IN GENERAL.

CHAPTER II.

OF RIGHTS AND OBLIGATIONS.

CHAPTER III.

OF PROPERTY.

CHAPTER IV.

OF THE LIMITATIONS OF PROPERTY.

CHAPTER V.

OF OUR COMMON RIGHT TO THINGS.

CHAPTER VI.

OF DERIVATIVE ACQUISITIONS BY THE ACT OF MAN.

CHAPTER VII.

OF DERIVATIVE ACQUISITIONS BY THE ACT OF THE LAW.

CHAPTER VIII.

OF PRESCRIPTION.

CHAPTER IX.

OF THE OBLIGATIONS ARISING FROM PROPERTY.

CHAPTER X.

OF THE RIGHT WHICH A MAN HAS IN HIS OWN PERSON.

CHAPTER XI.

OF PARENTAL AUTHORITY.

CHAPTER XII.

OF PROMISES.

CHAPTER XIII.

OF CONTRACTS.

CHAPTER XIV.

OF OATHS.

CHAPTER XV.

OF MARRIAGE.

CHAPTER XVI.

OF THE RIGHT OF DEFENCE.

CHAPTER XVII.

OF REPARATION FOR DAMAGES DONE.

CHAPTER XVIII.

OF PUNISHMENT.

CHAPTER XIX.

OF WAR.

CHAPTER XX.

OF SLAVERY.

BOOK II.

CHAPTER I.

OF SOCIETIES IN GENERAL, WHERE ALL THE MEMBERS ARE EQUAL.

CHAPTER II.

OF CIVIL SOCIETY, ITS NATURE AND ORIGIN.

CHAPTER III.

OF CIVIL POWER.

CHAPTER IV.

OF THE DIFFERENT FORMS OF CIVIL GOVERNMENT.

CHAPTER V

OF THE CHANGES WHICH ARE PRODUCED IN THE RIGHTS OF INDIVIDUALS, BY CIVIL UNION.

CHAPTER VI.

OF CIVIL LAWS.

CHAPTER VII.

OF INTERPRETATION.

CHAPTER VIII.

OF CIVIL SUBJECTION AND CIVIL LIBERTY.

CHAPTER IX.

OF THE LAW OF NATIONS.

CHAPTER X.

OF THE CHANGES THAT ARE MADE IN STATES, AND IN THEIR CIVIL CONSTITUTIONS.

INSTITUTES

OF

NATURAL LAW.

CHAPTER I.

OF LAW IN GENERAL.

I. *What is meant by a law.*—II. *Permissions are not laws.*—III. *In what respect they may be considered as laws.*—IV. *Why they have been thought to be laws.*—V. *Laws either natural or voluntary.*—VI. *Cause of obligation to observe natural laws is foreign to our present inquiry.*—VII. *A short account of the cause of obligation.*—VIII. *Voluntary laws either divine or human.*—IX. *Divine voluntary laws.*—X. *Difference between law of nature and divine positive laws.*—XI. *Human voluntary laws of three sorts. Civil law what.*—XII. *Human laws of less extent than civil law.*—XIII. *Law of nations.*

What is meant by a law.

I. A LAW* is a rule to which men are obliged to make their moral actions conformable. The word law has indeed a much more extensive signification: all rules, from which any beings whatsoever either will not, or cannot, or ought not to deviate, are so many laws to them. The rules, which God has set to himself to work by; the rules, which brute creatures are led by their instinct to obey; and the rules, which inanimate matter in its motions and operations cannot but observe, are usually called the laws of their several natures. But since it is not our business, in the following work, to inquire into the rules, which God, before all ages, has set down to himself, for himself to work by; or into those, which the instinct of brute creatures imposes upon them, or into those, which necessarily determine the motions and operations of inanimate matter; but into those only, which men are bound to observe; it was proper, in defining the word law, to restrain it to this sense. Neither are all the actions of men subject to the natural law, which we are inquiring after; but those only, which are called moral actions; that is, those only, in which men have knowledge to guide them, and a will to choose for themselves. This is the reason for restraining the law still farther, by defining it to be a rule for the moral actions of men. It was necessary likewise to include obligation in our notion of a law, and to define

* Grot. Lib. I. Cap. I. § IX.

it to be a rule, which men are obliged to observe; because all the rules, which men observe, even in their moral actions, are not laws. Counsel, or advice, which they may follow or neglect at their own discretion; rules of convenience or prudence, which they may observe or not, as their own inclinations lead them; if they are ever called laws, are called so improperly.

Permissions are not laws.

II. By making obligation a necessary part in our notion of a law, all* permissions are, as they ought to be, excluded from being laws. Though permissions may come from the maker of a law, and may be established by his authority, yet they are rather negations of law than acts of it: instead of being operations of the law, they are checks upon its operation.

Permissions are of two sorts, they arise either from the silence of the law, or from its express declarations. All laws are understood to permit such actions as they are silent about: we are permitted to do whatever the law does not forbid; we are permitted to neglect whatever it does not command. There can be no question, whether such permissions as these are to be called laws: for certainly the silence of the law can never come within the notion of law. And as to the other sort of permissions, those which arise from express declarations of the law; what are they but declarations, that the law is not designed to extend to the privileged case? Mankind, if they were under no law, would be at full liberty to act in what manner they pleased. But suppose a law to be made commanding them to do this, or that; the liberty of all, who are subject to the authority of such law, is then restrained, and they are obliged to act as the law prescribes. Suppose farther the same law to declare, that such particular persons, or that persons in such particular circumstances, are permitted to do otherwise; the effect of such a declaration is, that the privileged person, or that the persons in the privileged circumstances, are left in the same condition, as if no law at all had been made: they are, notwithstanding the law, at liberty to act in what manner they please. And it is not easy to imagine with what propriety such a permission can be called a law, as leaves them at their full liberty, and places them in the same condition, that they would have been in, if the law had done nothing either one way or the other. Such a permission comes indeed from the law-maker, and is established by his authority. But then it is plain how his authority operates. Its operation is to check the obligation of his law, and to prevent its extending to such persons, or to such cases as it would have extended to, if he had not checked it.

From what has been already said, it will appear, that, though we distinguish between permissions, which arise from the silence of the law, and permissions, which arise from the express declarations of it; yet both of them are nearly the same in their effect. The principal difference between them is in their extent. All men are at liberty to act as they please, where the permission arises from the silence of the law. But they only have this full liberty, to whom the permission is granted by the law, where the permission arises from its express declaration. Perhaps the following instance may help to make this matter more intelligible. Suppose the local statutes of any col-

* Grot. Lib. I. Cap. I. § IX.

lege in either of our universities neither to have commanded nor forbidden the fellows of such college to enter into holy orders, but to have been wholly silent upon this head. Every one will see, that those fellows are permitted to act in this respect, as they please, and are at liberty either to enter into holy orders or not, at their own discretion. The founder of the college, or other person, who has a right to change their statutes, alters his mind, and enjoins, that they shall all be in holy orders at a certain age, under the penalty of forfeiting their fellowships. They are then no longer at liberty to choose for themselves, but must either lose their fellowships, or enter into holy orders. After some experience this law is found inconvenient, and the same authority, which established it, repeals it. The fellows are then at liberty again as they were at first; they are permitted either to enter into holy orders or not, just as they please. And this permission is plainly owing, not to any new law, but to a repeal of that, which was formerly made. It arises indeed from an act of the law-maker; but it is from such an act as only makes void what he had done before. But suppose him, instead of having repealed his former law, to have granted a dispensation to two of the fellows to continue laymen, if they please. Such a dispensation is a permission arising from the act of the law-maker: but we cannot with any propriety call it a law, in respect of those two of the fellows, to whom it is granted. Its effect is plainly a repeal of the law in respect of them: and if a repeal of a law, where it is universal, cannot be called a law; there is no reason why it should be called so, where it is partial. A permission to all the fellows, arising from the silence of the statutes, is plainly no law. A permission to all the fellows, arising from the repeal of the statutes, is plainly no law. The only difference between either of these cases, and the case of a permission to two of the fellows, is, that only these two enjoy that liberty in this case, which all of them would have enjoyed in either of the other. And it will, I apprehend, be necessary to find out some other difference besides this, before any satisfactory reason can be shown, why permissions arising from the original silence or total repeal of the law, are not laws; but permissions arising from an express dispensation or a partial repeal of it, are to be looked upon as laws.

In what respect permissions may be considered as laws.

III. But though permissions do not operate as laws, in respect of those persons, in whose favour they are granted; yet they have the operation of laws, and ought to be considered as laws, in respect of others, who are bound not to hinder those persons from the full enjoyment of that liberty, which such permissions allow. Thus, in the instance just now made use of, the governors of the college are bound by the dispensation, granted to two of their fellows from entering into holy orders, to suffer these two fellows quietly to enjoy their places or fellowships, notwithstanding the general statute obliging the rest of them to be in holy orders at a certain time, under the penalty of a forfeiture; though the fellows, who are thus privileged, should continue laymen beyond the time so limited. Permissions therefore, though they are not laws in one view, are laws in another view. In respect of those persons, to whom, or in whose favour they are granted, they are checks upon the law: in respect of others, who, if no such permission had been granted, might have lawfully hindered these persons in the exercise of that liberty, which it allows, they are acts of the law. They are not laws, as far as they allow a liberty of action: they are laws, as far as they include the notion of obligation.

Why permissions have been thought to be laws.

IV. One reason why permissions, even in respect of those persons, who claim a liberty of acting in virtue of them, have been mistaken for laws, has probably been, that where they arise from express declarations of the law, they are established by the authority of the law-maker. But that his establishment of them will not be sufficient to give them the nature of laws will be evident, upon recollecting in what manner his authority operates in their establishment. It operates only so as to check itself, and to hinder the law from extending so far as it would have extended, if he had not granted the dispensation or privilege. And it may be questioned, whether a privilege or permission, in this view of it, can be properly said to be established: unless we mean, that by the grant of such privilege the liberty of those persons is established, which the law would have taken away, unless the privilege had been granted.

Another reason, why permissions have been mistaken for laws, is that privileges and rights are derived from them. And since privileges and rights are supposed to be positive things, it is imagined, that permissions, upon which they are founded, must be looked upon as positive acts, and not as mere negations of law. But then we must observe, that if there was no law at all, there would be no difference between privileged persons and others; all men would be equally at liberty to act in the same manner. It is therefore the restraint, which the law has laid upon others, and not the grant of any thing positive to the privileged persons, which puts the difference between these persons and others. And a privilege, in this view of it, can no otherwise be considered as a positive thing, than as it is a reserve of that liberty in favour of the privileged persons, which the law has taken away from others not privileged. But such a reserve as this is plainly no act of the law; it is only a check upon it, and hinders it from acting. Many of our rights, it must be allowed, are derived from permissions. But this can be no reason for esteeming permissions to be positive acts of the law: unless the silence of a law can be called a positive act of it. Since as many of our rights are derived from permissions, which arise from the silence of the law, as from permissions, which arise from its express declarations. A right is indeed nothing more than a liberty of doing certain actions, or of possessing certain things consistently with the law. We have therefore a right to do such actions as the law does not forbid us to do, and to possess such things, as the law does not forbid us to possess. And it seems impossible for any one to conceive, that the laws not forbidding us to do an action, or to possess a thing, should be an act of the law. This is the case, where our rights are founded upon permissions arising from the silence of the law: and it is much the same, where they are founded upon what are called positive grants, that is, upon such permissions, as the law expressly declares. An express declaration of what the law allows, is no more than an express declaration of what it does not forbid. In one view, indeed, a permission, upon which any right is founded, may be looked upon as an act of the law: though in respect of them, whose right it is, the permission is only a negation of law, yet in respect of others it operates as a law: because it restrains all others from interrupting them in the free enjoyment of what is so permitted.

Laws either natural or voluntary.

V. *Laws are divided into two sorts, natural and voluntary. Natural laws are those, which mankind are obliged to observe from their nature and constitution. Voluntary laws, or, as they are sometimes called, positive laws, are those, which mankind are obliged to observe by the immediate will and appointment of a superior.

Cause of obligation to observe natural law, is foreign to our present inquiry.

VI. As it is the principal design of the following treatise to trace out the rules, which mankind are obliged to observe from their nature and constitution; there does not seem to be any great necessity for entering into the question concerning the cause of our obligation to observe these rules; a question upon which moralists are so much divided in their opinions. However they may differ about the cause of obligation, they are agreed about the law, to which we are obliged; whilst they dispute about the reason of duty, they concur in establishing the same rules of duty. The moralists of one sect derive our obligation to observe the law of nature from instinctive affections, or an innate moral sense. Those of another sect maintain, that all our obligations of this sort arise from certain abstract relations or fitnesses of things. A third sect are of opinion, that we cannot be steadily and constantly obliged to the observance of that law, but from the assurance of being made happy, for observing it, by the will and appointment of God. And a fourth sect think it necessary to join all these principles together, in order to render the obligation perfect. But all these different sects agree in contending, that the law of nature, which we are obliged to observe, prescribes piety towards God; justice and benevolence in respect of mankind; and chastity and temperance in respect of ourselves. But as the rules of duty are the proper subject of our present inquiry, and all moralists are agreed about these rules, however they may differ about the cause, which obliges us to the observance of them; we might pass over this question entirely, without being liable to be charged with neglecting what necessarily belongs to our subject: or if we say any thing about it, those moralists, who are not of the same opinion with us, must own, that the proper subject of the following treatise is not affected by it.

A short account of the cause of obligation.

VII. But though it is not necessary to speak at large concerning the cause of moral obligation, and to enter minutely into the disputes which have been raised upon that head; yet it may not be improper to say something about it. I shall therefore endeavour to show, in as few words as I can, for what reason we are obliged to the duties of piety towards God, of justice and benevolence in respect of mankind, of chastity and temperance in respect of ourselves. It is, I suppose, an undoubted truth, that all men are desirous of happiness. And I shall farther take it for granted, that when any practice appears to be so connected with our happiness, that we cannot obtain the one without following the other, we are then as strongly obliged to that practice, as

* Grot. Lib. I. Cap. I. § IX.

we can be. Whatever rules therefore are, by our own nature and the constitution of things, made necessary for us to observe, in order to be happy, these rules are the law of our nature. Now man, as an individual, unconnected with the creatures of his own species, not joined with them in a common interest, having no other provision or conveniency but what his own labour could produce, having no prudence but his own to contrive for himself, and having no strength but his own to defend him, would be unable to obtain such a degree of happiness, as his nature prompts him to desire, and much more unable to obtain such a degree, as his nature is capable of. It is therefore the law of his nature, that he should live in society with others of his own species: by which I do not mean, that he should merely live in company with them, as many brute creatures are observed to herd together; but that he should join with them in a common interest, that he should bind himself to them in such a manner as to labour with them for a general good. For without such a connection of interests, he cannot make use of a joint or common wisdom to contrive for his own good, nor of a joint or common strength to secure himself in the possession of it. So that, although his own particular happiness be the end, which the first principles of his nature teach him to pursue; yet reason, which is likewise a principle of his nature, informs him, that he cannot effectually obtain this end without endeavouring to advance the common good of mankind; but must either be contented to enjoy his own happiness, as a part of the general happiness, or not enjoy it at all.

When he discovers farther, that there is a God, who made and governs the world, to whose power he owes his being, and to whose goodness he owes all the happiness that he either does or can enjoy; and when he learns besides, either by the use of his reason, or by express declarations from the maker and governor of all things, that he is not to cease to exist, when he passes out of this present life, but that his being will be continued to him in another; the same desire of happiness, which obliged him to pursue a general good, and to keep his interests by this means united to the common interests of his species, will oblige him to observe all these rules in his moral conduct, which he finds to be necessary, in order to secure the favour of his maker, and his own welfare in the life after this. He will plainly understand, that the most effectual way to secure the latter point, is to secure the former; that he is most likely to obtain this future happiness, by putting himself under the protection of that Almighty Being, who is the disposer of all things. Nor can he have any hope of engaging the protection of God, but by endeavouring to please him, or by obeying his will, as far as he can discover what his will is. But since, from a view of what is before him, it appears, that God has made his nature and constitution such, as requires him, if he would be happy here, to work for a general good, or for the common interest of his species; the most reasonable conclusion is, that God, who made his nature and constitution what it is, expects him thus to work; and that, by thus endeavouring to do the work, which God expects him to do, he takes the most effectual method of securing whatever happiness can be hoped for hereafter.

But besides the general desire of happiness, he finds within himself certain appetites, which lead him to some particular sorts of pleasure, and that a part of his happiness, whilst he is here, consists in the gratification of these appetites. But then he finds likewise, that, if he indulges himself to excess in such pleasures, the excess is attended with pains and diseases, and that, if he gives himself up to those pleasures, he becomes either useless or hurtful to his species. From either of these discoveries he may collect, that he cannot be as happy, as he naturally desires to be, or that he cannot obtain his greatest good, unless he takes care to restrain his appetites within proper bounds. For since the pain and diseases, which attend the too free indulgence of them, arise from his nature and constitution, excesses of this sort are contrary to his nature and constitution, and consequently are contrary to the will of that Being, who made his nature and constitution what they are. And since the same excesses interfere with the common good of his species, by making him either useless or hurtful, they are upon this account likewise contrary to his nature and constitution, which he finds to be such, that he cannot obtain his own particular happiness without endeavouring to promote the common happiness of his species.

Upon the whole, mankind are naturally desirous of making themselves as happy as they can; and whatever rules are by their nature and constitution made necessary for them to observe, in order to obtain this greatest good, are the law of their nature. And these rules have been shown to consist, first, in piety and reverence towards God, who is the maker and disposer of all things; secondly, in justice and benevolence towards one another, or in working for a common interest, by taking care to do no harm, and by endeavouring to do good; and, thirdly, in restraining their appetites by chastity and temperance, so as neither to hurt themselves nor others, by the improper indulgence of them.

In tracing out the obligation arising from the law of nature, to observe these duties, I have taken the expectation of a life after this into the account; without considering, whether we come to the knowledge of such a life by the use of our reason, or by some express revelation, which God has made to us. Nor do I think it necessary to enter here into any debate upon this head; because by whatever means we are informed of this fact, that there will be a future life, such a life is equally a part of our nature, and of the constitution of things; and all the consequences relating to our practice, which can be deduced from it, are equally the laws of our nature. It may perhaps be urged, that the law of nature is a law, which reason discovers to us, and that upon this account revelation cannot fairly be made the foundation of it. But whoever is disposed to make such an objection as this, should consider in what sense reason is said to discover the law of nature: it does not discover all the facts from whence it deduces this law. Many of them are learned by our own experience, and many more depend upon the experience of other men, and are conveyed to us by their testimony. Whoever would be truly and fully informed of the nature and constitution of the human species, must make use of these means: and after he is thus informed of the facts, his reason traces out from thence the rules, which such a nature and constitution obliges mankind to observe. The use of reason, in tracing out those rules, will, as far as I can see, be precisely the same, whether he is informed of the facts relating to the nature and constitution of man, by his own experience and the testimony of other men, or whether he joins to these helps the much surer testimony of God.

Voluntary laws either divine or human.

VIII. *As voluntary laws are rules prescribed to mankind, by the immediate authority of a superior, they must necessarily be either divine or human: because the only superiors, that we know of, are either God, who is the author of our being, or such of our own species as have a right to direct our conduct.

Divine voluntary laws.

IX. †Divine voluntary laws are such rules as we are obliged to observe by the immediate command and authority of God. These laws are either of partial or of general obligation; they are either such as oblige only one particular people, or such as oblige all mankind. We know of but one instance of a divine voluntary law, which was confined to a single people; and that is the law which God gave to the Israelites by Moses. It is evident, that the positive parts of this law were never obligatory upon any people, except the Israelites: both because the law is addressed to them only; and because the principal observances which it enjoined, and many of the rewards which it promised, were confined to the country where they lived. A voluntary law can oblige no farther than the law-maker intended that it should oblige: because all the authority that it has, is derived only from his will and intention: so that, wherever this will or intention stops, the obligation of the law must stop with it. Now the intention of God, in giving the Mosaic law, does not appear to have extended beyond the Israelites; for the law is addressed to them alone. Hear, O Israel, says the legislator, the Lord thy God is one Lord. And as the intention of the law-maker thus confined it to that one people, so the matter of the law and the sanctions of it are, in many instances, such as confine it in the same manner. Some of the feasts which it appoints, could not be celebrated; some of the sacrifices which it commands, could not be offered; some of the ceremonies which it prescribes, could not be observed, at any place, except at Jerusalem. The promises of living long in the land which God had given them; the promise, that when all their males went up to Jerusalem three times in a year, none of their neighbours should invade their country; the general promises that God would bless them more than any people, are all of them in their own nature limited to the Israelites; and some of them are limited not only to the Israelites, as a particular people, but as a people settled in that particular country.

As this law was never obligatory upon any other nation besides the Israelites, so, since the preaching of the gospel, it is not obligatory upon them. This was expressly declared by the council of the apostles at Jerusalem, and is frequently repeated by St. Paul in most of his epistles. We are to observe, however, that the Mosaic law may be distinguished into three parts; that many of its precepts are purely political, and were designed to regulate and establish the civil government of the Israelites; that many of its precepts are ceremonial, and were designed to settle the outward forms of religious worship; but that some of its precepts are moral, and are only parts of the law of

* Grot. Lib. I. Cap. I. § XIII. † *Ibid.* § XV. XVI.

nature. Now, whilst we affirm the Mosaic law to have been never obligatory upon any besides the Israelites, and not to be obligatory at present even upon them; we must remember, that the moral precepts of it did always oblige, and still continue to oblige all mankind; not because they are parts of the Mosaic law, but because they are transcripts of that natural law, which was, and always will be, of universal obligation to all men, as being derived from their nature and constitution.

Whatever positive laws were given either to Adam or to Noah, as the common parents of all mankind, would be of universal obligation, if we could come to the knowledge of them: because the commands of God to them, as the representatives of the species, one at the creation, and the other after the flood, necessarily extend to that whole species which they represented.

All such positive laws, as are contained in the gospel, are likewise of universal obligation: because the author of it, and they who first preached it by his appointment and under his direction, declare that all men are obliged to receive it.

There does not seem to be any occasion to prove, that we are obliged to observe such positive rules as God is pleased to prescribe to us, since. His authority over us, and his power to make us happy or miserable, are such apparent and effectual causes of obligation, that the most slight observer cannot want to have them pointed out or enforced.

Difference between law of nature, and divine positive laws.

X. Before we pass on to the consideration of human laws, it may not be improper to state and explain the difference between the law of nature, and the positive laws of God. *This difference will be best understood, if we consider what it is which makes any intelligible distinction between moral and positive duties. When the law of Moses, for instance, forbids murder, and when it forbids the Israelites to eat the flesh of such animals, as it determines to be unclean; what is it which makes one of these a moral and the other a positive precept? This point is not at all cleared up by saying, that one of these is a precept of the law of nature, and the other is not so: for this, instead of bringing us forward in removing the difficulty, only carries us back to the place that we set out from. We cannot say, that moral and positive duties are distinguished from each other by the different authority which establishes them: because the same God who binds us to the observance of the law of nature, binds us likewise to the observance of his own positive laws. Neither can we say, that they are distinguished from one another by the different sanctions upon which they are established: because happiness to those who obey them, is the common sanction of duties of both sorts. This is plainly the case, both in the gospel and in the law of Moses; where moral and positive duties are enjoined under like penalties. We cannot, therefore, look for the difference of these two sorts of duties here; unless we will maintain that every moral duty becomes a positive one, whenever God is pleased to establish such moral duty by any express promise of a reward to them who perform it.

The principal mark of difference is to be found in the matter of the duties. The actions of men are, in their own nature, either good, or

* Grot. Lib. I. Cap. I. § XV. XVI.

bad, or indifferent. Such actions as in themselves, or of natural consequence, tend to promote a common interest, or to prevent a common harm, are called morally good: they make a good part in the behaviour or morals of those persons who do them; because they are productive of good or happiness to mankind. Such actions, as in themselves, or of natural consequence, tend to hinder a common good, or to produce a common harm, are morally bad: they make a bad part in the morals or behaviour of those persons who do them. Such actions are indifferent, as do not affect the general good or welfare of others, either one way or another; such as in themselves, or of natural consequence, neither prevent harm nor do good; neither prevent good nor do harm. The law of nature, as has been shown already, enjoins all those actions which are morally good, and forbids all those which are morally bad. By this means the former become duties, and the latter crimes. And if God, in any express revelation of his will to mankind, has been pleased to recite any part of the law of nature, and to establish it by any new sanctions; still the nature of the duties so recited and established continues the same; and the actions thus enjoined, being morally good, are called moral duties. But when any actions, which are indifferent in themselves, are commanded or forbidden by any express revelation of God's will; those actions, likewise, which God thus commands, become duties; and those actions which he forbids, become crimes: however, as the actions in themselves, or in their own nature, affect the common good of mankind neither one way nor other, as they have nothing in them either morally good or morally bad; this sort of duties is called positive duties. Thus in respect of God, fear, and love, and reverence, are moral duties; because they tend to promote a common good, since the obligations that we are under to work for this end, depend upon our knowing it to be his will that we should so work; and unless we fear, and love, and reverence him, his will would not appear to be a law to us. But the particular forms or ceremonies; the particular times and places appointed for expressing these sentiments, are of a positive nature. Temperance and charity, as they tend to promote a common good, or to prevent a common harm, are moral duties. But any extraordinary restraints upon our appetites, which have not such a tendency, are duties of a positive sort. In short, since all such actions as are good in themselves, in the sense already explained, are called virtues; and all such as are bad in themselves, are called vices; we may say, in general, that all virtues are moral duties, and all vices are moral crimes; or that virtue and vice are the matter either of the law of nature, or of God's moral law, which enjoins the former, and forbids the latter. But such actions, as are indifferent in themselves, such as in their own nature are neither virtuous nor vicious, are the proper matter of God's positive law; they become duties when he commands them, or crimes when he forbids them.

I would not be understood to mean, that the observance of God's positive commands does not at all affect the general good of mankind, after he has been pleased to give those commands; or that the common interest is not concerned, whether they are observed or neglected. There is certainly thus much of morality even in all positive duties; that any habitual neglect of them is inconsistent with the fear, and love, and reverence, which are due to God, and which are the surest establishment of the whole law of nature: so that they, who pretend to despise all positive duties, as if they were of little or no importance, would do well to consider, that they may justly be looked upon as enemies to the general good of mankind; in as much as they lessen the authority of God, and weaken the firmest support of all moral virtue.

From the difference between the moral and the positive laws of God, in respect of the matter of those laws, another mark of difference arises in respect of the means by which we do or may arrive at the knowledge of them. The moral law of God commands all such actions as in themselves, or of natural consequence are productive of general good, and forbids all such as, in themselves, or of natural consequence, are productive of general harm. Now the experience and the reason of mankind may discover this natural difference between virtue and vice, or between good and bad actions: and consequently it is possible, in the nature of the thing itself, for mankind, by the use of their reason, to trace out the rules of moral duty. But then in respect of positive duties, which consist of such actions as are in their own nature indifferent, or of such actions as do not appear to us to be productive of either good or harm to mankind, our reason can be no guide to us. For certainly reason can never distinguish the duties from the crimes, without some express declaration of the will of the law-maker, where nothing but his will makes any apparent difference between those actions which are commanded, and those which are forbidden.

Though I have here said, that it is possible for mankind, by the use of their reason, to trace out the rules of moral duty, I would not be understood to intimate, that, in respect of our moral duties, all revelation is useless. In respect of these duties, revelation may and does answer very useful and necessary purposes. In the nature of the thing itself, such actions as are moral duties, may be distinguished from such as are criminal: because there is a natural difference between them. But then as this difference consists in the good or harm which arises from our actions; long experience, close attention, and accurate reasonings are necessary to discover it. So that however possible it may be in the nature of the thing itself, for mankind to trace out the rule of moral duty, without the assistance of revelation, it is in fact very unlikely that they should do it without some such assistance. The life of any one man is too short, his observations too few, his attention too much taken up with other matters, to search into the nature and consequences of all human actions, and by general reasonings to establish a rule of duty. This would be the case, supposing we were all of us to employ ourselves in this inquiry with as much diligence as the circumstances of human life would admit of. Even upon this supposition, we must have recourse to the experience and reasonings of those who have gone before us. But, in general, we have neither diligence nor skill enough, to go through such an inquiry: the bulk of mankind would never find out their duty if they were not taught it; they would never give themselves the trouble of looking for it, if it was not laid plainly before them. In this instance, therefore, revelation will be useful in respect of moral duties. It will help to teach the rule of duty, even to those who are the most diligent inquirers; because as the knowledge of God is infinitely superior to our own, his declarations about the nature and consequence of our actions will be a surer guide to us than our own experience and reasonings can be. And wherever he has been pleased to point out our duty to us, neither want of leisure nor want of skill can prevent us from seeing it. This, then, is the first use of express revelation in respect of moral duties. It assists the learned in their inquiries, and instructs the ignorant; who, without such instructions, would have known little or nothing of it. But such a revelation is of use, not only in publishing the rule of duty, but more especially in establishing the obligations of mankind to observe this rule, by instructing them in the full knowledge of God and themselves, by informing them what their true condition is at present, and by what means the wisdom and goodness of God designs to lead them to happiness hereafter. But I am entering too far into the province of theology, and must ask the reader's pardon for this digression.

Human voluntary laws of three sorts. Civil laws what.

XI. *Human voluntary laws are of three sorts; either the civil law, or a law of less extent, which is not derived from the civil power; or a law of greater extent than the civil law. The civil law is a rule established by the civil power, to which the subjects of any nation, who are under the authority of its civil power, are obliged to conform their behaviour. By the civil power, we mean that power which governs what, in Latin, is called *civitas;* in English, a state, a nation, or a civil community. And by a nation, or civil community, we mean a complete or perfect society of men who are in possession of their personal liberties, and have united themselves into one body for the purposes of securing their rights, and of promoting a common interest. The name *civil law* is now almost appropriated to the civil law of the Roman empire; as this has long been called so by way of eminence, whenever we speak of the civil law, we are supposed to mean this. But whenever I have occasion to speak of this law, I shall call it the Roman law, and shall use the words *civil law,* in the most extensive sense, for the law of the land in each particular nation or country, that is for the law, which the civil power in that nation or country has established.

Human law of less extent than the civil law.

XII. †Human voluntary laws, which are of less extent than the civil law, and are different from it, as not being derived from the same power, are the rules which any one, who has authority over others, different from civil authority, prescribes to those whom he has a right to command. Such are the rules which the master of a family prescribes to his children, or to his servants. The obligation of this sort of laws does not extend so far as the obligation of civil laws; for the former extends only to the family of which the father or the master is the head; the latter generally extends to all the members of the civil community. Or if in any instances the obligation of the civil law seems to be confined within narrower limits; yet, even in these instances, we may plainly distinguish it from the law that we are now speaking of; if we only attend to the authority from whence the law is derived. Thus military law, though it is confined to the army, is to be reckoned a part of the civil law, because it is derived from the civil power. The particular laws of any body corporate, which is but a part of the civil community, differs from the

* Grot. Lib. I. Cap. I. § XIV. † Grot. *ibid.*

civil law only as a part differs from the whole; because the power, which such a body corporate has to make laws for itself, is granted to it by the civil government.

XIII. The law of nations is a law of greater extent than the civil law, and is not derived from the civil power. By the law of nations, we mean such rules as nations or civil societies are obliged to observe in their intercourse with one another. There are several points, relating both to civil laws and to the law of nations, which want to be explained. But our business in this chapter was only to give the reader a general notion of laws, to show him the several sorts into which laws may be divided; and to bring him acquainted with the general matter of the law of nature. Such points as relate to civil laws, or to the law of nations, shall be explained in their proper place.

Law of nations.

CHAPTER II.

OF RIGHTS AND OBLIGATION.

I. *The word* right *sometimes signifies a law.*—II. *The same word sometimes means a quality in actions.*—III. *It commonly means a quality in persons.*—IV. *Rights perfect and imperfect.*—V. *Obligation and right are correlatives.*—VI. *Two maxims of natural law explained.*—VII. *What actions are void.*—VIII. *Rights are natural or adventitious.*—IX. *Rights are alienable or unalienable.*—X. *Things are corporeal or incorporeal.*

I. The word **right* is used in three different senses. Sometimes it signifies a law. Indeed, in our own language, the word has very seldom this meaning; perhaps it is used in this sense, when we say that natural right requires us to keep our promise, or that it commands restitution, or that it forbids murder. But the Latin word *jus*, which is supposed to answer to our English word *right*, is very commonly made use of in that language in the same sense as the word *lex*, to signify a law.

The word *right* sometimes signifies a *law*.

II. †The word right sometimes means that quality in our actions, by which they are denominated just or right ones. Though I think this quality is more usually called the rectitude, than the right of our actions. The definition, which I have here been giving of right when it is used for the quality of an action, is the same that Grotius has given. And we may observe upon it, that our author, when he thus defines it, does not inform us what this quality is. But if we call it *rectitude* instead of calling it *right*, we shall soon be able to inform ourselves what it is, and wherein it consists. The rectitude of an action can be nothing else but its conformity or consistency with some rule: particularly in morality, it is

The word *right* sometimes means a *quality* in actions.

* Grot. Lib. I. Cap. I. § IX. † *Ibid.* § III.

the conformity or consistency of our actions with such laws as we are bound to observe. It is from this conformity or consistency of our actions with the law, that they are denominated lawful, or just, or right. In explaining what is meant by the right or rectitude of actions, I have made use of the two words *conformity* and *consistency;* because if I had used only the former word, the reader might have been led to imagine that no actions are just or right ones, but such only as the law commands. Whereas, in truth, not only such actions as are conformable to what the law commands, but such likewise as are consistent with it, or are not forbidden by it, have all the rectitude that is necessary to make them just or right ones: for whatever actions are lawful, are just or right; and it is plain, that all actions are lawful which the law does not forbid.

All our actions, in reference to laws, are divided into such as are duties, such as are crimes, and such as are indifferent: those actions which the law forbids, are crimes; those which it commands, are duties; and those are indifferent about which it is silent, so as neither to forbid nor command them. This latter sort of actions the law allows of; and such allowance is sufficient to make them lawful. And as every action is called lawful, if it is not unlawful, so every action is called just or right, if it is not unjust or wrong.

It is no unusual mistake to imagine that such actions only are to be esteemed just as the law commands. And if what has been said already is not sufficient to guard against this mistake, and to show the difference between the notions of duty and rectitude, or between such actions as we are obliged to do, because the law commands them, and such as are simply just, because the law does not forbid them; we may observe, further, that the word *justice* itself, though it seems to mean a positive quality in actions, frequently means a negative one; or that actions are denominated just rather from what is not in them, than from what is. Such actions are unjust as have the quality of doing harm, or preventing good: and such actions are just as have not this quality. When, therefore, we say that the law of nature commands us to be just, the meaning is, that it forbids us to do harm, or to prevent good. And consequently, our actions are as just as this part of the law of nature requires, provided we are careful to avoid what the law forbids. So that, in this view, our actions are just, not only when they are such as the law commands; but when they are such as the law is silent about or does not forbid.

The word *right* commonly means a quality in persons.

III. *By *right* we commonly mean that quality in a person, which makes it just or right for him either to possess certain things, or to do certain actions. In this sense we use it, when we say that a man has a right to his estate, or a right to defend himself. By saying that *he has a right*, it plainly appears that we conceive this right to be some quality which belongs to him, or is inherent in his person. Now, in this definition, Grotius, instead of describing the quality itself, has only described the effect of it; instead of informing us what it is, and wherein it consists, he only tells us what it does, that it makes a man's actions or his possession just. However, we may easily discover what this quality is,

* Grot. Lib. I. Cap. I. § IV.

if we will only ask ourselves what it is which makes our actions and our possessions just? The obvious answer to this question is, that our actions or our possessions are just, where they are consistent with law: and consequently the right which any person has to do an action, or to possess any thing, is nothing more than his power of doing this action, or possessing this thing consistently with law.

Right and moral power are expressions of like import. A man's natural power extends to every thing which his strength enables him to perform, whether the law allows of it or not. But his moral power extends to such things only as his strength enables him to perform consistently with law. For, in a moral sense, or in reference to such rules as a man is strictly obliged to observe in his behaviour, he is not supposed to have any more power than what the law allows him to exercise.

Rights perfect and imperfect.

IV. *Rights are divided into two sorts, perfect and imperfect. He would be but an indifferent casuist, who, in explaining the distinction between these two sorts of rights, should only tell us that perfect rights are those which may be asserted with rigour, even by employing force to attain the execution, or to secure the exercise of them, in opposition to all such as should attempt to resist or disturb us: but, when reason does not allow us to use forcible methods, in order to secure the enjoyment of the rights which she grants us, then these rights are imperfect ones. If a man had any doubt concerning some particular right, whether it was perfect or imperfect; and was, upon making inquiry of his casuist, to receive only this description of the two sorts of right; instead of being resolved as to his present doubt, he would only be led to another; he would be sure, upon receiving this answer, to doubt whether the right was such an one as might be supported with rigour, and by the use of force or not; and his casuist would never be able to give him any reasonable satisfaction in this point, till he has given a farther and clearer explanation of the distinction between the two sorts of right than this before us.

We may, perhaps, see the distinction between perfect and imperfect rights more clearly, if we observe, that, where the things which we have a right to possess, or the actions which we have a right to do, are or may be fixed and determinate, the right is a perfect one: but where the things or the actions are vague and indeterminate, the right is an imperfect one. If a man demands his property, which is withheld from him, the right that supports his demand is a perfect one; because the thing demanded is, or may be, fixed and determinate. But if a poor man asks relief of those from whom he has reason to expect it, the right, which supports his petition, is an imperfect one; because the relief, which he expects, is a vague and indeterminate thing. As far as the bargain between a master and his servant has determined the service which the latter owes, and of course the command which the former has a right to give, the master's right to command is a perfect one. But though a parent has a right to expect esteem and reverence from a son that is of full age; yet as the measures of esteem and reverence which the son then owes to the parent, are not fixed and determinate, the right of the parent is, in this instance, an imperfect one.

* Grot. Lib. I. Cap. I. § IV.

If this account of the matter does not appear satisfactory, we may consider it in another light. Where no law restrains a man from carrying his right into execution, the right is of the perfect sort. But where the law does in any respect restrain him from carrying it into execution, it is of the imperfect sort. Or, in other words, our right is a perfect one, where we can carry it into execution, without breaking in upon the right of other men; but it is an imperfect one, if the rights of other men stand in the way of it; so that we cannot carry it into execution without breaking in upon them. Thus I have a perfect right to defend my life against those who have no right to take it away. I have a perfect right to make use of such means as are necessary for my defence; where the law does not prescribe the means to be made use of. I have a perfect right to keep my property; since my possession of what is my own does not violate the rights of any other man. When my property is withheld, my right to recover it is a perfect one; because no law restrains me, or no person has any right to hinder me from recovering it. My poverty may give me a right to expect relief from them that I have deserved well of; but I cannot carry this right into execution without breaking in upon the right which they have to their own property; the law, therefore, restrains me from carrying it into execution, and the right is an imperfect one. If I am well qualified for any office of trust and profit in a civil society, especially if I am better qualified for such office than my competitors, I have a right to expect it: but this right is only an imperfect one; because the office being in the disposal of the governors of the society, I cannot carry my right into execution without breaking in upon their right to dispose of it as they please; and the same law which gives them the disposal of it, hinders me from carrying my right into execution.

Obligation and right are correlatives.

V. Obligation and right are correlative terms: where any person has a right, some one or more persons are under an obligation which corresponds to that right: and, on the contrary, where any person is under an obligation, some other person or persons have a right which corresponds to that obligation. If the right is a perfect one, so is the correspondent obligation: if the right is an imperfect one, the obligation is so too.

This might serve for the explaining the distinction of obligations into perfect and imperfect. As a man's right to his life is a perfect one, we may be sure, if we know this, that the obligation not to take it from him is a perfect obligation. As the proprietor has a perfect right to demand his goods of us, when we happen to be in possession of them, we are under a perfect obligation not to withhold them. We are obliged to relieve the indigent; but our obligation is of the imperfect sort, because they have only an imperfect right to expect relief. When we have the disposal of places of trust or profit, we are obliged to give them to the most deserving: but this obligation, in respect of those who are most deserving, is an imperfect one; because their right to the places, which they ask for, is of the imperfect sort.

But, perhaps, we may be able to distinguish between perfect and imperfect obligations, without attending immediately to the rights which answer to them, by observing, that the obligations which arise out of negative precepts of the law, are perfect; and that those which arise out of affirmative precepts, are imperfect. For, since the matter of negative precepts is precise and determinate, such precepts allow of no liberty at all; they take away the whole moral power of acting, and consequently produce a perfect obligation. But the matter of affirmative precepts is not so precise and determinate: such precepts are to be complied with as we have proper opportunities; and our judgment is to direct us as to the opportunities: whilst, therefore, they direct us how to behave, they allow some liberty of choosing; and, upon that account, the obligation produced by them can only be imperfect. The law says—Thou shalt do *no* murder. The obligation here is of the perfect sort; for the matter of the law is so precise and determinate, as to leave no moral power of acting. The law says—Honour thy father and thy mother. The obligation here is imperfect; because, as the matter of the law is not precise and determinate, instead of leaving no power of acting, it supposes us to have such a power, and directs us how to make use of it as we have opportunity.

From what has been said already concerning the nature of justice, that it consists in doing *no* harm to others, it appears that the precepts of justice are, all of them, negative ones; and, consequently, that all of the obligations of justice are of the perfect sort. But as kindness ana favour consist in doing good, the precepts of benevolence are affirmative, and upon that account the obligations to any of those duties, by which any kindness or favour is done, are imperfect ones.

Two maxims of natural law explained.

VI. There are two maxims of natural law, which are often applied very injudiciously, and which want therefore to be explained. One of these maxims is, That no right can be founded on an injury. The other is, That what could not be done lawfully, is valid after it is done. To understand the meaning of these two general rules, and the proper application of them, it will be necessary to observe, that some actions, which are contrary to law, are not only wrong, but void; that is, the law considers them as if they never had been done, as to any moral effect that might have been produced by them: but some actions, which are contrary to law, are only simply wrong; they ought not to have been done; but after they are over, they produce the same moral effect as if they had been right. Where the obligation of the law is perfect, such acts as are contrary to it, are void; or no moral effect is produced by them. The law says, Thou shalt not steal. The obligation is of the perfect sort; and upon that account the act of theft, as to any effect which the possession of goods might have produced, is void; the thief gains no property in the goods which he has stolen. The reason of this is plain: in the use of our natural power we can break the law; but since the obligation, as it is a perfect one, has taken away the moral power of acting, the law does not suppose us to have any power left, and consequently does not suppose any thing to have been done with any effect, where we have made use of such natural power. Now an injury, properly so called, is a breach of justice; that is, it is a breach of a perfect obligation, and the production of a right is a moral effect. But since no breach of a perfect obligation can produce any moral effect, it follows that no right can be produced by an injury. Where the obligation of the law is imperfect, such acts as are done contrary to it, are simply wrong, and are commonly not void, but produce their proper effects as if they had been right. The law says, Obey your parents. A son of full age contracts himself in marriage, contrary to the commands of his parent: such a contract, though it is unlawful, is valid. The reason is, because imperfect obligations do not take away a man's power of acting, but only direct him in the use of it. And when the law supposes a power of acting, it cannot suppose nothing to have been done, where such power has been made use of. The act therefore is commonly not void, but will obtain its proper effect. Thus we see that these two general rules, though at first sight they may appear inconsistent with one another, are both of them true when they are properly applied. The former rule, That no right can be founded on an injury, is to be applied to cases of perfect obligation. The latter, That what was unlawful to be done, is valid after it has been done, is applicable only to those cases where the obligation is imperfect.

What actions are void.

VII. *We have already seen, that such actions as are contrary to any precepts of natural law, where the precept is of perfect obligation, are void; but that such as are contrary to precepts of imperfect obligation, though they are wrong, are however commonly valid. I say *commonly* valid, because in some cases, even such actions as these are void. The way to know whether actions, that are contrary to a law of imperfect obligation, are void or not, is to consider the effect of them. If the effect is consistent with the law, then the act is valid; because as the obligation was imperfect, there was a moral power in the agent; the act therefore does not want a valid foundation: and because the effect is consistent with the law, by the supposition, the law will not hinder its effect. But if the effect is illegal, as well as the act, then, notwithstanding, there seems to be no defect of moral power on the part of the agent, yet the act will be so far void as not to produce any effect: because the effects cannot proceed or take place where the law disallows them. The law says, Honour thy father and thy mother. The obligation is imperfect. But yet, in virtue of this precept, the marriage of a son with his mother will be void; because the effect of such a contract is as inconsistent with the law as the act is. The superiority which such a marriage would give to the son over his mother, is inconsistent with the honour which the law requires him to pay to her. This may be expressed otherwise. What is done contrary to a precept of imperfect obligation will be void, if the validity of the act would discharge us from the obligation of such precept for the future. Thus the law says, as above, Honour thy father and thy mother. A man vows that whatever he gives to his father or his mother out of his substance, shall immediately be consecrated to God, so as to make it unlawful for them to use it, or to receive benefit from it. Such a vow as this is a void one, notwithstanding the precept with which it is inconsistent, is only of imperfect obligation. The general reason is, because the validity of it would make void a precept of the law of nature. And, consequently, as no man can have a moral power of releasing himself from that law, no man can have a moral power of doing any act which will make that law void, or which, if it was to obtain its effect, would for the future release him from the obligation of observing that law. So that, in reality, even in these instan-

* Grot. Lib. II. Cap. V. § X.

ces, as in those where we transgress a precept of perfect obligation, the act is void from a defect of moral power in the agent.

VIII. Another division of our rights is into natural and adventitious. Those are called natural rights which belong to a man by the gift of nature; those which belong to him originally, without the intervention of any human act. Adventitious rights are such as presuppose some act of man from which they arise, and upon which they originally depend. The rights which a man has to his life, to his liberty, to his health, to freedom from pain, to the integrity of his body, to his good name, &c. are natural ones. Property, or the right which he has to his goods, either moveable or immoveable, sovereignty, or the right which he has to command others of his own species, and many more of the like sort, which arise from some previous bargain or contract, either express or tacit, are adventitious ones. But though some of our rights are thus called adventitious, and are by this means distinguished from natural rights; we must not imagine that only the natural rights of mankind are under the protection of the law of nature; or that it is no offence against the law of nature to violate such adventitious rights. This law equally forbids the violation of our rights of either sort: such things as we acquire consistently with the law of nature, are as much our own, as if nature had given us them originally: as much causeless harm, that is, as much injustice, is done to a man, by causelessly taking from him what he has fairly acquired a right to, as by causelessly taking from him what he had a right to by nature. And since the law of nature equally forbids every instance of injustice, it forbids not only the violation of men's natural rights, but of their adventitious ones too.

Rights are natural or adventitious.

IX. Some of our rights are alienable, others are unalienable. Those rights are alienable which the law does not forbid us to part with. Those only are unalienable which we cannot part with consistently with the law. There seems to be no other foundation, for such a distinction of our rights, but this. I know not how any one can show that any of our rights, either natural or adventitious, are unalienable; unless he can produce some law which forbids our parting with such right. Certainly where a man's right to possess a thing, or to do an action, is absolute, or is not restrained or limited at all by the law; he may part with it, if he pleases, either by giving it up entirely, or by transferring it to some other person. An absolute right is otherwise unintelligible: since the power of doing as we please, makes up the whole notion of such a right. This, therefore, may be laid down as a general and fixed rule, that none of our rights are unalienable but such as are, in some respects, restrained and limited by law.

Rights are alienable or unalienable.

X. Before we go on to consider the several rights of mankind, and the manner of acquiring them; it may be of use to us to observe, that things, in the science of natural law, are divided into corporeal and incorporeal. Our senses will best inform us what things are corporeal; for such things are called corporeal as are the objects of our senses. Of this sort are a man's cattle, his house, his furniture, his lands, his implements of husbandry, his money, &c. Incorporeal things are such, as cannot be seen or handled; they consist of rights, and no real thing exists without us, con-

Things are either corporeal or incorporeal.

formable to that idea of them, which is in the mind: only for better dispatch, we frequently speak of our rights as if they were real things. Thus sovereignty is spoken of as if it was a real thing; though there is no corporeal existence which answers to our idea of it: it consists wholly of a right to do certain actions, or to give and enforce certain commands. An advowson, which is a right of presentation or collation to a church, is an incorporeal thing. An ecclesiastical benefice is itself an incorporeal thing; there is no real thing existing, which answers to the whole notion of it; it consists not only in a right to receive certain profits, but in a right likewise to do certain actions.

Our rights being divided, *as above, into rights to possess certain things, and rights to do certain actions, we will go on to consider them under these two general heads.

CHAPTER III.

OF PROPERTY.

I. *Property what.*—II. *Things not appropriated originally.*—III. *In the community of goods, a right to use supplies the place of property.*—IV. *Inconveniences arising from a community of goods.*—V. *Property remedies these inconveniences.*—VI. *A conjecture about the first author of property.*—VII. *Property arose from compact.*—VIII. *This compact is either division or occupancy.*—IX. *Property now only to be acquired by occupancy.*—X. Mr. Locke's *opinion examined.*—XI. *Making a thing introduces no property but by occupancy.*—XII. *Acquisitions are either original or derivative.*—XIII. *Property either general or particular.*—XIV. *How far property ceases by dereliction or extinction of the proprietors.*

Property what.

I. Our †right to things is either such an one as is common to us with all mankind, or such an one as is peculiar to ourselves. Some things belong to us, because they belong to the species in general, and to us among the rest. Other things belong to us by such a right as excludes all the rest of the species from having any thing at all to do with them. Such an exclusive right to things is called property. Where things are thus fully our own, or where all others are excluded from meddling with them, or from interfering in any manner about them; it is plain that no person, besides the proprietor, who has this exclusive right, can have any claim either to use them, or to hinder him from disposing of them as he pleases. So that property, considered as an exclusive right to things, contains not only a right to use those things, but a right to dispose of them either by exchanging them for other things, or by giving them away to any other person, without any valuable consideration in return, or even of throwing them away, which is usually called relinquishing them.

* See § III.

† Grot. Lib. II. Cap. II. § I.

II. It does not appear that the *Author of Nature, when he provided for mankind such things as are necessary for the support or comfort of life, appropriated particular things to particular persons, or gave to any one a right to any part of this provision exclusive of the rest of the species. The world which we inhabit, the trees, herbs, and fruit, which the earth produces; the soil itself, from whence they are produced, the inferior animals, such as birds, beasts, and fishes, which supply us with food, or labour for us, or clothe us, or serve for our pleasure, were given to all alike. As the Author and Giver of these things stands in the same relation to all mankind; his gifts, as far as reason can judge, must belong to all alike: nor can we conceive any of them to belong originally to any part of the species or to any individual exclusive of the rest; unless we could find that he had made some express division and assignment of them. Now as reason can never collect such an express or positive division and assignment, so neither does revelation teach us that any such was made, either from the beginning of the world, or in any subsequent period of it, by the Lord of all things. We therefore conclude, that all things belonged originally to all mankind in common, and that the exclusive right of property was introduced by some act of man.

Things not appropriated originally.

III. If things had continued in this state of community, they would have been used and enjoyed by us only as we had occasion for them: each person might have taken out of the joint stock as much as he wanted, and no more; and might have applied to his own purposes what he had so taken, as long as he wanted it, and no longer. For these common goods are his in no other respect, and for no other purposes, but to supply his wants; and they belong to the rest of mankind in the same respect, and for the same purposes, as much as they belong to him. These purposes, therefore, limit his claim to them; since all his claim is only to use what he has occasion for. And consequently he can have no right to take more than is necessary, or to keep what he has so taken longer than is necessary. Whilst things continued in this state of community, the general claim of all mankind to use what they wanted, so far supplied the place of property, that each individual, though he could not accumulate possessions, had an opportunity of furnishing himself with the necessaries of life, and even with the conveniences of it too; provided no person had any occasion for what he had taken beyond what was barely necessary.

In a community of goods, a right to use supplies the place of property.

From hence we may understand, that a man might possibly be injured in respect of these common goods, even though, by the supposition of their being common, he had no exclusive right of property in any of them, but only a claim in common with the rest of mankind to use what he wanted. If they belong to him, as they belong to the rest of mankind, they, who hinder him from using what he wants, when they do not want it themselves, do him a causeless harm; he has a right in common with them to use what he wants, and they take his right from him.

IV. Such a community of goods as we have been speaking of, would necessarily become inconvenient as the wants of mankind increased, and as the love of jus-

Inconveniences arising from a community of goods.

* Grot. Lib. II. Cap. II. § II.

tice and equity decayed amongst them. The wants of mankind were increased by polishing their manners, and by introducing amongst them a civilized and elegant way of living. Savages, who could be contented to live in caves, to clothe themselves with bark or skins, and to feed upon nuts or acorns, or such other fruits as the earth produces without much culture, would have but few wants, and these wants would be easily supplied. But when men are civilized and improved in their way of living, they must have convenient houses, useful furniture, warm and clean clothing, and their food must be prepared and dressed for them before they can eat it. This increase of wants, arising from a civilized and improved way of living, would not be perceived, if nature furnished us with as plentiful a supply for these wants as for the ordinary wants of a savage. But materials to supply such wants as these, are not to be met with every where: nature has given us some of them so sparingly, that it requires much industry to collect them; and even those, which are collected most readily, are not fit for use till they are improved and manufactured with much art and labour. So that, even in these instances, where materials are plentiful, provisions would be scarce, if there were not able heads to contrive, and a number of hands to work.

But the increase of numbers will be an additional increase of the wants of mankind. Whatever way of life they may be in, the greater their numbers are, the greater plenty of provisions they will have occasion for. The same quantity of materials, or the same improvements which would produce plenty, if there were but few men to consume what is provided, would be too scanty to supply the demands of a multitude. When the wants of mankind, compared with the provisions for supplying them, were thus increased, it would become not only inconvenient, but inconsistent too with their peace and quiet, to continue joint partners of all things, as of a common stock belonging equally to all. For when the wants of them all, in such a scarcity of provisions, could not be supplied at once; when more men came at the same time to have occasion for the same thing, which could not however answer the purposes of more than one of them: in such a state of community, where each has the same claim to what all of them want, and but one of them can enjoy, disputes and quarrels would be endless.

This inconvenience would become more pressing, if mankind failed in the practice of equity and benevolence towards one another. Few would be willing to labour for the improvement of a common stock, where others are to enjoy in common with themselves the produce of their contrivance and industry; and few, even of them who were least able or least inclined to work, would be willing to take up with the rude and uncultivated supplies of nature, or be contented to use and enjoy nothing but what they had cultivated and improved themselves. Thus, on the one hand, the want of such benevolence as might incline us to labour for the good of the species; and, on the other hand, the want of such equity as might dispose us to be satisfied with the fruits of our own industry, would increase those disputes and quarrels which a scarcity of provisions had begun.

Property remedies those inconveniences.

V. The most effectual way of securing the peace of mankind, in these circumstances, is by introducing an exclusive property. As by this means the extent of each person's claim is ascertained, and the particular share out of the general stock, which belongs to him, is settled; he can have no just grounds of quarrelling with others for taking more than they ought to have, whilst they let his property alone: and they, on the other hand, can have no pretence to hinder him from using and enjoying what he has a right to use and enjoy exclusive of them. If his share is large enough to supply him with the conveniencies and elegancies of life, those who are more scantily supplied, have no just reason to complain that they are injured: and if the share, which is allotted to him out of the general stock, will afford him no more than the necessaries of life, he must content himself, as well as he can, with this small provision; because he knows that he can claim no more. This, then, is one advantage of an exclusive right above a community of goods; that, though it may sometimes be a question amongst several claimants, which of them has the right; yet these questions will seldom arise: and even when they do arise, they will admit of a decision: no two persons can have full property in the same thing; because the property of one effectually excludes the claim of the other. Whereas, in a state of community where all have an equal right to the same thing, it would be a continual question which claimant should use or enjoy the matter in dispute: nor could such a question be easily decided; because neither of the claimants could set forth such a right as would effectually overrule the pretensions of his competitor. But there is, besides this, another considerable advantage arising from the introduction of property. Such an exclusive right assigns to each person the part, or materials, in which he is to labour; and makes the improvements produced by his art and industry, entirely his own. Men will be more ready to make improvements when they are morally sure of enjoying them, than they would be, if others, who are unwilling to work, had any claim upon the fruits of their labour. These seem to be the reasons which determined mankind to change their right to things from a common claim, which belonged to all alike, into an exclusive claim of particular property.

A conjecture about the first author of property.

VI. If we look into the history of the first ages of the world, as it is recorded by Moses, in the book of Genesis, we may there, perhaps, meet with some account of the first inventor of property. Supposing the reasons for introducing this change to have been rightly assigned, we should look for the origin of property amongst them whose wants were the greatest; who were most scantily provided for, and who were least likely to practise the duties of benevolence and equity towards one another. All these circumstances concur in the posterity of Cain. Their *ancestor had killed his brother; and his fears, least the rest of mankind should punish this crime upon him and his posterity, induced him and his family to unite themselves together, and to build a city for their defence. By living in society, their manners were polished, and a refined way of living was introduced amongst them. This seems to be evident; because we find that they were the inventors of arts and sciences, both of such as are useful, and of such as administer to pleasure. Tubal-cain was the instructor of every artificer in brass and iron; and

* Genes. IV. 8, 17, 21, 22.

Jabal was the father of all such as handle the harp and organ. This family had separated themselves from the rest of mankind, and were shut up together within a narrow district: where, if there had been but a few of them, and they had been contented with coarse fare and ordinary clothing, they would have found it difficult enough to supply themselves. But the difficulty was rendered greater, not only by their elegance and luxury, but by the constant increase of their numbers. We have no reason to imagine that this family had any great sense of duty: it is much more likely, that, as they lived with a bad parent, the influence of his example had indisposed them to observe the rules of equity and benevolence in their behaviour towards one another. Here, therefore, we are to look for the beginning of property, or of an exclusive right to things. And the sacred historian informs us accordingly, that *Jabal was the father or inventor of possession. Our translators render it, *of such as have cattle.* But Jabal could not be the first who taught how to bring up and take care of cattle: because we read that Abel had, before this time, been engaged in this employment. The original word signifies *possessions* of any sort, acquired in any manner, and is not necessarily confined, as our translators confine it here, to possessions of cattle. If, therefore, we render this passage, as it ought to be rendered, that Jabal was the inventor of possessions; there will be some appearance of reason for concluding that he was the first projector of particular property. †Abel is indeed said to be a keeper of sheep, and Cain to be a tiller of the ground: but it is not necessary that each of these should have had property in his respective department; since they might, either by their own choice, or by their father's appointment, undertake to cultivate these two different parts of the common stock.

Property arose from compact.

VII. But let us return from this digression. ‡We have seen by what reasons mankind were led to introduce such an exclusive right as we call property, and are to inquire, in the next place, in what manner it could be introduced consistently with justice. The common claim which all men originally had to all things, is taken away by the introduction of property, as far as this exclusive right extends. Where one man has a right to exclude all others from the use or enjoyment of a thing, they cannot possibly have any claim of common right to use and enjoy it. Now it would be inconsistent with justice to deprive them of their common right without their consent. Property, therefore, could not be introduced, consistently with justice, unless mankind consented to it, either expressly or tacitly. But if they lawfully might, and actually did, give such consent; that is, if their common right was alienable, and they agreed to alienate it; no injury was done to them by the introduction of property. There is no reason to say, that this common right is unalienable: there is, indeed, no law of nature which commands the introduction of property; but neither is there any that restrains men from giving up their common claim, for the benefit of any one who has a mind to appropriate to himself what would belong to all in common, unless they had parted with their claim.

* Gen. IV. 20. † Gen. IV. 2. ‡ Grot. Lib. II. Cap. II. § II.

VIII. When mankind were few in number, and lived together in the same place, they could easily meet in order to divide their common stock, and to assign to each other his proper share by express consent, agreement, or compact. But after their numbers were increased, and they were settled in different parts of the world, very distant from one another, it became impossible for all of them to meet together. This method, therefore, of introducing property, by express consent, was rendered impracticable. Some consent, however, has been shown to be necessary to make the introduction of property consistent with justice; and a tacit one would be sufficient for that purpose. Such a tacit consent is called occupancy. Indeed occupancy is but one part of the act which is called by this name; but as it is the leading part, it has given its name to the whole act. What a man seizes upon, with a design to make it his own, or to appropriate it to himself, will become fairly his own, or will be made his property; when the rest of mankind, as far as they have an opportunity of observing him, understand what his design is, and show by their behaviour, in not molesting him, that they agree to let his design take effect. If they know his intention, and do not interrupt or contradict it, when they have it in their power, they tacitly consent to it.

This compact is either division or occupancy.

A man's bare intention of acquiring property in a thing, is not enough to make it his own, till that intention is known: for without the consent of mankind no property can be gained justly; and there can be no ground for presuming that they consent to what they know nothing of. Now the act of occupancy is the outward mark by which his intention is made public. And this act is, therefore, understood to give him property; because if the rest of mankind, that is, if the joint partners, who had before a right in common with him to the thing which he has seized, do not upon this notice of his intention, assert that common right, they are presumed to part with it. However, before a right of property can proceed upon the act of occupancy, one circumstance is necessary; which is, that the thing seized upon should be certain and determinate. No consent of mankind can be presumed to be given to what the occupant designs, any farther than that intention is or may be known to them. And if the thing seized upon is uncertain and indefinite, the act of occupancy leaves his intention doubtful and obscure; the rest of mankind do not understand what it is; and their consent cannot be supposed to reach any farther than their knowledge.

Upon the whole, then, property, as we have seen already, cannot be introduced consistently with justice, unless by the common consent of mankind. The consent which is necessary for this purpose, might either be given expressly, when all mankind could meet together, (and such an agreement is called division,) or else it may be presumed, in consequence of the future proprietors having, without molestation, taken and kept possession of the thing which he intends to make his own; and such a tacit agreement is called occupancy.

IX. But though either division or occupancy might give property in the first ages of the world, when all the joint commoners could meet together; the way of introducing property, by division, is now at an end. The great numbers of mankind, and their remoteness from one another, have rendered it impossible for them all to meet and to divide the common stock

Property can now only be acquired by occupancy.

of goods, or such parts of the common stock, as have not yet been appropriated. There is, therefore, at present, no other method left for beginning property but occupancy only; all things which were not appropriated formerly, must now be appropriated by occupancy, or not at all.

Mr. Locke's opinion examined.

X. Mr. Locke agrees with Grotius, that occupancy is the foundation of private property. But then he does not consider occupancy in the same light that Grotius considers it, as a tacit agreement between the joint owners of the common stock and the future proprietor. In his opinion, things which originally belonged to all mankind, in common, became the property of the first occupant; because, as he has a property in his own person, and consequently in the labour of his body, or in the work of his hands, by removing any thing out of the state in which nature placed it, he has mixed his own labour, or a personal act of his own, with it; and by thus joining to it something which is his own, he makes it his property. For this labour being the unquestionable property of the labourer; no man, but he, can have a right to what that is once joined to: at least, where there is enough, and as good left, in common for others. Thus, whilst he agrees with Grotius in words, they differ widely from one another when the sense of their words is explained.

I design to examine, at large, his application of what is here advanced. But, before we do that, let us stop awhile and inquire, whether his first principles are true. As every man has a property in his own person, the labour of his body and the work of his hands are properly his. Now the labour of a man's body or the work of his hands, may mean either the personal act of working, or the effect which is produced by that act. In the first sense, it must be allowed that a man's labour is properly his own: he has a right to exert his strength in what manner he pleases, where he is under no restraint of law. But it does not follow from hence, that the effect of his labouring, or that the work of his hands, in the other sense of these words, must likewise be properly his own. He has, you may say, mixed his own labour with what he removes out of that state in which nature had left it: but will you conclude, that by thus joining to it his act of working, he has made it his own? In order to strengthen such a conclusion, it would be necessary to show that the labour of one man can overrule or set aside the right of others. If I knowingly employ myself in working upon the materials of my neighbour, however I may have mixed a personal act, which is my own, with his property, this will never give me a reasonable claim to his materials. You may urge, that the cases are not parallel; because the materials, now in question, are not the property of any one; and, consequently, that, by working in such materials, we may gain property in them; though we could not gain it by the like act, where the materials were appropriated before. But the cases are parallel, as far as the point before us requires. It is allowed, that the materials do not belong to any person by an exclusive right of property; but then they belong to all mankind of common right. And if mixing my labour with the materials of an individual will not make these materials mine, in opposition to his exclusive right, I know not how any act of the same kind, or the mixing my labour with materials which belong to all mankind, should make them mine, in opposition to their common right. As setting aside the right of an individual, without his consent, is an injury to him; so setting aside the common claim of mankind, without their consent, is an injury to them: and if an injury cannot be the foundation of a right in one case, it will not be very easy to prove that a like injury may be the foundation of a right in the other case.

Mr. Locke has applied these principles to explain the introduction of property both in moveable and immoveable goods. And if we go on to examine what he says upon the subject, we shall find that he has mistaken the exercise of a common right, for the exclusive right of property. "*He that is nourished," says this writer, "by the acorns he picked up under an oak, or the apples he gathered from the trees in the wood, has certainly appropriated them to himself; no body can deny but the nourishment is his. I ask, then, When did they begin to be his? when he digested? or when he eat? or when he boiled? or when he brought them home? or when he picked them up? And it is plain, if the first gathering made them not his, nothing else could. That labour put a distinction between them and common: that added something to them, more than nature, the common mother of all, had done; and so they became his private right. And will any one say he had no right to those acorns or apples, he thus appropriated, because he had not the consent of all mankind to make them his? Was it robbery thus to assume to himself what belonged to all in common?" The answer here is obvious. When those acorns or apples are become a part of his body, we may, if we please, say that they are his: but the right which he then has in them, is the same which he has in his whole person; and is no more to be called a right of property, in the sense that we use this word, when we apply it either to moveable or immoveable goods, than the right which a man has in his leg or his arm, can be called by this name. When he gathered them, or when he boiled them, he had likewise a right in them; but it was just such a right as any one else might have had: a right, as one of the joint commoners, to use as much out of the general stock as he had occasion for. It is by no means necessary either to allow, on the one hand, that he had an exclusive right of property in them; or, on the other hand, to contend that it was robbery, thus to assume to himself what belonged to all in common. There is a middle opinion between these two, which is the opinion already mentioned; that when he gathered them, and was eating them, he exercised his common right of using and enjoying, out of the joint stock, what his occasions called for. Though, therefore, we contend that he could not acquire an exclusive right of property in them, or in any thing else, without the consent of mankind, either express or tacit; yet there is no fear of his being starved whilst he is waiting for this consent; because, in the mean time, the exercise of his common right will sufficiently provide for his subsistence.

That it is this common right which a man exercises when he separates a thing for his own use, and claims to use it because he has so separated it, will appear from the limitation which Mr. Locke himself puts upon what he calls property when it is thus acquired. "†God has given us all things richly, is the voice of reason, confirmed by in-

* Locke's Works, Vol. II. page 181. † Locke ut sup.

spiration. But how far has he given it us? To enjoy. As much as any one can make use of, to any advantage of life, before it spoils, so much he may, by his labour, fix a property in: whatever is beyond this, is more than his share, and belongs to others. Nothing was made by God for man to spoil or destroy." But, certainly, to take no more than we want, or no more than we can make use of, before it will be spoiled, is a limitation unknown to property: it belongs only to the exercise of a common right in a joint stock, where no one of the commoners has an exclusive right to keep but all and each of them have a joint right to use.

But Mr. Locke endeavours to take off this limitation, and to show us by what means, upon the same principles, property might be accumulated. "*The greatest part of things really useful to the life of man, and such as the necessity of subsisting made the first commoners of the world look after, as it doth the Americans now, are generally things of short duration; such, as if they are not consumed by use, will decay and perish of themselves: gold, silver, and diamonds, are things that fancy or agreement hath put the value on, more than real use, and the necessary support of life. Now of those good things which nature hath provided in common, every one had a right to as much as he could use and property in all he could effect with his labour; all that his industry could extend to, to alter from the state nature had put it in, was his. He that gathered a hundred bushels of acorns, or apples, had thereby a property in them; they were his goods as soon as gathered. He was only to look that he used them before they spoiled, else he took more than his share, and robbed others. And, indeed, it was a foolish thing, as well as dishonest, to hoard up more than he could make use of. If he gave away a part to any body else, so that it perished not uselessly in his possession, then he made use of it. And if he also bartered away plums that would have rotted in a week, for nuts that would last good for his eating a whole year, he did no injury; he wasted not the common stock; he destroyed no part of the portion of goods that belonged to others, so long as nothing perished uselessly in his hands. Again, if he would give his nuts for a piece of metal, pleased with its colour, or exchange his sheep for shells or wool, for a sparkling pebble or a diamond, and keep them by him all his life, he invaded not the rights of others; he might heap up as much of these durable things as he pleased; the exceeding the bounds of his just property not lying in the largeness of his possessions, but the perishing of any thing uselessly in it." But this writer seems here to take for granted the point in question. We contend, and he allows, that the right of him who gathered acorns or plums, extends no farther than to such a quantity of them as he can use before they are spoiled: and in showing how this limitation may be removed, he reasons as if there was no such limitation. How else should he, who had collected more plums than he could use before they were spoiled, or more sheep than he wanted to clothe or to feed himself, barter away the plums for nuts which would keep the year round, or for metal that would keep as long as he lived? The very notion of bartering implies property. Our author, therefore, must suppose the man to have property in what would spoil

* Locke ut sup. page 186.

before he can use it; or else he could not suppose him to barter it away: that is, since this contrivance of bartering was introduced, to show how property might be accumulated, or to take off the limitation of appropriating no more than can be used whilst it is good; in order to apply this contrivance, he must suppose the limitation to be taken off already, and the man to have property in plums or sheep, which he does not want, and which he could not use before they would perish in his hands. Indeed, if mankind would consent and submit thus to barter one with another, this consent would be sufficient to take off the limitation, and to introduce a true right of property. For if I knowingly and willingly bargain with another about my own goods, which are in his possession, as if they were his, this act of mine may well be construed as a tacit consent to make them his. And if, in like manner, mankind would bargain with one another about goods which belonged to all in common, as if they were the property of the possessor, they tacitly give up their claim to those goods, and so they become his property. But property, when introduced after this manner, is introduced by consent of parties, and not by the labour which the possessor or occupant has employed in separating the things which he possesses from the common stock.

In Mr. Locke's opinion, property in immoveable goods, such as the earth or soil, is acquired in the same manner and is governed by the same measure as property in moveable goods. "*As much land as a man tills, plants, improves, cultivates, and can use the product of, so much is his property. He, by his labour, does, as it were, inclose it from the common." But what is this again, but the exercise of a common right, instead of such an exclusive right as property is. For not to insist here upon the limitation of having property only in so much land as we can use, let us try the effects of this right, and see whether they are the same with the effects of property. Suppose then, that the man, after he has for some time tilled the land and cultivated it, was either by age or sickness to become incapable of tilling and cultivating it any longer: if the mixing his labour with it was his whole title to it; when his labour ceases, his title to the land must cease with it; the land can be his no longer than he can cultivate it; and when he is disabled for labouring, he cannot sell or let it to any other person: that is, it was his to labour in, but not his to dispose of as he pleases; and consequently his right could only be a right to use, and not an exclusive right of property. This Mr. Locke might have been sensible of, if he had attended to his own reasoning. "†He," says this author, "that in obedience to the command of God to improve the earth to the benefit of life, tilled and sowed any part of it, thereby annexed to it something that was his property, which another had no title to, nor could, without injury, take from him. Nor was this appropriation of any parcel of land, by improving it, any prejudice to any other man, since there was still enough and as good left, and more than the yet unprovided for could use." If then his title to the land which he occupies, rests upon this principle, that there was enough for others, besides what he had taken for his own use, it is plain that, unless there had been enough for others, his title would not have been a good one: and

* Locke ut sup. page 182.

† Locke ut sup. page 182.

from hence it follows, that all his title is no more than a common right to use what he wants, and not an exclusive right of property; because the right of property does not at all depend upon the convenience of others.

To strengthen this opinion, concerning the introduction of property, and to answer an objection which has been hinted at already, Mr. Locke compares the value of labour with the value of land; in order to show that the property which a man has in his labour, when he has mixed that labour with the land, overbalances the value of the land with which it is so mixed. "*Nor is it," says he, "so strange, as perhaps before consideration it may appear, that the property of labour should be able to balance the community of land. For it is labour, indeed, that puts the difference of value on every thing; and let any one consider what the difference is between an acre of land planted with tobacco or sugar, sown with wheat or barley; and an acre of the same land lying in common without any husbandry upon it, and he will find that the improvement of labour makes the far greater part of the value. I think, as he goes on, it will be but a very modest computation to say, that of the products of the earth, useful to the life of man, nine-tenths are the effects of labour: nay, if we will rightly estimate things as they come to our use, and cast up the several expenses about them, what in them is purely owing to nature and what to labour, we shall find that in most of them ninety-nine parts in a hundred are wholly to be put on the account of labour." But we may ask in return, what the value of pure labour is when considered merely as the personal act of the labourer? If neither the timber of his plough, nor the horses that draw it, nor the meat which they eat, nor the manure which he lays upon his land, nor the grain with which he sows it, are his own, what will you rate his labour at? Certainly you rate it much too high, if, upon comparing it with the value of the land, you set it at ninety-nine parts in a hundred, or even at nine parts in ten. But you will suppose all these materials to be his own. I ask, therefore, how he gained property in them? You answer, by his labour; and explain this labour to be only the act of taking them, or separating them from the common stock. Now this labour is of little or no value at all; and consequently you cannot say, in this instance, that the common right of mankind is overbalanced by the labour of the occupant. And if, in one instance, a labour, which is worth nothing when compared with the thing acquired, will give the occupant property, then we can have no reason to imagine that it is the high rate of labour, when compared with the value of land, which so overbalances the common right of mankind to the land as to give the labourer an exclusive right to it. You have only dazzled our eyes with this high account of the value of labour; since you must, in order to give it so high a value, suppose property to have been introduced beforehand by a labour which is of little or no value at all. We may go one step farther. The property of labour, you say, overbalances the community of land: because the value of it, when compared with the value of land, is worth ninety-nine parts in a hundred. Now if, by saying, that the property of labour overbalances the community of land, you only mean that labour is worth much

* Locke ut sup. page 184.

more than uncultivated land, we might allow it. But if you mean, that, because the value of labour is so much greater than the value of land, the labour of one man will overrule or set aside the common claim of all mankind, we must deny it. For suppose the labour of him who cultivates the land, to be worth ninety-nine parts in a hundred of the whole value of the land after it is cultivated, all that could be due to the labourer, upon this supposition, would be no more than the produce of his own labour: the ninety-nine parts which belong to him, would not swallow up the hundredth part which he had originally no exclusive right to. This hundredth part, that is, the land itself, must therefore still remain in common as it was before; he might labour in it again, if he pleased, as one of the joint commoners, but he would have no property in it. Let us try this reasoning in another instance. The landlord, as we call him, or the owner of the soil, after property has been introduced, has an exclusive right to some certain quantity of land; suppose, for instance, to an acre which bears twenty bushels of wheat: the tenant ploughs and sows this land; and besides the mere personal act of labour, he uses his own materials in cultivating the land. Now the labour of the occupier puts the chief value upon the land, and without this labour it would be worth little; for it is to this that we owe all its useful production. For whatever the straw, bran, bread, &c. of that acre of wheat is worth more than the product of an acre of as good land, which lies waste, is all the effects of labour. You see then how much the property of labour overbalances the property of land. But no one will be led to conclude from hence, that because, according to this reckoning in the value of an acre of land, ninety-nine parts in a hundred are owing to the labour of the occupier, the property, which he has in his own labour, will swallow up the property which the landlord has in the soil; and that the land, because he has cultivated it, will for the future become his own. But if the right of property in the soil, which in estimating the value of land, is but one part in a hundred, is not overruled or set aside by the overbalance in the value of labour, I can see no reason why the same overbalance should be supposed to set aside the common claims of mankind to land which was never appropriated. Let the right be what it will, whether it is a right of property or of common claim, if an overbalance in the value of the labour, which is joined to it, will not swallow up one of them, no good reason can be given why it should swallow up the other.

Making a thing produces no property but by occupancy.

XI. The most natural claim to a thing seems to arise from our having made it: for no one appears to have so peculiar a right in it as he who has been the immediate cause of its existence. This opinion, if it was true in the full extent of it, would overturn our general position, that division and occupancy are the only ways of introducing property. But *it is to be observed, that when we make a thing we do not produce the materials: these existed before, and all that we do is to give a new shape or form to them. Now the materials out of which a thing is made, are either our own property, or they are the property of some other person; or they are the property of no one, but are in common to

* Grot. Lib. II. Cap. III. § III.

all. If, before we made the thing, the materials were our own, it is plain that, by making the thing, we do not introduce any new or original claim, but only continue our former claim. The materials were our own before the thing was made; and nothing else is our own afterwards: they are still the same materials, but only in a different shape. If the materials were the property of some other person, the maker of the thing has naturally no claim to them, unless he makes amends to the owner of them, or unless the owner voluntarily gives them up. For it would be an injury to the owner of such materials to take away his property without his consent. But if the materials were in common, before the thing was made; that is, if they were not the property of any one, then by making a thing out of them, property is introduced: because, in this case, the maker is the first occupant. As far, therefore, as specification, or the making a thing, differs from occupancy, it does not produce property: and whenever it does produce property, it obtains this effect only because it implies occupancy.

Acquisitions are either original or derivative.

XII. When I say that property can be no otherwise acquired but by division or by occupancy, I must be understood to mean, that original acquisitions can be made in no other way. Our acquisitions of property are divided into original and derivative. Original acquisitions are such as introduce or begin property in things, which were before in common or had no owner. Derivative acquisitions are such as convey the property of things from one man to another: the things which are said to be alienated by the old proprietor, are derivatively acquired by the new one.

*We may observe by the way, that original acquisitions are made not only of such things as never had an owner, but of such things likewise as have had an owner, and by the ceasing of his property are become common again. Derivative acquisitions are but continuations of the same property in a different person. When, therefore, the property in a thing has ceased or been interrupted, the thing returns into the common stock; and whoever acquires it afterwards, begins or introduces a new property in it, just as if it had never before been in property at all.

Property either general or particular.

XIII. †Property is of two sorts, either general or particular. By general property is here meant the right which a body of men have to a thing, exclusive of the rest of mankind: and by particular property is meant the same exclusive right in an individual. General property is acquired by a general occupancy, or by occupancy in the gross. A number of men, uniting themselves into a collective body, are seeking for a place to settle in; and finding a large tract of land uninhabited, they seize upon it, and settle there. By such an act of occupancy the whole country becomes the property of this body of men. Though no single person in the body has a right to exclude any other single person, in the same body, from the use of any spot within the whole tract of land so seized upon; yet all and each have an exclusive right to the whole, and to every part of it, in respect of all other individuals, who are not members of this body, and in respect likewise of all other collective bodies whatsoever.

* Grot. *ibid.* § XIX.

† Grot. *ibid.* § IV.

After such a general property has been introduced in the whole tract of land, where this body of men has settled, something farther is requisite to give the individuals, of which the body is composed, particular property in the several parts of this tract. This particular property is introduced either by express division and assignment, or else by particular occupancy; that is, either the body by express agreement divides the whole country into parcels, and assigns to each individual the parcel, which is to be, and which is thus made his own; or else the body allows the individuals to seize upon such spots or parcels of land as they like best, and gives them, or rather allows them to have, an exclusive right to these spots or parcels so seized upon.

How far property ceases by dereliction, or by extinction of the proprietors.

XIV. *Property in goods may cease two ways. It ceases when the owners relinquish their right without transferring it to any one: and it ceases likewise when the owners are extinct; that is, when no person is left who has any right to the goods. Property in goods ceases by the owners' dereliction of them: because, as no one else had any exclusive right in them, upon his dereliction or quitting his claim, no one at all has any exclusive right in them; and consequently they become common to all alike. Property in goods ceases when the owners of them are extinct; because property and a proprietor are relative terms, so that one of them cannot subsist without the other: property is the exclusive right which a person has to such goods as are, upon account of this exclusive right, called his own or his property: if, therefore, the persons who had such right cease to exist, the goods are no longer the property of any one.

It is possible, however, that goods which are relinquished by their owners, or goods which cease to have any particular owner, may not so far become common as that any person who pleases, is at liberty to seize upon them, and by such occupancy to gain property in them. Where a body of men have seized upon a tract of land in the gross, and have by such occupancy acquired a general property in it; if the individuals of which this body is composed, acquire private or particular property afterwards in the several parts of this land, either by an express division and assignment made by the collective body, or by particular occupancy with the allowance and consent of such body, then upon the dereliction or failure of these particular owners, the land returns into the state in which it was before those individuals had acquired particular property in it; that is, it again becomes the general property of the collective body. No person, therefore, is at liberty to seize upon such parcels of land as have thus ceased to be in private property: because, though they have no particular owners, they have still a general owner; the collective body has the same exclusive right to them that it had before any of the individuals acquired private property in them.

This principle does not naturally extend to moveable goods. Though the land, and such immoveable goods as adhere to it, or may be considered as parts of it, were originally seized upon by the collective body, and are therefore matter of general property, yet each individual may well be supposed to have acquired property in many sorts of

* Grot. Lib. II. Cap. IX. § I.

goods before he settled with the collective body upon that particular tract of land. What plate or jewels, what money or clothes he brought with him, are his own; they are not parts of the land, and can scarce be supposed to have been acquired with it. If he had catched and tamed cattle for his use, his right to his sheep, or horses, or oxen, which he had so catched and tamed, is not derived from the collective body; these goods were his own, not only before he settled with such body, but perhaps even before he joined himself to it. When, therefore, such goods as these are relinquished by their owners; or when the owners of them fail, if the collective body of which they were members, has any general claim to the goods; that is, if these goods become the property of such collective body, so as not to be free for any person that pleases to seize upon them and make them his own; this effect must be produced either by the consent of the several owners, or else it must arise accidentally from the claim which the body has to the land. All foreigners, that is, all who are not members of this body, are excluded from seizing upon such moveable goods as have no owner, and are found upon that land in which the body has general property: because they have no right to come upon the land for this or for any other purpose of their own without leave. So again, when any parcel of land is returned to the public, upon the failure or dereliction of the private or particular owners, such moveable goods as have likewise no owner, and are found upon that parcel of land, will become the property of the public: because, as they have property in the land, no individuals, even though they are members of the public, can claim to come upon it in order to seize upon those goods, and by such occupancy to make them their own. But where moveable goods, having no owner, are found upon land which has an owner, if the owner of the land, being likewise a member of the collective body, may not seize them so as to make them his property by occupancy, he must be precluded by some express law of that body. If this law is considered merely as a positive one, the justice of it is to be defended upon the principle already mentioned, of its being established by the consent or agreement of the several individuals: or it may be considered as declarative, that the public grants out its general property in the land to individuals with this reserve, that whatever moveable goods, having no owner, are found upon it, they shall be seized for the use of the public, and not of the individuals.

CHAPTER IV.

OF THE LIMITATIONS OF PROPERTY.

I. *Property limited in respect of continuance, use, or disposal.*—II. *Limitations arise from the proprietor, or from some other person.*—III. *Limitations in respect of continuance.*—IV. *Services or limitations in respect of use.*—V. *Limitations in respect of disposal.*

Property limited in respect of continuance, use, or disposal.

I. Full property in a thing is a perpetual right to use it to any purpose, and to dispose of it at pleasure. Property, in the strict notion of it, is such a right to a thing as excludes all persons, except the proprietor, from all manner of claim upon it. No person therefore can, consistently with such a right, take the thing from him at any time, or hinder him in the free use of it, or prevent him from disposing of it as he pleases. If any other person can claim either to take the thing from him at any certain time, or to hinder him at all in the free use of it, or to prevent him from disposing of it as he pleases, he has not, in these respects, an exclusive right to it; that is, his exclusive right or property in the thing is so far limited. These then are the limitations to which property is subject; they are limitations in respect of its continuance, or in respect of the use of what we have property in, or in respect of the disposal of it.

Limitations arise either from the proprietor or from some other person.

II. A man's property may be limited in any of these respects either by his own act, or by the act of some other person. He limits it by his own act, if he consents either expressly or tacitly to give any one, besides himself, any claim upon what is his. If this is done by express consent, we call it a grant. If it is done by tacit consent, we call it usage or custom. His property is limited by the act of another, though not indeed wholly without his own consent; if he receives a thing by gift or by purchase, and the person from whom he receives it makes it over to him under limitations. The act of the person who makes the thing over to him, is principally considered; because the limitations are made at the motion and discretion of that person: but yet his own consent concurs with this act; for he was at liberty to have refused accepting the thing under those limitations, if he had thought proper.

Limitations in respect of continuance.

III. If lands are granted to a man for a term of years, with full power, whilst that term lasts, to use or to alienate them; he has property in these lands, but not full property; he has an exclusive right to use and dispose of them, but this right is limited in respect of its continuance. If a man grants away the reversion of his estate, and this grant is to take place at his death; he limits his property, in respect not only of its disposal but of its continuance too, by his own act. Indeed his property might have ceased at his death, though he had made no such grant; yet if it had not been made, there are natural ways by which, if he pleased, he might have continued this property in other persons, even after his death, to an indefinite time.

Services or limitations in respect of use.

IV. Limitations in respect of the use of things, in which we have property, are called services. If the owner of a thing has not the full and free use of it to himself; that is, if any other person, notwithstanding his property in it, can claim either to use the thing, or to hinder him from using it in what manner he pleases, the thing is then said to be charged with a service due to the person who has such a claim.

It may not, perhaps, be thought foreign to our present purpose, to take notice of the effects produced by some of those services which the goods of one man may owe to another. Services may be divided into two sorts, personal and real. *Indeed all services, when we con-

* Grotius, Lib. I. Cap. I. § IV.

sider them as rights, belong to persons: but then some of them belong to a person considered simply, or merely as a person; and these are what we call personal services, to distinguish them from others which belong to a person not considered simply, or merely as a person, but as a person possessed of some particular thing. This latter sort, though they belong to a person, as well as the former, yet because they do *rem sequi*, follow the possession of a thing, are called real services.

*The principal personal service is usufruct, or use and profits, which is a right to use the property of another and to enjoy the advantages arising from it, without impairing the substance of the thing so used and enjoyed. The fruits or advantages of a thing, which is a man's own, naturally belong to the owner of it: he may therefore, if he pleases, grant them away, provided they can be separated from the thing itself; and yet still retain a right to the disposal of the thing; that is, to the disposal of the substance of it, which is all that, after such a grant, belongs to him. But it is to be observed, that this limitation of property, which is called usufruct, can take place only in such goods as can be used without being consumed; such as lands, houses, slaves, horses, books, &c. For in things which are necessarily consumed in the using, the substance and the use, or the property and usufruct, if we may so call it, are inseparable from one another. There seems, however, to be something like a right of use and profits different from property in these things, which shows itself whenever they are lent. If, when wine, or grain, or money are lent, the full property in them was transferred by the lender to the borrower, a loan of such things as these would not differ from a gift. And yet, in the mean time, if the borrower had no sort of property in the substance of the thing made over to him, he could not use what he has borrowed; because the use and substance are so united to one another, that no use can be had of such things without breaking into the substance itself. Under the article of contracts this matter will be fully explained. At present it will be sufficient to observe, that where things, which cannot be used without being consumed, are lent, the borrower has a property in the things made over to him by the lender: but then this property is not full and absolute: it is limited in respect of time. His property continues only during the lender's pleasure, if no particular time of payment has been fixed: but if there is a fixed time for payment, then the property continues till that time comes. The other sorts of personal services, such as bare use, dwelling, work of slaves, as the Roman law explains them, are only more restrained instances of usufruct: and any of these are limitations in respect of use upon the property of him whose goods owe such services: he cannot have the full and free use of them, where others have any claims of this sort upon them.

Real services due to any person upon account of some estate which belongs to him, are certain advantages which the estate of another owes to his: and the other, whose estate owes such service, is limited as to his property in respect of the use of it. For if any person, besides himself, may lawfully claim to use what belongs to him, or if he may be lawfully hindered by any other person in using it himself, he cannot, in either case, be supposed to have the full and free use of it.

* Puffend. B. IV. Cap. VIII. § VI, VII, &c.

These services are divided into services of city estates, and services of country estates: But under the notion of city estates, the Roman law includes not only such as are actually in a city, but likewise all buildings, wherever they are situated, which are intended for the habitation of mankind, or for the exercise of commerce. Such are the services of bearing a burden, where my neighbour has a right of letting his house rest upon my wall, or my pillar: the service of receiving dropping water, where he has a right of conveying water through spouts or gutters, into my yard: the service of not receiving dropping water, where he has a right to hinder me from turning such spouts or gutters into his yard: the service of jutting or shooting out, where he has a right to extend his buildings in such a manner as to hang over my ground: the service of not raising a building higher, where he, for the profit or convenience of his house, has a claim upon me not to build beyond a fixed height: the service of lights, where I am obliged to admit his making windows into my yard or garden: the service of not hindering lights, when I can raise no building upon my own ground, so as to obscure his windows: the service of prospect, where I am bound to let my neighbour look freely into my estate: the service of receiving a water course, where I am bound to grant a passage to water-pipes through my house for the benefit of his: the service of sinks, where I am bound for the convenience of my neighbour's house to suffer his sink to pass through my grounds. Instances of services due from estates in the country, are path-way, drift-way, and road. A path-way is a right which my neighbour has of walking through my grounds, upon account of some particular estate which he is possessed of, and with which this right is connected. Drift-way is a like right, not only of walking, but likewise of driving his cattle or carriages through them. And a road is a right of passing, going, walking, driving, carrying, or drawing through them, either to a town, or to some highway, or to a ferry, or to a bridge, or to some estate of his own. In these, and many more instances of the like sort, the use of my property is limited: I cannot do what I will with a thing which belongs to me; because some other person has a claim upon me to submit to an inconvenience, or not to reap an advantage; which, if there had been no such claim, I should not have submitted to, or should have reaped.

Limitation in respect of disposal.

V. Though a man cannot be understood to have any property in a thing, when another person has a full right to dispose of it, yet property may be conceived to continue, where the proprietor has not a right to dispose of the thing as he pleases. This seems to be the case of an estate which is held in trust. For though there is commonly another limitation of such estates in respect of the use, by which limitation the trustee is obliged to dispose of the profits arising from them to certain purposes; yet are they attended, too, with a limitation in respect of the disposal of them, where the trustee is no more at liberty to dispose of the estate itself, at his own discretion, than he is to dispose of the use and profits of it. In the case of pledges, the property of the person, whose goods are pledged, is limited as to the disposal of such goods. Pledges are such goods as the debtor puts into the hands of the creditor, or assigns over to him as a security, that upon failure of payment, the creditor shall have property in the thing pledged. If moveable goods are pledged, they are called pawns; if immoveable ones, they are called mortgages. In both cases the owners' property is limited in respect of the disposal of the thing, till the debt is paid; because the creditors' right of security would be broken in upon, if the debtor was to dispose of it.

CHAPTER V.

OF OUR COMMON RIGHT TO THINGS.

I. *What things are still in common.*—II. *The ocean is not in property.*—III. *Some waters admit of property.*—IV. *Wild beasts, birds, and fishes are in common until taken.*—V. *The right to take wild beasts, &c. may be restrained as to its exercise.*—VI. *Right of extreme necessity sets aside property.*—VII. *This right is subject to three limitations.*—VIII. *Right of harmless profit, on what founded.*—IX. *This right is precarious in its exercise.*

What things are still in common.

I. *ALL things may be divided into such as are in common, and such as are in property. Such things are still in common, as either from their own nature never could be appropriated, or though in their own nature they might be appropriated, yet in fact never have been. We will consider the rights which belong to all mankind, in common, in respect of things of each sort.

The ocean is not in property.

II. †The ocean, either as to the whole, or as to the principal parts of it, does not admit of property, but remains still in common to all mankind, notwithstanding the introduction of property in other things. The first reason that we urge in proof of this, is only a moral or probable one. It is not likely that mankind should ever think of gaining an exclusive right to the ocean; because there was no reason for it; no cause or motive which might induce them to it. And though, where an act appears evidently to have been done, we could never disprove the existence of it by alleging that there was no reason for doing it; yet, where it is doubtful whether an act has been done or not, the conclusion is probable that it never has been done, provided no reason can be found why it should. ‡Now the general reason for appropriating other things is, that the same thing would not answer the purposes of all the joint commoners who might have occasion to make use of it at one and the same time. But the ocean, whilst it continues in common, is not liable to this inconvenience: it is large enough to answer the occasions of all mankind, either to sail upon, or to fish in, or to fetch water from. We therefore conclude, that it was never in the intention of mankind to appropriate it, or to acquire an exclusive right in it; because the general reason for acquiring such a right in other things, could, in respect of the ocean, have no weight with them.

* Grot. Lib. II. Cap. II. § I. † Grot. *ibid.* § III. ‡ See Chap. III. § V.

We may say the same of large banks of sand, which are sufficient to supply all men who want to use the sand, either for ballast, or for any other purpose. The same reasoning is likewise applicable to the air, as far as any use can be made of it, without making use at the same time of the soil or the water.

But besides this moral reason, arising from the want of intention in mankind to acquire an exclusive right in the ocean, there is a natural one, which shows that no such right ever could be acquired. *Occupancy cannot proceed so as to give property, unless in such things as are certain and determinate. The soil or land, though the parts of it are in continuity or join to one another, is distinguished into parcels by hills or mountains, by brooks or rivers: and where these natural boundaries are wanting, parcels of it may be distinctly set out by fences, or plantations, or other artificial land-marks. But the surfaces of fluids are, in their own nature, so smooth and yielding, as not to admit of being distinguished into parcels by any such natural or artificial boundaries. If they are thus set out at all, it must be by the banks or shores in which they are contained. Now the ocean is not contained within banks or shores: for it rather encompasses the land, the continent, as well as what are commonly called islands, than is encompassed by it. The natural uncertainty, therefore, of the thing, both as to the whole of it, and as to its principal parts, renders it incapable of being appropriated by occupancy. Mariners, indeed, and geographers divide and set it out by the artificial measure of degrees in latitude and longitude. But as these are not lasting and visible limits, they cannot so distinguish the ocean into parcels, as that one part of mankind should be able to find out what another part design to make their own, without express information; and consequently they cannot make the ocean capable of being appropriated, unless all the parties were to meet and enter into an express agreement about settling the limits of each other's property. Such an agreement as this is what we call division. But if property in the ocean cannot be introduced any other way than by division, no property can be introduced in it at present, †as has been shown already. And formerly, whilst mankind were few, and lived near together, so that they could readily meet, the ocean, or however far the greatest part of it, was unknown to them, and consequently could not, at that time, be measured, divided and assigned. Since, therefore, property in the ocean could not be introduced either by occupancy or by division, the necessary consequence is, that it is not capable of being appropriated at all.

Some waters admit of property.

III. The case of ‡rivers, bays, streights, pools, or lakes, is different from that of the ocean. For though, as fluid bodies, they are not set out into certain and determinate parcels, by any marks or limits upon their surface, yet, as they are contained within banks or shores, which are near to one another, they are by this means made certain and determinate enough to admit of property by occupancy.

Wild beasts, birds and fishes, are in common till taken.

IV. §Many things, which in their own nature admit of occupancy, so that an exclusive right to them may be acquired, have yet in fact never been appropriated;

* See Chap. III. § VIII.

† See Chap. III. § IX.

‡ Grot. Lib. II. Cap. III. § VII.

§ Grot. *ibid.* § V.

because no one has seized upon them for this purpose. Of this sort are wild beasts, birds and fishes, which have never been caught; or, after they are caught, have escaped from us; islands, which are uninhabited, or such tracts of land, either in islands or on the continent, as no person has yet settled upon.

As to wild beasts, birds or fishes, since they are part of the common stock, any person may of common right take them for his own use or diversion; and occupancy without interruption will give him property in them. But then this property is very precarious; because it continues no longer than possession. Whenever such animals have made their escape, the natural presumption, upon account of their wildness, is, that they can be recovered no more: and consequently their former owner must, in all reason, be understood to give them up or relinquish them. This property, however, as precarious as it is, seems to be more than the mere exercise of a common right to take and to use them: because, if he, who takes them, can make them tame, so that by loss of possession he does not lose all prospect of recovering them, his property in them will be fixed, even after they have escaped from him; and he may claim them wherever he finds them. And it farther appears that the right to such animals, when they are taken, is more than a common right to part of a joint stock; because no reason can be given, in the nature of the thing itself, why any person may not take more such animals than he wants for his own use: and as long as he can keep possession, what he has so taken are his own to dispose of in any manner that he pleases. His right, therefore, whilst possession continues, is not merely a right to use, but an exclusive right of property.

The right to take wild beasts, &c. may be restrained as to its exercise.

V. But though no reason, in the nature of the thing, can be given why any person may not lawfully take as many of these wild animals as he will, yet his right of taking them at all is limited, by a reason drawn from the consideration, that other men have property in such things as he must make use of, in order to take them. No man can hunt, or fish, or fowl, without using the soil or the water. If, therefore, others have an exclusive right to the soil or the water, which he has occasion to make use of in following these diversions; as he cannot claim to use their property, he cannot justly claim the liberty of hunting, or fishing, or fowling on such lands or such rivers as belong to them. It may, perhaps, be asked how he can justly be hindered from exercising a right which he enjoys by the law of nature, a right of taking and using, or even of appropriating such animals as do not belong to any one; since such a hindrance or interruption seems inconsistent with the law of nature? But to this we reply, that fishing, hunting, or fowling, are originally matter of natural right; not because the law of nature commands them, but because it does not forbid them. Now though no act of man can take away the liberty of doing what the law of nature commands, yet there is nothing that can prevent such act from taking away the liberty of doing what the law has left indifferent; provided the parties, to whom such liberty belongs, give their consent to it. This, in respect of hunting, fishing, or fowling, though it was not done expressly, was done tacitly, and of necessary consequence, by the introduction of property in the soil or the water. For it is unintelligible to suppose that one man has an exclusive right in the soil or the water, and yet that another may use them, if he pleases, to these purposes. To give any other person besides the proprietor such a claim after property is introduced, some reserve must be shown, and an express reserve too, of this liberty: for, otherwise, the common or general liberty of using the soil or the water for the purposes of hunting, fishing, or fowling, is as effectually given up by the introduction of property, as the general liberty of using them to any other purpose whatsoever.

Right of extreme necessity sets aside property.

VI. *It may seem strange, that we should inquire whether all mankind can, in any circumstances, or in any instances, claim of common right to make use of such things as are appropriated to particular persons. For, since property is an exclusive right to the things appropriated, it seems to have wholly superseded these common claims of mankind. We shall, however, find upon inquiry, that the fact is otherwise, and that in some circumstances our common right to the use of things remains, even after those things have been appropriated and have their distinct and respective owners.

Grotius maintains, that there are two instances of such a common claim: the first he calls the right of extreme necessity; the latter the right of harmless profit. In support of the right of extreme necessity we may urge with him, that when mankind first agreed to divide the common stock amongst them; or when, afterwards, they suffered any one to acquire property by occupancy; if they had been asked whether they consented so effectually to exclude themselves from what they agreed to appropriate, as never to claim any use of it, even though it should be absolutely necessary to their own preservation? It is most likely they would have answered, that they intended no such thing, but agreed to the introduction of property for the convenience of all, and not for the destruction of any. And since the claim, which the proprietor of a thing has to it, depends upon the consent of mankind, this claim must be subject to all the limitations which they designed to lay it under, and can extend no farther than they designed it should extend.

We may urge in support of the same right of extreme necessity, that no compact, either express or tacit, could so introduce property as to be binding without such a limitation. For, since the right which a man has to his life is unalienable, (as will appear hereafter,) he cannot alienate the natural right which he has to the necessary means of his own preservation. However, therefore, mankind may have consented that particular things should be possessed in property by particular persons, yet in whatever respect such things become absolutely necessary for the preservation of individuals, they still continue in common. So that extreme necessity sets property aside, or makes it lawful for persons, who labour under such necessity, to use those things in which others have property, as if the things were still in common. Thus, where a man must have starved otherwise, it is naturally no theft if he takes victuals which is not his own: because, though the owner of what is so taken has, in respect of all other men, an exclusive right to it, he has no such right in respect of the necessitous person. You may

* Grotius, Lib. II. Cap. III. § VI.

say, indeed, that it is not the property of the poor man who takes it; which we readily allow. But then we contend, that, in respect of him, it is not the property of the person from whom he takes it. If it was, you might easily prove this act to be theft, unless the owner consented to his taking it: because theft consists in taking away the property of another without his consent. But you should observe, that where there is no property there can be no theft. And if, in order to prove the poor man's act to be theft, you will assume that the person from whom the thing is taken has property in it, you either take the matter in question for granted, or else you are guilty of a fallacy. If, when you assume that the person from whom the thing is taken has property in it, you mean that he has property in respect of the poor man; or that, as the owner has a right to exclude all others from the use of the thing, so he has likewise the same right to exclude him, you take the matter in question for granted. But if, when you assume this in general, you mean only that he has property in respect of all others, you are guilty of a fallacy; you have more in your conclusion than is contained in your premises: you assume only that he has property in respect of some, and conclude as if he had property in respect of all.

To this head we may likewise refer the right which we have in case of fire, to pull down our neighbour's house in order to preserve our own; the right which we have to cut the nets or cables of another man, where our own boat is entangled with them, and must otherwise sink; the obligation on ship-board, which each person is under, in a scarcity of provisions, to bring out his own stock and to leave it in common: the right which, in a storm, all who are on board have to demand that each person shall throw so many of his goods into the sea, as would overburden the ship; and, lastly, the right which a nation at war has to seize upon and garrison a place of strength, in a neutral country, when it is morally certain that the enemy would otherwise get possession of it, and by that means be enabled to do them irreparable damage. For though, in some of these instances, the preservation of life may seem not to be immediately concerned; yet, at least, the reason upon which Grotius supports the right of extreme necessity, is applicable to all of them. It is not probable that mankind, when they consented to introduce property, should design to extend that claim to cases wherein such an exclusive right would force them to suffer what is beyond the ordinary patience of human nature.

The right of extreme necessity is subject to three limitations.

VII. *This right of extreme necessity is subject to such restrictions as will keep it from being abused, and from being made a pretence to encroach upon the property of others, where we have no claim. The restrictions are these three, which follow:

First, all other methods are to be tried as far as the necessity will allow of; such as a request to the owner or an application to the magistrate, before we make use of such things as are the property of another. The reason of this restriction is evident. No necessity can be called extreme, or in effect there is no necessity at all, where our occasions or calls may be answered by the use of such means as are in our power. Indeed in our own country, where the civil laws have provided for the

* Grotius, Lib. II. Cap. III. § VII, VIII, IX.

poor, there can be no necessity which the rigour of the law will allow to be a sufficient ground for taking and using such food or such clothing as are the property of other persons: because, as the law has made a provision for the supply of such wants, it cannot suppose them ever to happen. And yet if, in the execution of the law, it should appear, that, notwithstanding the legal provisions to the contrary, in some particular instance such an extreme case has happened, the magistrate would be wanting in natural equity if he did not mitigate the rigour of the law against theft, as far as he is able.

A second restriction of this right of extreme necessity is, that it fails when the proprietor is under as great necessity as the other claimant. For, where the necessity is equal on both sides, the claim of the possessor is the better of the two: because the effect of necessity is only to overrule the right of property, and to make the thing in question common to the parties concerned. But in the exercise of our right over such things as are in common, where the parties equally want to use them, the first occupant has the best right to use them first: and in the case now before us, the possessor stands in the place of the first occupant.

A third restriction is, that where we have taken things which were not our own, and have used them in virtue of this right of extreme necessity, we are obliged, if it ever is in our power, to make amends to the owners of them. This restriction seems to be so inconsistent with the right for which we have been contending, that some have imagined we must either give up the restriction, or give up the right. If I have a right to use the goods which my necessity calls for, where can be the obligation to restitution? since all obligations of this sort imply that I have injured another by taking from him what I had no right to. Upon supposition therefore of a right to use such goods, there can be no obligation to make amends for it. Or if, on the other hand, we will contend that there is an obligation to make restitution, we must allow that the person in necessity had no right to take and to use the goods which he stood in need of. But to this we may answer, that a right to take and to use such goods as we cannot do without, and an obligation to make restitution for the exercise of that right, are indeed so inconsistent with one another, that they cannot possibly subsist at one and the same time. So long as my right subsists, I can be under no obligation to make restitution upon account of my exercising that right. But then they are not so inconsistent as to prevent them from subsisting at different times. My right subsists as long as the necessity continues, which is the foundation of that right; and so long there is no obligation to make restitution. But as soon as my necessity ceases, the foundation of my right is taken away, and consequently my right ceases with it. And it is then, and not till then, that the obligation to restitution begins.

Right of harmless profit, on what founded.

VIII. *The right of harmless profit is the right of using another man's property for our benefit, where the owner suffers no harm by our use of it. This right may be easily made out in theory; but when we come to the exercise of it, we shall find it so precarious as to be in effect no right at all. To

* Grot. Lib. II. Cap. III. § XI, &c.

support this right, we must look back to the general reason for introducing property, which was the impossibility that the same thing should at one and the same time, answer the uses which all or many might have for it. Now the claim of property, or the exclusive right to a thing extends no farther than the intention of mankind extended when they introduced it: and their intention cannot be understood to have extended any farther than the motive or reason which engaged them to introduce it. Therefore one man's property in a thing does not exclude another's right of harmless profit; because this right takes place in those instances only where the owner suffers no harm; that is, in those instances only where the thing will answer all the purposes of the proprietor, notwithstanding the use which the other makes of it.

Such right is precarious in its exercise.

IX. But this claim, as well as it may seem to be established in theory, will be found, as to the exercise of it, to depend upon the will and consent of those who have property in the goods that we have occasion to make use of for our own benefit. No right of this sort can be pretended, unless where our use of what is another man's property will do him no harm. But the proprietor himself must determine how far such use of his goods will be harmless; because his right in the goods would have no effect, or would be no right, if he could not exclude us from using them whenever we pretend that he will receive no damage from such use. If therefore he is to determine how far he is likely to suffer any harm by the exercise of our right, before we can claim to exercise it, we cannot make use of his goods in virtue of such right, till we have his consent. This is plainly in effect no better than no right at all; because where there is no pretence of a right to use the goods of another man, we may in any instance lawfully use them if he gives his consent.

We may be farther informed about the precarious nature of this right, as to the exercise of it, if we go on to examine some of the principal instances of it, which Grotius has mentioned. Those, says he, who have occasion for a passage over our land, or upon our rivers, either to seek a new settlement, when they are driven from their own country, or to carry on any commerce, or to recover by a just war what has been taken from them, or for any other lawful purpose, have a claim to such passage. Let us see, therefore, how far such a demand can be justly supported against the proprietor. A nation which has jurisdiction over the soil or water, or which has property in them, might object in particular to the passage of an army, that they are afraid of suffering some irreparable damage, if they were to allow such a number of armed men to come amongst them. To this difficulty Grotius replies that your fears cannot take away my right. But it is to observed, that though such a general answer might be sufficient in other cases, yet it cannot remove the objection which is urged in the present case; because no use of my property can be called harmless to me if it exposes me to such losses, as I should have been in no danger of suffering without such use. It may be true that my fears cannot take away your right, but then it cannot be true without an exception of those cases in which the very being of your right depends, as this of harmless profit does upon my security. Perhaps, indeed, even in this sort of right, it might be more proper to say that my fears prevent your right, than that they take it away. But which ever of these two expressions is the more proper, the effect is the same: there cannot be any right of harmless profit over the property of another man, where the owner has good reason to apprehend that he shall be a loser by the exercise of such a right. Our author, however, urges farther, that sufficient caution may be given to the owner to indemnify him against any loss that he may be apprehensive of: he may, in the instance now before us, insist that the army shall pass in small companies, that the men shall not be armed, that a guard shall be hired for him at their expense, and that hostages shall be put into his hands, as a security for their good behaviour in their passage. Now the necessity which our author allows there may be for taking such cautions as these, and the right which the proprietor has to insist upon them, plainly proves that without this security there would be no claim to use his property. But since sufficient caution is a vague thing, and since the proprietor alone can be the judge what caution is sufficient, he has such an opportunity of disappointing this right in the exercise of it, as makes the right itself not worth having.

But Grotius goes one step farther, and maintains that men have not only a right to demand such a passage for themselves, but for their goods too, when they want to carry on any trade or commerce; because, as such an intercourse of any one nation with any other is for the general good of mankind, we can have no right to hinder it. But this reason, if we allow it all its weight, can only prove that by hindering this intercourse we shall not contribute so much as we are able to the general good of mankind. And if this be all, the right of passage is only a demand of the imperfect sort; and they upon whom it is made, are at liberty to judge for themselves how far it is convenient for them to allow it to take effect. How can we in this instance, says our author, be properly said to sustain any damage by their passage, since whatever benefit we might be able to make by carrying on that trade exclusively, which they want to have a share in, it is such a benefit as we could only hope for, and not such an one as we could claim of strict right. But, whether the loss of such a benefit can be called in strictness of speaking a damage or not, is not worth inquiring. Perhaps it is not properly a damage. Yet certainly if the situation of our country is such as gives us an opportunity of carrying on any branch of trade exclusively, by denying others the use of our land or the use of our rivers, they cannot claim such use as a matter of harmless profit; because whatever will make our property less beneficial to us, can never be reasonably looked upon as harmless to us.

We are obliged likewise, as our author adds, to allow those who are passing by us to stop for a while, and even to build temporary huts or pitch tents, if they have occasion to stop in this manner for the recovery of their health; for this is to be reckoned amongst the harmless uses which they may have from our property. But certainly it is not universally true that such an use of our property will be harmless to us. Suppose, for instance, that they should be ill with the plague or with any other infectious distemper; their stopping amongst us would not be harmless. We must, therefore, be allowed at least to have a right of being satisfied whether their distemper is infectious or not, before they can claim to stop for the recovery of their health. And if they cannot claim, till we are satisfied of this, their right will be so vague and so much in our power that it can only be reckoned amongst the imperfect ones.

CHAPTER VI.

OF DERIVATIVE ACQUISITIONS, BY THE ACT OF MAN.

I. *Derivative acquisitions are of two sorts.*—II. *Mutual and notified consent of parties necessary in those made by the act of man.*—III. *An alienation may be revoked before acceptance.*—IV. *Acceptance may go before alienation.*—V. *Property may be continued after death by a will.*—VI. *Aliens, how incapable of inheriting by will.*

Derivative acquisitions are of two sorts.

I. * DERIVATIVE acquisitions are made either by the act of man or by the act of the law. Where the property which one man has in a thing, is transferred to another, either the owner transfers it with his own consent, and then he who acquires it, makes a derivative acquisition by the act of man, or else the law takes the property in the thing from one of them and gives it to the other, and then he to whom it is so given, makes a derivative acquisition by the act of the law. When the property in things passes from one person to another by the act of the former, he who so parts with the things is said to transfer or alienate them, and he to whom they are so transferred is said to acquire them.

Mutual and notified consent of parties necessary in derivative acquisitions by the act of man.

II. † The proprietor or owner of a thing, when the law does not interpose to take it from him, cannot cease to have a right in it, unless he designs to part with it; an injury is done him if it is taken from him without his own consent. On the other hand, no property in a thing can be acquired without the design or consent of him who makes the acquisition; nothing can become his own unless he has a mind to make it so. From hence it follows that in all derivative acquisitions by the act of man, a design or consent to alienate the thing is necessary on one part, and a design or consent to accept it is necessary on the other part.

But besides the mere consent of parties on both sides, it is farther necessary that this consent should be sufficiently made known or signified by some outward sign or mark, such as words or actions or both. For a consent which does not appear, can no more fall under the notice of mankind than a consent which does not exist: and consequently the law of nature cannot allow that, in respect of mankind, a consent or intention which rests in the mind only and is not sufficiently declared, should produce any effect; such intention being as if it had never been, the property in a thing can neither be transferred nor acquired by it.

An alienation may be revoked before acceptance.

III. But since the declared consent both of the giver and receiver is necessary before any derivative acquisition can be made by the act of man, it follows that, though the giver has declared his consent, and so has done all that was necessary on his part towards alienating his property, yet such alienation may be recalled at any time before acceptance is declared on the other part; because, till acceptance is declared, the party to whom the giver designed to alienate his property, has no claim upon it. Perhaps it may be thought that, notwithstanding one of the parties gains no claim to the

* Grot. Lib. II. Cap. VI. § I. † Grot. ibid. § I. II.

thing for want of acceptance, yet the other party has, by alienating it as far as was in his power, lost his claim to it. But in order to clear up this mistake we should take notice of the difference between dereliction and alienation. Dereliction is the absolute giving up of property; so that he who relinquishes what is his, loses his right in it, though no other particular person acquires that right. But alienation is the giving up of property for the use or benefit of some other particular person, or in order that this other person may acquire property in it; so that if he, for whose benefit the thing was to have been alienated, fails of acquiring property in it, the alienation produces no effect, or is as if it had never been. He who made the alienation had no design of quitting his claim, but in order that a certain person might acquire it; and consequently, if this person either through his own default or by any other accident does not acquire it, his property continues in him, as it was before, this being the only purpose for which he had any design of parting with it.

Acceptance may go before alienation.

IV. When the property of one man passes by his own act to another, the most natural order is that acceptance should follow alienation. But this order, though it is most natural, is not necessary. For acceptance is sometimes understood to have been made before alienation, so that the transfer is complete immediately upon alienation, and cannot justly be recalled, though no acceptance should follow it. If I ask for a thing, I am plainly willing to accept it; and if, upon my asking it is given me, the transfer is complete without any farther acceptance; because I am understood to be still in the same mind as when I asked for it, unless I expressly declare the contrary.

Property may be continued after death by a will.

V. From the power, which a man has of alienating his property in what manner and upon what condition he pleases, it follows that he may naturally prevent his property from ceasing upon his death, *by making a will and disposing of it in his life-time.

He who has full property in a thing, may alienate it either absolutely or conditionally. As far as the law restrains him from doing this, his property is not full but limited. As he may alienate it conditionally, so likewise for the same reason, he may choose his own conditions. Amongst other conditions which he might have chosen, suppose him to choose that the alienation shall so depend upon the event of his own death, that whatever he says or does towards alienating his property shall be understood to be complete on his part, when this event happens, and not before. The effect of such a condition would be, that he might recall the alienation at any time before his death; because the transfer is so far from being completed by any acceptance on the other part, that the alienation itself is not complete on his part till this event happens. And if such a conditional alienation may be recalled at any time before his death, a new disposition of the thing so alienated may be made; he may, notwithstanding what he has done already, make a like conditional disposition of it to any person that he pleases, or he may sell it, or he may give it away absolutely. It is plain, therefore, that if he retains such a right in the thing after it is thus conditionally alienated, such an

* Grot. Lib. II. Cap. VI. § XIV.

alienation is so far from being inconsistent with his property in it, that it does not so much as restrain or limit such property.

Now an alienation of the sort that I have been describing, is a will or testament. For a will is nothing more than a conditional alienation, which is to take place upon the event of the testator's death, without affecting his property in the thing disposed of till this event happens. Supposing, therefore, property to be introduced, the right of making a will and of disposing of the things in which we have property, by such will, naturally follows from it.

However, we are to observe that this right may not only be regulated, but may even be taken away, either by express compact or by civil law. But, then, as far as it is either restrained or taken away, our right of property is limited: because, as has been seen already, the right of making such a conditional alienation is necessarily included in the right of full property.

Perhaps it may be asked, at what time the property in a thing, devised by will, is alienated by the testator. It does not appear to be alienated before his death, if we have given a true account of the nature of a will: and it cannot be alienated after his death; because after he is dead, he has no power of acting at all, so as to alienate his property, or to do any thing else. Nor can we properly say that it is alienated at the very instant when he dies; since the will, which is the instrument whereby he makes the alienation, was made before that instant. The fact is, that the alienation was made before his death, but made conditionally: he consented to transfer his goods to the person whom he appoints to be his heir, upon condition of his retaining the full property in them till the time of his death, and of the heirs' claim not taking place till this event happens. Now this latter condition suspends the effect of his alienation, or renders it incomplete till the event of his death: it was indeed so far perfect on his part, that, after the will was made, there was no occasion for any farther act of his to make it more perfect; nothing was wanting but that the event should happen upon which the heirs' claim, given him conditionally before, was to take place and become absolute.

It seems, indeed, to be necessary, by the law of nature, that the heirs' acceptance, without which he acquires no property in the thing devised by will, should be made before the testator's death. There will otherwise be an interval of time pass in which the goods will have no owner, and consequently will be open to the first occupant. This interval of time is what passes between the testator's death and the heirs' acceptance. The testator has then no property in the goods, because he is not in existence: and the heir has no property in them for want of acceptance. The occupant, therefore, who is some third person, cannot naturally be said to injure any one by seizing upon such goods. From hence it appears, that if a will obtains its effect, where the heir has not accepted before the death of the testator, it must either be accidentally, (because no third person has been before-hand with the designed heir in seizing upon the goods,) or else the will must owe its effect to the aid of some positive law, besides the mere will or appointment of the testator; which law takes the custody of the goods upon the death of the testator, and hinders all persons from seizing upon them, till it appears whether the heir will accept or not. We cannot suppose the testator's will to be of itself so far binding upon all mankind, as to become a law to them, and hinder them from seizing upon the goods devised by it; since it is well known that this will is no law even to the heir appointed in it, till he has accepted.

However, no acceptance of the heir, before the testator's death, will so far bind the testator as to make it naturally unlawful for him to make another will and appoint a different heir. For the heir can accept only upon such terms as the testator offers: and the terms of a will are, that the goods devised to you shall be yours upon the event of my death; under this restriction, that, in the mean time, the full property in them shall be mine: my design is to retain a right to dispose of them as I please, till the event of my death happens; but if, in the mean time, I make no other disposition of them, immediately upon that event they are yours. If the heir accepts, upon these terms, in the testator's life-time, though such acceptance is sufficient to make the goods his property at the testator's death, without any subsequent acceptance; yet, in the mean time, the conditions annexed to the testator's alienation are such as will leave the goods in his power to dispose of in what manner he shall think fit, as long as he lives.

Whenever I speak, hereafter, of the power of disposing of our goods by will, as naturally incidental to the right of property, without the aid of civil laws; the reader must remember that I mean a will under the circumstances just now described, where the heir has accepted before the testator's death.

Aliens how incapable of inheriting by will.

VI. Though the right of making a will is incidental to property, and consequently is coeval with it, yet such property in goods, as enables a man to give them away by will, must be full property; at least it must not be limited in respect of the disposal. There is one natural limitation of this sort not much attended to, which will prevent a will from obtaining any effect. When the occupancy of land and of all its appendages was made in the gross, so that the general property is considered as vested originally in that body of men, by which such occupancy was made; particular property is derived from thence to each individual, as he is a member of this collective body. But what belongs to a man, as he is a member of such body, cannot be his to dispose of to any person who is not a member of the same body. He cannot transmit his property upon any other terms besides those upon which he received it: and consequently, as the property which he has in the land was derived to him from the community, under the qualification of his being a member of it, he cannot transmit that land to any person who has not the same qualification. This is a natural bar against an aliens inheriting land by will: the bar may be considered as arising rather on the part of the testator than on the part of the alien; it arises rather from a limitation in the testator's property in respect of his right to dispose of the land, than from any incapacity in the alien to accept what the other devises to him. Where the testator has full property, as he has in his moveable goods, which are considered as of his own original acquisition, and not as derived from the general property of the community, such goods are naturally in his own absolute disposal, and he can transmit them as effectually to a stranger as to one who is a member of the same community with himself. But, then, though such goods as these are naturally in the testator's disposal, he may, notwithstanding this, be prevented by the civil law from disposing of them to an alien at his own discretion. For as the community has a general property in the land where such goods are, it may hinder an alien from coming to fetch them away upon any other terms than what such community shall agree upon. The only difference, then, in this respect between land and moveable goods is, that an alien cannot naturally inherit land by will, unless some express law has been made to enable the members of the community to transmit their land by will to aliens: whereas, they can naturally so transmit their moveable goods, unless some express law has been made to the contrary.

CHAPTER VII.

OF DERIVATIVE ACQUISITIONS BY THE ACT OF THE LAW.

I. *Grotius supposes two sorts of derivative acquisitions by the act of the law of nature.*—II. *Derivative acquisitions to satisfy a claim, how made.*—III. *The claim to succeed to the goods of an intestate depends upon conjecture.*—IV. *Intestate successions need some other support besides the law of nature.*—V. *Inheritance does not arise from a general consent of all mankind.*—VI. *A regard to a man's personal duty is the principle upon which intestate successions were introduced.*—VII. *The natural order of succession according to this principle.*—VIII. *Children why preferred to parents in intestate successions.*—IX. *The same principle governs the succession, where an intestate leaves no children.*—X. *Philo is mistaken in his interpretation of the Mosaic law.*—XI. *Order of succession may be varied by civil laws.*—XII. *The succession of children may be cut off by disherison.*—XIII. *Uncertainty of birth hinders a child from succeeding to an intestate parent.* XIV. *Infants, ideots and madmen, naturally incapable of property.*—XV. *Law of nations wrongly explained by Grotius.*—XVI. *Custody of the law supplies the place of property.*

Grotius supposes two sorts of derivative acquisitions, by the act of the law of nature.

I. WHEN the property of one man is transferred to another by the act of the law, this is done either by the law of nature, or by some positive law. Our subject does not require that we should consider any other transfers of this sort, besides what are made by the law of nature.

*Grotius maintains, that property is acquired derivatively by the law of nature in two instances; either to satisfy some claim of strict justice, or to supply an heir to a person who dies intestate. In the former of these instances, the acquisition is indeed made by the law of nature; but in the latter of them we shall find that it is not made effectually without the aid of instituted laws.

* Grotius, Lib. II. Cap. VII. § II.

Derivative acquisitions, to satisfy a claim, how made.

II. If any person has injured us by taking from us what is our own, or by withholding from us what in strict justice is due to us; the law of nature not only allows us to make reprisals, by seizing upon so much of his goods as is equivalent to what we have lost, where we cannot recover the very thing itself; but it gives us property likewise in the goods so taken. For the law of nature cannot be supposed to hinder us from prosecuting our just claims, or from endeavouring to recover what, by the same law, is due to us. But we have a claim upon him who has thus taken, or thus withholds our property from us, to the value of the thing detained. If, therefore, we cannot come at the thing itself, as we have naturally a claim to an equivalent, the law of nature will allow us it out of his goods. Now the bare possession of what may in itself be of equal value with the thing lost, is not an equivalent to the injured party; because, whatever may be the value of the goods so taken, considered in itself, yet the bare possession of them cannot make amends for the loss of property. The claim, therefore, cannot be satisfied, unless the law of nature, besides allowing us to take possession of goods, which are worth as much as what we have lost, makes over to us likewise the property in such goods.

The claim to succeed to the goods of an intestate, depends upon conjecture.

III. The property which any person has in his goods, naturally ceases at his death; and the goods, as having no owner, revert to the common stock; if he has not disposed of them by will, that is, if he has not in his lifetime made an eventual alienation of them, or transferred the property which he had in them, to some other person whose claim takes place immediately upon the event of his death. *When, therefore, a person dies intestate, (that is, without having made any will at all; or, at least, any that appears,) whatever claim his relations, or any one else, may have to his goods, either moveable or immoveable, it can have no other foundation in nature but a supposition or conjecture that he had disposed of them in his own mind; that he had designed to make them over to such claimant, though this design was never declared.

In support of this conjecture it may be urged, that, when a man foresees the necessity of dying, and of being by this means deprived of all benefit or enjoyment of his goods, in his own person, it is not likely that he would lose this opportunity of doing a kindness to such other persons as he had a regard for, but would suffer his goods to revert to the common stock, or to become the property of any one who should first seize upon them after his death. The consequence from this conjecture, supposing it to be well grounded, would be, that every man does in his own mind appoint a successor to his property; that he intends to convey his goods, when he is prevented by death from enjoying them any longer, to some one or more persons whose welfare he has at heart, and to whom he is desirous of showing all proper instances of kindness and regard.

Intestate successions need some other support besides the law of nature.

IV. However, if we suppose this conjecture to be ever so well grounded, yet those persons who claim to inherit an intestate's goods, must have some other law to support their claim besides the law of nature. The foundation of their claim is laid in a supposed inten-

* Grot. Lib. II. Cap. VII. § III.

tion of the intestate person, which he never declared. But according to the law of nature, *as has in another case been observed already, no effect can be produced by a mere inward design; the outward declaration by which the design is notified, is as necessary to make any transfer of goods valid, as the design or intention of transferring them. An intention which does not appear, can no more fall under the notice of mankind, and is therefore no more regarded by the law of nature, than an intention which does not exist.

† Even where a will has been made, if there is no acceptance on the part of the heir before the testator's death, it does not produce its effect without the aid of positive laws. Much less therefore can any natural effect be obtained by a mere conjecture about the design of the deceased; where, as the intention of the ancestor never was declared, it is impossible to suppose that the heir had ever accepted. When a man has made a will, his heir, if he knows of it, may be ready upon the spot, and though he has not accepted beforehand, may accept immediately upon the testator's death. But when a man dies intestate, it will commonly be uncertain for some time, whether a concealed will may not appear which no one knew of; and during this interval, if no positive law takes the goods into its custody, any person may seize upon them, and by such occupancy may gain property in them; since during that interval they have no owner. Nay, the conjecture itself, upon which the whole supposed claim to inherit the goods of an intestate person depends, is too precarious to be the foundation of any right, if there was no other objection to it. We may say on the one hand, that a man could scarce be supposed willing to have his goods become common to all mankind, or pass into the hands of a stranger, when he has an opportunity to dispose of them for the benefit of those whom he loved. But then we may say on the other hand with equal probability, that his neglecting to dispose of his goods amongst his relations or friends, when he had it in his power, is a sign that he did not care whether they were so disposed of or not.

Since then the claim, which any person may be supposed to have to the goods of one who dies intestate, depends upon a very uncertain conjecture; since this conjecture is such an one as for want of having been declared, the law of nature takes no notice of; and since, even if the law of nature should take notice of it, yet for want of acceptance the goods might be seized upon by some other person, before this law could convey the property in them to the relations of the intestate, recourse must be had to some other law in order to make out the claim of his relations to inherit his goods.

It may perhaps be imagined that a man's obligation to maintain his children extends itself to his goods, so as to give them a natural right to such goods after the death of their parent, though he dies intestate. But it is plain that the general claim to inherit in intestate successions cannot depend upon this principle. If this was the foundation upon which the claim of inheritance depends, such claim could extend no farther than to his children: his brothers or sisters, his uncles or aunts, or any other of his relations in what degree soever, could have no place in the intestate succession. But since where a man dies without chil-

* See Chap. VI. § II. † See Chap. VI. § V.

dren, the claim of inheritance is, in use and practice, extended to his other relations; we may be sure that this claim is supported upon some other principle, and not merely upon the duty which a parent owes to his children. We may go one step farther. The claim of the children themselves, where there are any, to inherit the goods of their intestate parent, cannot depend solely upon the duty of the parent to maintain them. Their claim reaches, at least in use and practice it is supposed to reach, to all his goods; whereas a claim founded in the parent's obligation to maintain them can naturally reach to so much only of his goods as may be necessary for their maintenance. If we examine this obligation of the parent still more closely, we may perhaps find that it is not only insufficient to give the children a claim to all his goods, but even to any part of them. As the parent's obligation arises from a personal act, whereby he became the cause of the children's existence, so it rests upon the parent's person, and does not directly affect his goods. A parent is obliged to maintain his children, but he is not obliged to apply this or that particular part of his substance to this purpose; nor does he hold any of his goods upon condition that he will maintain them. He has an absolute right in his goods, and may sell them or give them away, and when he has sold them he may squander away the money, nay at his death he may leave them from his children by will. If he has stripped himself of his goods in his life-time, or if, as may be the case, he had originally no goods, the obligation to maintain his children would still be the same. It would not indeed operate in the same manner, because whilst we suppose him to have goods, this obligation will affect them indirectly; those goods are then the readiest means which he can make use of for the discharge of his personal duty; but after he has those means no longer in his power, he must still discharge that duty, as well as he can, by his labour, or by some other means. But if the obligation of the parent to maintain his children arises from his personal act; if the right, which he has to his goods, is not the less absolute for his having children; and lastly, if this obligation is the same, whether he has any goods or not, we may reasonably conclude that the claim of the children to maintenance is upon the person of the parent, and not upon his goods; and the consequence will be, that since they have no direct claim upon his goods, even during his life-time, their claim of maintenance can give them no right to his goods after his death.

It is indeed very evident, that a parent ought to do the best that he can for the welfare of his children; and consequently, that he does not do his duty, if he suffers them, through any act or any neglect of his, to lose such goods as he had in his disposal, and as he might have secured to them after his death. But this duty is of the imperfect sort; the children have no strict right to the goods, and what is done contrary to this duty and to their imperfect right will only be wrong and not void. However, when a parent dies possessed of goods, and without any just reason gives them away from his children, or causelessly disinherits them, civil laws do well to interpose, and set that will aside; not because the children had naturally a strict right to inherit; for if they had, the will would be void of itself, without the interposition of any positive law; but the law, having authority over the person of the parent, does well to take care that he shall in all respects discharge his duty, or to discharge it for him where he has neglected it.

Inheritance does not arise from the general consent of all mankind.

V. We have already seen, that the law of nature does not convey an intestate's goods to any particular person, but leaves them in common, and subjects them to the claim of the first occupant; or that inheritance in intestate succession is not naturally incidental to property. *But it may still be questioned, whether inheritance has not been introduced and established by such a general consent of all mankind, as that which introduced and established property itself. In order to form a true judgment upon this question, it will by no means be sufficient to consider merely the claim, which the heir has to the goods of his ancestor, where both of them are members of the same community; because, though such heir in all civilized nations, should be found regularly to claim the goods of such intestate ancestor, yet it will be impossible to conclude from thence, that inheritance is established by any universal law arising from a general consent of all mankind. Each nation may have introduced inheritance amongst themselves, by their own particular consent, though all nations, as one great collective body of individuals, have not introduced such a claim amongst one another by a general consent. To determine whether a claim of inheritance, though such claim prevails in all nations, was the effect of a general consent of all mankind as one collective body, or of a particular consent of each nation for itself, we must consider how this claim operates, or whether there is any such claim at all, when the two parties, the claimant and the ancestor, are members of different communities. For certainly a claim of inheritance will hold universally, and operate uniformly, as well where these two parties are members of different communities, as where they are members of the same community; if it was introduced by the general consent of all mankind, establishing an universal law for all, and not by the particular consent or appointment of each nation establishing laws for itself.

The method of introducing general property in land, by occupancy in the gross, will naturally prevent a stranger, that is, a person who is no member of the community, in which such property is vested, from inheriting by will; and much more will it prevent him from inheriting by right of intestate succession. And where there is such a natural bar, the consent of mankind must be express, or at least the general use and practice of mankind must be very clear and uniform, before we can have any reason to conclude such bar to have been removed. But if on the contrary we find, as upon inquiry we should find, that in many, or rather in most nations, aliens or strangers are not allowed to inherit land; the conclusion must be, that inheritance, of land at least, is the effect of civil laws, and not of any positive law established by universal consent.

The property of individuals in moveable goods, as has been already observed, is more unlimited in respect of the disposal of it, than their property in land. But even such goods, in respect of inheritance, are accidentally subjected to the community, in whose territories, that is upon whose land, they are found; the claimants can by this accident be hindered from fetching them away, unless upon such terms, as the community has established. Now if all persons, who claim in an intestate

* Grot. Chap. VI. § V.

succession were to take such goods as these, according to the same rules, in the same order and under the same limitations, in whatever territories these goods are found, whether within the territories to which they themselves belong, or in any other whatsoever; such an uniform claim might lead one to suspect, that it had been introduced and established by the common consent of all mankind. But if, as the fact is, the rules, the order, and the limitations of succession to moveable goods, are determined by the civil laws of the community, within whose territories such goods are found, and the claimant must take them in such manner as those laws appoint, which laws and which manner are different in different countries; the obvious conclusion from hence is, that the claim of inheritance being under the regulations of the civil law of each community, is not the effect of universal agreement, but of civil law only. Distinct communities, as having a general property in the land of their respective territories, seem to have agreed in this only, to take the advantage, which such general property gives them, of excluding all from the claim of inheritance, unless they are willing to derive this claim from the laws of the community, and to enjoy the benefit of it as an effect of those laws.

In the introduction of intestate successions a regard is had to a man's personal duty.

VI. As far as a man has a right to dispose of his goods by will, he has an opportunity of doing good to others, without any inconvenience to himself; and since it is every person's duty to do all the good he can, whoever does not take care at his death to give away what he has in his power, and can no longer enjoy himself, does not discharge his duty so well as he ought. * If the law in introducing and establishing intestate succession proceeds upon the principle of doing a man's duty for him where he has neglected it, of taking care to do that good for him which he might have done himself, but has not done; we may trace out the persons, who, in successions established upon this principle, will naturally inherit an intestate's goods, and may point out the order in which the claims of those persons will take place. Though the right of inheriting is introduced and established by positive institution, yet this institution, like all others, will have a natural operation; and if we know the principle, upon which the institution proceeded, we may from thence be enabled to judge what its natural operation will be.

A man's children stand first in the succession.

VII. If the law introduced intestate inheritance merely with a view to the discharging a man's duty for him, where he had neglected to discharge it himself, the persons to whom this principle will direct us, in the disposition of an intestate's goods, are they, to whom he ought to have been kind. And the order in which such persons are to claim, will be determined by the different degrees of kindness, which the intestate owed them.

† The first duty of kindness which a man owes, is to his children: he owes them the duty not only of maintaining them, but likewise of doing his best endeavours towards putting them into such a condition as may make their life easy and comfortable to them. They are the principal objects of his regard, or have of all other persons the highest reason to expect his favour and bounty. Indeed, as he was the immediate cause of their coming into the world, it can scarce be looked upon as a mat-

* Grotius, Lib. II. Cap. VII. § III.

† Grot. ibid. § IV.

ter of favour and bounty in him, to make them as happy as he can, whilst they continue in it: he might rather very justly be charged with cruelty, if he was to do otherwise. This then being the principal instance of kindness that every person, who has children, is obliged to, their claim to inherit his goods, upon the principle already laid down, will stand first if he dies intestate.

*What we say of children, in the first degree of descent, may likewise be applied to those of the second or third degree, that is, to a man's grandchildren, or great-grandchildren. Where the immediate parent of such descendants is dead, and cannot inherit the goods of the grandfather or great-grandfather; the children, upon their remote parent's dying intestate, inherit his goods; not only because they stand in the place of their father, who would have inherited if he had been alive, but because it is the duty of the remote parent, as the remote cause of their existence, to show them all the kindness in his power.

Children why preferred to parents in intestate successions.

VIII. †But suppose it should happen, as it sometimes does, that a person who dies intestate, should leave children, and that his parents likewise should survive him. As he owed a duty to his children, so he owed a duty to his parents; his gratitude for the kindness, which he received from them in their bringing him up, would oblige him to make some return of kindness to them; it would in particular oblige him to provide for them as well as he could; if by age or infirmity, or any other accident, they were rendered incapable of providing for themselves. But then it is to be observed, that there is a natural reason, why parents should be left out in an intestate succession, at least where the estate is of ancient inheritance. Such estates may come to a man from some remoter relation by will; but the usual course of them is, that they come to him from his parents. If therefore the rule for disposing of them, where a man dies intestate, will be most natural, when it is most agreeable to the usual course of such estates; since the general presumption is that they came from his parents, the consequence will be, that in a general rule for disposing of them, as his parents cannot be supposed to be in existence, so no regard can be had to them. This rule may, by a reason taken from the common course of nature, be extended so far as to take no notice at all of a man's parents in any intestate succession, where he leaves children. In the common course of nature a man's parents, especially if he has lived long enough to have children of his own, do not usually survive him. If therefore his parents are entirely left out of an intestate succession, where he leaves children, it may be upon a general presumption, that he has then no parents in being.

The same principle governs the succession where an intestate leaves no children.

IX. ‡When an intestate person leaves no children, we are, in the disposition of his goods, to consider whether they came to him by inheritance, or were of his own acquisition. In either case a regard to his duty, considered as the principle upon which the claim of inheritance was introduced, is to govern the succession and to point out who shall be his heir. Such goods, as came to him from his ancestors, laid him under an obligation of gratitude to them, from whom they came. If they descended from his father, the return of gratitude is due to him; if from

* Grot. Lib. II. Cap. VII. § V. † Grot. ibid. § V. ‡ Grot. ibid. § IX.

his mother, it is due to her. And yet, though the duty which governs the succession, immediately respects his parents, some reasons already assigned will serve to show us, why they should be excluded from inheriting in their own persons; if the inheritance is ordered by such general rules as the course of nature would suggest to us. There is a natural presumption, that a man's parents do not survive him; and though such estates as we are now speaking of, might possibly have come to him by will from some other ancestor, and not from his immediate parents, yet the more usual descent in estates of ancient inheritance, is from the parents themselves. And since such general rules, as are to govern these successions, are to be taken from what is commonly the case, it follows that the parents of the intestate persons are very reasonably left out of the succession, where the estate to be disposed of is ancient inheritance, upon account of the general presumption, that such estate came from the parents, and consequently that his parents do not survive him. As it is presumed therefore not to be in his power to pay the debt of gratitude to them in their own persons, he can only pay it to their representatives; that is, to those whom his parents, if they had been living, would have valued in the next place to themselves. These representatives are the children of his parents, or his own brothers and sisters. The duty of gratitude, therefore, which he owed to his parents, for the estate of ancient inheritance, received from them, will point out his brothers and sisters to be his heirs.

But suppose that no brothers or sisters survive him, and consequently that it is not in his power to make a return to his parents in the persons of their representatives; we must then go another step backwards: the gratitude, which he owed to his ancestors, for the inheritance descended from them, would lead him to his remoter parents, to his grandfathers or grandmothers. However as there is more reason to suppose them to be dead than his immediate parents, he could only show his gratitude to these remoter parents in the persons of their representatives, who are his uncles or his aunts.

If there are no such representatives to take, in an intestate succession, the obligation of gratitude ceases, and estates of ancient inheritance are disposed of in the same manner with estates of a man's own acquisition. And we are next to consider in what manner the principle of doing a man's duty for him will lead the law to dispose of such estates as these when he dies without children.

*What a man has acquired himself is not chargeable with any debt of gratitude, as it did not descend to him by the favour of any one. So that in these circumstances he has no other duty to regard, but that of kindness or good will in general. Now the ties of friendship are often much closer in a man's own opinion, than those of blood; we have often a stronger inclination to be kind to our friend, than to our relations. But as the connections of friendship are arbitrary and accidental, whilst those of blood are natural and uniform; the former cannot be reduced to the same rule or come under the same general notice, that the latter do. Upon this account, whatever arbitrary or accidental affections a man, whilst he was alive, may have had for his friend, the most natural presumption is, that he loved his relations better than any one else, and

* Grot. Lib. II. Cap. VII. § X.

that he ought to have shown his kindness and good will to those in the first place, who were the nearest to him by blood. These, therefore, upon the principle already laid down, have the first claim to inherit what estate he has acquired himself.

Philo is mistaken in his interpretation of the Mosaic law.

X. The law of Moses says, *" Thou shalt speak unto the children of Israel, saying, if a man die, and have no son, then ye shall cause his inheritance to pass unto his daughter; and if he have no daughter, then ye shall give his inheritance unto his brethren; and if he have no brethren, then ye shall give his inheritance unto his father's brethren; and if his father have no brethren, then ye shall give his inheritance unto his kinsman, that is next to him of his family."

Philo maintains, that this law of intestate succession does not exclude the intestate's father: †" for it would be senseless to imagine, that the uncle should be allowed to succeed the brother's son, as a near kinsman to his father, and yet the father himself be denied the same privilege. But since, as this writer goes on, the law of nature appoints that children should be heirs to their parents, and not parents to their children, Moses passed this case over in silence, as ominous and unlucky, and contrary to all pious wishes and desires; lest the father and mother should seem to be gainers by the untimely death of their children, when they ought rather to be afflicted at it. Yet by allowing the inheritance to uncles, he indirectly admits the claim of the parents, in order both to preserve decency, and to prevent the estate from going to a stranger."

He here allows, that in the order of nature, parents are excluded from succeeding to their children; and this, one would think, is a sufficient defence of the law of Moses. He had however another point in view; he did not so much design to defend the law, as to explain it for the benefit of parents, and to show that the law, though it does not name them, allows them to succeed to the estates of their children. But any one who reads the passage here cited from the law of Moses, and compares it with what occurs in the same law upon the like subject, will find reason to think that the legislator has a particular view to estates of ancient inheritance. And we have already seen, that the general presumption of such estates coming to a man from his parents is a sufficient ground for leaving the parents out of the succession.

There is one disposition made by this law of succession, which differs from the general rules, that have been mentioned above; and that is the disposition of a man's inheritance to his sons, exclusive of his daughters; so that his daughters have no claim, unless he dies without sons. This part of the law was relative to the civil polity of the Jews; and the intent of it was to obtain a purpose, which the legislator had in view, of maintaining an equality of fortune amongst the people, by keeping the same quantity of land not only within the same tribe, but likewise within the same family. Now if the daughters had shared with the sons, they by marrying into other families would have carried a great part of the inheritance out of their own. The law therefore postpones their claim, and only gives them a claim in case there are no sons. And even then, though it cannot obtain its first intention of keeping the inheritance within the same family, it takes care to keep it within the same tribe, by enjoining, ‡ that

* Num. XXVII. 8, 9, &c. † De vit. Mos. III. page 689. ‡ Num. XXXVI. 6.

such heiresses should marry to whom they think best, only to the family of the tribe of their father.

Order of succession may be varied by civil laws.

XI. Though the order of succession, which we have been describing, is called a natural one, yet it is not for that reason so fixed and settled, as to make it unnatural or unreasonable for civil laws to call the relations of an intestate to inherit his goods, in a different order. If this is a natural order at all, it is only so upon these two suppositions; first, that civil laws have established intestate inheritance; and secondly, that in such establishment they proceeded upon the sole principle of taking care to discharge a man's duties of kindness for him, where he had neglected to discharge them himself. But civil laws have commonly some other principles in view, besides this, such as are relative either to the civil polity of the state itself, or to the conditions upon which the individuals hold their property. So that, notwithstanding the law may design in general to show that kindness to an intestate's relations, which he ought to have shown them, by disposing of his fortunes amongst them, a regard to those other principles may lead it to dispense this kindness in a different order from what we have been describing. We have just now taken notice of an instance of this sort in the Mosaic law, which though it calls a man's children to inherit in preference to all others, as they are the persons to whom he owed the chief regard, yet in view to the design of preserving the same lands in the same tribe, and as much as might be in the same family, it postpones the claim of the daughters and gives them no share in the inheritance, where there are any sons. Upon the whole, as it is an argument of a shallow insight into matters of this sort, to charge the civil law of any country with being arbitrary and unreasonable, where in the order of intestate successions they deviate from such rules as would arise out of that natural affection, which every man is supposed to have for his relations, according to their nearness to him in blood; so on the other hand, no reasons that can be assigned for such deviations will be satisfactory, unless they are taken either from the particular civil constitution of the country, and the purposes which such a civil constitution has in view, or else from the conditions upon which every individual who is a member of the civil community, is supposed to receive and to hold his property.

The succession of children may be cut off by disherison.

XII. *If a man by any public or solemn act has disinherited his children in his life-time, this act will naturally prevent their claim to his goods, where he dies intestate. For his declared intentions concerning his property are in effect his will or testament; so that a child thus disinherited, has no more claim to succeed to the estate of his parent, than he would have had, if such parent had expressly excluded him by will. Such an act of the parent in his life-time, or such a will made by him at his death, are contrary to the duty of a parent, if the child had not been guilty of any crime, which might deserve such usage. But if the parent had a full right to dispose of his goods as he pleased, the act of disherison, though it is contrary to his duty, will not be void, without the interposition of the civil law. It is, however, as we have before observed, very reasonable, that the civil law should interpose in these

* Grot. Lib. II. Cap. VII. § VII.

cases, and set aside his will, or make void his act of disherison, so as to dispose of his estate in such a manner, as he ought in duty to have disposed of it himself.

Uncertainty of birth hinders a child from succeeding to an intestate parent.

XIII. *There is a second exception against a child's succeeding to an intestate father; and that is, where proper evidence is wanting, that the person whose goods are in question was its father. Because if there is not sufficient ground to presume that the child is his own, it does not appear to have been his duty to provide for such child. Now the ground for presuming the child to be his own is, that it was born in marriage. For since by marriage the wife is placed under the inspection, and is in the custody of her husband, it is reasonable to suppose that he has kept all other men from her, and consequently that the children which she bears are his own. Nor does it appear that where the law has established a right of inheritance, such children could claim in virtue of their fathers acknowledging them by any public act, unless the same law had allowed of the validity of such acknowledgement. For instance, where adoption is allowed of, a man might as well adopt such children born out of marriage as any other persons; and then the effect of his having adopted them would be, that they might inherit as his children. But where adoption is an act unknown to the law, an established right of inheritance extends to them only, to whom, in the eye of the law, the intestate owed a duty; and these are such only as are known, by the legal evidence of a marriage with their mother, to have been his children.

Infants, ideots and madmen, naturally incapable of property.

XIV. Now we are speaking of the claim which children have, of succeeding to the estate of their intestate parent; it may be proper to inquire how far such children, if they are infants, and how far infants in general, are capable of making a derivative acquisition of property. I say a derivative acquisition, because I suppose it to be evident, from what has been said already, that they cannot possibly make an original acquisition. And since the case of madmen and of ideots is nearly the same with that of infants, we may take this opportunity of considering how far any of them are capable of acquiring property derivatively. No derivative acquisition, as has been shown already, can be made without the intention, design, or consent of the party who makes it, and without some declaration or notification of such intention, either by words or by actions. But since there can be no such intention, and no such notification where there is no use of reason; it follows, that infants who are not yet come to the use of reason, that ideots, who never will arrive at it, and that madmen, who have lost it, are naturally incapable of acquiring property.

There is indeed one question relating to madmen, in which infants or ideots are not concerned. Infants cannot acquire property, whilst their natural incapacity continues, and ideots can never acquire it, as long as they live: we cannot, therefore, ask whether they are capable of keeping or holding property, after they have acquired it. But since men, who were once of sound understanding and have passed their infancy, may lose their senses afterwards and become mad, we may ask

* Grot. Lib. II. Cap. VII. § VIII.

whether they, by thus losing the use of their reason, cease to have property in those goods, which they had before acquired. And certainly where the design of keeping property in goods ceases, where there is no intention of excluding others from the use or possession of them, the right of property is at an end; an intention to keep up this claim is as necessary to maintain it, as an intention to acquire such a claim is to begin it. But since this intention ceases with the use of reason, madmen by the law of nature are no more capable of keeping property than they are of acquiring it.

Law of nations wrongly explained by Grotius.

XV. * Grotius imagines, that infants, ideots and madmen are made capable of accepting and of retaining property by the common consent of mankind, which considers them as part of the human species; and by this fiction, that is, by considering them as part of the human species, they are looked upon to have so much reason, as will render them capable, like the rest of the species, to accept and to hold property. But then he observes, that though human laws, such for instance as what he calls the law of nations derived from the common consent of mankind, may suppose what is different from nature, yet they cannot suppose what is contrary to it. The right, therefore, of property in infants, or ideots or madmen, as far as it depends upon such a law, can extend only to the acquisition and possession of things, but not to the use of them, or to the power of alienating them. Now it does not appear to me, that a supposition of their capacity to use or to alienate their property is at all more contrary to nature, than a supposition of their capacity to take and to retain it. Reason is as necessary in one of these acts as it is in the other: he, that has not the use of reason, cannot indeed alienate his property, but neither can he acquire property; and if it is contrary to nature to suppose him to have the use of reason for one purpose, it must be as contrary to nature to suppose him to have the use of it for the other purpose. Since therefore it is granted, that the common consent of mankind cannot, without going contrary to nature, suppose infants or ideots or madmen, to have so much use of reason as to make them capable of using or of alienating their property, we may reasonably conclude, that neither is it any common consent proceeding upon this principle, which makes them capable of taking and holding it. Indeed an incapacity of using or of alienating is inconsistent with the notion of property, unless we suppose that property to be a limited one; because full property in a thing implies a power of using it, and disposing of it, in what manner we please. If, therefore, both by the law of nature, and by this supposed fiction of the law of nations, infants and ideots and madmen are incapable of using and of alienating goods, they must be deemed equally incapable of having full property in them.

Custody of the law supplies the place of property.

XVI. It is obvious to ask here, what is meant when we speak of the estate or the goods of infants or ideots or madmen? If they have no property in such estate or goods, why do we call them theirs? and since, if they have not property in the things so called, those things are either the property of no man, or where inheritance has been established, are the property of the next heir, who is under no incapacity; the next question will be,

* Grot. Lib. II. Cap. III. § VI.

why may not any one seize upon such estate, as being become common; or, however, why may not the next heir consider it as his own, if there is any such heir? Certainly this might be done, if no positive law interposed to hinder both the next heir in succession from entering in his own right, and to hinder all other persons from seizing upon such things as would belong to an infant or ideot or madman, if they were capable of property. But then these laws do not interpose by a fiction, that infants or ideots or madmen, as parts of the human species, are capable of acquiring and holding property; they interpose by taking those things into their custody, or by guarding them for the benefit of him, who would be the owner of them, if he was capable of property. And thus all other persons are prevented from making any acquisition of them, not in virtue of any supposed exclusive right in him, but merely by the authority and prohibition of such law.

In the mean time the things are called his, not because they are so, but because the effect of the law in respect of all other persons is the same with the effect of an exclusive right in him. I say in respect of all other persons; for in respect of himself, the effect is not the same; an exclusive right of property either real or supposed would give him the power not only of keeping, but likewise of using or of alienating his goods; whereas the mere custody of the law, though it hinders others from seizing upon them, does not produce any such power in the person, for whom they are kept.

When things are thus kept for the benefit of infants, they are in the custody of the law, till those infants arrive at the use of reason, and then their property begins. When they are kept in the same manner for the benefit of madmen, the custody is precarious and temporary; for since madmen are frequently known to recover the use of their reason, and are therefore always deemed capable of recovering it, their property can be in the guardianship of the law only till this event happens; and since it is uncertain at what time it will happen, the custody of their property is precarious. But when things are kept for the benefit of ideots, the custody is perpetual, that is, it lasts as long as the ideot lives, because ideots are such, as never had and never can have the use of reason.

CHAPTER VIII.

OF PRESCRIPTION.

I. *What Prescription is, and on what founded.*—II. *Why long possession is necessary to claim by prescription.*—III. *Why uninterrupted possession is necessary.*—IV. *Why honest possession is necessary.*—V. *Prescription extends to incorporeal things.*—VI. *Objection to the natural foundation of prescription.*—VII. *Some grounds to believe prescription to have been established by an universal consent.*—VIII. *What length of time gives an equitable claim by prescription.*—IX. *Prescription holds against persons unborn.*

What prescription is, and on what founded.

I. Prescription is a right to a thing acquired by long, honest, and uninterrupted possession; though before such possession some other person and not the possessor was the owner of it.

*This right in the possessor is founded upon the presumed dereliction of the proprietor. It is not indeed agreeable to the law of nature, that any moral effect, such for instance as the loss or the acquisition of a right, should follow upon the bare intention of the mind; but when the intention either of parting with, or of acquiring a right is sufficiently declared, it is natural, that such an intention should produce its effect.

Now our intentions may be made known either by words or acts. We may, indeed, falsify in our words, or we may dissemble in our behaviour; it is possible, that we may say one thing, when we mean another, or that we may behave in such a manner as to deceive mankind, and make them believe our designs to be different from what they are. There is, therefore, no strict and necessary connection between our intentions, and the signs whereby we testify them. It must, however, be allowed, that our acts may be as certain marks of our intention, as our words; which is all we need contend for. Thus we may release a debtor, not only by a verbal declaration, but by delivering up or by cancelling his bond; and in like manner what we throw away is as plainly relinquished, as if we had declared our design to relinquish it in so many words.

The acts, by which we may notify our intentions, are either positive or negative; that is, our intentions may appear either from our actions or our omissions. †When any thing is transacted, in which a man is concerned, if he is present at the time, and does not contradict it, the presumption from his silence is, that he consents to it. If goods are shipwrecked, or cattle have strayed, and the owner neither sends out to look for them, nor endeavours by any means to recover them, the most obvious construction of his neglect is, that he despairs of finding them, and disregards or gives up any claim, that he had to them. In like manner, if he suffers another to keep possession of his goods, without laying claim to them, when he both knows where they are, and is at liberty to claim them, this neglect is fairly presumed to be a mark of his intention to part with them; and when the owner has thus relin-

* Grot. Lib. II. Cap. VI. § I, II, III, IV, V. † Num. XXX. 4. 11.

quished them, they become the property of the possessor, as the first occupant of them.

It is necessary, however, to remember that in this, and in all other instances, where a man's neglect to claim is deemed a mark of his intention to relinquish his goods, it is requisite that his silence should not arise either from ignorance or from fear. If he does not claim his goods, either because he does not know what are his goods or who is in possession of them, or because he is under some restraint and is afraid to claim them; his silence in such circumstances can be no mark of his intention to part with them: such silence plainly arises from another cause, and therefore necessarily requires another construction.

Why long possession necessary to claim by prescription.

II. From what has been said it will appear, that prescription cannot proceed but upon long possession: not because length of time operates as an efficient cause to produce a right in the possessor; but because it is necessary in order to make the owner's silence a reasonable ground to presume that he intends to relinquish his property. If his neglect is of short continuance, it may be owing either to his ignorance or his fear: he might not know what things he had a right to, or he might not know who was in possession of them; or if he knew both these particulars, yet still he might be afraid to make his claim. But in the course of a long time, it is reasonable to imagine, that he might have come to the knowledge both of his claims and of the person who is in possession of what belongs to him, and that he might likewise by some means or other be able to remove his fears, or at least to find some opportunity of declaring his right without any danger. Length of time, therefore, determines his silence or neglect to be a mark of his intention to relinquish his right, as it affords a reasonable presumption, that such silence or neglect was not owing either to ignorance or to fear.

Why uninterrupted possession necessary to claim by prescription.

III. Uninterrupted possession is plainly necessary to give the possessor a right by prescription, because his right depends upon the presumptive dereliction of the owner, and there can be no presumption of his having relinquished, where by any claim of his he has interrupted the possession.

Why honest possession necessary to claim by prescription.

IV. It is to be farther observed, that prescription cannot proceed without honest possession. If the possessor came dishonestly by the goods, though his possession is ever so long or ever so quiet, he acquires no claim to them. We may several ways become honestly possessed of what belongs to another man, without having any right to it, when we are first possessed of it. Suppose, for instance, that the thing has been given us by any one, who was not the true owner of it, though we thought he was; suppose we have purchased it of any one, who had obtained it by force or by fraud, without our knowing how he obtained it; or suppose we have found it, and have endeavoured without success to find out the true owner; in any of these cases our possession is honest, though the thing possessed is not our own. Where possession of a thing begins after such a manner as this, without any dishonesty in the possessor, and has been continued for a considerable length of time without being interrupted, it will give him a right to the thing. But if his possession was dishonest in the first instance, he can acquire no such right. All dishonest possession implies, that some fraud or some violence was made use of in obtaining it. Where fraud is made use of, the owner is certainly ignorant of something, which he ought to know; and where violence is made use of, the owner is certainly in some fear. Now length of time affords only a presumption, that the ignorance or fear of the owner are removed; and consequently, since no presumption can prevail against a certainty, no length of time can so far take away the ignorance or the fear of the owner, in the case of dishonest possession, as to render his silence a sufficient sign of his intention to quit his claim. As his ignorance or his fear were certain at first, the same ignorance or the same fear must be supposed to continue till they are certainly removed. Length of time affords only a presumption, that they are removed. Therefore, length of time does not remove them sufficiently. But since as long as his silence is understood to arise either from ignorance or from fear, it cannot reasonably be looked upon as a sign of his intention to relinquish his right, and upon that account the right of the possessor cannot take place; it follows, that no possession, though for a great length of time and without interruption, can give a right by prescription, if it began dishonestly.

Prescription extends to incorporeal things.

V. When we say, that things may be acquired by prescription, we must be understood to mean, not only corporeal, but likewise incorporeal things. Jurisdiction or sovereignty may be acquired in this manner, as well as land or moveable goods. Laws may be repealed, customs may be established into laws, civil constitutions of government may be altered, subjects may enlarge their privileges, governors may extend their prerogative, not only by express appointment or compact, but likewise by such a tacit agreement as this of prescription. But it is not necessary to enter into this matter now, because there will be a more proper opportunity, when we come to explain the law of nature, as it respects civil societies.

Objection to the natural foundation of prescription.

VI. The principle, upon which the claim of prescription is founded, according to the law of nature, as far as we have yet explained it, is only presumption or conjecture. *The owner of the thing, which the present possessor claims, is presumed to have quitted his right to it, merely because he has been silent about it, and has neglected to claim it for a long time. Mankind indeed might by common consent establish such a silence into a standing mark of an intention to relinquish, in the same manner as, by a like common consent, they have affixed a certain and determinate signification to words, which in themselves, without such consent and establishment, have no signification at all. But without an establishment or consent of this kind, the owner's silence alone, though of ever so long a continuance, would be too precarious a mark of his intention to relinquish his right for any certain and uniform claim of the possessor to be founded upon it. Mankind, as far as we can learn what their inclination is by constant experience, are generally disposed to keep what they have gotten, and not to relinquish it without good and sufficient reasons for so doing. Any neglect therefore to claim what is their own, if we would interpret it agreeably to the nature of mankind, as we learn from constant experience what that nature is, cannot well be looked upon as a

* Grot. Lib. II. Cap. VI. § VIII.

mark of their intention to relinquish their right, unless some other good and sufficient reasons appear, why they should relinquish it: their general temper and inclination will rather lead us to suppose, that such neglect or silence may have been owing to ignorance or fear.

To support the right of prescription upon natural principles, it is sometimes explained in a different manner. This right is said not to take place, till a man has been in possession of the thing claimed for time immemorial, and that as no other proprietor can then appear, besides the present possessor, he alone is to be looked upon as the true proprietor; because a claimant, who does not appear, and a claimant, who does not exist, are in a moral view the same thing. Now if by time immemorial, is here meant such a length of time, that no memory can possibly go farther back, the possessor of the thing must, after such time immemorial, be undoubtedly the proprietor of it; but then he cannot well be said to have a right to it by prescription; because his right, upon this supposition, will not differ at all from a right by first occupancy. For certainly where there neither are nor can be any traces of any other owner, besides himself, he must necessarily be looked upon as the first owner. But if by time immemorial any time less than this is meant; if there are any traces of a former owner, though such former owner has not claimed for many years, it will be as difficult, upon this principle of possession for time immemorial, to make out the possessor's right to the thing so possessed, as upon any other, without having recourse to some positive establishment.

Some grounds to believe prescription to have been established by an universal law.

VII. The circumstances of mankind after the introduction of property, and after possession had been long lost by the old proprietor, and had long continued in some other person, would make such a claim as this of prescription, generally beneficial. For without such a claim, the difficulty of ascertaining the right of either party would be the occasion of endless disputes and of great hardships. Disputes arising, after possession on one side had been many years uninterrupted, could not easily be decided with fairness and honesty; because it would be difficult either for the successor or the other claimant to clear up their title. And it would be a hardship to turn the possessor out of what he had quietly enjoyed, till it was in a manner grown to his patrimony, especially since the former proprietor cannot in general be supposed to want it much, as he had been able to live so long without it, and to provide for himself by some other means. The usefulness of a claim is indeed no proof, that such claim has in fact been established. To prove this we must have recourse to the common opinion of mankind, as it appears in their constant practice. And since, when we look into their practice, we find, that not only such persons as are members of the same civil society, but those likewise, who belong to different communities, plead prescription against one another; nay, since we find that when one nation has been long possessed of what did formerly belong to some other nation, the possessor maintains his right to the thing by a like plea; and that such a plea, if it can be well supported, is generally allowed to be a good one; we have reason to conclude, that the claim of prescription has been introduced and established by a like common consent with that which introduced and established the claim of property. But because prescription is a sort of limitation or exception in the right of property, it is necessary to look a little farther than the bare establishment of such a right in order to see how we can reconcile it with the claim of property. And it is in this part of the question, that we have recourse to the principles already explained, to the presumption that he, who is silent for any great length of time and does not claim his right, is disposed to relinquish it.

What length of time gives an equitable claim by prescription.

VIII. It may perhaps, without some express appointment, be difficult to determine for what length of time a person must be in possession of a thing, to give him a claim to it by prescription. The foundation of this claim, as we have already explained it, will show us, that the time must be long enough for presuming the former owner of the thing was not hindered from putting in his claim either by ignorance or by fear, but must have had frequent opportunities of knowing both what his right is, and who was in possession of it, and frequent opportunities likewise of releasing himself from any restraints, which might have forced him against his will to be silent as to his claim. Possession however for time immemorial, if the meaning of the words is rightly explained, seems to be the most equitable time of possession for acquiring a prescriptive right.

The most obvious meaning of time immemorial is a time of such duration, that the memory of no man living can of itself, when unassisted by any external evidences, go back beyond it. A possession of no longer continuance than this would give a right by prescription too soon; because by the help of written evidences, the memory of man is assisted to go back into such periods of time, as have been long past; and such evidences will frequently show where the possession of the former owner ceased, and by what means the claimant by prescription got possession at first and continued it afterwards. But then on the other hand, if by possession for time immemorial we mean nothing less than so long a possession, that not only the unassisted memory of persons now living cannot go farther backwards, but likewise, that no written evidences, no memory assisted by the ordinary method of recording facts which are past, can make out any traces of any other proprietor, besides the present possessor; the claim of prescription would then be useless, and would not differ at all from the claim of first occupancy. For where would be the use of it, if there was no other claimant besides the present possessor? and what other claimant could there be, if there were no traces at all to be found of any right in any other person besides himself? He would upon this supposition have an indisputable title to the thing which he possesses, as the first occupant of it, because he appears to be the only owner that it ever had.

There is, however, a middle sense of time immemorial. If we understand it to mean so long a time, that though a former owner may be able to make out some sort of title, yet he cannot either by the memory of any person now living, or by any record of past facts, make out a clear and undoubted title to the thing in question; possession, for such a length of time as this, may fairly determine the thing to belong to the present possessor. A prescription gained by possession for a time thus limited, will be different, as it ought to be, from a right of first occupancy, and it will likewise be of benefit to mankind by deciding controversies, not easily to be decided otherwise, without taking place so soon as to be in danger of barring the claim of the true owner. Its use consists in barring a doubtful right; and its equity is preserved by a proper regard to all such rights as can be made out by the memory of man, when assisted by written evidences.

Prescription holds against persons unborn.

IX. What we claim by prescription, or in consequence of our having been possessed of it without interruption for time immemorial, must commonly have been in possession either of ourselves or our ancestors, for a longer time than the extent of any one person's life. So that prescription must most frequently be pleaded, not so much against the former owner as against his heirs. Now for great part of the time whilst this possession lasted, those heirs were not in being; they were not born when our own possession began, and possibly were not born, when our ancestor's possession had continued long enough to give a prescriptive right. *Shall we allow, therefore, that the claim of the ancestor, which was set aside by our long possession, will revive again in the person of the heir? If we allow this, prescription will be of little use; it will only serve to lay a dispute asleep for a while, but will suffer it to revive hereafter, when the question concerning the respective claims of the former owner and of the present possessor will have become more intricate, in proportion as we are farther removed from the original evidence, by which that dispute might have been settled. Shall we, therefore, on the other hand, affirm that a prescriptive right will bar the claim not only of him who first lost possession, but of them likewise, who are descended from him, and were not born at the time, when such prescription was going on and began to take place? Before we affirm this, we should consider by whose silence or neglect the right of property is lost. If it is lost by the silence of the heirs, who were unborn, a prescriptive right would have no foundation in reason, that might reconcile it with the notion of property. It is absurd to construe the silence of those, who were unborn, as a mark of their intention to relinquish their rights; because their silence will not only bear, but requires another construction; they were therefore silent and did not claim, because they were not born, and could not claim. But if we maintain, that they who were unborn, lost their right, not by their own silence or neglect, but by the silence or neglect of their ancestors; prescription against them seems to be founded in injustice; it is an injury to deprive them of what belongs to them, for the neglect of their ancestors, a neglect in which they were no way concerned.

What shall we say therefore? Shall we take away the benefit of prescription, by allowing that it does not hold good against the posterity of the former owner? or shall we, on the other hand, maintain, that it does hold good against his posterity as well as against himself, and so either make the claim absurd, by saying that the silence of his posterity, when they could not speak, is a mark of their intention to relinquish their right; or else shall we make it unjust by saying that they forfeit their right by the neglect of their ancestor? The truth is, that prescription holds good, not only against the ancestor, but against his posterity; not from their neglect, who were unborn, but from the neglect of those who went before them. And by taking this part, we have only the justice of such a claim by prescription to defend. It will be no very difficult

* Grot. Lib. II. Cap. VI. § IX.

matter to defend this part of the alternative, where inheritance has never been established; because the descendants of a man can have no injury done them in being kept out from inheriting what they had no right to inherit. But suppose a general right of inheritance to have been established; yet still the claim of prescription will stand clear of injustice. No injury can be done to a person, where no right is taken from him. But the posterity of a man, who loses his claim by the prescription of another, are not deprived of any right. Before they were born, they had no right at all; for as things, which are not in existence, have no natural qualities, so persons who are not in existence, have no moral qualities; and amongst other moral qualities they have no rights. If then the thing in question was lost by their ancestor before they were born, no right is taken from them by their being barred from claiming what he had so lost; because they have no right to inherit any thing from him, which is not his own at the time of his death; and whatever he has lost by long neglect, and another has acquired by long possession, has ceased to be his own. No injury was done to them, whilst the claim was acquiring; because then they had no right in the thing, if they were not in existence, and lost that right by their own silence, if they were in existence. And no injury is done to them by the possessor, after the claim is acquired, if he still keeps the thing, because it then belongs to him, and not to them; since they can have no pretence to inherit from their ancestor, what such ancestor himself had no right to at the time of his death.

CHAPTER IX.

OF THE OBLIGATIONS ARISING FROM PROPERTY.

I. *Property of one man obliges others not to hinder him in enjoying what is his own.*—II. *The right of property produces an obligation to restitution.*—III. *The natural fruits or advantages of another's property are to be restored.*—IV. *Honest possessor not obliged to damage himself by restitution.*—V. *No obligation to restitution where the thing has perished.*—VI. *Obligation to restitution does not extend to all advantages made by the possessor.*—VII. *No obligation to restitution of fruits neglected.*—VIII. *Or where a thing given is given away again.*—IX. *Or to restore the overplus of price where a thing bought is sold again.*—X. *Restitution to be made without reimbursement.*—XI. *Goods to be restored and not returned to the seller.*

Property of one man obliges others not to hinder him in enjoying what is his own.

I. The first and most obvious obligation, that we are under, towards any person upon account of his property in a thing either moveable or immoveable, is to suffer him quietly to enjoy it, and to dispose of it, in what manner he pleases, without attempting by force or by fraud, either to take it from him, or in any respect to make it worse. This obligation plainly arises out of the notion of property; for his right to exclude us from meddling at all with a thing would have no effect, or would be in reality no right; if we, notwithstanding such right, were at liberty to take the thing away from him, or to hinder him in the use and enjoyment of it, or by any means to impair and waste it.

The right of property produces an obligation to restitution.

II. *As the right of property, which any person has in a thing, obliges us not to take that thing from him dishonestly, so it obliges us to restore it to him, or not to keep it from him, when we have, even by any honest means, gotten it in our possession. When without any knowledge of the truth or any bad design on our part, a thing is given us, which belonged to some other person and not to the giver; when we purchase what some one else, and not the seller had a right in; when we find a thing, the owner of which is not known at the time of finding it; in such cases as those our possession of the thing is honest, till we have found out the proprietor; but as soon as we have found him, we are obliged, in virtue of his property, to restore the thing to him. For if we knowingly and designedly keep him out of what he has a right to, we do him the same harm, and consequently are guilty of the same injustice as if we had taken it from him.

The natural fruits or advantages of another's property are to be restored.

III. From this obligation to restore any person's property, when it is in our hands, another obligation is derived; an obligation to restore the natural fruits, produce or advantages, which have arisen from it, whilst we were in possession of it; because the natural produce of a thing, and all the natural advantages arising from it belong as much to the proprietor, as the thing itself. But it will be necessary, in determining questions of this sort, to distinguish between the fruits which come from the thing itself, and those which are produced by the labour and at the expense of the occupier. The former are what I call its natural produce; and of these only we speak, when we maintain, that there is the same obligation to restore the fruits of a thing, as to restore the thing itself; for certainly my property in a thing can never give me a right to another person's labour. Suppose the thing possessed to be common field land, which produces nothing, unless it is manured, tilled and sowed; if the honest possessor has a crop of corn upon the ground, at the time of discovering the true owner; he would be under no obligation of restitution as to the corn; because it was produced by his labour and at his expense: the corn is not the natural produce of the thing, which the other has a right to. But if it was a meadow with a crop of grass upon it, the possessor could have no claim to the grass; it is part of the meadow itself, or is the natural produce of it, and consequently belongs to the owner of the thing, and is not due to the labour of the possessor. In like manner the young of cattle, as they are their natural fruit or produce, belong to the owner of the cattle, and are to be restored to him. If the sire belongs to one of the parties and the dam to the other, the young naturally belong to the owner of the dam, after a very small satisfaction is made to the owner of the sire. For though the sire contributed to the production of the young, yet numberless accidents might have happened, after his act was over, to hinder the production. His

* Grotius, Lib. II. Cap. X. § I, II.

owner, therefore, has no right to more than what the chance, that young would be produced, was worth, at the time of his act.

Honest possessor not obliged to damage himself by restitution.

IV. As the obligation to make restitution, which we have been speaking of, guards against any injury that might be done to the owner of a thing; so it is reasonable, that such limitations should be fixed to this obligation, as will guard the honest possessor from suffering any injury. The general limitation is, that the possessor is not obliged to suffer any loss in what he has a right to, by making restitution. For since the owner's claim extends no farther than his property, the obligation of the possessor can extend no farther.

From hence it appears; First, that if the true owner cannot be put into possession without some expense, the honest possessor is not obliged to be at that expense; nor is he obliged to be at any more trouble in making restitution, than he is paid for; because the other has no more right to his labour than to his money.

Secondly, if the possessor has made any improvement in the thing, whilst he supposed it to be his own, he has a natural right to be paid for his labour and materials. Thus if he has built a house upon ground which he was honestly possessed of, the proprietor, as his claim reaches only to the ground, can have no natural right to the house, so as to hinder the other from pulling it down, unless he pays for the materials and workmanship.

Thirdly, though, as we have seen already, grass, whilst it is growing, is the natural produce of the land, yet if it has been cut and made into hay, the honest possessor's labour is joined to it, and he has, as in this instance, so in all others of the same sort, a natural right to be paid for his labour in collecting what is in itself the fruit of the thing possessed. But then this labour is all that he ought to be paid for; and however it might be urged, that the fruits would have been spoiled, and consequently would have been worth nothing, if he had not collected them; this will give him no right to the fruits themselves. For suppose, which is the strongest light the case can be put in, that the value of the labour is vastly greater than the value of the fruits; yet it cannot upon this account so overrule the claim of the proprietor, as to set it aside; since no satisfactory reason can be given, why, by joining a more valuable right of mine to a less valuable right of another man, the whole should be made my own.

No obligation to restitution where the thing has perished.

V. Grotius under this head has explained some particular cases relating to the honest possessor's obligation to make restitution. Some of these cases have been considered already; others do not belong to this head, and shall be considered in their proper places; the rest are these which follow: *First, if the goods, of whatever sort they are, and the natural fruits of them too, have so perished in the hands of the honest possessor, that no part of them remains, and no advantage has been made of them; he is under no obligation to make restitution merely because such goods and the fruits of them have passed through his hands. For since the proprietor's claim is a claim upon the thing only, and not upon the person, the obligation of the possessor extends only to the thing; and

* Grot. Lib. II. Cap. X. § III.

consequently if this and the fruits of it are not in being, the person of the possessor is not chargeable.

Obligation to restitution does not extend to all advantage made by the possessor.

VI. Secondly, *Grotius affirms in general, that if the possessor is at all richer by having had the property of another man in his hands, all the advantage which he has made, be it of what sort it will, is due to the proprietor; in particular, if the goods or the natural produce of them are consumeable, and the possessor has made use of them, he is bound to restore the value of them, provided he must have used as much of his own goods, if he had not been in possession of these; because, says our author, he has in this respect been a gainer by the other's property. Now of this there is some reason to doubt. For since the proprietor has a claim upon the thing only and not upon the person, his claim must be at an end, when the thing is no more; as such claim does not extend to the person of the possessor, there is no way by which it should charge any part of his property with the obligation to restitution. In the case of dishonest possession, as will be shown hereafter, we should have reason to determine otherwise; for there the dishonest act of the possessor lays an obligation upon his person to make restitution; the proprietor, as he has a right to the thing in virtue of his own property, so has he likewise a demand upon the possessor, on account of his crime.

No obligation to restitution of fruits neglected.

VII. Thirdly, †the honest possessor is not obliged to make restitution for the natural produce of the thing, where such natural produce has perished through his neglect to collect it. For here the fruits or produce, which are the thing in question, are not in existence; and consequently the claim of the proprietor, which, in case of honest possession is a claim to the thing only, must be at an end.

No obligation where a thing given is given away again.

VIII. Fourthly, if the thing was given to the possessor, and he gives it away again, he is not obliged to restitution. Unless, says ‡Grotius, it appears that he would have given away as much in value out of his own substance, if such thing had not been in his hands; because, in this case, he will have been a saver, or in fact a gainer, by the other's property. But here again our author has not applied the necessary distinction between a claim upon the thing and a claim upon the person. And since, where the possession is honest, there is no claim upon the person of the possessor, the proprietor's claim can extend no farther than to the thing which belongs to him.

No obligation to restore the overplus of price, where a thing bought is sold again.

IX. Fifthly, there is the same objection against the determination of §Grotius, that if the possessor bought the thing, and then sold it again for more than he gave for it, the proprietor has a right to the difference. The price, which the thing was sold for, is not the thing itself, and consequently is not the object of the proprietor's right; so that his claim cannot reach it, unless that claim affected the person of the possessor.

Restitution to be made without reimbursement.

X. Sixthly, the honest possessor, though he purchased the thing at a considerable expense, is bound to restore it, and cannot require the proprietor to reimburse

* Grot. Lib. II. Cap. X. § II. V. † Ibid. § VI. ‡ Ibid. § VII. § Ibid. § VIII.

him. *If the possessor could demand this, the owner's right of property would be nothing; since there is no value in a right which a man must pay for, before he can assert it. But we may add one exception to this rule, which is, that if the thing was in such hands before, that the owner could not have recovered possession, without some expense and trouble; actual possession is then a valuable consideration to him, and the honest possessor, from whom he receives his goods, may expect an allowance for it. Thus suppose the goods to have been purchased of thieves or pirates; or suppose them to have been found, when the owner had but little reason to expect that he should ever recover them; the honest possessor may demand salvage; because the right of the proprietor when it was so likely to be quite lost, is not to be valued to the full worth of it; the difference between its full worth, and the worth which he would have reckoned it of to him, when he was in so much danger of losing it, is due to the honest possessor, by whom it is saved.

Goods to be restored and not returned to the seller.

XI. Seventhly, †he who buys another man's goods of persons who have no right to sell them, cannot return them upon the hands of the sellers, in order to recover his money again; because, as soon as they were in his power, his obligation to restore them to the true owner took place. Indeed, if he had discovered that the goods did not belong to the seller, before he had completed his bargain, he would not be obliged to complete it, for the sake of being able to return them to the true owner; for no man can be bound in justice to part with his own money, merely that another may recover his right.

CHAPTER X.

OF THE RIGHT WHICH A MAN HAS IN HIS OWN PERSON.

I. *Right over persons reduceable to a right to do certain actions.*—II. *What is meant by a right to our liberty.*—III. *Law of nature the only original restraint upon a man's power of acting.*—IV. *Liberty, not unalienable.*—V. *Restraints upon liberty by the law of nature are of three sorts.*—VI. *Duty to God.*—VII. *Duty to mankind.*—VIII. *Several instances of a right in our own person.*—IX. *Duty to ourselves.*

Right over persons reduceable to a right to do certain actions.

I. In the general definition of right, we have only taken notice of a right to possess certain things, or to do certain actions. Our rights over persons are not particularly mentioned in that definition, because they are in effect only rights to do certain actions. Thus, the right which we have over others, is a right to command or direct them; and one of the principal rights which we have over ourselves is a right to act as we please.

* Grot. Lib. II. Cap. X. § IX. † Ibid. § X.

In some respects, indeed, the right which a man has in his own person, may perhaps more properly be reduced to a right in a thing; of this sort are the rights which he has to his limbs, to his health, to his life.

What is meant by a right to our liberty.

II. By liberty we mean the power which a man has to act as he thinks fit, where no law restrains him; it may, therefore, be called a man's right over his own actions. In the common way of speaking, every man is said to have a right to his liberty; but this expression is not so accurate as it might be. For since the notion of a person's liberty consists in having a right over his own actions, to say that he has a right to his liberty, is in effect to say that he has right to a right over his own actions. However, I shall neither quarrel with the expression, nor scruple to use it, as I have occasion; since custom has established it to import what is self-evidently true, that every man has an independent power to act as he thinks fit, where he is under no restraint of law.

Though liberty in the physical sense of it, is an independent power of acting, yet when we consider it in a moral view, our notion of it is less extensive. For if our nature and constitution, the circumstances that we are placed in, and the authority which our Creator has over us, oblige us to act in a particular manner; then, as far as we are under such obligations, we have not an independent power of acting as we please. Upon this account, in defining the word liberty, I have called it the power which a man has to act as he thinks fit, where no law restrains him. It may perhaps be difficult to prove, that man has physically an independent power of acting; but the difficulty does not arise from any uncertainty in the fact, but from the evidence of it; nothing being so difficult to prove as a self-evident proposition. If any one, therefore, doubts whether he has such a power, instead of attempting any formal proof of it, the best way is to refer him to his own experience for conviction.

The law of nature the only original restraint upon a man's power of acting.

III. The only restraint which a man's right over his own actions is originally under, is the obligation of governing himself by the law of nature and the law of God. Whatever right those of our own species may have over us, either to direct our actions to certain purposes, or to restrain them within certain bounds, beyond what the law of nature has prescribed, arises from some after-act of our own; from some consent either express or tacit, by which we have alienated our liberty or transferred the right of directing our actions from ourselves to them. Till this is done, they have no claim of superiority over us; nature has made no difference between one man and another; all, who are of full age, have reason of their own to direct them, and a will of their own to choose for themselves. And though, as men may differ from one another in the capacities of judging what is best to be done, it may be the safest way to take the advice of those who have more skill than ourselves; yet this is matter of prudence only, and not matter of duty. Our reason and our will belong as much to us, as their reason and their will belong to them; we must, therefore, naturally be as independent of them in directing our own actions, and in choosing for ourselves, as they are of us. I would not be understood to mean, that no man has a right to force us in any respect, till we have given him such a right by our own consent;

for it will appear hereafter, that in many respects men have a right to force us to comply with the law of nature. But such a right as this, implies no natural superiority in them; since in the like instances we have the same right to force them, that they have to force us.

Liberty not unalienable.

IV. There cannot well be any question, whether our liberty is alienable; at least it is a question which must at first sight be determined in the affirmative, unless some law can be produced, which forbids us to alienate it; because all our rights are alienable, as far as it is not contrary to any law for us to part with them. In fact, we find that in many instances our liberty is alienated, and no one questions whether it could be alienated or not; for certainly the obligations of promises and of contracts, where we bind ourselves to do what the law of nature would otherwise not have required of us, are wholly unintelligible, upon supposition that our liberty is the same, after we have made such promises or contracts, that it was before.

It may be said, perhaps, that no man can absolutely and without reserve, renounce his liberty, and transfer the full right of directing his actions to any one else; because this would be plainly throwing himself into a necessity of doing wrong, whenever the person, to whom he has thus subjected himself, shall think proper to command him. But the whole amount of this objection is, that no man can renounce or transfer a liberty which he never had. He has indeed a physical power of doing wrong; but his liberty, in a moral sense, is a power of acting as he pleases, where the law does not restrain him; he has not, therefore, the liberty of doing wrong, and consequently cannot transfer to any one the power of forcing him to do wrong; not because liberty is in itself an unalienable right, but because no man can transfer to another a right which he never had himself.

The restraints upon liberty by the law of nature are of three sorts.

V. In order to understand how far our liberty extends, or how far we have a right to act as we please, by the law of nature, previously to any obligations, under which we may have laid ourselves by any particular compact or agreement of our own, it will be necessary to consider what restraints that law has laid us under, in respect of God, in respect of mankind, and in respect of ourselves.

Duty towards God.

VI. We are obliged to obey the will of God, as far as we are able to discover it, because he is the sovereign Lord of the universe, who made and governs all things by his almighty power, and infinite wisdom; to whom we are indebted for all the happiness that we enjoy at present, and upon whom we depend for all the happiness that we expect hereafter. By the nature and constitution of things he is our superior; so that the right which we have in our own persons, particularly our liberty, or the right of acting as we think fit, is subject to his authority, and is limited by all the restraints which he is pleased to lay upon us.

From this account of the obligation that we are under to obey the will of God, the other parts of our duty towards him may be easily collected. The general name of this duty is piety, which consists partly in entertaining just opinions concerning him, and partly in such affections towards him, and such worship of him, as is suitable to these opinions.

It is the business of natural theology to demonstrate the existence and the perfections of God, to prove that there is an eternal omnipresent being, of infinite power, wisdom and goodness, who made and contrived the universe at first, and who still continues to govern and direct it. Where we have sufficient opportunities of informing ourselves rightly concerning the existence and the perfections of God, it is our duty to make use of these informations. We cannot obey his will at all, unless we believe that he is; and we cannot obey it as we ought to do, unless we have acquainted ourselves, as perfectly as we are able, with his nature and attributes. If, therefore, we are obliged to obey his will, we must for the same reasons be obliged likewise to form true notions and to entertain just sentiments concerning him; to believe his existence and perfections, to admire his wisdom, to adore his goodness, to reverence his power, to acknowledge our dependance upon him, and to honour him in all our thoughts and words and actions, as our maker, preserver and governor.

From hence it follows, first, that atheism, which consists in a disbelief of his existence; secondly, that blasphemy, which consists in attributing to God such imperfections as are inconsistent with his nature, and thirdly, that profaneness which consists in a wanton or disrespectful treatment of his nature and attributes, are all of them contrary to the law of nature.

But though we believe that there is a God, and have formed true opinions and entertain just sentiments of his nature and attributes, yet certainly we have not discharged the whole of our duty towards him, merely by avoiding atheism, blasphemy and profaneness. By avoiding these crimes we only take care not to dishonour him; but we are capable of doing more than this; we are capable of honouring him by our words and actions, as well as by our thoughts. Our words or actions will bring our pious sentiments into our own view, so as to strengthen and improve them in ourselves; and they will likewise bring them into public view, so as to excite the like sentiments in other men. Since, therefore, it is our duty to honour God, and since we honour him in the best manner that we can, by strengthening and improving our own pious sentiments of him, and affections towards him, and by exciting the like sentiments and affections in other men; it follows, that some external worship of him, both private and public, is a duty, and that irreligion or the neglect of such worship is a crime by the law of nature. If it was otherwise, I know not how we should be able to prove that the law of nature forbids idolatry, which consists in paying this external worship to a false god, or in attributing, by our words and significant actions, the power, wisdom and goodness of the creator to some of his creatures, to the work of our own hands, or to the inventions of our own imaginations; provided they, who pay such external worship to a false god, entertain in their minds just and proper sentiments of the true one. For, if external worship is an indifferent action, and is not due to God, he is not at all dishonoured, when we pay it to another. So effectually do they, who endeavour to set aside the obligations of prayer and thanksgiving, defend the worship of images, as it is explained at present in the church of Rome.

We may go one step farther. If God has at any time been pleased, by any positive revelation, to explain his nature, or to publish his will to mankind, and to afford us proper and sufficient evidence, that such revelation came from him, the law of nature will not allow us to treat it with contempt and ridicule, for this is profaneness. Nor are we at liberty to reject it without examining the evidence by which its pretensions to be a revelation from God are supported; because, as we are obliged to obey his will, and to entertain true and just sentiments concerning him, we cannot but be obliged to make use of our best endeavours to discover what his will is, and to inform ourselves rightly concerning his nature and attributes.

It will likewise be contrary to the law of nature to reject such a revelation, even after we have examined it, if God, who perfectly knows the extent and limits of the human understanding, who is fully acquainted with the just measures of credibility, and with the reasonable grounds of assent, has attested such revelation with what appeared to him sufficient evidence for convincing mankind of the truth of it. Whoever rejects a revelation so attested does not pay the obedience which is due, by the law of nature and the constitution of things, to the authority of God.

Duty towards mankind.

VII. Our right over our own actions is restrained in respect of mankind by the natural duties of justice and benevolence. We have seen already from whence our obligation to these duties is derived, and wherein the duties themselves consist. And since justice consists in doing no causeless harm to others, there must be as many sorts of injustice as there are perfect rights belonging to mankind, by the violation of any of which we may do them causeless harm.

Some acts of injustice have particular names given to them. Thus the causeless taking away a man's life is murder. If the person murdered was our parent, it is parricide. If we owed him any special obedience, such as a subject owes to his prince, a servant to his master, or a wife to her husband, it is treason. Injuring a man in his bed, or violating that right, which he has to the affection and to the person of his wife, is adultery. Injuring him in his liberty by causelessly taking it from him, is false imprisonment. Taking away his property against his consent, if it is done privately, is theft; if it is done publicly and by violence, it is robbery;—if great numbers are concerned in such an act of violence, it is rapine. If by some deceit or artifice he is led to give his consent to part with his property, when, if he had known the truth, he would not have parted with it, this is fraud. There are some acts of injustice, the names of which do not want any definition; because the name itself sufficiently expresses the nature of the act; of this sort are maiming, defacing, breach of contract, defamation, false evidence, &c.

We may likewise do injustice to a man, in respect of his property, not only by taking it from him unjustly at first, but likewise, as has been shown already, by keeping it, or not restoring it to him, though we at first came honestly by it.

Benevolence is a general word, and signifies a disposition of doing good to any person or in any manner. But this general disposition has a different name given to it, according to the different objects of it, or the different ways in which it exerts itself. When it is directed towards them who have been kind to us, it is called gratitude. When the distressed and afflicted are the objects of it, we call it pity. When our enemies share in it, we call it generosity. If it leads us to study the quiet of mankind by being mild in the judgments that we pass upon their conduct, and backward to censure their failings, we call it candour. If it is employed in checking our pride and in preventing us from being so much puffed up, either by the station that we are in, or by the good qualities that we possess, as to make others uneasy, we call it humility. If it exerts itself in relieving the poor and wretched out of our substance, it is liberality;—and the higher instances of liberality are called bounty. If it restrains our anger and resentment, it is patience, forbearance, or long-suffering. If it tempers the severity of justice and softens the rigour of our lawful demands upon such persons as are in our power, it is mercy. If it shows itself in an endeavour to make all men easy, who have any occasion to apply to us, by removing the difficulties of access to our person, and by conversing freely and openly with them, it is affability. If it goes one step farther and seeks for opportunities of showing such affability, it is courtesy. The obligation to these several duties, as they are parts of benevolence, has been made out in its proper place; and whatever power we have of acting for ourselves, yet in respect of mankind we abuse this power, and apply it otherwise than the law of our nature directs us, when we neglect them.

Several instances of a right in our own person.

VIII. Besides our liberty, or the right of acting in what manner we please, which has been mentioned already, we have several other rights in our own person. A man's life is his own, it is the gift of nature; and whoever deprives him of it, is guilty of injustice towards him. His limbs too, are his own, for the same reason; so that he is injured by being maimed. He has a right likewise to freedom from pain, as far as no law obliges him to submit to it; he is injured, therefore, if he is causelessly hurt by any blow or wound. He has still a farther right to his good name, that is, to all the advantages or all the satisfaction, which he can receive from being thought or spoken of, as he deserves; scandal therefore and defamation are injuries to his person.

Duty towards ourselves.

IX. But it is proper to consider how far we have a right to dispose of our person, or to manage it in any manner that we please; whether our liberty or the power of acting as we think fit, is, in respect of ourselves, under no restraint from the law of nature.

It seems to be self-evidently true, that no man can have a right to manage his own person, or to dispose of it in such a manner, as will render him incapable of doing his duty. For his duty is a restraint, which arises from the law of nature; he cannot, therefore, have any right to free himself from that, unless he has a right to free himself from all restraints which the law of nature has laid him under. The consequence of this is, that a man's right to his life or his limbs is a limited right; they are his to use, but not his to dispose of. As they were given him to use, whoever deprives him of them does him an injury. But then, as they are not his to abuse or dispose of, it follows that he breaks through the law of nature, whenever he renders himself incapable of complying in any instance with that law, which the author and giver of his life and limbs, has required him to observe.

Upon this account we have no right to maim ourselves, if by such an act we shall become unable to discharge any of the duties of justice or benevolence. And much less have we any right to kill ourselves, since by this means we become unable to discharge any duty at all. A duty which we can release ourselves from at pleasure, is unintelligible; it is in effect no duty: the law of nature could not in any respect be binding upon a man, if we suppose him to have such a right in his own person, that he may at any time, by his own voluntary act, lawfully release himself from the whole obligation of it, or in any respect render himself incapable of performing it.

Upon the same principles we may easily understand, that all such luxury or intemperance in eating or drinking, as either fills up too much of a man's time, and takes him off from his duty, or by disordering his understanding, clouding his judgment and impairing his health, incapacitates him for the performance of such duty, are not within the bounds of his liberty; his power of acting as he thinks fit, is restrained in these instances by the law of nature.

Some duties of chastity are plainly such as respect not only ourselves, but likewise other men; because a breach of those duties is an injury to others. Of this sort are adultery and rapes; to which we may add the debauching virtuous women; because those women are thus deprived of their credit and reputation, and the peace and quiet of their family and relations are broken in upon. The consent of the woman who is debauched, can no more excuse the injury than the consent of a person who is cheated out of his property, can excuse the fraud. To raise and inflame her passions till it is not in the power of her reason to control them, and then to take the advantage of that weakness, which he who debauches her has been the occasion of, is the same thing in effect, as to mislead a person's understanding, and then take the advantage of his ignorance to cheat him out of his property.

There are other breaches of chastity which the law of nature forbids, because they frustrate that end for which the desire of the sexes towards each other was implanted by nature. Amongst these breaches of chastity, besides those of the grosser sort, we may fairly reckon common prostitution, and the debaucheries of such as indulge their lusts with common prostitutes.

Having thus considered the rights which a man has in his own person, and the several restraints under which these rights are laid by the law of nature, we shall now pass on to the consideration of those rights which he has over the persons of others.

CHAPTER XI.

OF PARENTAL AUTHORITY.

I. *Right of parents, whence derived.*—II. *Father's authority superior to mother's.*—III. *Three parts of childhood.*—IV. *Parental authority in the first part of childhood.*—V. *Parental authority, properly so called, ceases in the second part of childhood.*—VI. *Honour due to parents in the third part of childhood.*—VII. *Variations in parental authority show the origin of it.*—VIII. *Natural minority, what.*—IX. *What right of punishment included in parental authority.*—X. *The law of nature may in some cases allow parents to sell their children.*—XI. *Adoption is different from purchase.*

Right of parents, whence derived.

I. We acquire a *right over the persons of others three ways; by generation, by their consent, or by their having committed some crime.

The right which parents have over their children, arises originally from generation, not as its immediate, but only as its remote cause. If we were to follow Grotius, and to assign generation as the immediate cause of parental authority, there are several incidents in this authority which we should not be able to explain. I choose therefore rather to consider generation as the remote cause, and the duty of the parents, which arises from thence, as the immediate cause of that authority which they have over the persons of their children.

It is the design of God, as far as we can collect it from his works, that the species of mankind should be continued; and as this cannot be done unless children, when they are born, have some care taken of them, it is the duty of mankind to maintain and provide for them. But since their maintenance and provision will necessarily be attended with some expense and trouble, such expense or trouble cannot justly be laid upon any other persons, but upon those who were the occasion of it; that is, upon the parents. They, therefore, because they produced the child, are obliged to maintain it, and to provide for it. Now it would be an injury to mankind to bring up a person in such a manner as to be hurtful or burdensome; and upon this account the parents are obliged not merely to maintain the child, but likewise to educate it in such a manner as to prevent its being hurtful, and to fit it for some useful employment, that it may not be burdensome. But the manners of the child could not be so formed as to render it useful, or even preserve it innocent, unless the parents have some authority over it. And since nature cannot be supposed to prescribe a duty to the parents, without granting them the means which are necessary for the discharge of such duty, it follows that nature has given the parents all the authority which is necessary, for bringing up the child in a proper manner.

Father's authority superior to mother's.

II. Both the parents have authority over the child, because the duty of maintaining and educating it belongs to both. However, if the commands of the father and of the mother should at any time happen to clash, the father is rather to

* Grot. Lib. II. Cap. V.

be obeyed; upon account, says *Grotius, of the excellence of his sex. And yet in his method of explaining the origin and foundation of parental authority, this reason can be of no weight; because upon supposition that generation is the immediate cause of the power which the parents have over the child, the mother, who contributes as much as the father, or more, if we consider the trouble and uneasiness of gestation, must have an authority equal to the father's, if not superior to his. But if generation is considered only as the remote cause, and the duty of the parents to bring up the child and to form its manners, is considered as the immediate cause of their authority, then the father's authority will be superior to the mother's, upon account of what may be called the excellence of his sex; for he is in general with good reason supposed to be better able than the mother to defend and to instruct it; and in proportion as his abilities are greater, his duty, and with it his authority, must be greater likewise.

Three parts of childhood.

III. †The whole time of childhood may be distinguished into three parts. The first is the age of infancy or minority; before the child has arrived at a perfect judgment to choose for itself. The second is that part of the child's life after it is past its minority, whilst it continues a member of the parents' family. The third is so much of the age of maturity as remains after the child has joined itself to some other family, or has erected a family of its own. For want of a better word, I have here made use of the word childhood in a more loose sense than it commonly is used, to signify all the time of a person's life that passes, whilst his parents are living.

Parental authority in the first part of childhood.

IV. In the first part of childhood, that is, during the infancy or minority of the child, all its actions are under the absolute authority of its parents. As it has then no reason of its own to judge, and no will of its own to choose what is best, the parents, whose duty it is to take care of it, are to judge and to choose for it. But no power can be more absolute than this, where the reason of the parents is the sole guide of the child, and where its will is concluded by theirs.

However, though the authority of the parents, as far as it reaches, is absolute as to the degree of it, yet it is not unlimited as to the extent of it. For since it arises out of the duty of the parents to provide for the good of the child, they have no authority knowingly and designedly to treat it or to dispose of it in such a manner, as will be hurtful to it. Their duty to maintain and to educate it can never be reasonably supposed to give them a right to maim, or to expose, or in any way to neglect it.

But whatever promises or contracts the child engages in, or whatever other acts it does without the consent of its parents, all such acts are void; it has no moral power of acting for itself, for want of reason and choice; and upon this account, whatever acts it does, will, as to any moral effect, be as if they had not been done.

Parental authority, properly so called, ceases in the second part of childhood.

V. In the ‡second part of childhood, that is, when the child is come to maturity of judgment but continues in the family of its parents, they have no parental authority, properly so called, over any of its actions. The au-

* Grot. Lib. II. Cap. V. † Grot. ibid. § II. ‡ Grot. ibid. § II.

thority of the parents arises from their duty to provide for the child and to take care of it whilst it is unable to govern and direct itself; this authority therefore must necessarily cease, when the duty ceases upon which it is founded; after the child is able to think and to judge for itself, it is no longer the duty of the parents to think and to judge for it; and consequently the will of the child is no longer under the absolute control of their will.

However, in this part of its life they have a demand upon it of gratitude, esteem and reverence; it is still bound to honour them, by showing them all marks of respect, and more particularly by paying a deference to their advice and direction; for as they, from their longer experience, are more likely to judge rightly than the child is; so their former care of it may convince it, that they are disposed to contrive for its welfare. But notwithstanding the child owes them this duty of honour, they have not, as its parents, such authority over it as will make void any acts which it does without their consent, or even against their commands; because the obligations to these duties are of the imperfect sort; the person who transgresses them does not use his liberty agreeably to the law of nature, but the law does not suppose him void of such a power of acting, as is sufficient to give a validity to what he does. If a man's parents have any more authority over him than what has been described, it is an authority which arises from his own consent, as a member of that family or community wherein he continues, and of which his parents are the head.

Honour due to parents in the third part of childhood.

VI. In the *third part of childhood, when the child has not only arrived at maturity of judgment, but has either joined itself to another family, or is become the head of a family of its own, the obligations of gratitude, deference and esteem still continue, as long as its parents live; for the reasons, upon which these duties are founded, are perpetual. But as in the second part of childhood, so much more in this, no acts of the child, however wrong they may be for want of the parents' consent, will upon that account be invalid.

Variations in parental authority show the origin of it.

VII. Grotius allows that these variations which we have been mentioning are incidental to parental authority. And such variations are easily accounted for, provided this authority arises immediately from the duty of the parents, and remotely only from generation; because as the duty of the parents, in the first part of childhood, is different from their duty in the second and third part of it, an authority arising from that duty and depending upon it, will naturally vary with the duty. Whereas, upon his own principle, that generation is the immediate cause of parental authority, it will be difficult to find out any reasons upon which these variations can be explained; because a relation, which arises from a personal act of the parents, cannot be changed, and consequently an authority which depends upon this relation as its immediate cause, must be uniform or continue always the same, as long as the person continues, from whose act the relation arose.

Natural minority, what.

VIII. †The law of nature cannot be supposed to fix any precise age at which the absolute authority of pa-

* Grot. Lib. II. Cap. V. § VI. † Ibid. Lib. II. Cap. XI. § V.

rents shall in all cases cease, and all persons universally shall be looked upon to be capable of acting for themselves. Persons are then arrived at maturity, when they come to the use of their reason. But this happens at different times of life in different countries: in some climates the mind ripens faster and attains to the use of reason sooner than it does in others. In the same country, too, it happens at different times of life to different persons; all who live in the same climate, do not come to maturity of judgment at the same age. No particular person, therefore, can be said naturally to have arrived at years of discretion, or to be capable of acting for himself, till we have observed how that particular person behaves in common life; when he shows by his behaviour that he has the use of his reason, then, and not till then, he is past his natural minority.

Civil laws do, indeed, usually fix some certain age as the limit of minority for all the subjects. But if these laws are intended to copy nature as nearly as general rules can copy it, in a point where there is naturally so much uncertainty, a different age must be fixed in different climates. Nor can the properest time be settled in the same climate till long experience and many observations have shown at what age the judgment of men in that climate is usually ripe. And since in the same climate some few arrive at the use of reason much sooner, and some few are much longer before they arrive at it, than the generality of the inhabitants, the laws of each country will copy nature the closest, if they fix the limit of minority neither at the earliest nor at the latest age, when any person has ever been known to arrive at maturity of judgment, but at the middle age between those extremes, at the age when the generality have been found to arrive at it. Extraordinary instances are not the proper measure of nature; they are not the standards whereby to fix a general rule, but are rather to be looked upon as exceptions from such a rule.

What right of punishment included in parental authority.

IX. The *authority which parents have over their children, implies a power to punish or correct them, as far as such a power is necessary for obtaining the end which that authority has in view. Since it is the duty of the parents to contrive for the good of the child, and to direct it to what is best for it, whilst it is incapable of judging and choosing for itself; as far as this end cannot be obtained without correction, they have a right to punish it, because nature cannot be supposed to enjoin an end, such for instance as the good of the child, to be pursued, without allowing such correction as is necessary for obtaining that end. But then the end, which is the good of the child, limits the right of punishing; the parents cannot upon this principle have a right to inflict any punishment but what is for the child's benefit.

From hence it follows, that the power of a parent to correct his children does not extend to the inflicting any capital punishment, because the child's good cannot be the end proposed in taking away the child's life; nor can such a punishment be in any manner consistent with the parents duty to take care of it, to bring it up, and to contrive for its benefit. Wherever parents have had any right of punishing more extensive than what has been described, in the second or third parts of

* Grot. Lib. II. Cap. V. § VI.

childhood, this right must have been derived from some other principle, and is no part of parental authority.

We may observe by the way, that as the power of parents to punish their children is limited to correction for their good during their minority, no fault of a child can justify the parents if they disinherit it so far as to deprive it of sustenance, where it is under age and unable to provide for itself; because such a disherison would in effect be a capital punishment, as it would leave the child to starve. After it is come to such an age as to be able to provide for itself, the faults which it commits may justify a disherison of this sort; not because the parent has then any more right to inflict a capital punishment than he had before, but because he is then released from the duty of maintaining the child, and may dispose of his own goods in any proper manner that he pleases.

The law of nature may in some cases allow parents to sell their children.

X. *Where parents from the birth of the child, or at any time afterwards, whilst it is under their authority, are unable to subsist it, there seems to be no reason against their selling it to any one who will undertake the expense and trouble of bringing it up. For nature, if it has prescribed to parents the duty of providing for the subsistence of their children, cannot disable them from making use of the only means that they have in their power of discharging this duty. Grotius, consistently with his own account of the origin of parental authority, maintains that the relation or habitude of a parent, which arises from the act whereby the parents become the authors of the child's existence, can no more be separated from the person of the parent than the personal act itself can. Yet in the mean time he contends that the child may be sold, in order to make a provision for it, when the parents themselves are unable to subsist it. But upon his principles, such a sale would be unintelligible; for unless the purchaser acquires at least the authority of the parents over the child so purchased, nothing is done by it; and it is impossible for him to acquire this or any other degree of authority, if this authority arises from a personal act of the parents, or from a relation depending upon that act, which is in its own nature inseparable from their persons. But upon the principles here laid down, the purchaser, by undertaking the duty of the parent, so far at least as to maintain the child, acquires with it the parental authority. The usual event of such a sale is the slavery of the child; which event neither is nor can be brought about by the sole act of the parent, unless some other accident intervenes. By what accident this event is brought about will hereafter be the subject of a more particular inquiry.

Adoption is different from purchase.

XI. In like manner, when a child is adopted, so that the parent who adopts it does by his own voluntary act take it for his own, or engage for the care of it, he does by this act, with the consent of the natural parent, acquire a parental authority over it; for this authority goes along with parental duty, and is inseparable from it.

I have not supposed the child's consent to be necessary in adoption; because, if it is under age, its consent is included in the consent of its parents. But if it is of such an age as to have reason and a will of its own, the consent of the party adopted is necessary, and adoption cannot proceed upon the sole act of the parents.

* Grotius, Lib. II. Cap. V. § V.

It may perhaps be asked, if the consent of the parents includes that of the child in case of adoption, why might not parents upon the same principle sell their children into direct slavery, or why is any thing else necessary to make the child a slave, besides the consent of the parents, when they sell it. The difference of these two cases will readily appear, if we consider that the parents' authority over the child arises from his duty to provide for its good; and consequently, where the good of the child is not the end proposed, this authority is nothing. Now adoption is for the child's benefit, and upon that account the act of the parent is binding upon it. But if the child should be supposed to receive any benefit by slavery, which scarce can be supposed, yet this benefit is not the end designed by slavery; the good of the master is the principal point in view; the good of the slave is merely accidental.

CHAPTER XII.

OF PROMISES.

I. *What obligations arise from declaring our future intentions.*—II. *Promises, what.*—III. *Promises of giving, the same in effect as promises of doing.*—IV. *Promises always relate to future time.*—V. *Promises do not affect the heirs of the promiser.*—VI. *No obligation from promises where there is no liberty.*—VII. *No promise obliges to an impossibility.*—VIII. *Unlawful promises not binding.*—IX. *A subsequent promise cannot bind, where it is contrary to a former promise.*—X. *Obligation of a promise may be in suspense.*—XI. *Promises not to be evaded by a supposed tacit condition of circumstances continuing the same.*—XII. *Promises of infants, ideots, and madmen do not bind.*—XIII. *Rash promises, in what sense binding.*—XIV. *Promises become binding by acceptance.*—XV. *Signs of consent in promises and acceptance.*—XVI. *Fear makes a promise void in some instances, not in others.*—XVII. *Erroneous promises, how made void.*—XVIII. *A man's agent may promise for him.*—XIX. *Voluntary agent does not oblige.*—XX. *What promises may, and what may not be recalled when they pass through a third hand.*—XXI. *Effects of acceptance by another, either with or without commission.*—XXII. *A man's heirs cannot accept a promise for him.*

What obligations arise from declaring our future intentions.

I. The rights which we acquire by promises or contracts or oaths, arise from the consent of those persons over whom such rights are acquired. And as none of our rights are more necessary to be rightly understood than these, it will be worth our while to consider them at large.

We may do good to other men, either by our property or by our actions; that is, either by giving them such things, or by doing them such services as will be of use to them.

When we intend to do them any good hereafter, which we either do not choose to do, or have not an opportunity of doing at present, the three ways which *Grotius mentions of expressing ourselves concerning such future intention, may be reduced to two.

First, we may merely declare what our present intentions are, by saying, that we design to give them such or such things, or that we design to do them such or such services. Here, says Grotius, all that is required to justify our declarations of this sort, is, that we speak the truth, or that, at the time of making the declaration, we have the same intentions which our words express. For the mind of man, as our author goes on, has not only a natural power, but a right likewise to change its design. But he ought to have added, unless it is under an obligation to continue in the same design. Now such a declaration as we have been speaking of, made in my favour, does not indeed give me a perfect right over the person of him who made it, or over the thing which he designs to give me; and consequently it does not lay him under a perfect obligation either of doing me the service or of giving me the thing: but yet it lays him under such an obligation as a wise or a good man will attend to. A wise man would not willingly lay himself open to the charge of levity of forming his designs by chance, and altering them again without reason. And unless the motives which engage him to change his designs are notorious and weighty, he cannot easily escape this charge, if he does not act up to what he has declared. Besides, we are apt to alter our schemes of life, to bring the expected profit or service into our plan of happiness, and to live as if we were to receive it. A disappointment therefore does not leave us in the same condition that we should have been in, if no such hopes had been raised: our pursuits will have been changed by them; and we shall perhaps have lost sight of what might have been obtained, if we had continued to pursue it, and had not been called off to another scheme of happiness by these delusions. What is still worse, we may have been led to live more expensively, in expectation of having our fortunes bettered, or to engage in difficulties, out of which we cannot extricate ourselves, in hopes of such services as would have enabled us to surmount them. This may be said in some measure to be our own fault; we ought perhaps to look upon all future events as uncertain, and never to depend so much upon them as to be hurt if we are disappointed. But allowing this to be always the case, a good man would never, if he can avoid it, be even the innocent cause of hurt to others. However, in fact, it is not always so. There are many favours which a man is not capable of receiving without changing his way of life: what therefore is he to do, where he is made to expect such favours as these? It would be imprudent in him, if he did not qualify himself to receive them, when declarations are made that such favours are designed him: and if he does change his way of life, or his course of studies, in order to qualify himself for them, a disappointment robs him of other advantages, which he might have expected by going on in his former pursuits, or of advantages which he was sure of, if such false hopes had not been raised in him, as engaged him in expenses, that his fortunes, without the expected improvement in them, were not able to bear. A wise man, therefore, for his own sake, or out of regard to his own character, and a good man for the sake of others, or out of tenderness to their

* Grot. Lib. II. Cap. XI. § II, III, IV.

welfare, will take care to keep his designs to himself, and to make no declarations about them, till he has well considered the matter, and finds no likelihood, that any thing will intervene, which may oblige him to fail in making them good. Or if he has been led to declare such favourable intentions, he will take care to abide by them, and to bring them into execution; unless the accidents which prevent him are such as may appear to the world, and such, too, as will justify him in the common opinion.

We may go one step farther in this way of speaking about what is future; we may not only declare what our present intentions are, but may add, that these intentions are not unsteady, that we are not only in earnest now, but will continue in the same mind when the time comes for putting these intentions in practice. This additional declaration does not confer any perfect right upon the person in whose favour it is made, or does not give him any strict demand upon us. But it strengthens our reasons for making our designs good; both because it would be an instance of greater levity to change what seems to have been thus fixedly and unalterably resolved upon; and because a disappointment to those who are made to expect our favours will be so much more hurtful, in proportion as their expectations were raised higher.

Promises what.

II. The second way of speaking concerning our present intentions of giving a man hereafter what may be useful to him, or of doing for him hereafter some beneficial service, is by making him a promise. This is not merely a declaration of our present intentions in reference to some future gift or service, with a sufficient sign of our being in earnest, and of our having determined with ourselves to continue in the same mind; but it contains likewise a declaration that we now design to give him a right to demand such gift or such service hereafter.

Promises of giving, the same in effect as promises of doing.

III. *Grotius seems to make a small difference between promises of giving and promises of doing, when he says, that the former are the first step towards the alienation of our goods, and that the latter are the actual alienation of some part of our natural liberty. But it would be difficult, if we follow this distinction closely, to show that any demand at all is conferred by a promise of giving: because it does not appear what it is which he, to whom we make such a promise, has a demand upon. The distinction does not seem to allow that his demand is upon the person of the promiser; for he is not understood to have alienated any part of his liberty; this being supposed to be the peculiar effect of promises of doing. Nor is his demand upon the thing promised; because the distinction supposes that the thing is not alienated, but only that the first step is taken towards the alienation of it. But if a promise to give a man a thing confers upon him no right either over the person of the promiser or to the thing promised, it cannot possibly confer upon him any right at all: and if he acquires no right by the promise, then the promiser cannot be laid under any obligation by it.

But, in truth, there is not in this respect any difference between promises of giving and promises of doing: the obligation of them both is upon the person of the promiser; and they are, either of them, alie-

* Grot. Lib. II. Cap. XI. § VI.

nations of his liberty. Before I make a promise of giving any particular thing to a man, I am at liberty whether I will give him it or not: but after the promise is made I have no moral power or right not to give; in regard to not giving I have parted with my liberty, by conferring upon him a right to demand, that I should act in such a manner as the promise expresses. He has no claim upon the thing promised, because I did not actually give him the thing, but only engaged that I would give him it; I did not make it his, but gave him a right to demand of me at some future time to do whatever act should be necessary to make it so.

Thus, promises of giving are in some sort promises of doing. The effect of them both is in one respect the same: they affect the liberty of the promiser, and tie him down to that particular action, which the promise contains or implies. If they are promises of giving they tie him down to the action of giving; if they are promises of doing they tie him down to the actions or services which are specified in them.

Promises always relate to future time.

IV. Promises are sometimes distinguished into such as are made in words of future time, and such as are made in words of present time. But this distinction is without foundation. What is called a promise in words of present time, can scarce be so explained as to give it the appearance of a promise: it is either an actual performance, or it is nothing at all.

Promises of giving in words of present time are actual performances. If I say that I now give you such or such a thing; what is so given does, upon your acceptance, immediately become your own; this act is a direct alienation of my property. I may indeed delay putting you into possession, by adding that I will deliver to you at some future time what is so given. This exception, as to the time of delivery, may make the whole matter have the appearance of a promise rather than of an actual performance: but then it is to be observed that, as far as this exception is concerned, the words will be of future and not of present time. However, if we consider the effect of such an exception, we shall find that it is in itself no promise; nor does the act of giving become a promise by the addition of it. Such an exception, instead of conferring any particular right upon you, limits your claim; it is added for my benefit, and not for yours. Upon my giving you the thing, you had a right to immediate possession: and by engaging to give you possession at some future time, I only postpone this right. This will be clear, if we observe that when the time of delivery comes, you will have no other right to the actual possession of the thing, but what you would have had at the instant of giving, if I had not added this limitation. And certainly as such a limitation confers no right, either perfect or imperfect, it cannot with any propriety be called a promise, or part of a promise.

As to promises of doing in words of present time, if we would endeavour to express them so as to distinguish them from promises of the same sort in words of future time, we shall find them unintelligible. I know not how to promise a man a present service, unless I am actually doing it; and a promise of it, whilst I am actually doing it, is ridiculous.

This distinction is sometimes applied to promises of marriage: but it will be very difficult to show that there is any such thing as a promise of marriage in words of present time, which is not an actual marriage. If the man promises to the woman, that he will marry her, this is promising in words of future time: if he declares that he does marry her, there is nothing naturally wanting but her acceptance to complete the marriage. It is only civil institution which prevents such a transaction from being looked upon in any other light. In almost all civil communities some particular forms and ceremonies are established for the celebration of marriage. And, consequently, if such forms and ceremonies are considered by the law as necessary to make the marriage binding upon the parties, the same law which makes them necessary, cannot call any act a marriage, where they have been omitted. Now, as a man's declaration that he does marry a woman is more than a promise of marriage; and yet civil laws, for the reason before mentioned, decline giving it the name of an actual marriage; a sort of middle name has been found out for it, and it has been called a promise; or because acceptance of such promise makes it mutual, it has been called a contract, in words of present time.

It may perhaps be apprehended that such a transaction is not called a marriage, but only a promise in words of present time, for want of consummation. But consummation in marriage is like actual possession in gifts. As in giving a thing by words of present time, the delay of actual possession does not change the act of giving into a promise; so neither does an agreement in words of present time between two parties, to take each other for man and wife, become no more than a promise by the delay of consummation.

In one view, indeed, all promises may be considered as expressed in words which relate to the present time. They declare a present intention of conferring upon the person to whom we make them, a demand upon us for some future performance. To tell a man that I will give him such a thing, or that I promise to give him it, or that I give him a demand upon me for it, are all of them expressions which the common use of language has made to be of one and the same import: and any of them confer on him a right over my person. They do not indeed alienate my property in the thing, or transfer it to him; but they alienate a part of my liberty, and bind me to the future performance of such an act as will transfer the thing to him. If I promise a man to serve him in such or such instances; if I say that I will do him such or such good offices; these and the like expressions tie me down to a particular way of acting; they give him a demand upon me so to act, or alienate the liberty which I had of acting in any other manner.

When promises of giving and promises of doing are thus explained, there appears to be little difference between them. Both of them are in effect promises of doing; since each of them conveys a right to the person that we make them to, of demanding that we shall act agreeably to what is expressed in the promise. If it is a promise of giving, the demand of those to whom we make it, and consequently the personal obligation which we are under, is that we shall do such acts as are necessary to transfer to them the thing promised: if it is a promise of doing, the demand on their part, and the obligation on ours, is that we shall do such acts, whatever they are, as are contained in the promise.

Promises do not affect the heirs of the promiser.

V. From hence, we may see the reason why the obligations of a man's promise do not of themselves descend to his heirs. They are alienations of his own liberty, and consequently, being obligations upon his person only, do not effect his property; even promises of giving confer no direct or immediate right to the thing promised, but only a demand upon the person of the promiser to give such a right hereafter. Where a man has charged his goods with any obligations, the heir, who cannot receive the goods in any other condition than what the ancestor leaves them in, is, by receiving the goods, involved in the obligations that are connected with them. But all obligations which reach no farther than the person of the promiser, cease with his person. And since the obligations of promises are of this sort, it is matter of bounty only when the heir undertakes to make good the promises of his ancestor.

No obligation from promises, where there is no liberty.

VI. Since a promise is an alienation of part of our liberty, by giving the person to whom we make it a demand upon us to act in such a particular manner, as we have engaged for, the consequence is, that we cannot oblige ourselves farther by promise than our liberty reaches; for since no man can alienate what does not belong to him, no man can give up that liberty to another either in whole or in part, which he never had himself.

No promise obliges to an impossibility.

VII. From hence it follows, first, *that no promise can oblige us to an impossibility. It is certain, indeed, that we could never perform such a promise; but when I say that it does not oblige us, I mean something more than this; I mean, that whatever folly there may be in making such a promise, there is no wrong or injustice in not performing it. For where a man has no demand upon us, we can do him no injury; and the person to whom we make a promise, can have no demand upon us, if the promise is void in its own nature. But since a promise consists in an alienation of a part of our liberty, it must be void, or must be as if there was no promise, where no such alienation has been made. Now we have not, and never could have, the liberty of doing what is impossible; we cannot, therefore, in respect of what is so, alienate our liberty; that is, we cannot make such a promise as will be binding upon us.

Unlawful promises not binding.

VIII. Secondly, †no unlawful promises can oblige those who make them. As they have not the liberty of doing what the law has forbidden them to do, they cannot alienate their liberty so as to give any person a demand upon them to do it. When I speak of unlawful promises, I do not mean those only by which we engage to give or to do what the law of nature forbids to be given or to be done by us; where the matter of a promise is forbidden by any other law, by the positive law of God, for instance, or by the law of the land, or by the commands of our lawful superiors, as far as they have a right to command us, such a promise is void; we have done nothing by making it, and consequently have not obliged ourselves to the performance of it. The reason why we have done nothing by making it is, because the law, as far as we owe obedience to it, has taken away our liberty, and we cannot alienate our liberty where we have it not.

* Grot. Lib. II. Cap. XI. § VIII. † Ibid.

IX. Thirdly, a second or any subsequent promise, which is contrary to one that was formerly made, cannot oblige us, or cannot make void the former promise. When we have once alienated a part of our liberty, it is not our own to dispose of again; when we have given one man a demand upon us to act in a particular manner, we have parted with our liberty in this respect, and cannot give another man a demand upon us to act in a contrary manner. What is here said of promises is equally true of all other sorts of voluntary obligations. Any former obligation takes away the liberty of the person who is engaged in it; and where he has no liberty, he can do no act which will be valid, and consequently none which can be binding upon him. Indeed, upon any other supposition, there would be no such thing as any possibility of a man's being obliged at all by his own act; which in morality is deemed an absurdity. For, if a second obligation could make void the first, then a third might make void the second, and a fourth might make void the third, and so on without end.

A subsequent promise cannot bind, where it is contrary to a former promise.

X. *If the matter of a promise is impossible or unlawful at the time of making it, but the circumstances of the promiser are such as may be altered, and a change in his circumstances would render it possible or lawful for him to perform his promise; it may be questioned whether a promise of this sort is binding; because it may be thought, that as the promiser engaged for what he had, at the time of engaging, no natural or no moral power to perform, his act was originally void; and that no accident, which shall happen afterwards, can give a validity to what was so void in the first instance. But here it should be observed, that the act is not so far void from the beginning, as that no future event can make it binding. Where a man's words can be so interpreted as to have any meaning, we are always to follow that interpretation which will give them a meaning. And if the promiser had any meaning at all, it must be this—that he would give the thing or do the act promised, whenever it should be in his power, or whenever by any change in his circumstances it should become lawful. This condition is sometimes expressed in promises of this sort; and when it is not expressed, the rule of interpretation before laid down naturally leads us to suppose that it was implied. But where such a condition is either expressed or implied, notwithstanding the present impossibility or unlawfulness in the matter of the promise, the promiser does something: he gives those to whom he thus engages, a demand upon his person not to use his liberty otherwise, upon a supposed event, than according to the terms of his engagement; he might upon this event have his liberty, but he alienates it beforehand; if the matter of the promise ever can be possible or ever can be lawful, his liberty of acting is his own in possibility; and as far as it is his own, he consents to part with it. The obligation of these promises is in suspense, and then only takes place when the event happens which renders the matter of them possible or lawful.

The obligation of a promise may be in suspense.

Sometimes it depends upon ourselves, whether it shall be possible for us, or not, to perform our promises; some act or some endeavours of our own may put us into such a situation as will make the performance pos-

* Grotius, Lib. II. Cap. XI. § VIII.

sible. A promise in this case binds us to the doing those acts, or to the using those endeavours; though such acts and such endeavours are not expressly contained in it; for he, who has obliged himself to the end, cannot but be understood to have obliged himself to the necessary means. Or rather, nothing can be properly called impossible for a man to do, which by his own acts or his own endeavours can be brought about. A promise therefore of this sort is binding from the beginning; and though we have not in express words bound ourselves to do those acts or to use those endeavours, yet if the possibility of performing what we have promised depends upon them, we are obliged to them in virtue of our promise.

Promises not to be evaded by a supposed tacit condition of circumstances continuing the same.

XI. Some have imagined, that all promises are to be understood to contain a tacit condition, that the promiser continues in the same situation, as when he promised. I do not mean a tacit condition of being obliged, only if the matter of the promise continues possible or lawful to him; for there is no occasion to suppose such a condition, since the obligation of the promise, in such a change of situation, would cease of itself without the help of any tacit reserve. But I mean a reserve that, when the time of performance comes, it shall be as convenient to the promiser to make good his word, as it was at the time of promising.

Such a tacit condition as this, if the promiser is allowed to explain it, will put it into his power either to be obliged or not obliged at his own pleasure. For it is next to impossible for the circumstances of any man to continue so exactly the same, as not to give him an opportunity of finding out some alteration in them, between the time of promising and the time of performance. And it would be absurd to suppose a condition to be tacitly annexed to any obligation, which is of such a sort as to leave the obligation to the discretion of the party obliged.

But if the party to whom the promise is made, is to be the judge of the other's circumstances; if it is left to him to determine whether such a change has happened in them, as to set the obligation aside, such a tacit condition will be of no use to the promiser; he must, notwithstanding this reserve, stand to the courtesy of the party to whom he is obliged, and he could only stand to his courtesy to be released, if we suppose no such tacit condition.

Men of loose principles are apt to pretend that they promised under this condition, though they did not express it; not only when the performance of their promises by a change in their circumstances is become a real hardship, and common benevolence would engage the other party to release them, but when they find that by breaking their word they may make some petty advantage, which they could not make by keeping it. If there was any way of convincing men of such a character, that their promises could not suppose any such tacit condition, it must be when in making them they have expressed some other condition. The surest way of making a promise absolute in all other respects, is by annexing some one express condition to it. Where one condition is expressed, the natural presumption is, that no other is implied or understood; because if there had been any other in the mind of the promiser, such a fair opportunity as that of mentioning one condition would in course have led him to mention that other; when he designed to make conditions, and was employed about making them, he mentioned only one; we have, therefore, good reason to believe, that he thought of and intended no more. Upon this account the strongest form of promising is to annex some slight condition to the promise, such as—If I live;—If I have my senses;—or some other of the like sort.

Promises of infants, ideots, and madmen do not bind.

XII. *No promise is binding, unless the person who made it, has liberty to choose for himself, and understanding to direct him in his choice. Without these faculties of liberty and understanding, he is no moral agent, or is not capable of doing an act so as to produce any moral effect by it. Upon this account the promises of infants, ideots and madmen are not binding; they are not moral agents, and are therefore unable to do any valid act.

Rash promises, in what sense binding.

XIII. If it should be inquired, whether a rash promise is binding, it would be necessary before we determine upon this question, to examine what is meant by a rash promise. The words are sometimes used to signify only a promise which is made unadvisedly, or without sufficient deliberation, and sometimes to signify a promise where the matter for want of such deliberation is unlawful. As to the latter sort of promises, they are void in themselves, without considering whether they are rashly or advisedly made; promises, if the matter of them is unlawful, are not binding, though they were made with ever so much deliberation.

Promises which are called rash in the former sense, merely because they were engaged in too hastily, if there is no other defect in them, are binding. Every act of a person who has liberty and understanding, must always be considered as the result of proper deliberation; if he has these faculties, the presumption is that he made use of them; and it was his own fault if he did not. If it was otherwise, if a man's having these faculties was not a sufficient ground to presume, even against his own subsequent declaration, that he made use of them, there could be no effectual obligation derived from any human act whatsoever, because the agent need only declare in any case after the act is over, that he did not act deliberately, and then the obligation would be void.

Promises become binding by acceptance.

XIV. †Before we go on to consider some other questions relating to promises, it may be proper to observe, that a promise is not binding till it is accepted. The party to whom it is made, does not without acceptance acquire any right or demand upon the promiser; for no right or demand of any sort can be acquired without the consent of him who acquires it. And unless some person has a demand upon the promiser, he is under no obligation.

‡From hence it follows, that a promise, after it is made, may be recalled without injustice, provided this is done before such promise is accepted; no right or demand is acquired, till the acceptance of the promise; and where there is no right, there can be no injustice. It ought, however, to be remembered, that as in alienations of property, so likewise in promises, it is not necessary for acceptance to follow the promise in order of time. When a person asks us to make him a promise, and we make it at his request, the promise becomes binding immediately; so that we cannot justly recall what we have done, upon pretence that he has not accepted it. His request is a sufficient evidence of his acceptance, though it

* Grot. Lib. II. Cap. XI. § V. † Ibid. § XIV. ‡ Ibid. § XVI.

went before the promise; unless, by any subsequent act or declaration of his, it appears that he had changed his mind.

*There may be some doubt, perhaps, whether mere acceptance is sufficient to bind the promiser, or whether it is not necessary that he should know of such acceptance. When the promise is made under either of these forms—I will that it shall bind me, when it is accepted—or I will, that it shall bind me, when I know it to be accepted; such precision leaves no room for this doubt. But when these forms are not observed, it seems to be the truer opinion, that in strict justice there is no obligation upon the promiser, till he knows of the acceptance; because an acceptance which is not made, and an acceptance which does not appear, are in respect of him the same thing. But yet if the promiser, without waiting a proper time to know the other parties' mind, should recall his word, he could not escape the charge of levity.

Signs of consent in promises and acceptance.

XV. The manner of promising or of refusing, when a request is made to us, and the manner likewise of accepting a promise, must be some external mark of the mind's intention. Nods may, indeed, bear the construction of consent, or shrugs, of refusal; but these are not established marks either of the one or the other; common usage has not sufficiently established their signification. The best established declarations of our mind are words either spoken or written. In some cases, indeed, our consent may be collected from our silence; but then there ought to be some special reason, why, if we did not consent, we should speak; for silence, when there was no such reason, will not easily bear this construction; in many instances we might fairly be supposed to have been silent only because we had no mind to speak.

Fear makes a promise void in some instances, not in others.

XVI. †Before we can determine whether we are bound by a promise which is extorted from us by force, or by threatening us with some great harm, unless we make such promise, it will be necessary for us to distinguish whether the force so made use of comes from the party to whom we make the promise, or from some one else; and if it comes from him, we must distinguish farther whether that force is just or unjust; that is, whether he has any right or not to threaten us with such an evil as is the occasion of our making the promise. If we were to determine that no promises which arise from fear are binding, and to ground our determination upon this principle, that the promiser, when such force is made use of as produces his fear, has not liberty to choose for himself, and is upon that account incapable of binding himself, it is plain the words of the question are what lead us to this determination, rather than the sense of it. Force is commonly opposed to liberty; and from thence we are induced to conclude too hastily, that where a promise is extorted by force, the promiser has not his liberty. But the force here supposed is not such as will leave the promiser no liberty of choosing for himself; he is forced indeed to choose one part of a disagreeable alternative, either to make the promise, or to suffer the evil with which he is threatened. But however disagreeable the alternative may be, yet, when he has two things to choose out of, he cannot be said to have no liberty. It must be a very ill-natured and inhuman doc-

* Grot. Lib. II. Cap. XI. § XV. † Ibid. § VII.

trine to teach, that the word of a person when he is in distress, and makes a promise in hopes of being relieved from it, is not as much to be relied upon, as when he is in full ease and happiness; and yet this must be the case, if a promise which we are induced to make from the apprehension of some great evil, is not binding upon us, merely because in such circumstances we have not a proper degree of liberty, as having only a disagreeable alternative before us, and being forced to choose out of two things, neither of which would have been the object of our choice if we had been in a better condition. Grotius was aware of this, and when he is considering only the situation of the promiser, he determines such an extorted promise to be binding.

His opinion, when he comes to speak of the other party, is very singular, and cannot be made intelligible. If, says he, the person to whom the promise is made, extorts it by bringing the promiser into any unjust fear, he is obliged to release such promiser; not because the promise was originally void in itself, but upon account of the unjust damage which he has done him. But how the promise can be valid, and the promiser not be bound by it, or how the promiser can be bound, and yet the other party have no demand upon him, or how this other party can have a demand and yet be obliged to give it up, is above my comprehension. An obligation on one part implies a demand or right on the other part. If, therefore, the promise is valid, or, which amounts to the same, if the promiser is obliged to performance, the party to whom such promise is made, must have a right to demand performance. But then, as a right to make such demand upon the promiser is inconsistent with an obligation to release him; it follows that one part of our author's opinion cannot be true; he must either allow the promise to be void, or must give up his notion of the other parties obligation to release the promiser.

To clear up this matter, let us return to our first distinction. If the promise is extorted by any unjust threatenings, and the party to whom it is made is the author of this unjust fear, such a promise is not binding; not upon account of the promiser's fear, but upon account of the other parties injustice. No right can be founded in an injury: every unjust act is void, as to all the moral effects of it, and consequently can never produce a demand in the person who is guilty of it. Now all obligations imply a right which corresponds to them. Therefore, if there is no right on the part of him who unjustly extorts the promise, there can be no obligation on the part of him from whom it is so extorted.

Upon these principles it will appear, that all promises which arise from fear, and from even unjust fear, are not void, though some are. If a magistrate by the fear of lawful penalties, forces me to make such promises or other stipulations, as I ought to have made without the use of force; my promise, notwithstanding the threatenings and fear from whence I am induced to make it, will be binding. There is nothing on my part, let the fear arise from what cause it will, which renders me incapable of binding myself; and if it arises, as is here supposed, from a just cause, there is no injustice in the other party, and consequently nothing which renders him incapable of acquiring a right. Nay, even where the fear is unjustly brought upon me, my promise will be binding, provided the fear arises from a third person, and the party to whom I make the promise is not concerned in the injustice. If I am afraid of being murdered because some one has threatened it, and promise a reward to a person for guarding me, though I am unjustly brought into this fear, yet my promise will oblige me. There is, as in all cases of fear, nothing on my part which disqualifies me from obliging myself; and as the guard to whom I make the promise, does me no injury, he is not disqualified from acquiring a demand.

When, therefore, we maintain that an extorted promise does not oblige, it must always be done under these restrictions, that we are unjustly brought into fear, and that the party to whom we make the promise is concerned in the injustice.

Erroneous promises, how made void.

XVII. *Where some mistake or error in the promiser is the only real and true cause of his making the promise, the obligation of such promise is void. When the supposed truth of a fact determines us to make a promise, where, if we had been rightly informed, we should have made none, we consent to be obliged upon supposition that the fact is true, and consequently the truth of the fact becomes a condition of our promise. If, therefore, the fact is false, the promise must be void; because all conditional promises are void, where the conditions are not made good, or because no man is obliged farther than he consents, and in the case now under consideration, we consent to be obliged no otherwise, than upon supposition that the fact is true.

It ought, however, to appear plainly from the promiser's words, or from the circumstances of the promise, or from the matter of it, that his error was the sole reason which effectually determined him to make it; because, if his obligation was to be void where this does not appear, it would almost always be in his power to make his promise void at his own pleasure. He might pretend that he was in some error, and that, if he had been well informed, he should not have engaged in such a promise. An error which does not appear, is of no more account in our dealings with one another, than an error which does not exist; the law of nature cannot allow any effect to be obtained by what does not fall under the notice of mankind. Caius is a candidate for a certain office, and I promise him my vote: at the time of making this promise, I supposed that Sempronius, to whom I have particular obligations, would not be his competitor; but before the day of election I find that he is. If this supposition of mine did not appear at all, if it was not plainly the reason which induced me to make this promise; it cannot affect the promise after it is made, so as to set it aside. I might not have this supposition in my mind, or if I had, yet since all men are not determined in their actions by principles of gratitude, I should perhaps have made the same promise, whether I thought about Sempronius as a competitor or not. But if, when I engaged to Caius, I expressly told him that I had great obligations to Sempronius, but believed his present situation to be such, as made me imagine he would not offer himself, a declaration of this sort plainly shows that I had this supposition in my mind, and that it determined me to engage myself to him. Or if Caius, when he applied to me, had said, that, notwithstanding my obligations to Sempronius, I might safely engage to him, because my friend would not oppose him, and in consequence of this assurance I promise my vote

* Grot. Lib. II. Cap. XI. § VI.

to him; though my own words might not show what supposition determined me to this promise, yet the circumstances would show it plainly enough to release me from any obligation, when I find afterwards that Sempronius is a candidate.

XVIII. *As we may bind ourselves by a promise which we make in our own person, so likewise we are obliged to stand to a promise which another person makes for us, where we have given him either a general commission to act for us in all things, or a particular commission to act in this affair. In either case, by such a commission, where he keeps within the bounds of it, we have made his act our own.

A man's agent may promise for him.

Where we have given a man a power or commission to act for us, as our proxy, though no restriction or limitation of such commission may appear, yet it frequently happens that we give some private instructions to such proxy or agent in what manner we would have him act, and how far he may go. Suppose him then to act contrary to these private instructions, and to go farther than we allowed him; we shall be obliged to stand to the promise which he makes for us, notwithstanding our consent seems to be wanting. For that act of our will, whereby he was appointed our agent, which is the only act of our will that is or can be known by the party to whom the promise is made, is sufficient to make what such agent does for us be considered as our own act. The private instructions which we gave him, cannot affect any one to whom they are not known, and from whom we were determined to conceal them; they cannot, therefore, so affect the party to whom the promise is made, as to prevent his claim upon us; the consent which appears to him, must, in respect of him, be looked upon as our true and full consent. If it was otherwise, there would be such room for collusion between the promiser and his agent, that it would be in their power at any time to prevent any obligation from arising upon promises thus made.

However, though our limitations or secret instructions, in respect of the party to whom the promise is made, are considered as not in existence, because they neither do nor can appear to him, and consequently cannot invalidate his claim, which arises from our public consent or apparent act; yet they will produce their proper effect upon the person to whom they are known. Our agent knows them, and the effect which they produce upon him, is to make him answerable for any loss or damage that we may sustain by his having exceeded them; because by undertaking to act for us under these restrictions, he has at least tacitly obliged himself not to act otherwise.

XIX. †When we have appointed an agent to promise for us, the agent may happen to die before he has transacted the business, and some other person who knew that he was our agent and for what purpose, may possibly undertake to make the promise without our appointment, which he was to have made if he had lived long enough to do it; in this case no obligation arises upon us from the act of such person. For want of our appointment, that is, for want of our consent to what he has done, it cannot be looked upon as our own act. If, indeed, our promise was contained in a letter, and the bearer to whom we entrusted the letter dies, but after his death this

Voluntary agent does not oblige.

* Grot. Lib. II. Cap. XI. § XII.

† Ibid. § XVII.

letter is delivered by some one else to the party to whom the promise is made, the promise then becomes binding upon acceptance. The first bearer of the letter was not our agent; the letter is to promise for us and is the instrument of our consent; and it is not at all material whether the instrument by which we designed to bind ourselves, comes to the hands of the party to whom we make the promise, by the hands of the first bearer to whom we entrusted it, or by the hands of any one else.

What promises may and what may not be recalled, when they pass through a third hand.

XX. Where a promise passes from the promiser to the other party through a third hand, we should consider whether this third person was appointed merely as a messenger to notify the promise, or as an agent to make it. If he was only a messenger to notify the promise, and the promiser recalls it before acceptance, but without acquainting his messenger that he has done so, such a revocation will have its effect; and though the messenger should afterwards notify the promise, and acceptance should be made upon such notification, the promiser is not obliged to make the promise good. The obligation of such a promise depends upon the will of the promiser, and not upon the will of his messenger; he had not bound himself to the messenger, and much less to any one else, to continue in the same mind or to abide by any act which his messenger should do. This is the decision of Grotius upon the case. But he should have added that the promiser, though he might have no opportunity of informing his messenger that he had recalled his promise, should take care to acquaint some others with his having done so; because his revocation, if it did not appear, can be of no more account than if it did not exist; and consequently without this precaution he could not in justice claim to be released.

But, when the person through whose hands the promise passes, was appointed to make it as the promiser's agent, then notwithstanding the promiser should recall it before it is made, yet unless his agent is made acquainted with what he has done, and for want of such notice makes the promise, it will be binding. The agent's appointment continues till he knows himself to be discharged, and the promiser by that appointment had transferred his power of acting in the case from himself to his agent.

Grotius, when he is taking notice of this distinction, applies it in passing to the case of gifts. Where I have made an actual donation, and have ordered a messenger to notify this to the person to whom I so alienate my property, in order for his acceptance; if I die before this notice is actually given, and he upon receiving the notice accepts; though this is done after my death, the donation is valid. It was complete on my part before my death; the messenger was not to make the donation for me, but to notify that I had made it; and as to the other parties acceptance by which the transfer is completed, this may as well be done after my death as before it; since I am no way concerned in this act of acceptance, nor is any farther concurrence of mine necessary towards completing the transfer than what I had given already. We should, however, observe, that such a donation can only take place as a will does, where no acceptance is made before the testator's death; it must be some positive law which, by taking the thing given into its custody, prevents it from becoming the property of the first occupant, between the giver's death and the other parties acceptance. But if, instead of making the donation myself, and ordering a messenger to notify what I have done, I appoint an agent to make it for me; then if I die before it is made, the donation will be void; though my agent, not knowing of my death, should make it afterwards. The donation in this case was not actually made before my death, but was only ordered to be made; and after my death, as I cannot act for myself, so neither can I act by any other person; the appointment of any other person to be my agent, or to do my acts for me, ceases with my life, as I am then no longer capable of doing any act.

But what is here said, relates only to actual donations, and not to promises of giving. Whatever may be the character of the person, through whose hands such promise is conveyed, whether he is a messenger sent by me, or an agent commissioned to act for me; if I die before acceptance, no subsequent acceptance can affect my heirs; since the obligation of my promise, even after it is accepted, is only personal, and consequently must cease at my death. A promise does not alienate my property in the thing promised, or give the party to whom I make the promise any claim upon the thing; it only alienates a part of my liberty, and gives him a claim upon my person to do such acts as will alienate the thing hereafter.

Effects of acceptance by another, either with or without commission.

XXI. *As we bind ourselves by promises, which another man who is appointed to act for us makes in our name, so likewise we may accept promises by our agent, and may acquire a right in virtue of a promise so accepted. But where a person who happens to be present when a promise is made, accepts for us, without having our commission for so doing, some doubt may be raised concerning the effect of such an acceptance. And it will be necessary in determining any doubts upon this head, to inquire whether the promise is made directly to the person who is present, though it is made for our benefit, or whether the words of it show that it was made to us who are absent, and that the person who is present at the time of making it is only appealed to as a witness of what has passed. Thus a promise relating to Titius, who is absent, may be made to Caius, who is present, under either of these forms.—I promise you, Caius, that I will give such a thing or do such a service to Titius,—or, I promise Titius to give him such a thing, or to do him such a service, and do you, Caius, take notice that I have promised it.

In the former of these cases, as the promise is made directly to Caius, though it is for the benefit of Titius, yet the acceptance of Caius binds the promiser; because the liberty which he alienates by it, is alienated to Caius, and it is he who acquires a right by this act over the promiser's person. It is, therefore, in his power to release the promiser at any time before Titius has accepted it. But after his acceptance, it is out of the power of Caius to release such promiser; because by his proposal of the affair to Titius, and by the acceptance which follows upon it, his right over the person of the promiser is conveyed to Titius. Suppose Titius should refuse the favour, this refusal releases the promiser, and he is no longer under the same obligation to Caius; because, as the benefit arising from the promise was a benefit to be received by Titius, upon his refusal to receive such benefit, the matter of the promise becomes impossible.

* Grot. Lib. II. Cap. XI. § XVIII.

In the other case, if the promiser says I engage to Titius, who is absent, that I will give him such a thing, or do him such a service, and do you, Caius, take notice that I have so engaged; then upon supposition, that Caius has a general commission to act for Titius, or a special commission to act for this purpose, his acceptance will make the promise binding upon the promiser. But if he has no such commission, and does not accept, then the promise will, notwithstanding his attestation of it, be in the power of the promiser, who may recall it if he pleases, at any time before it is accepted by Titius. Only as he had published the promise, it will be necessary for him to recall it publicly; otherwise, if the promise appears, but the revocation does not appear, the promise will stand good and the revocation will be nothing, for a reason which has been frequently mentioned and need not be repeated. Or lastly, suppose that Caius, who is so called upon to attest a promise made to Titius, should, though he has no commission to act for him, accept the promise; then if the promiser does not agree that he should accept it, his acceptance can have no effect; he is not appointed agent for Titius, and the promiser will not transact with him as if he had that character. But if the promiser consents that he should accept, then, notwithstanding he has no such appointment, this case will be reduced to the same state with the former case; the promise upon the acceptance of Caius will be binding till it appears whether Titius will accept or refuse the interest which he has in it; for it is the same thing whether the promiser engages to Caius for the benefit of Titius, or engages to Titius and allows Caius so far to stand in the place of Titius as to accept for him.

A man's heirs cannot accept a promise for him.

XXII. If a promise is made to a man and he dies before acceptance, the acceptance of his heirs does not bind the promiser. However the promiser might propose to alienate a right over his person to the deceased, it does not follow that he is willing to alienate the same right over his person to the heirs of the deceased. Nay, we may go one step farther; if a promise is made to a man and is accepted by him, but is not performed before his death, his heirs have no claim to performance, unless they were expressly included in it. If, indeed, it had been made to him and his heirs, his acceptance would be binding upon the promiser for their interest as well as for his own. But if they were not included in it, if it was made to him without mentioning them, though he had accepted, yet the right acquired by such acceptance is merely personal, and dies with him.

This is too plain to be questioned in promises of doing. I have promised a man who is candidate for a certain office, that I will give him my vote; he accepts my promise, but dies before the day of election, and his son offers himself as a candidate for the same office. No one would imagine that my promise made to the father binds me to vote for the son.

Nor can any reason be given why it should be otherwise in promises of giving, why if I promise to give a man a sum of money and he accepts the favour of my promise, but dies before performance, his heir, unless he was expressly included in the promise, should have any claim to the money. If, indeed, the money, instead of being promised, had been actually given, the benefit of the promise would have descended to the heir; but this is no reason why, if the money had not been given, he should have the same claim upon me that the deceased would have had. I intended to give to the deceased; it does not follow from thence, that I intended to give to his heirs; the benefit of my promise, if it had been performed, would indeed have descended to them; but this is accidental, and does not appear to have been in my intention, as they were not expressly mentioned in the promise. If I had actually performed my promise by giving the money, I could not upon his decease have demanded it again of the heirs; because by giving it, I had parted with all my claim to it, and the deceased had, before his death, acquired a right not merely over my person by a promise, but in the thing itself by a transfer of it. He might, therefore, have disposed of it by will, if he had pleased, or if he does not do this it will descend to his heirs in intestate succession.

Promissory notes for money lent do not come under this description. The form of such notes—I promise to pay; especially if I add, for value received,—shows them to be more than mere promises; it shows that he who gives such notes acknowledges that something was due to the person to whom they are given; and consequently instead of being gratuitous promises, they are evidences of a debt.

CHAPTER XIII.

OF CONTRACTS.

I. *What meant by contracts.*—II. *Contracts are either of immediate or future performance.*—III. *Contracts are either of partial or mutual benefit.*—IV. *Contracts are either of giving or doing, or both.*—V. *No man by contract parts with more than he intended.*—VI. *The nature and obligation of a loan of inconsumable goods.*—VII. *Of a commission.*—VIII. *Of a charge.*—IX. *Contracts of mutual benefit either share the matter or make it common.*—X. *Incapacity of either party to be obliged, voids the contract.*—XI. *What the equality required in contracts consists in.*—XII. *Equality in the previous acts relates to knowledge and freedom.*—XIII. *Equality in the principal act relates to knowledge of the price.*—XIV. *Equality in the matter relates to faults in the goods, or errors in the price unknown to either party.*—XV. *Want of an equivalent, how supplied in auctions.*—XVI. *Price of things or work, what it is and how varied.*—XVII. *Fair price is the market price.*—XVIII. *Extraordinary circumstances allow to exceed the market price.*—XIX. *Advantages by the introduction of money.*—XX. *Metals, the most proper materials for money.*—XXI. *Uses and rules of coining.*—XXII. *Use of money varies the price of goods.*—XXIII. *Buying and selling.*—XXIV. *Letting and renting.*—XXV. *Letting and hiring of labour.*—XXVI. *Loan of consumable goods.*—XXVII. *Interest for money, upon what principles to be defended.*—XXVIII. *Usury, why forbidden by the Mosaic law.*—XXIX. *Question relating to a loan.*—XXX. *Nature of insurance.*—XXXI. *Mixed contracts.*—XXXII. *Gain and loss, how adjusted in partnership.*—XXXIII. *Partnerships mixed with insurance.*—XXXIV. *Contract of one party's bearing the whole loss without any share in the gain.*—XXXV. *Work and money how compared in partnerships.*—XXXVI. *Contracts how dissolved.*—XXXVII. *Contracts of chance, their nature and obligation.*—XXXVIII. *Contracts with a man to do or give what we might claim, are void.*—XXXIX. *Contracts void where the matter is unlawful.*—XL. *Obligation how restored to void contracts.*

What meant by contracts.

I. In the last chapter we have considered at large the nature of promises. Where by promises I mean such acts, as lay an obligation on the party or parties concerned on one side, and convey a demand upon their person to the party or parties concerned on the other side. So that in promises, according to this description of them, there is no mutual obligation of the parties on both sides, each to the other; there is only an obligation on one part, and a correspondent right on the other part. *Such acts of mankind, as produce a mutual obligation, and consequently a mutual claim on the parties concerned on both sides, are contracts.

* Grot. Lib. II. Cap. XII. § VII.

II. Contracts are either such as are performed immediately, or such as we engage to perform at some future time. Those of immediate performance I shall call simply contracts, and those which we bind ourselves to perform at some future time, may be called promissory contracts.

Contracts are either of immediate or future performance.

From this description of promissory contracts, it will appear that we need not consider them particularly; for the questions which arise upon them, are either what may be determined from the rules relating to contracts in general, or from those which have been laid down relating to promises.

III. A second division of contracts is into such as *are of mutual, and such as are of partial benefit. All contracts, indeed, suppose a mutual obligation of the parties engaged in them; but we shall find presently that they do not all produce a mutual benefit.

Contracts are either of partial or of mutual benefit.

IV. A third division of contracts is into †contracts of giving, or contracts of doing, or contracts both of giving and of doing. For all the benefit arising from contracts, whether it is partial or mutual, must arise either from things or from actions, or from both. Only it is to be observed, that under the notion of things we here include not only goods but money likewise, and the use of either goods or money.

Contracts are either of giving or doing, or of both.

V. The fundamental rule in all contracts is, that no man by engaging in them parts with more than he designed to part with, or that the demand of one party cannot exceed what was in the intention of the other party to transfer or give up to him.

No man by contract parts with more than he intended.

By the design or intention of either party, is not here meant any secret or reserved design or intention, which he kept in his mind and never discovered. Such a design or intention as does not appear, is in cases of contracts, as in all other cases, of no more account than a design or intention which does not exist. But by the design or intention of either party, is meant such design or intention as may be fairly collected either from his words or his actions. In the intercourse of mankind one with another, no person can be supposed to design or intend what does not appear in one of these ways; because there is no evidence and can be no knowledge of his designing or intending any thing else but what does so appear.

There is a plain reason why no person's grant on one side, and consequently no person's just demand on the other side, as far as such grant is made or such demand arises from any contract, can ever extend beyond the design or intention of the person who makes the grant. If it was otherwise, he might lose a part of his property, or might be constrained to the doing certain actions without his own consent. But as all causeless harm done to a man either in his property or in his liberty, is injustice; and the taking from him his property or the constraining him to act in a certain manner without his own consent, is doing him causeless harm in these respects; it follows, that there can be no just demand either upon his goods or his person, any farther than he appears, or may be fairly shown to have had a design or intention of granting such demand.

* Grotius, Lib. II. Cap. XII. § II.

† Ibid.

The nature and obligations of a loan of inconsumable goods.

VI. We will first consider contracts of partial benefit, which may likewise be called gratuitous contracts, because there is a favour done on one side, and no return of benefit arises from such contracts.

*If one man makes over his goods absolutely to another, without reserving to himself any claim upon the goods, or upon the party to whom he makes them over; this is a gift, and does not come within our description of contracts; no mutual obligation arises from such an act as this. In like manner, if we find that any person has occasion for our assistance, and we do him the service which he wants, this is no contract; provided no mutual obligation of justice arises from such service. But where our goods are such as will not perish or be consumed in using, we have it in our power to dispose of the use of those goods, without alienating the property which we have in them; we may let a man have the use of our house, or land, or horses, or books, and still keep our claim to the things themselves. When this is done, without taking any valuable consideration of the person to whom we so make over the use, this is called a loan; and the act of our lending and his borrowing is a gratuitous contract. The act is plainly gratuitous; because he has a benefit from the use of our goods, and we receive no benefit in return: and it is a contract, because a mutual obligation upon the lender and upon the borrower arises from it.

The principal obligation on the part of the lender is to take nothing for the use of his goods. This is all which is contained in the general notion of a loan: neither the words nor the actions of a man, who says that he will lend another his house, or his land, or his books, or his horses, or any thing else which may be used without being consumed, and who does lend them accordingly, imply any more than this.

There may indeed be some other accidental obligations upon the lender: but they are such as are not included in the general notion of a loan, and can take place no otherwise than by having been particularly specified. Thus he may, for instance, have expressed particularly for what determinate time he made over the use of his goods; if he has done this, he is obliged not to call for them, and has no right to demand them till that time is expired.

The principal obligation on the part of the borrower is to return the goods in the same condition that he received them: except only as far as they must have been necessarily impaired by time or by the use which was granted to him. He is obliged to return the goods again, because the lender did not design to transfer the property of them to him: and by the general rule of all contracts, the borrower can demand no more than the lender designed to grant. If no time was fixed at first for returning the goods, it cannot be collected for what time the lender designed to part with the use of them: it must therefore depend upon his pleasure how long the borrower shall use them. But if any time was fixed when the goods were lent, the owner then agreed to let the borrower use them so long. However, therefore, the lender may want them in the meanwhile, the borrower can only be charged with ingratitude if he refuses to return them. He certainly cannot be charged with injustice in keeping the use of the goods for as long a

* Grot. Lib. II. Cap. XII. § II.

time as the other had given him a right to keep them. When the borrower returns the goods, he is obliged to return them in the same condition in which he received them; because otherwise he would take more than the lender designed to give him. The lender intended to grant only the use of his goods; but he loses more than this by the borrower, if his goods are returned to him in a worse condition than when they went out of his hands.

We ought however to consider whether the damage which the goods have received is such as they would have suffered, though they had continued in the owner's hands, or whether it is such as they have suffered through some fault of the borrower. In the latter case he is obliged to make good the damage, for the reason already assigned. But in the former case, as for instance, suppose the house to be burnt, or the land to be washed away by the sea, or the horses to die of some common distemper, the lender must in justice bear the loss; because if the borrower was to stand to all such hazards, and to make good all accidents which happen without his fault, and would have happened, though the thing had continued in the hands of the lender, there would arise from the contract a mutual benefit to the lender, which is contrary to the nature of a loan. There is indeed no injustice in bargaining with a man, that he shall ensure our goods from casualties for the use of them: and if he agrees to this, he will be obliged to stand to all damages, as well those which happen without his fault, as those which happen with it. But then this contract is not a loan: such conditions as these are not implied in the act of lending; and if we would claim to have them observed, we must take care particularly to specify them.

The nature and obligation of a commission.

VII. If a man undertakes to do business for me without any pay or reward; his proposal of this sort, and my acceptance of it, is a gratuitous contract, the general name of which is a commission. If the service which he undertakes to do me consists in taking the custody of my goods, this particular sort of commission is called a charge.

In a commission, the obligation on his part who undertakes it, is to transact the business without wages or any other valuable consideration, and to use the same care and diligence in it, as if it was his own. That he is to require no wages or reward for his work, is plain from the nature of this contract, which supposes him to undertake the business gratuitously, that is, to have declared his design of giving his time and trouble to the person for whom he undertakes it. The only question is, what degree of diligence is required of him. The degree mentioned above is the same that he would make use of in his own business, where it is of the same importance with that which he undertakes for another man; and it cannot be shown that the other has any right to claim a higher degree than this. Every man is supposed to manage his own affairs to the best of his abilities, as far as the matter in hand may deserve or require such management: and there can be no reasonable demand that he should increase his usual care, when he is to manage the affairs of another. But though a higher degree of diligence is not required, yet a lower degree would scarce be sufficient. It is better for us to pay for having our business well done, than to have it managed carelessly for nothing. Whenever, therefore, we entrust any person with a commission, we must reasonably be supposed to have some ground for believing that our affairs, when put into his hands, will be well managed: and the most obvious ground for believing this, is what we have observed ourselves, or have heard well attested by others, concerning his management of his own affairs. Since therefore his prudent management of his own affairs, as far as our observation or intelligence reaches, is the ground of our trusting him; we show by the very act of trusting him, that we expect he will manage as carefully for us as he is used to do for himself. And if this is our intention, which is made to appear by our act of trusting him; then he, by undertaking the trust, tacitly engages for this degree of diligence. However, unless there is notorious mismanagement, his kindness entitles him to our favour: it is not reasonable that any man should be a loser by his kindness in undertaking to give us his time and trouble in doing our business for us; and upon this account it is equitable to presume, in all doubtful cases, that the damages which we may suffer in such of our affairs as are in his hands, have not been owing to any indiscretion or neglect in him.

The obligation on our part, when such a commission is undertaken for our benefit, is to repay any expenses which he who undertook it, may be at, and to make good any loss which he may sustain in his own affairs, upon account of his having engaged in the management of ours. By engaging to give us his trouble, it appears, indeed, that he intended to give us thus much; but it does not appear that he intended to give us more. Therefore, by the general rule of all contracts, no more than this is due to us: and whatever he loses more than this by our means, or upon our account, he has a right to demand of us.

A guardian or executor of a will is engaged in a contract of this sort; where he undertakes the trust without being paid for it, or, which amounts to the same thing, where he receives a small acknowledgment that does not by any means answer his trouble, nor was intended as a sufficient payment. The ward or the heir is not the other party concerned in this contract with the guardian or executor: for he does not undertake the trust at their request or by their appointment. The other party is the testator, who requests and appoints him to be guardian or executor. This appointment was made by the testator before his death, and the contract is completed afterwards by the acceptance of the executor or guardian. Here then, it may be asked, since the ward or the heir is not a party in the contract, how comes the guardian's or executor's demand for such expenses as he makes, or for such losses as he meets with, to be upon the ward or heir? The reason is, that the guardian or executor, being entrusted with the management and disposal of the testator's goods, has a demand for his expenses or losses, not upon the person of the testator, but upon those goods with which he is so entrusted; and by this means the demand will terminate in the ward or heir, who receives the goods chargeable with such demand.

In intestate successions, where the heir is an infant, whoever voluntarily undertakes the management of his affairs has a like demand. Such inheritances are indeed introduced by positive laws, and the laws which introduce those inheritances, commonly take care to provide both for the benefit of the heir and the security of the guardian. But the claim of a guardian will appear still stronger, if we were to consider this case as it would stand by the law of nature. The guardian then would have a right to the goods as the first occupant: and if out of mere bounty he should afterwards give them up to any relation of the intestate person, there could be no question of his having a right to such a part of the goods as would repay him what expenses he had made, and would satisfy him for what losses he had sustained by taking the custody of the whole, till the intestate's relation was capable of receiving them.

The nature and obligations of a charge.

VIII. From this account of the obligations which arise from the general notion of a commission, we may easily understand what are the obligations attending that particular sort of commission, which is called a charge. If I undertake the charge of another man's goods, to keep them safe for him; I engage for nothing but my own diligence and fidelity. Whatever expenses therefore I may be at merely upon this account, he is obliged to repay me. In the mean time I am obliged to use the same diligence in keeping and securing his goods, that I would make use of in keeping and securing goods of the same value, if they were my own.

Upon this principle it will sometimes happen, that I ought to preserve his goods, rather than my own; not because a greater degree of diligence is due to him than to myself; but because his goods may be of more value than any which belong to me; and I am to use the same diligence in preserving his goods, that I would use in preserving my own, if they were of equal value. Thus, if I have a chest of gold or of deeds belonging to another man in my custody; I might be obliged, in case of fire, to secure those treasures, rather than any of my own common furniture.

On the other hand, if attempts have been made to break open my house, whilst I have the treasure of another man in my keeping, and I am therefore forced to hire a guard, not for the sake of securing my own common goods, which are not likely to have been the temptation; as this expense is undertaken upon his account, he is obliged to pay the wages of the guard.

There can be no question whether the nature of this contract allows me to make use of goods which are thus deposited in my hands, and which I undertook to secure. They were plainly lodged in my hands for the owner's benefit, and not for mine: they were to be kept for him, and not to be used by me. Neither can I claim the use of them, in return for my trouble in keeping them: if I had designed such a thing, I might have mentioned it at first; and then, if he had consented to it, I might have claimed the use of such goods so deposited with me. But in the mere act of undertaking a charge, no such claim is understood: the act in its own nature is beneficial to the owner of the goods only, and is gratuitous on my part, unless I have taken care to make any express reserve to the contrary.

Indeed, where goods will not be at all the worse for using, as for instance, if I have a piece of plate in my custody, and only set it on my sideboard for ornament; the owner might be thought too strict, if he complained of me for making such a use of his goods. However, my charge has certainly given me no right to use his goods, even for such purposes as these. And if by thus letting it be publicly known that I have goods of value in my hands, the future custody of them should become more expensive to me than it otherwise would have been; I do not see with what justice I could require him to bear these extraordinary expenses which I have brought upon myself, by doing what I had no right to do.

Contracts of mutual benefit either share the matter or make it common.

IX. *Contracts of mutual benefit are either simple or mixed. Simple contracts of this sort are either such as share the matter of them between the contracting parties, or such as make it common to the parties.

Such contracts, as share the matter of mutual benefit between the parties concerned in them, may be distinguished into three sorts, agreeable to the third general division of contracts, which has been already taken notice of. The only ways of benefitting one another, are either by giving things in exchange for things; or secondly, by doing useful services in return for useful services; or lastly, by doing useful services in exchange for things.

This division of contracts will be better understood by applying it in some few instances. We will begin with bartering. This is a contract of the first sort, in which goods are given on one part for goods given on the other part. The contract does not unite the goods into one common stock, but all the goods on each side being considered as the matter of the contract, it shares or divides this matter between the parties concerned in it. Bartering may be considered in two different views. This contract could not be very like buying and selling, before the invention of money. Goods might then indeed be exchanged for goods, as horses for oxen, or sheep for corn: but there could be no other way of comparing them with one another, no measure of the price of them on either side, but what was taken from the use which one party might have for the goods of the other. If one person had many sheep but no grain, and another on the contrary had much grain but no sheep; each of them would make his own want of the other's goods the measure by which to determine what quantity of his own he would be willing to give for what quantity of the other's. But since the invention and use of money, bartering approaches so near to buying and selling, that there is scarce any difference between them: in the exchange of goods for goods, the goods on both sides are valued in money, and are compared with one another by this standing measure. If a man exchanges sheep for oxen, or wool for wine; he does not determine how many sheep he will give for an ox, or what weight of wool he will give for a hogshead of wine, by considering how little he wants the sheep or the wool, and how much he wants the ox or the wine: but he estimates the value of the goods on both sides in money, which is the common standard of price.

There is another contract of the same sort, to which the name of exchange is appropriated, a contract of giving money for money. I do not mean, when money is given for a medal or some scarce coin, which is matter of curiosity; for this is buying and selling: but when current coin of one sort is given for current coin of another sort, as gold or silver coin for copper coin; or when current coin of any sort is given in one place for current coin of any sort to be paid in another place; as when I give a man a certain sum of monev at my own

* Grot. Lib. II. Cap. XII. § III.

home, and he is to give me, or to pay for my use, a certain sum of money in London or Paris.

Giving cash for bills cannot be strictly reduced to this head; because he who gives the cash and takes the bill, gives something more than the cash: he gives his trouble in negotiating the bill, and runs some hazard, if the several parties concerned in the bill should become insolvent whilst it is in his hands. So that if we consider the bill as money, he for this money gives his own money and his work besides, and does likewise in some sort ensure the bill.

The contract is still of the same sort when money is given for goods; and the name of this contract is buying and selling. The money and the goods are the matter of the contract; and the contract shares this matter, or divides it between the parties concerned, and gives each of them property in his particular share.

Of the same sort are those contracts, in which the use of goods is given for the use of goods: as if, for instance, a person has the use of my house in town, and I, in exchange, have the use of his house in the country. The use of the houses is the matter of the contract; and it is the business of the contract to share this matter between the parties, and to adjust their respective claims upon it.

In like manner the use of goods may be given for money: this contract is still of the same sort, and is called letting or renting. Nor is it a different contract when the use of goods is given for goods, as when I let my estate, and bargain to receive the rent of it in cattle, or wheat, or malt.

It is not possible to reckon up the several contracts which share the matter between the contracting parties, and fall under the second head of contracts, whereby useful services are exchanged for useful services. They are as numberless as the actions are, by which one man can promote the pleasure or profit of another. In general, we may observe, that in all these contracts, the work or service on both sides is the matter of the contract; and that the effect of the contract is to assign to each party the work which he is to do, and to give the other a claim upon him to do it. Contracts, therefore, which are purely of this sort, so that things are in no respect any part of the matter of them, are mutual alienations of liberty: each party obliges himself to do some work for the benefit of the other, or each party gives the other a demand upon his person.

Under the third head, where things are exchanged for beneficial services; though the beneficial services which may be performed are numberless, yet the things which are given for such services, must be goods either moveable or immoveable, or money, or the use either of goods or of money. The beneficial services and the things to be given for them are the matter of such contracts: and the effect of the contract is to assign each party his share of this matter, or to settle what things one of the parties shall have a right to claim, and what services in return the other shall be entitled to. When money is given by one party in consideration of the other party's undertaking to preserve his goods from accidents, it is called insurance. When money is given for common or daily work, it is called letting and hiring.

The second sort of contracts of mutual benefit are such as make the matter common to the parties concerned in them, or give the contracting parties a common claim to it. The general name of all contracts of this sort is partnership: and the matter of them may be either things or actions, or both. When two or more persons join money, or goods, or labour, or all of these together, and agree to give each other a common claim upon such joint stock, this is a partnership.

All wages, or gaming of any sort, come under the notion of partnership. The stakes, that is, the money or goods laid down on each side, are a joint stock, upon which the parties concerned in the wager or game have a common claim, till the wager is decided, or the game is over. This partnership was originally intended to be of no longer continuance: the parties agreed from the first, that some uncertain event should put an end to it in such a manner, that when it ends, the stock, which was in common before, shall not be divided, but shall become the sole property of one of them.

Lots, indeed, are made use of in other instances where there is no partnership, and no such common stock: but then in these instances there is no contract. If a nation should determine itself by lot in making choice of judges in the assigning of provinces, or in the disposal of any other offices, this is no contract; it is only the method which the public fixes upon for choosing one out of many competitors, in order to avoid the ill will of those who are disappointed: and the right which the fortunate competitor has to his office, does not arise from any other contract, but the appointment of the public.

Incapacity of either party to be obliged voids a contract.

X. Contracts are, in some respects, subject to the same rules with promises: all the parties contracting must have the use of their understanding and of their will, or otherwise the contract will be void. I say all the parties must have these qualifications: because, as a mutual obligation of the parties on both sides is essential to contracts, where one of them is under any incapacity of obliging himself, the other cannot be obliged. In what manner fear or error affects a contract will appear from taking a more particular view of the equality naturally required in all mutual contracts.

What the equality required in contracts consists in.

XI. *It has been shown already, that neither of the parties in a contract can claim any right by virtue of it, which the other does not consent to transfer to him. And it appears from the nature of contracts of mutual benefit, that neither of the parties has, or can be supposed to have, any design or intention of transferring any right to the other without receiving an equivalent. From hence it follows, that when either party has received more than he has given an equivalent for, he has received what the other never designed or consented should be his: and consequently, as he has no claim to what he has so received, the contract is either void or must be corrected, that so he who has too little may either have his own again, or else may have amends made to him.

It may indeed be said, when I have bought goods and have paid the money for them, that by my act of parting with my money and taking the goods, I plainly showed my consent to transfer my property in the money to the seller, upon condition of his transferring his property in the goods to me. But the answer to this is obvious: in buying and

* Grot. Lib. II. Cap. XII. § VIII.

selling, it is well known, from the very nature of the contract, though our words may not express so much, that neither the buyer nor the seller intend to give each other any thing as matter of mere bounty, but only upon supposition of each receiving an equivalent for what he gives. If therefore I buy goods, I transfer the property in my money to the seller, upon supposition, that I receive an equivalent for what I so transfer, and not otherwise. So that if this supposition fails, if I do not receive an equivalent, the condition fails, upon which alone I consented that the money should be his. For this reason, though he may be in possession of the money, he has no right to it: he can have no right to it, unless I consented to give him such right; and I never consented to give him such right but under the condition just now mentioned. In like manner, if I hire a house or lands, that is, if I purchase the use of them; my intention, according to the nature of this contract, is, that I will give the owner nothing without receiving an equivalent for it. There is nothing of mere bounty in contracts of this sort; each party designs to receive as much benefit as he gives. Whatever rent therefore the owner of the house or lands receives of me, I consent to make it his, upon supposition that I receive the value of it in the use of his estate. If then this supposition fails, though he may have gotten possession of my money, it is not his; because it cannot be his without my consent, and I consented to make it his only upon supposition of my receiving an equivalent, which I have not received. The same reasoning may be applied to other contracts. If I hire a man's work or service, this is not matter of favour or bounty on either side. The nature of the contract shows, therefore, that I design to receive an equivalent for the wages which I am to give him: and consequently that I consent to make the wages his, or to give him property in my money only upon this condition. Unless then I do receive an equivalent for my money, the condition fails upon which alone I consented to make it his: and upon that account he has no claim to the wages for which we bargained.

Now, in order, as far as may be, to secure an equivalent to each party, in contracts of mutual benefit, it is necessary that they should treat with one another upon an equal footing; and their thus treating upon an equal footing is what we call the equality required in contracts. This equality relates either to the acts or to the matter of the contract. The acts in which equality is required, are either those which are previous to the contract, or the principal act of contracting.

Equality in the previous acts relates to knowledge and freedom.

XII. *Before the contract is entered upon, it is previously requisite that each party should be equal to the other as to his knowledge, or that whatever faults one of them knows of in the thing or the service, concerning which they are about to bargain, he should discover them to the other. For any fault in the matter of the contract which either party designedly concealed from the other, will make the contract void, by preventing the other from receiving his equivalent.

You sell me goods at a certain price, which would indeed be the true price of the goods, provided they had no concealed faults, but you know that they have such faults, and do not discover them. The goods

* Grot. Lib. II. Cap. XII. § IX.

then are not worth the price which you set upon them: and as I designed to give you such a price for them, only upon supposition of their being worth it, I transfer the property in the purchase money to you only upon this supposition; and, consequently, as this supposition is a condition of the transfer, there is no transfer at all, unless the supposition is true; and if you keep the money, you keep what is not your own.

How far common practice in buying and selling may have prejudiced you against this conclusion, I cannot tell. However, to show you the reasonableness of it, I will apply it to a similar instance in another sort of contract. I hire you to do some particular work; you, at the time of letting yourself, labour under some distemper or other infirmity which you conceal from me, so as to be disabled by it from doing the work for which I hire you. It will, I imagine, be allowed, that as soon as I discover you to be disabled, the bargain will be void; that you have no claim to the wages for which we bargained; and that, if I paid you them beforehand, you ought in justice to return them. What then is the reason why you have no claim to these wages? is not it because your work is not worth what I supposed it to be worth, and consequently in this contract I cannot receive my equivalent? If this conclusion is well grounded when I purchase your work, what should make it doubtful when I purchase your goods? If you have imposed upon me by concealing their faults, and they are not worth what I give for them; you have then no more right to the purchase money than you would have had to your wages if I had hired you for work, and by any concealed weakness you were disabled from doing that work. You will say, perhaps, that in letting out your service you bargain for so much work, and consequently, that if you cannot do the work, the bargain is void, because you fail of performing your part of it. And I may reply, that in selling your goods for such a price as they would have been worth if they had been free from the concealed faults, you bargain for goods of such a value, and consequently, that if the concealed faults make them of less value, the bargain is void, because you fail of performing your part of it.

When the parties are equal as to their knowledge of the faults, either of goods to be purchased, or of the use of goods, or of beneficial services to be hired; and the purchaser or hirer is willing, notwithstanding what he knows about the matter of the contract, to enter upon a bargain; these faults, which are so known, cannot afterwards be a sufficient reason for setting the bargain aside.

We have hitherto supposed the inequality as to knowledge, to be on the side of the purchaser or hirer, and have shown by what means such inequality will make the contract void. But it is to be remembered that a like inequality on the side of the seller or letter will have the same effect for the same reasons.

If I know of advantages or perfections in a man's goods which he is ignorant of, and when I am about to bargain with him for those goods, or for the use of them, conceal from him what I know of the matter, and so give him less for what I purchase of him than the thing is worth; I have no more right to the thing so purchased, than he in the opposite circumstances would have had to my money.

As it is requisite, previously to the contract, that the parties should be equal as to their knowledge of the faults or excellencies of the thing about which they are going to bargain; so it is likewise requisite that they should be so far equal, as to their freedom of choice, that neither of them ought to make use of any unjust threatenings to force the other, through fear, to contract or bargain with him. In such an inequality as this the party by an act of injustice hinders the other from receiving his equivalent: and no act of injustice can give him a right to the difference.

If the fear of one party was just, or if, though it was unjust, it arose from some other quarter, and was not at all owing to the party with whom he bargains, I should then determine otherwise. Because, though the person who is in such fear, does not receive his equivalent in the special matter of the contract, such as the goods purchased, or the work hired, yet he receives the difference in being relieved from his fears: and as there is no injustice on the part of him from whom such relief comes, there is nothing to hinder him from claiming the difference.

Equality in the principal act relates to knowledge of the price.

XIII. *In the principal act, which is the very act of bargaining, it is requisite that the parties should again be equal in their knowledge as to the true price of the goods, or the use or the service about which they are bargaining; so that the purchaser may not impose on the seller, by underrating the thing to be disposed of, nor the seller, on the other hand, impose on the purchaser by setting too high a price upon it. If the seller, by being better informed about the true price of the thing than the purchaser is, should obtain more for it than it is worth; or if, on the other hand, for want of this equality in knowledge, the purchaser should give him too little; in either case one of them has not received his equivalent: and this want of an equivalent on either side is sufficient to make the contract void, for the reason so often alleged already: the party who has received too little, intended to transfer his right in the thing which he is disposing of, only upon supposition of receiving what is of equal value; his right in it, therefore, being transferred upon this supposition, and not otherwise, the party, who has not given him an equivalent, has gained no right by the bargain.

That a knowledge of the intrinsic faults or excellencies in the matter of a contract, is different from a knowledge of the true price; or that what Grotius calls equality in the acts previous to the bargain, is different from what he calls equality in the principal act of bargaining, will appear presently, when we come to consider by what means the price of goods or labour is varied, and to show, that though the particular intrinsic faults or excellencies of the matter may and do make a difference in the price; yet there are many other causes which will vary it, where those faults or excellencies are out of the question.

Grotius, when he is treating about the equality required in contracts, proposes to examine a question which Cicero has started, concerning a merchant, who had transported corn from Alexandria to Rhodes, at a time when the Rhodians were in great want of it, and corn sold very dear at their markets. The merchant is supposed to know, at the

* Grotius, Lib. II. Cap. XII. § IX.

same time, that a large fleet of merchant ships laden with corn were actually in their way from the same port, and destined for Rhodes. And the question is, whether, as the knowledge of this circumstance would have made the markets fall, he was obliged to discover it to the Rhodians, or whether he might take the advantage of their ignorance, and sell his own corn at a better price than it would have brought, if they had known that so large a supply was near at hand. Grotius determines, that, whatever kindness or benevolence might suggest to him, he might, consistently with justice, conceal this circumstance; because, though the seller is obliged to discover all the faults which he knew of, and the buyer did not know of in the goods themselves, yet there is not the same obligation upon him to discover all the accidental circumstances relating to them. But it seems very difficult to find out the difference between these two sorts of concealment: there appears to be the same want of an equivalent on the side of the buyer when the seller takes more of him than the goods are worth, whether this advantage is made by concealing any intrinsic fault in the goods themselves, or by concealing any accidental circumstances which would lessen the value of them to the buyer.

In fact, if Grotius had examined this question under its proper head, he would have determined otherwise upon it than he has done. He examined it when he was considering the requisite equality in the knowledge of the contracting parties in those acts, which go before the contract: and as this equality respects only the intrinsic faults of the goods themselves, it certainly does not include an equality in their knowledge of any accidental circumstances. But the proper place for examining this question is, when we are considering the equality of knowledge which is acquired in the principal act, or in respect of the true price of the goods. For if it is necessary that the price should be a fair one, it is necessary likewise that each party, in order to judge whether it is a fair one or not, should be equally informed about all the accidental circumstances upon which the true price of the goods depends. And if the merchant asked as high a price when he knew of the supply that was coming, as he would have asked if there had been no such supply near at hand, he knowingly asked more than, in those circumstances, his goods were worth, and more than the purchasers would have given him, if they had known as much as he did. The purchasers, therefore, if they gave him his price, did not receive their equivalent; and this is inconsistent with the nature of all contracts of mutual benefit.

Equality in the matter relates to faults in the goods, or errors in the price, unknown to either party.

XIV. *But suppose the buyer and the seller to have dealt fairly with one another, both in the previous and in the principal acts; suppose them to have been so far equal in their knowledge, as that neither of them has concealed any intrinsic faults which he knew of in the goods, nor has designedly rated them either too high or too low; yet still there may be an inequality in the matter of the contract; there might be faults in it which neither of them knew of, or they might either of them set a false price without designing it. By this means one of the parties will not receive his equivalent: and as he parted with

* Grot. Lib. II. Cap. XII. § XI.

his own right in the money or goods, and transferred it to the other, only upon supposition of receiving an equivalent; upon failure of this supposition nothing is done; he has parted with no right, and consequently the other has gained none by the bargain.

Want of an equivalent, how supplied in auctions.

XV. There are indeed some ways of buying and selling, as by auction or inch of candle, in which the want of an equivalent on either side will not affect the contract. But then this want is provided against by a tacit agreement of the parties beforehand. He who puts his goods up to auction, signifies, by so doing, that he will get as much for them as he can; whilst they, who bid for the goods, tacitly consent to his proposal. And though, in some particular bargains, he may perhaps receive too much; yet it is supposed, that upon the whole, this inequality will be made up: because, as his intention is to get as great a price as he can, so he is understood to signify, at the same time, that he will be satisfied with as little as the purchasers choose to give.

Price of things or work, what it is, and how varied.

XVI. *As one part of the equality required in contracts relates to the setting a fair price upon the things or the work that are to be disposed of by them, it may not be improper, before we go on to the farther consideration of contracts, to say something concerning the notion of price, and the variations of it.

The price of things is their comparative value in respect of one another.

The wants of mankind, either real or imaginary, are the foundation of the price both of things and of labour. Such things as no person either really wants or fancies himself to want, will have no value at all, and consequently can have no relative value in comparison with other things.

Now, since the want that mankind have of a thing, is the true cause of its having any price at all, the price of things must necessarily vary as the want of them varies: in proportion as mankind want them more or less, their price, that is, their comparative value in respect of one another, will be greater or smaller. We will first consider how the price of things varies, where mankind are in real want of them. Things are more or less wanted in proportion as they are more or less useful. Upon this account, if all other circumstances are equal, things which are the most useful will bear the highest price, and things which are the least useful will bear the lowest.

But then our want of such things as are of real use to us, does not rise or fall in proportion to their usefulness only, but in proportion likewise to the difficulty of obtaining them. For where two things are equally useful or equally necessary, so that in this respect our wants of them both are equal; yet, in another respect, our wants of them will be greater or less in proportion to the difficulty or ease of obtaining them: because, where the usefulness of a thing is given, our want of it will be greater or smaller in proportion as we feel that want more or less: and those wants are felt the most which are of the longest continuance, and those are felt the least which are of the shortest. But since that want, which is the most difficult to supply,

* Grot. Lib. II. Cap. XII. § XIV.

will commonly continue the longest, and will therefore be felt the most, it is upon this account the greatest; whilst another want, which may in itself be equal to the former, but is the most easy to supply, will commonly pass off the soonest, and being therefore felt the least, will for this reason be the smallest. But the comparative value or price of things rises or falls in proportion as our wants of them are greater or less. Therefore, where things are equally useful, those which are most difficult to be procured will bear a higher price than those which may be procured more easily.

The difficulty or ease of procuring a thing depends upon two circumstances; first, upon the scarcity or plenty of the thing itself, and secondly, upon the greater or smaller number of persons who want it at the same time. In a certain number of purchasers, if there is great plenty of a thing, it is easily procured, and this will make it cheaper; if there is not much of it, we shall find some difficulty in procuring it, and this will make it dearer. Where only a certain quantity of a thing is to be had, there will be more difficulty in procuring as much of it as we want when a great number want it at the same time; and this will raise the price of it: if there are fewer who want it at the same time, those who want it may be more easily supplied, and this will bring the price of it down lower.

Upon the whole, then, the want of a thing is the foundation of its price; and consequently the price will vary as the want varies. But either the want, or the price in consequence of the want, will depend partly upon the usefulness of the thing, and partly upon the difficulty of procuring it; and this difficulty depends partly upon the quantity of the thing, and partly upon the number of purchasers, or, which amounts to the same, upon the demand that there is for it.

What has been said of the price of things may be applied to the price of labour; in order to show that the comparative value, which is founded in the want that we have for it, will depend, ultimately, upon the usefulness of such labour upon the number of hands that may be procured, and upon the demand that there is for it. In proportion as the use of it is greater, as there are fewer hands to be procured, or a greater demand for what hands are to be gotten, the price of it will be higher: and so, on the contrary, in opposite circumstances, the price will be lower.

In the purchase of goods which have been manufactured, the price depends partly upon the price of the materials out of which they are made, and partly upon the price of that labour or work by which they are manufactured. But here again it is the want of such goods, and consequently of such materials and such workmanship, that is the original foundation of their price; and in what manner this want will vary their price has been seen already.

Under the head of real wants we include what is necessary for the support and common convenience of man's life, according to the rank or station in which each person is placed; as food, clothing, a dwelling, bedding, education, medicines, &c. But there are other wants which we may call ordinary ones: and under this head we include whatever may administer to a man's needless, but innocent pleasure or entertainment; as paintings, statues, plate, jewels, &c. These wants being presupposed, the price of such things as will supply them, or of the labour which must be employed about those things, is varied in the same manner and in the same proportion with the price of such things as are necessary to supply our real wants; and of such, labour as is of real use. Things of this sort will be dearer, as the taste for them runs higher, that is, as their supposed usefulness is greater, or as they are more difficult to be procured; that is, as the want of them is more felt; and the difficulty of procuring them will be greater, as the quantity of them which can be had is less, or as there are more persons who want them at the same time.

Grotius, amongst other circumstances which increase the price of things, reckons the trouble or expense of the merchant who procures them; for which, he says, allowance is to be made in the price of the goods so procured. But these two circumstances are not distinct from what have been mentioned already, and may easily be resolved into one or other of them. If the merchant is at any expense besides paying wages to those who are employed in procuring them, which wages are the price of labour; such expense is a part of the original purchase money, which he paid for them. And to say that allowance is to be made to him for expenses of this sort, is no more than saying, that as he buys dearer he must sell dearer. But what makes him buy dearer, unless it is either the usefulness of the goods, or the difficulty of procuring them, which difficulty depends upon their scarcity, or upon the demand that there is for them? so that at last, if the price of his goods is high, it is for one of the reasons already assigned.

Fair price is the market price.

XVII. None of these particulars, upon which the price of things or of labour depends, can be reduced to any mathematical certainty. It is impossible to determine with exactness the comparative degree of their usefulness, or of their scarcity, or of the demand that there is for them. The price therefore neither of goods nor of labour can be so precisely settled as to allow of no latitude. No one can say that this, or that, is so exactly what they are worth, that if the seller takes more, he takes too much; or if the buyer gives less, he gives too little. The general rule of price is what we call the market price, by which we mean the price that men, in that place, at that time, and in those circumstances, are commonly willing, and have been used to give. But this is a very lax rule; and the price of things, or of labour, when adjusted by it, may well admit of these three degrees, the highest price, the lowest price, and the moderate or middle price.

Civil laws, indeed, frequently interpose, and fix the price both of goods and of labour: and when their price is thus fixed, whatever exceeds that measure is too much, and whatever falls short of it is too little.

Extraordinary circumstances allow to exceed the market price.

XVIII. There are some extraordinary circumstances, which may reasonably allow us to fix a higher price upon our goods, than the market price. But even these extraordinary circumstances may be reduced to one of the principles already mentioned, the usefulness, under which I include the imaginary as well as the real uses, the scarcity, or the demand.

These principles appear in numberless shapes; and in whatever shape they appear, they vary the price of goods. You have goods which you want to dispose of, and which I have no occasion for; but, to oblige you, I am willing to buy them. It is plain, then, both that they are of no great use to you, because you desire to part with them, and that they are of no great use to me, by the supposition of my having no occasion for them. In this situation, I expect to buy them at a lower price than ordinary; and the reason why I should buy them so, is the small use of them either to the buyer or the seller.

You have goods which are very useful to you, and which would likewise be particularly useful to me: and you sell me these goods merely to oblige me. There is, by the supposition, some extraordinary usefulness of the goods, both to the buyer and the seller; and upon this account, you set an extraordinary price upon them.

You have an estate which came to you from your ancestors, and this circumstance makes you fond of it; the possession of it gives you more pleasure than if you had acquired it any other way. A particular fondness of this sort is, indeed, but an imaginary usefulness; but it is such an one that, if I want to buy the estate, you have no reason to part with it, unless I am willing to give you a higher price than you would have asked otherwise, or than the estate would have been worth, between buyer and seller, if it had not been attended with this circumstance.

If you could have made any particular advantage of your goods by keeping them yourself, or if you shall suffer any particular damage by parting with them; then, besides the ordinary price, you expect to have this advantage or this damage made up to you; and upon this account you ask an extraordinary price for your goods. Here again the price is raised by the particular usefulness of the goods to you.

It is some loss to you if I delay the payment of the purchase money, when I buy your goods: for till the payment is made you have no use of the money. Such delay of payment therefore is a reason for your selling your goods dearer than if I had made prompt payment. Money paid some time hence is not so useful to you as money paid just now would be: what therefore is wanting in the usefulness of money so paid, must be made up in the quantity of it.

Advantages by the introduction of money.

XIX. In bartering, where goods are to be compared immediately with goods, there is more difficulty in adjusting the price, than in buying and selling with money: because in such bartering the value of the goods on both sides is to be estimated. Whereas in buying and selling for money, the value of the money is already settled, and nothing is to be estimated but the comparative value of this standard, and the goods which are to be purchased. My meaning is, that such goods as are not frequently exchanged for one another, will be uncertain in their price: but money, which is in constant commerce, and is exchanged every day for goods of all sorts, will by such use have its comparative value so well settled, that we may without much difficulty, upon every occasion, not only determine how much goods we ought to receive in exchange for how much money, but may apply it as a common standard or measure to compare the value of goods of one sort with the value of goods of another sort. This we may reckon as one of the advantages arising from the introduction of money: the constant use of it in exchange makes it a standard of price by which the comparative value of goods is more readily adjusted than it could have been otherwise.

A second advantage arising from the introduction of money is, that by the help of it we may commonly procure such things as we want: whereas, if all our riches consisted in goods, though we had great plenty of one sort, we might want those of another sort, without being able to get them in exchange. I might have great plenty of corn; but if I had occasion for sheep or oxen, though you had plenty of them, you might not be willing to barter them for my corn: because you might have more corn of your own already, than you wanted. In the meantime you might have occasion for wine, and would be glad to exchange your sheep or oxen for it, if I had any. But as I have none, I am forced to keep my own corn, and cannot procure for it what I want, and what, if I had any goods which would suit your convenience, you would supply me with: in the meantime you are subject to the same inconvenience; if they, who have wine to spare, have no occasion for sheep or oxen. This inconvenience is remedied by the use of a current standard, which all men are ready to take, one of another. Though you would not part with your sheep or oxen for my corn, because you do not want it; yet you will readily part with them for my money, as you know, that they who would not let you have wine for sheep or oxen, will let you have it for this money, which they can pass off again in the same manner, and procure in exchange for it such things as they want.

A third advantage arising from the introduction of money is, that it lies in a little compass, and is therefore better fitted for commerce than bulky goods would be. I have great numbers of cattle, and should be willing to exchange them, if I could, for wine: but no person near me has any to dispose of; perhaps none is produced in the country where I live. If then I would have it, I must go from home for it: and it would be vast trouble, if indeed it was possible, to drive or convey my cattle to such a distance. But money lies in a less compass, and is easily carried from place to place: it will therefore make the exchange much easier to me. Though I could not convey my cattle so far, I can get money for them nearer home, and can easily convey the money to the place where I want to make the purchase of wine.

As it is one advantage arising from the introduction of money, that a great value lies in a narrow compass; so we may reckon it a fourth advantage, that we can reduce it into parts, which are of small value, much more readily than we can most sorts of goods. I have more horses than I want, but have occasion for a sheep, which is worth much less than any one of my horses. I cannot therefore get what I want, but at a great disadvantage: because I have nothing to give in exchange for it, but what vastly exceeds it in value. The introduction of money has removed this inconvenience. Though I could not divide the horse so as to give no more than the sheep is worth, yet I can, when I have sold him, divide the money and procure what I want, without giving too much for it.

A fifth advantage arising from the introduction of money is, that we may keep it more easily than we could have kept most sorts of moveable goods. When we have taken it in exchange, there is no danger of its wasting or perishing in our hands, before we shall have occasion to part with it again. Cattle would die; fruit would rot; corn or wine would spoil: but money may be kept for any length of time without being the worse for it.

Metals the most proper materials for money.

XX. If the advantages which I have been mentioning, were proposed in the introduction of money, we may easily determine what materials are the most proper to make it of. As it is designed to be the standard of price, a common measure, by which to compare the several values of other things with one another; the materials of which it is made, should be as steady as possible, in their own value; the usefulness of them, their scarcity, and the demand for them, should be as little liable to variation, as may be.

Secondly, money is intended to be current amongst all those who have any intercourse of commerce with one another, so that any person will readily take it in exchange for such goods as he can spare; because he knows beforehand, that others will take it in like manner of him again: for this reason the materials that it is made of, should be such, as in the opinion of those who have such intercourse, have some usefulness, and consequently some value, either real or imaginary. Paper or leather, or any thing else, which has no such intrinsic value, either real or imaginary, will be current no farther than the credit of the person goes who vents them, and makes himself answerable to take them at any time in exchange: nor will they be current even so far, unless he makes himself answerable likewise to exchange them for what will be current with every body. Suppose a man to circulate bills which were payable by him upon demand, but were to be paid when demanded, in corn, or in wool: those bills would not be current as far as his credit would go: all persons, who might otherwise be ready to trust him, would not be willing to take such bills in exchange: no one indeed would take them, who might possibly not be able to exchange them with any body besides the first drawer of the bills: because no one would care to be forced to take corn or wool, at a time when perhaps he may have no occasion for any, or may not know how to dispose of any, if he had it. If those bills were payable in money by the drawer, then indeed such bills will pass with all persons who know they may depend upon his promise to take them again. Such is the necessity that the current exchange amongst private persons should be carried on with such materials as have, in themselves, some real or imaginary value. The authority of civil government will reach something farther; it will be able to circulate useless materials in common exchange, as far as its jurisdiction extends. The subjects of the same government, in their contracts with one another, may be forced by the laws, or where the government has the right of coining, and will vent only base money; they may be forced by the necessity of the case, to take such money in the course of their common dealings. But then foreigners who are not under the same jurisdiction, nor under the same necessity, will not take their money; because it is worth nothing to them. Nor will such foreigners take bills upon the credit even of the government, unless those bills are payable in such materials as are worth something in themselves, and such too as they can circulate again upon account of some intrinsic value, either real or imaginary.

Since a third advantage, proposed by the use of money is, that what will fetch many goods in exchange may lie in a narrow compass, the materials of which it is made, should be such as have in themselves a high value, either upon account of their great usefulness, or their great scarcity. Such materials as have both these qualities, would not be proper for the purpose. A sufficient quantity of what is very useful, if it is likewise very scarce, could not be spared from the common occasions of life to be applied to the sole purpose of exchange: because as much as is applied to this purpose becomes useless to other purposes. And certainly such materials as have only the quality of great usefulness, but are at the same time very plentiful, will be of too small value to answer this design of introducing money, which we are now speaking of. The best materials therefore are such as have little real usefulness in themselves, and have their chief intrinsic value given them by some imaginary usefulness only; such as mankind can do very well without, but such as common opinion has made them desirous of having. Materials of this sort may be spared from the common uses of life to make money of. And if their value is raised very high by the scarcity of them, such a quantity of them as will lie in a narrow compass, will fetch many goods in exchange.

A fourth advantage, designed by the introduction of money, is, that it may be reduced into such small parts as to be exchanged without disadvantage for things of small value. It is proper, therefore, to use materials of different sorts, some of greater, some of lesser value: because as the last mentioned use of money requires that some should be made out of very dear materials, though the same materials might be made into pieces, some greater and some lesser, yet the lesser pieces would either be of too great value to be exchanged upon fair terms for cheap goods, or else they would be so small as to be in danger of being lost.

The fifth advantage proposed by the introduction of money, is, that it will keep without wasting or spoiling; so that he who takes it in exchange, is in no danger of having it perish in his hands. And in view to this advantage it is plainly requisite that money should be made of such materials as will not easily wear out, and as are not subject to perish or to be damaged by keeping.

*Metals, some of them at least, as gold or silver, will answer most of these purposes. Their intrinsic usefulness is not very great at any time; so that there is no danger of any such variations in this usefulness at different times, as will make their value uncertain; and the plenty or scarcity of them is at all times much the same, unless some very unlikely or unforeseen accident, such as the discovery of the West Indies, should make an alteration: and as the value of them is imaginary rather than real, the demand for them will commonly be much the same. But then this imaginary value being almost universal, they will be readily current every where in exchange for goods. And as it is high at the same time, a small quantity of them will bear a great price, or what is worth much will lie in a narrow compass. As this high value arises from opinion and scarcity, rather than from any real usefulness of them; what is wanted to carry on commerce may be made into money, without depriving mankind, in any degree, of what they want to use for the purposes of common life. And we may

* Grotius, Lib. II. Cap. XII. § XVII.

observe by the way, that if iron was as scarce as gold, it would not be so proper for the materials of money; notwithstanding the very high value which its known usefulness and its supposed scarcity would give it: because, if so little of it was to be had, by making money enough out of it to maintain a general commerce, more of it would be taken from the uses of common life, than could be well spared. But gold and silver alone will not answer all the designs of introducing money: their value is rather too high: pieces of these metals, if they were small enough to exchange, without disadvantage, for small quantities of cheap goods, would be in danger of being lost: and upon this account it is necessary to make use of some baser metal, such as copper, for pieces of smaller value. Any metals may pass from hand to hand without wearing out, and may be well enough kept, as long as we please, without being the worse for it: but gold and silver are the best upon this account, as well as upon others; because they are less hurt by keeping than the other metals are.

Uses and rules of coining.

XXI. After mankind have been led by such reasons, as we have been mentioning, to fix upon metals, as the standard of price, and the current matter of general exchange; it is plain, that without the aid of civil laws, the different value of this or that piece of any metal, as of gold, for instance, can depend upon nothing but the different quantity contained in the same piece, or upon what is the same in effect, the different weight of it. If a certain quantity of bullion is, in the course of exchange, worth two sheep, any civil legislator may order, if he pleases, that all persons under his jurisdiction shall take the same quantity of metal after it is coined, in exchange for six sheep. But this rule will be of force no farther than his jurisdiction extends: foreigners, who are free from his authority, will not regard such a law, and will estimate his coin only by the weight of it. And as in coining there must be some allay or mixture of baser metal, they will have a regard to this too, and will estimate a given weight of the mixed metal by its fineness; that is, by the true weight of pure gold in the coin.

However, as there would be much trouble and much time lost in weighing the metal every time it is exchanged, there is a great convenience in signifying by some stamp, upon every piece of metal designed for exchange, what the weight of that piece is. And this convenience gave occasion to the coining of metals.

Indeed, as there is some trouble and time saved to the trader by having every piece of metal which he is to receive so stamped; it is but reasonable that he should make some allowance for this convenience. So that a piece of money, when coined, is worth something more than the same quantity of bullion would be. This difference ought not to be greater than what may answer the convenience of the trader: because no one can be expected, or would be willing, in the course of exchange, to pay for more. An allowance for such a difference as this is reasonable on both sides; the coiner expects it, that he may be paid for his trouble; and the receivers, one after another, are willing to pay it, upon account of the convenience already mentioned. The coiner may indeed use more art and labour than is necessary for the purpose designed by coining; and if he does, he has no reason to expect that the receiver will allow him for it. Some art and labour however is necessary: a plain simple stamp would not well answer the purpose. Care must be taken to make the stamp such as is not easily counterfeited: because otherwise base metal, or metal under weight, might be made to pass as if it was pure and of due weight, by the help of such a counterfeit stamp. And care must likewise be taken to stamp or mark it in such a manner that no part of the metal, after it is once stamped, can easily be taken away without effacing the stamp, either in whole or in part, so as to discover the fraud. So much art and labour as this will be of use to the receivers, as the money passes from one hand to another: and therefore the coiner may expect to be paid for it. The value of this art and labour is what a piece of metal is worth when it is coined into money, more than an equal weight of the same metal would be worth in bullion.

As the stamp is designed to ascertain the weight of metal, and as money is designed to be the matter of general exchange, it is proper that the business of coining should be in the hands of persons of the most undoubted and of the most extensive credit. The stamp of a person of doubtful character would not induce any one to take money so stamped without weighing it: and the stamp of a person of good credit, if he was not much known, would induce only the few who did know him, to take it upon his authority. Upon this account money that is coined by national authority, or by the government of each nation, will best answer the purposes designed by coining.

My subject led me to say something concerning the price of goods and labour, and the grounds of its variation: and as this engaged me to inquire into the use and value of money, the reader will, I hope, excuse me, if this digression has been longer than he expected.

Use of money varies the price of goods.

XXII. The introduction of money occasions another seeming variation in the price of goods, besides those which we have taken notice of already. *Money, though it is used as the standard of price, by which the different values of goods or of labour are compared with one another, is not wholly invariable in its own price; that is, in respect of goods or labour it has not always the same comparative value. There is not always the same quantity of money amongst all mankind who have an intercourse of commerce with one another; and much less is there always the same quantity of it current in the same nation, or amongst those who, upon account of their nearness or other connections, have the most frequent intercourse of commerce. The scarcity of money raises its price, and the plenty of it sinks its price; in the same manner as the scarcity or plenty of any thing else varies the comparative value of that thing. If, when money is scarce, a small quantity of it is equal, upon the comparison, to a certain quantity of any sort of goods or labour; a greater quantity of it, when it is plentiful, will only be equal in value to the same quantity of the same goods or labour. A quarter of wheat, which at one time is worth no more than two shillings, may at another time, in the same plenty of wheat, be worth forty shillings: not because there is any alteration either in the intrinsic usefulness of wheat, or in the comparative value of it with other goods, such as sheep, cloth, wine, &c.; but because the quantity of money is altered so as to be twenty

* Grot. Lib. II. Cap. XII. § XIV.

times more plentiful at one time than at the other; and upon account of this greater plenty, twenty times any quantity of it, when compared with the same sort of goods, will be worth no more, or will bring in exchange no more of those goods than the simple quantity was worth or would have brought in a greater scarcity. In cases of this sort we usually say, that wheat or any other sort of goods is grown dearer: but the fact is, that money is grown cheaper. Only as money is looked upon to be the standard of price, and is therefore considered as invariable in its own price; goods or labour seem dearer or cheaper, in proportion as more or less money must be given for the same quantity of them.

Buying and selling.

XXIII. *Before we leave this subject of mutual contracts, it may be proper to say something concerning some of the most usual contracts of this sort. Buying and selling is a very common and well known contract. But the writers upon natural jurisprudence do not seem to have determined some of the questions arising upon it with sufficient exactness. It may be asked at what time the contract of buying and selling is complete? But before we can answer this question, it will be necessary, for those who ask it, to explain what they mean by the bargain's being complete. The bargain may be said to be complete, either when the parties are bound, each to the other, to do what they have agreed upon; or when the property of the goods is actually transferred to the buyer, and the property of the money to the seller.

In the first sense, the bargain is complete as soon as the parties have agreed upon the price: the seller has then agreed that he will part with such a quantity of goods for so much money; and the buyer has then agreed, that he will part with so much money for such a quantity of goods. The buyer, after this, can justly force the seller to deliver up the goods, and the seller can justly force the buyer to take the goods and to pay down the money. But if the matter rests here, it is only a promissory contract; the bargain is not so far completed as to have transferred what was the property of either party to the other. They agreed that they would transfer this or that; but they have not actually transferred it. The demand therefore is yet only upon the person, to force him to do what he had promised: there is no demand upon the thing, till the property is actually transferred. If, then, either the buyer or the seller was to die, before they had proceeded any farther, I do not see that the survivor would have any right over the goods or the money agreed for; nor, consequently, that he would have any right to force the heir of the deceased to stand to the bargain.

To complete the bargain so far as to give each a right, not merely over the person, but in the things of the other; some acts or words are necessary denoting a mutual consent of each to make an actual transfer of his property to the other. Such a transfer as this is sufficiently expressed by the mutual delivery of the goods and money. Or it may be expressed only by the delivery either of the goods or of the money on one part, and the acceptance of what is so delivered on the other part: because, as the seller, for instance, had agreed that he would give the buyer property in such or such goods, in consideration of so

* Grot. Lib. II. Cap. XII. § XV.

much money to be paid to himself; if the buyer pays the money, the seller, by accepting it, must be understood to do what he had before agreed that he would do, upon this consideration. Delivery in part, or giving earnest, has the same effect: it is designed on the buyer's part to signify his will to make an actual transfer of his property in the money agreed upon; and the seller, by taking earnest, is understood to give his actual consent to what he had before agreed to do, in consideration of receiving property in the purchase money. In the purchase of immoveable goods, such as houses or lands, the seller, though he cannot deliver the whole thing purchased, may by a negative act signify his consent to make an actual transfer of the property which he had in such goods. This negative act is his suffering the buyer, without interrupting him, to take possession by settling in the house, or by cultivating the lands, or by letting either of them to some other person, and receiving the rents or profits. The thing purchased may indeed be delivered in part by a positive act; as in the sale of lands by delivering a clod or a turf, and in the sale of houses by delivering the key. The parties may likewise transfer their property each to the other, in moveable or immoveable goods, or in money, by words either spoken or written; if instead of engaging in words of future time, that they will transfer, they expressly declare in words of present time, that they do transfer their property. Where such words of present time are made use of, the bargain does not rest in a promise; it does not merely give each a claim upon the person of the other, but gives actual property in the thing itself.

After the bargain of buying and selling is complete, suppose the thing sold to remain in the seller's possession, and whilst it is so, to perish, or to be any way lost or damaged; it is farther inquired whether the buyer or the seller is to bear the loss? Here again we are to consider what is meant by the bargain's being complete, that is, we are to consider what sort of a bargain it was, whether it was promissory only, so that in virtue of it the parties had each of them a right merely over the person of the other; or whether it was such a bargain as made an actual transfer of property from one to the other.

In the former case, where the bargain rests in a mutual promise, the goods are still the property of the seller, and the money is still the property of the buyer: the seller therefore must bear the loss or damage; because naturally all the loss or damage which a thing sustains, falls upon the owner of it. The buyer agrees that he will give such a sum of money for a house or for lands; but before the property is transferred, the house is burnt down, or the sea washes away the lands: the seller can then have no demand upon him for the money: the house and land were still the property of the seller; and the loss will naturally fall upon him.

If, indeed, either by delivery in part, or by the plain words of the contract, the property of the goods was transferred to the buyer, and before he has full possession of them, they perish or are damaged; the loss falls upon him as being the owner of the goods, and not upon the seller, in whose hands they happen to be.

It is true, that if such goods perished or were damaged through the fault of the seller, then the buyer has a demand for an equivalent: but this demand arises from another principle, to be explained hereafter, and not from the contract.

These particulars may be otherwise settled between the buyer and the seller by express words. But it would be endless to reckon up all the exceptions or conditions which they may add to their bargain: all that we can pretend to do is to show what rights arise out of the mere contract, where nothing else is agreed upon. Only it is to be observed, that where any express conditions or exceptions are added by the consent of the parties, each of them is obliged, by his own consent, to comply with such conditions or exceptions.

If I sell the same goods twice, it may be a question, which of the two purchasers has a right to the goods. Here we are to inquire, what sort of a bargain the first of the two was. If it was such an one, as gave the purchaser property in the goods, the second bargain will be void: because, as the goods, at the time of this second bargain, were not mine, I had no right to dispose of them. But if the first bargain was promissory only, so as to give the purchaser a personal demand upon me, but no property in the goods; then the second bargain, provided it was such an one as gave property, will be so far valid, that the second purchaser will have a right to the goods: this second bargain, though my former promise had made it unlawful, is not void; since, by the supposition, the goods were still mine, or I had still a right in them. In the meantime there is no reason for saying, that the validity of this second bargain will make void the first: the claim of the first purchaser will still continue what it was, a demand upon my person to the value of the goods, upon his paying me the sum of money which we had agreed upon.

Letting and renting.

XXIV. *Letting and renting is subject to nearly the same rules with buying and selling: for these two contracts are in all respects very like one another. The principal difference between them is, that in letting and renting, the owner or landlord sells, and the occupier or tenant buys the use of the thing: whereas, in buying and selling, the owner sells, and the purchaser buys the property in it. The consideration which is paid for the property in one of these contracts, is called the price: the consideration which is paid for the use in the other contract, is called the rent.

When a man has purchased the property of a thing, if the thing is lost or damaged, he is to bear such loss or damage. Suppose, therefore, instead of purchasing the property of the thing, that he had only purchased the use of it; then, if the use of the thing is lost or damaged, the loss or damage of the use seems naturally to fall upon him who is the owner of the use; that is, upon the tenant, and not upon the landlord, who has parted with the use, though he is still owner of the thing.

But this rule wants to be explained, in order to adjust the several claims of the owner and the hirer. The use of a thing may be lessened two ways. It may be lessened, though the thing continues in the same condition as when it was hired; or it may be lessened by some damage, which makes the thing worse in itself, than it was then.

* Grot. Lib. II. Cap. XII. § XVIII.

All losses in the use of the thing, which are of the first sort, or which happen without any damage in the thing itself, naturally fall upon the hirer. These are losses in the use only, which use he has made his own by purchasing it. Suppose I hire a shop which is well situated for trade at the time of hiring it, and consequently is worth a large rent: but before the time for which I hired it is expired, the course of trade alters; and my custom becomes, by that means, much worse than might reasonably have been expected at the time when I first entered upon the shop. In this case the use of the thing is damaged, without any damage in the thing itself. Since, therefore, the thing is no worse, the loss cannot justly fall upon the owner of the thing: it is the use only of the thing which is lessened, and this must naturally fall upon me, as the owner of the use.

But if the use is lessened by any damage which the thing itself has sustained, the loss will naturally fall upon the owner of the thing: because, as the damage primarily affects the thing itself, there can be no just reason given why any one else, in particular, why the owner of the use should bear the loss which happens to the other's property. This seems to be clear, in those instances, where the damage done to the thing itself is such as to destroy the very existence of it. I hire a house, and before the time for which I hired it is expired, the house is burnt down. No one can imagine that I am naturally obliged still to pay the rent of it. I hire lands, and before the time for which I hired them is expired, the sea washes them away. This event will naturally discharge me from the payment of rent. But suppose that the fire, instead of burning the house down, had made it so ruinous as to be uninhabitable: or that the sea, instead of washing away the lands, had overflowed them, and remained there, so that it could not be drained off again. There could be no more reason for my payment of rent upon this supposition than upon the former. Whatever damage affects the thing itself is naturally the loss of the owner of the thing: but if the hirer was still obliged to pay the same rent after the thing is perished or damaged, that he paid before; the owner would suffer no loss at all, the whole of it would fall upon the purchaser of the use. The country, in which a man has hired land, happens to be the seat of war: the enemy seizes upon the land and keeps possession of it; by which means the hirer of the land is hindered in his use of it. Here the land is lost to the owner; the damage sustained is properly in the thing itself; and consequently the proprietor can demand no rent of the tenant: because the tenant ought not to bear the loss of another man's property. But suppose the enemy, instead of seizing upon the land, had foraged upon it, and carried away the grass or corn that was growing there; this loss does not affect the thing itself, but the use of it only; and as it ought, therefore, to fall upon the tenant, he would be still obliged to pay rent.

There is one exception to the rule, which subjects the owner to the loss, and not the hirer, where the use is made worse by the thing itself becoming worse. This exception is, when the thing is made worse through the fault of the hirer. It would be unjust to make the proprietor suffer for the neglect or fault of his tenant. If a tenant hires land to sow with corn, and impoverishes that land by his bad management of it; though the use of the land here becomes worse, because the land itself is worse, yet he cannot expect any abatement of rent: because it is not so much the fault of the land as his own fault, that it is in so bad a condition: it would have been as good as it was, if he had taken such care of it as he ought to have taken.

The contract of letting and hiring, like that of buying and selling, is binding upon the persons of the parties concerned in it, as soon as they have agreed upon the rent. But something farther is requisite to give one of them a right to the money, and the other a right to the use. Delivery of the money, in whole or in part, gives the owner of the thing to be let a right to the money; and upon his acceptance, as he knows upon what consideration this payment is made, the hirer has a right to the use of the thing. In this manner the owner tacitly makes over the use. But he may likewise do it expressly by words of present time, either spoken or written.

The bargain even as to fixing the rent may possibly be tacit on both sides. As if I have hired a house or lands for some years, and after my term, for which I at first hired them, is out, I continue to live in the house, or to occupy the lands; as both parties knew what conditions they had agreed upon before; from this act of mine, and from the owner's giving me no disturbance, the reasonable and necessary presumption is, that we approve of the former conditions, and are still willing to abide by them.

Letting and hiring of labour.

XXV. In letting and hiring of labour, if we hire the labour of a man in general for a certain time; whatever accident may happen to him and disable him from labouring, he has a claim to his wages; provided he is willing, under such inability, to do us all the service he can: because what we purchased was his labour for that time: whether, therefore, his labour within that time is little or much, it is all that we can claim: and when our claim is satisfied, it will be unjust to diminish his. But if we hire him to do any particular work, and not merely for any certain time; whatever disables him from performing that work releases us from the obligation of paying his wages: because he has no claim to them, unless he performs the work for which he was hired.

*If I have hired out my labour for a particular purpose, and the same labour may be profitable to more persons besides the first hirer; nothing hinders me from taking as much of those other persons as my service to them is worth, without any abatement in the wages agreed upon between me and the first hirer. Each of them has here the valuable consideration for which the wages are due; and it is no damage to the first hirer that I can make an advantage of my labour, besides what I am to receive from him. I am hired to go a journey to do some particular business for the person who is to pay my wages: I can, in the same journey, do business for others, without neglecting his: whatever wages I am to receive from him who first hired me, will be due to me, notwithstanding the gain which I accidentally make of others, who take this opportunity of employing me: since my labour is not the less valuable to him for being serviceable to them.

Loan of consumable goods.

XXVI. †The loan of goods which cannot be used without being consumed, such as grain, wine, &c., and

* Grot. Lib. II. Cap. XII. § XIX.

† Ibid. § XX, XXI.

more especially money, is a contract of mutual benefit, and plainly belongs to that sort of contracts, in which things are given for things to be given again. The Latin expression for lending things of this sort, (*mutuo dare*) imports a mutual giving. In this respect it differs from (*commodatum*) a loan of such goods as may be used without being consumed: for a loan of this latter sort is a beneficial contract only on one side; the use of the things is given by one party, and nothing is given for it in return by the other party.

It is to be observed farther, that in such things as cannot be used without being consumed, the use cannot possibly be separated from the property, as it may be in other things. One man may either by free grant, as in a loan, or by purchase, as in letting and renting, have the use of houses, or lands, or cattle, or books, &c., whilst another man has the property in them, or the sole right to dispose of the things themselves. But no use can be made of grain, or wine, or money, without disposing of them: the grain must be sold, or must be spent in the family, or must be sown upon the land; the wine must be consumed in some such manner; the money must be laid out in purchasing necessaries, or in some way of commerce. But whoever has a right thus to dispose of the things themselves must have property in them. There is, therefore, in things of this sort no right of usufruct separable from property: but when a man lends them, he makes over the property in them to the borrower; since he, who grants the use, must grant the property at the same time, if there is no use separable from property.

This might occasion an inquiry, in what respect a gift differs from a loan, where the things given or lent are such as will be consumed in using; since he who lends them, grants the property of them to the borrower; and he who gives them seems to grant no more. The difference between them is, that a gift is a grant of property, without any condition of making a return: but a loan is a grant of property under a condition that either upon demand or at a certain time limited, the property in an equivalent shall be returned.

Interest for money, upon what principles to be defended.

XXVII. *We may here inquire whether it is unlawful to take interest, or any valuable consideration, for the loan of such goods as are consumed in their use, more particularly for the loan of money. I would not call the valuable consideration, which is taken for the loan of money, by the name of usury: because this word has by common custom been made to signify such an exorbitant consideration as is oppressive and unjust. I, therefore, choose to call it by the name of interest, which is a word of a milder signification, and has not by custom been made odious.

Grotius has mentioned three arguments, which are sometimes used to show that interest is unlawful, or that it is contrary to the nature of the contract between the lender and the borrower, for the former to take any consideration upon account of money lent, beyond the payment of the principal money itself. First, it is urged, that the nature of a loan, since it is a beneficial act, will not allow us to take interest or any valuable consideration for what we lend.—We might, indeed,

* Grotius, Lib. II. Cap. XII. § XX, XXI.

question here, whether a loan of such goods as are consumed in their use, is a beneficial contract or not: but to pass this over, we may observe, that the argument here urged against taking interest for money lent, if it proved any thing at all, would prove too much. The loan of such goods as may be used without being consumed, is a beneficial act; and if we will conclude, from the nature of a loan, that to take any consideration for the use of money is unlawful, we must, for the same reason, conclude it to be unlawful to take any rent for the use of houses or of land. In the meantime, however, it must be allowed, that when we take rent, the contract is changed from one of simple to one of mutual benefit; it is then no longer a loan, it becomes letting and renting. But though it is thus changed from a gratuituous contract to one of mutual benefit; it does not follow that it is changed likewise from a lawful to an unlawful one: the latter contract, when it is made upon fair and equal terms, is in its own nature as lawful as the former.—It may be urged, in support of this argument, that letting and renting, where the owner has made his bargain accordingly, is indeed a lawful contract, and that he, who has made such a bargain, may lawfully require the payment of rent: but that the loan of books or cattle, or houses, or land, is in itself a contract of simple benefit; and that he, who from the first, instead of letting, has lent any goods of this sort, has no just claim to rent, or to any valuable consideration for the use of such goods. He may, if he pleases, lawfully make such a contract at first as will entitle him to rent: but if he has originally lent his goods, he cannot afterwards lawfully demand any rent; because he cannot make such a demand consistently with his own agreement. Now this, it may be said, is the case of money; we lend it whenever we grant the use of it to another; the contract is, therefore, a loan from the beginning; and consequently we cannot, consistently with the nature of our first bargain, require any interest or valuable consideration afterwards. But this conclusion has nothing to support it besides the scantiness of language: whatever our bargain is in thus granting the use of money to another, we always indeed call it lending; because we have no other word to express it by. To make the conclusion a just one, they, who urge the argument, should show, that in lending money, it is unlawful from the beginning to agree with him to whom we lend it, that he shall give us a valuable consideration for the use of it.

A second argument to prove the unlawfulness of taking any interest or increase for money lent, is, that money is barren in its own nature; that no profit arises from it without the labour and industry of him who uses it; and, consequently, that this profit being due to the labour, is the property of the borrower, as his labour has produced it; and the lender, who has had no share in the labour, can have no claim upon the profits arising from it.—This argument again would prove too much, if it had any weight at all. Houses or arable land are profitless in themselves: the advantages arising from them are produced by the labour and industry of the occupier. And yet it is not deemed unjust that the landlord, notwithstanding he bears no part in the labour, should receive rent from the tenant. The fact is, that as in the use of houses or land, so in the use of money, the profit is due partly to the thing, and partly to the labour: because as the thing would have produced no profit without labour, so there could have been no labour, and, therefore, no profit of labour without the thing. The consequence of this is, that the person who labours, and the proprietor of the thing, have each of them a claim upon the profits, which arise from the use of it.

This answer will open the way to the third argument against taking interest for the use of money, and will show it in its full strength. I might urge, when you lend me a certain sum of money, that by granting me the use of it, you grant me at the same time the property of it; since the use of money and the property of it are inseparable. If, therefore, you demand any increase when I pay you the principal, you demand more than is due to you: what I received was the property of such a sum of money; I pay you the same sum of money; and, consequently, having paid you as much I received, I have paid all that you can fairly demand. You demand something more than the principal, in consideration of the use: but I reply, that the use and property are inseparable: if, therefore, your property is returned, what right have you to any thing more? especially if you consider that the profit of it being partly due to the thing and partly to the labour of the user, must be due wholly to me; since you made me the proprietor by lending me the money, and I was confessedly the user or occupier.—This argument would indeed be unanswerable; if you had not originally bargained for interest or increase: for since, by lending me the money, all you do is to make over the property of it to me for a certain time, I cannot see that this act considered by itself can entitle you to any thing more than your own property again, when that time is expired. Though the property of the money was mine only for a time, yet it was as much mine during that time, as if it had been mine for ever. If, therefore, you would secure your just claim to interest, you must take the matter higher; you must, from the beginning, make your bargain accordingly, and must show that a bargain originally made, to receive more than your principal in payment, is consistent with justice. It will appear that such a bargain would be a just one, provided you can show that you parted with any valuable consideration besides the principal money, in making over the property of it to me for any certain time: and this you may easily show; because in parting with the principal money, you parted with all the gain which you might have made of it during the time of its being in my hands, if, instead of lending it to me, you had employed it yourself in trade or in husbandry.

This then is the foundation of your claim upon me to receive interest for the money lent me; or rather the foundation upon which you are to justify making a bargain, from the beginning, to receive it. You claim such interest in consideration of the gain which you might have made by using your money yourself. Indeed your interest cannot fairly be equal to the highest gain which you could have made: you must allow something for the uncertainty of this gain; it might, by accident, have been less than you hoped for: and you must allow something for the trouble which you must have been at in making such advantage. When, from the usual gain which is to be made of such a sum of money, in trade or in husbandry, you have deducted a fair allowance for the uncertainty of your expectations, and a fair allowance likewise for the price of your labour; the remainder of the clear profits arising from the use of your money may be considered as due to you beyond your principal.

Something more than this may indeed be fairly claimed, where you run any hazard of losing your principal by my becoming unable to repay it; you may in these circumstances justly expect to be paid for such hazard. And upon this account it is, that you may fairly expect higher interest where your security is bad, than where it is good.

There is indeed one case in which interest may be demanded for money lent, though it was no condition of the original loan; and that is, when the money is not repaid at the time fixed for payment. At that time the borrower's property in the money ceases, and the lender may demand to be satisfied for whatever damage he sustains by not having his property restored to his possession at the time that it ought to be.

Usury why forbidden by the Mosaic law.

XXVIII. The authority of the law of Moses seems to weigh the most of any thing with those who maintain that interest is unlawful. Grotius urges upon this head, that the matter of the law which forbids usury, though it may not be necessary, is certainly commendable; and that, in this view, the law is binding upon christians, who are obliged by the gospel not only to observe the rules of strict justice, but to comply likewise with all the most perfect and exalted rules of moral duty. An Israelite, says he, was allowed indeed to take increase of a stranger, but was forbidden to take it of his neighbours or brethren. Now the gospel, as he goes on, has taught us to look upon all mankind as our neighbours or brethren. From whence he concludes, that whatever moral duty one Israelite owed to another; the same duty is owing from a christian to all mankind: so that no christian, consistently with his religion, can take interest or increase of any man for money lent.

Before I examine this argument, it may not be amiss to inform the English reader, that a passage in the book of Leviticus, relating to usury, is wrongly translated in our bibles. *The passage is this—And if thy brother be waxed poor, and fallen in decay with thee, then thou shalt relieve him, *yea, though he be* a stranger or a sojourner, that he may live with thee: take thou no usury of him or increase; but fear thy God, that thy brother may live with thee: thou shalt not give him thy money upon usury, nor lend him thy victuals for increase. This passage at first sight implies, that the Israelites might not take increase of a stranger or sojourner; if he was grown poor or fallen to decay amongst them: they are commanded to relieve their brother who was in such distress; not only if he was an Israelite, but though he was a stranger or a sojourner, they were to take no usury or increase of him. But it is to be observed, that the words, *yea, though he be*, are not in the original: and if we render the original literally it will be—Thou shalt relieve him, a stranger or a sojourner, that he may live with thee. There is something wanting to make the sense full; and instead of supplying it with the words *yea, though he be*, it should have been thus supplied—If thy brother is waxen poor, and fallen to decay with thee, then thou shalt help him, a stranger and a sojourner *shall help him*, that he may live with thee. In the common translation it is plain, that a stranger or a sojourner must be called the brother of an Israelite; which

* Levit. XXXV. 35, &c.

is so unusual in the other parts of the law of Moses, that this alone would be a sufficient reason for concluding, that our translators have missed the sense of this passage. The intent of the law in this place seems to be, that all persons who lived under its jurisdiction, whether they were Israelites or sojourners, should help a poor Israelite. This precept is, in this respect, like the fourth precept of the decalogue; it extends to all who dwelled in the land. And we may find a farther reason for preferring this sense to the sense which is expressed in our translation, if we compare this passage with another that we meet with in the book of Deuteronomy. *The law says there,—Thou shalt not lend upon usury to thy brother, usury of money, usury of victuals, usury of any thing, that is lent upon usury: unto a stranger thou mayest lend upon usury, but unto thy brother thou shalt not lend upon usury. Here is a plain difference made between those who are called brethren, and those who are called strangers. Nay, we find, that the Israelites were allowed to lend upon usury to strangers, though they were forbidden to lend upon usury to one another. And since, according to the common translation of the passage cited from Leviticus, they were alike forbidden to lend upon usury either to their brethren or to strangers, it is evident that our translators must have mistaken the sense of that passage; because the same law cannot expressly allow in one place what it expressly forbids in another.

If then it appears that the Israelites were forbidden to lend upon usury to one another only, and were, without exception, allowed to take usury of strangers; the consequence will be, that there can be nothing morally wrong in the practice itself: if there had, they would have been forbidden it in respect of foreigners, as well as in respect of one another: since what is wrong in itself, is as much so, when practised towards one set of men, as when practised towards another set. But if this practice was not forbidden to the Israelites upon account of any viciousness in it, then, notwithstanding the perfect morality which christians are obliged to, we cannot conclude from this precept in the Mosaic law, that it is unlawful for christians to take interest for money lent.

In fact this precept seems, from the distinction made between Israelites and strangers, to be of a political rather than of a moral nature: and no part of the merely political law of Moses is binding upon christians. The circumstances of the Hebrew nation, and the Mosaic constitution of government, will show us upon what policy this law was founded. They were not originally a trading nation, and consequently could make but little advantage by the use of money. And besides, by the Mosaic constitution, the land was equally divided between the several members of the community; and lest this equality should in process of time be broken in upon, no person was allowed to purchase land in perpetuity; whatever was bought, was to return again at the year of jubilee to the former owners. With the same view likewise, that the inheritance of one family or tribe might not pass into another, and the original equality of land be destroyed by accumulation, heiresses were commanded to marry within their own family or tribe. Since then, we may collect from these institutions, that the legislator intended to pre-

* Deut. XXIII. 19, 20.

serve an equality, and to prevent any one person or family from growing too rich; a plain reason appears why usury, especially in a nation without trade, should be prohibited. If it had been allowed of, those who paid it must have been impoverished; and those who received it, though they were in some measure prevented from realizing their fortunes by purchases of lands in perpetuity, would yet have grown more rich in proportion to their neighbours, than the law designed they should be.

Question relating to a loan.

XXIX. There is another question which may arise concerning a loan. If the value of money should alter between the time of borrowing and the time of paying, it may be asked, whether the payment is to be made according to the value of the money at the time of borrowing, or according to its value at the time of paying.

Before we can answer this question, it must be made a little more determinate than it is in this manner of stating it. Let us state the question thus:—Suppose I have lent a certain number of pieces of any particular denomination, and before the time of payment, those pieces change in their price, or in their relative value, when compared with pieces of some other denomination; as suppose, for instance, that I lend a hundred guineas, which, at the time of lending them, are each of them worth twenty-two shillings; but that, before the time of payment, guineas are each of them worth no more than twenty-one shillings; would it be a sufficient payment if the borrower was to return the same number of pieces of the same denomination, that is, to return me a hundred guineas again.

Here it would be necessary to know whether the intrinsic or the extrinsic value of the pieces in question had been changed, so as to make this alteration in the price of them. Certainly if their price had been altered by a change in their intrinsic value, there would be no reason to think it a sufficient payment.

The intrinsic value of guineas, or of any other pieces of money, can be made less only by making them of baser metal, or by putting a less quantity of pure metal into them. Suppose, then, that I lend a man a hundred guineas of a purer sort of metal; it seems to be self-evident that, if before the time of payment the guineas have been lowered in their intrinsic value, by making them of baser metal, he does not pay me what he borrowed by returning a hundred guineas made of this baser metal. I lend a man a hundred pieces of gold, which are called guineas: no one could think that he would make a full payment by returning an equal number of pieces of brass of the same shape and stamp. And it would be as plainly no full payment, if the pieces returned were a mixed metal of half gold and half brass: for what I lent was all gold, and what I receive is but half gold. You might say, indeed, that these are counters and not guineas. But this is not the true reason why I am not fully paid. It is not the denomination which gives the value to money, but its weight and fineness. The payment is short, not because what I lent were called guineas, and what I receive are called counters; but because the weight and fineness of what I receive is not the same with the weight and fineness of what I lent.

The second way of debasing the coin, is by making a greater number of pieces of the same denomination out of the same weight of pure metal. Thus, if a pound of gold makes forty guineas, and I lend forty such guineas; it would be a short payment, if I was to receive only forty guineas of such a size, that threescore of them would weigh no more than a pound. In this rate of payment, the number, and the denomination, and the fineness both of the pieces that I lend, and of the pieces that I receive, would be the same; and yet I should receive but two-thirds of my debt: because the weight of these forty guineas is only two-thirds of the weight of what I lent.

In reckoning money we are apt, where the denomination and number is the same, to consider the value as the same too; without considering that the way of estimating the quantity of money by the number of pieces is quite accidental. This way of reckoning proceeds upon a supposition, that all pieces of a certain denomination, with such a certain stamp upon them, have a certain degree of fineness and a certain weight. Upon this supposition, counting the number of pieces, comes to the same in the end as weighing them. But whenever this supposition has been taken away by keeping the denomination or stamp and changing the fineness or the weight of the pieces; those who are not forced to do otherwise by positive laws, will take the money by tale no longer; but will adjust its fineness, and estimate its weight, in order to determine the quantity of pure metal that they receive.

Where the intrinsic value of the pieces is the same, their extrinsic value in comparison of any other pieces, as of shillings, for instance, may be altered, either, first, by debasing the metal out of which those shillings are made; or secondly, by lessening their weight without debasing the metal; or thirdly, by the accidental variations in the quantity of silver and gold that are current. But naturally these alterations in the extrinsic value of gold, or of guineas made of gold, are of no account: because, naturally, gold is lent as gold, without any reference to silver. It is only civil institution which has given it this reference, by considering all the current coin of a nation as if it was of the same species; by considering, for instance, shillings as parts of a guinea, and halfpence as parts of a shilling, without regarding the difference of the metal that these several coins are made of. But naturally, if I lend a hundred guineas, each of which, in reference to silver, is then worth twenty-two shillings, and am to be paid again when, in the same reference, each is worth no more than twenty-one shillings; I shall be fully paid if a hundred guineas are returned me. The gold that passes between me and the borrower is to be estimated only by its weight and fineness, and not by its value in comparison with silver, any more than by its value in comparison with any thing else. It would be readily seen to be a very strange question, supposing I was to lend a guinea when it would buy five bushels of wheat, and was to be paid again when it would only buy four, whether a guinea would be full payment? And it is in the nature of the thing as strange a question, supposing I lend a guinea, when it would buy me twenty-two pieces of silver, and am to be paid again when it would only buy twenty-one such pieces, whether this is full payment? What has made us see the strangeness of the former question more readily than of the latter is, that guineas and wheat are considered by us as different species of things; so that in estimating the value of the one we do it without any necessary or customary reference to the other. But guineas and shillings in a nation where both of them are current coin, are looked upon as things of the same species, and as differing only as a part differs from the whole: by which means we are led to estimate the value of the one by the proportion which it bears to the value of the other. Suppose I lend two pounds and a half of gold in bullion, which compared with silver is at that time worth two thousand two hundred shillings: it would, I imagine, be thought full payment, if I received two pounds and a half of bullion again; though, perhaps, at the time of payment, it might be worth no more in silver than two thousand one hundred shillings. For the natural rule is, that in such things as are estimated by number, weight or measure, it is a full payment, if we return the same species in equal number, weight or measure. The coining these two pounds and a half of bullion into a hundred guineas before I lend it, would make no real difference in the two cases: for all that is done by coining is to denote by a certain stamp upon each piece into which the bullion is divided, what is the weight of that piece. Coining the bullion might indeed make such an imaginary difference as has occasioned all the difficulty in this question: the bullion being then changed into gold coin, we might by that means be led to consider it as of the same species with silver coin, and to judge of its value, not by its weight, but by its relative value in comparison with silver coin.

This reference of gold coin to silver coin in determining its value, as if they were of the same species, and differed from one another only as greater and less, is kept up in civil reckonings by referring both of them alike to some common and settled denomination: which denomination is so far imaginary, that it is quite accidental whether there are any pieces coined which answer to the several terms of such denomination or not. Thus, in England, our civil way of numeration is by pounds, shillings and pence. All our coin, in reckoning money, whether it is gold, or silver, or copper, is referred to this standing denomination; which is in itself only an imaginary one. There are, indeed, such pieces as shillings, which answer to one term in this common denomination: but it is quite accidental that there are such pieces: this term in the denomination was not taken from the coin which is called a shilling, but was itself the occasion that such pieces should be coined. And it is plain that this term might, in reckoning money, be as readily made use of as it is now, though there was no such coin as a shilling; since another term in the same denomination, the term of pounds, is well understood, and easily applied; though there is in fact no such coin as a pound.

As far as the civil law, for the sake of making all the coin that is in a nation circulate alike, requires it in all loans and all payments to be reduced to such a common standing denomination, the state of the question now before us would be changed, and the determination upon it must be changed accordingly. If I lend a man a hundred guineas when the value of each guinea is one pound two shillings; the sum that I lend is not to be called a hundred guineas, for guinea is no term in the national way of reckoning; it must be called one hundred and ten pounds. Here, if it be asked whether a hundred guineas, when each is reduced to the value of one pound one shilling, would pay me, the answer will be clear; if we consider what sum, according to the national way of reckoning money, a hundred such guineas would make.

They would make no more than one hundred and five pounds. And we cannot well imagine that one hundred and five pounds paid will be a full payment for one hundred and ten pounds lent.

We may put this question in another instance, where, perhaps, the matter will appear clearer. I lend a hundred crowns; and each crown, at the time of lending them, is valued by the law at five shillings; by which I do not mean that it is worth five such pieces as we call shillings, but that it is considered, in reckoning money, as a fourth part of a pound on one hand, or as equal to sixty pence on the other hand. Before the time of payment, the law reduces these pieces in their value, and reckons each to be worth no more than four shillings, that is, to be the fifth part of a pound, or equal to forty-eight pence. Would it be a full payment, if the borrower was to return me no more than a hundred such pieces? If there is any doubt about the true answer to this question, instead of calling them crowns, call them five shilling pieces when they are lent, and four shilling pieces when they are paid: and then, I suppose, it will be plain, that four hundred shillings paid is not an equivalent for five hundred shillings lent.

Now, if this be the case, when the pieces are called by such names as express their value in the national way of reckoning; it must be the same, when we are to count our money in that way, though the same pieces should have some other technical name. Thus, if, in like manner, instead of calling the pieces guineas, we call them one pound two shilling pieces when they are lent, and one pound one shilling pieces when they are paid; it is evident, that a hundred of the latter is not a full payment for a hundred of the former.

Upon the whole, where gold coin is estimated by its intrinsic value, no change is made in the value of it, but by a change in its weight and fineness: and, consequently, whatever quantity we borrow, a full payment is made, where the same quantity in weight and fineness is returned. But where, in estimating it, we refer it to any extrinsic standard, the value of it is changed, by a change in comparison with this standard, though its weight and fineness should continue the same: and, consequently, when we borrow any sum of it computed by this standard, the payment will not be a full one, unless the sum returned, when computed by the same standard, is equal to the sum borrowed.

Nature of insurance.

XXX. *A contract of insurance is void, if it is made either when the goods insured are perished, and the owner knows it; or when they are out of all danger or hazard, and the insurer knows it. There can be no contract of any particular sort, where there is no matter of such contract: and the matter of insurance is a possible but uncertain loss, against which the insurer undertakes to indemnify the owner: he engages therefore for nothing, unless there may be a loss, and unless that loss is uncertain. But if the ship, for instance, which the owner insures, is lost at the time of insurance, and he knows it, there is no uncertainty in the loss, because it has been suffered already: or if the ship is safely arrived in port, and the insurer knows it, there is no loss possible. Indeed such a contract would be void upon account of the inequality of it. The insurer en-

* Grot. Lib. II. Cap. XII. § XXIII.

gages his work, in consideration of such a price as his labour would be worth, if he could preserve the goods in the hazard which they run: but if the goods are actually perished already, he engages for a less consideration than his labour would be worth; because, in these circumstances, his labour would be worth the whole of these goods: if, therefore, he insures for less than the whole value of the goods, he has not his equivalent. On the other hand, if the goods are safely arrived in port, and the insurer knows this, but the owner does not know it; the owner, if he promises any thing at all, promises more than the insurer's labour would be worth to preserve his goods in such circumstances: and, consequently, the owner does not receive an equivalent for the price that he gives.

The work or labour of the insurer, which I have been speaking of, is only a supposed work or labour: for in most contracts of insurance he does not labour, nor ever intends it. But the form of the contract seems to suppose that he does—What will you give me to insure your house from fire? that is, what will you give me to make you sure that your house shall not be burnt? The making you sure that such an accident shall not happen, implies, that I will take care to prevent it, and that, if it is not prevented, you shall look upon the loss as owing to my neglect, and upon that account, shall require me to make it good.

The necessary equality is preserved in this contract, if the owner gives no more and no less than the insurer's labour, considering the hazard which the goods run, would be worth, supposing him able to preserve those goods from damages.

Mixed contracts. XXXI. In many instances we find two or more of these simple contracts, which have been already described, united into one act. *Thus, if I knowingly and designedly give a man more for his goods than they are worth; this is partly a gift, and partly buying and selling. This is one of the instances made use of by Grotius for explaining mixed acts: and, perhaps, it is more properly called a mixed act than a mixed contract; because that part of it, which is a gift, is no contract. If I bargain with a workman to make rings or vessels for me out of his own metal; this is partly buying his goods, and partly hiring his labour. Some writers, indeed, consider this as merely buying and selling; because, if I had bought the rings or vessels ready made, I must have paid in the purchase both for the materials and for the workmanship. And, certainly, the only difference is, that in this contract the labour is valued particularly, and is considered separately from the materials; whereas, in buying such rings or vessels ready made, we usually purchase the thing in its present state, without making a separate estimation of the materials and workmanship. The contract of insurance is sometimes mixed with a loan: as when a person lends a sum of money to a merchant for a certain premium, upon condition, that, if such merchant's ship returns safe, he shall receive his principal again, but shall loose his principal, if the ship is lost. This is called bottomry. As he lends the principal money for a premium, it is a loan with interest; and as his receiving such principal again depends upon what may happen to the ship, it is insurance.

* Grot. Lib. II. Cap. XII. § V.

XXXII. *In partnerships of trade, goods, or money, or labour, under which I include skill or management, are by the consent of their respective owners united into one common stock. Each partner has in view a benefit to be received, for a benefit which he gives. The separate stock of any of the partners alone might be too small to trade with, in the manner proposed; or the nature of the undertaking may require not only more goods or more money than any one of them could supply, but more labour or more skill than any one of them is equal to. The gain arising from the common stock of goods or money is the price obtained for the use of those goods or money; and the gain arising from their joint labour, is the wages obtained for such labour.

Gain and loss, how adjusted in partnership.

If we consider the gain in this view, it is easy to determine what proportion of it each partner ought to receive. In whatever proportion the use of one partner's goods is more valuable than the use of the other partner's goods, so much more of the gain belongs to the former, than to the latter. I do not mean, that in dividing the gain, any regard is to be had to the particular share of it, which arose accidentally from the goods contributed by this or that partner; but that after the goods are united in a joint stock by agreement, each partner has a claim to the gain arising from it, in proportion to what was the probable value of the use of his goods, if he had traded with them separately. And as the probable value of the use is in proportion to the value of the goods themselves; each partner's claim upon the gain will be in the same proportion. In like manner, where there is a joint labour, since the profits arising from it are the wages of that joint labour, each partner has a claim, not to that particular part of the gain which his labour earned, for then it would be no partnership, but to such a comparative share out of the common wages or gain, as is proportional to the value of his labour, when compared with the labour of the other.

As the gain of each partner, so likewise the loss of each ought to be proportionable to the value of what he contributes. As much as the goods which one partner contributes, exceed in their value the goods which the other contributes; so much greater is the claim of the former upon the joint stock, than the claim of the latter. Since, therefore, their respective claims upon the whole stock, are in proportion to the share of that stock which came originally from each of them; their claim upon each part of the whole must be in the same proportion. And, consequently, if any part of the stock is lost, each partner having a claim upon such part lost in proportion to his original share, looses a claim in the same proportion, that is, the loss of each is in proportion to the original share which he contributed towards the common stock.

This, then, is the rule for adjusting the gain and loss in partnerships, where no express agreement has been made to the contrary. Each partner is to receive such a share of the gain, or to bear such a share of the loss, as has the same proportion to what any other of the partners receives or bears, that the share contributed by the former has to the share contributed by the latter. The interest or claim of each upon the whole stock is in this proportion: and, consequently, the interest or claim of each in the increase or decrease of it, in any part ad-

* Grotius, Lib. II. Cap. XII. § XXIV.

ded to it by way of gain, or in any part taken from it by way of loss, ought to be in the same proportion.

Partnership mixed with insurance.

XXXIII. If the parties agree that one of them shall have a share in the gain, but shall bear no share in the loss; the contract is a mixed one: it is partly partnership, and partly insurance. As they are all of them to have a share in the gain, it is partnership: but he or they who are to bear all the loss, insure the principal stock of him who is to bear none of it.

To adjust the shares which each party, in such a mixed contract, is to receive in the gain, we are to consider what it is worth to insure his principal, who is not subject to any loss. And when the value of such insurance is deducted from the whole gain, and assigned to those who were to have borne all the loss, if there had been any; the remaining gain is to be divided in proportion to each party's share in the capital stock.

Contract of one party's bearing the whole loss, without any share in the gain.

XXXIV. It is generally maintained to be contrary to the nature of partnerships, that, where a capital stock is made by mutual consent, the parties so forming a capital stock should agree, that one of them should have all the gain, and the other bear all the loss. And certainly such an agreement is contrary to the nature of partnership; if we define partnership to be a contract, which gives the parties a common claim to the joint stock: because, where they have a common claim to the stock, they must, in consequence, have a common claim to the gain arising from it, and to the losses sustained in it.

But such an agreement, though it may be inconsistent with the nature of partnership, is not inconsistent with the law of common justice. A man wants five hundred pounds capital stock, to enter upon a certain branch of trade; he has only three hundred pounds of his own. I agree to let him have two hundred pounds to make up his capital, upon condition that he shall have all the advantage arising from the whole; that, if he saves the whole capital, my money shall be returned, but that, if any part of it is lost, I will bear the loss, as far as the two hundred pounds which I have advanced. There can, I think, be no question, whether the law of nature would allow of such an act of humanity as this. You may say that such an agreement is contrary to the law of partnership. I grant it is, and therefore am satisfied that it should not be called a partnership. I only insist, that the agreement is not contrary to the law of nature, and leave it to you to call it by what name you please. Perhaps you may have no name for it; but a contract is not the more unlawful for wanting a name.

Work and money, how compared in partnership.

XXXV. *In partnership, where work is contributed on one side, and money on the other, the partner, from whom the money comes, may contribute either the use only of the money, or the property of it.

If he contributes only the use of it, and still keeps his property in the principal, so that the joint stock is to be considered as made up of the labour of one partner and of the use of the other's money; it is plain, that, supposing the principal to be safe, it belongs to him, and that, supposing it to be lost, he alone is to bear such loss. The other

* Grot. Lib. II. Cap. XII. § XXIV.

partner who contributes work, since, as the case is put, he had no claim to the principal money, or to any part of it, cannot be obliged to make good any part of that loss, or to bear any share in it.

But if he contributes the property of his money, so that the joint stock, upon which each of them has a common claim, is made up of his principal money and of the other's labour; then the partner, who labours, has a claim upon the principal money itself: and, consequently, whenever the partnership is dissolved, if the principal money or any part of it is safe, he ought to have a share in it; and if the principal is lost, he is a sufferer by losing such share.

In the former case, where he, from whom the money comes, still keeps his property in it, and has a right to the whole principal, you may ask what it is which he contributes? But the answer is obvious. He contributes the use of his money; that is, he contributes the clear gain which he might probably have made of it himself. This however is not all. He contributes, besides this, the hazard of his principal; because, if the whole, or any part of it, should be lost, the loss is his. In order, therefore, to adjust the share which each partner ought to have in the gain, if there is any, you are to value the work of one, and the use and hazard of the other's money: and in proportion to the value contributed by each of them, upon such an estimate, their respective gains are to be settled.

In the other case, where he, from whom the money comes, contributes the property of it, and the other contributes his labour; in adjusting their respective shares of the gain, you are to value the money of one and the labour of the other. And when the comparative values of what each has contributed are thus settled, their respective shares in the gain are to be in the same proportion.

Contracts, how dissolved.

XXXVI. It is plain, from what has been said of contracts, that the obligation arising from them may be dissolved by the consent of the parties concerned in them. The same mutual consent, by which the obligation was originally produced, can destroy it again, without any injustice to either party: since, whatever claim the contract gave them, each of them agrees to give up that claim; whenever, by such mutual consent, they dissolve that contract.

The obligation, however, does not cease by any declaration of one of the parties alone, that he will not stand to his bargain, unless the other agrees to release him: an obligation which was produced by the concurrence of both their wills, cannot be destroyed again by the will of only one of them: he who declares that he will not stand by his bargain, cannot, by so doing, justly take away the right which the other had acquired by the contract; unless the other consents to part with that right.

Another way in which the obligation of a contract ceases, in respect of one of the parties, is by the non-performance of the other. In all contracts of mutual benefit, whatever obligation one party is under to give or to do it, is undertaken upon condition of his receiving the equivalent agreed upon. If, therefore, he fails of receiving such equivalent by the other's non-performance, the condition fails, upon which he consented to be obliged; and, consequently, he ceases to be under any obligation.

But it may, perhaps, be worth our while to be a little more particular in considering the several ways in which partnerships are dissolved.

First, partnerships are dissolved by the mutual consent of the parties concerned in them: for, as in all other contracts, so in these, an obligation arising from their mutual consent may be destroyed by the same cause that produced it.

Secondly, they are dissolved by the accomplishment of the business for which they were formed. If the partners consented to form a joint stock, and to give each other, by mutual consent, a common claim upon it, only for a certain purpose; this purpose limits their consent: and in consequence it limits the obligation arising from that consent. Whenever, therefore, the purposes are brought about, which led them thus to join together, the obligation of continuing so connected, is at an end.

Thirdly, partnerships, if they were formed only for a certain time, cease at the expiration of that time. The partners, in their original agreement, limited their obligation to one another, and the mutual claims which each has upon the things of the other; and by so doing, by consenting to stand thus obliged for a certain time, they plainly showed that it was not their design, or that they did not consent to be obliged any longer.

The renunciation of one partner, without the consent of the other, when the purpose of the partnership is not accomplished, or when there either was no time limited, or that time is not expired, is not sufficient to dissolve the partnership. No obligation can, in its own nature, be destroyed, but by the same cause that produced it: an obligation arising from the concurrence of the wills of two or more persons cannot be set aside by the single will of one of them. Indeed, the partner who renounces, has it in his power to make it impossible, by his perverseness, for the partnership to go on: but still, though he has a natural power to do this, he has no right to do it; the obligation of the partnership is in force, and will obtain its effect. The only way in which it can obtain its effect, in these circumstances, is by giving the other partner a right to satisfaction for any damage which may follow from such a breach of contract.

Neither does the death of one of the partners naturally dissolve the partnership, as far as goods or money are concerned. The goods or money of the deceased, which were part of the common stock, were subject to the claim of the survivor: and the heir can receive them in no other condition than what his ancestor left them in: he can receive them only as part of such common stock, subject to such claim. In respect of labour indeed the case would be otherwise. Labour is a personal act, and consequently the obligation to perform it, being merely personal, cannot descend to the heir. Upon this account, as most contracts of partnership are so fixed, that labour, or some personal act of industry, knowledge, or fidelity have a share in them, it is most usual for partnerships to cease upon the death of one of the partners.

Contracts of chance, their nature and obligations.

XXXVII. I have already spoken of all contracts of chance, such as wagers or gaming of any sort, as partnerships; and such they undoubtedly are, though not partnerships for trade.

To preserve an equality in wagers, if the stakes are equal on each side, the knowledge which each party has of the uncertain event that the wager is laid upon, ought to be equal. Each, by what he stakes, purchases an equal interest in right to the common stock, which consists of their joint stakes. The chance which each of them has of winning that whole stock, is their respective interests in fact. But if their interests in right are equal, as they are, where they stake equal sums, it is unjust that their interests in fact should be unequal. And their claims in fact will be unequal, if one of them knows which way the event had fallen out, where they lay upon a past event, or which way it will fall out, where they lay upon a future one; whilst the other in the meantime is ignorant of the matter, and looks upon the event as uncertain.

In games that depend upon skill or upon strength, whatever advantage one of the parties has in point of skill or strength above the other, so much he ought to stake more in proportion than the other stakes. The interest which he has in fact in the common stock made up of both their stakes, exceeds the other's interest in it, in the same proportion that his skill or strength exceeds the skill or strength of his antagonist. And the interest, which in right he has in the same stock, is in like manner proportionable to his stake, when compared with the other's stake. If therefore his stake exceeds the stake of his antagonist, just as much as his skill or strength exceeds the skill or strength of his antagonist, their interest in fact will be respectively as their interest in right.

In general, in all such contracts as depend upon chance, where the stakes are a common stock and the chance is to adjudge that stock to one of the parties; each party ought to deposit as much, that is to pay as much for his chance, as that chance is worth: and since the value of each person's chance, when compared with the others, rises in proportion to his knowledge, skill, or strength; it follows, that each party's stake, which is the purchase of his chance, ought, when compared with the stake of the other, to rise in the same proportion.

Contracts with a man to do or give what we might claim, are void.

XXXVIII. Those *contracts are void by which we engage to give money, or some other thing of value, or to do some beneficial act, in consideration that he to whom we so engage, shall give us, or shall do for us, what we might have claimed without any such contract.

Grotius considers this question under the head of promises, and determines such promises to be binding: because, says he, a promise is binding, though we make it of our own mere motion without any valuable consideration: and for this reason, though the promiser does not, properly speaking, receive any thing in return for what he is to give or to do, yet he is obliged to make good his engagement. He does not, properly speaking, receive any thing in return for what he is to give or to do; because what he receives was due to him, or was his own, without purchasing it, and cannot therefore be looked upon as a return for what he promises.

However, we should rather consider this as a contract than as a promise.—If you will let me have my goods, which you detain from me

* Grot. Lib. II. Cap. XI. § X.

unjustly, or if you, being to set as judge in my cause, will give a sentence in my favour, where the right is clearly on my side; I will give you such a reward. Here is money to be given, in one case for goods, and in the other case for work. And such contracts are void, if each party does not receive his equivalent. But how have I received an equivalent, if all that I receive was my own before? There must, in fact, be some force or some fraud in the person with whom I have to do; since no man, who designed honestly, would be concerned in selling me what, without paying for it, I had a right to.

Contracts void where the matter is unlawful.

XXXIX. *If money or any other valuable consideration, is promised in order to hire a man to do an act of injustice, such promise is void.

Grotius determines very singularly upon this point. If, says he, I promise any thing, in order to obtain the doing a criminal act, as suppose I promise money to hire a man to commit murder; such a promise is vicious; because it is an enticement to the assassin to commit the crime. And since this viciousness continues till the crime is over; and since all acts which have a continued viciousness inherent in them, or connected with them, are void; it follows, that till the crime is committed, this promise cannot be binding. But as soon as the crime is over, this viciousness ceases: because the promise can be no longer considered as an enticement to the commission of the crime. The obligation therefore of this promise, till the crime was committed, was in suspense: but as soon as the crime is over, the obligation exerts itself: for the promise was in reality obligatory from the beginning, but its obligation was prevented from taking effect, by a viciousness which accidentally adhered to it: consequently as soon as this viciousness is removed by the commission of the crime, the promiser is bound to make good what he engaged for.

Now this whole matter may well be set in a different light. The act of engaging to give wages for the doing a crime is plainly a contract: something is to be given for something to be done: and such contract is void on both sides from the beginning. A contract, which is void on one part, cannot be binding on the other part: because if one party is released from his obligation, the other must be released of course, as having no equivalent for what he is to give or to do, but merely at the pleasure or bounty of the former. But on the part of the assassin, that we may use the same instance with Grotius, the contract is void from the beginning; because he has engaged for such an act as he has no moral power of performing. If there is any doubt of this, let us suppose that the assassin had promised to commit the crime without any promise on the other part, of wages to be given for committing it. His promise would, I think, be clearly void; and whatever reason would make such a promise void, if it had been a gratuitous one, affects it equally, when it is made for a valuable consideration. But if the promise, on the part of the criminal, is void from the beginning, the promise of him who hires such criminal to do the fact is void too. As the promises in this case are mutual, the assassin has a claim to his wages only in consideration and upon condition of the other party's having a claim upon him to do the work: but the other party has no claim upon

* Grot. Lib. II. Cap. XI. § IX.

him to do the work: he therefore has no claim to his wages. The commission of the crime in this view of the case, can give him no claim: for if the contract was void from the beginning, and no other act passes in the meantime between him and his principal who hires him to do the work, his right to his wages will stand just where the contract left it; that is, it will be no right at all.

We may go one step farther. A promise of wages to do what is unlawful, though it is not an act of injustice, but only an act simply wrong, is a void promise. Here again the principal, who engages to give the wages, contracts with the accomplice to give them in consideration and upon condition that he, the accomplice, shall be bound to do what is not agreeable to the law. Now the accomplice cannot bind himself to this: not indeed because he has no moral power of doing what is simply wrong; since in cases of this sort the law does not take away the power of acting, but only directs the use of it: but he is however incapable or has no moral power of binding himself to such an act, because such obligation, if it was possible, would supersede the obligation of the law. If, then, the accomplice is not bound by his promise, neither is the principal bound by his. The accomplice therefore cannot pretend to have any claim grounded upon the promise of the principal: because this promise was void from the beginning.

Obligation how restored to void contracts.

XL. We have seen in what instances extorted or erroneous promises, contracts for want of equality, and either promises or contracts made by persons under age or out of their senses, are void. But when the fear is removed by means of which a promise was extorted, or when the mistake which occasioned a promise, is set right; when the minor comes to years of discretion, or the lunatic recovers his senses; or lastly, when the inequality in a contract is discovered; suppose the party whose obligation is void in any of these instances, is willing to abide by the obligation; what is required in order to bind him? Certainly his mere intention of binding himself is not sufficient; for a mere intention does not bind in any case: and from what has been proved already, his former act did not bind him. Some new declaration, therefore, or at least some outward, though tacit mark of this intention, is necessary. It does not indeed seem necessary, that he should go over the whole form of promising or contracting again. One would think, that he sufficiently shows his design either by acting in any instance, as if he looked upon himself to be still obliged, or even by neglecting, when any fair occasion offers itself, to declare that he does not acquiesce in the obligation.

CHAPTER XIV.

OF OATHS.

I. *An oath what.*—II. *Obligation to fidelity.*—III. *Obligation to veracity.*—IV. *What concealments consistent with this obligation.*—V. *Assertory oaths confirm an implied promise.*—VI. *The nature of an oath.*—VII. *Oath where God is not mentioned, how to be understood.*—VIII. *What security an oath gives to the truth of what is sworn to.*—IX. *Credit due to an idolater's oath.*—X. *Oaths may be taken by proxy.*—XI. *Oaths and vows, how distinguished.*—XII. *No effect of an oath, unless there are outward marks of an intention to swear.*—XIII. *Want of inward intention, where there is the outward mark of it, does not prevent the effect of an oath.*—XIV. *Oath is void, when the pact is so, with which it is joined.*—XV. *Oath to a robber binding.*—XVI. *Effect of an oath does not extend to the juror's heirs.*—XVII. *Oaths to do harm, not binding as vows.*

An oath what. I. *An oath is a solemn act by which we renounce our hope of God's mercy, or devote ourselves to his displeasure, if we are guilty of falsehood. It is sometimes defined to be a religious act, by which God is called upon, as a witness, to confirm what might otherwise be doubtful.

The doubts, which an oath is made use of to remove, are either such as relate to our fidelity in what we promise, or such as relate to our veracity, in what we affirm or deny. And oaths are accordingly divided into two sorts, promissory and assertory: the former are designed to ascertain our fidelity in promises; the latter to ascertain the veracity of our assertions.

But, in fact, all oaths seem properly to be promissory ones: for when a person is sworn to tell the truth; in such an oath, a promise to tell the truth is implied, and this promise is in reality what he swears to. When a witness is sworn in a court of justice, that the evidence which he gives, shall be the whole truth and nothing but the truth; he, by consenting to swear under this form, plainly consents, or in effect, promises to speak the truth. If he is sworn to give true answers to all such questions as shall be asked of him; his agreeing thus to swear contains or implies a promise, that his answers shall be true.

The distinction between assertory and promissory oaths is usually placed in the different time of the fact sworn to. All facts are either past, present, or future. Those only are called promissory oaths which ascertain the existence of future facts: and those are called assertory oaths, which ascertain the existence of past or present facts.

But neither will this distinction preserve a difference between them: for when the juror engages that he will tell the truth, as far as he knows it, in relation either to past or to present facts; though the oath may be said indirectly to ascertain the existence of such facts, yet what it ascertains directly is the future fidelity of the juror in relating those facts.

* Grot. Lib. II. Cap. XIII. § I.

II. Before we proceed any farther in our inquiry concerning the nature of oaths, and the obligation which arises from them; it may be proper to say something concerning the general reason of our obligations to fidelity and to veracity; that is, our obligations not to falsify either in what we promise, or in what we affirm or deny.

Obligation to fidelity.

The obligations to fidelity have been explained already, under the heads of promises and contracts: and the immediate cause of these obligations has been shown to be our own consent. Every breach of fidelity, either in promises or in contracts, is a violation of that right, which, by our own consent, we conferred upon him to whom we promised, or with whom we contracted.

It would be an idle question to ask, from whence the obligation arises to mean what we say, or to consent with our minds to what our words express. In our intercourse with mankind, the settled marks of our intentions are always understood to stand for our intentions themselves. The demands which others have upon us, do not arise from the mere intention of the mind, which can be known no otherwise, than as it is expressed in our words or in our actions: they arise from our intentions so made known: and consequently they extend as far as our intentions are made to appear by our words or actions. So that if we do not comply with what we have thus expressed, we are guilty of injustice towards them to whom we have given such demands, or, to speak more exactly, to whom we have given a right to make such demands.

III. The obligations that we are under to speak the truth in what we affirm or deny, have been rendered less obvious by the several supposed allowances of dissembling or falsifying. *Grotius supposes the general notion of a lie to consist in speaking, or in writing, or in using any other outward signs, in such a manner, that what we speak, or write, or otherwise signify, cannot be understood in any sense, but such an one as is different from our real thoughts. But then, as he rightly observes, something farther must be added to this general notion of a lie, to make it naturally unlawful: for there is nothing contained in this description of it, which will show it to be so. Indeed, words or gestures have their significancy given them by use or custom, which may be looked upon as a general agreement. The consequence of which is, that if I would have my mind known, I am under a necessity of using such words or such gestures, as by custom or general agreement, have been made expressive of my thoughts. But a custom or agreement which has done nothing more than give words or gestures their current significancy, can never bind me to make my mind known. The established meaning of certain gestures, or of the words of that language in which I speak or write, will force me to use those gestures or words agreeably to this established meaning, if I have a mind that the person to whom I use those gestures, or to whom I speak or write, should know my thoughts.

Obligation to veracity.

But this is not the question. The question is, why I am obliged to let him know my thoughts. The general consent which established the significancy of words or gestures, does not oblige me to this: be-

* Grot. Lib. III. Cap. I. § XI.

cause I can comply with this establishment, and yet can at the same time not only conceal my thoughts, but make him believe them to be different from what they are. I can use words or gestures according to that meaning which custom has given them, though it is even contrary to what I have in my mind. A man asks me, which way Titius went? I know that he is gone northward: if I have a mind that he should know it too, the general agreement, which has established the meaning of words or gestures, will force me to say, that he is gone northward, or to point that way. But if I have no mind that he should know it; that general agreement will not oblige me to use these words or gestures. I use such words and such a gesture as is consistent with this general agreement, if I point the contrary way, or say that he has gone southward; upon supposition, that I have a mind the inquirer should think that he went a contrary way to what I know him to be gone.

Now, the difference which Grotius adds to the general notion of a lie, to make it unlawful, is its inconsistence with some right in the person to whom I direct my discourse, to whom I write, or to whom I make use of any gestures, to which custom has given a significancy. Upon these principles all lies do not seem to be naturally unlawful; those only seem so, which are inconsistent with some right either perfect or imperfect in those persons with whom we are conversing. But because the word lie is so hateful, *Puffendorf, though he differs in fact very little from Grotius, distinguishes falsehoods of speech, not into lawful and unlawful lies, but into lies and untruths. A lie, says he, consists in making our words or other signs bear a different sense from our real conception; where the person, to whom these words or signs are directed, has a right to understand and to judge of those conceptions, and we, on our part, are obliged accordingly, to make him apprehend our meaning. Whereas, an untruth consists in applying our words or other signs in such a manner, that the person to whom they are directed, shall conceive from them a different sense from what we have in our mind; when that person has no right to know our thoughts, and no man is prejudiced by our concealing them.

It is allowed then by these two judicious writers, and cannot, I think, be denied by any one, that where the person, to whom we direct our discourse, has any right to know our real thoughts, it is unlawful to falsify. But when I direct my discourse to a man, or behave towards him, whilst I am discoursing, in such a manner, that all the world, who heard and saw me, would conclude that I designed to inform him of the truth; do not I, by such discourse and manner of behaviour, tacitly consent to inform him of it? Though, therefore, he might have no previous right to such information; yet this consent of mine gives him a right at the time: and I should act contrary to this right, so conferred upon him by my tacit consent, if I was to tell him a falsehood. This principle will leave but few untruths which are not to be ranked in the class of unlawful lies: it will reduce to this class of lies, not only such falsehoods as will directly injure a man, or hinder his innocent benefit: but all such falsehoods, likewise, as are inconsistent with that tacit consent to tell him the truth, which appears from our conversing

* Book IV. Chap. I. § IX.

with him, as if we designed to tell him it: because these falsehoods, as well as the other, will come under the description of being contrary to a right of his, either perfect or imperfect.

It may, perhaps, be asked, whether this right of knowing the truth, which is only conferred by our tacit consent in the manner that we have been describing, is of such a value, that it can be looked upon as an injury not to do what we have so consented to do; unless there is some other damage done to the man that we are conversing with, or to some one else, by our telling him a falsehood. Certainly, in some cases, it may be of no great importance to him, or to any one else, whether we deceive him or not. But then he who has engaged to another, is not at liberty to judge of that other's right: the party whose right it is to know the truth, may, if he pleases, release the speaker from this obligation: but without such a release it cannot be at the speaker's option, whether he will comply with the obligation or not, upon pretence that the hearer's right is of small value. To allow such a latitude as this, would effectually destroy, not only all obligations to speak the truth, but all obligations whatsoever: since the same latitude is full as reasonable in all other instances, as it can be in this.

What concealments consistent with this obligation.

IV. Let us now inquire what sort of concealments, or untruths, or dissimulation, this principle will allow of.

First, it is not unlawful to conceal, by our silence, what we have no mind to discover; provided the person who wants us to make the discovery, had no previous right to know the truth. Where he would not be injured, or lose any innocent advantage by not knowing the truth, he has no right to know it, unless we give him one by conversing with him: and, consequently, since our silence gives him no such right, we lawfully may be silent.

Secondly, it is not unlawful, even where we direct our discourse to a man, as if we designed to inform him of the truth, to speak what we know is untrue; provided we are sure that he waves his right of knowing it. This, I suppose, is the reason, why it should not be thought wrong for a prisoner, upon his trial, to plead—not guilty; though at the same time he is conscious of the contrary: because the court does not expect or desire to know the truth, unless they can make it out without his immediate confession of it.

Thirdly, where we have put ourselves absolutely under the direction or authority of another person, that this person may, by his authority over us, which we have so given him, obtain a certain purpose; our rights, as far as the necessity of this purpose requires, are at his disposal. Whatever right, therefore, of knowing the truth we might acquire by his professions of telling it, or by his directing his discourse to us, as if he designed to tell us it; the authority which we have given him supercedes this right, as far as it would hinder the purpose which he is to bring about. This is the case of physicians in respect of their patients, and of commanders in chief in respect of the soldiers who are under their authority.

Fourthly, as infants, or idiots, or madmen acquire no right by an express promise, so neither do they acquire any by our tacit agreement to tell them the truth when we are discoursing with them. Upon this account it is not thought unlawful to deceive them by our words or actions, either for their own benefit, or to prevent them from doing any harm.

Fifthly, it is the established character of history, to relate facts as they really happened: they, therefore, who undertake to write history, profess, by so doing, to speak the truth, and are for this reason obliged to speak it. But writers of fables, or relaters of parables, profess only to teach useful truths, under feigned stories or resemblances. They do, therefore, what they profess, and, consequently, what alone they are obliged to do; if they take care to make their fables or parables useful and instructing; they are not guilty of any unlawful falsehood, though the facts, which they relate in their fables or parables, never happened.

Sixthly, there are some actions or other signs, by which we profess nothing; they are directed to no person for his information; but all who see them are at liberty to take them in what sense they please. Whoever is deceived by such signs or actions as these, cannot charge them who make the signs, or do the actions, with falsehood. A student keeps his door shut, that he may not be interrupted. The appearance is the same as if he was not at home. But the judgment which any man would make, who found it shut, is not necessarily, that he is not at home, but either that he is not at home, or would not have any one interrupt him. Of this sort are several stratagems made use of in war. Whoever is deceived by any feints of his adversary, cannot charge such adversary with any unlawful falsehood: because, if he knows any thing, he must know, that his adversary never designed or professed to give him information.

Seventhly, when we direct our discourse to any one who knows the meaning of what we say, and a third person, who has no concern in it, listens to what passes between us, there is no unlawful falsehood in speaking so as to deceive him. He had no business to know what passed between us; and we did not address ourselves to him: he had, therefore, no previous right to be informed of the truth, and we gave him none at the time.

Eighthly, suppose a man inquires of me concerning some matter, which prudence would oblige me to conceal; because some damage might arise to me, or to some third person, from his knowing it: am I at liberty to falsify, in order to prevent him from knowing what I have such reasons for concealing? If he makes the inquiry inadvertently, there will be no great difficulty in the matter: by telling him that it is an improper inquiry, we shall get rid of him, without being under any necessity either of answering his question, or of giving him untrue information. But if he makes use of any unjust force or fraud to find out what he ought not to know; as such injustice would hinder him from acquiring any right, even by a direct promise; so it would much rather hinder him from acquiring any by the indirect and tacit promise of telling him the truth, implied in our addressing our discourse to him, as if we designed to tell him it.

However, it ought to be carefully remembered, that none of these concealments, untruths, or dissimulations are allowable when any causeless harm will be done, or any innocent advantage be prevented by them: because, in all such cases, the person who suffers such harm, or is hindered of such benefit, has a previous right to know the truth;

and though we were to give him none by directing our discourse to him, yet such previous right is violated, if we conceal the truth from him.

Assertory oaths confirm an implied promise.

V. It is plain, from the nature of promissory oaths, that they are designed to confirm some promise. And the same may likewise be said of assertory oaths, upon the principles that we have been explaining. The general obligation to speak the truth, in what we affirm or deny, arises from some right in the hearer to know it. This right may be prior to our discourse with him; he may have a right to be told the truth, if we tell him any thing: and then our addressing ourselves to him, as if we designed to tell the truth, is the mark of our consent that this right shall take place. Or if there is no such prior right, yet the very addressing ourselves to him gives him a right to know the truth; because it implies a tacit consent that we will tell it. All assertory oaths, therefore, being only designed to ascertain our veracity in what we affirm or deny, contain a promise either express or implied, that we will not falsify.

The general conclusion from what has been said is, that oaths of all sorts are designed as confirmations of some express or implied promise. We are next to consider in what manner such a confirmation is produced by calling God to witness to the truth of what we say or promise, or by renouncing his mercy, and devoting ourselves to his displeasure, if we falsify.

The nature of an oath.

VI. *The form of an oath, from whence alone we can learn what is the nature and essence of it, seems not always to be the same. Sometimes God is invoked as a witness to the truth of what we say; and sometimes he is invoked as an avenger to punish us, if we falsify. But these forms, though they differ in words, have the same meaning. To invoke God, either as a witness, or as an avenger, must, in effect, be the same thing: since what is doubtful can no otherwise be ascertained, by calling upon him to attest it, than because, as we are under his absolute authority, he can, and, as we believe, he will punish us, if we do not speak the truth.

If we would examine farther into this point, we must observe, that some writers have imagined what would have depended upon our own testimony only, if we had simply affirmed it; to be, therefore, rendered more certain, when we have sworn to it, or called God to witness to it, because the truth of it is then evidenced by the testimony of God. But this account of an oath cannot possibly be applied to such oaths as are promissory.

If I make a promise, and then call upon God to witness to the promise, supposing me to mean no more by this than barely to call him as a witness, I have done nothing towards rendering my fidelity less suspected than it was before. What is the effect of his testimony, considered merely as a testimony? Is it designed only to evince that I have made such a promise? This is needless; because the person to whom I have made the promise, wants no such evidence to prove the truth of this fact: he knows it already by the help of his senses, and cannot want to be made more certain of it than he is. The matter in doubt is, not whether I have made such a promise, but whether I will

* Grotius, Lib. II. Cap. XIII. § X.

faithfully keep it. And I confess that I cannot see how the testimony of God, considered merely as a testimony, can evince my fidelity; unless, when he is so called upon, he would show, by some miracle, that he knew I would not break my word.

But if, when I call him to attest my promise, I mean to make him a guarantee to see to the performance of it, and to punish me, if I break it; I have then given the person to whom I swear, a surer pledge, or a stronger assurance of my fidelity, than if I had simply promised without an oath. The fear of incurring God's displeasure, to which I have devoted myself by calling upon him to see to the performance of my promise, will make me less likely to break my word, than I possibly might have been, if I had not by an oath laid myself open to this fear.

Since then this notion of an oath, that God is merely invoked as a witness, cannot be applied to promissory oaths, so as to produce any effect in ascertaining what would be otherwise doubtful; since all oaths, even those which are usually called assertory ones, contain either an express or a virtual promise; and lastly, since an oath, according to the common opinion of mankind, is made use of to ascertain what might otherwise be doubtful; we may conclude that this notion of an oath is not agreeable to the common opinion or common sense of mankind.

But suppose we neglect the tacit or express promise in those which are usually called assertory oaths; I know not, even upon this supposition, how the truth of what is affirmed, concerning past or present facts, will be better ascertained with an oath than without it: if an oath is considered merely as an invocation of God to be a witness, either to the truth of the fact or to the veracity of the juror. I am in doubt about a fact: a person affirms the truth of it: I am still in doubt about it; because I doubt the veracity of the person who affirms it: he swears to the truth of the fact: if by so doing he only calls upon God to attest either the truth of the fact or his own veracity, my doubt will still remain. Can he say, that the truth of the fact, which was supported before only by his own testimony, is now supported by the testimony of God? or can he say, that the truth of the fact is still supported more immediately only by his own veracity, but that his veracity is now supported by the divine testimony? This is the point which I am now in doubt upon. I know, indeed, that he has, as he says, called upon God to attest either the truth of the fact or his own veracity; and if I had any evidence, that God did attest either of them, when he is so called upon, my doubt would be at an end. But there is no evidence at all of this: and consequently no more evidence, that the fact is true after he has sworn to it, than there was before; if this was the whole notion of an oath; if we were to look no farther than the supposed testimony of God, supporting either the truth of the fact or the veracity of the juror. I have no more evidence, that God gives testimony to what he affirms, merely in consequence of his having called upon him to give such testimony, than I before had of the truth of the fact, merely in consequence of his having affirmed it.

Perhaps he might say, that after he has done this I can have little or no reason to suspect his veracity; because it would be such an affront to the truth and to the majesty of almighty God, to be called upon to attest what is false, as all but the most abandoned villains would tremble at: his fear therefore of thus insulting and defying God, and of the punishment which every sober man is sensible will be the consequence of such behaviour, is a sufficient security to me, that what he affirms upon oath is true, to the best of his knowledge. If he says this, I shall plainly understand how much stronger security I have from his oath, than I should have had from his bare assertion. But then this is the very point which I want to make good: if the fear of the juror, when he calls God to witness, is the security which his oath gives me, of his telling the truth; then by calling God to witness, he understands, that God will punish him, if he falsifies; or that calling him in as a witness, and calling him as an avenger, amount to the same thing.

The most usual forms of an oath are expressed to this purpose. When oaths are administered amongst us in this country, the juror has the gospels in his hand, and one of the usual forms of an oath is, that after repeating the matter to which he swears, he concludes with saying—so help me God, and the contents of this book; that is, may I receive the favour of God, and have a share in the mercies of the gospel only upon condition, that I observe my promise or speak the truth. The latter part of this form, and the contents of this book, is frequently omitted: but as the juror has his hand upon the gospels, when he repeats the shorter form, so help me God;—this gesture explains the meaning of his words, and shows it to be, that he is willing and desirous to be admitted to those helps or that favour of God which the gospel has promised, only upon condition, that he does not falsify. These forms plainly show, that the juror devotes himself to the displeasure of God by a solemn renunciation of his mercies in general, and of his mercies promised by the gospel in particular, if he does not make good what he swears to; whether it is to perform a compact, or to tell the truth. There are two forms of an oath mentioned by Livy, which may serve to show us, that the jurors amongst heathens, as well as amongst christians, were understood to devote themselves to the anger of their gods, if they broke their oath. In establishing an agreement between the Romans and the Albans, Sp. Furius devotes the Roman people, if they first broke the agreement—*If the Roman people fail to make good this agreement; do thou, O Jupiter, smite them upon that day, as I now smite this swine; and smite them so much more as thou art greater in power and might than I am—and having said this he struck a swine which he held in his left hand, with a stone which he held in his right. Hannibal, just before the battle with the Romans at the river Ticinus, having promised large rewards to his soldiers, confirmed his promise with an oath of much the same form. †He held a lamb in his left hand, and a flint in his right; and whilst he prayed to Jupiter and all the gods, that, if he failed, they would slay him, as he then slew that lamb, he struck the head of the lamb with the flint.

Oath where God is not mentioned, how to be understood.

VII. ‡It was not uncommon amongst the ancients, for persons to swear by other things, without the mention of God, as by the sun, the stars, or the heaven; by their own life, the life of their children, or the life of their prince. Oaths by the sun, the stars, or the heavens, seem to have been introduced, when these were imagined to be divinities. But such an oath in the mouth of a christian looks like profaneness: and I should

* Liv. I. 24. † Liv. XXI. 45. ‡ Grot. ut sup. § XI.

not so much inquire whether he was guilty of perjury in not keeping it, as whether he was not guilty of affronting God in taking it. Unless indeed where a person, out of reverence to the name of God, abstains from using it, and means, when he swears by heaven, to swear by that God, whom we have been taught to call our father, who is in heaven. *Sanderson imagines, that to swear by our own life, or the life of our children, or the life of our prince, is tacitly swearing by that God, from whom these blessings were received. But certainly, amongst the ancients, who used these forms, this was not supposed to be the import of them. The juror meant, indeed, to invoke the divine vengeance upon himself, if he falsified; but he did this by devoting to destruction what was, or what he pretended to be, of all things, most dear to him. This, which is the opinion of Grotius, appears to be true, from some passages that †Puffendorf has cited from the ancients, for this purpose. When Regulus, as the story is related by Pliny, had persuaded Verania that she would recover from her illness; she called for her will, and made Regulus her heir: it appears, from the sequel, by what sort of an oath he had attested the certainty of her recovery: for when Verania was, soon after this, in her last extremities, she exclaimed against him as a perjured villain, who had foresworn himself, by the life and safety of his son. Pliny's reflection upon it, explains the intent of such an oath. Regulus, says he, makes use of this stratagem not more frequently than wickedly; whilst he, every day, deceives the gods, to whose wrath he has devoted this unhappy son of his. ‡Lysias, in one of his orations, introduces the daughter of Diagiton and widow of Diodotus, offering to swear, by the children both of her former and her second marriage, that Diodotus had committed to the trust of Diagiton five talents; to which she adds, I am neither so abandoned nor so covetous, as to leave the curse of perjury upon my children, for the sake only of leaving them a maintenance. When the king of the Scythians is sick, he sends, says §Herodotus, for three of the most approved public diviners, to inquire into the occasion of his distemper: and their usual answer is, that such or such a person has forsworn himself by the royal palace: for amongst the Scythians, this oath, by the king's palace, is reckoned, of all others, the most sacred. From this last mentioned form, we may collect, both that swearing by the king's palace, was understood to be the same as swearing by the king's person; in like manner, as our Saviour interprets an oath by the temple, to be an oath by him, that dwelleth therein. And we may, from thence, collect, likewise, that such an oath, by the king's person, was understood to devote his person to some calamity, if the juror falsified.

What security an oath gives of the truth of what is sworn to.

VIII. It may, perhaps, be asked, what greater security we have of a man's veracity or fidelity, in respect of what he promises or affirms upon oath, than we should have had, if he had only affirmed or promised the same thing without swearing to it. Falsehood and perfidiousness are crimes against the law of nature, as well as perjury. If, therefore, either the love of what is right, or the fear of being punished for doing

* De juram. oblig. præl. I. § 4.
† Book IV. Chap. II. § III.
‡ Lys. edit. Tayl. p. 509, &c.
§ Herod. L. IV. p. 243. edit. Gronov.

what is contrary to the law of God, is what restrains any one from falsifying, when he is upon oath; will not the same love of what is right, or the same fear of being punished for what is contrary to the law of God, equally restrain him from being false or perfidious, when he is not upon oath?—The great security which an oath gives us of his veracity or fidelity, who takes it, arises, indeed, as is here supposed, from his fear of offending that almighty being, by whom he swears, if he is guilty of falsifying. And it must be farther owned, that a wise and a good man will be afraid of falsifying, even though he has taken no oath; lest by so doing he should offend the same almighty being. But then these are different degrees of fear: the fear of perjury is, upon two accounts, naturally greater than the fear of simple falsehood. First, because perjury is the greater crime of the two; since falsehood is only a breach of the laws of God; whereas, perjury is a direct insult upon him, and sets him at defiance. And, secondly, because he who is simply guilty of falsehood, has room to entertain hopes of forgiveness: whereas, he who is guilty of perjury, has devoted himself to the displeasure of God, and precluded himself from all such hopes of forgiveness by renouncing his mercies.

IX. *From considering the principle upon which our assurance of a man's fidelity or veracity depends, when he is upon oath, we may be able to judge what credit is to be given to any one who has sworn by a false god. Credit due to an idolater's oath.

But in determining this question, it will be necessary to inquire, whether the juror believed the being, by which he swore, to be the true God. If he did not, then he certainly would not be afraid of offending what he knows has no power to hurt him, if he does offend: his oath, therefore, would not in the least ascertain his fidelity or veracity. He might, too, perhaps, if he should falsify, acquit himself of the guilt of perjury: but then he should remember, that though it could not properly be called an insult upon God, and a defiance of his power to break such an oath, yet it was the highest insult upon him to swear in this manner. It was in fact nothing less than idolatry: for an oath is an act of religion, which implies, that we acknowledge the being, upon whom we call as an avenger of our falsehood, to have infinite wisdom and infinite power; such wisdom, however, as can search into our thoughts, and know whether we do falsify or not, and such power as can finally exclude us from all happiness, if we do. He, therefore, who swears by a false god, knowing it to be such, ascribes by this act such knowledge and power to the being, by whom he swears, as belongs only to the true God, and as cannot, without the crime of idolatry, be ascribed to any other being.

But if the juror is firmly persuaded that the being by which he swears, is the true God; we have, notwithstanding the idolatry, both of his general persuasion and of his particular act, the same assurance of his fidelity, that we should have of a christian's fidelity, who believes in the true God, and has sworn by him. The christian's fear of the consequences of perjury is our security that he will not falsify, and is the foundation of that credit, which he obtains upon his oath: and as the pagan, from his persuasion of the wisdom and power of the being,

* Grot. ut sup. § XII.

by which he swears, is under the same fears; we have the same security of his not falsifying: his oath, therefore, deserves upon the same foundation to obtain the same credit.

Whether the true God will punish a pagan for perjury, when he has foresworn himself by a false god, is a question of theology rather than of natural law, and is certainly, however divines may decide it, quite foreign to the point now before us. Our assurance of the pagan's veracity rests upon the same foundation, in whatever manner this question is determined: it rests upon the persuasion of his own mind, and upon his fears, which arise from that persuasion; and not upon the future sentence to be passed upon him by the true God, of whom he is ignorant, and whose counsels never come into his deliberation, when he considers the consequences of his perjury.

Oaths may be taken by proxy.

X. It is most convenient that the juror should take the oath in his own person, and not by proxy: because by going through the solemn outward acts, with which an oath is commonly attended, and by repeating the words of execration ourselves, we are more likely to be affected with a due sense of what we are about; than if another person was to go through the form, and to repeat the words for us. But otherwise there is nothing naturally wrong in allowing an oath to be taken by proxy: since, as I could renounce the divine mercy and imprecate the divine vengeance in my own person, so I can empower another to do it for me: and what he does, who is so empowered, is as much my act, and binds me as effectually, as if I had done it myself.

Oaths and vows, how distinguished.

XI. Before we go any farther in our inquiries concerning the nature and effect of oaths, it may be proper to take notice of a distinction between oaths and vows.

By what has been said already concerning an oath, it appears that by an oath, God is called upon to see to the performance of what we promise, or to the truth of what we affirm, and to punish us, if we are found to be perfidious or false. So that an oath does not properly contain in it any new and distinct obligation, but only confirms the obligation of some other act. If I make a promise to a man and he accepts it, I am obliged to performance. If he is doubtful about my fidelity, and, in order to remove his doubts, I swear to my promise; I do not, by this act, lay myself under any new or distinct obligation, but only strengthen the obligations, under which I had laid myself before: and this I do by introducing the deity as a third party in the obligation, or rather as a guarantee of the pact, to see to the performance of it. The effect then of an oath is to annex a peculiar penalty to some other obligation: the juror renounces God's mercy, or devotes himself to God's displeasure, if he does not make good that other obligation.

This effect of an oath is what we mean by the obligation of it. So that when I speak of the obligation of an oath, I would not be understood to mean any separate or distinct obligation, but only the effect of it in strengthening some other obligation, to which it is joined.

But a vow is a pact, in which there are no others concerned besides God and the person who makes the vow. It is a promise made directly to God himself, and is, therefore, such an act, as produces a distinct obligation upon the maker of it.

Some oaths may, indeed, from the form of them, produce an obligation, where the juror would otherwise have been under no obligation. This is the case in assertory oaths, where the person who takes the oath might otherwise have been silent, and consequently would not have been obliged to tell the truth, if he had not sworn to tell it. But then in forms of this sort we must observe, that, besides the oath itself, there is a promise contained, and such a promise, as would have been obligatory, if it had been expressed in such words as would have separated it from the oath. So that the oath introduces an obligation no otherwise, than by being accidentally included in the same form of words with the promise, from which the obligation properly arises. A form of words, which is suited to the purpose of my swearing to tell the truth, contains both a promise, that I will do so, and an oath confirming such promise.

No effect of an oath, unless there are outward marks of an intention to swear.

XII. *An oath produces no effect, where it is not attended with such outward circumstances, as plainly show, that he who goes through the form of it, intends to swear. How far his want of inward intention may affect his obligation, shall be considered presently.

This seems to be so certain, as to make it ridiculous to imagine, on the contrary, that he who repeats the words of an oath, when the occasion of doing this, or the manner of doing it, show him to have no intention of binding himself, should, notwithstanding this, be bound merely by repeating those words: as if the words of an oath acted like a charm, and could not pass through a man's mouth, upon any occasion, or in any manner, without binding his conscience. A clerk in court dictates to me the very words which I am to say in taking an oath, and without mentioning my name, speaks throughout in the first person, because I, who am to repeat the words after him, am to speak in this person: the occasion of his doing this would sufficiently show, that he had no design of swearing himself; that I, and not he, am the juror; and that whatever is the matter of the oath, I, and not he, am bound to the performance of it.

However, in most cases, all ambiguity of this sort is effectually provided against, by speaking in the second person, and telling the juror what he is to swear, without making him repeat the words: or, because, where the oath is long and the matter of it various, it may be the better impressed upon his mind, if he is made to repeat them, his name may be inserted to ascertain that he is the juror. And in either case, in the solemn form of an oath, besides repeating the words, some act likewise is to be done by the juror, such as holding the gospels, kissing the book, lifting up his right hand, putting his hand under the thigh of him who imposes the oath. Such oaths as these, from the corporal act of the juror himself, are called corporal oaths: and this act, whatever it is, sufficiently fixes who the person is, that intends to swear.

Want of inward intention, where there is the outward mark of it, does not prevent the effect of an oath.

XIII. †But may it not be asked, whether the juror is obliged by his oath, or incurs the guilt of perjury in breaking it, supposing him to go through all the formality of swearing, as to the outward acts, in such a manner, that all who see and hear him, would conclude that he intends to swear, but to have, in the meantime,

* Grot. Lib. II. Cap. XIII. § II.

† Grot. Ibid. § III.

a reserve, of not intending to swear, in his own mind. A simple promise, in the same circumstances, would undoubtedly be binding: because those outward signs, which either nature suggests or custom establishes for expressing or publishing our intentions, stand in the place of the intentions, which they so express. The juror, therefore, notwithstanding his inward reserve, is certainly under the obligation of his promise. And the only doubt that there can be, in regard to the effect of his oath, arises from hence: mankind have no way of knowing one another's thoughts, but by means of the outward signs, which are made use of to express those thoughts: upon that account, our obligations or our claims, arising from consent, can be ascertained no otherwise than by the intention, which appears; and no regard can be had to any other intention. But the case may at first sight appear to be otherwise in respect of God. He knows the innermost thoughts of our heart, though we express them by no outward sign at all; nor can he be misled to judge them to be what they are not, though we should make use of such outward signs as custom has made to signify what is directly contrary to our meaning when we use them. Since, therefore, the effect of an oath, like all adventitious obligations, depends upon our intention, as far as it is known to the party with whom we are concerned; and since the party, with whom we are concerned in oaths, is God, who knows the true intention of our hearts; it may seem at first sight, that the want of an inward intention to swear, will prevent the oath from producing its effect; notwithstanding we make use of such words or other signs, as might make us appear outwardly to have an intention of swearing. But here it is to be remembered, that the effect of all oaths is to confirm some human pact, some contract or some promise, either express or implied, between man and man. God is called in, not in order to produce any new obligation, but only to strengthen the obligation of such human pact. It is to be remembered farther, that, in the very oath itself, the juror agrees with the person, who imposes or who accepts the oath, to call God in as a party to their obligation. Thus then an oath, in all views of it, though it calls in God as a party, is in itself only part of a human pact: and, consequently, as in all other pacts between man and man, so likewise in an oath, the outward declarations stand in the place of the juror's intention; and if he falsifies in respect of what is expressed by such outward declarations, he is guilty of perjury, whatever secret reserves he might have in his own mind.

Oath is void, when the pact is so, with which it is joined.

XIV. From what has been said it sufficiently appears, that the proper matter of all oaths is some other obligation. What we swear to, is some promise or contract, either expressed or implied: and the obligation of such promise or contract, which the oath is intended to confirm, is the matter of the oath. When, therefore, the promise or contract is void, which the oath was made use of to confirm, there can be no effect of the oath; or, to speak in the common language, there can be no obligation arising from it. For where there is no obligation from such promise or contract, the oath has no matter, and of course can produce no effect. We swear to make good some particular obligation: therefore, where that obligation is void, or where there is no obligation, we swear to nothing.

*Upon this principle, all oaths which are obtained b, fraud are void; if the fact, in which the juror is deceived, was the whole ground or reason of his swearing: for we have seen already, that such erroneous pacts are void in themselves. In like manner all oaths to the performance of what is impossible or unlawful are void: because the pacts are so, which such oaths are made use of to strengthen. For the same reason, where an extorted promise is void, the promiser, though he should be sworn to performance, is not affected by the oath.

But in the case of oaths, which arise from fear, we must distinguish, as we did in the case of promises. Whenever a promise, which arises from fear, is binding upon the promiser, an oath, arising from the same cause, and applied to confirm such a promise, will have its full effect. All oaths, therefore, which are extorted by any just fear are binding; and so likewise are all such as arise even from unjust fear; provided the person, to whom we swear, had no hand in the injustice.

Oath to a robber is binding.

XV. †It is sometimes inquired, under this head, whether we are bound by an oath, which we swear to a robber. Those, who maintain such an oath not to be binding, are apt to confound two other questions with this; though they are very different from it. They either invent some unlawful matter for the oath, and then conclude it to be void; or else they set aside the obligation of it upon an arbitrary supposition of its having been unjustly extorted. But in the true state of this question the matter of the oath and the manner of procuring it are no way concerned. It is one thing to inquire, whether an oath to this or that purpose is binding; and another to inquire whether an oath, without considering the purport of it, is therefore void, because the person, with whom we are concerned, is a robber. The former inquiry relates to the matter of the oath, the latter relates only to the character of the person to whom we swear. So again; it is one thing to inquire whether an oath unjustly extorted is binding; and another to inquire, whether an oath is binding, merely because the person, to whom we swear, is a robber, without considering whether he extorts it or not. The stress of the present question, when stripped of all circumstances, which do not belong to it, rests upon this single point; since a robber is a common enemy of mankind; can any oath, though the matter of it should be lawful, and though there is no particular injustice in the manner of obtaining it, oblige the juror? The character of the person, to whom we swear, is the only circumstance to be considered: and the question is, whether, as there is no intercourse of social ties between him and the juror, he can have any claim in consequence of the juror's oath.

When the question is thus stated, the obvious answer seems to be, that such an oath is binding, notwithstanding the character of him to whom we swear. If there is nothing unlawful in the matter of the oath, nor any injustice in the manner of procuring it, the character of the robber does not at all enter into it, and for that reason cannot at all affect it. To urge, that he has broken all social ties, and that consequently he can have no claim arising from the natural connections of mankind with one another is nothing to the purpose: because the claim in question is not such an one as naturally arises out of any social con-

* Grot. Lib. II. Cap. XIII. § XIV.

† Grot. Ibid. § XV.

nections with him, but such an one as we give him by the particular act of swearing to him voluntarily for some lawful purpose. He may, indeed, by having, as it were, declared war against all mankind, have deprived himself of all his former claims: but it does not appear from hence, that it is become impossible for him to acquire any claim, though we are ever so willing to give him one, and though there is no injustice either in our giving him such claim, or in his procuring or accepting it.

*Grotius, indeed, carries this matter farther, and maintains, that if our oaths are not directed to man, but to God; that is, if our engagements are properly vows and not oaths; or if they are indeed such, as tend to confer a claim upon them, to whom we swear, but any thing can be objected to that claim, so as to set it aside; which is the case where an oath is extorted; we are then obliged to make good what we have sworn to, not in virtue of their right, to whom we swear, because, by the supposition, they have no right, but in regard to God, by whom we swear. If this reasoning was just, an oath given to a robber, not only when he has procured it fairly, but when he has extorted it by unjust fear, would be binding upon the juror.

To clear up this matter we will first suppose our engagement to be properly an oath: where, besides the appeal to God, there is the appearance of some right or claim conferred upon the party, to whom we swear. If this right or claim is void in itself, or if any thing can be opposed to it, which would set it aside, so that the promiser, if he had not sworn, would not have been bound to performance; yet, if he has sworn, the oath, says our author, will bind him. Now, this decision plainly proceeds upon this false principle, that the oath is a distinct covenant in itself, and not a part of the pact, which it is intended to confirm. But the true notion of an oath, as already explained, shows that it is no such distinct covenant, that it does not properly contain in it the notion of an obligation, if we separate it from some other obligatory pact with which it is joined: the obligation of it amounts to no more than the addition of an extraordinary penalty, if we falsify in that pact. If, therefore, we take away the obligation of the pact, to which such penalty has been annexed by swearing to it; what becomes of the penalty; that is, of the obligation of the oath? I make a promise or engage in a contract: by this act I oblige myself to do or to give something. I swear to this pact; the oath strengthens this obligation, by subjecting me to an extraordinary penalty, if I do not act conformably to my obligation. But by some flaw in the pact there happens to be no obligation arising from it: how, therefore, do I incur the penalty annexed? I am subject to it, if I do not do what I was obliged to: but I am, on account of that flaw in the pact, obliged to nothing; and, consequently, let me act as I will, I am clear of the penalty.

If we suppose, what is not true, that the oath is an obligatory act distinct from the promise or contract confirmed by it; the obligation of an oath, in this view of it, is between God and the juror; so that it will, in effect, amount to a vow. We shall, therefore, see how the case would stand upon this supposition, if we consider what would be the effect of a vow in such circumstances. Suppose, therefore, a vow

* Grot. Lib. II. Cap. XIII. § XIV.

to be unjustly extorted; does such vow bind the person, who is thus forced to engage in it? To determine upon this question, it will be necessary to observe, that as a promise made to a man does not oblige, unless he, to whom it is made, accepts it; so neither does a vow, which is a promise made to God, oblige, unless God accepts it. Whenever, therefore, we have sufficient reason to believe that God does not accept a vow, such vow is not binding. Now the case supposes some damage to arise from the vow to the party engaging in it; which damage is the effect of the other party's injustice, who extorts it by the use of force. I cannot, therefore, see what grounds there can be to imagine, that God accepts such a vow, unless we would make him a party in the injustice, and suppose that he consents to the damage, which must be sustained by the performance of it.

Effect of an oath does not extend to the juror's heirs.

XVI. *Whatever effect there is in an oath, merely as an oath, or as it subjects the juror to the guilt of perjury if he falsifies, this effect does not descend to the heirs of the juror. It has, indeed, been shown elsewhere, that as far as any contract, which has been confirmed by an oath, affects the goods of the juror, such contract will bind his heirs. But then it does not bind them under the penalty of perjury: because an oath is a personal appeal to God; it is an act, by which the person, who makes this appeal, imprecates the divine displeasure upon himself, or renounces for himself the divine favour, if he does not perform what he swears to: and, consequently, the penalty of incurring the divine displeasure, or of forfeiting the divine favour, if the oath is not kept, is merely personal, or does not affect the juror's heirs.

A man may endeavour to extend this penalty farther, by wishing a curse upon his heirs, by imprecating the divine displeasure upon them, or by renouncing the divine favour towards them, if they do not perform what he has sworn to. But whatever fear superstition may produce in them upon account of such an execration; it is very evident, that reason and religion would show it to be impossible for any one to renounce the favour of God and the hopes of his mercy for any one but himself; and, consequently, that the penalty of perjury is confined wholly to himself, however he might endeavour to extend it to his heirs.

Oaths to do harm not binding as vows.

XVII. When we threaten to do any causeless harm, and swear to put those threatenings in execution; it is plain that such an oath confers no right at all upon any one. It certainly confers no right upon the person who is to suffer this harm; or if we could imagine it to confer any, we may be sure it is such a right as he very readily gives up; because we are sure that he, like all other men, is desirous to keep free from suffering harm. And if we have engaged to do him this harm by a promise made to some third person, which promise we have sworn to; this promise is void. If, therefore, we apprehend ourselves to be bound under the penalty of perjury to do such harm, it must be by an obligation to God, in the way of a vow. But the matter of such oaths, even in this view of them, will always be sufficient to set them aside; since we may be certain that God does not accept them. So that the juror, though he is guilty of profaning God's name by thus swearing, is not guilty of perjury by not doing what he has sworn.

* Grot. Lib. II. Cap. XIII. § XVII.

CHAPTER XV.

OF MARRIAGE.

I. *Marriage, what.*—II. *Polygamy inconsistent with the notion of marriage.*—III. *The case of polygamy under and before the Mosaic law.*—IV. *Polygamy forbidden by the gospel.*—V. *Divorce forbidden by the law of nature.*—VI. *In what manner adultery dissolves marriage.*—VII. *Ill usage does not make a marriage void.*—VIII. *A second marriage is a nullity, where a former subsists.*—IX. *Want of consummation, in what instances it voids a marriage.*—X. *Marriages between relations, how made invalid.*—XI. *Force may make a marriage a nullity.*—XII. *The effects of an error in the contract of marriage.*—XIII. *Want of parents' consent not always sufficient to make a marriage void.*—XIV. *Husband's authority, whence it arises.*—XV. *What concubinage is a good and valid marriage.*

Marriage, what.

I. MARRIAGE is a contract between a man and a woman, in which, by their mutual consent, each acquires a right in the person of the other, for the purposes of their mutual happiness, and of the production and education of children. Little, I suppose, need be said in support of this definition; as nothing is affirmed in it but what all writers upon natural law seem to agree in. I have mentioned, indeed, no more parties, than a man and a woman: but I would not be understood by this way of expressing myself, to take it for granted, in the definition of marriage, that it is naturally unlawful for the same man to marry more women than one: this expression is consistent enough with such polygamy; because, if he marries ever so many, each contract is only between a man and a woman. I have defined marriage to be a contract; because mere cohabitation is never, that I know of, called by this name. And the ends or purposes which I have assigned; the mutual happiness of the parties, and the production and education of children; seem, on all hands, to be looked upon as the most natural ends of this contract. We will, therefore, proceed to consider what determination this notion of marriage will lead us to, in some of the principal questions relating to it.

Polygamy inconsistent with the notion of marriage.

II. *The chief points, about which moralists differ, are polygamy and divorce. Some contend, that the law of nature does not make it necessary, for only one man and one woman to be parties in the marriage contract, but allows the same man to engage, in this manner, and for these purposes, with as many women as he finds convenient. And they contend, farther, that the same law does not require this contract to be perpetual, but allows it either to expire at such a time as the parties shall agree upon at first, or to be dissolved at any time by their mutual consent. Others maintain, on the contrary, that the law of nature forbids polygamy, or does not allow a man to marry a second wife, whilst the first is living; and that the same law likewise forbids divorce,

* Grotius, Lib. II. Cap. V. § IX.

or does not allow the contract of marriage either to be made temporary from the first, or to be dissolved at the discretion and by the consent of the parties afterwards.

We will first examine the question concerning polygamy. And in order rightly to understand this matter, it will be necessary to observe, that whatever is inconsistent with the right, which each party gives to the other, by the contract of marriage, is inconsistent with the contract itself, and cannot be considered as a part or condition of it. And since the law of nature forbids us to break our contracts; it follows, that supposing polygamy is inconsistent with what we agree to in the contract of marriage, with the right which each party gives the other in his or her person, then polygamy must be inconsistent with the law of nature. The man and the woman, who are the parties in a contract of marriage, give to each other a mutual right in their respective persons. What right the man naturally has in the person of the woman, or the woman in the person of the man, is to be determined by the natural ends or purposes, for which this mutual right is given. If, then, upon examining this right by those ends or purposes, it shall be found to be inconsistent with polygamy; the consequence will be, that by entering into a contract of marriage, or by giving each other such a right, they have precluded themselves from polygamy by the very act of marrying, though they should not preclude themselves in express terms. Because it is impossible to suppose them to will or intend contrarieties at one and the same time: if they have a will or intention to give each other such a mutual right in their respective persons, this will or intention effectually precludes them from willing or intending, at the same time, whatever is contrary to such right. We may go one step farther. As the liberty of polygamy is tacitly taken away by the contract of marriage, when nothing is particularly said about it, supposing that upon inquiry we find such liberty to be inconsistent with the mutual right conferred by the parties; so likewise, upon the same supposition, the parties cannot give each other this liberty by any express conditions annexed to the contract for this purpose at the time of making it: because if the contract itself is binding, all conditions which are inconsistent with the obligations of such contract, are void; or if, on the other hand, these conditions are considered as binding, then they will set aside the contract or make that void: so that wherever there is a valid marriage, it takes away the liberty of polygamy or makes it unlawful; and wherever the man and the woman have so contracted as to allow of polygamy, if I may call it so, there is no valid marriage. In order therefore to show, that polygamy is naturally unlawful, or that the parties, by their mutual consent in marriage, have precluded themselves from the liberty of marrying any one else, whilst this contract continues in force; we are to show, that it is inconsistent with the mutual right which each of them has consented to give the other in his or her person.

Polygamy may be considered as of two sorts; it is either a contract of marriage of one woman with any number of men more than one; or a like contract of one man with any number of women more than one. As to the first sort of polygamy; I do not find, that the writers who favour polygamy the most, undertake to defend it. They seem to be agreed in maintaining, that the same woman ought not, at the same time, to have more husbands than one; or that, in marriage, the woman is naturally obliged to give the man such a full right in her person, for the purposes of marriage, as not to leave herself at liberty to dispose of her person, for the same purposes, to any one else, whilst he is living. We may therefore take it for granted, that a woman, when she marries a man, binds herself not to have children by any one else, and to contrive only for his happiness as a husband, exclusively of all others; that she binds herself to admit none besides him to share in her bed, or in her conjugal affection. This then being allowed to be the obligation on the woman's part, there cannot at first sight, one would think, appear to be any reason for imagining the obligation on the man's part to be different from it. When two people give each other a mutual right in their respective persons; the most natural conclusion is, that the right given is equal on both sides; if there is no express reserve to the contrary. Whatever liberty the woman parts with for the benefit of the man; it is natural, that she should receive an equivalent from him, or that he should part with as much liberty for her benefit. Unless, therefore, some exception is particularly agreed upon between them; he must be understood in marriage to give her the same right in his person, which she gives him in hers; that is, a full right to it for the purposes of having children, and of their mutual happiness; so as to make the effect of the contract the same on his side, and on hers, by binding himself not to admit any besides her, to share either in his bed, or in his conjugal affection.

It may be said, indeed, in reply to this conclusion, or rather to the premises from whence it is deduced; that the reason which lays the woman under restraints in this particular, does not extend to the man. She is not allowed to have more husbands than one; because if she had, amongst many husbands, it would become uncertain, to which of them any child or children of hers belong. Whereas there is no danger of any uncertainty, in the issue, from a man's having more wives than one: because each of the wives cannot but be sure which child is her own, and which is another's. But when this is urged as a reason, why, though the man has naturally an exclusive right to the person of his wife, yet we cannot from thence conclude, that the woman has likewise naturally an exclusive right to the person of her husband; they who urge it, should remember, that ascertaining the issue of the man, is so far from being the only end, that it is not the principal end, which even he proposes; and much less can we imagine the woman to have no other end in view but to make the man certain what children are his. And nothing is plainer than that the nature of an obligation, arising from a contract, can never be determined by a consideration, which is but a secondary one in the intention of one of the parties, and which never entered at all into the intention of the other. The principal end of each party is the production of children from the body of the other, and the happiness which each expects in the conjugal affection of the other. But if these are the ends, which they mutually propose in contracting to be man and wife, it can never be shown, that the woman, exclusive of all others, has not the same right to have children of his body, and to enjoy his conjugal affection, that the man, exclusive of all others, has to have children of her body, and to enjoy her conjugal affection. The happiness of the woman is of as great importance to her, as the happiness of the man is to him: and she is under no previous obligation to consult his happiness either solely or principally, any more than he is to consult hers. There is, therefore, no natural reason for imagining, that the contract of marriage should have his advantage more in view than hers, or give him a greater advantage, than it gives her. If each party has an equal advantage in view, they consent only upon condition of obtaining an equal advantage: and their consent upon these terms will not make the obligation of one of them different from the obligation of the other.

The only way, therefore, that is left to make polygamy lawful on the man's part, is by some express condition annexed to the contract. But such a condition, if it is inconsistent with the ends proposed in the contract, cannot be annexed, so as to be binding upon the woman, without destroying the contract. Now the happiness of the parties in their married state is one of the principal ends of marriage. But if domestic happiness for herself is the end which the woman proposes, and which engages her to enter into the contract of marriage; she consents no otherwise to give the man a right to her person, but upon condition of his obliging himself to contrive for her quiet and happiness in the married state, as far as he is able. It is unnatural and absurd to suppose, either that the woman has not this in view, or, if she has, that she should consent to give him a right to her person upon any other terms. And if the man consents to take her upon these terms, it is evident what obligation arises on his part from such consent. Now no reason can be given, why the contract of marriage should not be so far like other contracts, that whatever discharges the parties on one side from their obligation, should at the same time discharge the parties on the other side from theirs, and make the whole contract a nullity. But this is the effect of a liberty of polygamy granted to the man, even with the express consent of the woman: it releases him from the natural obligation of promoting her domestic happiness, as far as is in his power: and consequently, by releasing him from his obligation, it makes the contract itself a nullity from the beginning. So that, notwithstanding where there is such a liberty, there may be cohabitation, there can be no marriage. I need not, I suppose, set forth the jealousies and quarrels, which are almost unavoidable, where the same man has more wives than one: the fact, without enlarging upon it, is evident enough to convince us, that he, who shall thus cohabit at the same time with a number of women, is far from making the best provision that he can, for the domestic happiness of any one of them. Taking then this fact along with us, we may see how little force there is in what is sometimes urged in favour of polygamy; that no injury is done to the former wife by marrying a second in her life-time, if she has consented to it; since the husband cannot do her an injury by giving her only a part of his affection, when she has beforehand agreed to let him divide his affection between her and others. The effect of allowing such a liberty to him would not be to make it lawful for him to enter into a second marriage, the first still continuing in force, but to set the first marriage itself aside from the beginning, and to make it no marriage at all. We are misled by calling it a consent to be satisfied with only a part of his affection; it is a consent to give him the power of making her happy or unhappy, just as his own interest or caprice shall direct him. If we put a liberty of polygamy, allowed by the woman to the man, into these terms, the effect that it would have upon a contract of marriage, by being joined to such contract, will appear more evidently. The man and woman in the contract of marriage have their mutual happiness in view, and this mutual happiness is the end, which determines them to enter into such a contract: each party therefore is understood to give the other, by the contract, a right in his or her person upon condition only, that each shall be bound to promote the happiness of the other: but the woman in the meantime consents, that the man shall be at liberty to follow his own humour, and to make her happy or unhappy, as that humour shall lead him. Such a condition as this is so plainly contrary to his part of the obligation in marriage, that it is impossible for the marriage and the condition to subsist together: if the marriage is valid, the condition must be void; if the condition is binding on her part, who grants it, the marriage must be a nullity.

I say farther, that the woman is bound in conscience to stipulate for the entire affection of her husband, and that she puts it out of her power to do her duty, if she consents to be his wife upon any other terms. Her consent to be his wife certainly implies, that she consents to have children by him. And as the production of children is necessarily attended, on the part of the mother, as well as of the father, with the duty of providing for them, and educating them in the best manner, that she can; she puts it out of her power to do her duty, if she agrees to have children upon any terms, which will put it out of her power to provide for them and educate them, so well as she might have done. But certainly she will not be able to provide for them and to educate them, so well as she might have done, if she consents to let him divide his affections between her and other women, and consequently between her children and theirs. Upon this principle, a liberty of polygamy, annexed to a marriage, must at first sight be wrong: and perhaps, upon a closer inspection, such a condition will be found to be void. The duty of the mother to provide for and educate her children, may indeed be supposed to be of the imperfect sort; and if it is, a simple transgression of such duty in any act would not be sufficient to make that act void. But in the case supposed, the mother does more than simply transgress her duty; she takes from herself the power of discharging it: and the law can never allow the validity of an act, by which the agent, if the act was valid, would be no longer obliged to obey the law.

Before we leave this subject, it may be worth our while to look back to their opinion, who contend, that polygamy on the part of the woman is unlawful upon this principle, that if she was to have more husbands than one, the issue would be uncertain, and the man might place his affection, or employ his care, or bestow his goods upon children which are not his; or might, on the other hand, be wanting in some of those duties to his own children; as not having sufficient evidence, which children she had by him, and which by some other of her husbands. It is strange, that this should be thought a sufficient reason in the nature of the thing to bar the man against allowing the woman a liberty of having more husbands than himself; and yet that a like reason should not be sufficient to bar the woman against allowing a liberty of the same sort to the man. If it is matter of duty in him to secure all the benefits in his power to his own children; it must be as much matter of duty in her to secure all the benefits in her power to her own children; which, as we have already seen, she does not do, if she allows him, whilst she has a right in his person, to have children by another woman.

What is most apt to mislead us in this inquiry is, that only two persons are concerned in each separate contract of marriage; for which reason we conclude, that they may model the contract as they please, without injuring any one: no other person is injured by any conditions, which they two agree upon; because no other person has any thing to do in the contract, or in any conditions, which relate solely to themselves: and neither of them can be injured by such conditions or reservations; because they are supposed to be made with the joint consent of them both. If, then, there is no injury done to any person by polygamy, it may be thought impossible to prove, that the law of nature forbids it. But in this way of reasoning in defence of polygamy, there is a great mistake. In order to show, that the law of nature forbids it, there is no occasion to show, that any person is injured in the first instance by a liberty of practising it. Instead of attempting to show the unlawfulness of it in this method, we compare such a liberty with the notion of the marriage contract; and if we find, that polygamy and the marriage contract are inconsistent with one another; the conclusion is, that the nature of this contract so forbids polygamy, that the contract of marriage and a liberty of polygamy cannot subsist together. The consequence of which is, that though the woman endeavours by her consent to make the man's subsequent marriage lawful, it is not in her power: as the former contract between them two has taken from him the liberty of entering into a second marriage, so it has taken from her the power of giving him such a liberty. They must either agree to make their former marriage void: or otherwise this former marriage, if it continues in force, will make his subsequent marriage with any other woman a nullity. Whether they could by mutual consent dissolve their marriage is another question: but whether they could or not, polygamy would still be inconsistent with the marriage contract, and would, by the nature of that contract, be rendered impossible: for if they could dissolve it, then the second woman that he takes, would be his only wife; and if they could not dissolve it, he could have no wife besides the first, as long as she lives.

I am aware it may be objected here, that allowing all which has been urged, to be true, it would only prove the impossibility of polygamy, and not the unlawfulness of it. But we may observe in answer to this objection, that if it proves thus much, it proves enough for our purpose; it proves that the law of nature does not allow the same man to marry a second woman, whilst his first is living and continues to be his wife; and consequently, that his cohabitation with such second woman, under the pretence that she is his wife, must be unlawful. However, it is to be remembered, that one of the arguments, by which we have shown that it is not in the power of the wife, even by her own consent, to grant the husband a liberty of polygamy, was taken from the unlawfulness of such consent, from the inconsistence of it with the duty to her future children, which duty she undertakes by consenting to have children: for we showed that her consent to a condition of this sort would therefore be void, because it has a continued viciousness adhering to it; as it takes away her power, or sets aside her natural obligation of providing for her children and educating them in the best manner that she can.

The case of polygamy under the Mosaic law, and before it.

III. The authority of the law of Moses, the practice of the patriarchs, who lived before that law was given, and of the Israelites, who lived under it, are commonly urged in favour of the natural lawfulness of polygamy. It would however be necessary for them, who urge the authority of the law of Moses in this question, to inform themselves, how far the precept, which they commonly produce as an evidence of its allowing polygamy, relates to this practice. The law says,—*If a man have two wives, one beloved and the other hated, and they have borne him children, both the beloved and the hated; and if the first-born son be hers, that was hated; then it shall be, when he maketh his sons to inherit that which he hath, that he may not make the son of the beloved first-born, before the son of the hated, which is indeed the first-born: but he shall acknowledge the son of the hated for the first-born, by giving him a double portion of all that he hath.—As the law seems here to make a provision against an inconvenience, which might arise from the practice of polygamy, they, who favour the natural lawfulness of such practice, infer, that the Mosaic law must have allowed of it; since no law can be supposed to guard against the consequences of any practice, if it did not allow the practice itself. But in this inference from the passage before us, they plainly take for granted, that the beloved and the hated wives must both of them be living at the same time: whereas neither the words nor the design of the law make such a supposition necessary. The inconvenience here guarded against might as easily happen, and might be as proper to be guarded against, if the wife, whom he hated, was dead before he married the other whom he loved; as if both of them were alive together. It may be said, indeed, that such an interpretation of the passage inverts the order in which the wives are mentioned: for the beloved wife is mentioned first in the precept; whereas the interpretation supposes her to have been the second. But this is a very weak objection: there is no reason for supposing, that the lawmaker, in mentioning the two wives, must necessarily observe the order in which the man was married to them: nay, the fact, as it is here stated, seems rather to imply, that he was first married to the hated wife; for the eldest son is supposed to be hers.

This interpretation will appear the more probable, if we compare this precept with another, that is to be found in the same law.—†Neither shalt thou take a wife to her sister to vex her, to uncover her nakedness besides the other in her life-time.—This passage is rendered in the margin—Thou shalt not take one wife to another, &c.—And the least acquaintance with the original language will inform us, that the words will very well admit of this marginal translation. Indeed, if we attend to the precept itself, we shall find, that the best rules of interpretation require us to translate it in this manner. The reason of the law extends, not only to the marriage of the first wife's sister, but to the marriage of any other woman, besides the first wife. The reason of the law is, that the first wife might not be made unhappy. And certainly

* Deuter. XXI. 15, &c. † Levit. XVIII. 18.

she would be at least as likely to be made unhappy by his marriage with a woman, who was not at all related to her, as by his marriage with her own sister. If then the obligation of the law ought to be extended as far as the reason of it extends, we must look upon this passage as a prohibition of polygamy. Another rule of interpretation is, that a law ought to be understood in such a sense, as will give some meaning to all the words of it. But if we suppose this precept to relate only to the marriage of two sisters, and the law elsewhere forbids such marriage universally, without considering whether the former sister is living or dead, the words—in her life-time—will have no meaning, or a very improper one. Unless they imply, that a man, after the death of his wife, might marry her sister, they will have no meaning: and if they imply this, their meaning will be an improper one; because it will make this precept inconsistent with what is to be met with in other parts of the law. But if this precept relates to polygamy, the words have a clear meaning; they were added to show, that, though a man might not marry a second wife in the life-time of the first, yet the lawmaker did not design to forbid his marrying a second wife, after the first was dead. It must be owned, indeed, that the law does not elsewhere expressly forbid the marrying of a wife's sister, supposing the wife to be dead; but it forbids such marriage by necessary consequence. In the *book of Leviticus the several degrees of consanguinity and affinity, which bar marriage, are enumerated; and all of them are described on the part of the man; that is, the law declares that a man shall not marry a woman, if she stands in such or such a relation to him. But we may infer, by necessary consequence, that whatever degree of consanguinity or affinity renders it unlawful for a man to marry a woman, the same degree would, in the intention of the lawmaker, render it unlawful for a woman to marry a man. Thus, for instance, the law says—Thou shalt not uncover the nakedness of thy father's or thy mother's sister; that is, a man shall not marry his aunt—must not we conclude from hence, though the law has not expressly said it, that it was equally unlawful for a woman to marry her father's or her mother's brother; that is, to marry her uncle? In like manner, when the law says,—Thou shalt not uncover the nakedness of thy brother's wife; that is, a man shall not marry his brother's wife;—the necessary consequence is, that it must be equally unlawful for a woman to marry her sister's husband: because, whatever relation there is between a man and his brother's wife, there is just the same relation between a woman and her sister's husband.

If, indeed, we were to interpret the law of Moses by the practice of the Israelites, who lived under it, we might, at first sight, be inclined to think, that it had no where forbidden polygamy. But then, if on the other hand, we consider, in how many instances their history informs us, that they neglected to observe their law, we shall find their practice to be far from a certain rule of forming any opinion about the meaning of the law, so as to judge from thence either what that law forbids, or what it allows.

The example of the kings of Israel, in marrying many wives, and in taking many concubines, is urged here, not so much to show what

* Levit. XVIII. 6, 7, 8, &c.

was generally supposed to be the tenor of the law upon this head, as to carry us back to the law itself, which seems to tolerate them in this practice, when it only commands them not to *multiply wives: for as multiplying wives implies taking a great number, a law, which only forbids too great a number, cannot reasonably be construed to bind them to have no more than one. But whoever attentively reads the passage here referred to, will find some grounds for believing, that when the law forbids the king to multiply wives, we are not to understand by the word—multiplying—merely the increasing of them to too great a number. If this was the true import of the word, what can the law mean, when it goes on to forbid him *greatly* to multiply silver and gold? If not multiplying silver and gold means not increasing them to too great a quantity, the word *greatly* was here added without any meaning at all. †A truly learned prelate of our church has abundantly shown, that the law, when it forbids the king to multiply horses, must be understood to forbid his keeping more horses, than was consistent with the spirit of their polity. And as they were taught, through their whole law, that their state was under the immediate protection of providence, it was inconsistent with a persuasion, that God would fight their battles, to carry into the field an army of horsemen, in which the strength of an armed force is supposed to consist. If we observe the same rule in interpreting this other command of not multiplying wives, the meaning of it is, that their king was not to have more wives than the law allowed of. So that, instead of applying this passage to settle the meaning of the other parts of the law, we must search the other parts of the law to ascertain the precise meaning of this. By following this interpretation we shall see why the law forbids the king *greatly* to multiply silver and gold. The spirit of their polity had determined, that an armed force of horsemen was not to be brought into the field, and the letter of their law had forbidden a man to take one wife to another. When, therefore, the legislator says, that the king shall not multiply horses or wives, the spirit of their polity in one instance, and the letter of their law in the other, had sufficiently determined how far he might go, and where he must stop in these two particulars. But neither the spirit of their polity, nor the letter of their law had determined what quantity of riches a man might accumulate: something, therefore, was in this instance to be left to the prudence of the king; the boundary, how far he might go, and where he must stop, could not be precisely fixed; he was to take care only, that he did not go too far, and was commanded, in general, not *greatly* to multiply to himself silver and gold.

We are told farther, that, when Nathan was sent to David to expostulate with him, in the name of God, concerning his crime of adultery and murder, in the case of Uriah, Nathan, amongst other blessings which David enjoyed, mentions, particularly, that God had given him his master's wives. Grotius takes notice of this as an argument in favour of the lawfulness of polygamy under the Mosaic dispensation: but as he does not explain himself, I cannot tell whether he concludes this fact to make for his purpose, from the gift of many wives being called a blessing; or from Nathan's saying, that God had given David

* Deuteron. XVII. 16, 17, 18.

† Sherlock's Dissertation, IV.

these many wives. As to the number of his wives being called a blessing, it affords us no grounds for concluding, that the marrying many wives was agreeable to the strictness of the law: because, when David was to be reproached with not being satisfied with what he already enjoyed, it was natural to call that a blessing, which he looked upon as a part of his happiness, whether the enjoyment of it was tolerated by the law or not: nay, there was more reason for reproaching him with it, if it was an indulgence to him, beyond what the law, according to the rigour of it, would allow; than if it had been a general permission, which the law had granted promiscuously to every one. But if the strength of the argument rests upon its being said, that God had given David those wives; it has but little to support it. Our author, if he had read three verses farther, would have found that the enjoyment of what God is said to give, is not, therefore, to be looked upon as lawful, because he is said to give it. God there threatens, that he would give David's wives to his neighbour, who should lie with them in the face of the sun. This threatening was accomplished, when Absalom spread a tent upon the house top, and lay with his father's wives there. But Grotius, I suppose, would not conclude, that Absalom's act was lawful, from Nathan's having said, that God would give him his father's wives.

The patriarchs, before the law of Moses was given, undoubtedly practised polygamy. But this is no evidence that the law of nature allows of it; unless any one could first show, either that the patriarchs were so much wiser than their contemporaries, as to have traced out exactly, all the precepts of the law of nature; or that God had been pleased, by some express revelation, to teach them this law in all its branches. Though we should allow that they were ready to obey this law in all respects, as far as they knew it; yet, unless their own reason, or some divine revelation had made them complete masters of all its precepts, their practice might, in some instances, not be conformable to it. And I know not by what arguments it can be shown, either that the patriarchs had, by their own skill and application, investigated the whole law of nature; or that God, when he was beginning to call mankind to obedience, laid open to them, at once, all the parts of this law.

Polygamy forbidden by the gospel.

IV. Before we leave this subject, it may not be improper to give the reader a short view of what the gospel determines upon it. Our Saviour, though he does not mention and condemn this practice in so many words, has sufficiently taught us, that it is unlawful. *He declares, that whosoever should put away his wife, unless for fornication, and should marry another, is guilty of adultery. But if a second marriage, after such divorce, has this character, we may be sure, that it would not fall short of the same character, where there had been no divorce: if it is unlawful to marry a second wife, after the first has been put away, it must be at least as unlawful so to marry, before she has been put away. St. Paul's authority is express to this purpose: †he commands, that every man who marries at all, should have his own or his peculiar wife; and that every woman in like manner should have her own or her peculiar husband. He has likewise assigned the natural reason, why neither the husband

* Luke XVI. 18. † 1 Cor. VII. 2. 4.

is at liberty to dispose of himself to a second wife, nor the wife at liberty to dispose of herself to a second husband, in the life-time of the first partners of their bed: the reason is, that each has an exclusive right to the person of the other; the wife, says he, hath not power of her own body, but the husband, and likewise, the husband hath not power over his own body, but the wife.

Divorce forbidden by the law of nature.

V. The second inquiry concerning the marriage contract is, whether the law of nature allows of divorce, or requires that the contract should be perpetual, so as naturally to continue during the joint lives of the parties.

It seems to be evident, at first sight, that this contract, like all others, cannot naturally be dissolved, at the discretion of one of the parties, without the consent of the other; whatever may be the effect, where both of them consent. As the obligation is produced by their joint consent, nothing less than a like joint consent can destroy that obligation: whatever right one of the parties has in the person of the other, such right cannot justly be taken away without the consent of the party, whose right it is.

I choose to take particular notice of this, in order to correct their mistake, who imagine, that, *as divorce was permitted by the law of Moses, it cannot but be agreeable to the law of nature. Whereas, whoever will be at the trouble of looking into that law, and of considering it with any degree of attention, will find this permission to be far from decisive: because he will find, that under the law of Moses, divorce proceeded at the discretion and upon the authority of one of the parties. The husband, if his wife displeased him, wrote her a bill of divorcement and put her away. I should, therefore, think it impossible to prove from this permission in the law of Moses, that divorce is, in itself, agreeable to the law of nature: since the divorce, which the law of Moses permitted, is plainly contrary to the law of nature. I would not be understood to mean, that where such a liberty was allowed to the husband by sufficient authority, it would be unjust in him to make use of it: for certainly when the law had tolerated this practice, the woman, though she did not expressly consent to the divorce, at the time of putting her away, must be understood, as she knew what the law was, implicitly or tacitly to have consented to it, at the time of marrying. She was aware, that her husband had a legal power of putting her away, if she displeased him; and as she knew the conditions upon which she made herself his wife, she could not but be supposed to agree to those conditions. By these means, then, in consequence of the established and known toleration, the divorce would, in this respect, become natural; as it proceeded upon the declared intention of the husband, and upon the implied consent of the wife. But what I contend for is, that this toleration itself was not natural, or that the law of nature could not grant it. And if divorce, as it was allowed of by the law of Moses, would, without such an authorized and express toleration, have been inconsistent with the law of nature; I know not how any one can infer from the toleration of such a sort of divorce, that the law of nature allows of divorce. Either this conclusion, as drawn from the Mosaic law, must be given up; or else they, who de-

* Deut. XXIV. 4.

fend it, must go as far as the Mosaic permission will lead them, and conclude not only, that a marriage may naturally be dissolved by the consent of both parties, but that naturally every woman takes her husband upon such conditions, that he alone, by his sole authority, may put her away, whenever he chooses it.

One would think, indeed, that the authority of *Christ was sufficient to have determined, that no regard was to be had to this permission, in our inquiries, whether the law of nature allows of divorce or not; when he declares, that though Moses allowed the Israelites to put away their wives, yet from the beginning it was not so, and that this practice was tolerated for no other reason, but because they were too stubborn to be called back at once, from their long received customs, to a full obedience to the will and design of their Creator.

When we examine this question, concerning divorce, by the law of nature, we must consider, in the first place, what sort of a contract the ends of marriage make necessary; whether they can be effectually obtained by a contract, which will expire of itself after a certain time, or may be dissolved by the act of the parties at any time; or whether they require, that it should be perpetual from the beginning, and incapable of being dissolved afterwards. For, certainly, where a man and a woman consent to be husband and wife; that is, where they enter into a contract of marriage, the ends which they must, from the nature of the contract, have in view, determine what sort of a contract it is, that they agree to. If those ends require it to be a perpetual and indissoluble one, their consenting to it, for the attainment of those ends, implies, whether they express so much or not, that they consent to be husband and wife for ever. Nay, if the ends of marriage require such a contract, though they should annex to it any express condition of being released, after a certain time, or of being at liberty to release themselves by joint consent at any time; yet such condition would be void. If they have a will to enter into a contract, which is, in its own nature, perpetual; they cannot, at the same time, with any effect, will any condition, which should make that contract not perpetual. Such a contract and such a condition, cannot possibly subsist together.

Now the ends of marriage are the mutual happiness of the parties, and the production of children. And we are to inquire what sort of a contract these two ends, which the parties contracting have in view, will make necessary. †Dionysius Halicarnasseus commends an institution of Romulus, by which one sort of marriage was rendered perpetual, and incapable of being dissolved: and upon this occasion he makes an observation which will help to show us, how much the happiness of the parties depends upon their entering into such a contract as this. "This law, says he, engaged the wives, who had no other resort, to yield a ready compliance to the temper of their husbands: and it obliged the husbands, on the other hand, to treat their wives as a necessary possession, which they could not, on any account, relinquish." Undoubtedly each party will be more ready to comply with the temper of the other, and to correct, likewise, what is amiss in their own, when they are under a necessity of continuing together for life, than if they had the refuge of a divorce, whenever they grew disagreeable to one another.

* Mat. V. 32.

† L. II. p. 95.

As to the other end of marriage, which is the production of children, it includes in it the duty of maintaining and educating them in the best manner that the parties contracting are able: so that they who engage in a contract of marriage with a view to this end, must naturally be understood to bind themselves to this duty; the care of educating the future children in the best manner that they can, becomes, by marriage, the joint duty of the husband and wife. But this duty cannot be carried on by their joint care, unless there is an union of affections and interest: nor can there be such an union, when they know from the beginning, that at a certain time their mutual affections are to be withdrawn from each other, and their interests to be separated: and much less can there be any effectual union, when they are at liberty to withdraw their affections from each other, and to separate their interests at any time.

Since then one of the ends of marriage, and the duty, in which the other end of it engages the parties, require that the contract should be perpetual; the consequence is, that where a man and a woman enter into the contract of marriage, they must, from the nature of the act, consent to make that contract perpetual; because it is absurd to suppose, that they have a will to contract for such purposes, as require their obligation to each other to be perpetual and unalterable, and yet, that at the same time, they have a will to make that obligation temporary or precarious.

It has, I know, been inquired, why this contract, as its obligation is derived from the will of the two parties concerned in it, should not, like other contracts, be capable of being dissolved by the will of the same parties. I like a horse of yours, and as you are willing to sell him, we agree upon the price: and after we have so agreed, you take my money, and I take your horse. After a few days or weeks are past, we are both of us sorry for having made such a bargain; you are desirous of having your horse, and I of having my money again. Whatever obligation we were under from the bargain, that had been made between us; if one of us proposes to set it aside, and the other agrees to this proposal, as there was no third party concerned in it, and consequently no one is injured by setting it aside, the effect of our so agreeing, would be to make the bargain void. Nay, suppose we had gone farther at first, and had agreed that the bargain should be perpetual, that the horse should be mine, and the money be yours for ever, that neither of us would at any time make a proposal of setting the bargain aside, nor neither of us accept such a proposal, if the other made it: the effect would still be the same; whenever one of us, though we had agreed to the contrary, should offer to set the bargain aside, and the other, though in opposition likewise to the first agreement, should close with the offer; there would be an end of the contract, and no injury would be done to any one. Why then should not the case of marriage be the same? A man and a woman agree to give each other a mutual right to one another's persons; they agree, likewise, to make this contract a perpetual one: but after they have lived with one another for some time, they find reason to repent of their bargain, and both of them wish to be released: as no third party is concerned in the contract, or injured by dissolving it; why should not their consent to release each other, as naturally and as effectually dissolve this contract, as it would a contract of buying and selling? The short answer to this difficulty is, that the law of nature, which requires one of these contracts to be perpetual, does not require the other to be so. For, certainly, if the law of nature makes it necessary from the first, that when two parties will marry, the contract of marriage, into which they enter, shall be perpetual; the same law will for ever continue to forbid them to dissolve that contract, after they are entered into it. There is an absurdity in saying, that a contract, which is perpetual in its own nature from the beginning, may lawfully be dissolved at any time by the consent of the parties who are engaged in it. But a common bargain of buying and selling is not perpetual in its own nature; it is not only made but modelled likewise, at the discretion of the parties; and as not only the obligation itself, but all the qualities of the contract are the effects of their joint consent, a like joint consent will change the qualities of it, and dissolve its obligation. The objectors, when they suppose the buyer and the seller to have agreed, that the obligation of their contract shall be perpetual, put the case as strong as they can: but in the meantime, they do not attend to a material difference between a contract, that is perpetual in its own nature, whether the parties will or no, and a contract that is made perpetual only by the act of the parties themselves. A man and a woman are at liberty, whether they will marry or not: but if they will marry, they are not at liberty, whether they will enter into a perpetual contract or not; if they will marry, they contract for such purposes, as force them to contract for life. You and I are not only at liberty, whether we will bargain for the horse or not, but we are at liberty, likewise, when we are determined to bargain for it, to model our bargain as we please, and may either agree or not, that the bargain shall stand good for ever. Now, since the former of these contracts is perpetual in itself, or since this quality of being perpetual is necessarily connected with, and inherent in the contract; it is not left to the discretion of the parties, after they have engaged in the contract, to change this quality, by any act of theirs, and so to make the contract temporary or precarious. A quality, which was not originally produced, is not liable to be destroyed again, by an act of their will. Whereas, in the contract of buying and selling, the quality of being perpetual is derived wholly from the will of the parties; and because it is derived from thence, and not from the nature of the contract, it may be destroyed again at their discretion, by the same cause which at first produced it.

I have instanced in this contract of buying and selling, because others, who favour the contrary side of the question, have made choice of this instance to illustrate their opinion. But otherwise, a contract of partnership, for trade, or for any other purpose, has a much nearer resemblance to marriage. However, the principle here laid down is equally applicable, either to partnerships, or to buying and selling. Though the partners should agree to trade together, they are neither obliged, from the beginning, by the nature of their contract, to make the partnership perpetual; nor are they so far bound to continue in partnership for their joint lives, as not to be able to release one another by joint consent; notwithstanding they bargained at first, that the contract should be perpetual. Because this perpetuity, considered as a quality of the contract, is not, like the perpetuity of the marriage contract, derived from the contract itself; and in consequence, necessarily connected with it: the perpetuity of partnerships, to which the partners agree, is the creature of their own wills, and as it was at first produced only by their joint consent, so it may naturally be destroyed again in the same manner by a like joint consent.

In what manner adultery dissolves marriage.

VI. But though the contract of marriage cannot naturally be dissolved by the mutual consent of the husband and wife; yet it happens in this, as in all other contracts, that the contract will become void, if either party deprives the other of what such contract has given him or her a perfect right to: where the agreement is broken on one side, the obligation ceases on the other. Now, by the contract of marriage, each party has an exclusive right in the person of the other for the purposes of producing children. Adultery, therefore, which deprives one of the parties of this right, or is a breach of the agreement on one side, releases the other party, or makes the obligation void on the other side. It is necessary, however, to observe, that adultery does not so dissolve a marriage, as to release the adulterer from the bond of it, without the consent of the injured party. The contract of marriage is, in this respect, like other contracts: however, one of the parties may be injured; yet, if he knows of the injury, and is willing to submit to it, the contract will remain in force: if he chooses to continue under his former obligation, the party, who has done the injury, can, by such injury, acquire no claim to be released from hers.

It is upon this account that the husband, if he receives the wife to his bed after adultery, cannot divorce her, till some fresh crime of the same sort has been committed. By this act he has shown it to be his desire, that the marriage should continue: and as the contract, notwithstanding the adultery, was binding on her part, nothing was wanting, but such a declaration, on his part, to re-establish it. It may, therefore, perhaps, more properly be said, that adultery makes a marriage voidable, than that it makes it void: for if no act of the injured party follows the adultery, by which it appears that such party designs to be released from the marriage, if the husband, for instance, does not divorce the adulterous wife, but continues to live with her upon the same terms, as before the adultery, the contract remains in force.

If wilful desertion is not allowed to have the same effect in dissolving a marriage, that adultery has; the only reason for not allowing it must be the difficulty of fixing what is desertion, without some overt act of adultery. This, however, is certain, that nothing less than such a desertion as is properly wilful and obstinate can be deemed a sufficient cause for dissolving a marriage. The wife, for instance, may be forcibly driven away by her husband, or she may be compelled to leave him by bad usage, which is in effect a force upon her. And as desertion in cases of this sort is not her voluntary act; it cannot justly take from her the right, which she has in his person. It is farther necessary, that the party, who deserts the other, should continue obstinate; because, where the wife, who deserts her husband, is willing to return to him again; his right in her person is not withholden from him, though the use of it may have been suspended for a time. And the difficulty of determining, without an overt act of adultery, what desertion is sufficient to dissolve a marriage, rests upon this point; it cannot well be determined what length of time, or what refusals of returning, are sufficient to make the desertion obstinate.

Ill usage does not make a marriage void.

VII. It is a question, upon which people are much divided, whether ill usage on either side is naturally a sufficient reason for the party which suffers, to claim a release from the bond of marriage, or to divorce him or herself from the person who is the author of such usage.

Certainly the happiness of the parties is one of the principal ends which each of them proposes in marriage. But this is so far from being a reason, why ill usage after marriage should be sufficient to make the contract void, that it proves the direct contrary; it proves, that the marriage contract must, in its own nature, be of such a sort, as is most likely to secure this end, and that it excludes all such conditions as are likely to prevent this end from being obtained. And if the nature of the contract requires this to be the intention of the parties, they cannot be supposed, at the same time, to design, that the contract should be void, if either party found themselves less happy after marriage, than they expected: because such a condition as this would plainly make the happiness of the married state precarious. Whoever wanted to get rid of a present wife, that he might be at liberty to marry another, would be sure to use the former ill, that he might, by these means, compel her to give him his liberty. Whereas, if ill usage is likely to occasion no disturbance but in his own family, and he is upon that account under a necessity of feeling some of the effects of it, without being able to bring about any of his private purposes; he will be much more likely to use his wife well, and to endeavour, as much as he can, to promote her happiness, when he finds his own so closely connected with it. But if this is the nature of the contract, then whatever unhappiness either or both parties may meet with, after they have entered into it, they must look upon such unhappiness as a natural misfortune, and must either submit to it with patience, or endeavour on each side, by good behaviour, to soften the temper of one another, and lessen or remedy that evil, which they can remedy no otherwise, consistently with their contract.

But as the contract itself gives each party a right to the person of the other, for the purposes of producing children, so the condition, under which each of them makes over this right to the other, gives each of them likewise a right to good usage from the other; it may, therefore, be asked, why a violation of the latter right, by ill usage, should not have the same effect upon the marriage contract, that a violation of the former right by adultery would have upon it. In answer to this inquiry, we must observe, that the law of marriage, in one respect, is—Thou shalt not commit adultery.—The law of it in the other respect, is—Husbands, love your wives; and let the wife see that she reverence her husband.—The right arising out of the former law is a perfect one; because the precept is negative, and the matter of it for that reason is precise and determinate: whereas, the right arising out of the latter is imperfect, as the precept is affirmative, and consequently the matter of it is more vague and uncertain. As there is no medium between committing adultery and not committing it; no one can be at a loss to determine, when the right, which each party has to the person of the other, is violated. But good or bad usage admits of many degrees; some of which are so slight, that it would be ridiculous to mention them as sufficient reasons for dissolving a marriage. And where there is so much latitude, it would be difficult, if not impossible, to settle the precise degree which is sufficient for this purpose.

It would be an equitable and a natural temperament in this matter, to relieve the party aggrieved by allowing a separation, without dissolving the bond of marriage, as far as that bond hinders any second marriage. This is an equitable temperament, because where there is a real grievance, it would be a hardship to compel the party aggrieved to live miserably. And it is a natural temperament; because it is most agreeable to the nature of marriage, that the bond should be perpetual, as for other reasons, so for this in particular, that a perpetual bond is, from the first, the most effectual means of securing to each party good usage from the other.

A second marriage is a nullity where a former subsists.

VIII. Having seen what will dissolve a marriage, after it is contracted, we are next to inquire what will make it a nullity from the beginning. One cause, which will make it so, has been already explained at large. *No second marriage can be valid, whilst a former marriage is subsisting. A man or woman, under the bond of a former marriage, have no power to dispose of their persons to any one else for the same purposes: because their persons are then not their own to dispose of; the right which they had in them, was made over to the first partner of their bed. It is needless here to ask, whether a pre-contract in words of present time will invalidate a subsequent marriage of one of the parties concerned in it, with any other person besides him or her with whom such pre-contract was made. The law of nature knows no distinction between a contract of marriage in words of present time and an actual marriage. The formalities which distinguish such a contract from what is commonly known by the name of marriage, are of positive institution. If a man and a woman have agreed to live together in an union of affections and interests, and each of them has given the other a perpetual right in his or her person for the purposes of producing children; this is naturally a good and valid marriage; and as long as there is no divorce upon account of adultery, such a contract is sufficient to set aside all subsequent marriages of either of them with any third person. A mutual promise of future marriage is not an actual making over a present right to each other's persons; it is only an agreement that they will make over such a right hereafter. This too may be called a contract, but then it is only of the promissory sort: and any subsequent marriage of either of the parties, engaged in such a promise, to a third person would be valid, notwithstanding the prior promise. For each party has still a right in his or her own person; and this will be sufficient to make the subsequent disposal of it binding. The promise however is not without its effect; for, as in the case of buying and selling, it entitles the party to whom it was made, to all such damages as may be suffered by the breach of it.

We said, indeed, in speaking of promises, that a promise gives a right over the person of the promiser: and since an actual marriage conveys no more than a right to the person of him or her, who engages in it,

* Grot. Lib. II. Cap. V. § XI.

we may be asked what difference there is between a marriage in words of present time, and a promise of marriage in words of future time. What hinders us from immediately seeing the difference is, that in marriage contracts the person and the thing are confounded: if, instead of saying that a contract in words of present time gives each party a right to the person, we say, that it gives each party a right to the body of the other for the purposes of marriage; we shall more clearly see the difference between such a contract and a promissory one. A contract in words of present time gives each party a right to the body of the other: whereas a promissory one gives each a right only over the liberty of the other, as to the future disposal of their bodies.

Want of consummation, in what instances it voids a marriage.

IX. The contract of marriage is so far complete as to be binding upon the parties, when each has consented to give the other a present right to their bodies respectively for the purposes of marriage. Consummation is no more than taking actual possession of what, by the previous contract, each had a right to.

We are however to observe, that this contract, like all others, is binding conditionally: so that a failure of performance on one part releases the obligation on the other part. Impotency therefore on the part of the man, or incapacity on the part of the woman, will set the contract aside. The man and the woman have in words made over a right to their persons respectively for the purposes of marriage: but making over this right is in effect making over nothing, where one is impotent or the other incapable.

This seems to be what has led some to imagine that a marriage is incomplete, till after consummation. As an impossibility of consummation will set the marriage aside, they conclude it not to be complete by the mere contract. But we have shown already, that it is so far complete, as to be binding upon the parties; and that properly the want of consummation, arising from impotency or incapacity, rather invalidates by non-performance a marriage, that was otherwise complete, than makes it a nullity from the beginning by any defect in the marriage itself.

However, though the law of nature gives each party a perpetual right to the person of the other; it does not determine how long the use of that right must necessarily continue: and upon this account the imperfections which are sufficient to set a marriage aside, must be from the first: whatever imperfections arise afterwards will not produce this effect.

Marriages between relations, how made invalid.

X. *Marriages between persons, who are nearly related to one another either by consanguinity or affinity, are generally held to be null from the beginning. We call those relations by consanguinity, who are relations by birth; such as parents and children, brothers and sisters, uncles and nieces. Relations by affinity are relations in consequence of some former marriage; such are fathers or mothers-in-law and their children-in-law, a man and his brother's wife, or a woman and her sister's husband.

In our inquiries upon this head, it will be necessary to distinguish between kindred in the direct line, as parents and their children, and

* Grot. Lib. II. Cap. V. § XII.

kindred in the collateral line, as brothers and sisters, uncles and their nieces, or aunts and their nephews.

There is a plain reason in nature, why marriages between persons related by consanguinity in the direct line, should be void from the beginning. The difference of age, which some have assigned as the reason, is not satisfactory: because where the parties are not related one to another, though the difference of age between them should be the same as is usual between parents and their children, or even between grandparents and their grandchildren, such marriage is not looked upon as a nullity. But all acts are void, if the validity of them would set aside the obligation of a law of nature; it being impossible to suppose, that the law of nature can allow what would destroy its own authority. Now a marriage between a mother and her son, or a father and his daughter, is not merely contrary to that natural duty of honour which children owe to their parents, but would, if it was valid, supersede the duty and set it aside: such a marriage would make the children equal to their parents; and the necessary familiarities, which marriage supposes, are wholly inconsistent with that reverence which is implied in the notion of a child's honouring its parents.

It will be more difficult to find a natural reason, why persons who are related to one another by affinity, or by consanguinity in the collateral line, should be under an incapacity of contracting a valid marriage. If we have been brought up from our infancy in an opinion, that it is unnatural for a brother to marry his sister, we shall be surprised to hear it asserted that no reason in the nature of the thing itself can be found, which will render such a marriage unlawful; and much less can any be found, which will make it void. Our surprise, however, at hearing this asserted, will probably be abated, if we recollect the history of the creation; from whence we may learn, that the sons of Adam could have no wives but their own sisters. And we cannot imagine that God would have contrived to place mankind in such circumstances as must either have put an end to the human species at once, or else have laid them under the necessity of doing what the law of nature forbids.

Some moralists indeed tell us of a natural abhorrence of such mixtures as these: they say, that every man's own inward sense or instinctive feeling is, in this instance, a law to him, and informs him what he may and what he may not do. One would be apt to question whether there is such an abhorrence implanted in us by nature; when we find nothing which can be called by this name, except in countries where people are bred up in an opinion, that these marriages are unlawful: in other countries where the law or custom allows of them, there seem to be no traces of any such abhorrence. In fact, if this instinct was the only cause, why a man might not marry his sister, I do not see how such a marriage could in any particular instance ever be shown to be unlawful. Whatever other men may feel, it may fairly be presumed, that the man who actually marries his sister, is not sensible of any such abhorrence. And however unlawful marriages of this sort may be supposed, where the parties have this instinct; I see not how such an instinct, where it is not felt, can make them unlawful. Unless the sense or feeling, the desires or aversions of one man, are the proper standards by which to regulate the conduct of another.

It is farther urged against marriages between two persons who are nearly related to one another; that a man enlarges his interest by marrying out of his own family: he is already connected with his own kindred; and if he marry with them, it will be of less benefit to him than if he had taken care to create new connections by marrying into another family. This however can be only matter of prudence. The most we could prove from this consideration is, that such a marriage will sometimes be less beneficial, than another might have been. But it does not by any means follow from hence, that the marriage is unlawful. All acts which are contrary to a man's immediate interest, are not for this reason to be always looked upon as criminal.

But though we may be at a loss to find out a natural reason, which renders the marriages of persons related in the collateral line unlawful; yet it seems to be very certain, that such marriages are unlawful to all mankind. *These incestuous marriages are particularly mentioned as a part of the guilt of the Canaanites, and as one reason amongst others, why God was pleased to cast them out of their land, and to give it to the children of Israel. There is not the least reason for imagining, that God had ever given any positive law about this, or any other matter, to the Canaanites in particular, exclusive of the rest of mankind. But if he had not done this, and yet the Canaanites were obliged to observe such a law, and were represented as sinners for not observing it; the plain consequence is, that this law must have been universal, so as to have obliged all mankind. But because it was an universal law before the coming of Christ, and yet was no part of the law of nature; it must have been a positive law given either to Adam or to Noah. Now from the necessity that Adam's children were under to marry with one another, we cannot well imagine any such law to have been given to him by the same God who had laid them under this necessity, by making no provision for them to marry with any one else. We must, therefore, conclude, that some positive law forbidding incestuous marriages was given to Noah, and in him to all his descendants.

This observation may help to explain a difficulty in the apostolical decree upon the question, whether the converted Gentiles ought to be circumcised. The apostles determined, that those Gentiles were free from the yoke of circumcision, but required them to abstain from fornication, from things offered to idols, from things strangled, and from blood. As three of these articles forbid things which are in themselves indifferent; the difficulty is, why the other article should forbid fornication, which the law of nature had already made criminal. One would expect, that the decree should be uniform, as to the matter of it; especially since we see no occasion for the apostles to interpose their positive authority to provide against a practice, which was naturally and in itself unlawful. †Mr. Hooker here refers us to what are called the seven precepts of the sons of Noah, one of which is—" To abhor all unclean knowledge in the flesh.—This precept he understands to relate to unlawful marriages, such as Moses in the law reckons up; and declares, that for his own part he thinks the apostolical canon is rather to be understood of these, than of fornication, according unto the sense of the law of nature. Words, says he, must be taken according to the

* Lev. XVIII. 24, 25, 27.

† Book IV. § II.

matter whereof they are uttered. The apostles command to abstain from blood. Construe this according to the law of nature, and it will seem, that homicide only is forbidden; but construe it in reference to the law of the Jews, about which the question was, and it will easily appear to have a clear other sense, and in any man's judgment a truer, when we expound it of eating, and not of shedding blood. So if we speak of fornication, he that knoweth no law, but only the law of nature, must needs make thereof a narrower construction, than he, which measureth the same by a law, wherein sundry kinds even of conjugal copulation are prohibited as impure, unclean, unhonest. And *St. Paul himself doth term incestuous marriage fornication."

However it is to be presumed, that this positive law, forbidding incestuous marriages, had some general convenience attending it. Though such marriages do not appear to do any injury to any one, and consequently are not naturally unjust; though they do not disqualify a man for doing good, or hinder him from doing it, any more than any other marriage; yet it is to be presumed, that some benefit must arise from avoiding them, if not to the public, yet to the individuals, who do avoid them; for we can scarce imagine that what is of no use at all, in any view of it, would ever be established by a divine command. The reason of this law is commonly supposed to be, that near relations live together in such a free and unobserved manner, as would tempt them to be guilty of much unchaste practice, if they were not kept, as it were, at a distance and checked in their desires by a law, which forbids them to marry with one another. But it seems to be evident, that the Mosaic law had some other reason in view: for it prohibits a man from marrying his sister, †whether she was born at home or abroad. Her being born at home implies, that there were opportunities of free intercourse between her and her brother: but her being born abroad implies, on the other hand, that there might have been no such opportunities. So that the law in effect says—Thou shalt not marry thy sister, whether there has or has not been any opportunities of familiar intercourse; whether thou hast or hast not lived with her in a free and unobserved manner.—It appears to me to be much more probable, that the legislator intended, by this provision, to leave mankind as free as possible to choose for themselves in marriage. A father or mother might consult some particular conveniences of the family, rather than the inclination of their children; and whatever interest or caprice determined them to bring about a marriage between two of their children, they would easily be able to accomplish such marriage, if the brother and sister could make a valid marriage: because both the parties are under their authority and direction, and might not only be unduly influenced by such authority, when they were arrived at maturity, but might, even during their minority, be contracted to one another by the act of their parents. Indeed, where the parties are children of different parents, their respective parents may possibly be determined, by some interest or caprice of their own, to influence such children to engage in a marriage disagreeable to themselves. But when the parents are of different families, the parties are not under the authority of the same common power; they are each of them under the authority of their own

* 1 Cor. V. 1.

† Levit. XVIII. 9.

parents only. And as these parents have no other common interest, but what arises from the proposed marriage; they will be much more likely each of them to consult the inclination and interest of their respective children, than to join in using their authority to drive their children into a marriage, which, as it was disagreeable to them from the first, was likely to end in nothing but misery.

Force may make a marriage a nullity.

XI. Unjust force, if either of the parties are concerned in making use of it, will be sufficient to prevent the obligation of marriage; in the same manner as it prevents the obligation of other contracts: because, as in them so in this, injustice can be no foundation of a right in the person who is guilty of it, and can therefore produce no correspondent obligation upon the person who suffers it. Indeed, if voluntary consummation follows such an extorted marriage, the marriage is then binding: because this is a plain indication that the person who suffered the unjust force, is willing to abide by the contract. Consummation by force, in consequence of such an extorted contract, is a rape.

The effects of an error on the contract of marriage.

XII. We have seen that some errors will be sufficient to invalidate promises or contracts: and what has been said concerning other pacts is applicable to marriage, under such restrictions as the nature of this contract requires.

If a man stipulates for one woman, and another is imposed upon him, instead of her that he agreed with; such a marriage is voidable at the man's discretion: because in fact he never consented to marry the woman thus imposed upon him. However, if he acquiesces in the fraud, after it is known, as Jacob did in the case of Leah; by such acquiescence the marriage becomes valid.

Most of the other errors, concerning which any question has arisen, whether they prevent the obligation of a marriage and make it a nullity, will be found upon inquiry to imply such conditions as are inconsistent with the nature of the contract, and cannot therefore either be supposed to be contained in the contract, if they are not expressed, or to produce any effect at all, if they are. Such are the questions, how far an error in regard to the woman's fortune, or in regard to her virginity, will make a marriage void. A man may indeed stipulate in this form—I consent to marry you, provided you have such or such a fortune. But then the contract must stop here, till he has informed himself whether she is worth what he requires or not. He gives her no right to his person, and consequently has no right to hers, till this condition is satisfied. But if, without inquiring any farther, he proceeds to act, as if he had a right to her person; as he does, if he proceeds to consummation; he tacitly owns, that she has a right to his: and consequently by so doing he must be understood to relinquish the condition. The marriage therefore will continue in force, notwithstanding he should afterwards find, that she is worth less than he stipulated for. If he could have any claim at all, in virtue of the condition, which he originally annexed to their contract, it must be a claim to be released from it by divorce. But the law of nature will not support such a claim. For the condition was not, that if you have not such or such a fortune, I will divorce you after marriage; but, if you have such or such a fortune I consent to marry you, and not otherwise. The terms, therefore, of this condition, however they might justify him in not marrying her, would not justify him in divorcing her afterwards. And if he was to annex the former of these conditions to his contract with her; either such condition would be made void by the nature of the contract; or if the condition was valid, it would make the contract a nullity; as has been shown already, when we were speaking of divorce.

An error concerning the woman's virginity, or concerning any natural infirmities, which modesty or decency will not allow a man to inform himself about, till the contract is completed, and each has taken possession of the other's person, cannot hinder that contract from binding, or make it a nullity from the beginning. A man may stipulate in this form—I consent to marry you, provided you are a virgin.—But this condition must be expressed: for the marriage contract does not naturally imply any such condition. And if it is expressed, I do not see, that it would hinder the natural effect of the contract, though the man should afterwards discover, that she is no virgin: because he must not only complete the contract, but must give her possession of his person by taking possession of hers, before he can make the discovery: and by so doing he gives up his conditions, and binds himself absolutely. The form of the stipulation did indeed make the marriage conditional; so that, as long as such condition remained in force, she could not demand him as her husband. But before he knew whether the condition would be satisfied or not, he made himself her husband, and consequently gave up the condition, by taking possession of her person. It may however be asked, whether such an error as this, though it does not make the marriage a nullity, may not be a sufficient cause for a divorce; whether the contract, though it is not void in itself, may not upon this account be rescinded afterwards. In answer to this inquiry, we may say the same that we said in answer to the other inquiry, whether an error concerning the woman's fortune is a sufficient cause for rescinding a marriage. It will be a sufficient cause, provided divorce in general is lawful, but not otherwise. When other contracts are rescinded upon account of any error in them; this rescinding of them is not the setting aside a valid contract, but is the effect of a declaration of one of the parties, that he will not abide by a contract, which from the beginning laid him under no obligation. But we have seen, that in the marriage contract, consummation precludes a man from declaring this, notwithstanding any error either in the fortune or in the virginity of the woman. And consequently a marriage, where there is such an error, can be rescinded no otherwise, than by setting aside a valid contract. So that, if divorce is unlawful in general, marriages after consummation cannot be dissolved, upon account of these or the like errors on either side. The Mosaic law indeed allowed an error in the woman's virginity to be a sufficient cause for dissolving a marriage: but this allowance is consistent with the principles here laid down; since we know that the same law allowed of divorce in general.

Want of parents' consent, not always sufficient to make a marriage void.

XIII. *The full use of reason is necessary in marriages, as in other contracts, to make them binding. So that a marriage contracted between persons who are under age, and have not yet arrived at the use of reason, will be void for want of the consent of parents. Or if only one

* Grot. ut sup. § X.

of the parties are upon this account incapable of binding themselves, the marriage will produce no obligation upon the other; because there is no obligation at all in any contract, unless such obligation is mutual. We may here observe, by the way, that the want of reason is naturally sufficient to make the marriage of an ideot or lunatic a nullity from the beginning.

Where persons are of full age, the want of their parents' consent does not invalidate a marriage. The law of nature does indeed enjoin, that children should honour and reverence their parents. For which reason it is undoubtedly the duty of children, not only to advise with their parents, but likewise to let their advice have its due weight, in all affairs of moment. And since nothing can be of more moment to the advantage and welfare as well of the family in general, as of the child in particular, than the marriage of the child; it cannot be denied, that such marriages as are contracted without the consent or against the commands of a parent, are contrary to the duty of the child; and that consequently the parent cannot be blamed, if he takes less notice of such a child, than he takes of the rest of his children, and chooses to dispose of his favours amongst those who have been more observant of their duty towards him. But then, on the other hand, marriages so contracted are not invalid, provided the child is of a proper age to think and act for itself. At this age he has a power of binding himself, and is not under the authority of his parents; except in such things, as relate to the interests and order of that family, of which he is a member, and of which the parents are the governors. And even this authority ceases, as soon as he separates himself from the family of his parents. The interests of the family are indeed greatly concerned in the marriage of the children: but then the child is, by marriage, separated from the family; and thus an end is put to such authority of the parents, as arose from this consideration.

Husband's authority, whence it arises.

XIV. It does not appear from any thing which is contained in the contract of marriage, that the husband has any other authority over the wife, than what arises from the general presumption, that he has more skill and experience than she has: which is a consideration that will make it prudent in her to leave the chief direction of the family to him. And this is no more than what he might expect from her; as she is obliged to contrive for their mutual happiness, as well as she can: which she does not do, unless she willingly commits the management of such affairs to him, as he is likely to manage to greater advantage than she could.

But, yet, when it happens otherwise; when her skill is the greater of the two; it will be equally prudent in him to let her have the management. The scriptures have indeed taught us, that the wife is in subjection to her husband; and have given such an account of her duty, as makes it proper for her to promise obedience in the very contract of marriage. But then they teach us, at the same time, that such subjection is not her natural state, but was appointed, by positive institution, as a punishment for that crime, into which the first husband was seduced by the first wife; that it might be a standing lesson of humility to all future wives, reminding them, that through the weakness of their sex, a curse has been entailed upon the whole species.

What concubinage is a good and valid marriage.

XV. *A concubine, according to the sense in which the word is now commonly used, is a woman who cohabits with a man without any stipulations of conjugal faith. And when, by concubinage, we mean such a cohabitation as this, it differs little, as to the unlawfulness of it, from a vague lust.

But the scriptures use the word concubine in such a sense, that those women, who are there called by this name, are such as the law of nature allows to be wives; for as far as appears, they were joined to the man, with whom they cohabited, by a marriage contract, and were no otherwise distinguished from wives, than either by their own condition, or by the condition of their children. If the woman was originally of servile condition, and was not raised by the marriage to an equal condition with her husband; and if the children, which she should bear, were understood to have no claim to inherit; she was then called a concubine. Thus, Hagar, who was of servile condition, was Abraham's concubine. She was originally a slave; and we find by the authority, which Sarah had over her, that her cohabitation with Abraham had not made her of equal dignity with her mistress. Her son Ishmael was indeed designed by Abraham for his heir: but then his claim was founded upon his being adopted by Sarah, and was not derived from the marriage of his mother. In like manner Bilhah and Zilpah were of servile condition: and their marriage with Jacob did not change their condition; for they are called handmaids even after their marriage: nor did the children, that were born of them, inherit any otherwise than in virtue of their being adopted by Rachel and Leah: for. Bilhah's children were considered by Rachel as her own; and so were Zilpah's children considered by Leah. After marriage, they were indeed sometimes called wives; but it is plain, they were not wives of the same sort with Leah and Rachel, not only because they were still sometimes called handmaids, and because their children were not considered as their own, nor inherited in their right; but likewise because Jacob had obliged himself, by oath, to Laban, not to take any wife besides his daughters. Bilhah, therefore, and Zilpah, though they are called wives, seem to have been concubines. And from this instance, as well as from that of Keturah, who is sometimes called Abraham's wife, and sometimes his concubine, it appears how little a wife differed from a concubine. As to the essential parts of the contract, they seem indeed not to have differed at all. Only in the contract with a concubine, some disadvantageous conditions were added, in respect both of herself and of her children. But as these conditions were not inconsistent with the contract, the law of nature would not have disallowed of such concubinage, as we read of in the scriptures, if it had not been attended with polygamy.

* Grot. Lib. II. Cap. V. § XV.

CHAPTER XVI.

OF THE RIGHT OF DEFENCE.

I. *Right of defence, in what founded.*—II. *Indefinite in its extent.*—III. *Not confined to injuries.*—IV. *How affected by benevolence.*—V. *Defence of life.*—VI. *Defence of limbs or of chastity.*—VII. *Defence against slighter personal injuries.*—VIII. *Honour, what.*—IX. *Mistakes in matters of honour, whence they arise.*—X. *Defence of our goods.*

Right of defence, in what founded.

I. Amongst the other principles, from whence any one man may derive a right over the person of any other, I mentioned some crime or injury on his part, over whose person such right is acquired.

*Now the rights, which are derived from hence, may be divided into such, as arise from an injury before it is committed, and such as arise from it, after it is committed.

Those rights which arise from an injury, before it is committed, are called the rights of defence.

The injuries which any one designs to do us, are such as relate either to our person, or to our property. Of the former sort, are murder, rape, maiming, wounding, slander; of the latter sort, are theft, fraud, robbery, burning, or otherwise destroying or wasting our goods. And our natural right of defence is nothing more than the liberty which the law of nature allows us, of taking such measures, as may guard against any injuries which we are likely to suffer in our persons or property. The great question concerning this right of defence is, how far it extends; what liberty the law of nature allows, or what may lawfully be done, in order to prevent an injury, which any one designs to do us.

†Before we can determine any thing with certainty upon this question, it will be necessary to inquire into the true principle, upon which the right of defence depends. A right to our life, or to our goods, means no more than a liberty of preserving them or keeping possession of them: we are, therefore, said to have a right to any thing, because the law of nature does not oblige us to part with it; or because our possession of it, and our endeavours to keep such possession, are consistent with that law. Now our endeavour to keep possession of a thing, when any one attempts to take it from us, is the defence of ourselves in the possession of it: and since, where the thing is our own, or where we have a right to it, this endeavour is consistent with the law of nature; it follows, that where we have a right to a thing, our defence of ourselves in the possession of it is lawful; or that a right of defence is implied in the very notion of our having a right to a thing. In short, the true principles upon which our right of defending either our persons or our goods depends, is this; the law of nature does not oblige us to give them up, when any one has a mind to hurt them, or to take them from us: and that the law of nature does not oblige us

* Grot. Lib. II. Cap. I. § II.

† Grot. Ibid. § III.

thus to give them up, is evident; because our right to them would be unintelligible, or would, in effect, be no right at all, if we were obliged to suffer all mankind to treat them, as they pleased, without endeavouring to prevent it.

Right of defence indefinite in its extent.

II. If this then is the principle, upon which the right of defence depends; we cannot expect to find that the law of nature has exactly defined how far we may go, or what we may lawfully do, in endeavouring to prevent an injury, which any one designs and attempts to do us. *The law allows us to defend our persons or our property: and such a general allowance implies, that no particular means of defence are prescribed to us. We may, however, be sure, that whatever means are necessary must be lawful: because it would be absurd to suppose, that the law of nature allows of defence, and yet forbids us at the same time to do what is necessary for this purpose.

From hence it follows, that he, who attempts to injure us, gives us an indefinite right over his person, or a right to make use of such means to prevent the injury, as his behaviour and our situation make necessary.

Right of defence not confined to injuries.

III. †Though we speak of the right of defence, as a right to guard against injuries; the word injuries must not here be confined to its strict and proper sense, as implying some criminal malice in the person, against whom we have a right of defending ourselves. The principle upon which this right is founded, will extend it to all cases, where we are likely to suffer any causeless harm; even though there is no criminal design on the part of the assailant or of him, who, unless we were to prevent it, would be the immediate, though, perhaps, the innocent cause of our suffering such harm. For the law of nature no more obliges us to undergo any causeless harm, when it arises from an innocent person, than when it arises from a malicious design: our right of defence is not founded in the crime of him who attempts to hurt us; but in the liberty which the law allows us, by not obliging us to submit to any harm which we have not deserved.

How benevolence affects the right of defence.

IV. Before we go on to apply these general principles to particular instances, it may not be improper to inquire, whether the right or liberty of defence is not restrained by the dictates of benevolence, notwithstanding there is no precept of strict justice, which takes it from us.

If, indeed, the law of nature had commanded defence, the least degree of patience or submission to any causeless harm would be criminal. But since the defence of our person or of our property is just, only because it is not unjust; since we are only allowed, and not commanded to defend ourselves, or to guard against injuries; defence seems to be a matter of indifference. Will not, therefore, the regard, which we ought to have for the welfare of others, be a check upon us, and engage us to submit to an injury; as there is no want of injustice in submission; rather than suffer us to make use of the right, which we have over the person of him, who attempts to hurt us; as the exercise of this right may argue a want of benevolence or compassion, a want

* Grot. Lib. II. Cap. I. § X.

† Grot. Ibid. § III.

of that tender regard, which is due to his welfare? This reasoning will certainly prove to demonstration, that there is great room for benevolence in the exercise of our right of defence; and that proper abatements, in the rigour of it, by patience and submission, are by no means inconsistent with any precepts of justice. But in the meantime, though benevolence may lead us to regulate our right of defence, and to make it as consistent as we can, with the welfare of others; we have no reason to imagine that the same virtue of benevolence will oblige us wholly to give up that right, or to be satisfied with the use of such means of defending ourselves, as would render it wholly ineffectual. The highest degree of benevolence seems to be that of loving others as well as ourselves; of being as tender of their welfare as we are of our own; or of paying an equal regard to an equal degree of happiness, whether it is our own happiness, or the happiness of another man. But even this degree of benevolence cannot require us quietly to give up either our life, or our liberty, or our limbs, or our goods, without endeavouring to preserve them; merely from the apprehension, that he, who attempts to deprive us of them, might suffer some hurt, if we were to defend them. By so doing, we should do more than the law of benevolence imports; we should pay a greater regard to his happiness, than to our own; whereas the law only requires us to pay the same. As there is, therefore, no want of justice in standing upon our defence, so neither is there, in the first instance, any want of benevolence. The consequences of our doing this may indeed be fatal to him, who attempts to injure us: but then these consequences are chargeable upon himself, and not upon us. We only desire to secure what is our own: he sees what may be the event, if he obstinately persists in endeavouring to take it from us: and if, notwithstanding this, he is obstinate enough to persist, the consequences must be considered as arising from his own act rather than from ours.

V. These general principles will, perhaps, be better understood, if we apply them to some particular instances. Defence of life.

* If a man is attacked with a plain design to kill him; as the law of nature does not oblige him to part with his life, he is at liberty to stand upon his defence, and has a right, against the aggressor, to do whatever is necessary for preserving himself from the hurt intended him. If the aggressor suffers any harm, if he is wounded, or maimed, or killed, this cannot be looked upon as unjust or causeless harm: because he, who did it, was providing for his own security; he was doing what the law of nature allowed him to do, and killed the aggressor, because he could not avoid it. The end, therefore, was lawful in itself, and the means were made lawful by being unavoidable. You may say, indeed, that the means were not unavoidable, provided he would have consented to part with his own life. But this is nothing to the purpose: for whatever is absolutely necessary for obtaining an end, which the law will justify him in pursuing, must, in the judgment of that law, be unavoidable. It might, perhaps, be possible for a person, who is thus assaulted, to save his life by running away from the danger. The assailant, however, has no right to demand, that he should do this. As the law of nature allows the person assaulted to secure himself; it

* Grotius, Lib. II. Cap. I. § III.

leaves him at liberty to judge what means are necessary for this purpose; whether, for instance, he can preserve himself by running away, or must necessarily stand upon his defence. Benevolence may persuade him to choose that method of providing for his own safety, which will be attended with the least hurt to the aggressor. But where the danger is instantaneous, the mind is too much disturbed to deliberate upon this head; and if it was more calm, there is no time for deliberation. I see not, therefore, any want of benevolence which can be reasonably charged upon a man in these circumstances, if he takes the most obvious way of preserving himself: though, perhaps, some other method might have been found out, which would have preserved him as effectually, and have produced less hurt to the aggressor, if he had been calm enough, and had been allowed time enough, to deliberate about it.

* The danger which our life is in, may be less immediate; a person may have threatened to kill us, whenever he meets with a fair opportunity; he may have taken some steps towards putting this design in execution; he may have hired assassins, or may have laid in wait for us himself. In such remote dangers, there is more leisure for deliberation, and the suggestions of benevolence may be better attended to. But even in these circumstances defence is lawful. If they, who live out of civil society, should kill a man, in their endeavours to get security of him against their suffering the evil, which they foresee to be otherwise unavoidable, there would be no injustice in such defence: and the circumstances might be such, as would clear the fact from the charge of inhumanity. If the person, against whom there is this design, is morally certain of it, he has a right to demand security; the public authority would interpose and take care that he should have security, if he lived in a state of civil society: and if there is no magistrate, no public authority, the law of nature will allow him to do, what in a state of civil society, the magistrate would have done for him: it will allow him to get security for himself, and to make use of force in order to obtain it, when it cannot be obtained by any other means. This law cannot be supposed to oblige a man to expose his life to such dangers as may be guarded against, and to wait, till the danger is just coming upon him, before it allows him to secure himself. Whatever degree of assurance he has, that he shall lose his life, if he does not take care to guard it; he may reasonably demand the same degree of assurance, that the design against him is laid aside, and will never be put in execution. His right is only to demand such security, as is necessary for this purpose: and if they, whom he had reason to be afraid of, will give him it, he can ask no more. But if they refuse this, his right still subsists; and consequently he may lawfully make use of force to compel them: because the right, which he has to be secured against their ill designs, would, in effect, be no right at all, if he might not support it by all necessary means. If then they should make resistance to such force, and in making resistance should be killed, it is their fault, and not his: they lose their lives, not through any want of benevolence in him, but through their own injustice. He would have been satisfied with suffi-

* Grotius, Lib. II. Cap. I. § V.

cient security, that he should not be hurt by them: and if they oppose this demand, and are killed in the struggle; there is no breach of justice on his part: because he was supporting a just demand by the means which they had made necessary: and there is no breach of benevolence; because no rule of benevolence requires him to set a greater value upon their life, than upon his own; as he certainly must have done, if he had exposed himself to their designs, rather than endeavoured to obtain such security for himself, as he has a right to.

*It is possible that a man may make an attempt upon my life, and yet be innocent in so doing; notwithstanding I have not deserved death from him, or from any one else. He may walk in his sleep; or he may be out of his senses; or he may mistake me for some one else, or he may be employed to fight against me in what appears to him to be a just cause, though it is not so. In such cases as these, though he is not chargeable with any crime, I may lawfully defend myself against him, and may make use of all such means of defence, as the circumstances that we are in, have made necessary. For though we consider the right of defence as arising from a crime not yet committed, but designed and attempted; yet the principle upon which we show that there is such a right, extends farther than those cases, where the assailant is, properly speaking, guilty of a crime. The right which I have against the assailant's person, is the liberty, which the law of nature must necessarily be understood to allow me, by not obliging me to bear any causeless harm; whether there is any crime or not, on the part of him who attempts to do me such causeless harm.

But suppose a person, without any design of hurting me, should happen, when I am assaulted by another, to stand in my way, and hinder me either from making my defence, or from providing for my security by flight; might I ride over him, or push him down a precipice, or otherwise dispatch him, in order either to clear the way for my flight, or to remove the hindrance which he is of to my defence? Certainly this would be unlawful, if nothing but injustice, as injustice, could give me a right to take away the life of another man for the preservation of my own. But if my right of defence which I have even in cases of injuries, arises from the liberty which the law of nature allows by not obliging me to submit to any causeless harm; this principle will extend the right of defence to all cases, where I am likely to suffer any causeless harm, if I did not take care to use the necessary means of preventing it. Whatever, therefore, an innocent person may accidentally suffer, whilst I am doing what I am at liberty to do, it must be looked upon as a natural misfortune. There is no injustice on my part, if he only suffers what is unavoidable, without my submitting to what the law of nature does not impose upon me. Nor is there any want of benevolence; unless benevolence obliged me to have a greater regard to another man's life, than to my own.

Defence of limbs or of chastity.

VI. †When a man is in danger of being maimed, or a woman of being ravished; the manner in which Grotius accounts for the right of defending themselves against these injuries, would lead one to imagine, that in his opinion, the measure of what we may lawfully do in the defence of our person, is to be taken from

* Grot. Lib. II. Cap. I. § III.

† Grot. Ibid. § VI. VII.

the evil which we should suffer, if we were not to defend ourselves. The reason which he gives, why the assailant may lawfully be killed in such attempts as these, is, that one of our principal limbs, or our chastity, is of equal value with our life. As if, upon supposition, that what we are likely to lose is not of equal value with our life, it could not lawfully be defended at the expense of his life, who endeavours to take it from us.

But I have already shown, and Grotius, upon another occasion, acknowledges, that he who attempts to injure me, gives me an indefinite right against him, a right which knows no measure, besides the attainment of the end, for which the law of nature allows it. Since we are not obliged to submit to such injuries as we have just now been speaking of, we are at liberty, that is, we have a right to defend ourselves against them: and the law, which allows this liberty, cannot be supposed to forbid any of those means, without which such liberty would be ineffectual.

But the observation of Grotius concerning the value of what would be lost in an attempt to maim or to ravish, though it is of no weight at all in settling the justice of defending ourselves to the utmost extremity, may be of use to show, that it is not inconsistent with benevolence to repel such an attempt at the expense of the assailant's life: because no rule of benevolence obliges us to love another better than ourselves; which must be the case, if we were ready to spare his life, though, with the loss of what is of as much value to us, as his life is to him.

Defence against slight personal injuries.

VII. *Strict justice would allow a man to repel the slightest injury to his person, such as a blow or a box on the ear, by any means which the aggressor makes necessary. The principle so frequently mentioned already is applicable to this case. As the law of nature does not oblige a man to submit even to such injuries as these, he is naturally at liberty, or has an indefinite right to repel them. But where the suffering is so slight to the person attacked, and the much greater evil of death would be the consequence to the aggressor, if defence was carried to the utmost rigour of strict justice; natural benevolence would teach a man rather to bear the injury, than to ward it off at so great an expense to the aggressor, as that of his life.

Honour, what.

VIII. †We hear it, indeed, frequently maintained, that a man's honour will require him to kill his adversary if he can; not only that he may ward off such an affront, but even that he may revenge it, after it has been received. And it may not be altogether foreign to our purpose to take this opportunity of inquiring into the meaning of the word honour, and into the rules of conduct which this principle is supposed to suggest.

It is no very easy undertaking to explain a word which is used by all men very unsteadily, and by most without any meaning at all. Grotius says, that honour is the opinion of our worth or excellence. He does not tell us whether he means that any man's honour is the opinion which the man himself has, or the opinion which other people have of his worth and excellence. In the former sense, the definition of honour,

* Grot. Lib. II. Cap. I. § X.

† Grot. Ibid.

as it signifies a principle of action, is not true; and in the latter sense it is unintelligible. The true definition of a word may always be substituted instead of the word itself. Try, therefore, to substitute the definition which Grotius gives of the word honour, instead of the word itself; when you affirm that your honour will not suffer you to do such or such an action, or that your honour requires you to do such or such another action. Do you mean that your opinion, or the judgment which you make, concerning your own worth or excellence, is the principle which influences you to do or not to do this or that action? If this be the case, then every thing is consistent with a man's honour, which he can reconcile to his own opinion, whatever the rest of the world may think, or whatever the rules of right reason may determine about it: and a man who had debased his mind and corrupted his judgment, would easily prove to you, that cowardice and treachery are as consistent with a principle of honour, as courage or fidelity. Grotius, however, when he speaks of honour, as consisting in the opinion of our worth and excellence, did not mean a man's own opinion of these qualities in himself, but the general opinion of mankind concerning them. But if honour has such a reference to the opinion of others, as this definition supposes, it will be nonsense for a man to talk of his own honour, unless we add something to the definition, which will give it likewise a reference to himself. If it is considered without any such reference to himself, merely as the opinion of other men, he cannot speak of it as a principle within his own heart. If we call it a sense of the esteem or regard of mankind, a desire of raising and preserving in them an opinion of our worth and excellence; the definition will be intelligible. And I will endeavour to show, that this is the true notion of honour, as far as the word is used with any steady meaning, or with any meaning at all.

When the word honour is made use of by those who call themselves men of honour, to denote a principle of action which influences their conduct; if any analogy of language is observed, or if it signifies any thing like what the same word is used to signify upon other occasions, we may judge what this principle is by attending to the import of some very common expressions. What do we mean, when we say, that we honour a man? The plain sense of such an expression is, that we think highly of him, or that we regard and esteem him. What is it then to behave honourably, but to behave in such a manner as to deserve to be honoured; that is, in such a manner as to deserve the regard and esteem of mankind? Now there seems to be no difference between behaving honourably, and behaving with honour: so that to behave with honour, and to behave in such a manner as to deserve the regard and esteem of mankind, are the same thing.

If this is the fundamental rule of honour, it will be easy to see what principle it is, which puts a man upon observing such a rule. Nothing but a desire that mankind should think well of us, or a sense of reputation, can lead a man to behave in this or that manner, merely because mankind will esteem and regard him for such behaviour. One would think that such a principle of action as this could seldom mislead us: because the general opinion of mankind, though it is not a demonstrative standard, must be allowed to be at least a probable standard of what is right and virtuous. General opinion is nothing else but the common sense of mankind, or the common judgment of reason: and it is not likely that mankind should universally approve any thing which is generally hurtful, or any thing, indeed, which is not generally beneficial.

Mistakes in matters of honour, whence they arise.

IX. The mistakes in this matter arise either from our making use of a wrong standard in judging what is honourable, or else from our applying the true standard in a wrong manner.

We make use of a wrong standard, whenever our sense of reputation is confined to a few, and does not extend itself to all; whenever we desire to be thought well of by a small party of men, instead of desiring to be thought well of by mankind in general. A few men may easily be mistaken in their judgment, a small party may be determined, by caprice or private interest, to regard and esteem us for such qualities or such conduct, as would make the rest of mankind think meanly of us. And, in fact, there is scarce any conduct so scandalous, but some will be found to countenance and encourage it. If then we mean by our honour, only a sense of reputation amongst the few, that we converse with amongst people, whose humour or interest is the same with our own; it is no wonder, if honour and virtue should sometimes be found to differ from one another. But this notion of honour is plainly a partial one, and may, for that reason, be justly called a false one. He cannot be said to act upon a true principle of honour, who is esteemed or thought well of by only an inconsiderable number of men; whilst he appears to the rest of the world to act meanly or basely.

Suppose, however, that we make use of a true standard of honour, and look upon no actions to be consistent with our honour, but such as are in general esteem; we may possibly be misled in our judgment by a partial application even of this standard. If an action consists of several different parts, or may be considered in several different views; some one part of it, taken separately from the rest, may deservedly be had in general esteem; the action, when we view it only on one side, may be such as mankind would approve, that is, it may be such as a true principle of honour would suggest. And whilst we attend to this part of the action, or whilst we consider it in this single view, we may look upon it to be consistent with our standard of honour: whereas, if we had attended to all the parts of the action, or had viewed it on all sides; we should have seen such a mixture of meanness or baseness in it, as would have convinced us that it could never either obtain or deserve a general esteem, and that no sense or desire of approving ourselves to the common judgment of mankind could ever lead to it. The same partial application of the standard of honour, which misleads us in judging of actions, misleads us likewise in judging of the characters of men. We attend so much to some striking part of their conduct, as not to observe the rest of it.—And it is only by this means, that many have had the credit of being men of honour, who, if their whole conduct had been as much attended to, would have been found to deserve contempt, and would justly be ranked amongst the meanest and basest of the species.

There is one very common mistake about the notion of honour, which may perhaps not be thought to arise either from the use of a partial standard of honour, or from a partial application of the true standard. The mistake, which I mean is, that courage and honour are by many people looked upon as one and the same thing. Men who are soon provoked, who carry their resentment, upon the slightest occasions, to the utmost extremity, and are prodigal of their lives to gratify their revenge, have assumed, and would appropriate to themselves, the title of men of honour; though they have scarce any one good quality that can give them any pretensions to it. The case seems to be this: men of true honour, that is, men who have a sense of esteem, and a desire to obtain the general good opinion of mankind, are tender of their reputation, and make it a principal part of their happiness to behave in such a manner, as to deserve to be well thought and well spoken of. Upon this account they cannot bear to have their character lessened, and would rather hazard their life, than submit to any causeless aspersion. Thus, as a true principle of honour naturally produces courage, or as men of true honour are commonly men of courage, the quarrelsome and the revengeful have mistaken the matter, and have imagined that the converse must be true too, that men of courage must be men of honour. They have this advantage on their side, that no prudent man chooses to call their title to this character into question: and they are, therefore, weak enough to please themselves with fancying that their title is a good one. Courage, indeed, is, in some stations of life, an useful part of a man's character. A soldier could not discharge the duties of his station, if he did not maintain a general opinion of his being possessed of it. The rule of benevolence would scarce dissuade a man, who is placed in such circumstances as make courage a necessary or valuable part of his character, from doing what justice allows of, if he could not avoid doing it without a general imputation of cowardice: not because the law of benevolence does not bind him, or does not command him, as well as other men, to sacrifice his own lesser happiness to the greater happiness of another; but because the good which he is enabled to do in his station, by preserving the reputation of courage, is greater than the good which he would do by submitting to injuries, where he cannot submit to them without forfeiting that reputation. But if they, whose station and circumstances have not made courage a necessary or useful part of their character, will resent or guard against slight affronts with the utmost rigour, that strict justice will allow of; it is their business to consider how well they comply with the natural dictates of benevolence; it is much too difficult a task for me to undertake.

Defence of our goods.

X. As the law of nature does not oblige us in strict justice to part with our lives, or our limbs, or our chastity, and does, by not obliging us to part with them, allow us to defend our persons; *so neither does it oblige us to give up our goods to those, who would unjustly rob us of them. And from this natural liberty of keeping our goods, in opposition to those who would unjustly take them from us, our right of defence arises, that is, our right over their person, as far as such a right is necessary for preventing their attempt.

It is plain from the foundation of this right, that it must be an indefinite one, or that we are not naturally debarred from proceeding to extremities in the defence of our goods; where the obstinate injustice of

* Grot. Lib. II. Cap. I. § XI.

such as would take them from us, makes this behaviour necessary. For as the law of nature does not oblige us to part with our goods, it cannot be supposed to prescribe any particular means of defending them: since to prescribe such means, as the only lawful means, would in effect be obliging us to part with our goods when those means fail. And such injunctions as these, would plainly make property nothing, or would give all persons who had a mind to deprive us of our goods, a power of doing so; provided they only took care to render the prescribed means ineffectual for the security and preservation of them.

Grotius, indeed, in order to justify killing a man in defence of our goods, observes, that the inequality of value between his life and our goods is made up by the favour of the law towards our innocence, and its aversion towards his injustice. But he was led to think this observation necessary by a principle, from which he reasons elsewhere upon a like question: it seems to have been his opinion, that the evil which the law of nature allows us to do in our own defence, ought not to exceed the evil, which we should suffer, if we were not to defend ourselves. This principle has already been shown not to be true: and it is the more to be wondered at, that Grotius should proceed upon it, since in speaking of what may be lawfully done in defence of our persons, he maintains, that they who attempt to injure us, give us, by such an attempt, an unlimited right against them; as far as such a right is necessary for preserving ourselves from the harm, which they design to do us. And it is plain from hence, that he was aware both of the true foundation of our right of defence, and of the true extent likewise of this right.

*But he had a favourite principle in his mind, that we ought not to take away any one's life immediately or directly for the sake of preserving our goods. He allows, however, that we may defend them, till our own life is in danger, and then we may justly kill the robber: because in these circumstances, the robber loses his life, immediately or directly, for the sake of preserving our own life, but remotely only, or indirectly, for the sake of preserving our goods.

Upon this principle, as he imagines, we are to account for the distinction which the laws of Moses, of Solon, of Plato, and of the twelve tables, have made between a thief who robs in the day, and a thief who robs in the night; when they allow the latter to be killed, but forbid killing the former. Witnesses, he says, can scarce be supposed present in the night, to explain how the death of the thief happened: and for that reason the law supposes favourably, that the person who killed the thief, did not do it merely for the sake of preventing the loss of his goods, but that, whilst he was defending his goods, his life was brought into danger, and that he was forced to take this method of preventing himself from being killed. Whereas in the day time there can be no room for such favourable presumption: when others are present or could readily come in, if they were called for; it would easily appear, whether the person who kills the thief, was in danger of his life or not: and since the law, when witnesses are to be had, presumes no more in his favour than he can make out, it forbids the killing a thief so robbing in the day time, because it intends that no man should lose his life directly for the sake of preserving another's goods.

* Grot. Lib. II. Cap. I. § XIII.

The allowance, which these laws granted to kill a thief in the night, can scarce be reconciled with what Grotius here supposes to be the intention of the lawgivers. But in order to reconcile such an allowance with such an intention, he makes use of several arguments to show, that those laws presumed the person who killed a night thief to be in danger of losing his own life. The chief of these arguments depends upon what he observes concerning the law of Moses, that it required the thief to be found with such an instrument as is used in stabbing: and urges, that if the law allowed him to be killed, only when he was found so armed, it must in this permission proceed upon the presumption, that he attempted to make use of the weapon with which he was found. But suppose, instead of calling the instrument with which he was found, an instrument for stabbing, we were to call it an instrument for breaking through; this evidence for the presumption, which Grotius supposes the law to proceed upon, will be taken away at once: no one from finding that the thief brought him with a crow-iron, or a file, or a saw, or any other instrument of this sort, which might help him in getting into the house, would think this any evidence, that he had been making an attempt upon the life of the master of such house. And perhaps after all, the word which Grotius translates an instrument for stabbing, and which I have translated an instrument for breaking through, may be very properly rendered by our English translators, when they describe the thief as being found, not with any particular sort of weapon, but in the act of breaking through.

However, without being at the trouble of examining into this nicety, we need only read the words of the law in order to inform ourselves of the reason, upon which it proceeded, in making a distinction between the two sorts of thieves. *The law says,—"If a thief be found breaking up, and be smitten, that he die, there shall no blood be shed for him: if the sun be risen upon him, there shall be blood shed for him; for he should make full restitution." The plain reason why the law did not allow a day thief to be killed, is here given: he ought not to be killed, because he should have made full restitution. The law had an opportunity of coming in to assist a person who was robbed in the daytime, and of taking care that proper justice should be done between him and the thief. And if this was the reason why a day thief was not allowed to be killed, we may easily infer from thence what was the reason, why this was allowed in the case of a night thief: the ordinary penalty of theft could not readily be inflicted; and men might therefore be encouraged, by the hopes of impunity, to steal in the night time, if some other method was not made use of to deter them. With this view, the law, when it could not come into a person's aid, left him to his natural liberty, and gave him leave to defend himself, by whatever means he should find to be necessary.

It may here be asked, why the law of Moses, which did not punish theft with death, if the thief was taken, should indulge private persons in a license of proceeding farther than it would proceed itself. †Puffendorf affirms in general, that none of those lawgivers, who permitted a night thief to be killed, decreed any capital punishment against theft, if the thief was taken. This, however, though it is true of the Mosaic

* Exod. XXII. 2. † Book II. Cap. V. § XVII, XVIII.

law, is certainly not true of all the rest. The law of the twelve tables decreed a capital punishment against a slave for theft. And the laws of Solon made theft capital, where the value of the thing stolen exceeded fifty drachmas, or where the theft was committed in a bath, or in a place of exercise; that is, where persons laid aside their clothes or other things of value, which they usually carry about with them, and were otherwise employed, so as not to be upon their guard, it was capital to steal.

We may, from hence, make two observations in passing. First, when the law of the twelve tables, or Solon's laws, allow a person to kill a thief in the night, but forbid the killing a thief in the day; the lawgivers could not proceed in this latter prohibition upon the principle, which Grotius imagines them to have had in view, the principle of not taking away any one's life directly upon account of our goods: because the Roman law punished theft in a slave, and Solon's law punished theft of goods to a certain value, and in certain circumstances, with death.

And if the lawmakers proceeded upon no such principle, it will be difficult to show, that, in the former permission of killing a night thief, they proceeded upon the presumption, that such a thief was killed, whilst the person, whose goods he was endeavouring to steal, was brought into danger of his life.

Our second observation relates to that part of Solon's law, which punishes theft in a bath with death, and to the apparent reason of this law, which has been already assigned. Where the owners of the goods stolen are not upon their guard, nor can be supposed to be so, the penalty of theft is greater, than where goods of the same value are stolen in other circumstances.

We may apply this to the cause of a night thief. Men are less upon their guard, and are less able to take care of their goods in the night, than in the day. It was necessary, therefore, for the law to give them a better security against being robbed in the night, by making the consequence of such theft more dangerous than the consequence of stealing in the day. And this seems in general to be a prudent rule in making laws to guard against such crimes as are most easily committed, by the highest penalties; and to take care, that the security, which is wanting in the nature of the thing, may be supplied by the severity of what the law threatens.

This leads us to the true answer to that inquiry from whence we have digressed. The law of Moses, though it does not punish theft with death, where the circumstances are such as to give the injured person what the law calls full restitution; yet in other circumstances it grants the best security, that it could, by allowing the injured person to defend his goods as he can. What the Mosaic law says concerning a night thief, cannot properly be called the establishment of a penalty: it only leaves a man in this instance to his natural liberty. In the case of a day thief the law appoints a certain penalty, forbids the person, upon whose goods the attempt is made, to kill the thief, and declares him to be guilty of murder, if he kills him. But in the case of a night thief, it does not command that he should be killed, but only says, that, if he should be killed, no notice shall be taken of it. In respect, then, of a day thief, the natural right of defence is abridged by the law; but in respect of a night thief, the words of the law are merely permissive, and may be looked upon as a declaration, that every man was at liberty to defend his goods against such a thief, in any manner that he pleased.

If we consider the law as it relates to a night thief, in this view, that is, as a simple permission, it will lead us to conclude, that the author of the law of Moses looked upon the defence of our goods, even at the expense of the life of the thief, as consistent with the law of nature. The law gives a man no authority to kill a night thief, which he would not have had, if no law had been made about a thief of either sort: it only supposes, that such a thief may happen to be killed, and then declares, that the man who kills him, shall not be punished for it. As this is a simple permission, it leaves men to the liberty of nature: and as the law exempts the person who thus defends his goods, from any punishment; it plainly shows what sort of defence was looked upon by the lawmaker to be justifiable, where men were left to that liberty.

Since, then, such a defence of our goods, as may end in the death of him who endeavours to take them from us, has been shown to be consistent with natural justice; the only remaining inquiry is, whether it is consistent with benevolence, or whether, for the sake of preserving the life of the robber, we ought not, in tenderness to his welfare, though not in strict justice, to part with the goods which he endeavours to deprive us of. But the question, when it is thus stated, does not take the matter far enough back. The first inquiry ought to be, whether benevolence, or a tender regard to the welfare of the robber, obliges us rather to part with our goods than to defend them at all: because all the consequences of such defence are to be charged to his account, and not to ours: it arises wholly from himself and not from us, that the loss of his life should come in competition with the loss of our goods. If the preservation of our goods was, in the first instance, consistent with benevolence, and we take no other measures to preserve them, than what his violence, or the manner of his attack upon them makes necessary; whatever event may happen to follow from our defence of them, it must be considered as his act, who pushes us to extremities, and not as ours, who had no design of doing more than benevolence would have warranted. Supposing, therefore, the matter in question to be of no great importance to our happiness, but to be such as we can well spare, without any considerable damage either to ourselves or to those, whom we are bound in duty to take care of, and to provide for; benevolence would persuade us to sacrifice it to mutual peace, to part with it rather than to engage in any contention about it. But if we are in danger of being plundered of all that we are worth, or of losing what is necessary to our own happiness, and to the proper discharge of that duty, which we owe to our relations and dependents; benevolence, which not only teaches us to show our first kindnesses to them, who have deserved the best of us, but which requires no more of us towards any one than to love him as well as we love ourselves, would not oblige us to part with it.

We find, that even the gospel, when it commands us not to resist injuries, has explained this precept in such a manner as to show, that we are to understand it of lesser injuries only. * " If any man will sue

* Matt. V. 40.

thee at the law, and take thy coat from thee, let him have thy cloak also." Though the precept, not to resist injuries, is delivered in general words, the instance made use of to explain it is an evidence, that he, who gave it, did not design to extend it to all instances of property. If he had illustrated his meaning by instances of the highest injuries, we might have been sure, that the precept included all lesser injuries: but as he chose to illustrate it by an example of a slight loss, there is by no means the same ground for concluding, that he designed to include all greater losses.

One thing, however, benevolence seems strongly to recommend to us, which is, to give the robber as good notice as we can, and as the disturbance into which he throws us, will permit us to give him, that we are determined to defend our property, by all such means as he shall make necessary: and when we have done this, if he persists in his design, the fault will be entirely his own, and no want of kindness to him can reasonably be charged upon us, whatever may be the consequence of his violence.

The liberty of defence, which we have now been explaining, is greatly abridged, where the parties concerned are members of the same civil society. But I shall defer considering in what manner it is abridged, till I come to speak about the nature of civil society, and of the effects which are produced in our natural rights, by the institution of it.

CHAPTER XVII.

OF REPARATION FOR DAMAGE DONE.

I. *Damage and fault, what they mean.*—II. *Right to reparation, whence it arises.*—III. *Imperfect right, no foundation for demanding reparation.*—IV. *Perfect and imperfect rights are sometimes confounded.*—V. *Some rules to be observed in estimating damages.*—VI. *Accessaries to an injury obliged to make reparation.*—VII. *Damages, how to be demanded from a number of principles.*—VIII. *Reparation due for the consequences of an unlawful act.*—IX. *Reparations for unjust death.*—X. *For maiming, wounding, beating, unjust imprisonment.*—XI. *For adultery, or for debauching a woman.*—XII. *For theft.*—XIII. *For slander.*—XIV. *Reparation due, where there is no malice.*

I. An *injury, after it is committed, produces a right in them who have suffered any damage by it, to demand reparation of such damage, from the authors of the injury; and it produces, likewise, a right of inflicting punishment.

†By damage we understand every loss or diminution of what is a man's own, occasioned by the fault of another. And by a fault we understand every lawful action or omission.

* Grotius, ut sup. § II. † Grot. Lib. II. Cap. XVII. § II.

It is proper to observe here, that though every unlawful act or neglect is a fault, yet every such act or neglect does not lay the person, who is in fault, under an obligation to make reparation: no such obligation is produced, unless the fault occasions some damage, that is, unless it occasions some loss or diminution of what some other person has a strict right to. A man is chargeable with a fault, that is, he is chargeable with behaving unlawfully, whenever he does not comply with the law. But in many instances he may behave unlawfully, and yet be under no obligation to make reparation to any one. All actions or omissions, which are contrary to the several duties included in the general virtue of benevolence, are faults; but such faults as these give no person any right to demand reparation. The notion of reparation is unintelligible, where no damage has been done: and whatever want of benevolence there may be in not giving to a man what he had reason to expect, or what he had an imperfect right to, there can be no damage in it: because damage is some loss or diminution of what is strictly and properly his own.

It is to be observed farther, that the definition of damage extends the notion of it beyond a man's goods. His life, his limbs, his liberty, an exemption from pain, his character or reputation, are all of them his own, in a strict and proper sense: so that the loss or diminution of any of them gives him a right to demand reparation from those, by whose fault they have been lost or diminished. Nor is the notion of damage confined to the loss or diminution of such things, as are a man's own by the immediate gift of nature, or by such a general compact of all mankind, as that is, which introduced property. It is a damage to him, if he suffers any loss or diminution of such things, whether corporeal or incorporeal, as any particular compact, or any positive laws may have made his own. Thus a servant, by withholding the service, which his bargain has given his master a right to, does damage to his master. And a guardian by neglecting to take such care of the affairs of his ward, as either the nature of the trust which he has undertaken, or the positive laws of his country oblige him to, does damage to such ward.

Right to reparation, whence it arises.

II. As the law of nature forbids us to hurt any man, it cannot allow any act of ours, whereby another is hurt, to stand good, or to obtain any effect. But the law, if it does not allow such act to stand good, or to obtain any effect, must, after we have done it, require us to undo it again. The only way of undoing it again, or of preventing the effect of it, that is, the only way of satisfying the law, is to make amends for what any person has suffered who was hurt by it, or to make reparation for the damages, which such person has sustained. The same law, therefore, which guards a man from being hurt, by requiring others not to hurt him, gives him a demand upon them, when they have done him any hurt, to undo it again, or gives him a right to demand reparation of damages.

If such reparation is refused, the law, which gives him a right to it, allows him to support this right by all such means as are necessary for that purpose: because a right which he is not at liberty to enforce and bring into execution, is, in effect, no right at all. He, therefore, who has suffered any damage by the fault of another, may, consistently with the law of nature, by the use of his strength, that is, by force, endeavour to obtain satisfaction by making reprisals upon the person who has done the damage, to the value of what he has lost.

We have already seen by what means and upon what account the property in such things, as are so taken in reprisal, will be transferred from their former owner to the person who takes them.

Imperfect right no foundation for demanding reparation.

III. * An imperfect right, as was just now observed, can be no foundation of a claim to reparation. We cannot properly be said to suffer damage in what is not our own: however reasonable our expectations of receiving a thing or a service may be, the most we can say, where they are refused us, provided they were matter of favour, and were not due to us in strict justice, is, that we are hardly or unkindly used. Indeed, in common language, a man who is very hardly or very unkindly used; who meets with no reward or encouragement of his merit from such as ought to reward or encourage him; who is not relieved in his distress by such as ought to relieve him; is said to be injured, or not to have justice done him. We sometimes go farther, and say, that his merit or his sufferings give him a claim to such or such instances of encouragement and assistance. But when we make use of these or the like expressions, upon occasions of this sort; the words injury, or justice, or claim, must not be understood in their strict and proper sense. Nothing is due to a man in strict justice; he has no strict and proper claim to any thing but what is his own: and whatever pretensions either his merit or his sufferings, may give him to the favour and assistance of others; however others may transgress their duty by not showing him such favour, or by not giving him such assistance; those pretensions, on his part, amount only to a reasonable expectation, that they should give him something which is not strictly his own, till they do give him it: and consequently the neglect or omission, on their part, cannot, in propriety of speaking, be called an injury.

Perfect and imperfect rights are sometimes confounded.

IV. But in many questions concerning what a man has suffered, whether it gives him a demand for reparation of damages or not; it will be necessary to attend carefully to the matter in dispute: because he may, in many instances, appear to have only been disappointed in what he had no more than an imperfect right to, when in fact he has been deprived of what was properly his own, and has suffered a real injury.

If we would not be misled in questions of this sort, we must distinguish between a right to a thing, or a service, and a right to ask for, or to be capable of receiving such thing or such service. The former may be an imperfect right; the giving us the thing or doing us the service may be matter of favour in the persons who have the disposal of them; so that no damage would be done us, if, upon our application, we should meet with a refusal; though it might be ever so reasonable on our part to expect; and though they might not discharge their duty as they ought to do, by not granting us what we ask for. But in the meantime the latter right, the right to ask for such favour, or to be capable of receiving it, may be a perfect one; so that whoever unjustly hinders us from asking, or renders us incapable of receiving, does us such a damage as would entitle us to reparation. If I am ever so well quali-

* Grot. Lib. II. Cap. XVII. § III.

fied for any particular office or employment, and my competitor is ever so far inferior to me in the necessary qualifications; yet if the person who has the disposal of such office, may give it to whom he pleases; it is in some sort matter of favour, that he should give it to me: and if he was to give it to my competitor, I could only complain of being unkindly used, or unfairly rejected; I should have suffered no such injury as would entitle me to reparation. But suppose that either by force or by fraud I had been hindered from applying for this favour; they, who hindered me, would have done me an injury, properly so called: my liberty of applying, or not, was strictly my own; and they who have unjustly taken it from me, or prevented me from using it, have done me damage. Indeed, in estimating this damage, I could not rate it at the full value of the favour, which I might have asked for, if they had not prevented me: because, if I had asked for it, I might possibly have been refused. What I have lost, therefore, by their injustice is not the favour itself, but the chance which I had for obtaining it: and the damages which I have sustained, are to be rated according to the value of that chance. It may be matter of favour, that a person should leave me a legacy: and however reasonable it might be in me to expect it, and however unkind or even ungrateful in him to disappoint my expectations; yet the disappointment would be no damage. But if unjust force or fraud is made use of by any one else to prevent him from doing it; he, who thus prevents him, does me an injury: the capacity of receiving this favour was my own; and to take it from me by unjust force or fraud, is properly a damage, and reparation is to be made for it. In some instances more persons than one may suffer by the same act; and though it may, in respect of some of them, be only a hardship, yet in respect of the rest it may be a real injury. If I have the care of a minor's estate as his guardian, and unkindly or unreasonably remove the steward of that estate, who had deserved well of me in all respects, and was particularly well fitted for his employment, in order to put in some other person; this would be no injury to the steward so removed, nor would it entitle him to damages: because, as the giving him this office at first was matter of favour, so it is matter of favour likewise to continue him in it. But if by this act of mine the ward is a loser; such loss is properly an injury to him: and if I did it knowingly, he would have a natural claim to reparation for the damages that he suffers by it.

Some rules to be observed in estimating damages.

V. *In estimating the damages which any one has sustained, where such things as he has a perfect right to, are unjustly taken from him, or withholden, or intercepted; we are to consider not only the value of the thing itself, but the value likewise of the fruits or profits that might have arisen from it. He, who is the owner of the thing, is likewise the owner of such fruits or profits. So that it is as properly a damage to be deprived of them, as it is to be deprived of the thing itself. But it is to be considered whether he could have received these profits without any labour or expense: because if he could not, then in settling the damage, for which reparation is to be made, the profits are not to be rated at the full worth of them; but an allowance is to be made for the labour or ex-

* Grot. Lib. II. Cap. XVII. § IV.

pense of collecting or receiving them; and when the labour and expense is deducted from their full worth, the remainder is all that he has lost, and consequently, is all that he has any right to demand.

Grotius, in estimating these damages, makes another allowance, which does not appear to have any reasonable foundation. He thinks that in making reparation for the profits arising from a thing, where the thing itself is restored, a deduction ought to be made for any improvements which it has received, whilst it was withholden from the owner. But certainly in the case of dishonest possession, whatever improvements the possessor makes in a thing, whilst he unjustly detains it from the true owner, they must be understood to be made against the consent of such owner: for it is against his consent that the other has the thing in his possession, and has an opportunity of improving it: and it would be an injury to force him to pay or to allow for what was done against his consent.

* In rating the damage which a man has sustained, we are to estimate something more than the present advantage which he has lost: for the hope or expectation of future advantage is worth something: and if such hope or expectation is cut off by the injury, the value of it is to be allowed him. We must, however, in estimating this hope, be careful not to estimate it as if the advantage had been in actual possession: proper deductions are to be made for the accidents which might have happened to disappoint his expectations. And in proportion as these accidents are greater, or more in number, or more likely to happen, a greater abatement is to be made in consideration of them. In general, the longer time there is to pass before the expected advantage can arise, the more room there is for accidents to prevent its being obtained. And for this reason, other circumstances being equal, the more remote a man's hope is, the less it is worth. Thus, in general, all other circumstances being the same, a field of corn, when it is destroyed in the blade, is worth less than if it had been in the ear.

Accessories to an injury obliged to make reparation.

VI. † Besides the person who immediately does the injury, others may be so far concerned in it, as to be under an obligation with him of making good the damages arising from it.

As far as we concur in what another man does, so far the act is our own; and the effects of it are chargeable upon us, as well as upon him: if he is considered as the principal party, we, by our concurrence, make ourselves accessories in the injury.

We may make ourselves accessories to what another man does two ways, either by our acts, or by our omissions: and in either of these ways we may be accessories in a higher or a lower degree.

They who have authority over him, that does the injury, and command the doing it; they who give their consent, when the injury could not have been done without such consent; they who assist the principal party in doing it; or they who protect and screen him after it is over, are, any of them, accessories to the injury in a higher degree, and make themselves so by their acts.

They who were obliged, in justice, to make use of their authority in forbidding the injury, and have not forbidden it; they who were

* Grot. Lib. II. Cap. XVII. § V.

† Grot. Ibid. § VI, VII, VIII, IX.

obliged, in justice, to assist him who has suffered the injury, and have not assisted him, are accessories likewise in a higher degree, and make themselves so by their omissions.

Accessories in a lower degree, are such as advise the injury, or commend and encourage him who does it. These become accessories by their acts.

Such, likewise, are accessories in a lower degree, as do not dissuade the commission of the injury, when they ought to dissuade it, or do not discover it, when they ought to discover it. These become accessories by their omissions.

Any of these, as far as they contribute towards the fact, by which the damage is done, are obliged to make reparation for it: because, so far the fact is their own, and the damage arises from them.

Damages, how to be demanded from a number of principals.

VII. *A number of men may so concur in doing damage, as to be all of them principals. In this case they are obliged, all and each of them, to make it good, if the act is such an one, as arises from each of them alone, though they happened to be altogether, when it was done, and all contributed towards the doing it; that is, if the damage which they have all done by a joint act, would have been the same, though only one of them had been concerned in it. But, if in the whole damage which is done by them all, only one part arose from one of them, and another part from another of them; then each of them is obliged for no more than his own share of the damage: because the rest of it did not arise from him.

We may explain this rule farther by distinguishing between indivisible and divisible acts. Those are called indivisible acts, in which many persons may concur: but the whole act would have been the same, though only one of them had been concerned in it. Thus, if a number of people join in setting fire to a man's stacks of corn, or in cutting a bank to drown his lands, the whole damage arises, indeed, from their joint act; but the single act of each of them would have produced the same damage. The person, therefore, who has been injured, has a demand for the whole damage upon each of them: because the whole would have been produced by the same act of each: and he has a demand for no more than the whole upon all of them together. So that if all of them can be come at, they are obliged to join in making reparation: or if only one of them can be come at, he alone is to make the whole reparation.

Where the act is a divisible one, that is, where part of the damage is done by one of the persons concerned, and part by another; so that the part which was done by the one, can be distinguished from the part which was done by the other, and without the concurrence of them all, the loss would not have been the same; in this case all of them together are obliged to make good the whole damage; but each of them alone, considered as a principal, is not obliged to make good more of it, than what arose from himself. If a man is attacked upon the road, and one person wounds him, whilst another kills his horse; the whole damage arises from both of them together, but not from each of them

* Grot. Lib. II. Cap. XVII. § XI.

alone: each, therefore, as a principal, is not obliged to make good more of the damage, than what arose from his share in the act.

Reparation due for the consequences of an unlawful act.

VIII. *Not only the damages which a man sustains from an unlawful act, are chargeable upon them who do the act; but those damages are likewise to be made amends for, which are the consequences of such act; though perhaps these consequential damages might not originally have been intended. If it was otherwise; if he who does an unlawful act, was not accountable for all the harm which arises from it, either immediately or in consequence; the whole obligation to reparation might, in most instances, be set aside, upon a pretence, that what the author of the damage originally intended, was little or no harm to the sufferer, and that all the rest arose merely from accident. A man sets fire to a tree or to a stack of straw, and in the event a house is burnt: if he was not accountable for this consequence of his act, as well as for the act itself, he might easily pretend that he did not design to do this harm, even though he did design it: and thus, for want of being able to disprove the truth of this excuse, the sufferer might lose reparation for such losses as the incendiary did really intend. His intention ought, therefore, to be judged of by what appears: and by this rule of judging, there will be reason to conclude, that such consequences of his act as might have been foreseen, and ought to have been guarded against, were in his intention, as well as the act itself.

We may put this matter in another light. All the harm that we are obliged to prevent, is justly chargeable upon us, if we do not prevent it. We are obliged to prevent all the harm that arises in consequence from an unlawful action; because we are obliged not to do the action itself. Upon this account, therefore, all the harm that arises from such an action, though by consequences which we did not directly intend, is chargeable upon us; and the reparation to be made for such harm is to be made by us who do the action.

Reparations for unjust death.

IX. †Grotius has applied these general rules concerning reparation to several particular instances. He who kills another unlawfully, is obliged to defray such expenses as the person killed may have been at in endeavouring to have his wounds cured. He is obliged likewise to make amends to those who had a right to be maintained by the deceased; such as his wife, his children, or his parents; according to the value of what they might have expected to receive from him, considering his age, his fortune, or his employment.

It may perhaps be questioned, whether they had a strict right to such maintenance or other benefits, as they might have received from the deceased: and if they had not, it may be asked, what restitution can be due for the loss of that maintenance or of those other benefits? But to this we answer, that however they might have been disappointed in their expectation, yet the expectation itself was their own, and it is a real injury to take it from them. All, therefore, which can be proved from this objection, is no more than we allow, that the reparation is to be estimated, not according to the worth of their maintenance, or of their other probable benefits, but according to the worth of their expectation.

* Grot. Lib. II. Cap. XVII. § XII.

† Grot. Ibid. § XIII.

Grotius here distinguishes between the murder of a free man and the murder of a slave: the life of the former cannot, he says, be reckoned in settling the damage done by his death; because no person has any claim to it besides himself: but the life of the latter is to be reckoned; because, if the slave had been alive, the master might have sold him; and consequently his life itself is of value to the master. But if we observe that the life of the slave can no otherwise be looked upon as the master's property, than as he had an interest in it, we shall find that there is no occasion for this distinction: since, as far as the relations of a free man had an interest in his life, the person who murdered him is obliged to make them reparation. So that in either case, in settling the damage, the life of the deceased is estimated according to the interest which those who survive him might have in it.

Reparation for maiming, wounding, beating, unjust imprisonment.

X. * He who has maimed another, does not make him full reparation for the damage sustained, unless he pays for the cure, and gives him, besides such payment, the value of what he has lost by being rendered incapable to earn so much by his labour, as he otherwise might have earned, if he had not been maimed. But these particulars, which are all that Grotius mentions, do not include the whole of the damage. He ought farther to pay for the loss of the person's time whom he maimed. Our author, indeed, adds, that if the person maimed is a slave, amends is to be made to the master for any scar or blemish, which will make the slave worth less when sold; but that in estimating the damage done to a free man, no regard is to be had to such blemish. Grotius should here have taken another particular into the account, which would have set him right in this respect, by showing him that satisfaction is to be made to a free man, as well as to the owner of a slave, for any scar or blemish arising from their being maimed. The person who is maimed has a right to freedom from causeless pain; and he who has hurt him has injured him in this right. He may, therefore, demand smart-money, or some consideration in amends for the pain which he has unjustly suffered. Now, under this head, we may fairly include any blemish which remains, after the first smart or pain is over: for as far as the injured person had a right to be free from such blemishes, or from the uneasiness which any deformity will occasion to him, he has a right to be paid for having them brought upon him. If the person who has been ill treated should escape without losing his limbs, or the use of them; yet, if he has been wounded, the expense of cure, the loss of time, the pain which he has felt, are all of them damages, for which reparation is due. Or if he has been only beaten, so that there has been no expense of cure, and no loss of time, he has still a demand of smart-money, or of satisfaction for the pain that he has felt.

What has been said concerning maiming, wounds, or blows, will be sufficient to show what sort of amends is due to a man who has been deprived of his liberty by unjust imprisonment. His loss of time is one article in the account, but it is not the only one; the mere uneasiness of such a situation, under which we may include the disgrace attending it, is a damage to him.

* Grot. Lib. II. Cap. XVII. § XIV.

Reparation for adultery, or for debauching a woman.

XI. * Grotius, in the case of adultery, takes notice of no other reparation, except that of indemnifying the injured husband from maintaining the spurious offspring, and that of securing the legitimate children against the loss which they would sustain, if the others were to share with them in the possessions of the family. But certainly neither of these particulars can be looked upon as reparation for the damages which the adulterer has done: they are rather cautions against any future damage, which might arise in consequence. The adulterer has deprived the husband of his wife's affections, has disturbed the peace and order of his family, and has brought disgrace and infamy upon it. These are the articles to be estimated in determining what reparation is to be made for the damages that have been done already.

If a woman is debauched, says our author, either by force or by fraud; he, who has so debauched her, is obliged to make amends for the advantage which she might otherwise have made by some future marriage, if he had not hurt her character. He adds, that if the man debauched her under a promise of marriage, he is obliged to make his promise good. But this obligation, one would think, arises rather from the promise itself, than from the damage done. He could not, indeed, object her want of chastity as a sufficient reason to release him from his promise: because, as her want of chastity has been owing to his own act, he cannot make use of this pretence to her disadvantage, unless he pays her, not only for having hurt her prospect of marriage in general, but likewise for her loss in not marrying him in particular.

Reparation for theft.

XII. † A thief or robber is obliged to restore what he has stolen, or an equivalent for it, with all its profits, and a compensation for the loss which followed, or the gain, which ceased to the owner for want of possession. In estimating the value of the thing and of the profits, Grotius lays it down for a rule, that they are to be rated neither at the highest, nor at the lowest, but at the middle price. However, he gives no reason, and it will be difficult to find any reason, why such a degree of favour should be shown to a man who has been guilty of theft.

Reparation for slander.

XIII. A man may be injured in his person, not only by death, imprisonment, maiming, wounds, or blows, but by scandal or defamation, which deprives him of his reputation, and casts a blemish upon his character. These damages are repaired by asking pardon, by a public acknowledgement of his innocence, and by such payments as will make him amends for the loss that he has sustained by any false aspersions.

Reparation due, where there is no malice.

XIV. The obligation to make reparation for damages done by our means, is not confined to those actions only, which are criminal enough to subject us to punishment. Though there is no degree of malice in an action, by which another is injured, yet it may arise from some faulty neglect or imprudence in him who does it, or is the occasion of its being done; and when any person has suffered damage, for want of his taking such care as he ought to have taken; the same law which obliged him, as far as he was able, to avoid doing harm to any man, cannot but oblige him, when he

* Grot. Lib. II. Cap. XVII. § XV.

† Grot. Ibid. § XVI.

has neglected this duty, to undo, as well as he can, what harm he has been the occasion of; that is, to make amends for the damage which another has sustained through his neglect.

Those faults, which consist in neglect, are sometimes divided into three degrees; a great fault, which is such a neglect, as all men may well be supposed, and ought to guard against; a small fault, which is such a neglect, as discreet and diligent men are not usually guilty of; and the smallest fault, which is such a neglect, as the most exact and most prudent take care to avoid.

Indeed, in many instances of gross faults, it is so difficult to distinguish between a mere neglect and a malicious design, that, besides the demand of reparation for damages done, some punishment may reasonably be inflicted upon the person so offending.

Sometimes, and especially in what may seem faults of the lower degrees, the damage, which arises from our supposed neglect, will be found, upon inquiry, to have been rather owing to the neglect of the person who suffers it; and then we are not only clear from all guilt that may subject us to punishment, but from all blame that might oblige us to make reparation.

A man professes some art or calling, in which he is not completely skilful, and through his want of skill, they, that employ him, suffer damage: or, supposing him to understand his business, they that employ him, may suffer the like damage, through some gross neglect of his: in either case he is obliged to make reparation. This is the case when a physician destroys his patient by administering improper medicines through ignorance, or suffers him to perish by neglect and desertion. Such faults as these are of the grosser sort, and approach so near to ill design, as not easily to be distinguished from it. * If others suffer by us, whilst we are engaged in any sport or diversion, as if a man was to be killed or maimed by our discharging a gun; notwithstanding we had no design of doing hurt to any one, and can make this appear, yet we are bound to make reparation: because we ought to have been so careful, in following our own amusement, as to prevent any damage that might happen to others, from what is merely matter of pleasure to us. If a soldier is exercising himself in an improper place, and does any hurt with his arms, it is his fault, and he must repair the damage. It would have been otherwise, if he had been in the place appointed for this purpose; because then what hurt was done by him would have been owing to their fault, who knowingly or negligently came in his way. A feller of wood kills a man who is passing upon a road or near a town, with the limb of a tree, which he is cutting down, without giving notice that it was falling: this is his neglect, and reparation is due from him. But if he did give notice, and the person, upon whom the limb of the tree fell, neglected to get out of the way, he is not chargeable with the damage done. Nor could he have been chargeable with it, even though he had given no notice, if he had been felling wood at a distance from the road or in the middle of the field: because the other person would have been in fault for having been there. The damage which a man's servants do, is, in many instances, chargeable upon himself: because he ought to take care that they

* Puffendorf, Book III. Cap. I. § VII.

should behave better. If a traveller loses goods in an inn, where he lodges; the master of the house ought to repair the loss: because a discreet and diligent man would take care to provide himself with honest servants, and would prevent whatever was under his charge from being stolen. If the traveller had locked up his goods in his own apartment, there would not be the same reason for charging the loss of them upon the master of the house: because the traveller has then taken the care and security of them upon himself; and if they are lost, it is but reasonable to consider them as lost through his own neglect: especially, as there would otherwise be room for collusion between him and others, who might take them away with his privacy. When any thing which is thrown out from a window, does any damage to persons passing by in the street; the master of the house, from whence it is thrown, is chargeable with it: he is certainly in fault, if he threw it out himself: and he is in some fault, though some one else threw it out: because he ought to take better care of the behaviour of his family. The damage which a man's beasts do, may reasonably be looked upon as done by himself: because it is his business to take care that they shall be kept in good order. Indeed, if they were put into their proper place, and have gotten into the grounds of another man, because this other does not keep up his fences; the damage is done through the neglect of the owner of the grounds, and not through the neglect of the owner of the cattle. In like manner, if a man was passing through grounds where there was no common path or way, and where he had no business, and should be wounded or maimed by a horse or an ox which were in the pasture of their owner; the fault is in the person so hurt; because he ought not to have been there.

CHAPTER XVIII.

OF PUNISHMENT.

I. *Punishment, what.*—II. *Justice of punishment depends upon the ends of it.*—III. *What those ends are.*—IV. *The justice of punishment explained.*—V. *Extraordinary tortures in capital punishments unjust.*—VI. *Obligations arising from a crime, what.*—VII. *The justice of punishment is negative.*—VIII. *Who may punish in a state of natural liberty.*—IX. *What crimes punishable by man in the liberty of nature.*—X. *What guilt is.*—XI. *How guilt is estimated.*—XII. *Measure of punishment, how adjusted.*—XIII. *Mercy or clemency, how exercised.*—XIV. *How the goods of a criminal are affected by punishment.*—XV. *Accessories to a crime punishable.*—XVI. *Those, who have no share in a crime, not punishable.*—XVII. *Obligation to punishment does not descend from the ancestor to the heir.*

Punishment, what. I. * A CRIME, as it does damage, obliges the criminal to make reparation; and as it shows a disposition to do harm, it makes him liable to be punished.

* Grotius, Lib. II. Cap. XX. § I.

By punishment, we understand some evil of suffering, which is inflicted upon account of some evil of doing. It is some pain or uneasiness, some loss or harm, which he, who has designedly occasioned any pain or uneasiness, any loss or harm to others, is made to undergo.

Justice of punishment depends upon the ends of it.

II. * Grotius lays it down as a self-evident principle, that he, who has done evil, may justly be made to suffer evil. If this principle was as clear and indisputable, as our author supposes it to be; one of the greatest difficulties relating to punishment would be removed. It would be ridiculous to inquire, why it is just to punish a criminal; if the justice of making a man suffer harm, who had done harm, was self-evident.

† He does not seem, however, to be quite satisfied in his own mind, that this principle will entirely justify us in punishing criminals. The most that he thinks can be proved from it, is, that no injury is done to a criminal by punishing him: but yet, he says, it does not follow from hence, that criminals are to be punished.

It is not very easy here to understand his meaning. If by saying it does not follow from this principle, that criminals are to be punished, he means, it does not follow, that we are obliged, in duty, to inflict punishment upon criminals; this is very certain. But his inquiries concerning punishment, might, notwithstanding this difficulty, have stopped at this first principle, if the principle had been self-evidently true: it may not, perhaps, be sufficient to prove, that inflicting punishment is a duty: but let him carry his inquiries as far as he will into the ends of punishment, he will still find the same defect, if it is a defect, in all other principles. Neither the supposed self-evidence of its being lawful to make them suffer evil, who have done evil, nor any of the ends proposed in punishing will prove that we are naturally obliged, in duty, to punish a criminal. But if, when he says, it is no consequence of his principle that criminals are to be punished, he means, that notwithstanding there is no injury in making those suffer evil, who have done evil, it is no consequence, that they may be punished, consistently with the law of nature; he plainly contradicts himself: if there is no injury in punishing criminals, it must, undoubtedly, be consistent with the law of nature to punish them.

To reconcile him with himself, we must suppose him to mean, that though the punishment of a criminal is self-evidently consistent with the law of justice, yet we ought to inquire farther, whether the law of benevolence or humanity does not forbid it: because, as some pain or loss is contained in the notion of punishment; such pain or loss would be a sufficient reason against inflicting it; if no advantage arose from it, or no beneficial purposes were answered by it.

But then these beneficial purposes are as necessary to be taken into the account, in order to reconcile the notion of a right to inflict punishment with the duties of justice, as to reconcile the actual inflicting of it with the duties of humanity. All causeless harm or loss, that we bring upon another, is unjust: and if punishment is not intended in its own nature to obtain some useful end; I see not how we shall be able to show, that the loss or harm implied in it is not causeless harm. Upon the whole, then, it seems necessary for us, in vindicating the justice

* Grot. Lib. II. Cap. XX. § I.

† Grot. Ibid. § IV.

of punishment, to consider the ends which are proposed by it: since the principle, which Grotius lays down as a self-evident one, cannot be shown to be true, without having recourse to the purposes, which punishment is is designed to answer.

The ends of punishment, what they are.

III. * Our author takes notice of three ends, which are designed to be brought about by inflicting punishment; first, the benefit of the criminal himself; secondly, the benefit of the person who has suffered by the crime; and thirdly, the benefit of mankind in general.

The two last of these may well be included in the single end of preventing the criminal from offending again: for by this means the benefit either of the injured person, or of the rest of mankind, is produced as effectually as the punishment of the criminal can produce it, if we look no farther than the criminal himself.

Punishment has, indeed, sometimes a farther view, and is designed, not only to prevent or discourage the criminal who undergoes it, from offending again, but to deter others likewise from following his example, for fear of meeting with the same treatment, that he has met with. But this is only a secondary end of punishment; it may, where a criminal has deserved to suffer, make it prudent not to pardon him, and may engage us likewise to punish him in a public manner. But if our right to punish had nothing else to support it, we should never be able to reconcile it either with justice or with humanity. For certainly to bring any harm or loss upon one man, that we may not suffer the like from others, is, in respect of him upon whom it is brought, no better than a causeless harm or loss.

The first end of punishment, which Grotius mentions, is likewise but a secondary one. If there is no other reason for inflicting punishment, besides the amendment of the criminal; this alone is not sufficient to justify it, when men live out of civil society. In the liberty and equality of nature every man's interests are in his own hands; he may pursue his own good, or he may neglect it, at his own discretion. Others may advise him what course to take, as most for his benefit; but if he should choose to neglect his own benefit, they have no right to force him to pursue it; unless by his neglecting it they suffer some injury. Thus far, indeed, in the equality of nature, the amendment of the criminal comes within the view of them who punish him: they have a right, as we shall show presently, when he has done them any injury, to hinder him from doing so again: and as his amendment will answer this purpose, they may endeavour to correct his bad disposition, or may compel him to follow his own interest, in order to restrain him from breaking in upon theirs.

From what has been said it will appear, that the primary end of punishment is to prevent the criminal from offending again. And that the two secondary ends of it are to amend the criminal, and to deter others from following his example.

The justice of punishment explained.

IV. Whilst a man takes care to live innocently, whilst he observes his duty so as not to hurt any one; we have no pretence to demand any security of him, that he will not hurt us. The law of nature is our security: he shows,

* Grot. Lib. II. Cap. XX. § VI.

by his behaviour, that he is sensible of his obligation to observe this law, and that it has authority enough with him to prevent him from doing wrong. But when he has once done wrong, when he has transgressed this law, and has shown, by doing so, either that it has no authority at all with him, or not sufficient authority to secure us against suffering by his means; it then becomes lawful for us to punish him; that is, it then becomes just, upon account of the evil which he has done, to inflict such evil upon him, as will prevent him from doing the like again. We cannot suppose the law of nature to forbid our taking such measures with a man, as his conduct has made necessary for us to take, in order to obtain the end, which the law itself has in view. The law of nature intends to secure us against injuries. When, therefore, a man has shown us, by his conduct, that he is disposed to injure us; this law leaves us at liberty to use such means as are necessary to prevent him.

The ways, by which we may prevent him from doing harm again, are by taking from him either the will to do it, or the opportunities of doing it, or the power of doing it. If we make him undergo some corporal pain, submit to some disgrace, or suffer some loss; this may discourage him from offending again, or may take from him the will to do harm. If we shut him up in prison, or employ him in constant labour, or force him to live at a distance from us, which in a state of civil society would be banishment, he will have few or no opportunities of hurting us. Death, which is called capital punishment, effectually puts it out of his power to offend.

The reader, I imagine, does by this time see clearly, what sort of a right over the criminal our right of punishing is, and for what reason some previous crime is requisite to give us such a right. Our right of punishing is nothing more than a liberty of using such means, as are necessary to secure us against suffering any farther harm from a person, who, by having done harm already, has shown himself disposed to do it, if we do not take care to prevent him. But till he has shown himself to be thus disposed by what he has done already; that is, till he has committed a crime, we have no such right over him. All force that we make use of against him, all harm that we designedly do him, upon pretence of compelling him to observe his duty, when he always has observed it, or of preventing him from transgressing his duty, when he never has transgressed it, is unjust force, and causeless harm.

Upon the whole, as on the one hand, no punishment can be just, where there is no crime; so, on the other hand, it would be impossible to show, even after a crime has been committed, that we have a right to punish, or that punishment is just, unless we show it from considering the end, for which it is inflicted.

Extraordinary tortures in capital punishments unjustifiable.

V. If the right of punishment is what I have represented it above; if it is a liberty of using such means as are necessary to secure us against suffering any farther harm from a person, who, by having done harm already, has shown himself disposed to do it, unless we take care to prevent him; it will be no easy matter, where we punish capitally, to justify any extraordinary tortures in the manner of taking away the criminal's life; such as impaling, crucifixion, or breaking on the wheel.

The corporal pain, which a criminal is made to undergo, is not unjust, where his life is spared: because such pain may correct his bad inclination, and, by taking from him the will to do harm, may serve to secure us against his doing any for the future. But, certainly, when we take away his life, any pain that we give him, which might have been avoided, is so much causeless harm done to him. There is no occasion for this sort of discipline to be used in order to correct his evil diposition, when, by putting him to death, we take away from him the power of hurting us. The only use, that can be pretended in defence of such cruelties, is, that they will be a terror to others, who seeing what they are to suffer, if they do as he has done, will be more likely to be kept from doing so. And it must be owned that this purpose, where we find it necessary to be pursued, will be sufficient to justify us in carrying our right of punishing to the utmost extent; in not pardoning, where we should otherwise have been disposed to pardon; in allowing the criminal as little time, as may be, to fortify himself against the apprehension of death; in making his punishment as public as possible; in exposing his body or mangling it, after it is dead or insensible, and is by that means incapable of suffering any real harm.

But however we may design to terrify others; a right to use such means, as the criminal's behaviour has made necessary for us to use, in order to secure ourselves against any future harm which he may do us, cannot possibly be construed to be a right to use him in such a manner, as we may think necessary, in order to secure ourselves against any future harm which other men may do us. Nor do I see upon what other principle such a practice can be justified; unless it could be shown, that a right to punish is a right to treat a criminal in what manner we please.

Obligation arising from a crime, what.

VI. We have seen what right arises over a man's person upon account of his having committed a crime: and it is plain, from the nature of the right on one part, what obligation it lays upon him on the other part. A right in others to use such means as are likely to hinder him from doing harm again; that is, a right in them to punish him, implies an obligation on him to submit to punishment: for if he had any right, or was naturally at liberty to resist punishment, they could not naturally have any right to inflict it.

The justice of punishment is negative.

VII. * When justice is divided, as Grotius divides it, into expletive and attributive; it may be a question to which of these two sorts punishment belongs. If the whole notion of justice is included in this division of it, our common ways of speaking seem to imply, that punishment belongs to one of these two sorts, or that either expletive or attributive justice is exercised, when we inflict punishment. There is, certainly, the appearance of exercising some sort of justice, when we say, that punishment is justly due to a crime, and that we have done justice by inflicting it.

Now, expletive justice, or justice properly so called, consists in satisfying a man's strict demands, or in taking care that he shall have what is strictly due to him. And attributive justice, which differs little or nothing from benevolence, consists in giving him all that he has

* Grot. Lib. II. Cap. XX. § II.

fair and reasonable grounds to expect from us, though he cannot properly demand it.

Punishment can scarce be thought to belong to this latter sort of justice; not only because there is no appearance of any benevolent affection in punishment; but likewise because punishment, instead of giving the criminal what he could not claim, takes from him something, which he otherwise might have claimed; it takes from him his life, or his liberty, or the use of his limbs, or his natural freedom from pain.

One would rather be inclined to think, at first sight, that it belongs to expletive justice; the common ways of speaking about it already mentioned, would lead us to think so. And yet we shall find, upon inquiry, that these are rather improper ways of speaking: because the criminal has no claim to punishment, or such a claim as we may be sure he very willingly gives up; so as to make it no injustice to him, no withholding of any thing which he demands, if we were not to punish him. If expletive justice is done to any one in punishing, it is to them, who inflict the punishment, and not to him, who undergoes it: their right and not his is satisfied by what he suffers.

The fact is, that justice, in the original notion of it, is a negative duty; it consists in doing no causeless harm, and implies rather the not doing what is wrong, than the actual doing what is right. But out of this negative duty, a positive one arises: the same law which forbids us to do any causeless harm, must be understood to command us, where any one has suffered such harm by our means, to make him reparation. Now, though expletive justice, in its full extent, comprehends both the negative and the positive duties of justice; yet it is more commonly used to signify the duties of the latter sort, those duties of justice, in which we are active. And in this sense we may venture to say, that expletive justice is not exercised in punishing; the act of punishing does not satisfy any demand which the criminal had upon us. The justice of punishment is rather of the negative sort; it is called just only because it is not unjust; it is rather the not doing what is wrong, than the doing what is right. But as the inflicting punishment implies some action, and is not merely a forbearance to act: we are apt to consider the justice of it, as of the positive, and not as of the negative sort; to call it doing justice upon the criminal, or giving him what is his due, though in fact it is no more than not doing him injustice, or not taking from him any thing, which his crime has left him a claim to, if we have a mind to take it from him.

Who may punish in a state of natural liberty.

VIII. If it was at all necessary, that he, who punishes a criminal, should be superior to the criminal, it must, in a state of natural liberty, have been unlawful for any one to punish another; or though there is no injustice in the notion of inflicting punishment, considered in itself, yet in the equality of nature, no person, for want of the necessary superiority, could justly have inflicted it: however lawful the action of punishing might be, when considered abstractedly from the agent; yet the institution of civil authority would be necessary to make it lawful for any person to do that action. But from what has been proved already, it will appear, that no such superiority of the person, who inflicts punishment over him, who suffers it, can be naturally required to make the action of punishing lawful in respect of the agent. Mankind in general, and he in particular, who has suffered by a crime, have an interest in restraining such injustice, as they are all likely to suffer by at another time, if it is not restrained. It is for the common good, that whoever will not listen to the dictates of reason, and obey the law of nature, in consideration of its ordinary sanctions, should be compelled to do his duty, or be prevented from transgressing it, either by being made to feel such pain and inconvenience, in consequence of the mischief which he has done, as will incline him to behave better, or by being deprived of the opportunities or of the power to do otherwise. From this beneficial end of punishment we have shown, that the law of nature allows of punishment, or leaves all mankind at liberty to inflict it: and it is impossible, that all mankind should be at liberty to inflict punishment, and yet that it should, at the same time, be unlawful for any of them to inflict it.

* Some inconveniences might probably arise in the exercise of this universal right to punish, when the punishment is inflicted by the person, who is the immediate sufferer by what the criminal has done. His passions may be so much inflamed by what he has felt, as to mislead him in judging of the fact, and in proportioning the punishment to the guilt of it: or if he should be more calm, and not be transported by the more violent passions; yet he would be liable to be biassed in his judgment by some selfish regards; few men being so little prejudiced in their own favour, as to be fair judges in their own cause.

Nor would the exercise of this right be without its inconveniences, if it was left promiscuously to others, who are not so immediately affected by the crime. A promiscuous right to punish is not likely to be duly exercised; even setting aside the consideration of passion and selfishness. It requires more dilligence to search into the fact, more prudence to weigh all its circumstances, and more equity to proportion the punishment to it, than most men are masters of. Besides, as it would be unjust to punish a man twice, or oftener, for the same offence; that is, to restrain him by force from offending again, when he has been restrained already; so amongst a multitude of punishers it would be unlikely, that he should escape with being punished only once: because it is unlikely, that where all have an equal right, the rest should acquiesce in what any one of them has done; or that they should all pay such a deference to the diligence, and prudence, and equity of any one, as not to dispute his pretensions to inflict the punishment in preference to themselves.

But the inconveniences which may attend the exercise of a right, are no evidence, that such a right does not subsist: men may have a right of acting, notwithstanding it is possible for them frequently to abuse this right. If it was otherwise, we must be beholden to civil institutions, not only for the right of punishing, but for the rights of defence, and of demanding reparation: since either of these two rights are as likely to be abused as the right of punishing, where men are judges in their own cause. All that will follow from its being more probable that the right of punishing should be abused in the liberty of nature, than in a state of civil society, is no more than what might be

* Grot. Lib. II. Cap. XX. § VIII, IX.

proved by many other arguments, that the institution of magistrates, with civil power, is for the general benefit of mankind.

What crimes are punishable by men in the equality of nature.

IX. We shall find, in our future inquiries, that many actions become so criminal, in a state of civil society, as to be punishable, which in the equality of nature men have no right to punish. At present we shall consider only what crimes are punishable by man, in a state of nature, before any civil connections were made, or any positive laws were instituted.

* If the foundation of our right to punish has been truly laid, it will be obvious, that no crimes are punishable by mankind, but such as do harm; that is, none but such as contain in them some notion of injustice towards mankind. From whence it follows, that the only actions which we have a right to punish in the liberty of nature, are those, which are naturally unjust.

If a man is void of benevolence, or wholly disinclined to do us good; this is a breach of his duty indeed; but it is such a breach, as must be left to the great author of the law of nature to punish, who will undoubtedly take effectual care to vindicate the authority of his own laws: for what right can we have to make a man suffer for not doing what we had no right to demand of him: however reasonable it might be for us to expect it from him?

The law of nature commands men to be chaste and temperate; and he who established that law, will punish the breach of it. But if a man's lewdness or intemperance were to hurt no one but himself, it does not appear, that any man has a right to restrain him by force from following such evil courses.

The existence of a God is written throughout every part of nature in such legible characters; and the duty of honouring him is so plain to every capacity; that they, who disbelieve his existence, or deny him that honour, which is due to him, cannot but be understood to offend against the clearest precepts of the law of nature: they must be wilfully blind, if they do not see their duty, and perversely criminal, if they do not practice it. But till we have a right to demand, that men should believe this obvious truth, and practice this plain duty; that is, till we are some way or other hurt, or some real injustice is done us by the contrary; it does not appear, that we have a right to punish those who disbelieve the one, or refuse to practice the other. Civil connections, when we are united into societies, may give us this right, as shall be shown in its proper place, they may make either atheism or irreligion punishable by us; but it will be difficult to make out, that we have any such right in the liberty of nature.

Indeed, whenever a man's want of benevolence changes, as it commonly does, into a want of justice; whenever his lewdness is attended, as it almost always is, with some harm to mankind; whenever his intemperance leads him to injure them; and whenever his irreligion is attended with its usual consequence of making him hurtful to them; as even in the liberty of nature they have a right to demand a contrary behaviour of him, they have a right likewise to use such means, as are necessary to make his behaviour what it ought to be, or to prevent it from being otherwise.

* Grot. Lib. II. Cap. XX. § XVIII, XIX, XX.

Grotius maintains, that one man is not punishable by another for any criminal intentions of any sort, not even when these intentions come to be known by some subsequent confession. And certainly the reason of the thing is on his side. The mere intentions of a man, whilst he keeps them to himself, cannot be punishable; because they are not known. And a subsequent confession of such intentions implies, that they are laid aside, before they are made public: in which case there can be no right of punishing; because there can be no right to restrain a man from doing an injury, where we have sufficient evidence, that he has already restrained himself.

We may add, that if by any means we come to the knoweledge of his intentions; whilst they subsist, but have not yet been put into execution; we have no right to punish him for them: because the proper notion of punishment is an evil inflicted upon account of some crime, which has been actually committed: and whilst the crime remains in the intention, it is not actually committed, it is only beginning. However, in these circumstances, though we have no right of punishing, we have a right of defence, which is a right of doing much the same thing under a different name.

Our author mentions another sort of crimes, which he says, are not punishable by man, and calls them such crimes, as human nature cannot avoid. It is not easy to imagine what crimes he had in his mind, when he gave them this general character. No action can be criminal, if it is not possible for a man to do otherwise. An unavoidable crime is a contradiction: whatever is unavoidable is no crime; and whatever is a crime is not unavoidable. If, indeed, he only meant, that where a criminal act is proposed to a man, though he may have a natural power of avoiding it, yet, if he is threatened, in case he will not do it, with such an evil as human nature cannot well bear up against, this circumstance will greatly abate, if not wholly remove the guilt of his compliance; this opinion can scarce be contradicted. But then an inquiry of this sort would have been made more properly, where he is treating of the manner, in which the guilt of a crime is to be estimated, than where he is enumerating the several sorts of crimes, which are not punishable by man.

What guilt is. X. Guilt is sometimes defined to be the obligation, which a man is under, to submit to punishment, in consequence of any crime that he has committed. But this, one would think, cannot be a true definition of it; at least it does not suit at all with our common ways of speaking about guilt. We commonly speak of guilt, as if it was capable of being greater or less: whereas, the obligation to punishment does not admit of degrees; there is no medium between being obliged and not obliged. And certainly, if this is all that we mean by guilt, many propositions relating to punishment, which we frequently hear, and which seem to have some sense in them, must be very trifling and uninstructive. When a man is said to deserve punishment upon account of his guilt; the meaning would be, if this was the true notion of guilt, that he deserves punishment, because he is obliged to submit to it. And it would be still more uninstructive to say, as we sometimes do, that a man is obliged to submit to punishment upon account of his guilt: for this would amount to no more than if we had said, that he is therefore obliged to submit to punishment, because he is obliged to submit to it.

Let us try, whether we cannot find out some other definition of guilt, which will explain the notion of it with more exactness. Now, it seems to be an agreed point, that guilt is that quality in a criminal, which deserves punishment, or which gives mankind a right to punish him. By attending, therefore, to the foundation of our natural right to punish, we may, perhaps, be able to find out, what that quality in the criminal is, which makes him deserve it. Mankind have a right to punish any person, or he deserves punishment at their hands, when his actions have shown them, that he has a disposition to injure them, or to do them harm, unless they take care, by forcible means, to prevent him from doing it. This disposition, therefore, is what makes the criminal deserve punishment: and, consequently, as far as men are concerned in punishing, we may define guilt to be a disposition to do harm, which has shown itself by some actual harm already done.

How guilt is estimated.

XI. *The guilt of a man is greater or less in proportion as his disposition to do harm, appearing from some harm already done, is stronger or weaker. Now, there are two ways of judging how strong or how weak this disposition is; first, from considering the nature of the crime itself, and secondly, from considering the circumstances of the criminal.

Guilt, according to the notion of it just now explained, is undoubtedly a personal quality; because the disposition to offend is in the criminal, and not in the crime. However, for the sake of speaking more distinctly upon this subject, I shall take the liberty, when we estimate the guilt of a person from considering the crime itself, which he has committed, to call it the guilt of the crime; and when we estimate it from considering the circumstances of the person who commits a crime, I shall call it the guilt of the criminal.

In general the guilt of a crime is estimated by the evil or harm which it does; not because guilt properly consists in such harm; but because any person's disposition to do harm is stronger or weaker in proportion to the greatness or the smallness of the harm which he can bring himself to do. The harm which others suffer by the crime of any person, is the immediate reason, why he should not have committed it: so that he who does more or greater harm, breaks through stronger reasons forbidding what he does, than he who does less harm: and the stronger reasons there are against offending, the stronger disposition to offend there must be in him, who can get over them. In short, there is so little difference between a disposition to do great harm, and a great disposition to do harm, that one of them may very well be looked upon as the measure of the other. Since, therefore, the guilt of a crime consists in the disposition to do harm, which the criminal shows by committing it; and since this disposition is greater or less in proportion to the harm which is done by the crime; the consequence is, that the guilt of a crime follows the same proportion; it is greater or less, according as the crime, in its own nature, does greater or less harm. Thus, as murder deprives a man, not only of all his present happiness, but of the possibility likewise of obtaining any fu-

* Grot. Lib. II. Cap. XX. § XXVIII, XXIX, &c.

ture happiness in this world; it does him the greatest possible harm, and is, therefore, considered as a crime of the greatest guilt. The divine author of the Mosaic law places adultery in the next degree of guilt to murder; as it does a man the greatest harm that he can suffer, next to that of losing his life, by robbing him of all his domestic joy and comfort. Theft, which takes from a man some of the means of happiness by taking from him his goods, implies much harm in it towards him who suffers such a loss, and consequently a disposition to do much harm in them, who are the authors of it: the guilt, therefore, of this crime being estimated by the rule here laid down, though it does not rise so high as that of murder, is little inferior to that of adultery. False aspersions, by which a man is injured in his character or credit, may, and frequently do produce considerable harm to him; they are, therefore, crimes of some guilt: but because the harm is less certain, the guilt of such crimes is less than that of the crimes before mentioned.

There are some circumstances attending the criminal act itself, which will aggravate the guilt of it; such as impiety towards a parent, inhumanity towards a friend, or ingratitude towards a benefactor. The want of piety, or of humanity, or of gratitude, does not, indeed, seem to be punishable in itself, where men live in the liberty of nature: but if murder, or adultery, or theft, or slander, are attended with such circumstances; the guilt of these crimes is reasonably esteemed to be much greater than it would have been otherwise: because, where the same harm is done, a man's hurtful disposition must be greater, if he not only breaks through the obligations of justice, but such obligations likewise, as would, if he had listened to them, have engaged him to hold directly the opposite conduct, to advance the good and welfare of those, to whom he has done evil.

Thus far we have seen how the guilt of a crime is to be estimated: in which estimation we consider only the act itself, and the circumstances of it. But when an act is done by some particular person, in order to determine his degree of guilt, regard must be had to the situation and circumstances of the agent, as well as to the nature and circumstances of the act. What is chiefly to be considered in respect of the agent, relates either to his knowledge, or to his freedom. As his understanding is more clearly informed, and enables him to see his duty more plainly; or as his will is less forcibly restrained, and enables him to perform his duty more readily; his guilt, in transgressing that duty is so much the greater. He must have the strongest disposition to offend, who offends against the clearest evidence, and with the fewest restraints upon his freedom of choice. On the contrary, as entire and invincible ignorance of what ought not to be done, or an absolute impossibility of doing otherwise, would clear a man of all guilt; so in proportion as he is nearer to such a state as this, his guilt will be less. That where the same crime is committed by different persons, their guilt should be considered as greater or less, in proportion as their knowledge and freedom were greater or less, seems to be agreeable to the common notions of mankind. When a person is driven by some great provocation to commit a crime, or when he is tempted to commit it in order to avoid some great evil, which he could not otherwise have easily avoided; these are generally looked upon as circumstances in his favour, which lessen his guilt. But if a reason was to be asked, why these circumstances should have such an effect; no reason can be given for it, but what is taken from the principle here advanced: the provocation which he received, or the temptation which he was under, have, either by clouding his understanding, prevented him from seeing his duty, or by putting a force upon his will, prevented him from performing it. And in proportion as his view of what he is obliged to is less distinct, or his liberty of doing it is more restrained, his acts, however criminal they may be in themselves, have so much the less guilt in them, when considered as done by him in these circumstances: because they do not arise so much from any disposition in him to do harm, as from his ignorance, or his restraint, from his want of understanding, or his want of freedom.

But then it is to be remembered, that if ignorance or restraint are admitted in alleviation of a man's guilt, as rendering his act in some sort the result of necessity, rather than of his own disposition to offend, this ignorance or restraint must be such as have not originally been owing to himself. An involuntary act, if the necessity which drives us to it, was brought upon us at first by our own free choice, must, in all reason, be considered as a voluntary act. Thus, though madness might clear a man from any guilt in what he does, yet drunkenness, notwithstanding he, who is drunk, may be really mad for the time, would be no alleviation of it. If a man is provoked by blows and other ill usage to kill the person, from whom he receives them, whilst the smart is upon him; such a provocation may be thought to lessen his guilt; but if he, by striking the first blow, was the occasion of what followed; his guilt would not be lessened by what he felt himself at the time of committing the fact, and by the provocation to commit it, which he brought upon himself.

Measure of punishment, how adjusted.

XII. By these rules we may be assisted in judging how far the guilt of one person exceeds the guilt of another, not only where they have committed different crimes, but likewise where they have committed the same crime. But in judging what punishment should be inflicted upon a criminal, another comparison may be thought necessary, a comparison between the guilt of the criminal and the evil which is to be inflicted upon him; that we may from thence be enabled to proportion the punishment to the guilt.

It is commonly said to be a proper rule of justice, that as much as the guilt of one person exceeds the guilt of another, so much the punishment of the former should exceed the punishment of the latter. If there was no other exception to this rule, yet it certainly does not come up to the point in question. For in this proportion guilt is compared with guilt, and punishment with punishment: whereas, the question is, what rule we are to observe in comparing guilt with punishment. However clear we may think it, that of two persons who have committed different crimes, and in different circumstances, he is to bear the greater punishment, whose guilt is the greater, and he the less punishment, whose guilt is the less; this rule will never help us in determining what particular sort or degree of punishment is to be inflicted upon either of them. We may know, certainly, that theft is a crime of greater guilt than slander; and, consequently, that in like circumstances, a thief may justly be punished more than a slanderer.

But after we know this, the most material inquiry still remains undetermined: it will still be a question, whether theft is to be punished with death, or maiming, or slavery, or imprisonment, or whipping. There seems likewise to be a farther exception against this rule, which will prevent it from being universally applicable. The exception is, that amongst many crimes, all of which deserve death, the guilt of some is greater than the guilt of others. And if death is a just punishment for the least of these crimes, it is impossible to apply this rule in punishing the others, which are greater: for the rule directs us to rise in our punishment, as the guilt of the crime increases: whereas, when the lowest of these crimes is punished with death, it will be impossible to rise higher in our punishment, though the guilt of the other crimes is greater. If theft deserves death, how are we to punish a murderer? if murder deserves death, how are we to punish parricide?—you may think to answer this objection by surmising, that no crime is to be punished with death except murder. But certainly there are many other crimes which betray such an evil disposition in the person who commits them, that nothing less than capital punishment can secure us against him. And if you have a due regard to the authority which established the Mosaic law, you will find that your surmise is not well supported, and that God himself directed other crimes, besides murder, to be punished with death. Or if neither of these considerations will show you, how little is to be said in favour of your opinion, you may ask yourself, whether murder is in all cases a crime of the same guilt? or to speak more properly whether the guilt of parricide is not greater than the guilt of simple murder? If, then, simple murder is to be punished with death, we may go back to the question just now asked, how will you punish parricide? It is to be hoped that you, who are so mild in your opinion, as to the proper punishment of other crimes, would not be so cruel in punishing parricide, as to think of adding tortures to death. Or if you should think of doing so, you ought to be informed that your rule, if it would lead you to this, can never be a just one. We may torture, where we spare life, in hopes of amending the criminal's bad disposition; or we may take away life, where there is no hopes of his amendment: but to take away life, which is an effectual security against his offending again, and at the same time to torture, when death has made it impossible for us to amend him, is no better than an unwarrantable cruelty.

Another rule which seems, in some sort, to be drawn from the primary end of punishment, is, that the evil which the criminal is made to suffer, should be equal to the evil which he has done. As the end of punishing him is to prevent him from doing the like again; we may think it likely, that by putting him into the place of the sufferer, and making him feel what he has made the other feel, he may be taught, by his own experience, how grievous it is to be born, and may by these means be brought to do so no more. It is, I suppose, some such rule as this, which they may have in view, who seem to be of opinion, that no crime, besides murder, ought to be punished with death. And as they seem to think it a merciful or rather a favourable rule, so there are others, on the contrary, who charge the law of Moses with excessive cruelty for establishing retaliation in some few instances. When these latter speak of the penalty of an eye for an eye and a tooth for a tooth, of burning for burning, wound for wound, stripe for stripe; they ask, in their usual style of declamation, whether any thing can be imagined more inhuman, than for a man who has lost his eye or his tooth in the heat of a quarrel, to go in cool blood and thrust out the eye or the tooth of his neighbour? But before they impeach the Mosaic law of inhumanity for establishing such a penalty, they would do well to inform themselves, whether by that law it was not necessary, that there should be some malice in the criminal who had defaced a man, in order to subject him to the penalty of retaliation: and if this was necessary, we may reply to them, not only that what they talk about the heat of passion can be no more than declamation; but that other law-makers have found great reason to carry the punishment for crimes of this sort much higher, and to make the malicious maiming or defacing a man capital. But be this as it will; certainly retaliation, however proper it may be in some instances, cannot be the universal standard of punishment. In some instances such a punishment is impracticable, in others it would be indecent and criminal. An incendiary, who has no houses or but few goods of his own, cannot be made to suffer the same evil which he has brought upon those, whose houses or whose goods of great value he has maliciously burned. Forgery of a will, in the liberty of nature, or treason against the state in civil society, could not be punished by retaliation. The same may be said of an adulterer, who has no wife of his own; and if he had one, this sort of punishment, whilst it endeavoured to correct a crime in one person, would engage others in the same crime. We need not enumerate any more instances: these, that have been mentioned, will be sufficient to satisfy the reader, that we must look for some other measure of punishment, besides this of retaliation.

We cannot easily find a better measure than what the end of punishing suggests to us. Where we have sufficient evidence from previous facts, that a man is disposed to injure us; the law of nature allows us to provide for our future security, by enforcing the criminal's duty upon him, or by so restraining him, as to leave him either no opportunity or no power to transgress it. This is the end proposed in punishment, which justifies us in inflicting it. And certainly the measure or degree in which we may punish, can only be determined by that end, which justifies us in punishing in any degree. Such degrees of punishment, therefore, are consistent with the law of nature, as are found to be necessary for obtaining that security against the criminal, which the law of nature allows us to require. The proper degree of punishment, if it is to be regulated by this principle, plainly admits of some latitude. The law of nature does not fix any precise point, below which we cannot fall, without inflicting it in too low a degree, and above which we cannot rise, without inflicting it in too high a degree. On the one hand, indeed, there is no hazard of doing wrong: for as punishment is only allowed and not prescribed by the law of nature; a man's right to inflict it, in the liberty of nature, is entirely his own to make what abatements in it he pleases. But on the other hand, by inflicting too high a punishment we may exceed what is allowable: because we are allowed to inflict no more than our future security against suffering by the criminal requires: the right of punishing, though it is a man's own, to make such abatements in it, as his prudence and clemency may recommend to him, is not his own to carry to any rigour or severity, that passion or revenge may prompt him to.

Mercy or clemency, how exercised. XIII. * There are two ways in which mercy or clemency may exert itself in regard to the punishment of criminals. It may either remit the whole punishment, and then it is called forgiveness or pardoning; or else, in the latitude of punishing, it may engage us to try the lowest degree, in order to see how far this will answer the purpose, before we proceed as far as we lawfully might.

If, indeed, the law of nature enjoined, that punishment should follow a crime, it would be contrary to our duty to pardon a criminal. But since this law only allows us to punish; or since punishment is naturally just, only because the law of nature does not forbid it; we are left at liberty to judge for ourselves, whether we shall inflict or remit it.

It is a mere fallacy to urge, that punishment is naturally due to a crime, and consequently that a just man, as he gives all men their due, cannot, consistently with this character, remit a punishment, or withhold it from the criminal. For when punishment is said to be naturally due to a criminal, we certainly cannot mean that the criminal has a right to demand it: we choose, indeed, to speak affirmatively, and say, that it is due to him in justice; whilst our meaning is a negative one, whilst we only mean, that no precept of justice is transgressed, nothing which is due to him is either taken or withholden from him, when he is made to suffer for what he has done. A just man, therefore, may be obliged, if he would act up to this character, so to give all men what is their due, as not to withhold from them any thing which they have a right to demand: but it does not follow that he is obliged to punish a criminal who is in his power; because, as the criminal has no right to demand punishment, it is not due to him in this sense. If any one has in this case a right to demand; he, who inflicts the punishment, has a right to demand, that the criminal should suffer it; he who suffers it has no right to demand, that the other should inflict it. The right then of punishing, as it is wholly his, from whom the punishment comes, may, if he thinks proper, be waved or given up. By giving it up he uses this right as his own, and in the equality of nature is not accountable to any one for so doing.

Indeed, a criminal, in this equality of nature, is not very likely to escape punishment. Where all have a promiscuous right of calling him to an account; it is a great chance, though one may pardon him, whether all will be equally inclined to clemency. † Cain seems to have been sensible, how little security he had in this respect; when, after the murder of his brother, he declares himself to be afraid, that every one who met him would kill him.

If this branch of clemency is consistent with the law of nature, there can be no question whether the other branch, which consists in punishing in a low degree, is so or not. For if we are at liberty to wave our right entirely, we must certainly be at liberty to wave it in part; that is, to make such abatements in it as we see convenient. Humanity towards the criminal will commonly persuade us to exercise this part of mercy, to be satisfied with the least degree of punishment that may seem sufficient to restrain or correct his bad disposition.

* Grot. Lib. II. Cap. XX. § XXXIV, XXXV, &c.

† Gen. IV. 14.

Some circumstances either of the criminal himself, or of the crime committed by him, may justify us in not exercising this branch of mercy. The principal circumstance of the criminal, is his having repeated the offence frequently, after he has been punished in these lower degrees: because this is an evidence, that these slighter punishments are not sufficient to answer the purposes which are designed to be brought about by them. His having repeated the offence without ever having been made to suffer for it at all, ought, however, not to check our humanity towards him; since it does not then appear that slighter punishments would not have amended him if they had been tried.

The principal circumstances of the crime which will justify us in not being satisfied with punishing in the lowest degree, are its being common, or its being obvious. When few people are likely to follow the criminal's example, or to do as he has done; we have nothing more to consider than his particular case: he stands, as it were, alone; and if we have reason to hope that the slighter sort of penalties may correct what is amiss in his disposition, we need proceed no farther than to inflict such slight penalties. But when many run into the same crime, and custom may seem likely to establish the practice of it, if care is not taken to prevent it; there is the greater necessity for being as severe as justice will allow us to be, in order to deter others, who might be encouraged to offend, if they saw that a man could offend either with impunity, or at the expense of only a small punishment. The facility of a crime, or its being obvious to be committed, does not increase the guilt of it: there is no more guilt in offending where it is easy, than where it is difficult; nay, in fact, the facility of a crime, considered in itself, may rather seem to lessen than to increase the guilt: because he who can take the pains to offend, where great difficulties are in his way, shows a stronger disposition to offend than he who meets with few or no difficulties to oppose him. But the guilt of a crime being duly adjusted, the facility of it is a reason why we should carry our punishment of it as high as justice will allow of. For where a crime is easy and open, it is more likely to be committed than where it is difficult. And if we punish, in order to secure ourselves, primarily indeed, against the person offending, but secondarily against all others; there is more reason for punishing with all just severity, where we are guarded by nothing but the fear of punishment, than where we are guarded by the very difficulties which any person would meet with who should attempt to injure us.

We may observe that in civil society law-makers have this rule in view, when they appoint and establish the penalty for breaking a law. As the mercy of an individual, in the liberty of nature, shows itself in the gentleness of the penalty which he inflicts; so the mercy of the law shows itself in the gentleness of the penalty which it appoints. And it is usual for civil laws to forbid those crimes which are the most easy to be committed, under higher penalties than those of the like guilt, which are not to be committed without greater difficulty. The mercy of some laws has restrained the natural license of punishing theft with death, and has established the penalty of restitution with increase, where the theft is committed in the day time; or with slavery, when the thief has not wherewithal to make such an ample restitution as is required of him. But in the night time, those laws leave the thief to the discretion of the person whom he robs: that so, where it is more easy to offend in this way, the person offending may run the hazard of suffering a higher penalty. Stealing cattle from the pasture, and stealing them from the stall, are crimes of much the same guilt. But the former is a crime more easily committed than the latter: and upon this principle the Mosaic law punishes the former with more rigour, and the latter with more clemency. Five oxen are to be restored for an ox, and four sheep for a sheep, in one case; but a double restitution is made the penalty in the other case. The law says, *"If a man shall steal an ox or a sheep, and kill it or sell it, he shall restore five oxen for an ox, and four sheep for a sheep. If a thief be found breaking up, and be smitten that he die, there shall be no blood shed for him. If the sun be risen upon him, there shall be blood shed for him; for he should have made full restitution: if he have nothing, then he shall be sold for his theft. If the theft be certainly found in his hand alive, whether it be ox, or ass, or sheep, he shall restore double." The supposition of his being found breaking up, when, if the theft is in the day time, only a double restitution is required, shows that the cattle so stolen were supposed to be in some place of security.

What has been here said concerning mercy or clemency is applicable only where men live in the liberty and equality of nature, or where the right of punishing is every man's own, so that he may abate the rigour of his demands, or entirely give them up at his own discretion. But in civil society, where the magistrate punishes, he exercises the right of the public. His mercy, therefore, is to be guided by what he reasonably presumes to be the will of the public, and not by what he might be willing to do if he was exercising only his own private right of punishing.

How the goods of a criminal are affected by punishment.

XIV. As we have here had occasion to mention a punishment by double or four-fold, or five-fold restitution, it may be proper for us to stop a while in order to consider, whether in the liberty of nature the person who punishes, particularly if he is likewise the person who has suffered by the crime, has any right to take possession of the criminal's goods, or acquires any property in them, in consequence of the right to punish beyond what is sufficient to make him satisfaction for such damages as he has sustained. In civil society punishments by fines, or by confiscation, are very usual; and in some countries, the law may direct that what is thus taken from the criminal shall go to the sufferer: as we find the Mosaic law provided in the instances just now taken notice of.

How the civil magistrate comes by the general power of punishment, and how he comes by this particular power over the criminal's goods, will be the proper subject of some of our future inquiries. At present we are only to inquire how a criminal's goods are affected by the right of punishing in the liberty or equality of nature; where there is no magistrate in whom the exclusive right of punishing is vested, but this right belongs promiscuously to all.

It is plain, that loss of goods may bring about the ends of punishment several ways. Such a loss as this, like any other evil which the

* Exod. XXII. 1, 2, &c.

criminal is made to feel, may teach him to behave better for the future, for fear of suffering such another loss, if he has still any thing left to lose. Where many of his goods are taken from him, so as to reduce him to a low condition; he will have fewer opportunities of offending than he had whilst he had enough to maintain him in idleness. And these opportunities will be more particularly lessened, if his riches, whilst he had them, were either the principal motives to his crime, or the chief instruments that helped him or gave him the power to commit it. Since then the ends of punishing may thus be answered by deprivation of goods; if we have any right to make a criminal suffer at all for these ends, we must have the same right to make him suffer in his goods, as to make him suffer directly or immediately in his person.

But the great question is, when the criminal is deprived of his goods, who has the property in them? They cannot naturally pass to his children or relations, if inheritance is not a right of the law of nature. Nay, though inheritance was supposed to be natural, or though it had, in a state of nature, been introduced or established by general consent; yet even then his children or relations could not, in virtue of such a right, claim to inherit the goods which he loses. For inheritance is not a right to claim property in such things as belonged to the ancestor, whenever his property in them ceases; it is only a right to claim property in such things as he leaves the heirs in possession of when his own property ceases by death. So that before his death, there can be no claim of inheritance upon any of his goods; and at his death there can be no claim of inheritance upon such of his goods as he does not leave them in possession of. And he certainly no more leaves them in possession of those goods, which he has been justly deprived of in his lifetime, than he does of those which he has sold, or given away.

As the heirs of the criminal have no claim to such goods, as he loses in the way of punishment; so neither has the injured person any, considered merely as the injured person. He has, indeed, a right to so much of the criminal's goods as will make him amends for the damage which he has suffered: but no reason can be given why he should have a right to more; unless some positive law has given him such a right. The ends which justify punishment, will by no means extend his claim any farther than this. The criminal, by suffering in his goods, may be discouraged or prevented from offending again: but a design to discourage or prevent him from offending again, can be no ground for that person, whom he has injured by offending once, to claim property in the goods which he is deprived of. The ends of punishment may be answered by taking the criminal's goods from him: but these ends do not require that the property, which he loses, should be vested in the person whom he has injured.

The person who punishes, whether it is the same that has been injured, or any one else, seems most likely to have, or rather to acquire a right in such goods: not because he is at the trouble of punishing; but because, when he deprives the criminal of his property in them, he has the fairest opportunity of being the first occupant. The person who undertakes to punish a criminal, has another opportunity, besides this, of acquiring a right in the criminal's goods. Most of the evils which the criminal can suffer in his person, may be estimated in money or in goods; and he probably would willingly submit to lose as much money, or as many of his goods, as would make the evil, which he should feel by such loss, equal, or nearly equal, to the evil of some other punishment. Suppose, for instance, the punisher might imprison him, and he would readily give a sum of money rather than lose his liberty: in this case, by his own voluntary act, he might give the punisher a certain sum of money, in order to redeem himself from imprisonment; that is, he might choose to bear one sort of punishment, rather than another: and, in consideration of the punishers being willing to change the sort of punishment, he might make over his right to that sum of money, or to any other of his goods of the same value.

After a number of men have originally acquired a general property, as a collective body, in all such things as are distributed afterwards by that body amongst the particular members of it, and so become the private property of each individual, to whom they are thus distributed and assigned; we may, notwithstanding this, suppose each individual, in respect of punishment, to be still in a state of nature; that is, we may suppose the right of punishing to belong, promiscuously, to each of them. Whoever, in these circumstances, punished a criminal with loss of goods, could have no right to these goods, unless by way of commutation. If nothing has passed between the punisher and the criminal, except that the former has merely deprived the latter of his goods; such goods have then no particular owner: and if the punisher could claim them at all, he must claim them as the first occupant. But where a right of general property in the public or collective body obtains; such goods as have no particular owner, do not cease to have any owner at all; they revert to the public or collective body, and are not so in common, as that any one who pleases, may lawfully seize them for his own, and acquire property in them by such occupancy. Suppose such a collective body of men to have approached a little nearer to the forms and institutions of civil society, and to have made over their general property to some one or more particular persons: then, as all goods which have no other owner, so those amongst the rest, which a criminal is deprived of in the way of punishment, will become the property of such person or persons; that is, in the more common way of speaking, the goods of a criminal will, as a punishment for what he has done, be forfeited to him or them; when deprivation of goods is the proper punishment of his crime, and any one thinks fit to inflict that punishment.

Accessories to a crime punishable.

XV. We have seen that justice will allow us to punish the person who commits a crime: but it may still be asked, whether we can, consistently with the same justice, punish any others besides him. *This question relates to two sorts of persons; to such as are parties in a crime, though they are not the immediate doers of it; and to such as have neither done the criminal act, nor are any ways concerned in it.

As to the first sort of persons, those who are parties in the crime, they are plainly liable to punishment; not for the guilt of another man, but for their own guilt; not because a criminal act has been done by some one else, but because they had a share, or were accessories in what that other person has done. The several ways, by which we may

* Grot. Lib. II. Cap. XXI. § I.

so far make ourselves parties in doing an injury, as to become parties, likewise, in the obligation to make satisfaction for the damages arising from that injury, have been already explained. By the same ways a man may make himself so far a party in a crime which another commits, as to be justly liable to be punished for it. They, who command a crime, who consent to it, when, without their consent, it could not have been committed, who assist the immediate actor in committing it, or who protect him after it is committed; they who are, in strict justice, obliged to forbid the crime, and do not forbid it, who are in like manner obliged to assist the sufferer, and wilfully neglect to assist him; they, who advise, or encourage, or countenance what is done; and they who ought to dissuade the crime, but do not dissuade it, or who ought to make it known, but conceal it; any of these are parties in it, or accessories to it: and if they have such a share in it, as evidences any evil disposition, they become liable to punishment.

It is, however, to be observed, that a man may be so far accessory to a crime, as to be obliged to make good the damage arising from it, without being liable to share in the punishment due to the guilt of it. Every neglect of justice, though in the slightest instances, obliges him to make reparation: because justice, even in the slightest instances, is what all mankind may claim of him. But punishment is inflicted to correct a bad disposition, or to prevent it from breaking out into future acts of injustice: and it is very possible, that through inadvertence, or by accident, a man may be the occasion of harm to others in the lower instances, without having such a bad disposition as to stand in need either of correction or restraint.

In punishing a criminal and his accessories; when they, by whose authority, or at whose instigation he committed the crime, can be found out, and are in our power; it is generally thought reasonable, that we should be more ready to mitigate or to remit his punishment than theirs. The crime is supposed to begin from them; and we are willing to hope, that unless they had commanded or instigated him to do what he has done, the fact might never have been committed. But certainly this rule will, in many cases, be a very improper one. He, who is under the strongest temptation to commit a crime, has the least guilt; and whether we consider him as an object of our mercy or not, yet in point of justice he deserves the least punishment. Now, it frequently happens, that his provocation, from whom the crime begins, is much greater than his, who carries it into execution. I may have provoked a man by some extreme ill usage, which puts him upon hiring an assassin to murder me: the guilt of the assassin, who is prevailed upon by a small reward to commit the fact, is plainly the greater of the two: for he, who can be brought so easily to commit a crime, must have a worse and a more dangerous disposition of mind, than he, who does not appear likely to have thought of committing it, if he had not been under the influence of a great provocation.

Those who have no share in a crime, not punishable.

XVI. * The principles already established, concerning the ends and the right of punishing, will sufficiently prove that they, who are no ways concerned in a crime, cannot, with any appearance of justice, be punished for

* Grotius, Lib. II. Cap. XXI. § IX, X, XI, XII.

it. If punishment is justifiable upon no other principle, but a design of correcting or restraining a disposition to hurt mankind; then where there is no crime to evidence such a disposition, that is, where there is no guilt, there can be no justice in inflicting punishment.

We do not, indeed, maintain, that no punishment can be justly inflicted upon a criminal, which shall, in any manner, or by any accident whatsoever, affect an innocent person. Mankind are so connected with one another, that, if this was a true principle, it would be almost impossible to punish a criminal at all: for there is scarce any punishment which can be inflicted, but what, by some accident or other, will, in its consequences, affect other persons besides him, upon whom it is inflicted. No one is so much a solitary individual, as to be, in all respects, quite detached from the rest of his species: either our interests are mixed with the interests of others, or, at least, there are some, with whom we are connected by ties of affection. The death of a parent will commonly hurt his children; both upon account of the interest which they had in his life, and upon account of the affection which they had for his person. He cannot be maimed or imprisoned without their feeling it: they lose at least that pleasure, which they enjoyed from his company or his welfare, and are, perhaps, deprived of that maintenance, which they received from his labour. Even any corporal pain, though he is the immediate sufferer, affects them: it is a pain to them that he should be hurt: and what is a disgrace to him, is, however we may reason about it, a disgrace to his family, in the opinion of the world. Where a man is not attached to others by natural affection, he has many other connections which will extend the consequences of his punishment to them. If he is in debt, and has no way of satisfying his creditors, but either by his labour, or by his going on in some gainful employment, which he had entered into, and which they, perhaps, had hazarded their money upon; his death, or his imprisonment, or his banishment, will be a loss to them. If he is a slave, his master will be a sufferer; if he is a master, his dependents will be sufferers; when any of the higher punishments are inflicted upon him. But the losses or evils which any of these innocent persons undergo, in consequence of a criminal's punishment, is not a punishment to them. They suffer, indeed; but they must look upon what they suffer as a natural misfortune, which was brought upon them, not directly by the design of those who inflict the punishment, but in consequence only of their accidental connections with the criminal, upon whom it is inflicted. All punishment may, indeed, be considered as some loss to them, who suffer it: but then all loss is not, on the contrary, to be considered as a punishment. Whatever loss we designedly and directly bring upon a man, if we do it upon account of some crime that he has committed, it is a punishment; if we do it without any previous crime, it is an injury. Nay, even such loss as we bring upon a man in consequence of what we do, is an injury; if the act from whence this loss arises is an unlawful one. But the loss which an innocent person suffers by the punishment of a criminal, upon account of the accidental connection that there is between such person and the criminal, is not of either of these sorts. It is not directly or designedly brought upon him: nor is it the consequence of any act, which is in itself unlawful. He suffers it in consequence only of our doing what, in respect of the criminal, we had a right to do.

What has been already said may help to clear up the question, whether a criminal may justly be deprived of his goods, since they are by this means prevented from descending to his children, notwithstanding these children have no share at all in the guilt of his crimes. This punishment is, in this respect, no more exceptionable than any other punishment would be: since, as we have seen, in almost every other sort of punishment, his children, and all others who are connected with him, must, in some degree or other, suffer with him. And upon the same principles, that we justify any other sort of punishment, we may justify this, in which the loss suffered by the children is not directly or designedly brought upon them, but only in consequence of our doing an act in itself lawful.

I am aware, however, that this explanation of the matter is open to an objection. It may be asked, whether in calling the act a lawful one, which is attended with this consequence, we do not take the point in question for granted? The loss which the children sustain, though we do not think fit to call it a punishment, may yet be an injury: as all losses are, which any innocent person suffers in consequence of our doing what we ought, in justice, not to do. And to say that our act of punishing a criminal by deprivation of goods, is in itself a lawful one, is taking it for granted that the act is lawful, notwithstanding the certain consequence of it is, that an innocent person will be hurt by it. However, this objection is not a very formidable one: for when we say that the act is in itself a lawful one, we consider it as detached from this consequence. In the first place, we may affirm, what has been proved already, that it is lawful to punish a criminal. And in the next place we may affirm, that if a criminal was a solitary individual, who had no children and no relations at all, to whom his goods would descend at his death; it would be lawful to punish him by deprivation of goods. And if the act is lawful thus far; the consequences, which are not directly designed by him who does it, but follow by the accidental connection between the criminal and his relations, are not chargeable upon him as an injury to those relations.

Children have a right to maintenance from their parents; they have a right likewise to the pleasure which they receive from the company, the safety, and the welfare of their parents. Now, there is scarce any sort of punishment, but what will, in some degree or other, affect the children, when it is inflicted upon the parent. And yet we never hear the same complaints about the injury which is done to the children, by punishing the parent in any other way, that are usually made about the punishing of him by deprivation of goods. Every one seems to be aware, in other instances, that the loss sustained by the child is accidental, and that the view of what it must suffer, by the punishment of its parent, is not sufficient to make such punishment unjust. Though, in fact, the loss which is suffered by the child in other instances, affects what may, with more propriety, be looked upon as its right, than the loss which it suffers in the instance of taking away the parent's goods. For the child has no more than an expectation of succeeding to his goods; and this expectation depends upon the condition of his keeping those goods till he dies. So that by depriving the parent of his goods, instead of taking away any right from the children, we only intercept the condition, without which they can have no right at all to them. *Puffendorf, after he had come to this conclusion, goes on to observe, that it was, however, as Buchanan calls it, a truly unjust and barbarous law, which was made by Mogaldus, king of Scotland, that all the goods of condemned criminals, were to be forfeited to the crown, excluding their wives and children from any part of them. If he does not use the word *unjust* in its strict and proper sense, it will be easy to reconcile what he here says, with his former conclusion. For though the rigour of justice will allow of this; yet it might still be his opinion, that tenderness and humanity would persuade us to let the wife and children of the criminal enjoy, if not the whole, yet however some part of his goods.

But, perhaps, he had in his mind another objection to such a law as this; an objection, which does not seem to have been much attended to. Though deprivation of goods may be justified, even against any supposed injury to the children of the criminal, when this is the only punishment which he is made to suffer; yet it is still a question, whether he may be punished by death and by deprivation of goods too? All the reasons, upon which the justice of punishment is supported, are satisfied by the death of the criminal. He is effectually prevented from offending again, when his life is taken from him. And as we showed before, upon this principle, that all unnecessary torture, that is, all pain which might have been avoided in putting the criminal to death, is an injury to him; so here it may be asked, whether the accumulated punishment of death and deprivation of goods is not upon the same account to be looked upon as an injury?

If this was the whole of the objection, we might easily reply, that deprivation of goods added to death is not like unnecessary torture added to it. The criminal feels the unnecessary torture; and because he is then capable of feeling it, he is likewise capable of being injured by it. But deprivation of goods is more like exposing or mangling his body, after it is become insensible: if it is at all to be called taking his goods from him, it is taking them from him, after he has no longer any occasion for them, and can no longer feel the loss of them.

But here the case of the children returns, and gives new force to the objection. If they have a claim to inherit what their father dies possessed of; then to seize upon the goods of the father at his death, though it is no injury to him, will be an injury to them: because, in this case, seizing his goods is not merely intercepting the condition, upon which the children had a claim to them; it is taking the goods away in opposition to their claim.

Shall we say, that it is of great use for men to have a punishment of this sort before their eyes: since, though they might be hardy enough to offend, where they themselves are to suffer alone; yet their affection for their children will probably prevent them from offending, where they foresee, that if they do offend, these children must suffer with them? But when we are inquiring about the justice of inflicting a punishment, after a crime is over; it is nothing to the purpose to give an answer drawn from the expediency of threatening a punishment

* Book VIII. Chap. III. § XXXI.

before the crime is committed. It might be of great use to threaten, that if a man committed such or such a crime, his children should be tortured, or be put to death before his eyes; and, doubtless, to inflict a punishment of this sort, in some instances, might be of great use in preventing others from offending. But the expediency of such a proceeding would never show the justice of it. However just it might be, in respect of the parent, who, upon account of his crime, is made to suffer the anguish of so horrid a spectacle; yet, certainly, it never could be thought just, in respect of the children, who are thus made to suffer torture or death, notwithstanding they are clear from the guilt of their parent's crime.

Shall we say, that inheritance is an instituted right; and that consequently, in a state of natural liberty, no injury is done to the children in cutting them off from inheritance; because they had no right to claim it; and that in a state of civil society, those who institute the right of inheritance, may model it as they please, and may convey the goods of the father to his children, upon such conditions, as seem to them to be most convenient. They may, therefore, in view to the expediency of such establishment, appoint, that, where the father has been guilty of such or such crimes, all inheritance, as derived from or through him, shall be cut off; and then, in consequence of this establishment, what, in the first instance, was expedient only, becomes just: the child is not injured by this bar of his claim to inherit; because, if the same laws, from which this bar arises, had not given him a claim to inherit, he would have had no such claim at all. This answer may be a satisfactory one, where the children have no right to the goods of their parents, but by intestate succession. But it is plainly an insufficient answer, if the parent, or other ancestor, has been careful enough to make a will. For however inheritance in intestate succession may be the creature of civil institution, inheritance by will is coeval with property.

Shall we say, therefore, that property itself, and all the incidents of it, the power of making a will, amongst the rest, is the effect of civil institution? This would be saying what cannot well be proved to be universally true.

But where property is considered as acquired in the gross, and as derived from the public to the individuals, in whom separate or private property is vested; the public might, certainly, make the grant of it to such individuals, upon such terms, and under such conditions, as seemed to be most expedient, or most conducive to the common good.

But even then, it is to be remembered, that a general grant of property to the individuals, can never be understood to be any bar to their disposing of their goods by will; unless this limitation is particularly mentioned. For, as the right to dispose of our goods by will is naturally incidental to property; whoever grants the one, does, at the same time, grant the other, if no express condition is annexed, which may prevent it.

Upon the whole, then, we may come to these conclusions. Where a criminal is punished with death, supposing inheritance in intestate succession to be the creature of civil institution, the children, or other relations of such criminal, have no claim to his goods, in the liberty of nature; and, consequently, deprivation of goods can have no injustice in it. It cannot be unjust, in respect of the criminal; because, after he is dead, he does not feel the loss of them. And it cannot be unjust in respect of the children; because, in respect of them, it is not properly deprivation; it does not take from them any thing which they had a right to; it only prevents them from possessing what did not belong to them, any more than to any other person.—But though inheritance in intestate succession is supposed to be introduced by civil society, and to be established by positive laws; yet, inheritance by will, is incidental to property and coeval with it: and, consequently, where a criminal is punished with death, in the liberty of nature, whoever claims his goods by will would be injured, if they were hindered from succeeding to them.—And though we consider civil society as in its infancy, which is the case where a body of men have the property of lands in gross, and individuals derive their private property from the grant of such body; yet this principle would not be sufficient to justify depriving the heir of a claim under the will of the ancestor; unless where it was otherwise provided by some express conditions annexed to the grant.

However, we are to observe farther, that in civil society the established laws, to which, as we shall see hereafter, all the subjects consent, either mediately or immediately, operate in the same manner with such express conditions. Whether those conditions are made at first, or are introduced with consent of parties afterwards; there is no injury on the side of the community, which makes use of them, as a restraint upon the behaviour of the subjects. So that in civil society, by virtue of the laws, the power of making a will may, consistently with justice, be taken away from criminals, who are punished capitally.

There is another case, in which such persons as are innocent of a crime, seem to be punished for it; and that is where the guilt of the criminal is the remote cause, but some act of their own is the immediate cause of the evil which they suffer. He that engages, either for the appearance of a criminal, when he shall be called upon, or for his future good behaviour, becomes answerable for such appearance or such behaviour, and makes himself liable to undergo the penalty, under which he engaged for either. The guilt of the criminal arising from some crime formerly committed, which made him liable to be called upon, in one instance, or his guilt arising from some future misbehaviour, in the other instance, is the remote cause, which subjects the sponsor to undergo what he voluntarily engaged to undergo, upon condition the criminal failed of appearing, or of behaving well. But the immediate cause, which involves the sponsor in the obligation to undergo such evil, is his own voluntary act of engaging under this condition.

It is evident, that what the sponsor suffers, is owing to his own voluntary act, and not to the guilt of the criminal; because the measure of what he is to suffer is determined by his own engagement, and not by the other's guilt. Whatever may be the guilt of the criminal; this consideration does not affect the sponsor: what he is to undergo is neither more nor less than he voluntarily engaged to undergo. Upon this account it is, that he, who thus gives security for another, cannot forfeit his life as a penalty; when the conditions that he engaged for are not made good. He cannot forfeit his life, because he can forfeit no more than he had pawned or pledged as a security: and he can pledge nothing, but what he has a right to dispose of. Now, a man's life is not his own to dispose of: and, consequently, as he cannot pledge it in security, he cannot forfeit it; when the conditions which he engaged for fail of being performed. The ancients seem to have been of another opinion: the sponsor might, in their judgment, suffer capitally. And there is a plain reason why they might be of this opinion, notwithstanding they acted upon the principle here laid down, that the sponsor suffers immediately on account of his own engagement, and not on account of the criminal's guilt; and, consequently, that he can forfeit no more than he pledges, and can pledge no more than he has a right to dispose of. For, in the meantime, they looked upon every man to be absolute master of his own life, not only to keep or preserve it, but to dispose of it too, as he pleased. They allowed the sponsor, therefore, if he thought fit, to put himself, in all respects, into the place of the criminal, so as to subject himself to suffer capitally; if it appeared, upon inquiry, that the criminal deserved so to suffer.

Obligation to punishment does not descend from the ancestor to the heir.

XVII. * We have already had occasion to observe, that the children or heirs of a criminal cannot justly be punished, upon account of the guilt of their parent or ancestor; provided they have no share in this guilt. It may not be amiss, before we leave this subject, to take notice of the reason, why the obligation to undergo punishment does not, like some other obligations, descend from the ancestor to the heir. Guilt, or a disposition to do harm, is a personal quality; and, consequently, the obligation which arises from it, must be merely personal. As the guilt is in the person and not in the goods; the heir, to whom those goods descend, receives them without that obligation of punishment which the ancestor was under. But though the heir stands clear of the punishment itself; that is, though, if the punishment was not inflicted, or, at least, was not settled and determined, before the death of the ancestor, the heir will naturally not be liable to it; yet, if it was inflicted, or however was fixed, before his death, the heir will, in consequence, be affected by it, as far as it affects the goods of his ancestor. For the heir can receive these goods in no other condition than the ancestor leaves them: so that if any fine or any forfeiture has diminished them, he can claim no more than the remainder: or if the fine or forfeiture has been settled in the ancestor's life-time; though the one has not been actually paid, nor the other actually seized on; they are due from the goods of the ancestor; the obligation no longer rests upon his person, but is extended to his property. Consequently, the heir, to whom such property descends, receives it charged with this obligation, and is bound to give up what he can have no claim to, because his ancestor had none.

In explaining this matter, I have supposed the heir to be affected by the consequence of the ancestor's punishment, not only when the punishment of a fine or a forfeiture has been actually inflicted before the ancestor happens to die, as where the one is actually paid, and the other actually seized upon; but likewise, when such punishment has been settled and determined, though it has not been actually inflicted,

* Grot. Lib. II. Cap. XXI. § XIX.

But, in the liberty of nature, this latter supposition cannot well take place: for where there is no common judge to decree the fine or forfeiture, they cannot easily be settled and determined any otherwise, than by an actual payment of the former, or an actual seizure of the latter. It may, indeed, possibly be otherwise; the punisher and the criminal may, by mutual agreement, have settled this matter: and then the supposition will take place, even in the liberty of nature. Though the criminal has not actually been deprived of the possession of such goods as he had agreed to give up in the way of punishment, or rather in the place of other punishment, yet the obligation arising from his crime, is, by such agreement, extended beyond his person, and affects his goods.

This may frequently happen in a state of civil society. After the magistrate has decreed the fine or forfeiture, whether the criminal directly agrees to it or not, they become due, so as to affect his goods, and to make the heir answerable; if it should happen, that the sentence is not put in execution before the ancestor's death.

CHAPTER XIX.

OF WAR.

I. *War, what it is.*—II. *Private war, what.*—III. *War is naturally lawful.*—IV. *Who may lawfully engage in making war.*

War, what it is. I. WAR* is a contention by force. When we call war a contention, we must not be understood to use this word in so restrained a sense as to mean by it only the act of contending. Nations are said to be at war with one another, not only when their armies are engaged, so as to be in the very act of contending; but, likewise, when they have any matter of controversy or dispute subsisting between them, which they are determined to decide by the use of force, and have declared, by words, or shown by certain actions, that they are determined so to decide it. War, therefore, in the common use of the word, signifies, not only an act, but a state or condition. And, upon this account, the word contention, in this definition of war, is to be understood to signify the state or condition of those, who, though they are not actually making use of force, have some matter of dispute subsisting between them, which can be decided by no other means, and who are, therefore, determined to take every fair opportunity of using these means for the decision of it.

Private war, what. II. † If this is the notion of war, it is plain that there may be war, in the liberty of nature, before the institution of such civil societies as we call nations. War of this sort is private war: because, antecedently to the forming civil societies or bodies politic, which bodies are called public persons, the parties concerned in war must be private persons. Even after such public persons are formed,

* Grot. Lib. I. Cap. I. § II.

† Grot. Ibid. § II.

the right of private war is only abridged, and is not wholly taken away; as will be shown in its proper place.

Our principal inquiries at present, are contained within a narrow compass: they are only these two; first, whether, in the liberty of nature, individuals may lawfully make war upon one another; and secondly, supposing such war to be lawful, who are the persons that may lawfully engage in it.

War is naturally lawful.

III. * What has been proved already, concerning the right of defence, the right of recovering reparation for damages done, and the right of inflicting punishment, will serve to show, that an injury will justify men in making use of force, both before and after it is committed. An injury justifies the use of force, before it is committed, in order to guard against it: and it justifies a like use of force, after it is committed, in order, either to recover what is lost by it, or to hinder him, who has done it, from doing the like again. Now, the use of force is war: and, consequently, the law of nature, since it allows the use of force for any of these purposes, allows of war.

Who may lawfully engage in making war.

IV. †Though the war, which we are now speaking of, is the war of individuals against each other; yet the law of nature does not hinder any number of individuals from taking part in it. The person, whose interest is immediately concerned, either to defend himself and his property, or to recover reparation of damages, or to inflict punishment, is not the only person who may lawfully make use of force for his own security. This has been proved already in the instance of inflicting punishment. For, as the right of doing this, belongs, promiscuously, to all who may suffer by the criminal, if he is not restrained; any number of persons, where any one, or some few of them, have not force sufficient to inflict the punishment, may join their force together for this purpose: what is lawful to each of them separately, is equally lawful to all of them, when they are thus united. In respect, likewise, of defence or of reparation, though it is more particularly the interest of him, who is in danger of suffering, or who actually has suffered, to guard against the injury, in one case, or to enforce the demand of reparation in the other case; yet, where he is engaged in such a lawful act, as either that of defending himself, or that of recovering damages, no rule of justice can forbid or restrain others from giving him their assistance. Nay, where his sufferings are likely to be very great, or have been very great already, and his own abilities, either to ward off the evil which threatens him, or to redress it, after it is over, are but small; benevolence would rather persuade those, who have an opportunity of being serviceable to him, not to refuse or withhold what help they are able to give him. From hence it appears, that war is lawful to two sorts of persons; either to him, whose interest is immediately concerned, or to them, who voluntarily give him assistance.

But there is still a third sort, concerning whom, it may be inquired, how far they may lawfully engage in a war: and these are such as have no interest in the occasion of it, and, if they were left to choose for themselves, would take no part in it; but being under the authority of him, whose interest is immediately concerned, they are commanded

* Grot. Lib. I. Cap. II. § I.

† Grot. Ibid. Cap. V.

by him to give their assistance. The case of such persons as these, will come more particularly under our consideration in the second part of this work, when we are to inquire into the effect of civil jurisdiction upon our natural rights. Only we may here observe, by the way, that as a son, who continues in his father's family, or a servant, who has bound himself by agreement for this purpose, is obliged to obey the lawful commands of the father or the master; the consequence is, that when such father or master undertakes a lawful war, the son or the servant may lawfully assist him, and are, indeed, obliged to assist him, if he commands them.

CHAPTER XX.

OF SLAVERY.

I. *Perfect despotism and perfect slavery, what.*—II. *Difference between despotism and parental power.*—III. *No man is naturally a slave.*—IV. *Causes of slavery.*—V. *Limitations of despotism.*—VI. *Slavery, how the consequence of just war.*—VII. *Children of slaves, why they follow the condition of their mother.*

Perfect despotism and perfect slavery, what.

I. * GROTIUS, in defining perfect slavery, calls it an obligation to give all our labour for a supply of the bare necessaries of life.

But the common notion of perfect slavery does not seem to be fully expressed in this definition of it. We usually understand the master or owner to have, not only a right to direct such actions of the slave as may properly be called labour, but a right, likewise, to direct all his other actions. And from this right to direct all the actions of the slave, there arises a right by gift or sale, to dispose of the slave's person; that is, to transfer the power over him. For the slave being supposed under the absolute authority and direction of his master, must, in consequence, be obliged to submit to the authority and direction of another, whenever his present master is pleased to order that it shall be so.

Perfect despotism seems, therefore, in the common notion of it, to be an alienable right to direct all the actions of another. And, consequently, perfect slavery is an obligation to submit to be thus directed.

Difference between despotism and parental power.

II. The different ends to which the power of a master and the power of a parent are directed, will sufficiently distinguish them from one another: though both of them are absolute; and though one of them extends to all the actions of the child, as the other extends to all the actions of the slave. The good of the child is the end, to which the authority of the parent over the child is directed: and the good of the master is the end, to which the authority of the master, over the slave, is directed. The parent has no right to command the child, but in view to the benefit of the child itself: the master has a right to command the

* Grot. Lib. II. Cap. V. § XXVII.

slave to do such actions, as are for the master's benefit: so that however the slave may find his account in obeying his master's commands, this is merely accidental; since the master's right to give these commands, has another purpose principally in view.

But though the master's power is not directed to the same end, and, consequently, is not tempered by the same limitations with parental authority, yet it is subject to several other limitations. We shall best understand what these limitations are, after we have considered the original of the master's power and the slave's subjection.

No man is naturally a slave.

III. Though it may be possible for a man to be a slave from his birth, yet no man is naturally a slave. They who are slaves from their birth, must have been made such by some accident, which happened before they were born; slavery is by no means their natural condition. Nature has, indeed, made a difference between the parts and capacities of mankind: some are better able to judge for themselves, and to pursue their own good, than others: but, though this difference of parts and capacities may have made it more convenient for some to be directed, and for others to direct; yet it cannot possibly be looked upon as a sufficient reason, why the former should be slaves, and the latter be their absolute masters. Those, who stand in need of the direction of other men, and are willing to have recourse to such direction, stand in need of it for their own benefit, and are led to have recourse to it by the hopes of advancing that benefit. But slavery is an obligation upon a man to be directed in his actions, in view to their benefit, who direct him: it cannot, therefore, be founded in that difference of parts or abilities, which makes it convenient for him to have recourse to their direction, in view to his own benefit.

As men are naturally endowed with different degrees of understanding and judgment, so are they, likewise, naturally possessed of such different degrees of bodily strength, as will make it possible for one man, who is stronger, to subdue another, who is weaker, and force him to obedience. But whatever superiority in bodily strength we may be born to, though it gives us the physical power, it does not give us the right of compelling another to obey us. The weak man's mind and his body, and, consequently, all the faculties of his mind, such as his judgment and his will, and, likewise, all the powers of his body, are as much his own, as if nature had given him greater strength, and enabled him to make a more effectual struggle in his own defence. We cannot, therefore, claim a right to dictate to him; nor can we act as if we had a right of forcing him, against his inclination, to pursue our interest in such manner as we shall direct, without doing him an injury, without doing violence to that judgment and will of his mind, and to those active powers of his body, which nature has made his own.

Children are born in a natural subjection to their parents. But this subjection has been shown already to be, in its own nature, very different from slavery. And as it is distinguished from slavery by its nature, so, likewise, it is by its duration. The master's power over the slave is perpetual: the parent's authority over the child ceases, when the child is able to think and to act for itself.

But if neither superior understanding, nor superior strength, nor parental authority, is a natural foundation of despotism; we may safely conclude, that no man is naturally a slave: for there does not appear any other condition of human nature, which can possibly be imagined to give one man such an absolute right over another, as is implied in the notion of despotism.

We may form a general argument to show, that nature gives no man a just title to despotism, upon the principles already made use of to show, that no just title to it can arise from a superiority in bodily strength. If nature has made any thing a man's own, his mind and his body are so. At least, it is evident, that whatever right one man has in his mind and body, another man must have the same right in his; that is, as far as we can judge from any appearance in nature, each man has an equal right in his own mind and body respectively. But no man's mind and body can be his own, unless the faculties of both, that is, his judgment, his will, and his powers of acting are so. Now he, who has a right in his faculties of judging, of choosing and of acting, is no slave. And since nature, which gave every man a right in his own mind and body, gave him a right likewise to these faculties; the consequence is, that nature has not placed any man in a state of slavery.

Causes of slavery. IV. But slavery, though it is not the natural state of any man, may be introduced consistently with the law of nature. First, a man may come into a state of slavery through the act of his parents. The law of nature obliges the parents to maintain their child. But it is possible for them to be in so low a condition, as to be absolutely unable to discharge this duty in their own persons, and to be under a necessity either of suffering the child to perish, or of procuring some other person to discharge it for them. In these circumstances, if civil laws had made no better provision, the law of nature seems to allow them rather to put the child into the hands of any one, who would, upon his own terms, undertake to preserve its life, than to suffer it to perish for want of common necessaries. Nature, indeed, gave the parents authority over the child, in view to the child's benefit: and he, who undertakes to maintain it and bring it up, upon condition of its being his slave, has his own benefit principally in view. It may, therefore, well be asked, whether the parents have authority to dispose of the child upon these terms. To this, it may be answered, that the parents, through want and infirmity, being under a necessity of leaving their child to starve, or of accepting these conditions, provide for its benefit, as well as they can, by delivering it up to any person who will undertake to subsist it, even upon the condition of its being bound to act for his benefit, as long as it lives. There may, however, be a farther question, how it is possible for the temporary right of the parent over the child, to produce a perpetual right in the master over it as a slave. And, undoubtedly, if there was no other cause of the master's power besides the parent's act, the slavery of the child would cease, when it comes to years of discretion. As the authority of the parent ceases at that age, the power of the master, if it was derived solely from that authority, could subsist no longer. But the master undertakes, from the first, to maintain the child, in view to his own benefit; and, consequently, its maintenance is not to be considered as a bounty bestowed upon it by the master. If then he does not give the child its maintenance, the child must be his debtor for such maintenance: and, upon account of this debt, he claims a right to direct its future actions for his own benefit. Nor will the labour of the child, after it is grown up, discharge this debt, so as to redeem it from slavery: because its future labour will be due to its master for its future subsistence: and the original debt will, upon this account, still remain unsatisfied. This original debt may, indeed, be greater than what arises from barely maintaining the child, whilst it was unable to work: for, as the parents, though they were under a necessity of disposing of their child to some one, were at liberty to dispose of it to whom they pleased; the master may have given them money to engage them to let him have the child, rather than any other person. And whatever he has thus paid to the parents is to be placed to the child's account, and becomes a part of the debt which it owes to the master.

We may observe, by the way, that when we speak of parents selling their child into slavery, nothing more can be meant by it, than that the purchaser, as we call him, gives the parents some valuable consideration to engage them to let him, rather than any other person, acquire a right to the service of the child, by maintaining it in its infancy, whilst it is unable to earn its own living. For, certainly, as the child is not a slave to its parents, they can have no immediate right of making it a slave to any one else: nor can they, properly speaking, so sell it, as that the purchaser shall immediately by their act acquire a right to direct all the actions of the child for his own benefit.

Secondly, slavery may arise from a man's own consent. As the law of nature allows him to give another a temporary right to direct him in some of his actions by contract or agreement; so it will be difficult, if not impossible, to prove, that the same law does not allow him to make this right perpetual, and to extend it to all his actions. It is not very material to inquire whether any person has ever consented thus to part with his liberty: we are rather concerned to know what may be done of right, than what has been done in fact. And as every right which a man is possessed of, may be alienated, if no law forbids him to alienate it; we may venture to conclude, that his liberty is alienable in whole as well as in part, unless some law of nature could be produced, which, though it allows him, in numberless instances, to let out his service for hire, yet forbids him to make a slave of himself. It may, perhaps, be urged, that despotism implies a right to dispose of the life of the slave at pleasure, and to compel him to do such actions as the law of nature forbids; and that consequently, as no man has a right to dispose of his own life, or to do what is unlawful, he cannot give any one else such an authority over him, as is implied in the notion of despotism. But the ready way of answering this objection is to deny the first principle that it proceeds upon. Despotism does not imply a right either to dispose of the slave's life at pleasure, or to compel him to do what the law of nature forbids. And the reason why it does not imply such a right, is the same which the objectors here give: no man is at liberty to dispose of his own life at pleasure, or to act contrary to the law of nature; and consequently no man can put his life into the arbitrary disposal of any one else, or subject himself to be compelled to do what the law of nature forbids. But though a man cannot alienate a liberty which he has not, it does not follow, that he cannot alienate a liberty which he has. And he who has alienated all the liberty which he has to some other person, makes himself a slave; whilst he, to whom it is so alienated, acquires such an absolute authority, as we call despotism.

Thirdly, slavery may arise from damages done, where the person who did it, has no other way of making reparation. The obligation to make reparation operates like a debt, and gives the creditor a right to direct all the actions of him, who has done the damage, to his own benefit; if this is the only way in which he can obtain satisfaction for the damage sustained. But suppose the debtor's labour will be of no use to the creditor, yet the obligation to make reparation will still subsist: and if this obligation can be satisfied in any other way, either in whole or in part, the creditor has a right to demand such satisfaction. Now, though the debtor's labour would be of no service to the creditor himself, yet it may be serviceable to some other person, who would be willing to pay for a right to demand this labour. And as the creditor's damages may, at least in part, be repaired, though not by using the debtor as his own slave, yet by selling him for a slave to the person who wants him; the right to demand reparation, would, for this reason, terminate in a right so to sell the debtor; where this is the only way in which the creditor could obtain any reparation.

Fourthly, slavery may be produced by guilt, consistently with the law of nature. Amongst the other methods of restraining a criminal from offending again, this is one: he will have few opportunities of offending, where all his actions are under the absolute authority and control of another. And this loss of liberty may be either temporary or perpetual, according as the guilt of the criminal deserves a less or a greater penalty. The punishment of a criminal may likewise end in slavery, where the guilt is such as to deserve death. They, who are to punish him, may, if they find it proper, remit the rigour of the penalty, and give him his life, upon condition of his becoming their slave.

Limitations of despotism.

V. From whichever of these causes slavery begins, it does not appear that the master, merely upon account of that right, which we call despotism, has a right to dispose of the slave's life at pleasure.

When slavery is derived from the act of the slave's parents, it is certain that act cannot immediately, and in itself, give the master any arbitrary right over the life of the slave. The parents themselves had originally no right of this sort: and they cannot give a right to another, which they themselves never were possessed of. Perpetual slavery, where the parents sell the child, is produced, indeed, as we have just now seen, not by the immediate act of the parents, but by the debt which the child contracts, before it is able to earn its livelihood. And that this debt cannot give the master any power to dispose of the slave's life at pleasure, will plainly appear, when we have considered the effect of slavery, arising from damage done, or a debt contracted.

Secondly, slavery, arising from a man's own consent, gives the master no absolute power over the life of the slave. The slave could not, by his own act, give the master any power, which he himself was not possessed of; and no man has a right to dispose of his own life at pleasure.

Thirdly, though damages done or debts contracted, as they give the creditor a right to every valuable consideration in the debtor's power, may, by this means, end in slavery; yet they give the creditor no absolute right over the life of the debtor. His life is, indeed, a valuable consideration to himself: if he loses it, he loses what is of the greatest value to him. But it is no valuable consideration to the creditor; that is, the creditor, by taking it from him, would gain nothing. The law of nature, therefore, notwithstanding it gives the creditor a right to whatever may satisfy his demand, can give him no right to the life of his debtor. He has a claim to whatever he can get from the debtor, which may be beneficial to himself, till his damages are fully repaired. But then his claim extends no farther: it does not extend to a right of taking what the debtor will be hurt by losing; if what is so taken will not help towards making him amends for the damages which he has sustained. One might here ask, how the imprisonment of a debtor, for no use or purpose whatsoever, can be reconciled to the law of nature. He may, indeed, lose his liberty by being confined to work for the benefit of his creditor: because this is an amends for the damages which he has done, or for the debt which he owes. But the loss of liberty, if it is merely confinement in a prison, is no more a satisfaction for damages, than the loss of life would be. Where men live in civil society, if the debt, by the instituted laws of the society will not give a full claim upon the debtor's lands, but only upon his moveable goods; in these circumstances, if the debtor has no moveable goods, and refuses to pay out of his lands what he owes; imprisonment may be a very proper way to bring him to a proper sense of his duty, and to make him willing to give up his lands in payment. But if he has neither lands nor moveable goods; such imprisonment seems to have but little foundation in natural justice. And yet in a country where slavery is unknown, and imprisonment for debt is frequent, the prejudices that men have been brought up in, will probably make them wonder to hear that slavery is a more natural and a more reasonable consequence of damage, or of debt, than imprisonment.

Fourthly, if slavery is the punishment of a crime which deserves no higher punishment; the power of the master or punisher stops here: it would be unjust to inflict death where the proper punishment is slavery. The master, therefore, has, in this case, no absolute right over the life of the slave. Indeed, where the crime deserves capital punishment, the person who inflicts the punishment, has, in the first instance, a right over the criminal's life to take it away if he pleases. But if he has agreed to mitigate the punishment by changing it into slavery, this right is at an end: he parts with this right by consenting to take the criminal as his slave. So that even in this case, though the punisher had originally a right over the life of the criminal, yet the master will have no right over the life of the slave.

It is no objection to what is here advanced, that if a slave commits a capital offence, his master will have a right to punish him with death. This right belongs to him as a man, and not as the master of the slave. Any one has the same right over the slave in this respect, that the master has: and if the master is to be employed, rather than any one else, in inflicting the punishment; it is only because he has a better opportunity of doing it than any one else, as the slave is in his custody.

We need not be particular in proving what has been mentioned above, that despotism gives no right to the master of compelling the slave to do any act which the law of nature forbids. A man's own consent, the obligation to repair damages, or the obligation to undergo punishment, are the natural occasions of slavery: and it cannot be thought, that the master can derive such a right from any of these principles. We may, indeed, prove, by a general argument, that it is impossible for him to have such a right. The law of nature cannot allow any person a right of forcing another to disobey its own precepts: every pretence, therefore, of the master to such a right, is inconsistent with the law of nature.

Perfect slavery seems, in its own nature, to put an end to property; at least it will make the slave's property worth nothing. For if he is bound in all his actions to work for his master's benefit, if the master has a right to direct him to this purpose in whatever he does; he can neither keep, nor use, nor dispose of any goods, either moveable or immoveable, for his own benefit, or at his own discretion, but only for the benefit, and at the discretion of his master.

However, if his master has allowed him to have property; his property held under such allowance is not rendered precarious, merely by his being a slave. The goods which he has acquired, are as much his own to keep, to use, and to dispose of, as if he had been free. In effect, the allowance of having goods of his own, is a grant of so much of his liberty as is necessary for these purposes: the very notion of his having property in such goods implies, that he has this liberty in its fullest extent; unless the master, when he allowed him to have goods of his own, has made some express reserve, so as to abridge this liberty.

The consequence of this is, that, when the slave dies, he may give his goods away by will; or if intestate succession has been received in the place where he lives, they will descend to his heir, and the master will have no claim to them; unless he has expressly taken care to reserve such a claim. It may happen, indeed, that his children are slaves; and for this reason, are unable to claim either under his will, or in intestate succession. But then it is their incapacity which prevents them from claiming, and not any defect in his right, to whom the goods belonged.

Slavery, how the consequence of just war.

VI. From what has been said concerning the origin of slavery, we may see in what manner it may arise from a just war.

It is lawful to make use of force either to recover satisfaction for damages sustained, or to inflict punishment upon such as have deserved to be punished. And since the slavery of the party who has done the injury may be the only satisfaction that can be obtained for the damage which he has done, or may be the proper punishment of his guilt, a just war may end in slavery. Despotism may thus be the consequence of conquest.

But then the power of the conqueror does not arise immediately from conquest: he has no right to command the vanquished to act for his benefit, merely because he happens to be stronger than they are, and has subdued them. Those who call war an appeal to * heaven, have given too much countenance to this opinion. It is obvious to conclude, if war is an appeal to heaven, that victory is a divine decision in

* Locke's Works, Vol. II. p 179. 225.

favour of the conqueror: and the probable inference from hence would be, that he has, I know not what divine right of despotism over the vanquished, without considering whether he had any original right to make use of force at all. Whereas, in truth, though despotism may follow victory, the right of the conqueror over the vanquished does not arise immediately from victory: he must have had this right before, or his superior strength could never have given him it. All that his strength can do, is to enforce his claim of damages, or his right of punishment. This claim, or this right, might have been unjustly prevented from taking place, if his adversaries had happened to be stronger than he is. And if, when it is said, that conquest gives a right to despotism, all that is meant by it is, that it supports a right, which might otherwise have been hindered from obtaining its effect, the expression must be allowed to be at least very inaccurate.

Slavery produced by an unjust war is a manifest injury, notwithstanding such war is attended with conquest. The slaves, however they may be subdued, and be forcibly deprived of their liberty, continue in a state of war with their conqueror. They have still a right to their liberty, and may assert that right whenever they have an opportunity.

If, indeed, his victory has been followed by any express agreement between him and them, to confirm to him what, in the first instance, was obtained unjustly; such agreement may be binding. But it will, certainly, be no otherwise binding, than upon supposition, that the unjust force was removed. If the same unjust force, by which they were subdued at first, is made use of afterwards to extort their consent, such agreement will be a nullity. An express agreement is necessary, even if the unjust force is removed: long submission, without any efforts to free themselves from slavery, will not give the conqueror a claim by prescription; since no prescription can take place where the original possession was unjust.

The reader should observe, that the war and the despotism which we have here been speaking of, are private war in a state of nature, and private despotism, or the power of a master over his slave. The effects of conquest, in respect of civil power, will come more properly under consideration in another place.

Children of slaves, why they follow the condition of their mother.

VII. * Since liberty is the natural state of mankind, it may be asked, whether the children of slaves are free? to which we may answer, that if it is otherwise; if the children of slaves are not free; the slavery of such children is not entailed upon them by nature; it is not derived from their parents, as their temper, their constitution, or their complexion sometimes are: some other principle, besides the condition of their parents, will be necessary to explain their slavery.

If the condition of the parent is the occasion of the child's slavery, it is only the remote occasion of it; some other accident is the immediate cause, which deprives them of their liberty. When a child, which has been sold by its parents, is grown up, and is itself become a parent, its offspring, unless disposed of in the same manner as the parent was,

* Grot. Lib. II. Cap. V. § XXIX.

is not affected by what was done long before its birth, and so done as not to include its liberty in the bargain.

When a man enslaves himself, Grotius contends, that he may, at the same time, enslave his future children, if he has no other possible way of providing for them. But then those children are slaves; not merely because their parents are so, nor, indeed, because their parents have thus disposed of them; but by another accident, which has been already explained at large. However, slavery thus produced must stop here: the children's children will not be affected by what has passed between the master and their remote parents; and in respect of them the question will return, whether they are slaves or not; and if they are, what made them so?

Thus, slavery arising either from the act of a man's parents, or from his own act, will not descend to his remote offspring: and much less will it descend to them, when it is a satisfaction made for damages which he has done, or a punishment of any crime which he has committed. The child of a man, who has injured another, may be bound to make reparation; because the obligation to make reparation affects, not only the person, but the goods, likewise, of him who did the damage; and the child, by taking the goods, is involved in all the obligations with which those goods are charged. But where there are no goods, or what goods there are will not be sufficient to make reparation; that is, as far as the obligation affected only the person of him, who did the damage, so as to subject him to slavery; the child, if it was neither a principal nor an accessory, is no way involved in that obligation. We have seen, upon another occasion, that guilt is a personal quality; and, consequently, that, if the child stands clear of the parent's guilt, it cannot justly share in the slavery, or in any other punishment which is inflicted on the parent.

Nor can it here be objected, that, as the child may justly lose those goods, which, if the parent had not been deprived of them, would have descended to it; so it may, for the same reasons, be deprived of that liberty, which, if the parent had been innocent, would have been its birthright. These two cases are widely different from one another. Liberty is the child's right; the parent's goods are only its conditional expectancy. Though we may, therefore, justify cutting off the child's expectancy where it had no right; we cannot, upon the same principles, nor upon any other, justify taking from it what is properly and strictly its own.

If, then, none of all the ways, by which despotism over the parents is acquired, will naturally affect the children, we are still to inquire by what accident the slavery of the parent should make them slaves. Grotius, to make this inquiry more easy, supposes both the parents to be slaves. The child then, he says, as soon as it is born, is maintained at the expense of their master, before it is able to earn its own livelihood by its work. By this maintenance the child contracts a debt, which its future work cannot discharge; because its future work will be due for its future maintenance. This debt, therefore, will remain as long as it lives, and will give the master of the parents a right to every valuable consideration in the child's power.

Our author's principle, as here explained, may, perhaps, account for the child's slavery after it is once in the master's power. But the inquiry may be carried one step farther back, by asking, how the child comes to be a slave rather to the master of the parents than to any other person; since any other person seems to have as good a claim, upon this principle, as he has, to undertake the maintenance of the child, in view to the benefit which may arise from its service? And, in truth, Grotius has not shown, either that the master of the child's parents, or that any other person has such a claim. As far as appears from what he lays down as the foundation of the child's slavery, it is as much in a state of freedom at the time of its birth, as it would have been upon supposition, that neither of the parents were slaves.

We cannot, indeed, maintain, on the contrary, that the children of slaves are naturally born slaves: but there seems to be an accident previous to their birth, which fixes them to this condition. If the mother is a slave, her owner, during the time of gestation, and during the time of her illness, occasioned by the birth, loses her work, and is likewise at an extraordinary expense in taking care of her. As this loss and these expenses are owing to the child, they make it, from its birth, a debtor to the mother's master; and upon this account, he has an immediate claim to every valuable consideration that he can receive from the child, as far as this debt extends. It is a slave, therefore, from the beginning, not because the slavery of the parent naturally entails slavery upon it, but because the slavery of the mother made the child from the beginning a debtor to her owner.

The original debt is, indeed, increased by its maintenance during its infancy: and, in this respect, the principle laid down by Grotius, has some effect in its future slavery: though this principle is not sufficient in itself to explain the occasion of its coming at first into this state.

From hence we may see the reasons why the offspring should naturally follow the condition of the mother, and not of the father: why, if the mother is a slave, the child will be so, though the father is free; and why, if she is free, the child will be so, though he is a slave. For, if she is free, no one has any property in her work, nor is put to any extraordinary expense upon her account, so as to acquire any original claim upon the child. In another respect, likewise, the child follows the mother: it belongs to her master, if she and the father are both slaves, and have different masters. For the loss of her work and the extraordinary expense which the child occasions during the time of gestation and birth, fall upon the master of the mother and not upon the master of the father.

It was necessary to say thus much concerning slavery, that we may be enabled, in the following book, to distinguish this sort of subjection from civil subjection, and private despotism from civil power.

We have been hitherto employed in considering the rights and obligations of mankind, the principles from whence they are derived, and the rules by which they are governed in the liberty of nature. And though mankind are at present united into distinct civil communities, yet these points are not now become matter of mere speculative amusement, but are still as necessary to be known, in order to ascertain our respective rights and obligations, as if we had continued to live in a state of nature.

For first, though mankind are now united into civil communities, and are become subject to the positive laws of such communities, so that these laws are, in most instances, the support of their rights, and the measure of their obligations; yet all mankind are not united into one and the same civil community; they are not all subject to the same positive laws; and, consequently, these laws cannot ascertain all their claims, or regulate their conduct in all instances. Not only different civil societies, when each society is considered as one collective person or body politic, but, likewise, individuals, who are members of different civil societies, are still in the liberty of nature, and must have recourse to that law of nature which respects mankind, as they are individuals, in order to determine what is just and fit to be done in respect of one another.

Secondly, even they, who are members of the same society, are upon many occasions, left to their natural liberty: sometimes, because the civil laws of that society, either through their silence or their imperfection, have not provided for the case in question: sometimes, because either an express or an equitable permission has replaced them, as it were, in a state of nature, and given them leave to defend themselves, when the danger, which threatens them, is so imminent, as to make it impossible for the civil laws to come in to their assistance: sometimes, because the civil laws, from the apprehension that some rights which are acquired consistently with the law of nature, might be abused, would set such rights and their correspondent obligations aside, provided the persons so obliged think proper to be released from them: but those persons are left, in the meantime, to judge for themselves, whether, in good conscience, they ought to comply with such obligations or not.

Thirdly, civil laws are, in some particulars, transcripts of the law of nature; they are only such rules as individuals, in the liberty of nature, are obliged to observe in their conduct towards one another. An acquaintance, therefore, with these rules, will be of great use towards enabling us to understand such laws rightly, and to apply them properly.

Fourthly, in interpreting and applying civil laws, when they are not mere transcripts of the law of nature, as it respects individuals in a state of natural liberty, a thorough knowledge of this law is commonly necessary: because, though such civil laws derive their obligation from civil authority; yet this authority does not always settle the precise manner of their operation in each particular case, but leaves them to operate according to the nature and reason of things.

Fifthly, as the authority, by which civil laws themselves are established, is derived from the consent of those who are subject to such laws; it will be necessary to inform ourselves of the rights and obligations of mankind, as they are individuals; not only that we may trace out the origin of this authority, but that we may understand the nature and settle the extent of it, may determine what adventitious rights and obligations are introduced, what original rights and obligations are either superseded or altered, and in what manner either of these effects are naturally produced by it.

BOOK II.

CHAPTER I.

OF SOCIETIES IN GENERAL, WHERE ALL THE MEMBERS ARE EQUAL.

I. *A society, what.*—II. *What acts of a society bind its members.*—III. *Upon an equality of votes, nothing is done.*—IV. *Natural majority, what, and how to be reckoned.*—V. *Absent members have a right to vote by proxy.*

A society, what.

I. A SOCIETY is a number of men united together by mutual consent, in order to deliberate, determine, and act jointly for some common purpose.

What acts of a society bind its members.

II. In every * society, where all the members are equal; that is, where one has no more authority than another, whatever is determined by the whole or by the greater part, is binding upon each of the members.

There can be no question, whether the act of the whole is binding upon each of the members: because each of the members is naturally bound by his own act; and the act of the whole is only the joint act of each individual member. The chief doubt is, whether the majority can naturally, by any joint act of theirs, bind, not only themselves, but the whole society, even those who are in the minority, and different from such act. This seems, at first sight, to be inconsistent with a well known rule, that, as all men are naturally equal, no person can be obliged by the act of another, without his own consent. But it is to be remembered, that when a man joins himself to a society, which is formed or instituted for the sake of carrying on some certain purpose, he either expressly consents, or must, by thus joining himself to such society, be understood tacitly to consent, that this purpose shall be carried on. He obliges himself, therefore, by his consent, either express or tacit, to whatever is necessary for carrying on this purpose in such a manner, as is consistent with reason and equity. Now there are but three ways in which a number of persons can do business jointly: it must be managed, either according to the sentiments of the whole body, or according to those of the greater part, or according to those of the lesser part. In all matters of a doubtful nature, or of an uncertain event; especially where the number of persons concerned is very great; it is next to impossible for all of them to agree in the same sentiments. The purposes, therefore, for which a society is formed, could not be carried on, if nothing less than the full agreement of all the members was sufficient to determine what was to be done, so as to bind each of them to concur in the same measure. But each member, when he joined himself to the society, consented, that this purpose should be carried on, and, consequently, consented to be bound in some reasonable and equitable manner; though the whole society should not happen to agree. This then being the case, the next question will be, whether it is more reasonable and more equitable, that the minority

* Grot. Lib. II. Cap. V. § XVII.

should be bound by the act of the majority, or the contrary? The answer to this question is obvious. It is plainly most consistent with reason, that the sentiments of the majority should prevail and conclude the whole: because it is not so likely that a greater number of men should be mistaken, when they concur in their judgment, as that a smaller number should be mistaken. And this is likewise most consistent with equity: because, in general, the greater number have a proportionably greater interest, that the purposes of the society should succeed well, and have more at stake, if those purposes should miscarry or be disappointed. This, then, being the most reasonable and the most equitable way for a number of men to do business jointly, when they are not all agreed upon the same measures; and each member of the society having originally consented, that the purposes, for which it was formed, should be carried on in the most reasonable and the most equitable manner; it follows that each member has consented to have the business of the society done according to the opinion of the majority; where there is not an unanimous agreement of the whole.

From hence, it appears, that, although no person can naturally be obliged but by his own consent, yet each person, who votes with the minority, is obliged, by the act of the majority. He does not, indeed, give an explicit consent to such act at the time of voting: but there was a prior consent, from whence this obligation arises: when he became a member of the society, he consented, either expressly or tacitly, that he would, in all instances, conform himself to what should be the sense of the greater part of that society, to which he joins himself, so as to become a member of it.

Upon an equality of votes nothing is done.

III. *Where the members of a society are equally divided in their opinions upon any point; there is no more weight of reason or of equity on one side than there is on the other. No business, therefore, can be done: and consequently all things must, upon such an equality of votes, continue in the same state that they were in before, without having any change made in them. For this reason, says Grotius, where judges are equally divided in their opinions, as to acquitting or condemning a criminal, such criminal is acquitted. And in like manner, where they are equally divided upon a question of property, the possessor keeps the thing in dispute.

But after he has thus assigned the true principle for these determinations, he goes on to observe, from Seneca, that, when one judge acquits, and another condemns, the milder or more favourable opinion prevails. It is true, in fact, that where the judges are thus equally divided upon the question, whether a person accused of a crime is guilty of it or not, the milder opinion does prevail. But this is merely accidental. The natural reason why it prevails, is, not because it is the milder opinion, but because nothing is done. A person accused of a crime is not properly a criminal, till the crime is proved upon him in the opinion of his judges. Unless this is done upon his trial, he is deemed innocent, and is, of course, acquitted; there being no middle condition, after trial, between being criminal and being innocent, between being acquitted and being condemned. If, therefore, where the

* Grot. Lib. II. Cap. V. § XVIII.

judges are equally divided in their opinion, nothing is done; the necessary consequence is, that the person accused is acquitted: because he has been tried, and is not, in the opinion of his judges, proved to be guilty.

In like manner, upon a question of property, the possessor naturally keeps the thing in dispute, if the judges are equally divided; not because it is the milder opinion, but because nothing is done, and things continue in the same state that they were in before the matter was litigated. As the possessor, therefore, had the thing before, so he keeps it afterwards; an equality of voices not having such a weight against him as to disturb his possession.

The fact, indeed, which Grotius alleges, as the ground of this determination, might, in many instances, be questioned; I mean, it might be questioned, whether the continuance of possession is the milder opinion. But allowing it to be so; this is not the principle which decides in the possessor's favour. If this was the leading principle, then, in all cases, where there is an equality of voices, the more favourable opinion would take place, as well as in these two cases, which Grotius mentions. Amongst other cases which might be produced, where it is otherwise, we have one in our own university. If a person petitions the senate for a degree, and the house is equally divided, his petition is rejected. This is certainly a determination on the less favourable side, and proceeds upon the other principle of doing nothing, where there is an equality of votes. He had no degree when he petitioned; and as an equality of votes does nothing, he continues in the same state: such an equality not being sufficient to produce any change, is not sufficient to give him a degree.

But though naturally the business of a society must stop, where the society is equally divided in opinion; yet, by mutual agreement, this case may be provided for several ways. Some one member of the society, either by express agreement, or by custom, which is a tacit agreement, may have a casting voice. Or the business, when, for want of a majority, it cannot be done by the whole society, may, by positive institution, devolve to some particular members of it: and where such institution gives these select members this power, their act, or, if it is so appointed, the act of the majority of them becomes binding upon the whole: because each person, when he consents to be a member of the society, is understood to agree to all the rules or institutions of it. In some lesser societies a farther provision is sometimes made: when a majority cannot be procured within the society, the business devolves to some one or more persons, who are not members of it. And where such provision has been properly established, the determination of such person or persons is binding upon the society: not because such a provision is naturally incidental to a society; but because, when it has been made and established as a standing rule of the society, all who become members of such society, if they do not consent to it expressly, are understood, by the act of making themselves members, to consent to it tacitly.

Natural majority, what, and how to be reckoned.

IV. * From what has been already said, the reader will easily understand, that the natural majority in a society, where no agreement has been made to the con-

* Grot. Lib. II. Cap. V. § XIX.

trary, is a major part of the whole. A society may be divided into three or more parts of as many different opinions: and though there may be a greater number of one opinion than of either of the other two; yet, unless that greater number is a majority of the whole society, it is not such a majority, as will naturally, or without some particular agreement, conclude the whole. If the members, who are of the other two opinions, when they are taken together, would make a majority of the whole society, neither the equity nor the reason is with the third party. The equity is not with them; because this third party has not a greater interest at stake: and the reason is not with them; because this party is not more likely to judge rightly, than the other two, which differ from it. But as this may be urged equally against any one of the three parties; in such circumstances all business must stop; unless some method has been contrived, and particularly settled, for carrying it on. Some of the methods already mentioned, by which the business of a society may be carried on, when there is an equality of votes, may be made use of here. Or it may have been particularly provided, either by express consent or by custom, that whatever is agreed upon by the greater number, whether such greater number is a majority of the whole or not, shall be conclusive. And though it is not naturally incidental to a society to be determined by such a majority as this; yet an express agreement for this purpose, or long custom, which is a tacit agreement, are natural means of obliging the members to be concluded by such a majority.

It may happen, that, when a society is divided upon any question into three or more parties, though none of the parties, taken separately, make a majority of the whole society, so as to determine upon the whole question; yet two of the parties may so far agree, upon part of the question, as to make a majority for determining that part. And if these two parties are reckoned together for this purpose; then the remaining part of the question is to be determined by a second vote or scrutiny. Thus, if a society of judges are divided into three parties, one of which condemns a criminal to death, another condemns him to banishment, and a third acquits him; the two former parties agree that he is guilty, and may be reckoned, together, to make a majority against those who acquit him. This part of the question, then, is determined conclusively: the third party is overruled by the majority, which have agreed, that he is to be punished, and is, therefore, obliged, upon a farther scrutiny, to join itself to one of the other two parties, so as to make a majority of the whole for settling what his punishment shall be. Suppose one party of the judges to condemn the criminal in a fine of ten pounds; another party to condemn him, in a fine of five pounds; and a third party, to acquit him: those who condemn him in a fine of ten pounds, agree with the second party, that he is to be fined: but though the lesser fine of five pounds is included in the greater, yet this is no reason why the fine should be settled at five pounds. The two parties agree, or say the same thing, thus far, that he is to be fined: but then they do not agree entirely: they, who set the fine at ten pounds, may be understood to say, that he shall be fined five pounds; but this is not all, that they say; they say this and more. We cannot, therefore, in order to procure a majority of the whole society, follow the opinion of Grotius, as Gronovius has explained it, and settle the fine at five pounds, but must, as in the former instance, proceed to a second scrutiny. The majority have determined, that the criminal shall be fined; they, therefore, who were for acquitting him, are concluded thus far, and must upon the other part of the question; how much the fine shall be? agree with one or the other of the two parties.

These difficulties may, however, in most instances, be avoided, if care is taken in stating the question, to divide it originally into all its parts, and then to put each part to the vote separately. Thus, in the first instance that we have been mentioning, if, instead of voting from the beginning, what in general was to be determined concerning the person accused, the judges begin with voting, whether he is guilty or not; they can only divide themselves into two parties. If this question is determined in the affirmative, they may next vote, whether he is to be punished capitally or not; and here, again, there can be but two parties. They may proceed in the same manner through the several sorts of punishment, and may thus, without much difficulty, come to a clear decision.

* The foundation of a society may be some real possession, in which the several members of the society have unequal shares. Thus a joint stock of money may belong to several proprietors; and some of these proprietors may have ten times, some four times, some three times as great a share in the capital as others. In such societies, Grotius is of opinion, that the weight of each person's vote, in regard to the management of the joint stock, should be estimated in proportion to his share in that stock; or that, if he, who has one share, has one vote upon any question; he, who has two shares, should have two votes; and he who has ten shares, should have ten votes. The equity of the case seems to be on this side, as it is equitable to allow each person a weight, in determining upon any question, proportionable to the interest which he has, that the whole stock should be rightly managed. But the reason of the thing is on the other side: since there is no more likelihood that a man should judge rightly about the management of such stock, because he has ten shares in it, than there would have been, if he had been possessed of no more than one share. We cannot, therefore, from the nature of such societies, determine either one way or the other: and this uncertainty makes it necessary, that the point should be settled by particular agreement. In fact, we find, that some societies of this sort have settled this point one way, and that others of the same sort have settled it the other way.

Absent members have a right to vote by proxy.

V. † When a society meets to do business, the absent members of it have a natural right to vote by proxy; that is, to appoint agents, who shall vote in their stead: because, what a man does by another is naturally as much his own act, as if he had done it in his own person. But when we speak of the right of voting by proxy, as a natural one, we must not be understood to mean, that it is an unalienable one, so that the members of a society cannot, by agreement, bind themselves either to vote in person, or not to vote at all: we only mean, that, where no such agreement has been made, either expressly or by custom, it is not incidental to society that no member should have a right to act by another: every one has, in

* Grot. Lib. II. Cap. V. § XXII.

† Grot. Ibid. § XX.

this instance, as in all others, a right of appointing a proxy to act for him, unless he has consented to part with that right.

A society may, indeed, be so formed, that each member may be represented in it, though he has no particular proxy. To such societies as these, it is naturally incidental, that the absent members of them should have no right of appointing any particular proxies: because they are represented without having any. Thus, if a society, which is too large for all the members of it conveniently to meet together for doing business, chooses a select number or smaller society out of the whole, and delegates a power to this smaller society to do business for them; each member of this committee or smaller society, being likewise a member of the whole, has had his vote already in the choice of such committee, and, consequently, is represented in it. If, therefore, he should at any time be absent when the rest meet, he has no right of voting by any particular proxy of his own immediate appointment; because, by this means, he would be twice represented; once by the committee, which he had a share in choosing, and once by such proxy so appointed.

But in all societies, where there is no right of appointing proxies, and even in those, which allow this right, if any member is absent, without appointing his proxy; such members, as are present, conclude the whole: because those who are absent, are, by their not attending either in person or by proxy, understood to devolve their power of voting, upon those who do attend.

CHAPTER II.

OF CIVIL SOCIETY, ITS NATURE AND ORIGIN.

I. *Civil society, what.*—II. *The motives which lead men to form civil societies.*—III. *All mankind are not one civil society.*—IV. *The manner of forming civil societies.*—V. *Occasions of forming civil societies.*—VI. *How men become members of civil societies.*—VII. *Members of a civil society, not to leave it without consent of the public.*—VIII. *How far allegiance to a civil society is due from its banished members.*

Civil society, what. I. A civil society, or, as we usually call it, a state, has* already been defined to be a complete assembly of men of free condition, who are united together for the purposes of maintaining their rights, and of advancing a common good. These two purposes, which civil society has in view, point out to us the mutual claims of such society and of its several members.

Each individual, who associates himself with others, so as to form with them one civil society or body politic, does it with a view of obtaining their assistance in the maintenance and support of his rights; that is, he proposes to himself the advantage of being protected against such injuries, as he might have been exposed to, if he had continued in

* See Book I. Chap. I. § XI.

a state of nature. On the other hand, the body politic, to which he joins himself; that is, the other individuals, with which he associates, expect in return, that, as he is protected by them, he shall agree with them in whatever is necessary or conducive to their common benefit.

Now, as these are the known purposes which the body and each of its members have respectively in view, in associating with one another; the very act of associating, though there should be no express stipulation between them, implies, that the society, considered as a body, agrees to the terms upon which each individual joins himself to it; and that each individual agrees to the terms upon which the society admits him as a member. And thus the society obliges itself to protect its several members; and each member obliges himself to pay allegiance to the society; that is, to conform himself to whatever such society shall judge to be for the common good.

The motives which lead men to form civil societies.

II. Under the notion of protection two things are implied; first, the ascertaining our several rights, and consequently the several duties that correspond to them; and secondly, the use of such force as is necessary to prevent those rights from being violated. The law of nature considers all mankind as one great society, and obliges them, in this view, not to hurt one another, and mutually to do for one another all such kind offices as are in their power. And if all mankind were fully informed of the several particulars included in this general rule, and were ready to act accordingly, they would have no inducements to separate themselves into lesser communities, or to form civil societies. But though the general rule of duty may be plain and obvious, yet all men are not able to apply it to particular instances of practice, and even amongst those, who can apply it, few are willing to act up to it. * The law of nature has, indeed, provided a remedy against injuries in the equality of nature: any person, who is either in danger of suffering an injury, or has actually suffered one, may make use of force either to defend or to redress himself. But this remedy will frequently be insufficient, when he has no force but his own to carry his claims into execution, and to support him in the enjoyment of what he has a right to. If those who unjustly oppose or attack him are stronger than he is, his right will avail but little against their superior strength. He might, indeed, defend himself; but he is not able: he might demand reparation of what damages he has sustained; but he is too weak to enforce this demand: he might inflict punishment upon them, who have done wrong, and so secure himself for the future; but they are stronger than he is, and refuse to submit to it. However, we are to observe, that not only the person who has suffered an injury, but those likewise, who have done one, have sometimes occasion for more strength than they are masters of, to secure what they have a right to. As the sufferer is apt to be too much blinded by passion and biassed by prejudice, to see how far his duty will allow him to go; there is commonly occasion for some less prejudiced understanding than his own, to lead him to what is right, and for some superior strength, to oppose itself to his passions and prevent him from doing what is wrong.

* Book I. Chap. XV. XVII, XVIII.

* All men may, indeed, in the liberty of nature, join their force to support the practice of justice: but then they are not obliged to do so; they are not so far bound to make themselves parties in the quarrel of another, as to give him any right to demand it of them. And even if he could demand their assistance, he would many times have no benefit from it; unless he had strength enough to compel them: and it is only for want of such strength that he has any occasion for their assistance.

Here, then, are sufficient motives to engage mankind to enter into civil societies, that every one may, by the joint understanding of many, be informed of his duty, and that every one may, by the joint force of many, be compelled to practise it. Nor can we well conceive any other motives that should lead mankind thus to associate, but what may be reduced to one or other of these two heads: because all would be as happy as they could wish to be, or at least as the condition of human nature would allow them to be; if all were fully informed of their duty, and all were willing and ready to comply with it.

All mankind are not one civil society.

III. The motives which we have been speaking of, would not engage any man to associate himself with all his species. What he is chiefly concerned in is, that they who live near him, or with whom he has the most frequent intercourse, should have their duty ascertained, and should be held to the performance of it by such a force, as is sufficient to restrain or to correct them. His interest will be secured, as far as he wants to have it secured, provided they, who are most likely to hurt him, or to hinder his benefit, are informed what they ought to do, and what they ought to avoid; and provided he associates himself with such a number, as will have force enough to guard him against the injuries which he fears, or to redress the injuries which he has suffered. As good care is taken of his happiness, as he has occasion for, by joining himself to a part of mankind: if they, to whom he is joined, are properly informed of their duty, and have strength enough both to enforce the practice of this duty amongst themselves, and to repel the injuries of all, who are not associated with them, it is of no importance to him to join himself in this manner to any more, and much less to form the same sort of connexion with all mankind.

It is necessary, that the number of persons thus uniting themselves should not be very small: because, though others who are at a distance from them and have but little intercourse with them, are not very likely to injure them at all, or at least have not an opportunity of injuring them frequently; yet, since what is not very likely to happen often, may possibly happen sometimes, it is convenient to have such a number united as will be able, not only to restrain them who are members of the same society from doing what is wrong to one another, but to repel likewise the violence of others, who are not associated with them. But in the meantime the ends which men propose to themselves in forming civil societies, are so far from leading them to associate in this manner with their whole species, that in such a bulky society these ends could not be conveniently and effectually answered. The common understanding of such an extensive body could neither be collected nor made known, so as to guide all the parts of it: and such an un-

* Book I. Chap. XIX. § IV.

wieldy body would be unable to exert its joint force. There would, indeed, be no exercise of a common force wanting to repel the external enemies of this vast community; because, by the supposition, all mankind are included in it. But, then, as the several parts of it have such inconsistent humours, and such different interests; some or other of them would set up for themselves, and would be daily forming lesser bodies with an interest of their own, separate from the interest of the rest. And as the joint force of the whole could not exert itself to repress such parties, after they were formed, those parties would be able to do what they pleased; unless the force of their nearest neighbours was sufficient to repress them. But as this neighbouring force would not always be sufficient for this purpose, the parties so formed would sometimes establish themselves into a separate society. It would, therefore, not only be useless, as to the ends of engaging in civil society, to form one of such a vast extent; but even, if such an one was formed, it would be impossible for it to subsist long, without being broken to pieces, and resolved into such smaller bodies, as can be directed by the common understanding or general sense of their respective wholes, and can exert such a joint force, as is necessary, not only to guard themselves from foreign enemies, but to reduce their several constituent parts to obedience, and by this means to keep themselves together.

The manner of forming civil societies.

IV. What has been already shown, in the former part of this work, concerning the natural rights of mankind considered as individuals, will serve to teach us by what means civil societies must be formed, in order to make them consistent with those natural rights. * Every man has naturally a right to think and to act for himself. The law of nature has indeed restrained him from doing what is unjust, and has subjected him to proper checks to prevent him from causelessly hurting others, and to proper punishment, if he does causelessly hurt them: it has obliged him likewise to advance the happiness of mankind, as he has ability and opportunity; but then it leaves him to judge and determine for himself in what instances he can conveniently advance their good, and to choose for himself the means of doing it. When he becomes a member of a civil society, the public or body politic claims a right of pointing out to him what is just and what is unjust, and of directing him likewise what good he is to do, and in what manner he is to do it. There is no way of making such a claim as this, consistent with his natural right of thinking and choosing for himself; unless by his own consent, either express or tacit, he has waived this right, and has voluntarily agreed to be so guided and directed. Every man has naturally a right to make use of his own force, either for his own defence, when he is in danger of being injured, or to obtain reparation and to inflict punishment, when he has been injured. But the civil society, to which he is joined, claims a right to judge both upon what occasions any force is lawful, and what force is lawful upon these occasions. And as it takes him and all its other members under the protection of the common force, and considers him as a part of the public; it does not allow him to exert his own force, but in concert with the public, and requires him so to exert it, whenever it is wanted. Here again the claim of civil society, upon the in-

* Book I. Chap. X. § III.

dividuals that compose it, cannot be reconciled with the natural rights of mankind, unless each individual has, either by express or tacit, by explicit or implied consent, parted with such rights, and agreed, that, where the public force can defend or redress him, he will never make use of his own, but in such manner as the public shall direct. Thus the liberty of individuals is abridged in a state of civil society: the community has such a claim upon them in respect both of the rules, which they are to follow, and of the manner in which they are to make use of their force, as the same men that compose the society would not have had, either severally or jointly, if they had continued unassociated, or had remained in that state of equality in which all mankind are naturally placed. And as it would be an injury to take any part of their natural liberty from them without their consent, the consequence is, that civil societies could not be formed, consistently with natural justice, by any other means than by the joint consent, either express or tacit, of those who compose them.

Each individual who thus consents to give up a part of his natural liberty, obtains however more than an equivalent for what he gives up. If he submits to be guided in his duty by the public understanding or general sense of the community to which he joins himself, those, who are near him, and with whom he has the most frequent intercourse, submit in return to be guided in the same manner. And as by this means he is less likely to transgress the duty which he owes to others, so he has good reason to expect that others will be less likely to transgress the duty which they owe to him, than if both they and he had continued in a state of natural independency. As he parts with his independent right of using his own force according to his own discretion, either to defend or to redress himself, and gives the public a claim upon him to join his force with theirs, who are associated with him, whenever his assistance is wanted; so in return he is assured of the protection of the community, and has the advantage of a stronger force than his own, to defend and to redress him when he has a reasonable occasion for it.

As this principle of forming a civil society by the mutual consent of those who are members of it, is sufficient to reconcile the obligations which each member is under to the public, with their respective natural rights; so it will likewise show us, that their associating themselves together in this manner is not contrary to the rights of others, who are not associated with them, and to the obligations which they are under to the rest of their species. The claim which the public has upon the liberty of each individual who is a member of it, arises originally from his own consent. This * claim, therefore, can extend no farther, than such individual had a power of binding himself or of alienating his liberty. Now, each individual who joins himself to any civil society, is under a prior obligation to observe the laws of nature, and to make them the rule of his conduct towards all mankind: and as he has not the liberty of transgressing those laws, he cannot alienate a liberty which he never had: and consequently he cannot give the society a right to require him to transgress them. When, therefore, a number of men have united themselves together for the purposes of maintain-

* Book I. Chap. X. § IV.

ing their rights, and of promoting their common good; what they have done in order to obtain these purposes, is no injury to the rest of mankind. The individuals who are thus associated, are still under the same obligations towards all such as are not associated with them, that they would have been under if they had still continued in the liberty of nature. Whatever adventitious obligations arise from the civil connexion of these individuals with one another, they must be such as are consistent with the duties which they naturally owe to the rest of mankind, who are not joined to them by any connexions of this sort. Those who are members of the same civil society, acquire new rights and are laid under new obligations in respect of one another. But then, since these rights and these obligations must be consistent with the law of nature, all who are members of the same civil society, are still bound to observe the law of nature towards the rest of mankind; their rights and obligations in respect of all such as are either members of different civil societies, or remain in the liberty of nature, are the same that they would have been if no such civil connexions had ever been formed.

Occasions of forming civil societies.

V. The occasions of forming or beginning distinct civil societies have been various. A number of individuals, falling into distress at one and the same time, and hoping by their joint force and mutual assistance to mend their condition, have in many instances been the founders of new civil societies. Thus a multitude of the Heneti, who had been driven from Paphlagonia, joined themselves to Antenor, and settling with him on the coast of Italy, founded the state of Venice. It may perhaps be denied, that there ever was a time when all mankind lived in a state of nature. But be this as it will, there certainly have been many persons who at one and the same time have been broken off from societies already established, and have been forced to shift for themselves independently of one another. Individuals in these circumstances are properly in a state of nature, and have no other connexions with one another, besides what they make by joint consent: and their common distress is a natural occasion of endeavouring to form such connexions for their mutual relief and support.

But distress has not always been the occasion which led men to unite together and to form a common or civil interest. They have sometimes been brought together by their birth, that is, by having arisen from the same common parent. I would not be understood to mean that parental power is the same with kingly power; and that the children of the same parent were under any natural obligation to submit to such parent as their civil governor, after they were grown up. They were subject indeed to his parental authority whilst they continued in the state of infancy; and this might induce them to place themselves afterwards by their free consent under his civil jurisdiction. But if no such * consent had intervened, then as soon as they were grown up, and were able to think and to act for themselves, they were naturally at liberty either to continue in his family, and so to become subject to his power, as the head of this little community, or else to withdraw themselves from it, and to begin other families or communities of their own. Their children, again, when they came to years of discretion, would enjoy

* Book I. Chap. XI. § V.

the same liberty; they might either remain with the original ancestor, and so increase the family; or they might separate themselves from this community and set up for themselves. If the children of the same parent, and their descendants after them, chose to remain united together under the direction of the common ancestor; such a number of free men so united by their own consent, in order to secure their respective rights, and to advance their common interest, would form a civil society. I call them free men; notwithstanding the subjection to their common ancestor, which began from their birth, might be continued during the life-time of such ancestor: because when they were at age to judge for themselves, they were free to separate themselves from his family: and if their subjection to him as their civil governor continued, it was the effect of their own act. His authority as a parent ceased when they attained to the use of their reason: and whatever authority, properly so called, he might have over them afterwards, as parts of his family, it was derived from their choosing to continue in this family, of which he was the head. If any of the immediate or the remoter descendants of this common ancestor found reasons to leave the family, those who so separated themselves from it, acted as consistently with the law of nature, and consequently had as good a right to do what they did, as the others who remained in it. For the law of nature, after children are arrived at a proper age, ties them to no other duty in respect of their parents, besides those of gratitude and reverence: and these are duties which will not confine them to live under the jurisdiction of their parent; they are duties which imply no such subjection as will oblige the children to continue in the parent's family, and to submit themselves to his civil authority.

The * Jewish state arose from such a beginning as this. The descendants of Abraham, in those branches of the family, which were derived from Isaac, and after him from Jacob, continued together, till they were so increased as to become a multitude; and till their family connexion ended in a civil union. In the meantime, Ishmael and Esau, with their respective descendants, separated themselves from the rest of the family; and each of them founded distinct bodies politic. They became wholly unconnected with the rest of their brethren, and with each other, and had no other connexion with their respective parents, besides the ties of filial love and reverence. We have an instance of this filial love in Ishmael, when he joined with his brother Isaac† in burying their common parent. And I choose to take notice of this circumstance, that the reader may not imagine the son's duty of filial reverence to be inconsistent with his civil independency: for it is plain, that Ishmael, notwithstanding this act of filial reverence, had no civil dependence upon his father Abraham: because he was then separated from the family of Abraham, not only by his own choice, but by the act of Abraham himself, and, consequently, was so entirely free from all proper jurisdiction of his parent, as to have a full right to dispose of himself in what manner he pleased. It is farther observable in this patriarchal family, that a son, by being separated from the family of his parent, not only ceases to be under the jurisdiction of this family with the parent at the head of it, but may even acquire civil jurisdic-

* Gen. Chap. XVI, XVII, &c. † Gen. XXV. 9.

tion over it. Joseph was accidentally separated from the rest of his brethren, and began a family of his own in Egypt; where he was advanced to civil authority, not only over the native Egyptians, but over all strangers, who were permitted to settle in that country; amongst whom we find his father and his brethren. No one can reasonably deny, that, in these circumstances, he had as good a natural right to found a distinct society, as his father Jacob had. Any positive command of God to keep all the children of Jacob united together is here out of the question. As we are now considering how civil societies may begin, and what may give occasion to the founding of them consistently with natural right; we might be excused from taking notice of whatever is matter of positive institution. However, we find, that even in this family, which was kept together by such positive command, the descendants of Joseph were looked upon as parts of a new family, exempt from the patriarchal jurisdiction, till they were recalled into it by* adoption or consent of parties. So little ground is there for concluding, that, because family connexions have, in some instances, been the occasion of civil union; therefore, civil power is naturally derived from parental authority, without the consent of those who are subject to such civil power.

The reader, if he attends to the history of Abraham's family, will be able to deduce these consequences from it. First, civil societies may frequently begin from family connexions: the children and descendants of the same common stock, having been connected with one another originally, may choose to continue united, and by such a voluntary union, which their original connexion led them to, may form a body politic. But then secondly, though every child is born under a natural subjection to his parents; yet he becomes independent of them as he advances in years, and is able to think and to act for himself. He is, therefore, at liberty either to separate himself from his brethren, to remove himself from under the jurisdiction of his parents, and to begin a family or society of his own, or else to continue with his brethren, to remain under the jurisdiction of his parents, and so to make a part of that community, of which his parents are the head. If the child separates himself from the family of his parents, their authority over him is at an end; nay, he may even acquire civil jurisdiction over them. He still owes them, indeed, the duties of gratitude and esteem; and as the instance of Ishmael, already mentioned, will serve to teach us, that these duties are consistent with the civil independence of the child, so the behaviour of Joseph towards his father is an evidence, that the duty of filial piety is so far from subjecting the son to any civil jurisdiction of the father, that it is consistent even with the son's civil jurisdiction over the father. If the child remains in the family of the parent: then, indeed, the parent's authority over him continues after he is come to years of discretion: but it is continued no otherwise, than by the choice and voluntary act of the child: it is his own consent, either express or tacit, which produces civil jurisdiction, when paternal authority ends.

If any one doubts, whether civil society arose at first from mutual consent, and his doubts proceed from a notion, that mankind were never actually in a state of equality, because all men were born in a natural

* Gen. XLVIII. 5, 6. 16.

subjection to their parents; it will now be easy to clear up this difficulty. The subjection of a child to the authority of his parents continues during his infancy: but after he is come to years of discretion, he is then, as to any jurisdiction or authority, properly so called, equal to his parents, and is, therefore, in respect of them, so far in a state of nature, as to be at liberty either to join with them in the same society, or to begin a society of his own. Suppose it, therefore, to be true, in fact, that civil society is as ancient as the race of mankind, and that the natural connexions of the first family gave occasion to the first civil society; yet this supposition will be no objection to what has been said concerning the means, by which civil societies are formed. These family connexions might give occasion to civil union; but such union could never be formed consistently with that natural equality and independency, to which all men are born, without some express or tacit consent of the individuals so united. Notwithstanding the first man's parental authority over his children, he would have had no natural right to keep them in subjection, after they became capable of thinking and acting for themselves; if they had not agreed to submit to him as their civil governor.

It is probable, indeed, that the first civil societies were nothing else but so many distinct families with their respective parent at the head of each of them. But then we cannot well imagine, that in these first rudiments of civil society, or these first attempts to form bodies politic, every thing was immediately as well regulated, as we find it at present. There is not the least appearance of reason for believing that the ties, by which the several parts of these bodies were united to one another, were the same then, that we find them to be now. We must, on the one hand, be but little acquainted with the history of mankind, or of the beginning of nations, if we can persuade ourselves, either that the first civil society was formed by a regular meeting of a number of men, who had before lived in a state of nature, and then agreed to unite into a body politic, which arose at once from such agreement, complete in all its parts, as well methodized as the ends of forming such bodies require, as the light of reason could suggest, or the law of nature admit. On the other hand, if we are aware, that the first rudiments of civil society were laid amongst the children of the same parent, and amongst the families descended from the same common stock; we must have made but few observations upon the gradual improvements in all other human inventions, if we can persuade ourselves that societies were from the beginning kept together by the same ties which keep them together at present. One would rather think that a common affection for their parent, a deference to his judgment, a sense of his regard for them, and the inconvenience of leaving him, were the bands, which at first kept his descendants together. As these bands would be broken by his death, the several families, which were derived from him, would then be at liberty to separate from one another. Thus the several sons of the same parent, who continued in a sort of temporary society whilst he lived, would be in a state of nature after his death, and might either by a subsequent consent, continue united under such a form of government as they could agree upon, or else might each of them assert his own independency, and begin a society from that branch of the family, of which he himself was the head.

We meet with something like this in the history of Jacob and Esau. * Though Esau complained of having been defrauded by his brother; yet, whilst they continued in the family of Isaac, he considered himself as under the jurisdiction of their common parent, and did not propose immediately to punish the act which he complained of, but resolved, that, after Isaac's death, he would assert his own independency, and would kill his brother Jacob. His † convenience, however, led him afterwards to separate from his father, and to set up for himself, before this event happened. By this means he became independent of the little society to which he formerly belonged, and was advanced to be the head of such another society of his own forming. Jacob was aware of this; and knowing that his brother Esau was no longer under the jurisdiction of their common parent, he did not think himself safe under Isaac's protection, but sought for other means of security, and endeavoured to purchase the friendship, or at least, to appease the anger of Esau by a present.

It is not necessary to suppose, that all civil societies were increased, till they became as large as we now find them, by the constant addition of fresh descendants from the same original parent. As the sons of one common parent, and the families derived from those sons who had consented to remain united together under the jurisdiction of such parent, as long as he lived, were at liberty after his death either to continue in a like union, or to separate from one another; so the sons of different families, and their descendants with them, in consequence of such a liberty as this, might join with one another and form larger bodies, which did not come originally from the same common stock. Such unions may frequently have been occasioned by the want of a settlement, or by the fear of unjust violence. The fear even of just punishment has undoubtedly sometimes increased the multitude in a society thus joined together: and Rome itself would have begun from smaller numbers than it did, if its founder had not opened an asylum to screen criminals from justice. Nay, there is some reason to believe, that the first society which we read of, owed its original to such an occasion as this. ‡ The first city that history makes mention of, was built by Cain. And if Cain does not show what motive led him to this undertaking, when he declares his apprehension, that every one who found him would kill him; yet we may learn it with some degree of certainty from what Lamech is recorded to have said to his two wives. He did not choose to be shut up with his brethren, but was desirous to live at large like the rest of mankind: and to encourage his wives not to fear, that the crime of their ancestor would be punished upon them, he clears himself from the guilt of it, and assures them that there was no danger in leaving their present way of life, and in trusting themselves abroad. This will be the most obvious meaning of what he says to Adah and Zillah, if we render the words as they may be rendered: Have I slain a man to my wounding, and a young man to my hurt? If Cain shall be avenged seven-fold, truly Lamech seventy and seven-fold.

* Gen. XXVII. 41. † Gen. XXXII. 3, 4, &c. ‡ Gen. IV. 17. 23.

How men become members of civil societies.

VI. The condition of mankind is at present something different from what it was formerly, when civil societies first began to establish themselves. Such societies are now established in almost all parts of the world that are inhabited at all: they are no longer in their first rudiments, as they were whilst separate families were making attempts to settle themselves, and to collect a force sufficient to repel injuries, but are founded upon steady principles, and unite their several members together by firm and lasting ties. And yet even in the present circumstances of mankind, numberless individuals have an opportunity of setting themselves free from these ties in such a manner as to be at liberty either to found new civil societies, or to unite themselves to such new societies as others have begun.

It will be necessary, for the better understanding this matter, to consider by what means men naturally become members of any particular nation or civil society; and by what means, after they are so become members, they may be at liberty to separate themselves from it again. Civil societies, in general, are willing to consider persons who are born amongst them, as members of those societies where they are born. It is plain, that they are considered in this light; because if they were looked upon as aliens, till they have been formally admitted to be members, they would, like all other aliens, be incapable of inheriting immoveable goods. But then this is matter of favour in the society; and persons so born seem to be naturally at liberty either to make use of this favour or to refuse it. There does not appear to be any natural reason why a child, though he is born of parents who belong to any particular nation or civil society, and is born likewise within the territories of that nation, should be obliged, after he is come to years of discretion, to continue in it. Positive institutions may indeed have ordered it otherwise: but he appears to be naturally at liberty either to make himself a member of that society, if it will receive him, or to join himself to any other, or to begin a new one in any part of the world not yet inhabited. He may, indeed, part with this liberty, after he is capable of thinking and of acting for himself, either by express or by tacit consent. If any express stipulations for that purpose pass between him and the society in which he was born, he makes himself a member of it, and is no more at liberty, after such stipulations, to leave this society, than he is to depart from any other contract, by which he has bound himself. But without any formal or express stipulations, he may unite himself effectually to the society, in which he is born, by tacit consent. After he is arrived at maturity of judgment, if he continues to make use of the protection of that society, and to pay it such allegiance as it requires of its members; his conduct must necessarily be understood as an evidence on his part, that he is willing or consents to be a member of it, and on the part of the society, that it consents to receive him. Amongst other instances of tacit consent, we may reckon his taking and holding such immoveable goods, as are in the jurisdiction or general property of the society. As *aliens cannot naturally take and hold such goods, it is plain, that the society by allowing a native to take and hold them considers, or however is willing to consider,

* Book I. Chap. VI. § VI.

a native as a member. And whoever makes use of this favour declares by so doing, that he is willing or consents to be considered in the same light in which the society considered him. And it may be worth the while to observe, that though he should afterwards relinquish his goods, or dispose of them by sale or by gift, he does not cease to owe allegiance to the society: because the jurisdiction of the society over him did not arise merely from the possession of such goods, but from his consent to be a member of it, of which consent his so taking and holding these goods was an evidence.

The only natural difference between a native and a foreigner, in respect of their becoming members of any particular civil society, is, that the native was certainly never united to any other society; whereas, the foreigner may possibly have been united to some other, before he came to settle within the territories of this. The effect of this doubt, concerning the possibility of the foreigner's being a member of some other civil society, is, that he cannot become a member of the nation in whose territories he settles, without some express stipulations by which he engages his allegiance to this nation, and is formally received by it. If he continues there any time before he makes these express stipulations, and before he is formally received as a member, he is obliged to behave himself peaceably and to submit to the laws of the country; because the society would not suffer him to stay within its territories upon any other terms. This peaceable behaviour therefore is no evidence on his part, that he owes no allegiance any where else: and the society by allowing him to stay within its territories, before this point is cleared up, cannot be understood tacitly to receive him as a member. In the meantime he cannot unite himself to the society by taking and holding such land, as is under its jurisdiction: because as long as he is considered as an alien, that is, till he is formally admitted into the society, he is naturally incapable of taking and holding such land. These principles, however, are not applicable to foreigners, who have been brought by their parents into the territories of any nation, and have settled there, whilst they were in their infancy. For at that time of life, they could naturally owe no allegiance elsewhere. And consequently, if any distinction is made between such foreigners and natives, it must be derived merely from positive institution.

But notwithstanding the close ties by which, in the present constitution of civil societies, men are generally understood to be connected with those particular societies of which they are members; it is possible for them to recover a natural right of founding and establishing new societies independent of that to which they formerly belonged. Where the territories of a nation are small, or where the inhabitants even of a large territory become very numerous, especially if they have not the skill or the opportunity of supplying themselves with necessaries by husbandry, or by trade and by manufactures; it will be for the convenience of all parties, that companies of adventurers should be sent out to seek their fortune. Sometimes a powerful faction in a state think it for their interest to drive out their weaker antagonists. Sometimes a lawless tyranny, usurped over the religious or civil rights of the subjects, leaves them only the alternative either of submitting to oppression and cruelty, or of freeing themselves by a voluntary exile. Sometimes by war or other calamities a civil society, which was formerly established, may be broken in pieces. In any of these cases, and in many others of the like sort, which the reader's own imagination, or his acquaintance with the history of mankind may suggest to him, there are individuals enough restored to the liberty or equality of nature to begin new societies in any part of the world where they can gain a settlement, and under any form of government that is agreeable to themselves. And as individuals, when they are in these circumstances, are at liberty to found a civil society of their own, if they have numbers sufficient for such a purpose; so are they at liberty to join themselves to any civil society which is already established, and is willing to receive them.

Members of civil society not to leave it without consent of the public.

VII. *Grotius is inclined to think, that individuals, after they are become members of any particular civil society, are at liberty to withdraw themselves from it at any time, even without having first obtained the consent of that society. The principal, or indeed the only reason which he offers in support of this opinion, is, that though such a liberty might be inconvenient to the society in respect of the members which it loses, yet this inconvenience may be balanced by the general consideration, that, if this is the case in all civil societies whatsoever, each in its turn would be as likely to gain new members from others, as to lose old members of its own. But the determination of this question does not depend upon prudential reasons, which can only give occasion to positive institutions; but upon such reasons as are drawn from those mutual ties between the body politic and its several members, which necessarily result from the nature of civil society.

Grotius himself makes such concessions upon this head, as will be sufficient to overturn his own opinion. In the first place he allows, that it is inconsistent with the nature of civil society for its members to withdraw themselves in great numbers at one and the same time. For we cannot suppose civil society to form itself upon such principles as naturally tend to its own destruction: and consequently we cannot suppose the nature of it to be such as will allow the members to withdraw themselves in great numbers at once; because such a liberty as this tends to destroy it. From this concession we may reason in the following manner: If any one individual is at liberty to withdraw himself at any time from the civil society of which he is a member, without having first obtained the consent of that society; any other individual has the same liberty. If any two individuals may thus leave the society whenever they please, any other two may leave it in like manner. And what is naturally lawful for any four individuals, must upon the same principles be equally lawful for any four hundred, or any four thousand, or any other number of them. We cannot, therefore, maintain that a single member of a civil society may leave the society to which he belongs, whenever he pleases; unless we will maintain farther, that any number of members may leave it at any time. But our author allows, that it is inconsistent with the nature of civil society for great numbers thus to withdraw themselves: and consequently he ought, upon his own principles, to allow that it is equally inconsistent with the nature of civil society for any single member to leave it till he has first obtained the consent of the society.

* Grot. Lib. II. Cap. V. § XXIV.

Grotius allows farther, that where the society has any particular interest in keeping all its members together; suppose, for instance, that the public is in debt, so that the burden of paying the debt will be less felt, in proportion as there are more persons to bear a part of it; or suppose that the state is engaged in a war, or any other undertaking, the success of which depends upon its numbers; no person can leave the society consistently with his obligations to it, unless he has taken care to satisfy the interest, which it has in his continuing united to it. Now, if this is a true principle, if no member of a civil society is at liberty to withdraw himself from it, where the society has a particulai interest in his not withdrawing himself; the consequence is, that no member can leave the society, till he has first obtained the consent of the public: unless we maintain that each member has naturally a right to judge and determine between himself and the public, how far it is interested in his staying or withdrawing himself.

If each individual was at liberty to leave the state to which he belongs whenever he pleases, civil society would be nothing but a rope of sand; it would be impossible for a common good to be effectually promoted, or for a common mischief to be effectually guarded against. Every member of the society would be at liberty either to continue in it, and endeavour to advance the general interest, or to leave it, in order to advance a separate interest of his own. And in times of public distress, whoever could shift for himself would be at liberty to do so, though he left the other members of the society to perish for want of his assistance. But the great end of forming civil societies is to promote a common good, and to guard against a common mischief. Certainly, therefore, the nature of civil society can never allow such a liberty as this to its members: because it is inconsistent with the end which a civil society proposes to itself. Each particular member, indeed, proposes to advance his own interest, to obtain his own benefit, and to guard himself against such dangers, as he would be exposed to in a state of nature. But this design of any individual, though it is the motive which engaged him to join himself to the society, is not the measure of the obligation which he is under towards it. The other individuals, who are associated with him, as each of them had the same view for himself that he had, would not have joined with him for these purposes of promoting his benefit, and of securing him from violence, unless he would consent to join with them for the like purposes, for the purposes of promoting their benefit, and of securing them from violence. So that if each member is considered in his turn as an individual joining himself to society, and the other members are considered as the society to which he joins himself; the ends proposed on each part are their respective benefit and security. And as these are the terms upon which they associate; the very act of associating implies, that they agree to these terms, that each individual consents to join in promoting the common interest, and in maintaining the common security of the rest. The end, therefore, which each proposes, is a particular good to himself: but he cannot pursue this end by the help of civil society; that is, the society will not receive him as a member upon any other terms, but those of consenting, and, consequently, of obliging himself by such consent, to join with it in promoting a general good. Protection is the end which he proposes; and as the society, by receiving him, agrees to this end, it becomes the measure of the society's obligation towards him. Allegiance is what the society expects in return; and as he, by joining himself to it, agrees to these terms, they become the measure of his obligation towards the society. But in this mutual obligation thus derived from mutual consent, as in all other contracts, where there is no failure in performing the conditions stipulated on one part, it would be unjust not to perform the conditions stipulated on the other part; unless the parties contracting have released one another by a like consent: as long as the society grants the protection which it owes to the individual, he cannot justly withdraw the allegiance which he owes to the society, unless he has the consent of the society for so doing.

There is, however, no reason for maintaining, in the meantime, that every person, who is a member of any civil society, must necessarily continue a member of the same society, unless the public expressly consents to his removal from it. Where an individual of little or no importance to the state removes, and is neither stopped at first, nor reclaimed afterwards; this may be looked upon as a tacit consent; the public may be presumed to agree to what it does not hinder. And thus far the opinion of Grotius may be admitted to be true; that though a single member, of no importance, may thus remove, in times of peace and security, without the express leave of the state; yet no individual of great importance, nor a great number of individuals, who are made of importance by their numbers, nor any individual in times of public distress, when the situation of affairs makes every one of importance, can presume upon the consent of the state, but in order to justify their removal, they ought to have its express consent: not because an inconsiderable person, in times of peace and security, has any more right to withdraw from a society without its consent, than he would have in times of public danger; or than an important person, or a number of persons of any sort would have at any time; but because the consent of the society, though it is not expressly granted, may be more reasonably presumed in one case, than it can be in the other.

This obligation, upon every individual who is a member of any civil society, not to leave it without either the express or the tacit consent of the public, is no exception to an instance, just now mentioned, of persons freeing themselves from lawless tyranny and oppression by a voluntary exile: since the withdrawing protection on the part of the society, and much more such lawless tyranny and oppression, as is not only inconsistent with the notion of protection, but is directly contrary to it, must necessarily be looked upon as a discharge from allegiance on the part of its members. For in this contract between the members and the body, as in all other contracts of a like sort, when one of the parties refuse to discharge their part of the obligation, this is naturally a release to the other party.

How far allegiance to a civil society is due from its banished members.

VIII. A civil society, says * Grotius, has no claim of allegiance upon its banished members. And certainly this must be true in general: because the obligations of protection, on the part of the society, and of allegiance on the part of its members being mutual; whenever the society judges

* Grot. Lib. II. Cap. V. § XXV.

the crimes of any one of its members to be such as will discharge it from affording him protection any longer, and will justify it in forcing him to leave it, the natural consequence of its withdrawing protection is, that such member will be discharged from all claims of allegiance, which the society had upon him. We might as reasonably maintain, on the one hand, that the public owes protection to the individual, when he has withdrawn his allegiance, as on the other hand, that the individual owes allegiance to the public, when it has withdrawn its protection. All that can be said to make these two cases appear different is, that if the individual is banished for any crimes committed by him, the public has a just cause for putting him out of its protection; whereas, if he has left the society without its consent, he has not justly withdrawn his allegiance. But this difference is not at all material to the point in question. If, indeed, we maintained, that where protection is withdrawn by the society, allegiance may be withdrawn by the member in the way of reprisal; it might be something to the purpose to urge, that in the case of banishment, the state has a just cause for putting the member out of its protection: because then it would follow, that where the society has done no wrong to the individual by banishing him, he could not justly make the reprisal of withdrawing his allegiance. But this is not the way in which his obligation to allegiance ceases: it ceases of natural consequence: his right to protection and his obligation to allegiance correspond to one another; and when he loses the right, whether justly or unjustly, the correspondent obligation is at end. However, the opinion of Grotius upon this head, though it is true in general, ought to be so explained as to admit of its natural limitations. A member of civil society is commonly said to be banished, when he is compelled to leave that part of the society's territories, in which he was settled, and had made all his connexions before, and to remove to some distant, and perhaps inconvenient part of them. Such a removal as this, though we usually call it banishment, is not properly a banishment from the society, but only from his own habitation: he still continues within the territories, and consequently is still subject to the civil jurisdiction of the society. So, likewise, we call the temporary removal of a man from under the protection of that society, of which he is a member, by the name of banishment. He is sai to be banished if he is compelled to leave the territories for seven or fo ten years. In the meantime the protection of the society is suspended, and of consequence, his allegiance must be suspended with it. But then, at the expiration of the time, his own state will have the same claim of subjection upon him, that it would have had if he had never been banished: because, as such a banishment is not a final excision of him; the nature of it shows, that the state intended to receive him under its protection again, and to reclaim his allegiance. But where the banishment is not limited to any particular time; or where it appears from the beginning to be a final excision of the member; the regard which he may show to the authority of such society, after he has left it, is merely voluntary; the hopes of being recalled may lead him, but the nature of civil society will never oblige him to pay it.

CHAPTER III.

OF CIVIL POWER.

I. *Civil power is legislative or executive.*—II. *Origin of civil power.*—III. *Legislative power implies a power of altering and repealing laws.*—IV. *Legislative power implies a power of enacting penalties.*—V. *Legislative power implies a power of taxing the subjects.*—VI. *Executive power is either external, or internal, or mixed.*—VII. *Judicial power is internal executive power.*—VIII. *External executive power is military power.*—IX. *Appointment of magistrates is mixed executive power.*—X. *Prerogative, what.*—XI. *Civil and military power, how distinguished.*

Civil power is legislative or executive.

I. If we attend to the motives which lead men to unite into civil societies, they will help to give us some insight into the nature of civil power, that is, to inform us what sort of power naturally arises out of such an union. As men are originally led to unite themselves into distinct civil societies, with a view of having their several rights and duties ascertained by a joint or common understanding, and with a view likewise of forming a joint or common force, so as to act with it for their security; we cannot suppose them to have united together, without designing at the same time to establish such powers as would be necessary for obtaining these purposes, which they had in view. The natural consequence therefore of men's forming a civil society, is the establishment of a power in such society, to settle or ascertain, by its joint or common understanding, the several rights and duties of those who are members of it, and of a power likewise, to act with its joint or common force for their defence and security. The former of these is called the legislative, the latter is called the executive power. No other powers besides these are requisite for obtaining the ends which mankind propose to themselves in forming civil societies; no other powers, therefore, besides these are necessary for governing such societies: and consequently civil power, which we have defined to be the power that governs a civil society, consists of these two branches, and of these only.

Origin of civil power.

II. After what has been * said, it will be needless to stop here and inquire from whence civil power is derived. For since this power, in both its branches, naturally arises from the establishment of civil society, the same consent or agreement of mankind, by which they form themselves into distinct societies, must necessarily be the principle from whence civil power is derived.

Legislative power implies a power of altering and of repealing laws.

III. The legislative power, as it is here defined, implies a power not only of making laws, but of altering and repealing them. As the circumstances either of the state itself or of the several individuals which compose it, are changed, such claims and such duties as might once be beneficial, may become useless, burdensome, or even hurtful. If, therefore, the legislative power could not change the rules which it prescribes, so as

* Book II. Chap. II.

to suit them to the circumstances of the body politic, and of the members of that body; it could not answer the purposes for which it was established; it could not at all times settle their claims and their duties in such a manner as is most conducive to the good of the whole, and of the several individuals which make up that whole.

Legislative power implies a power of enacting penalties.

IV. The legislative power implies, farther, a power of establishing laws in such a manner as to make them effectual; that is, in such a manner as to secure the observance of them. For it would answer no purpose at all to show men what their duty is, if they were afterwards to be left at liberty either to discharge or neglect it at their own discretion, without apprehending any particular inconvenience to themselves from not complying with the rules which the common understanding of the society has enjoined. It is possible, indeed, that, in some instances, the share which any individual might promise himself in the general good, would lead him to comply with those laws which he sees will be productive of such a good. It is possible, too, that, in some instances, where he either did not see the general usefulness of laws, or did not apprehend that he should have any share in the general good which they produce, he might be willing to comply with them, out of a proper regard and deference to the public understanding; especially if he found no particular inconvenience to himself from such compliance. But even where the laws made by the public are conducive to a general good, in which the several individuals will probably have a share; many are so selfish as not to be satisfied with such a remote and seemingly small advantage, and are desirous of grasping at what they think will be of greater and more immediate benefit to themselves, however inconsistent it may be with the benefit of the public. Even where men would feel no particular inconvenience from complying with the laws, which the common understanding has thought fit to establish; many are so conceited and petulant, that, instead of obeying a law, because it has been established by the common understanding, they would look upon this as a reason why they should disobey it, as far as they safely can.

Something farther, therefore, is necessary to secure the observance of such rules as the legislative power establishes, besides the mere establishment of them: especially since the advancement of the general good will frequently require not only such laws to be made, as will be productive of more benefit to each individual, than he could obtain without observing them, or such as all may observe without any inconvenience to themselves; but such, likewise, as may cut off many individuals from some private benefit which they might otherwise have obtained, in order to advance the greater benefit of other individuals and of the public in general. One method, therefore, of securing the observance of laws, is to establish them under some penalty; the view of which may check the petulance of those who would otherwise have transgressed them without any reason at all, and may give a proper turn to the selfishness of those who would otherwise have transgressed them upon reasons of private interest. Whether this is the only method or not, shall be considered hereafter.

We may take this matter still higher. All mankind in the liberty of nature have a promiscuous right of punishing criminal actions. But those who are united in a civil society, have agreed to put themselves under the conduct of the common understanding, to have their duties regulated, and their rights adjusted by the legislative power of that society. And as this power, when it makes laws, regulates the duty of the several individuals, by declaring what actions appear to the common understanding to be contrary to their duty, and are to be treated as crimes; so the same power, when it enacts penalties, adjusts the right of punishing such crimes, by declaring or appointing what punishment is to be inflicted on those who are guilty of them. So that the power of making laws and of enacting penalties, is only one and the same power exerting itself upon different objects: in making the law it exerts itself in ascertaining the rules of duty; in enacting the penalty it exerts itself in adjusting the right of punishment.

Legislative power implies a power of taxing the subjects.

V. As it belongs to the legislative power of a civil society to direct the several members of it what they are to do for the common good; so it belongs to the same power to direct them, likewise, what they are to give for this purpose; that is, the power of raising money to answer the expenses which the society must make in its political capacity, or in pursuing the ends for which it was formed, is a branch of the legislative power.

The payment of such money as these purposes require, is an obligation which each individual lays himself under, when he becomes a member of civil society. He tacitly agrees, by this act of becoming a member, to contribute his endeavours towards advancing and securing the general good. And since the general good of the society cannot be advanced and secured, nor even the society itself be kept together without a public revenue, this agreement binds him to pay his share towards such a revenue. This then is a duty of every individual who is a member of civil society. And, consequently, it belongs to the legislative power to settle what share each is to pay: because it belongs to the legislative power to adjust and ascertain the duties of each.

This right of the legislative power over the property of the subjects is not a right to take the whole, or, indeed, any part of it, from them causelessly and arbitrarily. The preservation of each man's property is one of the ends which he proposed to himself in entering into civil society. But it is absurd to suppose, that he would give up the whole of his property for the sake of preserving it. And the right which the society has, either over his person or over his property, is to be measured by what he may reasonably be presumed willing to give up for the sake of obtaining those ends, which he proposed to himself in becoming a member of such society. It is, indeed, reasonable to presume, that each individual would be willing to give up a part of his property for the sake of enjoying the rest in peace and security. It is, therefore, the business of the legislative power to consider and to direct what part of each man's property it is worth to have the rest secured to him. Now, the security which he has in view, depends upon the preservation and welfare of the public. And for this reason the legislative power, in settling what each person is to pay, should consider how much of each person's property it would be worth to him to preserve the state and advance its welfare: because, whatever appears to the common understanding to be necessary for these purposes, is what every person who belongs to the state, is naturally presumed to be willing to part with. Upon this account the burden of those payments which are called taxes, or duties and customs upon goods both moveable and immoveable, ought to be proportioned, as near as may be, to the value of each person's property: because the more a man's property is worth, the more he is naturally willing to pay for the security of it. From hence we may see the reason why these payments are naturally made higher in times of public danger, than in times of peace and quiet: the more a man's property is exposed to danger, and the more expense the society is at in defending and securing it; the more he is reasonably bound to pay for having it secured.

It might, perhaps, be of public benefit, if the state could get possession of a private man's lands. The society may want them for enlarging their roads, for erecting fortifications, or other public works of general utility. The principles here laid down will show us that the right which the legislative power has in the property of individuals, will not justify the taking such a man's lands from him, without making him amends. Such a tribute as this would not be a tax which all the members pay in proportion to their property; it would be a payment exacted of one man for the benefit of the whole, and would, therefore, be contrary to the nature of civil society, which requires, that the burden of all such public payments should be borne by the several members, in proportion to the interest which their property gives them in the general utility. But though the public should force him to give up his land, the burden is borne by all the members, if amends is made to him for it.

Some taxes or duties are paid, indeed, rather for the security of a man's person, or for the quiet enjoyment of some personal conveniences, than for the security of his property: such are poll-taxes, duties upon marriages, and many others of the like sort. But the same principles, with very little variation, are applicable to these payments. They are a part of a man's property, which he is presumed to be willing to give to the society, for the defence of his person, and for the quiet enjoyment of these personal conveniences. The chief difference between these taxes and others, is, that since such advantages as these are of equal value to all, the tax, which each pays to the public for securing them, may reasonably be an equal one: whilst other taxes, which are paid for the security of each person's property, follow the value of that property, or are proportionable to the worth of it.

Executive power is either internal, or external, or mixed.

VI. The natural use of the joint strength which a civil society forms, is either to preserve the rights and enforce the duties of the members of such society, in respect of one another, and of the public; or else to protect the whole and the several parts of it against such injuries as other civil societies, or other individuals, who still continue in a state of nature, or who are members of other civil societies might do them; to prevent such injuries from proceeding, where they are begun; or to procure reparation, and inflict punishment, where they are completed.

Now, the executive power is a power of acting with this joint strength, in order to obtain the purposes for which such strength was formed. And, consequently, the executive power is either internal or external. We may call it internal, when it is exercised upon objects within the society; when it is employed in securing the rights, or enforcing the duties of the several members, in respect either of one another, or of the society itself. And we may call it external executive power, when it is exercised upon objects out of the society; when it is employed in protecting either the body or the several members of it against external injuries, in preventing such injuries from being done, or in procuring reparation, or in inflicting punishment for them, after they are done. These two branches of the executive power, may, if we like these names better, be called civil and military. Civil executive power is a name which will very well express all that is meant by internal executive power. And the only objection against calling external executive power by the name of military executive power, is, that something more is included in this branch of power, besides what is strictly called military.

Judicial power is internal executive power.

VII. Judicial power is the internal or civil branch of executive power exerting itself under such checks and controls as the legislative power has subjected it to, in order to prevent its deviating from the purposes for which it was formed. A legislative power, without an executive one, would be of no great use. It might, indeed, ascertain the rights, and determine the duties of the subjects; but unless the common strength of the society comes in to its assistance; that is, unless the executive power interposes to support those rights, and to enforce those duties, the laws might fail of obtaining their effect; it would depend upon the virtue, or upon the humour of the subjects, whether they should obtain it or not. On the other hand, an internal executive power, which is under no checks or controls from the legislative, would be more dangerous than useful: it must be either a brute force, uninformed and unguided by any intelligent principle, or else a discretionary power in the hands of them, who are entrusted with the management of it. In the former case the wrong or the right application of it would be merely accidental; and in the latter case it would probably be oftener made use of as an instrument of private interest and undue favour of avarice or oppression, of revenge or cruelty, than as the means of doing justice to the public, and to the several members of it.

But in matters of internal jurisdiction, the executive power will plainly appear to be such an one, as is calculated to answer its proper purposes; if we consider it as acting, in this instance, under the direction and conduct of the legislative. Now, as the legislative power adjusts and settles the rights of the several members of a civil society, it naturally belongs to this power to determine how far, and upon what occasions, they shall have a right to the interposition of the common force; that is, it naturally belongs to this power to direct the use and extent of the internal executive power. Effectual care will be taken about the due use of this common force, if provision is made, that it shall not be put in motion in criminal matters, unless the fact to be punished is first made evident in the eye of the law; that is, in the judgment of the public understanding, speaking by the law; and unless the fact, when so made evident, is such an one as the law has declared to be punishable: and if a farther provision is made, that, after the fact is clear, and the legal guilt of it is apparent, no other use shall be made of this common force, besides what the law allows; that is, that no other punishment shall be inflicted but what the law has prescribed. The like care is taken, if a like provision is made, in matters of claim for restitution or damages done; if the law does not allow the claimant to have any assistance from the common force, till his right is made evident in the same manner; and then allows him no farther assistance from it, than what the law has determined to be sufficient to enforce his claim, or to obtain satisfaction.

We may observe here, that the judicial power is divided into two branches; one is called civil judicature, and the other criminal or penal judicature. The former acts with the common or joint force of the society to obtain restitution of what is unjustly withholden, or reparation for damages done. The latter acts in like manner to inflict punishment for the guilt of crimes committed.

The name of judicial power, which belongs to this power in both these branches, has probably been what leads many writers upon this subject to distinguish it from executive power. Having determined the notion of executive power to consist in a power of using and applying the joint force of a civil society, they do not immediately see how it could ever be called by the name of judicature; since judicature implies an act of the common or public understanding, and not a mere exercise of the common force. In the meantime they are aware, that judicature and legislation are different things; that the former is the application of such laws as are derived from the authority of the latter. And thus, as they distinguish the judicial from the executive power on the one hand, so they distinguish it likewise from the legislative power on the other hand. The consequence of which has been, that they consider the civil power as consisting of these three several parts, legislative, judicial and executive. Whereas, in fact, the province of judicial power is plainly to direct and apply, to actuate or restrain, the public force of the society; and in this view it can be nothing else but a branch of the executive power. All the formalities which precede this application of the public force, are so many checks and controls which the legislative has fixed, to prevent an undue application of it. Courts of judicature are the means by which the legislative controls the executive. Their proceedings are settled by the direction of the legislative, and the executive acts under their direction. The name of that power, which such courts exercise, regards them indeed as the instruments of the legislative, rather than as the principal agents of the executive; as checks of the common understanding upon the common force, rather than as the springs which put that force in motion, and direct its application. But in whatever light the judicial power might be considered by them who gave it this name, its efficacy and the use that it is of to civil society, arise from its being executive in its nature. Courts of judicature might meet, might hear causes, and might give sentence upon them, as the laws direct; but these sentences would be nothing; they could neither redress injuries nor inflict punishment, if such courts had not either an original or a delegated power of acting with the joint force of the society to put their sentence in execution.

External executive power, or military power.

VIII. The second branch of executive power, which is called external executive power; or may, if we like the name better, be called military power, is the power of acting with the common strength or joint force of the society to guard against such injuries as threaten it from without; to obtain amends for the damages arising from such injuries; or to inflict punishment upon the authors and abettors of them. The force of the society, as it is employed upon these objects, is called its military force. And the only objection against calling this whole branch of the executive power by the same name is, what has been *hinted already, that this external branch of executive power, or rather the persons vested with it, are employed, not only in the actual use of the common force, but in regulating, abating or stopping it. Thus, if the society is attacked, or any of its rights are infringed by foreign enemies; it is the usual province of them, who are vested with this power, not only to make war upon such enemies, but likewise, as the circumstances of the case may require, to suspend the war by a truce, or to end it by a peace. Nor is this usually the whole of their province. As a civil society may be attacked by more or by stronger enemies than it can conveniently, or perhaps than it can at all defend itself against by its own strength, there is frequent occasion to call in the assistance of others to help it. And because the procuring and engaging such assistance, as well as the actual use of it, when procured, is usually considered as an act of the common force; this is looked upon as a part of external executive power. Farther still; as this power acts with the common force of the society against its foreign enemies, where those enemies infringe its rights, and likewise stops or suspends its action, where the purposes of using it are answered, or are likely to be answered; the power of adjusting the rights of the society in respect of foreigners is commonly connected with external executive power, and is considered as a part of it. Hence it is that, when we are speaking of external executive power, we are supposed to include under that head, not only what is properly called military power, but the power likewise of making war or peace, the power of engaging in alliances for an increase of strength, either to carry on war or to secure peace, the power of entering into treaties, and of making leagues to restore peace, where there has been a war, and the power of adjusting the rights of a nation in respect of navigation, trade, &c. by conventions or agreements.

However, though these several powers are usually connected with external executive power, by being lodged in the same hands, they are not naturally essential parts of it. These several powers are rather acts of the common understanding, than of the common force; and therefore seem, in their own nature, to be parts rather of the legislative than the executive power. But where the legislative and the executive power are lodged in different hands, and especially in those civil societies, where the former of these powers resides in the whole body, or in a considerable number of representatives, the usual practice is to allow some degree of discretionary power in respect of war or peace, to him or to them, who are entrusted with the right of putting the military force in motion; especially in those instances where the legislative body cannot act with such readiness and expedition as the occasions or opportunities of war require. And since war is the means by which, in the last result, all the rights of the society in respect of foreigners must be defended and maintained; it is usually thought convenient that

* Book II. Chap. II. § VI.

those rights should, in some measure, be under the inspection and management of the same person or persons who are employed in looking after and managing the occasions and opportunities of war. So that, where the public understanding cannot direct by settled rules, which have been established beforehand, but must act, if it acts at all, as occasion offers, and particularly where this public understanding is the joint sentiment of a great number of men, and cannot for that reason be collected or made known on a sudden; in these cases, and in others which are naturally connected with them, it has in most civil societies been thought convenient to allow those a discretionary power of acting who have the external executive power, or to substitute their judgment in the place of the public understanding.

This, however, though it may be convenient, is not necessary: for the legislative body, where no positive law of the constitution forbids it, may appoint its own agents, distinct from those who actuate the common force: it may naturally not only make war or peace by its own authority, but may send its deputies along with the army, to control its operations even in war. Except, indeed, in the heat of action; where, unless there is a discretionary power lodged in the hands of those who have the military command, it would be impossible for them to do their duty. If the right of doing this is naturally implied in the notion of a public or common understanding, formed for the purpose of directing a civil society; that is, if a right to direct such affairs as relate to external jurisdiction, is naturally implied in the notion of legislative power; the consequence is, that in those particular civil societies, where by the constitution of government, they who are entrusted with the external executive power, act in any instance of external jurisdiction at their own discretion, without any immediate control from the legislative, this discretionary power must be considered as originally connected with the legislative: it must be so considered, in this sense at least, that though the fundamental laws of the constitution may make it unconstitutional in after times for the legislative body to take this power to themselves, yet there was from the beginning no natural reason, or no reason drawn from the nature of civil society or of civil power, against their preventing any such discretionary power from being established by general consent, or from establishing itself afterwards by long usage and custom.

In short, the external executive power, in its own nature, is no more an independent power of acting without being controlled by the legislative, than the internal executive power is. Even in those civil societies, where the particular constitution has left this power discretionary in some instances, it does not suffer it to be so in all. And by the checks, to which it is subject, in other instances, we are naturally led to judge, that, if the positive will or appointment of the legislative power, considered as acting originally in modelling the civil constitution, had not from the beginning established the contrary, it would have been subject to the like checks in all.

These checks appear principally in those instances where, without any great inconvenience to the society, the external executive power may be directed by general and standing laws, or rather in those instances where it could not, without great inconvenience, be left independent. Thus the legislative power, notwithstanding the executive is in some other respects left independent, determines what number of the members of the society shall be armed, in order to join their force for repelling or subduing its external enemies. It determines to what laws or to what sort of military discipline they shall be subject, who are thus armed. It determines in what manner they shall be maintained or paid, in order to make them amends for giving up other employments and engaging in this, to which, as members of the society, they were no more obliged than the other members. In alliances, leagues, or conventions, if they bind any of the members to give up their private claims, or to do any thing which is inconsistent with the civil laws then in being, its authority makes them void of course, unless it interposes to establish them. In particular, if such agreements cannot be made good without money, to be raised by a tax upon the property of individuals; if new duties are to be imposed upon any commodities, or duties established already are to be abolished; such agreements are not valid by any discretionary act of the executive power, but may either be made void or confirmed by the legislative. These are plainly natural checks of the legislative power upon the executive, and are sufficient to show, that the latter is not a discretionary power, but is in itself under the control of the former. So that wherever it is otherwise, in whatever nation we find a discretionary executive independent in any instances upon the legislative, we may conclude that it owes this independency to civil constitution or positive appointment, and does not derive it from its own nature.

Appointment of magistrates, mixed executive power.

IX. By magistrates I would here be understood to mean such persons in a civil society, as put the common force of it in motion, or act with that common force. I use the word, therefore, in a more extensive sense than it is commonly used, to mean not only such persons as act with the common force in the judicial or internal branch of the executive, but such persons likewise as act with that force in the military or external branch. The name of magistrate, in the usual sense of the word, is appropriated to the former: the latter are generally called officers, where the executive power is purely military, and ambassadors, ministers, envoys, &c. in the rest of that branch of the executive power, which is external. According to this notion of magistrates, they are the agents of the executive power; and consequently the appointment of them belongs to this power. But because their province is partly internal and partly external, the power of appointing them belongs partly to one branch of the executive and partly to the other; so that it may not be improper to call this mixed executive power.

It is necessary, however, to take notice of a difference between internal and external magistrates. The judicial power, which belongs to internal magistrates, is under the constant and steady control of the legislative; their power of acting with the public force is regulated and limited by standing laws. And consequently the nature of their jurisdiction is defined or settled by the legislative; though the power of exercising such jurisdiction is derived from the executive: it so far belongs to the legislative to erect or appoint courts of judicature, as to appoint, that magistrates with this or that particular power, may or shall be erected; notwithstanding the persons themselves are chosen or nominated, and the powers which they exercise are derived from the executive. This would be the case, likewise, of external magistrates, supposing this branch of the executive power to be under the like uniform control of the legislative. But in most civil societies, where the legislative and executive are in different hands, the constitution leaves the latter, in some instances, a discretionary power, as to the external branch of it. And for this reason such magistrates, as have their province in this branch, not only derive their power from the executive, but are likewise under the regulation of the executive, as to the degree or extent of their power.

* Grotius divides civil power into the five following parts; first, the power of making, altering, or repealing laws, both such as concern sacred, and such as concern other matters, as far as the former relate to or affect the state. Secondly, the power of making war or peace, of engaging in treaties, leagues, alliances, or conventions. Thirdly, the power of establishing taxes, customs, or duties to be paid out of the property of individuals for the public use and service. Fourthly, the power of hearing and effectually determining all matters of controversy, which arise between individuals. And fifthly, the power of appointing magistrates, ambassadors, or other officers. Though I have not kept to this division, the reader will be able to see, without much trouble, that all these several parts of civil power have been taken notice of, and been reduced to one of the two general heads, into which I have divided it; they are all of them branches either of the legislative or of the executive.

X. If we continue to speak of the legislative and executive power in the abstract, it will be difficult to explain rightly what is meant by prerogative. It cannot properly be called discretionary executive power; because the executive power, in the nature of the thing, is not discretionary in any part: wherever it acts at discretion, this privilege, unless it arises from the necessity of the case, as in the heat of military action, comes from the legislative, either by original establishment, or by long usage and custom, or by occasional permission. We shall be better able to understand what prerogative is, if we speak of the legislative and executive power, not in the abstract, but as lodged or entrusted by the state, in the hands of some one or more persons. Where the person, so entrusted with the executive power, is left by the legislative to act in any instances at his own discretion, to direct by his own understanding the public force, which is naturally under the direction of the public understanding, such a discretionary power in him is called prerogative. Thus, in penal cases, if the legislative forbids the public force to be put in motion for the punishment of any action, till the fact itself is proved to the public understanding in such a manner as the law appoints, and then will not suffer this force to be used but under the conduct of the law, so as to inflict only the legal penalty; thus far there is no prerogative, or no discretionary power in him, who is entrusted with the executive. But, then, if the legislative, instead of reserving to itself the right of judging whether such legal punishment is to be suspended, or whether the criminal is to be wholly pardoned, leaves it to him to pardon or not, as he thinks proper, such a discretionary power entrusted with him is called prero-

Prerogative, what.

* Grot. Lib. I. Cap. III. § VI.

gative. In cases of external jurisdiction, if the society makes war or peace, as he thinks convenient; if it is bound by such leagues or conventions as he engages it in; if its military force, when appointed and established, is under his command, and is to act as he directs; these are instances of a discretionary power: and where the person entrusted with the executive has such a discretionary power, it is called prerogative. If he, who is entrusted with the executive, has a discretionary power of calling the public together to act in its legislative capacity, or of calling the representatives of the public together, where it acts in this capacity by its representatives; or if it is left to him to appoint the time and place of its meeting; this, though it is not properly any branch of executive power, yet if it is so entrusted with him, who has the executive power, will come under the notion of prerogative. But should the legislative ever have limited him in this respect, and tied him down to call them together at any particular time or place; so far this prerogative is at an end; and the act of calling them together, though it might once be an act of prerogative, and so may still retain the name, becomes in its nature ministerial.

We may, from hence, learn, that in those nations, in which there is any struggle between the legislative body, and the person or persons who are entrusted with the executive power, this is not a struggle between the legislative and the executive powers. The provinces of these two powers considered abstractedly, or as they are in themselves, are marked out distinctly enough for any one to see their respective limits. It belongs to the legislative power, considered as the common understanding, or joint sense of the body politic, to determine and direct what is right to be done: and it belongs to the executive power, considered as the common or joint strength of the same body, to carry what is so determined and directed into execution. But in those particular civil societies, where the legislative and executive power are lodged in different hands, it is usual, especially if the legislative body is a large one, to allow those who have the executive power, to act discretionally in some cases; that is, it is usual for them to have, in some instances, such a discretionary power as is called prerogative. And the only subject of dispute about prerogative that can be intelligible, is between the executive body and the legislative body, concerning the instances where this discretionary power takes place, or else concerning the extent of it in some particular instance; that is, they may possibly dispute, either how far, in settling the constitution of government, such power of acting at discretion, vested in the executive body, was designed to extend, or how far it may be proper and convenient for the public, that it should extend.

The reader may, perhaps, have met with some difficulties in this chapter for want of having attended to a necessary distinction between the legislative power of civil society in general, and the legislative body of any particular society, and to a like distinction between the executive power, and the person or persons with whom such power is entrusted. The following chapter is the place, in which the subject will lead us to explain this distinction. And when it is explained, some passages in this, which may have appeared difficult, will probably be better understood.

XI. The force of a body politic, as it is employed in matters of internal jurisdiction, is called the civil force; and as it is employed in matters of external jurisdiction, it is called the military force. The civil force is what the judicial or internal executive power acts with; and the military force is what the external or military executive power acts with. These two forces, therefore, though they may appear to be the same, when they are considered only as the joint force of the same body politic, are distinct from one another in respect of their objects. The civil force is employed in putting the laws in execution; that is, in maintaining and supporting within the society what is right in civil matters, or in inflicting punishment in those which, though they are of a civil nature, are distinguished by the name of criminal matters. The military force is employed in defending the society and its several members against injuries from without.

Civil and military force, how distinguished.

This, which is a distinction between these two forces in respect only of their objects, leads us to a distinction, which may, in some societies, be made between the forces themselves; when we consider one of them as the force with which the internal executive power acts, and the other as the force with which the external executive power acts. For the internal executive power is under the constant and uniform control of the legislative: whereas, in most civil societies there is something of a discretionary power joined with the external executive. The consequence of which is, that the civil force, or force employed to maintain justice within the society, is under the same control with the internal executive power: but the military force, or force employed against injuries from without, may, in some instances, be a discretionary force, not guided so much by the legislative body, as by the judgment of them, who are entrusted to act with it.

If the constitution of government has introduced such a distinction in fact; that is, if the military force is actuated by a discretionary power; there is an evident reason why this force does not, in its own right, come in, where only the members of the society are concerned, in order to carry the laws into execution: because the force employed for this purpose ought to be such an one, as is under the checks and control of the laws, and not such an one as, in any respect, acts at discretion.

The force, indeed, which the society establishes to carry the laws into execution, is commonly a small one. What is done in this particular is considered as done by the joint force of the whole, though the whole, instead of rising for this purpose, acts by such civil officers, as the public understanding has thought sufficient. These are commonly but few; because few are sufficient to give a person possession of such rights as the law has adjudged to him, or to inflict punishment, after a legal sentence. However, if this small force is found insufficient, these civil officers usually call in any of the members of the society to their assistance in order to increase their force. They sometimes call in the assistance even of the military force: upon which occasion it is considered, not as the military force, or not as having in any respect a discretionary power, but as a part of the civil force acting under the direction of the civil magistrate. So that perhaps it might be more proper to say, that the civil magistrate upon some occasions, where he apprehends the usual force employed by him to be too weak to answer his purpose, calls in the soldiery to his assistance; than that he calls in the military force. The persons which are usually employed by him are either too few or too unskilful to withstand the resistance which he is likely to meet with. Therefore, as there are many members of the society who are the instruments of the external executive power, and who are trained up to oppose such violent resistances as frequently come from without; he has recourse to them, and uses them as his instruments, subject, when they are so called in by him, to his control; and consequently subject, as he is himself, to the control of the law.

CHAPTER IV.

OF THE DIFFERENT FORMS OF CIVIL GOVERNMENT.

I. *Sovereign and supreme power, what.*—II. *Legislative and executive power compared.*—III. *Civil constitution, what.*—IV. *Origin of civil constitutions in respect of the legislative.*—V. *How a civil constitution becomes fixed, as to the legislative.*—VI. *Executive body, how formed.*—VII. *Despotic constitution, how produced.*—VIII. *Executive body, how fixed.*—IX. *National constitution a question of fact.*—X. *Monarchical constitutions not more natural than others.*—XI. *Monarchical constitutions not impossible.*—XII. *Constitutions not necessarily democratical.*—XIII. *Titles or appearances do not determine the nature of a constitution.*—XIV. *Tenure of civil power to be distinguished from the power itself.*—XV. *Promise or oath of a king may limit his power.*—XVI. *Mixed constitutions.*—XVII. *Civil constitutions may be altered.*

Sovereign and supreme power, what.

I. When we speak of sovereign power, or of supreme power, we are led into some mistakes, by using these words indiscriminately. When we call any power supreme, the expression seems to be relative to some other subordinate powers: to call any power the highest of all, is not very intelligible, if there are no other powers below it. Sovereign power is likewise a relative term; but then it has not a necessary relation to subordinate powers. To call any power by the name of sovereign power, does not necessarily imply that there are any other powers in subordination to it. Whatever power is independent, so as not to be subject to any other power, though it has in the meantime no other power subject to itself, may with propriety enough be called by this name. In short, that power may well be called sovereign, to which none is superior: whereas, none can be called supreme, unless there are others inferior to it.

*Grotius, indeed, has not observed this distinction: he defines supreme power, as I should define sovereign power, to be such an independent power of governing a civil society, that no acts which are done

* Grot. Lib. I. Cap. III. § VII.

by it, can be made void by any other human power. In this sense, every state, in reference to all other states, has supreme, or, as we might better call it, sovereign power within itself: it governs itself independently, and no other state has authority to make its acts of government void. A society of men, by whatever ties and for whatever purposes they may be united to one another, is not complete in itself, if it has not within itself an independent power of government; but is, either in its legislative or in its executive, subject to be controlled by any power from without. Such a society, therefore, though formed for civil purposes, is no civil society; it can at best be only a part of some other state, and is usually called a province to that state in particular, from which it receives its laws, or by which its public force is put in motion and made to act.

Every individual, in the liberty of nature, is his own master, and has an independent or sovereign power over himself. The consequence of which is, that when a number of such individuals are united together, so as to form a society, this society is naturally its own master, and has an independent or sovereign power over itself. Since no person, and no collection of persons, out of the society, has naturally any authority over any individual within it; the consequence is, that no other civil society can have any authority over a body politic, made up of such individuals.

If, indeed, any one body politic has consented to submit itself to the authority of any other body of the same sort, it ceases to be its own master; it has no longer an independent or sovereign power of its own. *But then it ceases at the same time to be a state, and becomes a province. No assembly of men is called a state, unless it is complete in itself: and no assembly of men, united for the purposes of advancing a common utility, and of securing their rights, can be complete, if it has not within itself whatever is necessary to answer those purposes; if, instead of having a legislative and an executive power of its own, it is obliged to have recourse to some other society or assembly of men, to ascertain the rights and to prescribe the duties of its members, or to maintain those rights when they are ascertained, and to enforce the observance of those duties, when they are prescribed.

Legislative and executive power compared.

II. The not having attended to the distinction already taken notice of, between the notions of sovereign and supreme power, and the promiscuous use of these two words, may possibly have been one occasion of a seeming difference in opinion between those, who, if they were to explain their meaning, might possibly be found to agree. The executive power in any state may undoubtedly be called sovereign power: because, in reference to all other states, it is an independent power. It is not naturally subject to the restraint, or to the direction of any power out of the society. Where it is subject to any such external restraint, there is no state, but a province only, a part or member of some other society. Now, as the terms sovereign and supreme power are used indiscriminately, we are apt to conclude, that the executive, because it may in this sense be called sovereign power, is likewise to be considered as supreme power. But then the inquiries upon this head are usually carried something

* Grot. Lib. I. Cap. III. § VII.

farther. The legislative and the executive power in the same society, are sometimes compared together: and then the question is, which of these two is to be looked upon as the supreme power. It is not uncommon to imagine here, that executive power, because it is called sovereign, and is therefore looked upon as supreme in one reference or comparison, may likewise be called sovereign, and be looked upon as supreme in this other reference; so that if the legislative power is not subordinate to it, they must at least be independent one of the other.

The distinction of the two names sovereign and supreme, if it was attended to, would correct this false conclusion. The executive power of any one civil society in reference to the civil powers, either legislative or executive of any other civil societies, may indeed be called sovereign power: because it is independent of them, and does not act under their direction. But then in this reference it is not very proper to call it supreme power; because, though such foreign powers cannot of right direct or control it, yet they are not subordinate to it. And if, by proving the executive power of any particular society, to be sovereign power in this reference, it does not follow that it is to be called supreme power in the same reference; much less will it follow, that we are to look upon it as supreme power in reference to the legislative of the same society.

Indeed, there is in almost every state, what may be called supreme executive power, in reference to some other powers within the state itself. When an executive body is fixed by the constitution of government in any civil society; whether this body consists of one person or more, there are usually many other subordinate persons, or bodies, who have such a derivative and inferior jurisdiction, as commits the public strength of the society to their management in many instances. These inferior magistrates, therefore, have an executive power: but as it is derived from the person or persons with whom the executive is originally entrusted; this power is inferior or subordinate to his: and in this reference his executive power may be called supreme. But this again is no evidence that the executive power, either in itself or as it is entrusted in his hands, is superior to the legislative, or even independent of it. There can certainly be no ground for concluding that the executive power in his hands is supreme, when compared with the legislative; only because it is supreme, when compared with the executive power in other hands.

If we consider the nature of these two powers, there will be no great difficulty in judging which of them is supreme, when they are compared with one another. The legislative is the joint understanding of the society, directing what is proper to be done, and is therefore naturally superior to the executive, which is the joint strength of the society exerting itself in taking care that what is so directed shall be done.

As legislative power is thus found to be superior to executive, when they are considered in the abstract, we are apt to conclude, too hastily, that in every civil society the legislative body is in all instances superior to the executive body. Whereas, in fact, the constitution of government may, in some instances, have lodged * a discretionary power in the executive body: so that, though in general the public understand-

* See Chap. III. § X.

ing speaks by the legislative body, yet, in these instances, the understanding of the executive body may be designed to stand in the place of the public understanding, and to direct what is to be done as well as to see to the doing of it. For the existence of a legislative body is not wholly inconsistent with the notion of prerogative.

Civil constitution, what.

III. By the civil constitution of government in any nation, is meant the established form of exercising the supreme or governing power within that nation, which we have just now proved to be the legislative power of it. The simple constitutions of government are commonly reduced to these three; monarchy, aristocracy, and democracy: by which we are to understand, that there are three different sorts of legislative bodies; any of which may be established in any nation; and each of which may be called simple, because each of them is uniform or alike in all its parts. The constitution is democratical, when the legislative power is exercised either by the collective body of the people, or by representatives which they choose from time to time. It is aristocratical, when this power is exercised by the nobles; that is, by a small and select body of men, who, after their original designation to this office, are elective no longer, but transmit their power to their heirs, or to other established successors. It is monarchical, when this power is exercised by a king; that is, by a single man; whether upon his demise it is transmitted to his heirs, or to other established successors, or to such successors as shall, upon that event, be chosen. We cannot, indeed, properly say, that in this last form of government all the parts of the legislative body are alike; because the whole body consists of only one person: the form, however, is a simple one; because there is no mixture or diversity of parts in it.

The constitution of government is called a mixed one, when two or more of these simple forms are compounded, or joined with one another. Thus the legislative body may consist either of the whole body, or of a representative body of the nobles and of the people; or of the king and the people; or of the king and the nobles alone; or of the king and the nobles, with the representatives of the people.

The mixture, in this last form, will be a little varied, if the king is entrusted with the executive power in such a manner as to have any prerogative joined with it: or if the representatives of the people claim a right of establishing any sort of laws, whether relating to the public revenue or to any other matter, and the consent of the other two parts of the legislative body to such laws is considered as a thing of course, which they are not to refuse. In either of these cases the form is still a mixed or compound one, though the composition is not quite the same. In the former case it approaches towards monarchical, and in the latter towards democratical.

Origin of civil constitutions, in respect of the legislative.

IV. When a number of persons, who are equal to one another; that is, who are free, * as all men naturally are free, from any jurisdiction or authority over one another, have united themselves into a civil society; the natural result of such an union is a legislative power. But then there is originally no legislative body distinct from the collective body of the

* See Book I. Chap. X. § III.

society. * All and each are obliged to conform themselves to whatever the whole or the major part shall agree upon: but as no one person, nor any select number of persons, can have any right to prescribe to the rest; so neither is this collective body of men naturally obliged to elect or settle a number of representatives, who shall have authority to act for them, or to determine what is to be done, and what to be avoided. Each member of the society has originally a right to act for himself, as a member; that is, to deliberate with the rest, and to give his suffrage upon such points as come before them. It is necessary, therefore, to look farther than the compact, by which men unite themselves into a civil society, in order to find out the origin of any other civil constitution of government, besides such an one as is popular or democratical in the fullest extent of that word.

There is, indeed, an original † legislative power in every civil society; but some farther act is necessary, besides the mere union into such a society, before this power can be naturally vested in any one part of the society exclusive of the rest; before a king or the nobles can have a right of making laws, which shall bind the whole; or before the people shall be obliged to act by representatives, or to be concluded by the sense of any part of the society, instead of acting in their collective capacity, so as to be concluded by nothing less than the general sense of the collective body. All men, before they are considered as members of a civil society, are equal to one another, and are likewise independent of one another; each has naturally a right to think and to act for himself. This independency is, in some measure, limited by their entering into civil society. If there is no express agreement, yet the very act of entering into such society is a tacit agreement, which makes them so far dependent upon the general sense and will of the whole body politic, that they are from thence obliged to conform themselves to that general sense and will. But if they are considered merely as members of a civil society; if nothing more is supposed to have passed, besides that agreement, either express or tacit, by which they united themselves into such a society, they would still have a civil equality; this union, though it has produced a legislative power, has not lodged it in any particular hands; it leaves each member as free to act for himself in a civil capacity, as he before was in a natural capacity. From hence then it follows, that the obligation of being subject to a legislative power in any one man, or in any body of men, though this body is within the society, if it is different from the whole collective body, is a farther abridgement of natural liberty, than what arises merely from the agreement, by which mankind unite themselves into civil societies. But every abridgement of liberty, which is made without our consent, either express or implied, is contrary to the law of nature. No civil constitution of government, therefore, which is not purely democratical, can be established consistently with the law of nature, without a farther agreement between those who are members of the same civil society: we may, indeed, say, that without such an agreement, no constitution of government that we know of, or read of, could have been formed: because there does not appear ever to have been any constitution so entirely democratical, as to allow every mem-

* See Book II. Chap. I. § II.

† See Book II. Chap. III. § I.

ber an equal suffrage in all matters of legislative power. In the most popular forms of government, persons of no fortune, women, and such as are in their civil minority, whether they are in their natural minority or not, are usually excluded from having any share in the exercise of the legislative power.

There is no great difficulty in conceiving, that no single person can claim the legislative power in a civil society, in consequence of that compact only, by which the several members united themselves into one body, with a view of preserving their rights and of advancing a general good. An exclusive legislative power in a king must plainly be the effect of some farther compact. Nor is it more difficult to understand, that there cannot, without such farther compact, be any such thing as an aristocratical constitution of government. There is not naturally in any civil society, merely as a civil society, any select and standing body of men with an exclusive legislative power. Whenever a power of this sort is lodged in such a legislative body, it must, in order to be consistent with the natural rights of mankind, have been lodged there by some other act, besides the original agreement, upon which the society was formed. The necessity of supposing such a subsequent act is not so apparent in democratical constitutions. But yet it will, upon inquiry, be found necessary to suppose such a compact; if we consider what constitutions are called democratical. In many constitutions, which are so called, the legislative power is vested in the representatives of the people, and is not exercised by the collective body. Here then we plainly find another compact, besides that which formed the society: at least we find an act of electing such a representative body, and of delegating the legislative power to it: which act is different from the original compact, that joins the several individuals into one civil society. Suppose that each member of this representative body is chosen for life, and that upon every vacancy by the death of any member, the collective body has the right of filling up such vacancy: we may ask, on the one hand, how each member came to have a right to make a part of the representative body as long as he lives? that is, why the collective body has not a right of displacing him, so as to make a vacancy, till he dies? It will be impossible to show that he has any such claim against the collective body, from the nature of civil society, without having recourse to some farther act, besides that which formed the society, by uniting the several members of it into one collective body: and this farther act I have here called a compact. If there had been no such compact or settlement; no reason can be assigned from the mere nature of society, why the legislative power should be vested in the representatives of the people, rather than be exercised by the collective body; or why, if such representatives are once chosen, they should continue for life, rather than for a certain number of years, or rather than during the pleasure of their constituents. Suppose again, that the legislative power is vested in representatives chosen for a certain term of years; this is so far from being a form of government, which arises immediately from the nature of civil society, or from the original compact, by which such societies were formed, without the aid of any farther agreement, consent or compact, that a form of government of this sort would be precarious; it could, in its own nature, last no longer than during the term of years, for which the appointment of the representatives was made, but must, upon the expiration of this term, be continually renewed by such consent or compact. For, when the term is expired for which the representative body with legislative power was chosen, the legislative power would naturally return to the collective body in which it was originally vested. And this collective body would then be at liberty to act as they please in regard to the future exercise of that power. The people in general might either keep it and exercise it themselves, or they might choose a representative body which should continue either for the same, or for a different term of years; or during the lives of each representative member: or they might appoint a body of nobility, and give legislative power to them and their heirs, or to them and such successors as should be then settled; or lastly, they might delegate the legislative power to one single person, and so introduce a monarchical constitution.

Even in constitutions which approach as near as any, that we know of, to perfect democracies, some farther compact, besides that which formed the society, must be understood to have intervened in order to settle the legislative body. The nature of civil society does not exclude women from having a suffrage in making laws; that is, it does not exclude them from being a part of the legislative body. If, from observing either our own manner of choosing representatives, or the manner of making laws in other forms of government, where the people act in a seemingly collective body, and not by their representatives, we have been led to imagine that women are by the nature of civil society excluded from a share in the legislative; we may correct this notion by considering that * women, as well as men, have a natural right to their liberty, before they join themselves to civil society; and have, as well as men, a right to act as members of such society, after they have so joined themselves to it. The consequence of which is, that till some act of the society, subsequent to the forming of it, has by general consent excluded women from a right of suffrage, they might naturally claim it. But perhaps the reader may be more readily led to correct his mistake, if we only ask him, whether he has never heard of a queen upon the throne, in those countries where, by being seated there, she has a share in the legislative power, or makes a part of the legislative body? No civil laws, no civil constitution of government could give, or even allow such a power as this to a woman, if it was contrary to the nature of civil society for a woman to have a share in matters of legislation. If then the reader, from such facts as these, is informed that it is not contrary to the nature of civil society for women to have a share in the exercise of legislative power, we may next ask him, by what means it comes to pass, that, in the most popular forms of government, they should not be considered as a part of the collective body in the business of legislation? Nothing but compact or agreement can have justly excluded them. If, therefore, when the people are supposed to act in their collective body, whilst they exercise legislative power, the women, who are members of the society, make no part of that collective body; even such a democratical constitution as this must have been settled by some farther agreement, and did not naturally or necessarily arise out of that compact, by which the society was formed. What we

* See Book I. Chap. X. § III.

have said of women may, without much variation, be applied to persons who are * naturally at years of discretion, but yet are excluded from the right of voting in matters of legislation, even in the most popular forms of government, because they are not arrived at that period of life which the civil laws of the country have fixed as the limit of minority. It will, I know, be thought a very obvious answer to this difficulty, to say, that the laws have excluded them. But this answer does not take the matter up high enough: for we are not inquiring how they came to be excluded, after a legislative body was formed, in which they have no share; but how such a legislative body came to be formed at all. Allow me only, that, till such laws as exclude them, were made, they had a right of suffrage, as parts of the collective body; and this concession will be enough for my purpose. For if they are not excluded from such a right by the nature of civil society, the consequence is, that they never could have been justly excluded at all, if there had been no compact or agreement of the whole collective body, by which they were excluded. The same sort of reasoning is still farther applicable to persons who are in their own power; that is, who are not slaves, and yet are not considered in the most popular forms of government, as parts of the collective body, only because they are possessed of little or of no land within the territories. The †nature of civil society does not exclude such persons from being parts of the collective body. If, therefore, they are excluded in the most popular forms of government; even such popular forms must have owed their establishment to some farther act, and cannot have immediately arisen out of the compact, by which men are considered as uniting themselves into civil society.

I have been the more particular in explaining this matter, because it does not seem to have been well attended to: and for want of understanding it, we are led into many hasty and mistaken conclusions in several questions relating to civil government. The point which I have been endeavouring to make out is, in short, that, besides the compact, which unites a number of persons into a body politic, and gives them an original legislative power, as a collective body, it is necessary that there should be some farther act of mutual consent, in order to settle any other legislative body; that is, in order to establish a form of government in any civil society whatsoever. Unless, indeed, we could find a society where the government is popular in the fullest sense of the word; a society where all persons of free condition, who are old enough to be naturally capable of acting for themselves, whether they are men or women, poor or rich, have a share in the legislative power, and act by themselves, and not by their representatives.

But whilst we maintain, that to form a civil society, and to settle a civil constitution of government, two compacts, or, however, two distinct acts of consent are necessary; there is no occasion to maintain that these two acts should be done at different times. When we speak of that act, which produced the constitution of civil government, and formed a legislative body, as subsequent to the compact which formed the civil society, and produced an original legislative power in the collective body, it is not necessary that one of these acts should be subsequent to the other in order of time: for there is no reason in the nature

* See Book I. Chap. XI. § VIII. † See Book I. Chap. I. § XI.

of the thing that should hinder them from being done together. But still in the order in which we conceive them, the compact that establishes a legislative body, different from the collective body of the whole society, must be considered as subsequent to the compact, which forms the collective body itself: because we cannot conceive a legislative body different from the collective body to be settled; unless we first conceive that such collective body has itself been formed.

Neither is there any reason for maintaining, that the compact which settles the form of government or establishes the legislative body, must necessarily be an express one. As men may unite themselves to a civil society by tacit agreement, so likewise, when they are so united, they may by tacit agreement settle a form of government. Any of our alienable rights may be lost, and what we so lose others may acquire, by usage, custom or prescription. The right of sharing in person in the exercise of legislative power, which originally belongs equally to every member of civil society, may not only be lost by the particular and express consent of each, but by the joint act of the majority, or by the long forbearance of all other members to use it, except those who, by such long forbearance of the rest, are established into the legislative body.

We may now, perhaps, understand what *Grotius means, when he tells us, that what he says in regard to kingly power in those countries where the legislative or supreme power is lodged in the hands of one man, is equally applicable to the power of the nobility in aristocratical states, and even to the power of the people in democratical governments. For, as a king, invested with legislative power, is to be considered as a legislative body, appointed by the consent of the collective body of the whole society, so the nobles in aristocratical states are a body of the same sort appointed in the same manner: and even in democratical states, since the legislative body is usually a part of the people, and not the collective body of the whole society, the legislative power of such body must be derived from the same principles, and must rest upon the same foundation with kingly power in monarchical constitutions.

How a civil constitution becomes fixed, as to the legislative.

V. Since the power of any legislative body within a society, whether such body consists of one person, or of more, depends ultimately upon a compact or agreement of the collective body; it is plain, that every constitution of government, where either the whole legislative body, or some part of it, is not always in being, must naturally be precarious. For there can be no compact but between two parties at least: and if one of the parties ceases to exist, the obligation of the other party is at an end. If, therefore, the power of the legislative body arises from consent, agreement or compact between such legislative body and the collective body of the whole society, whenever the legislative body ceases entirely, the collective body is free to act as it pleases. This has already been taken notice of, when we were speaking of civil societies, which act by such representatives as are chosen only for a term of years.

In those forms of civil government, where the people have a share in the legislative power, and act by representatives chosen for such a term, the constitution may, however, be so established as not to be preca-

* Grot. Lib. I. Cap. III. § VIII.

rious; provided that those representatives of the people do not compose the whole legislative body, and that the other part of this body is conceived to be always in being. If there is no such part of the legislative body in being, the compact or agreement upon which the constitution depends, will be no more than a compact between the people and themselves; a compact which they may revoke at pleasure, because there is no other party in it. But if, when the term expires for which the representatives of the people were chosen, there is still a king, who is a part of the legislative body; such a mixed constitution will be a settled one. He is the other party in the compact; and as on the one hand the constitution, or rather the compact by which the constitution was regulated, does not allow him a full legislative power in his own person, but ties him up from exercising such power without the representatives of the people; so, on the other hand, the same compact obliges the people to go on in the same manner that they have done before; that is, to exercise their share in the legislative power by representatives, and not to change the form of government in any respect, by any act which they may do in their collective capacity.

In an elective kingdom, if the king is the legislative body of the society during his life, the legislative power will, upon his death, return to its first origin, to the collective body of the people: and there will be nothing which can properly be called a civil constitution, to hinder them, when it is so returned, from making what alteration they please in the future form of government. Their choice of the former king was a compact between him and them, by which the legislative power was entrusted with him, to be exercised for the general utility, and for the security of the rights of the society, and of its several members. But upon his demise, there is but one party in the compact remaining, and this party is the collective body of the people. They are, therefore, released from their obligation to continue under such a form of government as they had once introduced, and may either renew that form, or introduce any other, as they, at that time, shall judge to be most convenient. It will be otherwise, if any part of the legislative body remains during the interreign. If there is, for instance, then in being, a standing body of nobility, who are at all times a part, and only a part, of the legislative body; such a body of nobles has no constitutional right to act independently of the collective body of the people in any instance, without a king at their head; they cannot, therefore, consistently with the compact, which settled the constitution, make any change in that constitution. And as the same compact binds the collective body of the people to them, this collective body cannot, consistently with such compact, introduce any change in the constitution without their concurrence.

It will be nothing to the purpose to urge here in general, that the laws of every society are sufficient to continue the constitution, to lay the collective body of the people under an obligation of renewing their representatives in democratical states, or of appointing a new king in elective monarchies; even though during the interreign, there is no legislative body, or no part of a legislative body in being, besides the collective body of the people. For, certainly, if the society continues during the interreign, there must, even in that interval of time, be a legislative power in existence: and as there is then no particular legislative body, such legislative power must be vested in the collective body. The consequence is, that during this interval, the collective body may make or alter laws as they please, by their general consent. And if they then agree to introduce a new constitution of government, such an agreement effectually repeals all those laws, by which the old constitution is supposed to have been established.

The constitution of civil government in a nation, may, indeed, be said to be settled by law; and, perhaps, the word may be a more proper one than the word compact. But then if we trace such constitution up to its first source, we shall find that the law which settles it, must be ultimately derived from the joint consent of the society; that is, from the legislative power, not of any particular legislative body within that society, but of the whole collective body. The particular form of government in any society consists in the particular sort of legislative body, by which that society is governed, or in the particular sort of body, to which the legislative power of the collective body is given. To say, therefore, that the form of government is settled or determined by any law which is made by any particular legislative body of a society, different from the collective body, is the same in effect as to say, that the legislative body makes a law, by which it gives itself legislative power; or that it makes a law, before it has any power to make one. If we apply this to monarchical governments, we shall readily see the absurdity of it. One single person, in a civil society, makes a law, by which he gives himself legislative power. But how can this law be binding upon the society, if he had not legislative power when he made it? He must have derived his legislative power from some law, which was not of his own making, or else he could have no right at all to make this any more than any other law. Can we say in aristocratical governments, that the select few, who are but a part of the society, have a legislative power over the whole, in virtue of a law which they themselves established? If we would say any thing in defence of their right to any legislative power, we must go up to a higher source of law, to a legislative power vested originally in the collective body of the society, which settled in this particular legislative body, all the power that they have of making laws, so as to bind the whole. In like manner, we may ask, in democratical states, where the legislative body consists of representatives, or where it consists of any thing less than the whole collective body; by what law was this form of government settled? Certainly it could not be settled by any law which was made by such legislative body: because the law that we are inquiring after, must have been made before they were a legislative body: it being a law which established them into such a body, or which gave them a legislative power over the whole community.

Upon the whole, as the law, which determines the civil constitution, is derived from the original legislative power of the whole society; so no constitution, though it has been once determined, can be any otherwise fixed and permanent, than by such a provision as will prevent the legislative power from returning again to the collective body: because, if it ever does so return, the same legislative power which determined the constitution at first, may either continue it, or new model it at pleasure. And such a provision is made in fact, where, by the original constitution, the legislative body, or some essential part of it, is continued always in being. We have already seen that this may be done in mixed forms of government; and that for want of it even democratical governments and elective monarchies may be precarious constitutions.

But though such constitutions of government, as have provided a standing legislative body, either in whole or in part, are here called fixed or permanent ones; yet it is not necessary, that they should continue for ever, or should be unalterably the same, as long as the society continues. They are called fixed or permanent constitutions; only because they are not variable in their own nature. But yet we shall find in some of our future inquiries, that there are many ways, in which even such civil constitutions as these, are subject to alterations.

What I have now called a law is what I before called a compact, subsequent, in the order of our conceptions, to the compact, which unites the several members of a civil society into one body. For the first agreement or consent of a number of individuals to unite together and form one body politic, though it produces a legislative power, does not vest such power in any particular part of the body, but in the whole. It does not give a legislative power to any single person, as in monarchies; or to a few select persons, as in aristocracies; or to representatives chosen by the people; or, indeed, to any part of the people exclusive of the rest, as is commonly the case in what are called democracies. The original legislative power of the whole society cannot be vested in any particular legislative body within that society, any otherwise than by means of a law, which is the effect of that original legislative power: and, as we shall see hereafter, such a law is followed by an agreement or compact between the collective and the legislative body. When the society has agreed to vest its legislative power in a certain person, or in a certain number of persons; this person, or these persons so appointed, become the legislative body of that society, in consequence of their acceptance of this power, and of their agreement to exercise it in a body of such a form as is then settled.

Executive body, how formed.

VI. Though we principally regard the nature or form of that body, in which the legislative power in any nation is vested, when we denominate the constitution of government in that nation, monarchical, or aristocratical, or democratical, or mixed; yet, in order to form a full and distinct notion of such constitution, we must consider in what sort of a body the executive power is vested. This, which is the power of exerting the joint strength of the society, is originally vested in the whole collective body. If we look no farther than the first compact, which united the several individual members into one society; though an executive power would arise out of such a compact, yet this power could not, by this compact alone be lodged any where else than in the collective body of the society. The public will is the active principle, which puts the public force in motion: and if nothing has passed between the several individuals which compose it, besides the general agreement of uniting themselves into a civil society; the public will of such society is naturally the joint will of the whole.

If the executive power is lodged any where else; if the will of any one person, or of any number of persons, less than the majority, puts the public strength in motion, and is understood to have a right of acting with this public strength; such right must be founded in some farther agreement, compact, or law, and could not naturally arise out of that compact or agreement, which merely produced the society by uniting the several members of it into one body. Every individual in the liberty of nature has a right to exert his own strength for his own defence and security: but each, by becoming a member of civil society, acquires a farther right of acting with the common force of such society for these purposes: and in order to acquire this right, he consents to use his own force no otherwise, than as a part of the common or public force. In this situation, as long as nothing else has passed, his will has as much influence in actuating the common force, or putting it in motion, as the will of any other individual, who is a member of the some society with himself. This force does not, indeed, immediately operate upon his authority, or by the direction of his will; but then he has as much authority, his will has as much influence in exciting its operations, as the authority or the will of any one else has. As there is a natural equality amongst mankind before they unite in civil society, so there is a social equality amongst them, after they are united: the mere act of thus uniting does not give any one particular person, or any number of particular persons, authority over the rest. This act binds each individual to submit himself in judging of his duty, to such rules as the common understanding prescribes, and to conform his will, in using any force for his own defence or security, to the common will of the society. But the same act which binds him to this, gives him a right to have his understanding considered as a part of the common understanding; that is, it gives him an equal right with any of his fellow-citizens to deliberate and determine concerning the rules of duty; and it gives him, likewise, a right to have his will considered as a part of the common will; that is, it gives him an equal right with any of his fellow-citizens to excite the public force, or to put it in action. The consequence of this is, that an executive body in a civil society, if it is not the whole collective body of such society, can be no otherwise naturally formed than the legislative body is: as some compact, agreement, or law, besides that which binds the society together, is necessary to give any particular person or persons the authority of prescribing rules of duty to the rest, or to establish a legislative body; so a like compact, agreement, or law is necessary to give any particular person or persons the authority of acting with the public force, exclusive of the rest, or to establish an executive body. By the mere consent to unite and form a civil society, a legislative power, and an executive power are produced: but if no other act has passed within the society which is so formed, the collective body is the natural seat of both these powers. Whenever, therefore, we find either a legislative body or an executive body distinct from the collective body; such legislative or such executive body must have been created by some farther act of consent: they are formed by some farther compact between the collective body, in which these powers were originally vested on the one hand; and the legislative or executive body, in which the constitution vests them on the other hand.

Despotic constitution, how produced.

VII. Though we here consider the legislative and executive bodies as distinguished from one another, by being employed about different objects, or in different provinces; yet it is not necessary that these bodies should be different from one another in fact. Whatever prudential reasons there may be, there does not appear to be any reason in the nature of the thing, against supposing that both these powers may possibly be vested in the same person or in the same body. Where the compact, by which these powers are conveyed, has established both of them in the same person or in the same body, whether that body consists of one person or of more, the constitution is called despotic. If they are both vested in one man, it is an absolute or despotic monarchy: if in a select body of nobility, it is a despotic aristocracy; if in the representatives of the people, or in any part of them, which is not a majority of the whole, acting by joint consent, it may properly enough be called a despotic democracy; and lastly, if they are both vested in a body compounded of any two or all of these parts, the constitution, though a mixed one, will still be a despotic one. In all these cases, the same body which prescribes what is to be done, having the public force in its hands to compel the execution of it, is subject to no constitutional checks or controls: it is possessed of the whole power of government, and consequently is as absolute as it is possible for civil power to be. I say, as it is possible for civil power to be; because civil power, when it is vested any where, unless in the collective body of the society, however absolute it may be in some respects, is not so in all: we call it absolute, where the constitution has provided no constant and uniform control of it; that is, we call it absolute, when it is so in respect of any constitutional restraint. But still, as it is only civil power, it will be limited by its own nature: for, as this is a power formed for certain purposes, it cannot in its own nature be so far absolute as to be free either to promote those purposes or to prevent them. What means of redress are to be used when despotic governors, be they monarchical, aristocratical, democratical, or mixed, act contrary to the nature of that power, with which the constitution has entrusted them, will appear in some of our following inquiries.

Executive body, how fixed.

VIII. The executive power continues where the first agreement of the individuals to unite into a civil society naturally placed it, in the collective body of the society; if the magistrates, who put the public force in motion, or act with that force, are appointed by the people, and continue, whilst in office, so far accountable to their constituents, that the people in their collective body are the last resort; that is, if in judicial matters an appeal lies to the people against the sentence of any magistrate, and in matters of war or peace, conventions or alliance, nothing can be finally determined without the concurrence of the collective body. But though the magistrates are originally appointed by the people in their collective capacity, and though this appointment is only temporary, so that at the expiration of the term for which their office was given them, the executive power will again revert to such collective body; yet if, in the meantime, what those magistrates do is final, and no appeal lies from them to the people, the executive power is vested in their hands.

Such an executive body will indeed be of short continuance in itself; and the constitution will, in this respect, be liable to frequent changes: because upon every expiration of the term for which the magistrates were appointed, the executive power reverts to the people in whom it was originally vested: and they are then as much at liberty as they were from the beginning, either to exercise it for the future in their collective capacity, or to dispose of it in the same manner that they did before, or in any other manner that shall then appear to them to be more convenient. If, instead of appointing a number of magistrates, they have appointed only one, and have left the appointment of the rest to him, he cannot be considered as the executive body, if the public force of the society cannot, upon all occasions, be exerted by his sole authority, without the express concurrence of his constituents. When such a magistrate is appointed, as acts independently of the collective body of the people, and is commissioned by them to exercise the public force by his own authority, without their express concurrence, he then becomes the executive body of that society. But if he has this power only for a term of years, or if this power lasts even for his life, but no standing provision is made to continue the like magistrate, either by making the office hereditary in his family, or otherwise, the constitution will be only temporary. At his death, or at the expiration of his term, the executive power reverts as before; and the people being bound by no law or no compact to go on in the same manner, may either renew the same, or introduce a different sort of executive body, as they shall judge most convenient. Where the executive body, after it is once appointed, continues always in being, as it does, either if it consists of a number of persons, some of which remain, though others die, or go out of office; or if it consists of only one person, and is made hereditary, so that upon his demise, his heir succeeds immediately into his right; there is then a perpetual obligation arising from the compact, by which such executive body was formed: because there is then a party always in existence, to whom the collective body of the people are bound by that compact. The constitution is by this means as fully established as the nature of the thing can admit of. It may, indeed, be changed, but it is not variable in itself: such a consent, as introduced it at first, may alter it afterwards; or as it is founded in compact, a breach of that compact on the part of the executive body will give the collective body, if not a constitutional, yet certainly a natural right to alter it.

National constitution, a question of fact.

IX. The point in which each particular person seems to be most interested, is, to be able to judge what is the particular form of government in the nation to which he belongs. For, as he owes obedience to the sovereign power, he cannot either know to whom his obedience is due, or settle the proper measures of it, till he has first informed himself to what person or persons the society has entrusted this power. But as the forms of government, which may possibly be established, are very various, there does not seem to be any way of determining what form has been established in any particular nation, but by acquainting ourselves with the history and the customs of that nation. A knowledge of its present customs will inform us what constitution of government obtains now; and a knowledge of its history will inform us by what means this constitution was introduced or established. This seems to be self-evident, upon the principles already laid down.

The sovereign power, both in its legislative and in its executive part, is originally seated in what * Grotius calls the general subject of such

* Grot. Lib. I. Cap. III. § VIII.

power; that is, in the society itself considered as one collective body. If, therefore, there is within the society what he farther calls a particular subject of such power; that is, if there is any legislative or executive body which does not take in the whole collective body; this legislative and this executive body must have been established either by express or by tacit compact; and the terms or conditions of such compact cannot be found any where else but in the history, records, or standing customs of the nation.

Some, indeed, who are better pleased with amusing themselves in speculations, than with inquiring into facts, have endeavoured to settle our notions of civil constitutions by abstract reasonings: as if such reasonings alone would be sufficient to teach us universally what form of government is established in all countries, without attending to the history or customs of any. As this method favours the idleness of superficial politicians, it is no wonder that these abstracted philosophers should have many followers. Most men are willing to be thought very knowing in all questions which relate to the constitution of civil government in their own country; and few are willing to take so much pains as is necessary to give them a tolerable insight into such questions. It would be a great expense of time and labour to read history, to collect and consider usages or customs, to search records, to examine and compare facts. But such abstract arguments are easily invented, as will serve to puzzle both the inventor and his disciples; though they should neither be convincing to himself, nor to any one else. This seems to be the reason why most of those who write or talk about the constitution of civil government in our own or in any other country, should deal more in metaphysical reasonings, than in arguments drawn from facts and observation, and should choose to learn their political principles, rather from the subtilties of schoolmen than from records and history.

Sometimes we are told, on the one hand, that monarchy is the best form of government; that it must be a natural form, because the providential government of the world is of this sort; and that, as it arises necessarily out of parental authority, no other form can possibly be established of right, whatever may have been done in fact. On the other hand we are told, that supreme civil power is naturally and unalienably in the collective body of the people; and that consequently all establishments, which suppose a supreme power any where else, must be mere usurpations.

Monarchical constitutions not more natural than others.

X. What is generally urged to prove that monarchical constitutions are the only natural forms of government, is scarce worth examining. *We have already seen, at large, how little reason there is for imagining that monarchical power arises naturally out of parental authority; or at least for imagining that it should so arise without the aid of compact. And if children, after they are come to years of discretion, are not subject to any civil power of their father, till they have consented to it, they might naturally have withholden their consent, so as to continue in that freedom and independency to which they were born; or might, by giving a like consent elsewhere, have established any other civil

* See Book II. Chap. II. § IV.

government, either of the same form with what would have arisen in their own family, if they had agreed to remain under the civil power of their father, or of any other form which they like better.

Notwithstanding the providential government of the world may be called monarchical, this is no reason why mankind should be bound to establish the same form in civil societies. Nor is it even an inducement to copy this form, till human monarchs can be shown to have the same knowledge, to contrive for the benefit of their subjects, and the same goodness to dispose them invariably to pursue this benefit, that God has to contrive for and to pursue the benefit of all his creatures.

As to the superior advantages of monarchical government above any other form, it must at least be allowed, that they are very far from being self-evident: and consequently, even supposing them to be greater than they really are, it is very possible for a nation, in establishing its civil constitution, not to be aware of them. And since the collective body of the people is originally at liberty to introduce what form they please, it is possible for them to make choice of another. However, all these supposed advantages would be found, upon inquiry, to be at least balanced, or rather to be outweighed by many inconveniences, which would probably determine any nation to choose another sort of constitution: if they were not misled for want of proper deliberation, or were not driven by distress to fix upon what, in better circumstances, they would not have chosen.

Politicians are, however, very well employed in comparing and balancing the advantages and inconveniences of each form of government with one another. For, though the result of their inquiries will never determine what form it is, which any particular nation has agreed to establish, yet it may serve to show every nation what is the most desirable form, and may lead them, as they have opportunity, to make such alterations in their own, as will bring them nearer to that point, if they cannot quite reach it. Certainly our * English poet has but little reason on his side, when he represents such an inquiry as the business of fools, and maintains that the only difference between civil constitutions of government consists in the better or worse administration of them: for that constitution is in his judgment to be called the best, let it be what it will, which is best administered. Whatever public benefit depends upon the character of the persons in power, it is derived from their wisdom and goodness, and not from the nature of the form of government. So that, to call that form the best, which is best administered, seems to be speaking improperly. Or if we will call it the best, we must, in the meantime allow, that it is the best by accident only, and not in its own nature. In the common course of human affairs, it is almost impossible to prevent the civil power from coming into the hands of weak and bad men, whatever the constitution is. That form of government, therefore, is best in itself, which guards most effectually against this evil; or if this evil ever does happen, which lays the persons in power under such checks and restraints, as are most likely to prevent them from abusing their trust; or, lastly, if this trust is abused, which has provided the readiest means for correcting the abuses. An absolute monarchy is a constitution which has so little title to these

* Pope's Essay on Man. Epis. II. lines 305, 306.

characters, that it can have no pretension to be thought the only natural, and much less the only possible form of government, upon account of its being the best form.

Monarchical constitutions not impossible.

XI. But yet it does not appear on the other hand, as Mr. Locke* maintains, "that a monarchical government is inconsistent with civil society, and so can be no form of civil government at all. The end of civil society being, he says, to avoid and remedy those inconveniences of the state of nature, which necessarily follow from every man's being judge in his own case, by setting up a known authority to which every one of that society may appeal, upon any injury received, or controversy that may arise, and which every one of that society ought to obey; wherever any persons are, who have not such an authority to appeal to, for the decision of any difference between them, there those persons are still in a state of nature. And so is every absolute prince in respect of those who are under his dominion. For he being supposed to have all, both legislative and executive power in himself alone, there is no judge to be found, no appeal lies open to any one who may fairly and indifferently, and with authority decide, and from whose decision relief and redress may be expected, of any injury or inconvenience, that may be suffered from the prince or by his order: so that such a man, however entitled, czar, or grand signior, or how you please, is as much in the state of nature, with all under his dominion, as he is with the rest of mankind. For, wherever any two men are, who have no standing rule and common judge to appeal to on earth, for the determination of controversies of right betwixt them, they are still in a state of nature."

Though we should not be able to show why this reasoning is inconclusive, yet we may be sure that it is so, if it proves too much; that is, if it proves some proposition to be false, which we are sure is true. Now, the same argument which he here urges to prove, that absolute monarchy is inconsistent with the nature of civil government; and consequently that it cannot possibly be a form of civil government, will equally prove that any other form of government is likewise inconsistent with civil society, and consequently that there can be no such thing as any form of civil government.

Let us try this argument in another instance. Wherever any persons are who have no authority to appeal to for the redress of any injury which is received, or for the decision of any controversy which may arise between them; there those persons are still in a state of nature. And so is every legislative body in respect of those who are under its dominion. For this body being supposed to have all the legislative power in itself alone, there is no judge to be found, no appeal lies open to any one, who may fairly and indifferently, and with authority decide, and from whose decision relief and redress may be expected, of any injury or inconvenience that may be suffered from such legislative body or by its order: so that such a body, if it does not consist of the whole society, however it may be entitled, senate, or assembly of estates, or how you please, is as much in the state of nature, with all under its authority or dominion, as it is with the rest of mankind.

It will scarce be replied here, that we have not supposed the execu-

* Locke's Works, Vol. II. p 198.

tive power to be vested with the legislative power in this body, as they are both vested in an absolute monarch: because Mr. Locke would scarce allow the executive body, if it is distinct from the legislative, to be an authorized judge for deciding any controversy between the legislative body and the rest of the society, from whose decision relief and redress may be expected of any injury or inconvenience that may be suffered by any person in the society from such legislative body. And if the executive body is not such an authorized judge, there will not, in point of wanting an authorized judge, appear to be any difference between the situation of an absolute prince in respect of his subjects, and the situation of a legislative body in respect of the rest of the society. To suppose the executive body to be such an authorized judge, is to suppose its power to be superior to that of the legislative body; since, giving the former such an authority as this, would be giving it authority to set aside the acts of the latter. Nay, the executive body is so far from being a judge, with authority to relieve and redress any inconvenience that may be suffered by any person within the society, from the acts of the legislative body; that, if it is vested with no power but what its name imports; that is, with none but executive power, it is not so much as a check upon the legislative body. For, as the legislative power is the supreme power, so the executive body, if it is possessed of no other power than what is merely executive, is naturally ministerial to the legislative. And it will be very difficult to find any difference between a prince who has all, both legislative and executive, power in himself alone; and a legislative body, which has in itself alone all legislative power, and to which the executive body, with all executive power, is wholly ministerial. To make the executive body a check upon the legislative, we must suppose it to be possessed of some prerogative, and to be such a necessary part of the legislative, that nothing can be done by the legislative body without the consent of the executive. Yet even in such a constitution as this, it will scarce be maintained that the executive body is an authorized judge to give relief and redress of any injury or inconvenience that any person may suffer from the legislative or by its order.

It may, indeed, be said, that such a legislative, especially if representatives chosen from time to time by the people are a constituent part of it, can do no injury; because what is done by their authority is properly the act of the people whom they represent. But neither will this make any difference between the two cases. For in whatever sense such a legislative body is said to be incapable of doing any injury, an absolute monarch may be said likewise to be incapable of doing any. As the representatives of the people are commissioned to act for the people; so an absolute monarch, as his authority is originally derived from the same source, is likewise commissioned to act for them. And, consequently, if it is supposed impossible for the people to be injured by what their representatives do, it will, for the same reason, be impossible for them to be injured by what an absolute monarch does: because both the representatives and the monarch are commissioned by the original consent of the people to act for them; so that the people's consent is as much implied in what one of them does, as in what the others do. As a civil society has the common good of the public in view, so the natural end of that legislative power, which arises from civil union, is the common good. The power, therefore, which is committed to a legislative body, being the legislative power of the society, is in its own nature limited to this purpose: as the society had no other legislative power to give, so the legislative body can have no other vested in it. Whilst, therefore, it continues to use the power which was given it by the consent of the society, it can do no injury. But the question is, whether, if it acts for any other purpose, it is impossible for it to injure the society? and if it does so injure the society, the next question will be, who is the common judge between such legislative body, and the body of the society?

Mr. Locke has shown us, that these questions may be applied with as much propriety to a mixed legislative body, as to an absolute monarch. * "Governments, he says, are dissolved, when the legislative body acts contrary to its trust. He puts the case of a legislative body consisting of three distinct parts. First, a single hereditary person having the constant supreme executive power, and with it the power of convoking and dissolving the other two, within certain periods of time. Secondly, an assembly of hereditary nobility. And thirdly, an assembly of representatives chosen from time to time by the people. As any other sort of legislative body, so such an one as this, acts, he says, against the trust reposed in them, when they endeavour to invade the property of the subjects, and to make themselves, or any part of the community, masters or arbitrary disposers of the lives, liberties, or fortunes of the people. For since it can never be supposed to be the will of the society, that the legislative body should have a power to destroy that, which every one designs to secure by entering into society, and for which the people submitted themselves to legislators of their own making; whenever the legislators endeavour to take away and destroy the property of the people, or to reduce them to slavery under arbitrary power, they put themselves into a state of war with the people, who are thereupon absolved from any farther obedience, and are left to the common refuge, which God has provided for all men against force and violence." Who then are the common judges between the legislative body and the collective body of the society, when the former thus injures the latter? Shall we say, that, as long as the legislative body discharges its trust, there is no occasion for such a common judge, and that, when it abuses its trust, the government is dissolved? May not we, therefore, say the same, where a single hereditary person is the legislative body? As long as he discharges his trust, there is no occasion for any common judge between him and the body of the society, and when he abuses his trust, the government is dissolved? The people do not feel the want of a common judge, either where the legislative body is simple, or where it is mixed; till the trust committed to such body is abused. But if we consider, as Mr. Locke does here, what the situation of the people is, in respect of their legislators of either sort, when there is a notorious abuse of this trust, we shall find that there is, in fact, no more a common judge in one constitution of government than there is in the other. The consequence of which will be, that, if absolute monarchy is an impossible form of government, because it is inconsistent with the nature of civil society; a mixed

* Locke's Works, Vol. II. page 237.

legislative, or any other legislative will be an impossible form of government, for the same reason.

The institution of a legislative, Mr. Locke says, is an umpirage provided by the members of the same society for the ending all differences that may arise amongst them, and is a bar to the state of war. He does not tell us, whether he means here the institution of a legislative power or the institution of a legislative body. If by legislative he means a legislative body, it is not necessarily true, that where no legislative has been instituted different from the collective body of the society, there is no standing umpirage which may decide all controversies, and be a bar to the state of war amongst the members of the same society. Civil union naturally creates a legislative power; which is originally vested in the whole body of the community. But whilst it resides there, it is as natural a bar to the state of war, as if it was vested in a particular part of the society, or in a legislative body, either simple or mixed. Such a body, upon the institution of it, may be considered as having the standing umpirage, which bars the state of war. But between whom has it this umpirage? Between the several members of the collective body; and not between itself and this collective body. If then in a mixed constitution, we may say, that by the standing umpirage of the legislative body, there is a bar to the state of war; we may say the same in a monarchy. Or if in a monarchy, the legislative body and the people must be considered as in a state of nature with one another, for want of a standing umpirage between such legislative and the people; we must, for the same reason, consider a mixed legislative and the people as in a state of nature; since there does not appear to be any standing umpirage between them. This reasoning is equally applicable to all forms of government, except such a perfect democracy, as we scarce any where find to have been established.

It may, perhaps, be urged, that a mixed legislative body is not likely to abuse its trust; especially where an essential part of it consists of persons who are chosen from time to time by the people, and who are at all times so far considered as a part of the people, as to be subject to all laws made by their own concurrence, and to the same laws, that the rest of the people are subject to. This is undoubtedly true: and the necessary consequence is, that such a mixed constitution is vastly preferable to a monarchy. But this consequence does not affect the point in question. We are not endeavouring to prove that a monarchy is as good a constitution of government as any other; but only that it is at possible as any other: not that it is as unlikely to be abused, but that it is as consistent with the nature of society as any other. And the great use to be made of this point, when it is established, is to show that the abstract argument by which Mr. Locke endeavours to prove, that no government can be monarchical, will be of little service to those lazy politicians, who think they have sufficient grounds to conclude the civil constitution of their own country to be popular, from general reasonings upon the nature of civil government, without having recourse to records and history, to custom and usage; without looking back to the manner in which their civil constitution was begun at first, and to the changes which it has since undergone.

But after it has been thus shown, that Mr. Locke's reasoning is inconclusive, it may still be asked why is it inconclusive? We say, that the want of a common judge between the body of the society and its monarch, can be no reason for concluding that these two parties are necessarily in a state of nature; because there is the same want of a common judge between the government and the body of the society in all constitutions whatsoever, except such, if there be any such, as are perfectly democratical: so that, if we were to admit the truth of this principle, we should be led to conclude from it, that, in all other constitutions whatsoever, the constitutional governors, and the rest of the society, are in a state of nature. Either, therefore, it must be allowed, that this principle is a false one, or else it must be maintained that all constitutions of government are alike inconsistent with the nature of society. But though we are sure that no principle can be true, if it necessarily leads to a consequence which is confessedly false; yet still it may not be thought enough to prove in this manner, that it is not true, unless we can show why it is not; that is, unless we can show how two parties can possibly be considered as not in a state of nature, though they have no common judge to decide in disputes between them.

Now, it is certain that persons in a state of nature, have no standing judge of controversies, who can decide between them with authority: but till it is shown, that the having such a judge is the only effect of society, the converse will not be as certain; it will not be certain, that where there are two or more persons without any judge who can so decide, those persons must be in a state of nature. Indeed, in civil societies, all individuals in matters of private right or obligation, have a standing judge, vested with authority to decide finally: and this judge is the legislative body, or *rather the executive body, acting under the checks and controls of the legislative. But then the existence of such a judge, in some instances, necessarily implies, that there can be no such judge in other instances. For no decision can be final, unless the contending parties choose to acquiesce in it, where there is a farther judge to appeal to. If, therefore, there is a standing judge whose sentence is final, the existence of such an authority necessarily implies that there can be no farther appeal, or that there is no standing judge between this final one and the parties in controversy. A state of society, however, though in controversies between the legislative body and the community there is no standing judge, may easily be distinguished from a state of nature. The very existence of such an authority, as is lodged with the legislative body, is sufficient to make the distinction: because in a state of nature there is no such authority. Thus much, indeed, must be allowed, that, when there is occasion for a common judge between these two parties, between the legislative body and the rest of the society; that is, where the former have usurped a power which does not belong to them, these two parties are then so far reduced to a state of nature, that they will have no means of deciding the controversy between them, but that force or strength which nature has given them. But when this happens, the constitution of government does not subsist, but is dissolved.

Upon the whole, the reason why a monarch and the collective body of the society are not in a state of nature, is because this body has entrusted him with such an authority over it, as the state of nature knows

* See Book II. Chap. III. § VII.

nothing of. His authority, indeed, is not an arbitrary one of doing what he pleases with the people that he governs: though there are no constitutional checks and controls provided for his restraint, the authority entrusted with him is a limited one in its own nature, as being intended for the security and advancement of the common benefit. He and the society will, indeed, be in a state of nature when he abuses this trust. But this, instead of proving that a monarchical constitution necessarily places the monarch and his people in a state of nature, will only prove, that they come into such a state when the constitution is dissolved.

All constitutions not necessarily democratical.

XII. What I have here principally in view is to convince the reader, that the only reasonable method of learning what is the constitution of government in any nation, is to read the history of that nation, and to collect from its most authentic records, such facts as relate to the forming the constitution as far back as we can go; and such, likewise, as relate to any sudden or to any gradual changes which have from time to time been made in it. I have with this view examined already some of the abstracted arguments by which it has been attempted to prove, on the one hand, that all constitutions, except such as are monarchical, are unnatural; and, on the other hand, that a monarchical constitution is inconsistent with the nature of civil society.

We may now go on to consider and explain what Grotius says upon this subject; and, perhaps, when his opinion is thoroughly examined and placed in a true light, it may be found less exceptionable than at first sight it appears to be. * Grotius maintains it to be a false and dangerous opinion, that in all civil societies, without exception, the sovereign power is vested in the people, so as to make them the constitutional judges, whether their kings or other governors abuse their authority; and to give them a constitutional right of restraining or punishing those governors where they are chargeable with such abuse. His commentator here accuses him of stating the question in a false and insidious manner. No one, says Gronovius, ever thought that the supreme power is, every where, and without exception, lodged in the hands of the people, so as to give them a right to restrain and punish their kings whenever they misuse their power; or if any one ever has thought so, we can by no means agree with him. Thus far, therefore, the commentator and the author seem to be of the same opinion. But Gronovius goes on to inform us, that this is not the point in question. The true state of the question is, whether a people that have a government lawfully established; whether a people that have once agreed to be governed by a king, or by a senate of nobles, or by an assembly of the estates, may not change the government, and even punish their governors, when the greater part of the society perceive such established government to be destructive of the common good; when their king is plainly become a single tyrant; or their senate of nobles is degenerated into a body of tyrants; or their assembly of estates is changed into a confused meeting of seditious factions. This, indeed, which Gronovius proposes, is one question: but he had no reason for charging Grotius with stating it insidiously, if it is not the question which Grotius here

* Grot. Lib. I. Cap. III. § VIII.

designed to examine. It is one question, whether the collective body of the people have, every where and without exception, a constitutional right to restrain and punish their kings, or their nobles, or their standing representatives; that is, whether all constitutions of government must necessarily be perfect democracies. And it is another question, whether the people, whatever form of government they may have consented to establish, have not a natural right to judge when that constitution is broken; and when it is, to introduce, if they are able, a new form of government; to put the civil power under other regulations, and to restrain or punish those who have abused it, if they shall attempt to establish their unconstitutional usurpations by force. If the latter question had been what Grotius here designed to examine, he might indeed justly be charged with stating it insidiously. But if he designed to examine the former, he seems to stand clear of this charge. And certainly his words plainly show us, that he had the former of these two questions in his mind. Or if his words are not a sufficient evidence, we may have fuller evidence by attending to *the arguments which he tells us are made use of in defence of the opinion which he rejects: for those arguments, if they prove any thing, would prove that the collective body of the people have every where, without exception, a constitutional right of restraining and punishing the legislative body, and not that they have a natural right of doing themselves justice, where the civil constitution is dissolved by unconstitutional usurpations of power. There is still a farther evidence, that he had no thoughts of examining into the latter of these two questions in this place: for it is scarce likely that he should undertake to examine it twice; and we find, that he does examine it in †another place.

What our author has said upon the point before him, will be the more readily admitted, if we attend to his principles in their full extent. Though he explains himself in the instance of monarchical government, his principles, ‡he says, are intended to be general, so as to be applicable to the sovereign body, whatever the form of that body is; whether it consists of a single person, as in monarchies, or of a senate of nobles, as in aristocracies; or of any select part of the people, as in most democracies; or is compounded of all these, as in mixed constitutions. And if we suppose the sovereign body to consist of a single hereditary person, having the constant supreme executive power of an assembly of hereditary nobility, and of an assembly of representatives chosen from time to time by the people; it will scarce be thought an error in political principles to maintain, that the collective body of the people have not a constitutional right to restrain and punish such a body as this.

All that our author maintains more than this is, that monarchical government is possible; that it is possible for the collective body of the people to vest the supreme power, both legislative and executive, in the hands of one man. And even what he alleges in support of this opinion has been the more blamed for want of considering, that his arguments upon this head are as applicable to all other forms of government, as they are to monarchical ones: since it will scarce be possible to show,

* Grot. Lib. I. Cap. III. § VIII.

† Grot. Lib. I. Cap. IV. § VII.

‡ Grot. Lib. I. Cap. III. § VIII.

that the collective body of the people can vest such a power in any number of persons of what sort soever, less than the majority, if they cannot vest it in a single person.

Our * author's topic, from which he sets out, when he is to prove, that the whole civil power, legislative and executive, may be entrusted with a single person, has been the ground of some exceptions to his whole opinion. The law of nature, he says, allows an individual to dispose of his own person, so as to make himself a slave: and he appeals to the Mosaic and to the Roman law in support of this principle. From whence he argues, that a number of individuals, though formed into a civil society, may, consistently with the law of nature, subject themselves in such a manner to the civil power of any one man, as to retain to themselves no part of that power, either legislative or executive. The reader has already seen, in one instance, what abilities Gronovius was possessed of as a commentator; and his manner of treating this argument will give us another specimen of them. He first mistakes our author's meaning, and gives him a very exceptionable one, and then grants the whole argument to be conclusive in the mistaken and exceptionable sense, in which he understood it. Many, who read Grotius, fall into the same mistake with him, as to the author's meaning: but then they are wise enough to see, that, if Grotius meant what they imagine him to mean, his argument would not be conclusive. He is generally supposed to reason in the following manner:—Since the law of nature allows an individual, by his own act, to make a slave of himself, or to subject himself to the private despotism of his master; the same law must necessarily allow a number of individuals, by their own act, to make slaves of themselves, or to subject themselves to the private despotism of their civil governor. Thus he is supposed to conclude from what may be done in one case, that the same may be done in the other. Whereas, in fact, his argument is such an one, as the logicians call *a majori ad minus;* he reasons from the possibility of doing more, to the possibility of doing less. Since the law of nature allows an individual, by his own act, to part with so much of his liberty, or so much of his power over himself, as to become a slave; it cannot but allow a number of individuals to do what is less than this, to part with so much of their power over themselves in their social capacity, as to retain no constitutional civil power. If the law of nature allows a man, by his own act, to subject himself to private despotism by making himself a slave; it cannot but allow him, by his own act, to do less than this, to part with his liberty in a less degree, and subject himself to civil despotism, by giving up all the share which he had, as a member of civil society, in the legislative and executive power.

It may be necessary here, just to mention the difference between slavery and civil subjection on the one hand, and between private and civil despotism on the other. The slave is bound to make the good of his master the end of all his actions, and, consequently, to conform himself, in all things, to the will of his master. The subject is bound to preserve and advance the good of the civil community, and, consequently, to conform himself to the will of such community, in all things which relate to the general good. Private despotism, therefore,

* Grot. Lib. I. Cap. III. § VIII.

implies a right in the master to direct all the actions of the slave for his own benefit. Civil despotism implies a right in the civil governor, to direct such actions of the subjects, as relate to the general good or benefit of the society. From hence, we may understand, that our author's reasoning is conclusive, when it is considered, as he intended it, only as an argument, *a majori ad minus;* from what is greater to what is less. If the act of an individual can bind him to submit all his actions to be directed by the will of his master, for the interest of his master; a like act can bind any one individual or any number of individuals to submit such of their actions, as are relative to the society, of which they are members, to be directed by the will of their civil governor, for the common interest of the public. Certainly, if mankind are incapable of laying themselves under such an obligation as this, there can be no such thing as an established form of government, unless it is a perfect democracy: for this is the subjection which the individuals who are members of civil society owe to the legislative body; whether that body consists of one man, as in monarchies, or of a select body of hereditary nobility, as in aristocracies, or of any part of the people less than the majority of the whole society, as in all democracies, but those which are perfect ones; whether such part is considered as the representatives of the rest; or whether it is a part, which acts collectively, instead of the whole. We may observe, by the way, though it does not relate to our author's reasoning, that even private despotism is not such a sort of power, as it is commonly supposed to be. *It is not a right in the master to do what he pleases with the slave. It is naturally subject to several limitations; and as the slave is injured when any of these limitations are broken, he has a right to seek for redress. A single slave, indeed, may be too weak to have the means of redress in his power: but a nation of slaves, if Grotius had supposed any such thing, would have strength enough to support their rights, if they were willing to use it. However, Grotius does not suppose any such thing; but whilst he contends for the possibility of a people's committing the whole civil power, both legislative and executive, to a part of the society, as, for instance, to a king in some constitutions, to the nobles, or to the assembly of the estates in others, he considers the power in the hands of this part, only as civil power, and not as private despotism; and he considers the people as in a state of civil subjection, and not as in a state of slavery. If he had not this distinction in his mind, his whole reasoning here would be inconsistent with the first principles which he lays down †elsewhere, when he defines a nation to be an assembly of men of free condition, in opposition to a family of slaves. And whether this civil subjection is due to one man or to more, it is still but civil subjection: the power acquired by it is only civil power; that is, a power of directing and of compelling the subjects to promote the common good and benefit in all such actions, as relate to the peace and welfare of the society. This power is not tyrannical in itself, and does not imply, that they who are entrusted with it, have any right to compel the subjects to pursue any other end. If they should, under the colour of this power, pretend that they have such a right, I do not find that our author maintains it to be unlawful for the people to

* See Book I. Chap. XX. § V.

† Grot. Lib. I. Cap. I. § IX.

make use of such means as they can, to prevent themselves from being enslaved.

After Gronovius has supposed his author to be contending, that a number of individuals uniting into a civil society, may, consistently with the law of nature, make themselves slaves to their governor, and has granted the whole force of the argument in this mistaken sense of it, which no one else but himself would have granted; he asks, what is the farther consequence? and then amuses himself with contending, that, though such nations, as have thus enslaved themselves, may be slaves if they please; yet the consequences of this argument are not applicable to any nation in Europe. As if Grotius had here been endeavouring not only to prove that any subjects, considered as members of civil society, may be as much at the arbitrary disposal of their civil governors, as slaves are at the arbitrary disposal of their masters; but that some or all the nations in Europe have, in fact, thus enslaved themselves. As our author had no intention to prove, in general, that subjects, as members of civil society, may be slaves; so he had much less any intention of proving this to be the case, in fact, of any nation whatsoever. The point, which he has in view, is only to show, that all constitutions of government are not, in the nature of the thing, purely democratical; that the collective body of the people, though the supreme legislative and executive powers begin from them, and are originally vested in them, may so far have parted with these powers, as not to have a constitutional right of deliberating upon what the legislative and executive bodies do; and of restraining or punishing the persons who compose these bodies. He instances, at first setting out, in the case of a monarchy, and endeavours to show, that the constitutional, legislative and executive powers may be given up by the people, and be entrusted by them to a single person: but he observes, before he concludes what he had to advance upon this subject, that he designed his reasoning should be general, and should be extended to all other forms of government whatsoever. Nor does he attempt to prove, even whilst he dwells upon the instances of monarchies, that any such constitution, as he there describes, is actually established in any country whatsoever. If such a constitution is possible, in the nature of the thing, it is enough for his purpose. And his unthinking commentator, whilst he designed to oppose his principles, grants him not only this, but much more than this; he grants, that the members of a civil community may, by their own act, make themselves slaves to their civil governors.

We may judge how well this commentator was qualified to write upon civil power, if we attend to his manner of proving, what Grotius never denies, that there is no kingdom in Europe, where the subjects are under the absolute power of a monarch. The Germans, says he, elect their emperor. The French originally chose their kings in the first establishment of the three lines of Meroveus, Charlemaine, and Hugh Capet. And the Spaniards received the house of Austria, upon the title of marriage and compact. It is not worth the while to inquire how far, in the last of these instances, a claim to govern, under the title of having married one who had a right to govern, can, without any intervening act of the people, be called a compact. But in general we may observe, that, if all which he contended for here, is granted; if these several kingdoms were obtained by election or by compact, it will by no means follow, that the kings are not absolute: since, upon our commentator's principles, compact may not only give a king such an absolute civil power over his subjects, as shall be under no constitutional control, but may give him likewise even private despotism, so as to make them all slaves. And if we grant still farther, that none of these monarchs have absolute civil power, it will not follow that Grotius is mistaken, when he maintains that an absolute monarchy is a possible form of civil government.

Gronovius, indeed, asks, what occasion there is for concerning ourselves, in Europe, with such a question as this? But the answer is obvious. We have as much to do with this question in Europe, if we have a mind to understand the origin and nature of civil constitutions, and to settle the measures of that obedience, which we owe to our civil governors, as if we lived in Asia. For certainly the measures of constitutional obedience to our governors, be they monarchs or nobles, or our own representatives, with legislative authority, will not be the same, if the people in their collective body have not every where, and without exception, a constitutional power of restraining and punishing their governors, that they would be, if this collective body had such a constitutional power.

It was not material whether our author examined this question in the instance of an absolute monarchy, or in the instance of any other form of a legislative body. Though, perhaps, what he says upon it would have been less objected to, if he had made choice of some other instance: and he would, besides this, have had the farther advantage of not being led to explain the occasions of establishing absolute monarchies; upon which subject he has advanced some positions that most of his readers are displeased with.

The point which he wants to establish, when it is stripped of this circumstance, is, that, unless in perfectly democratical societies, there is in some one man, or in some body of men, within the society, a civil despotic power lodged, which, though it is originally derived from the collective body of the people, is exercised afterwards so far independently of them, as not to be subject to any constitutional restraints from that body. Despotic power is a bad name indeed, because it is commonly used to convey the notion of what is arbitrary and tyrannical. But this bad meaning will be taken off, if we call it civil despotism, which is the civil power originally inherent in the community or collective body itself, but entrusted by their consent, either express or tacit, with the governing part of each community. What Grotius principally contends for is, that this power may be so delegated by the collective body, as to leave that collective body no share in it. When this has been done, the people, he says, have no constitutional right to restrain or punish those governors who are entrusted by them with this power. But then, where the constitution is broken, or where the constitutional governors pretend to and make use of a power which does not belong to them, a power of causelessly and arbitrarily oppressing the people, which is no part of civil power; our author, as far as appears, does not contend, that in these circumstances the people have no natural right of doing themselves justice. And certainly we ought very carefully to distinguish between a constitutional right in the people to interfere in the affairs of government, to direct or restrain the legislative and executive bodies in the exercise of the power that is entrusted with such bodies, and a natural right in the people to maintain the constitution, as it was at first settled, when any attempts are made to alter it; to resume the legislative and executive power, when the constitution has been broken; or to defend themselves against all unsocial or unconstitutional oppression.

Grotius, as I observed before, having chosen to explain what he has to say upon this subject, in the instance of monarchy, was led to say something concerning the possibility of introducing such a form of government, not only in the nature of the thing itself, but in fact too. As to the possibility, in the nature of the thing, of entrusting the whole civil power, both legislative and executive, in the hands of one man, so as not to subject him to any constitutional restraints from the collective body of the people; the general consideration by which such a constitution of government is shown to be consistent with the nature of civil society, is the same that must be made use of to show that any other form of government is possible; that the legislative and executive power are subject to no constitutional restraints from the collective body of the people, when they are entrusted with any number of men, of any denomination whatsoever, less than the majority of the community. It might be objected, indeed, that we cannot well presume that any nation would ever consent to trust the whole civil power with any one man, for reasons which have been taken notice of already. * But to this our author replies, that the objection is nothing to the purpose of the point in hand: for we are not inquiring what form of government may be presumed to have been established, where the matter is doubtful, but what form may be established consistently with the nature of civil society. You may urge, that this form is attended with many inconveniences: but all the inconveniences which attend it, as they will never prove it to be impossible in fact, so much less will they prove it to be impossible in its own nature. All forms of government have some inconveniences attending them. And if the inconveniences of one form would prove it to be impossible, the inconveniences of all other forms would prove them all to be impossible. As there are many ways of setting out in common life; many different trades, professions or occupations for men to choose out of, and some are in themselves preferable to others, mankind, in determining what way of life they shall enter upon, do not always fix upon that way which may appear most eligible in itself. Sometimes their situation will not allow them to engage in the profession which they would otherwise have liked best. Sometimes they choose wrongly for want of deliberating at all. And sometimes they are misled in their judgment when they do deliberate. Just so it happens, where a nation is to choose its form of government. Distress may compel it to take up with such a form, as in better circumstances it would not have chosen. It may sometimes establish a form of government too hastily, without deliberating which is best. And sometimes, even though it should deliberate, it may be mistaken in its choice. So that, notwithstanding it is true, that absolute monarchy is not only attended with some inconveniences, as all other forms of government are, but

* Grot. Lib. I. Cap. III. § VIII.

that it is attended with more than any other; yet this is no reason why it should be impossible for such a form ever to be established in fact. The nation, where it is established, may have chosen this form, though they knew it was a bad one: or they may have chosen it, because, either for want of consideration, or for want of reasoning upon right principles, they thought it to be a good one. In our endeavours, therefore, to find out whether it is this, or any other form which has been established in any nation, we are not to consider the excellence or advantage of this or of that form, but to attend to the matter of fact, and to inquire what form appears to have been actually established by the consent of the people, either express or tacit. Grotius mentions particularly the motive of distress, when he supposes it possible for a nation to be in danger of being destroyed by war, if it does not put itself under the absolute command of some able and experienced leader; or to be in danger of perishing by want, if it does not give up its general right in the civil power to some person who will supply its wants upon no other terms. He supposes, farther, that an owner of large tracts of land, may grant the land out to such persons as are willing to settle there, upon condition of his having the constitutional power of governing all those persons, considered as united into a civil society; or that one, who has private despotic power over a great number of slaves; that is, of persons who are bound to work solely for his benefit, may give them their personal liberty, so as to form them into a civil society, upon condition that they shall still be subject to his civil despotism, or be obliged to promote a common good, in such a manner as he shall direct.

It is not worth our while to examine how far these supposed cases may ever happen in fact. The great point that we want to prove is, that all governments are not necessarily democratical; and that among other forms of government, which are not so, and yet are possible in the nature of the thing, an absolute monarchy is one. And if it should be thought farther necessary to show, that such a form is possible in fact, the considerations already mentioned may be sufficient to show it: I mean, that the distressful circumstances of a nation may compel the people to choose this form; or they may choose it capriciously, without deliberating; or they may choose it mistakenly, even after they have deliberated.

What our author says, in regard to the possibility of establishing this or any other particular form of government by conquest, is more exceptionable. But I shall pass it over here; because we shall have an opportunity, in another place, of examining into this matter more at large.

However, before we leave this part of our present inquiry, it may not be amiss to remind the reader, that after this or any other sort of civil constitution is established, it is not necessary that the same constitution should remain for ever. Since it is derived originally from a compact, either express or tacit, between the legislative and executive bodies, on the one hand, and the collective body of the people on the other; though both parties are bound by this original compact as long as it subsists, yet we shall find hereafter, that its obligation may be dissolved, or that its conditions may be altered.

If we go on to examine the arguments, which Grotius says are commonly urged against his opinion, we shall perhaps be better informed what that opinion is; and shall see, that instead of inquiring here, whether the people have a natural right to resist any unconstitutional oppression or injury arising from the legislative or the executive bodies, his design was to inquire whether they have necessarily such a constitutional right of restraining or punishing these bodies, that no form of government can be consistent with the nature of civil society, which does not vest the sovereign power ultimately in the collective body of such society.

* First, it is alleged, in contradiction to our author's opinion, that the king, or the hereditary nobles, or the representatives of the people, are all, or any of them, originally appointed by the act of the people, and derive their power, whatever it is, from the joint consent of the civil society over which they preside. But since in the very notion of an appointment to any office, the constituents are superior to those who are so appointed, the consequence will be, that, in every civil society, the people must naturally be the superior party, or that the constitutional sovereign power is naturally lodged with them. In reply to this argument, Grotius, indeed, insinuates that, in some instances, particularly in that of conquest, the power of governing may possibly not arise from the appointment of the people. But, as this part of his answer is not true, so neither is it what he lays the chief stress upon. He insists rather, that the principle upon which the argument proceeds, does not hold good universally, that a person who is appointed to an office, is not upon that account necessarily inferior to his constituents. Indeed, where the appointment is precarious; where he holds his office only at the will of his constituents, and may, by the particular nature of such appointment, be removed at their pleasure; he is at all times so dependent upon them, that the power which they reserve to themselves of displacing him, renders them, in point of authority, superior to him. But where, though the appointment arose originally from their will, the effect of it is afterwards necessary; so that he is no longer dependent upon their will for his continuance in the office, which they at first gave him; his having been appointed by them does not imply that they have any authority over him. If we, therefore, set out upon the principle, which Grotius seems to doubt of, without any good reason, (I mean, that the governors of a civil society derive their power from the appointment of such society,) yet it does not follow that the constitutional power of the people is necessarily superior to that of the governing body, of what sort soever it is, merely upon account of their having been the original constituents of that body. In order to prove this, they, who urge the argument, instead of reasoning from the general nature of appointments to any office, should reason from the particular nature of an appointment to the office of civil government, and should show, that such an appointment must always leave in the hands of them who make it, a constitutional power of displacing their civil governors at pleasure. It is not sufficient to show, that, where the constitution is broken, or where the governors are guilty of great and notorious oppression, the people have a natural right to redress themselves. This would only prove, that the people, as one of the parties in the compact, by which the constitution was established, are naturally obliged to

* Grot. Lib. I. Cap. III. § VIII.

nothing but what is contained in that compact: it would not prove, that they have, by that compact, a constitutional right to check and control their governors in the exercise of the power, which such compact lodged in their hands.

The principle upon which the second argument, that Grotius examines, proceeds, is, that all government is intended for the benefit of those who are governed, and not for the benefit of those who do govern; and, consequently, as civil government, according to this principle, is intended for the benefit of the people, they must necessarily be considered as the superior parties in the contract, which establishes the form of government: because we cannot imagine, that in any contract the chief regard would be had to the interest of any but the superior party. Our author objects, in the first place, to the principle, upon which the argument proceeds: he does not allow it to be universally true, that all government is designed for the benefit of those who are governed, rather than for the benefit of those who do govern. For, in his opinion, the benefit of the party who does govern, is, in some instances, the end of introducing the government. Thus, the good of the master is the end or purpose of that authority, which he has over the slave; and though it may be possible, that the slave should be benefited by this authority; yet this benefit of his is accidental; it is not the end, which the authority of the master has in view. In other instances, the mutual benefit of both parties is the proper end of government; particularly, it is so in that authority, which a husband has over his wife. But Grotius was aware, that if we make a very small alteration in the principle here laid down, so as to restrain it to civil government in particular, instead of extending it to government in general, these instances would be nothing to the purpose. If we say, that all civil government has the good of those who are governed, and not of those who do govern, for its principal end; the argument will stand clear of any exceptions that may be drawn from these examples: it will then be nothing to the purpose to urge, that it is not so in other sorts of government, in that of a master, or in that of a husband.

Our author, therefore, goes on to offer his reasons, why this principle should not be looked upon as necessarily true even in civil government. Where civil power, he says, is acquired by conquest, the end, which the conqueror has in view, when he establishes himself in the possession of such power, is his own benefit. And yet such an establishment is not necessarily a tyranny: because there may, possibly, be no injustice, either in the establishment of this power, or in the exercise of it, after it is established: and the word tyranny, as it is commonly used, includes the notion of injustice. We will not stop here to inquire, how far such a power may be established by conquest, nor how far it may be exercised without injustice; for without entering into these questions at present, we may observe, in reply to what our author here advances; that, if he will not allow us, on the one hand, to call a power of governing, introduced with a view only to the governor's benefit, by the name of tyranny; we cannot allow him, on the other hand, to call it civil power. Where the benefit or interest of the governor is the chief end proposed; so that they, who are under his authority, are obliged to direct their actions to the advancement of this end; the power, by whatever means acquired, or however lawful, is private despotism, and not civil power. We might, therefore, notwithstanding this instance, still maintain, that all civil government is introduced rather for the benefit of those who are governed, than of those who do govern.

This principle, however, though Grotius has not disproved it, is not true, in the manner in which it is here expressed. Civil government, though it is intended for the good of those who are governed, cannot be intended solely for their good: it is intended for the common interest of the whole society, both of those who are governed, and of those who do govern, and not for the separate interest of either, exclusive of the other. Civil power, in the first original of it, results immediately from civil union. And this power, if it was to continue in the hands where it is first lodged; that is, in the collective body of the people, is undoubtedly designed to promote the same end with civil union; that is, the common benefit of the whole body politic, and of the several parts of that body. But when any civil society has gone farther; when it has, by a subsequent compact, introduced some other form of government, which is not purely democratical, and has vested its civil power in the hands of some particular part of such society, as in a king, or in the body of the nobility, or in a body of representatives; these established legislators do not cease to be a part of the society: and, consequently, their benefit is as much in the view of civil power, as the benefit of any other persons who belong to it. The original end of civil power is the common benefit of all: and the nature of it is not so altered by being committed to a select part of the body, as to confine the benefit, designed by it, to those other parts, who have given up their share in it. The collective body of the people might, perhaps, be induced to commit the sovereign power to some particular legislative body, in expectation, that it would be exercised more to their advantage, when so disposed of, than if they had retained it in their collective body. But they would have little reason to expect such advantage, if, by this act, they designed to separate their interest from the interest of the legislative body, considered as a part of the society, whether it consists of a king only, or of a number of hereditary nobility, or of representatives, who are chosen for a term of years, or of all these together. I say, considered as a part of the society; because, though the end of civil society is the common benefit of all its parts, as much of the governing as of the governed part; yet when the governors set up a separate interest of their own, as if they were not parts of the society; neither the end of instituting a form of government, nor the end of uniting into a civil society, can bind the people to pursue this separate interest to the hurt of the public welfare.

Grotius, however, allows, that the good or welfare of those who are governed, is principally regarded in most instances, when civil constitutions of government are established: but then he denies it to be a consequence of this principle, that the people are, in every such establishment, the constitutional superiors. The power of a guardian, as he observes, is given him for the benefit and interest of his ward But no one can infer from thence, that the ward is superior to the guardian. The very notion of a right in the guardian to direct the ward, implies the guardian to be the superior; notwithstanding he is obliged, by the nature of the compact, which gave him this right, to use it to the advantage of the ward, by directing him to his own good. But our author is aware, that his own instance of guardian and ward may be urged against himself. It may be said, that, as the guardian, if he abuses his trust, may be removed from it, because he was appointed, and had this trust committed to him, for the benefit of his ward; so, likewise, it seems reasonable, that the governors of a society, of what sort soever they are, should be removed from their trust, when they abuse it. Our author replies here, that this may be the case of the guardian, because, in the society, of which he is a member, he has a superior: but in civil governors it cannot be the case; because there cannot be an infinite progression of civil governors, one superior to another, but must be somewhere a last resort, either in some one man, or in some body of men, who have no superior but God. This reply, however, does not clear up the matter; it does not show, that the constitutional governors have no constitutional superior; and particularly, that the collective body of the people is not this superior: since we may suppose this without being reduced to the necessity of supposing farther an infinite progression of civil governors, one superior to another. This collective body may be the last resort; it may be this assembly, which has no superior but God.

We shall be the better enabled to form a judgment upon the question now before us, if we attend to the distinction already mentioned, between a constitutional superiority in the people, or a constitutional right in them to restrain or punish their established governors, and a natural right of defending themselves against any unsocial or unconstitutional injury or oppression brought upon them by such governors, under the pretence of exercising that civil power only, with which the people had entrusted them. No one will imagine, that upon every supposed mismanagement of the public affairs, or even upon such real mismanagement, as human nature exposes a man to in every station, the people have a right to dethrone their king, to degrade their nobles, to discharge their representative body, before the term for which that body was chosen, is expired, and to take the civil power again into their own hands, to new model the constitution, or to continue the old form of government in a different set of men. Yet this must be the necessary effect of supposing a constitutional superiority in the collective body of the people, under any form of government, either simple or mixed. The common benefit of the whole, which is the end of civil society, as well as of every sort of civil constitution, may, indeed, be a sufficient foundation of a natural right in the collective body, to oppose unconstitutional oppression, or to release themselves from that compact, by which they committed the civil power to their established governors, when these governors have so far broken this compact, on their side, as to make their continuance in power plainly and notoriously inconsistent with such common benefit. If this is all that is meant by saying, that in monarchical constitutions, the people are superior to their king, we may allow it. But we should observe, at the same time, that this right is called by an improper name: for instead of being a constitutional superiority, whilst the compact, which introduced and established the form of government subsists, it seems rather to be a natural equality, when that compact is broken.

Others, says our author, have supposed such a sort of mutual subjection between the king and the people, that the people are obliged to obey him when he governs well; but that he, in his turn, becomes inferior to them when he governs otherwise. He is here speaking of monarchical constitutions in particular; but what he says will be applicable to all other constitutions, if we only change the word king for the words constitutional governors. If they who maintain this opinion, only meant that, where such governors command any unjust actions, the people are not bound to obey them, he allows that they would be in the right; but he observes at the same time, that such a liberty in the people does not imply any civil or constitutional superiority in them. In some constitutions we find the sovereign power actually divided between the king and the people: but where such a division is designedly made, the most usual and the best method of making it is, to assign certain and determinate limits to their respective jurisdictions; to give the king authority in some affairs, or over some parts of the territory, or over some certain persons; and to give a like authority to the people in other affairs, over other parts of the territory, or over other persons. But the good or bad management of affairs in any instance, especially in matters of civil policy, is so problematical; so much may be said, in any instance, in opposition to any particular measure, or in defence of it, that this can by no means be fixed as the proper limit of the respective jurisdiction or constitutional superiority of the king and the people. Such an uncertain limit as this, would occasion endless confusion: it would be always impossible to know which party was uppermost, and which party was vested with the sovereign power, whether the king or the people: one party having always an opportunity of pretending that the measure in question was a good one; and the other having a like opportunity of pretending that it was a bad one. But if so much confusion would follow from such a sort of mutual subjection as this; we can have no reason to imagine it to be of the essence of civil government, that there should be such a mutual subjection: because, as civil government was designed for the common peace and benefit of the society, nothing can be of the essence of it, which would necessarily introduce confusion. Thus our author reasons upon this point. But it will, perhaps, be made most intelligible, if we keep to our former distinction, and maintain that the king, in a monarchical form of government, has the sovereign power granted to him by compact, which power makes him the constitutional superior of the people. But then, if he breaks this compact, there is no necessity, in order to support the right of the people, to maintain that they become his constitutional superiors; it is sufficient, if such a breach of compact leaves them at liberty to redress themselves by such means as they have in their power.

Titles or appearances do not determine the nature of the constitution.

XIII. What has been already said may be more than enough to show, that whoever would form a true judgment concerning the constitution of civil government, in his own or in any other country, must consider it as a question of fact, and must make use of the helps of records and history, instead of amusing himself with abstract reasonings. But it will be necessary, even in using these helps, to observe some cautions: because, when the facts, by which he is to form his judgment, are before him, it is possible for him to form a wrong one.

*The first caution to be observed is, that, in judging what is the civil constitution in any country, we ought to be careful that titles or appearances do not mislead us.

The titles of emperor, or king, or prince, or duke, for instance, are commonly supposed to imply different degrees of civil power in the person to whom such titles are respectively given. When we find that the chief magistrate in any nation is called an emperor or a king, we are apt to imagine that sovereign power goes along with these titles; and, consequently, that the constitution must necessarily be monarchical. On the other hand, if he is called a prince or a duke, these are looked upon as inferior titles: and if we were to attend to the title, rather than to the truth of the fact, the inference might perhaps be, that the chief magistrate, who has only one of these inferior titles, has not sovereign power, but that the constitution is either mixed or popular. But these titles, however they might be intended at first, are now used indiscriminately. The lowest of them is frequently given to persons who have sovereign power; and the highest to persons whose civil power, within their own territories, is not sovereign.

In like manner, where we find a senate or parliament, by which the people are represented, we are apt to conclude from such an appearance, that the people have at least a constitutional share in the sovereign power, if not the whole of it. Such a conclusion, however, is not always well grounded. Before we can determine whether it is or is not well grounded, we must attend, not only to the existence of such a body, but to the business in which it is employed. It may be designed only to give the king an opportunity of knowing the state of the nation better than he could have known it otherwise; to acquaint him with such public grievances as he could not by any other means have been so well informed about; or, perhaps, by his own appointment, to register his acts in order to make them known to the people in the most ready and most authentic manner. If this is all that they have to do, they do not seem to have any civil power, except what he delegates to them. And the existence of such a body of men would be a very weak argument to prove that the constitution is not absolutely monarchical. But if, on the other hand, their business, when they meet, is to raise money for the support of the government; to settle the uses to which such money shall be applied; to exercise a part of the legislative power, by deliberating concerning the expediency of making any new laws, or of repealing any old ones, and to act with such authority in this point, that nothing can be done effectually without their concurrence; these are instances of sovereign power, and will at least prove the constitution to be a mixed one.

Tenure of civil power to be distinguished from the power itself.

XIV. †Secondly, the claim which the king has to the civil power; that is, the tenure by which he holds this power, or so much of it as the constitution gives him, ought to be carefully distinguished from the power itself.

Other things are held or possessed by three sorts of tenure; that is, there are three sorts of claim which the owner may have to them. A man may have full property in corporeal things; or he may have a claim of usufruct in them; or they may be his by a temporary tenure. Of

* Grot. Lib. I. Cap. III. § X.

† Grot. Lib. I. Cap. III. § XI.

these three sorts of tenure, that of full property is the highest in degree, and may, therefore, be called the supreme tenure. The other two, an usufructuary, or a temporary tenure, are of an inferior sort. In corporeal things, the claim of the owner, or the tenure, by which he holds them, is plainly different from the things themselves: it is impossible to confound the field which a man claims as his own, with the right by which he claims, or the tenure by which he holds it. The same field may at different times belong to one man in full property; to another, by usufruct; and to a third, for a term of years. But it is plain, that the field and the tenure, by which it is held, are distinct from one another: since the field is still the same, whilst the claim to it has undergone these several changes. The same observation is applicable, likewise, to incorporeal things, in *which number civil power is to be reckoned. And the caution which our author here recommends, is, that we are not to judge of the power of a king from the tenure by which he holds it, or by the nature of his claim to it. He may have the supreme claim to it, or may hold it in full property, and yet the power so holden may be less than sovereign: or he may hold it by usufruct, or for a time only; and yet, though the claim is of the inferior kind, the power may be supreme.

It is questioned, indeed, whether any one can have full property in civil power; whether a kingdom can be patrimonial; or whether the right to govern a civil society can possibly be alienable, at the discretion of the possessor, as his right to any other estate, or to any other part of his patrimony is. Certainly, when the people have vested civil power in any particular man, or body of men, this grant of theirs does not imply that such power is alienable; that the man, or the body of men in whom it is so vested, have a right either to exercise it themselves, or to alienate it to any one else, at their own discretion. Since a power to govern does not imply a power to choose and appoint a governor; a king may be invested even with the sovereign power of governing, without having full property in that power, or without having a right to alienate it: because transferring this power from himself to any one else, is, in effect, choosing and appointing a governor.

But this is not the point in question. Grotius no where supposes, that whoever is possessed of civil power, must necessarily have a right to alienate that power. On the contrary, the distinction which he makes, between the power itself, and the claim to such power, sufficiently shows it to have been his opinion, that a king may be possessed even of absolute power, without having full property in it. It is granted, therefore, that there is nothing in the nature of civil, or even of sovereign power, which will necessarily give any person, in whom such power is vested, a right to alienate it. If nothing more is done, than merely to lodge that power in his hands, he will have no patrimonial right to it; for the reason already mentioned: a right to govern by no means includes or supposes a right to appoint another governor. But though a grant of civil power, from the people to their king, does not imply, that he shall have a right to alienate such power to whom he pleases, and, consequently, though there is, in the original settlement of a constitution, no occasion for the people expressly to stipulate,

* See Book I. Chap. II. § X.

that the sovereign power shall not be alienable by him or them, to whom they entrust it; yet it may still be a question, whether it is impossible for the people to make it so; whether it is inconsistent with the nature of the thing for the people, when they vest the civil power in the hands of a king, or of a body of nobility, or even of their own representatives, to give them, at the same time, a right to dispose of their power, either to exercise it themselves, or to alienate it to some one else.

The general objection against the notion of a plenary right in civil power, which * Grotius mentions, does not seem to be decisive against his opinion, that such a right is possible. Free men, such as the members of a civil society must be, are not, it is said, matter of commerce, they cannot be bought and sold, or alienated and acquired, as slaves are. This is, undoubtedly, true. When the civil government is transferred from the present possessor to some one else; he, who acquires the power so transferred, cannot acquire the same power, which the purchaser of a slave acquires over the person of the slave. But this is no reason why he may not succeed by an act of his predecessor into the same power which his predecessor had. It is not possible, that by such act he should succeed into more: and if he does not, the subjects will be just as much free men, under the new governor, as they were under the old one. To suppose, that, if a king has a right to appoint his successor, or to alienate his kingdom, he must, necessarily, have a right to change the constitution, to give such successor a greater power than he had himself, or, perhaps, a power even of joining it as a province to dominions of his own, is supposing what is by no means contained in the notion of a patrimonial kingdom, and what Grotius particularly designed to guard against in this caution; where he has taken care to observe, that plenitude of property is so far from implying plenitude of power, that, if we were to inquire into facts, we should find the inferior sorts of civil power, as marquisates or dukedoms, to be more frequently alienable than sovereign power.

We, indeed, in this kingdom, have been brought up under such a constitution of government, as will make us wonder at the notion of any kingdoms being patrimonial, if we have never looked beyond what passes amongst ourselves. But whoever has looked abroad, and has considered, with the least degree of attention, what has passed in other kingdoms, even in Europe, will find that, in the common opinion of mankind, kingdoms may be alienable, in like manner as other inheritances are. It can scarce admit of any question, whether they are so in themselves. † Mr. Locke's reasoning upon this head seems to be decisive. "The legislative cannot transfer the power of making laws to any other hands. For it being a delegated power from the people, they, who have it, cannot pass it over to others. The people alone can appoint the form of the commonwealth, which is by constituting a legislative, and appointing in whose hands that shall be; and when the people have said, we will submit to rules, and be governed by laws made by such men, and in such forms, no body else can say, other men shall make laws for them; nor can the people be bound by any laws, but such as are enacted by those whom they have chosen and author-

* Grot. Lib. I. Cap. III. § XII.

† Locke's Works, Vol. II. p. 215.

ised to make laws for them. The power of the legislative being derived from the people by a positive voluntary grant and institution, can be no other, than what that positive grant conveyed; which being only to make laws, and not to make legislators, the legislative can have no power to transfer their authority of making laws, and place it in other hands."

But, then, though a king with legislative power, cannot, in virtue of such legislative power, alienate his kingdom, so that sovereignty in government, does not imply such sovereignty to be alienable, or plenitude of power does not imply plenitude of property in such power; yet there is still a farther question, whether the people who delegated the sovereign power, could not, likewise, confer a right upon the person or persons, to whom they delegated such power, of making it over to others? whether, as they gave the legislative power, they could not, likewise, give a right of transferring that power? If they could, then kingdoms, though they are not patrimonial in themselves, may be made so by the consent of the people, not only by a concurrence, at the time of transferring the sovereign power from the present possessor to his successor, but by a prior grant, at the time of delegating the sovereign power to such present possessor, or at any other time.

There are, certainly, many inconveniences, which would, probably, attend such an establishment as this; but none of them show it to be impossible. The danger which a nation is in, of being made a province, is one of these inconveniences, and has been mentioned already. And, upon that occasion, we observed, that plenitude of property, in civil power, would not give a king, or any other governing body, a right to do this: because, though they may have a right given them to alienate the power which they have, it is no consequence, that they have a right to transfer a power which they have not. The successor can have no right to any thing, which his predecessor had no right to: so that, if the nation was no province under the predecessor, it cannot, of right, become one by the transfer of civil power to his successor. Another inconvenience, attending such an establishment as this, is the possibility of the government's coming into improper hands, of its being alienated to such persons, as are neither agreeable to the people, nor fit for the office. This inconvenience, however great it seems to be, though it may show, that no nation would be likely to agree to such an establishment; if they were in so good a situation, as to be able to procure a better; yet will never prove such an establishment to be impossible, in the nature of the thing. An inconvenience of the like sort may be apprehended, where the constitution has made even a limited, and much more, where it has made an absolute monarchy hereditary. In the course of succession, the civil power may come into the hands of a person, who is neither agreeable to the people, nor fit for the office. And yet the apprehension of such inconvenience would be looked upon as a very weak argument to prove, that all laws, which have entailed civil power upon such a particular person, and the heirs of his or of her body, are inconsistent with the nature of civil society, and, consequently, that such laws, however they are made in fact, are, in right, no laws at all.

It seems to be true, in general, that what the collective body of the people do by another, whom they have appointed to act for them, is as much their own act, as if they did it themselves in a full assembly. In a kingdom, made hereditary by law, whether the king is limited or absolute, if there is a vacancy of the throne, either by abdication or otherwise, the choice of a successor, and the future settlement of the constitution would, undoubtedly, be binding upon the whole society, if such choice and settlement were made by persons entrusted for that purpose by the people; though this choice, and this appointment were not made in a full assembly of the whole collective body. We see, therefore, that the people may depute persons to choose governors for them, whether such governors have only a share in the legislative power, as in limited monarchies, or have the whole of it, as in absolute ones. And if it is not impossible, in the nature of the thing; that is, if it is not inconsistent with the nature of civil society, for the people to delegate their right of choosing legislators; it can scarce be thought impossible, in the nature of the thing, for the people to delegate such a power to the legislative in present possession. So that, though a king or a legislative body, merely as such, can have no right of appointing their successors, or of transferring their power to such successors; yet there does not appear to be any reason, why the collective body of the people may not, if they think proper, delegate or convey this right to their king or legislative body. And, consequently, though no kingdom, however absolute the power of the monarch may be, is, in its own nature, patrimonial; yet a kingdom may be made patrimonial by the consent of the people: it is possible for them, not only by their immediate concurrence to make a transfer of the power of governing them from the present possessor to any other person, whom they shall expressly approve at the time; but it is possible for them, by some former act of consent, to have given the present possessor a right to transfer that power to such person, as he shall approve of: and such a former act of consent will make his choice, in effect, their own.

Our author's caution, about this matter, may be proper to be repeated here; he observes, that this tenure of civil power, which we have called plenitude of property in it, and which is the supreme or highest tenure possible, is no evidence that he, who holds by it, has plenitude of civil power, or that his power is sovereign: for the tenure, by which the power is held, and the power itself, are different things; so that a power, which is patrimonial, may as well be an inferior sort of civil power, as sovereign or absolute civil power.

On the other hand, civil power may be sovereign or absolute; notwithstanding it is held by a tenure, which is inferior to plenary property, by a claim of use and profits, or by a temporary claim. Where the constitutional laws of a civil society have settled the succession to the crown, and have determined beforehand to whom it shall descend upon every demise; the present possessor, as our author says, holds his power by a tenure of usufruct; the use and profits of it are his to enjoy, but the thing itself is not his to dispose of. In like manner, where the crown is elective, and upon every vacancy, the people have a constitutional right to choose the successor; the present possessor holds by a claim of use and profits.

Perhaps in this latter instance, the tenure may rather appear to be temporary: since the right continues only for a certain term, for the life of the present possessor, and no longer. Whereas, in the former instance of hereditary kingdoms, the right continues to himself and such heirs as the laws have limited; so that those heirs, by the aid of such laws, claim in intestate succession: and consequently the thing so claimed seems to be his by more than a temporary right; it is transmitted from him to his heirs by the aid of the law, though he has no right to transmit it by his own act to whom he pleases.

It is not, however, worth the while to inquire particularly whether the tenure in elective kingdoms is of the temporary, or of the usufructuary sort. All that is necessary for us to observe here is, that an usufructuary claim to civil power, is no evidence that the power so held is not of the highest sort. The right by which a thing is claimed, is different from the thing itself: the nature of the claim, therefore, does not determine the nature of the power which is claimed: and he who should know that the civil power in any country belongs to the king by a claim of use and profits only, and not by a claim of full property, will have gone but a very little way towards determining whether the constitutional power of such king is absolute or limited; whether the sovereign power is vested in him, or in the people, or in the nobles, or in all together. For, as patrimonial civil power may be of the inferior sort, so usufructuary civil power may be sovereign.

If we look upon the power of an elective king to be temporary, this might serve as an instance to show us, that it is possible for civil power, though it is given only for a time, to be absolute as long as it lasts: since it is possible for the people, though they choose their king only for life, to make his power absolute as long as he lives. Grotius here makes use of the instance of the Roman dictator's power, in the beginning of that commonwealth, before the Horatian law had made it capital to create any magistrate that should not be subject to appeal. Nor can it be maintained, in opposition to this instance, that the dictator's power, before this law was made, could not be absolute, merely because it was only temporary: since the nature of a thing does not depend upon the time of its continuance. If civil power may be absolute, when it continues for the lives of a man and of his heirs, it may likewise be absolute when it continues only for six months. The way to judge whether it is so or not, is to consider the effects of it. Now, the effects of sovereign power are such, that no other civil power within the state can make them void. And as the effects of the dictator's power were of this sort, as long as that power lasted; the power, which produced these effects, could not be less than supreme, notwithstanding the claim to it was only temporary. If, indeed, we consider the majesty or dignity of the person who is invested with such temporary power, instead of considering the power itself, it must be confessed, that a temporary magistrate has less of that majesty and dignity, than one who is perpetual: not because his power is less in itself, but because the people cannot readily bring themselves to pay as much respect and reverence to one, who, though he is now their superior, will soon be reduced to a level with themselves, as they willingly pay to one, who will be their superior as long as he lives.

Promise or oath of a king, may limit his power.

XXV. * Grotius has mentioned a third caution, which is to be observed in forming a judgment upon the civil constitution of government in any nation, and of the

* Grot. Lib. I. Cap. III. § XVI.

power, which the people have lodged in the hands of their king. The caution is, that the power of the king may be sovereign, so as not to be constitutionally subject to the control of the people, notwithstanding he bound himself to the people by some promise or oath, when he accepted the crown, not merely to observe the law of nature or the law of God, which he would have been obliged to observe without such engagement, but to observe some other rules, or to act under some other restrictions, which otherwise would not have been binding upon him.

We shall the better understand whether we can allow this caution to be well grounded, if we consider it both where the promise or oath is required of him by the immediate act of the people, or by some fundamental law of the society, as a necessary condition of his receiving the civil power, with which he is about to be invested; and, likewise, where such promise or oath is wholly voluntary in him, and is matter of his own mere grace and bounty.

In the former case, if the constitutional laws require him to promise or swear to observe certain rules in his future government; or, where there are no such laws, if the people, when they make over the civil power to him, impose this promise or oath upon him, and will not lodge it in his hands upon any other terms; I do not see, how such a promise or oath can be consistent with the notion of his civil powers being in all respects superior to that of the people. A promise or oath of this sort is plainly a stipulation between him and them, and is the method which they make use of to ascertain their own constitutional rights, as well as to bind him not to exercise any power which shall violate those rights. But if they have a constitutional authority to require, that he shall promise or swear to observe certain rules in his future government, it seems absurd to suppose, that they have no constitutional authority to enforce the observance of those rules, and to see to his performance of such promise or oath. And how such an authority as this, in the people, is consistent with full or absolute sovereignty in him, is more than I can understand. If, indeed, any one chooses rather to say, that, where a promise or oath of this sort is not observed, the constitution is broken, and the people have, though not a constitutional, yet a natural right to resist him in the exercise of any power which is contrary to his promise or oath; it will scarce be worth the while to enter into a dispute upon this point: since the king and the people will, in effect, be in the same situation, if the people have a right to resist the exercise of such power, whether this right is to be called constitutional or natural; whether it arises from a superiority of constitutional power on their part, or from a breach of the constitution on his.

It is only to such a promise or oath, as is matter of mere bounty, that a nice distinction, made by our author, can possibly be applied: this distinction, if it was ever so just, is by no means applicable to constitutional oaths or promises. Let us, however, examine the distinction itself; and, perhaps, we shall find that it has no foundation. An oath or promise, says Grotius, which is taken by a king, when he comes to the government, may either be such an one as restrains him in the exercise of his civil power, in some instances, or such an one as gives up the power itself in the like instances. Suppose him to promise, that he will confine certain offices of profit or trust to persons of such a rank, or of such qualifications as the promise specifies; or that he will not raise any taxes, or impose any new tolls or customs, but such as have been used to be paid. By a promise of this sort he restrains himself, according to our author's opinion, in the exercise of his power, but does not part with the power itself. Whatever, therefore, he does afterwards, which is contrary to such a promise as this, will be wrong. But then, says our author, as he has retained the power of acting, though he has limited himself as to the exercise of it, what is so done will not be void. And from these principles Grotius concludes, that such a promise, or oath, does not make his civil power less than sovereign, as it does not appear to affect the validity of his acts at all, and much less does it imply, or create in the society, any power superior to his own. But suppose, as our author goes on, that his promise or oath is conceived in such terms, as to contain not merely the rules by which he engages to act in certain instances, but a renunciation likewise of the power of acting otherwise, than the promise or oath expresses: whatever is done contrary to a promise or oath of this sort will indeed be void. But then Grotius reminds us, that civil power is sovereign, when none of its acts can be made void by any other power within the society; and that, in the instance before us, the acts of a king, which are contrary to such promise or oath, are not made void by any other power within the society, but are void in themselves, upon account of a defect of power in him who does them. His conclusion, therefore, is, that the invalidity of these acts is no evidence that there is any power within the state superior to his own, and consequently is no evidence that his power is not sovereign. But there does not seem to be any foundation for distinguishing here between a promise or oath, which limits the king in the exercise of his power, and a promise or oath, by which he renounces the power itself. Every promise, if it has any effect at all, must be a renunciation of power, as far as it extends. A promise, in its own nature, affects the liberty of the promiser, by obliging him to act in a particular manner: and it is impossible to conceive, how he should have obliged himself to act in a particular manner, without having given up his liberty or power of acting in any other manner. All promises, therefore, or oaths, though they are voluntary on the part of the king, are renunciations of his power to govern by any other rules than those which he has promised or sworn to observe. The consequence of which is, that all such acts, as are contrary to these rules, will be void.

This, Grotius allows to be a diminution of his power, as to the extent of it; though he thinks it still continues the same as to its degree. To clear up his meaning in this second distinction, we will suppose the two following cases of a promise or oath. First, the future king may merely renounce his right to do certain acts, which, by virtue of the civil authority, vested in him, he might otherwise have done. Or secondly, he may not only renounce his right to do those acts, but may give the people a right to control him, if ever he does them, by agreeing, that they shall never be done without their consent, signified either by themselves, or their representatives. Whatever he does contrary to his promise, in either of these instances, will be invalid. In the first of them, it is, that Grotius supposes what he does to be invalid, without any diminution of his sovereignty, as to the degree of it; because his acts, done contrary to his promise, become invalid, by a defect of power in himself, and not by the superior power of any one else. In the second instance, his power cannot well be thought sovereign, because he vests that power in the people, which he renounces for himself; and by that means, establishes a power within the society, by which his own acts may be made void. When our author allows, that the promise or oath of a king, in the first of these cases, diminishes his power, as to its extent, but not as to its degree; he seems to mean, that where the king, before he enters upon his office, has, as the case is put, merely renounced the power of doing some acts, which he otherwise might have done, without vesting the power so renounced, in the hands of the people; his power is necessarily abridged as to the extent of it; because some acts, which he does, will be void, in consequence of his promise, though they would not have been void, if no such promise had been made. But then, in the meantime, his power is not diminished as to the degree of it; unless he transfers to the people, what he renounces for himself; because, unless he does this, there will be no power in the state superior to his own.

Yet, after all, this second distinction is of no weight in the present question. The whole civil power is originally in the body of the society. Suppose, therefore, that they either elect a king, and would vest the whole civil power in his hands; or suppose, that they have, formerly, made such a delegation of civil power to their king, and have established it by law, to his heirs after him; if any promise of such king to the people, when he takes the government upon him, is considered as a renunciation of any part of the civil power, it must naturally give, or rather return such power to the people, from whom it originally came. It is impossible for the civil power not to exist somewhere in all its parts: if he has it not, the people must have it. Certainly, therefore, if the constitution of government, in any country, was at its first establishment, designed to be absolutely monarchical; such a promise prevents it from being so: and if this form was once established, such a promise, from any subsequent monarch, must change the constitution, and restore to the people so much of the civil power, as is contained in the promise.

Mixed constitutions.

XVI. After what has been said already, we need not enlarge upon the fourth caution, which * Grotius proposes to be observed in judging of a civil constitution: the caution is, that though sovereign power seems, in its own nature, to be simple or indivisible, as being the act of the common understanding, directing what is to be done; yet it is not necessary, that this should be the understanding of any one man, as in monarchies, or of any single body of select men, as in aristocracies, or of the representative body of the people, as in democracies: it may be the joint understanding of a mixed body composed of any two, or all of these. So that all civil constitutions are not, necessarily, one of the three simple sorts: and in most nations we should find it very difficult; in some nations we should find it impossible to reduce the constitution to one or other of these sorts, and should form a wrong judgment about them, if we imagined them capable of being so reduced.

* Grot. Lib. I. Cap. III. § XVII.

Civil constitutions may be altered.

XVII. To these cautions we may add a fifth, which is, that when, in reading the history of a nation, we have discovered what its civil constitution was in any former period of time, we must not, from thence, conclude it to be the same at present: because civil constitutions, like all other things, are subject to alterations. The means, by which alterations may be produced in them, shall be inquired into hereafter.

CHAPTER V.

OF THE CHANGES WHICH ARE PRODUCED IN THE RIGHTS OF INDIVIDUALS BY CIVIL UNION.

Rights of mankind, how changed in civil society.

I. The rights of mankind, when we consider them as members of a civil society, are different, in many instances, from what they were in a state of nature. This difference arises either from civil union, or from civil laws. Some of the rights of mankind, when they are united into a civil society, are made different from what they were in a state of nature, by the immediate operation of that compact, which forms or unites them into such a society. Whilst some of them undergo no immediate alteration by this compact, but only are subjected by it, in general, to the authority of civil laws: so that such actual alterations, as they undergo afterwards, are produced immediately by these laws, and only remotely by civil union. After a number of individuals have agreed to join together into one body, for the purpose of securing one another, by their common force, against injuries, they are not so free to act for themselves for this purpose, at their own discretion, and by their own private force, as they were before they made this agreement. * But since many of the rights of mankind consist in nothing else but in the liberty of doing certain actions; it follows, that, in whatever instances their liberty of acting for themselves is restrained by such an agreement, their rights, by this act of civil union, become different from what they

* See Book I. Chap. II. § III.

were in the liberty of nature. But mankind form themselves into civil societies, not only for the purpose of securing themselves against injuries, but for the farther purpose of advancing a general good. The compact, therefore, which forms or unites them into such a society, binds them to act for the general good, by following such rules, as the common understanding of the society shall judge to be necessary for obtaining it. In consequence of this obligation, their liberty of acting is liable to be restrained by these rules; that is, by the civil laws of the society, in many instances, where the mere act of civil union had laid it under no particular restraint. All such restraints upon their liberty, as arise from this cause, are so many changes produced in their rights, by the immediate operation of civil laws.

Right of private defence, how restrained in a state of civil society.

II. Civil union lays the foundation of all the alterations, that are made in the rights of individuals, after they are become members of a civil society, by subjecting them to such future restraints as shall arise from the laws of that society. But the rights that are actually altered by civil union only, without the aid of civil laws, are chiefly such as arise from an injury, either before or after it is committed. * We have already seen at large what these rights are: so that it will be sufficient here, only just to mention them. Individuals, in a state of natural liberty, when they find themselves to be in danger of suffering an injury, have a right, before it is committed, to defend themselves against it at their own discretion, and by their own force. They have, likewise, after an injury is committed, a right to use the same means, both to obtain reparation for the damages, which they have sustained by it, and, likewise, to inflict punishment upon the authors of it. Some alterations are made in each of these rights by civil union: and we are now to inquire what those alterations are.

Individuals are restrained by the act of civil union, from defending themselves against an injury, by their own private force, and at their own discretion; and are obliged to apply to the society, or to the civil magistrate, acting for the society, to defend them by the use of the common force, under the conduct of the common understanding. It is the more necessary to inquire into the manner, in which this restraint upon the right of private defence is produced; because most of the writers upon natural law, seem rather to take it for granted, that there is such a restraint, than to explain the cause of it.

This inquiry might be soon brought to a conclusion, if it could be shown, that individuals explicitly renounce their right of defence, and transfer it from themselves to the civil magistrate, by the social compact; that is, by the compact which unites them into a civil society. By this compact all the individuals bind themselves to act with their joint force, for the preservation and support of their rights: and all of them bind themselves, likewise, to advance and secure the general good, by following such rules as the common understanding shall prescribe to them for this purpose. These two parts make up the whole of the social compact: and, whatever may be implied, there is, certainly, no renunciation of their right of private defence, nor any transfer of it from themselves to the civil magistrate, explicitly contained in either part of it.

* See Book I. Chap. XVI, XVII, XVIII.

After the civil laws of any nation have commanded the several members of it not to defend themselves by their own private force, but to apply to the civil magistrate for this purpose; their right of private defence will then undoubtedly be restrained. For one part of the social compact subjects mankind, in a state of civil society, to the authority of civil laws, by binding them to follow such rules, as the common understanding shall prescribe for the advancement and security of the general good. But this does not come up to the point in question, nor to the common opinion about it. We are not inquiring, whether the right of private defence may be restrained by laws, which become binding, in consequence of civil union; the point in question is, whether it is not restrained by the mere act of civil union, without the aid of such laws. And the common opinion about this point is, that mankind, considered merely as members of civil society, have no such right of private defence; whether any express laws have been made to restrain it, or not.

The other part of the social compact places each individual under the protection of the whole body, by binding them all to act with their joint force for his defence. But if we look no farther than his right to protection, it will be no direct consequence, that by acquiring this right, his own right of private defence is lost or restrained. For there is no direct inconsistency between his having a right to prevent or to repel an injury by his own force, if he thinks it safe and prudent to act alone, and his having a right to be assisted by others, if he finds himself too weak to prevent or to repel it, without their assistance.

We have* elsewhere had occasion to mention a second social compact, by which, after a civil society is formed, some particular civil constitution or form of civil government is introduced and established. It will be needless to stop here, and inquire, whether this is properly a compact or a civil law. We shall have an opportunity of examining into this matter hereafter: and though, if it should then appear to be a law, any restraint, that it may lay upon the right of private defence, would rather be a restraint arising from civil law, than from civil union; yet as we have hitherto called it a compact, we will still suppose it to be properly a compact, and will call it so in the present question. By this second compact, which we here consider as a joint agreement of the several members of the society, amongst other effects, which it produces, civil magistrates are appointed for the purposes of doing justice to all, who are under the protection of such society.† It may, therefore, be imagined, that their agreement to appoint civil magistrates, for the purpose of defending them, implies their consent to transfer their right of private defence from themselves to such magistrates. But not to insist again, upon what has been mentioned already, that their acquisition of a right to be defended by others, whether by the collective body of the society, or by the magistrate, does not directly imply the loss of their right to defend themselves; we may observe, that a civil magistrate, or an executive body, acting under the checks of the law, is nothing else but a part of the society, which is appointed to act for the whole of it. The right, therefore, which this second compact conveys to the magistrate, though it may be less, cannot possibly be greater

* See Book II. Chap. IV.

† Grot. Lib. I. Cap. III. § I.

than what the first compact had given to the collective body of the society: so that, unless we can show, that the first compact gives the collective body such a right, or such a power, as is inconsistent with a right of private defence in the individuals; the second compact can convey no such right or power to the civil magistrate.

There is a plain reason why the society will interpose and hinder a man from making use of his own force, upon any occasion and in any manner that he pleases, against those who are under its protection. The society, by receiving them under its protection, obliges itself to take care, that they shall suffer no causeless harm. And this obligation requires, that it should not allow him, or any one else, to act against them at discretion, even for his own defence: because he might possibly do them an injury, under the notion of defending himself from suffering one. He might pretend that they designed, or were preparing to injure him, when there was no ground for such a pretence: or even if they did design to injure him, yet he might be unjust, both in his demands of security, and in the manner of enforcing those demands. But this restraint upon his right of private defence, is a restraint rather in fact than of right: though the society is obliged to secure them, who are under its protection, against all causeless harm; yet he, in the meantime, if he is no party to this obligation, will have a right to defend himself at his own discretion, and by his own force. Such a body of men will be stronger than he is, and will, therefore, be able to hinder him from using his right: but this is no evidence that his right does not subsist: because it is no evidence, that he is obliged to submit to be so hindered, if he was strong enough to help it, and thought himself to be doing nothing but what the law of nature will justify. Such a restraint as this upon his right is no other than what he might have met with in the liberty of nature; if the individuals, that he had to deal with, happened to be stronger than himself: they might have stopped him from using his right of private defence, till they were satisfied that his defence was lawful: but in the meantime he would not have been obliged to submit to their determination upon this head, but would have been at liberty to determine upon it for himself. And as he had a right in a state of equality to judge for himself, whether the occasion of defending himself, and the means that he made use of for this purpose, were justifiable or not, and to act accordingly; notwithstanding the individuals that he happened to have to deal with, might be stronger than he, and might force him to submit to their judgment; so, likewise, in a state of civil society, though such society may, in fact, stop him from defending himself, at his own discretion and by his own force, against any persons who are under its protection; yet if we consider it as doing this, only in consequence of its obligation to guard those persons against suffering any causeless harm, without any consent on his part, he will still have the right to judge for himself, and to act accordingly.

We have now seen, where any person is in danger of being injured by others, that neither the obligation of a civil society to protect them against causeless harm, nor the right which he has to protection, will take away his liberty of private defence; if the obligation of the society and his right are considered separately. But if his right to protection is a right to be protected by the same society, which is obliged to protect them, and we consider this right, or rather the conditions, upon which he acquired it, and the obligation of the society together, we shall then find, in this view of the matter, that the same act of social union which gave him a right to protection, put his liberty of private defence into the hands of the public, or of the civil magistrate, who acts for the public. The obligation of the society towards them, if he is no party to it, will produce only a restraint in fact, and not a restraint in right, upon his liberty of private defence. But whatever act of his makes him a party in this obligation, either as such act declares, or as it implies his consent, that as far as he is concerned, the society should protect them; this act of his gives the society such a right, as restrains his liberty of private defence in respect of them. The act of civil union, or the act of putting himself under the protection of a civil society, is an act of this sort: it implies his consent, that, as far as he is concerned, the society should guard all others, who are under its protection, against suffering any causeless harm. And the reason why his act of civil union, or his act of putting himself under the protection of the society, must be understood to imply, that he consents to these conditions, is, because the society, being from the nature and design of it obliged thus to guard all others who are under its protection, could not consistently with this obligation, take him under its protection, unless he consented, and was willing to make himself a party to the same obligation.

Upon the whole, an individual is understood, by the act of civil union, to part with his right of private defence; not merely because this act places him under the protection of a civil society, but because it places him under the protection of a civil society, which stands engaged to protect those who are about to do him the injury, as well as to protect him, who apprehends himself to be likely to suffer it. This act implies, not only that he is willing to acquire a right of being protected by the common force against any causeless harm, which they might possibly do him, but, likewise, that he consents to their having a right of being protected by the same force against any causeless harm which he might possibly do them: it must be understood to imply such consent; because, without consenting to their right of protection, he could not acquire a right of protection for himself.

From hence it follows, first, that the jurisdiction which a civil society has over any individual in respect of the right of private defence, supposes both the individual who is in danger of being injured, and them likewise, who are about to injure him, to be under the protection of one and the same civil society: because it is his consent to their right of protection, which restrains his own right of private defence; and this consent of his is given no otherwise than by his acquiring a right of being protected by the same society which is obliged to protect them.

Secondly, it follows from hence, that the jurisdiction of a civil society over the liberty of private defence, is a right to restrain one member from acting against others by his own force and at his own discretion, as far as such a liberty of acting might expose them to any causeless harm. And, consequently, the society has a right, not only to judge whether the occasion of defence is just, but likewise to take care that nothing is done unjustly even upon a just occasion. After he has made it appear to the society that he is in danger of suffering an injury, the jurisdiction of the society over his right of defence does not stop here: he might, if he was left to himself, demand such security as he has no right to; because he might demand such as he had no occasion for; or he might do them more harm in obtaining the security to which he has a right, than he ought to do them; because, he might do them more harm than is necessary to obtain it. He is, therefore, not at liberty to make use of his own private force, or of any other force which is managed at his own discretion, but is obliged to make use only of the common force, which is under the direction of the common understanding.

Origin and nature of civil jurisdiction.

III. * Notwithstanding mankind are now united into civil societies, yet the right of private defence still subsists, where civil jurisdiction ceases. The reader will be better able to understand, both in what cases civil jurisdiction ceases, in respect of the right of private defence, and why, in those instances, this right should subsist, after civil union, if we first inquire into the nature and origin of civil jurisdiction.

By civil jurisdiction, we mean a right which a civil society, acting either by its collective body or by its magistrates, has to determine any matter that is in dispute between two or more persons, and to compel them by the public force, to submit to its determination, if they do not submit to it of their own accord.

Jurisdiction is divided into two sorts: a jurisdiction over persons, and a jurisdiction over things. Indeed, all jurisdiction is ultimately over persons, for it consists in a right to determine controversies between two or more persons, and to compel the persons concerned in such controversies to submit to the determination. But a civil society may have this right, either upon account of some purely personal circumstances of the parties contending, or upon account of the thing about which they contend: and to distinguish these two cases from one another, the former is called a jurisdiction over the persons, and the latter a jurisdiction over the thing. Where the persons concerned in a dispute are obliged, from their personal circumstances, if they cannot adjust it amicably, to have recourse to the public for a determination of it; the right of the society, which corresponds to this obligation, is a jurisdiction over their persons. Where they are obliged thus to have recourse to the public, not merely because their own personal circumstances oblige them, but because the thing in dispute is in the power of the society, and can be no otherwise claimed by either of them, than by the consent and under the direction of the society; the right in the society, which corresponds to this obligation, is a jurisdiction over the thing. Thus, if we consider only the immediate cause of jurisdiction, as it arises either from the personal circumstances of the parties contending, or from the situation of the thing in dispute, it may be distinguished into these two sorts: but if we consider its operation, as it binds the parties to submit to the determination of the society, all jurisdiction, in this view of it, may be said to be over persons.

The foundation of all civil jurisdiction over persons, is laid either immediately or remotely in such a civil union as places the persons concerned on one side, in any controversy about matters of right, under the protection of the same society that is to protect the persons concern-

* Grot. Lib. I. Cap. III. § II.

ed on the other side. We have seen *already, that this is the origin of civil jurisdiction in matters of defence; and shall see, presently, that it has the same origin in matters of reparation and of punishment. Many rights of mankind, indeed, are not brought under the jurisdiction of society immediately by the act of civil union, or merely upon account of the common protection which the same society owes to the persons in controversy. But the obligation of civil laws is derived from civil union: and those laws, where the general good requires it, may restrain such of their rights as were not restrained by the immediate act of civil union; and may, by this means, give the society a jurisdiction in many instances, where the mere act of civil union had not given it any. Civil jurisdiction over the persons of individuals, must either immediately or remotely have its foundation in civil union, or in some act which is equivalent to it. For, since all men are †naturally equal, and are naturally at liberty to judge and to act at their own discretion, no civil magistrate and no civil society can have any right to judge and to act for them, or to restrain them from judging and acting for themselves, unless they have some way or other consented to give the magistrate or the society this right. And this consent appears no otherwise, than by their joining themselves to the society, or, however, by their putting themselves or their rights, by some means or other, under the protection of the society. The jurisdiction which a civil society has over things, as far as it affects any person who is not under the protection of that society, may be thought an exception to this rule: but we shall see, presently, that this is rather a natural, than a civil jurisdiction. It may be called a civil jurisdiction, as it belongs to a civil society, but it is in fact no other right than what, in some sort, individuals have in the liberty of nature, and arises rather out of property than out of civil union.

When ‡a number of individuals have united themselves, by consent, into one body, and have settled upon any tract of land, such a collective body, by this act of settling there, or by this occupancy in the gross, acquires a general property in the land. This general property of a civil society, is like the particular property of individuals in a state of independency. As the particular property, which an individual has in a parcel of land, after he has seized upon it, is a right of such individual to exclude all other individuals, whether they are few or many, from having any thing at all to do with this small parcel of land, so the general property which a civil society, or a number of individuals united into one body, and acting together, acquires by occupancy in the tract of land, where it settles, is a right of such collective body to exclude the rest of mankind, all other civil societies, and all other individuals, who are not members of this body, from having any thing at all to do with this large parcel of land. This exclusive right of general property in a civil society, as it is distinguished from the private right of the same sort which the several members have in their separate shares or estates, is called the jurisdiction of the society over the land: and that whole tract of land, which is thus under the jurisdiction of the society, or in which the society has such an exclusive right of general property, is called its territory. §One immediate and necessary effect

* See § II.
† See Book I. Chap. X. § III.
‡ See Book I. Chap. III. § XIII, XIV.
§ See Book I. Chap. VI. § VI.

of this jurisdiction, as has already been shown, is, that no alien is capable of having private property in any part of the territory; or, rather, that no member is capable of transferring such private property to an alien, without the express consent of the society. We have, likewise, taken notice of an accidental effect of this jurisdiction in respect of aliens; which is, that, since no alien can have any right to come within the territories of the society, if the society chooses to hinder him, it follows, that no alien can take even moveable goods, which are within the territory, though they are no part of it, if the society has forbidden it. In general, the jurisdiction of a society over its own territory, subjects all the rights that any person may be supposed to have to any thing, which is either a part of the territory, or within it, to be regulated and governed by the society: even the rights of aliens are subjected by it to be thus regulated, notwithstanding such aliens, as to their persons, are neither members of the society, nor have ever put themselves under its protection. In the meantime, this is no more inconsistent with the natural liberty of such aliens, than it is inconsistent with the liberty of an individual in a state of nature, if he chooses to accept of a part of any other individual's private estate, to be bound to accept it upon such terms as the owner of the estate shall prescribe; or if he chooses to *hunt upon the soil, or to fish in the waters of another, to be bound not to hunt such beasts, or not to kill such fish as the owner forbids him to meddle with. For, as the right of the individual, in one case, depends upon the will of the owner, so the right of the alien, in the other case, depends upon the will of the society. The particular property, which the owner has in the land, makes it lawful for him to keep it to himself, and not to give any part of it to the other; and his particular property in the soil or the water, makes it lawful for him to hinder the other from using them at all. No injury, therefore, is done to this other, if the land is not given him, or if the use of the soil and the water is not allowed him upon his own terms, but upon such terms only as the particular owner thinks proper. In like manner, the general property, which the society has in its territory, makes it lawful for such society to confine all private property to its own members, without granting an express allowance to any aliens to have any land, which is a part of the territory: and the same general property makes it lawful for the society to hinder any alien from coming into the territory to take away such moveable goods as are found within it. No injury, therefore, is done to such alien, if he is not allowed to acquire private property there, or to take any moveable goods from thence, upon his own terms, but upon such terms only as the society, which is the general owner, thinks proper. But if the society, upon account of its general property, has a right to hinder those, who are neither members of it, nor under its protection, as to their persons, from taking such things as are either a part of its territory, or are within such territory, it necessarily follows, where any dispute arises concerning such things, that though some or all the parties, concerned in the dispute, are otherwise not under the protection of the society, so as to give the society any immediate jurisdiction over their persons; yet, in consequence of the jurisdiction which it has over the thing in dispute, it will have a

* See Book I. Chap. V. § V.

right to compel them either to take it according to the sentence which the society gives upon the dispute, or not to take it at all.

We may call this right by the name of civil jurisdiction, if we please; but it can be called so no otherwise, than as it belongs to a civil society: for it is a sort of jurisdiction which does not arise out of civil union. And, indeed, though it may belong to a civil society, yet it is not confined to a civil society: it is a right which is incidental to property, either general or particular, and may as well belong to an individual in a state of natural liberty, as to a number of individuals united by social compact into one body. Or suppose this sort of jurisdiction to belong only to a body of individuals so united into one civil society; it would still be improper to say, in respect of those who are not members of this body, that this jurisdiction, as it affects them, arises from civil union. Though we should suppose, what is not true, that civil union is necessary, before any such jurisdiction can subsist; yet it cannot be civil union which extends this jurisdiction to aliens: because aliens are not in civil union with the society which has the jurisdiction. But after all, those who are not under the protection of the civil society, and are, therefore, clear of its direct jurisdiction over their persons, may, if they please, avoid any indirect jurisdiction of this sort, arising from its general property, by not endeavouring to obtain such things as are within its jurisdiction. And since their endeavouring to obtain them is their own act, even this jurisdiction over things becomes a jurisdiction over their persons no otherwise than by their own consent. We cannot, indeed, say, that both or all of the parties, if they are more than two, who contend about a thing which is in the jurisdiction of the society, must necessarily, as to their persons, be under the protection of such society, or that the society will otherwise have no jurisdiction. But still the notion of common protection is so necessarily connected with the notion of jurisdiction, that the society could have no right to decide the contest, and to compel the contending parties to submit to the decision, if the rights of all of them, as far as this dispute is concerned, were not under its protection.

But we have no occasion to enter any farther into this inquiry concerning the jurisdiction which a civil society has over its own territory, or over such moveable goods as are within its territory. The jurisdiction of a civil society, as it restrains the right of defence, is a direct jurisdiction over the persons; and is founded partly in the protection which he, who is to be defended, has acquired a right to, or rather in his consent to be restrained in his liberty of defence, which consent he must be understood to give by the same act which gave him a right to protection; and partly in the protection which the same society owes to them, against whom he is to be defended.

How civil jurisdiction ceases.

IV. * Civil jurisdiction may cease, either in fact, or of right. It ceases, in fact, where any person has a right to the protection of the society, but the society cannot, in fact, give him protection. What has been † already said concerning such civil jurisdiction, as restrains the right of defence, will serve to show us, that where he, who is to be defended, is not under the protection of the society, the jurisdiction, which the society has over him, must, necessa-

* Grot. Lib. I. Cap. III. § II.

† See § II.

rily cease. For civil jurisdiction, in respect of the right of defence, supposes this, and more than this; it supposes that both he, who is to be defended, and they, likewise, who are about to injure him, are under the protection of the same civil society. Notwithstanding, therefore, he may have a right to be protected by the society, yet if, in fact, the society cannot protect him; the civil jurisdiction of the society, though it subsists of right, will cease in fact.

When civil jurisdiction thus ceases in fact, it may cease either for the present instant only, or for some indefinite length of time. A person, who has a right to be protected by a civil society, cannot, in fact, receive protection from it; sometimes, because the society cannot interpose at the instant, when he wants its protection, though it might be able to interpose afterwards, when its protection would come too late; and, sometimes, because it cannot interpose, either at the present instant, or at any determinate time hereafter.

Civil jurisdiction ceases, of right, where there is no civil jurisdiction at all; that is, where no civil society has any right to interpose and restrain a man from acting for himself, by his own force, and at his own discretion.

This division, though it is different from our author's as to the form of it, is the same with his, in substance. He first divides the cases, where civil jurisdiction ceases, into those, where it ceases only for the present instant, and those, where it ceases for an indefinite length of time. And then he goes on to divide the cases, where it ceases for an indefinite length of time, into those, where it ceases in fact, and those, where it ceases of right. But because civil jurisdiction can cease no otherwise than, either in fact or of right; and because it does not appear in his division, whether it ceases in fact or of right, when it ceases only for the present instant, I have, therefore, chosen, whilst I kept to the substance of that division, to change the form of it.

Where civil jurisdiction ceases, either in fact or of right, there can be no doubt of a man's having the same liberty to defend himself by his own force, and at his own discretion, notwithstanding he is a member of a civil society, that he would have had, if he and all mankind had still continued in the liberty of nature. For civil jurisdiction, in respect of the liberty of private defence, is the right, which a civil society has to restrain a man from deciding his own quarrel, and to decide it for him: and, in all instances, where the right of any civil society to restrain him from acting for himself ceases, he must necessarily be as much at liberty to act for himself, as if no society had ever been formed at all.

Right of defence, where civil jurisdiction ceases in fact.

V. Civil jurisdiction ceases, in fact, for the present instant; when the injury, which threatens us, is so immediate, that the public, or the civil magistrate for the public, cannot come to our assistance time enough to prevent or to repel it; that is, when we are in such circumstances, that we cannot possibly be defended at all, unless we defend ourselves by our own private force.

But yet, if we consider any person as a member of civil society, we shall find, that, even in these circumstances, it is not every injury, which will justify him in proceeding to extremities. I do not mean, that the injury, with which he is threatened, may be so remote, or so uncertain, as to give him time to apply to the society, and to obtain the assistance of the public to guard him against it. There can be no doubt of his being obliged, as a member of civil society, to have recourse to the society, where the injury is of this sort: because, in respect of such injuries as these, its jurisdiction subsists, both of right, and in fact. He has a right to the protection of the public; and has, in fact, an opportunity of obtaining protection. But what I mean is, that the injury, though it is both immediate and certain, may be too small, in its own nature, to justify him in taking away the life of the aggressor, or in doing him any grievous harm, in order to prevent him from putting his design in execution. This is not merely matter of humanity or benevolence; but when he is considered as a member of civil society, it seems to be what the society may claim of him. Lesser injuries, where men live in a state of society, may commonly be repaired, after they are over. The magistrate, perhaps, has not an opportunity of repelling the harm, but he may, and commonly will, have an opportunity of interposing afterwards, to take care, that full amends shall be made to the person, who has suffered it. In respect, therefore, of such lesser injuries, as may easily be repaired, civil jurisdiction cannot properly be said to cease; however immediate, and however certain they may appear to be. The members of the same civil society seem to be as effectually protected against one another where they are sure of being made amends for the injury that they have suffered, as where they are guarded beforehand against suffering it at all.

The loss of life, indeed, or the loss of chastity, are, in their own nature, irreparable injuries. If the public cannot interpose to guard those who are under its protection, against such injuries as these, they are as much at liberty, in a state of society, to defend themselves, by all necessary means, as they would have been in a state of natural equality; even though the aggressor's death should be the consequence of their defence: because it is to no purpose for the public to interpose, after the injury is over; if no amends can be made for the loss that has been sustained.

Sometimes injuries of a lower sort, though they are not irreparable, in their own nature, are irreparable by accident. And there is the same reason, why a man should be at liberty to defend himself against these, as there is, why he should be at liberty to defend himself against the other; where he can have no assistance from civil jurisdiction. Of this sort, we may reckon the loss of goods, where the person, who attempts to steal them, is unknown; or where, though he is known, there is a moral certainty, that the public can never interpose, so as to obtain the restitution of them. The rules, that ought to be observed in these circumstances, are the same that ought to be observed in a state of nature. And where the law of nature would justify a man, considered as an individual, in proceeding to extremities, the same law will justify him in taking the same measures, though he is a member of civil society.

When civil jurisdiction ceases, only for the present instant, the danger must be immediate. But both the notion of an * immediate danger, and the notion of the present instant, are to be understood with some latitude. Every danger is an immediate one, as to the purpose of al-

* Grotius, Lib. II. Cap. I. § V.

lowing the members of any civil society to defend themselves against one another, if such danger is so near, that it cannot be avoided by any other means. And the present instant, as to the same purpose, is not a single point of time, that has no duration; it is understood to continue as long as the impossibility of obtaining the assistance of the magistrate continues. If a man has been threatening to kill you, and is seizing a sword or some other weapon, with a plain design, as far as you can judge, of putting his threats in execution; the danger is immediate enough to justify your defence of yourself, at your own discretion, without waiting till the weapon is at your breast. Suppose that you and the aggressor had closed with one another, and had struggled together for some time before you were able to get such an advantage over him, as to make your defence effectual by despatching him; though this length of time cannot strictly be called an instant, yet your right of private defence continues during the whole of it: because there is in every part of it the same impossibility of your being assisted by the civil magistrate, or protected by the public.

*Grotius asks here, whether it would be lawful to secure our own life, by killing a person, who attempts to take it from us by such means as we are sure will operate effectually in the end, if we suffer him to go on with his design, though they do not produce their effect immediately? If, for instance, we are certain, that he lies in wait for us himself, or has conspired with others to take the first opportunity of destroying us by such means as shall offer themselves, or by such means as they have contrived, by assassination, by poison, by a false accusation, false evidence, or an unjust sentence in a trial for any capital offence; may we lawfully kill him, to prevent such a remote injury as this? Before a question of this sort can be properly answered, it ought to be stated more precisely, than it is stated here, by distinguishing between the case of persons who live in a state of nature, and of persons who are under the protection of the same civil society.

Grotius, by mentioning false accusations, false evidence, and an unjust sentence, seems to suppose the parties concerned in the question, to be members of the same civil society: because, in other circumstances, the notion of accusations, evidence, and a judicial sentence, are unintelligible. And certainly, if they are in a state of civil society, the person who apprehends such a remote injury, though he is ever so well assured that it will come upon him, unless he takes care to guard against it, has no right to defend himself by his own force, and at his own discretion. The reason why he has no such right, has been given already: he has time enough before him to apply to the public for protection: and where he has time enough for this purpose; that is, where civil jurisdiction does not cease, he is bound, as he is a member of civil society, to make use of the protection of the public for his security against all who belong to the same society with himself.

But if we attend to the point, which our author had before him in this place, we shall find reason to think, that he designed to extend the question farther than this, and to inquire, not so much whether mankind have such a right of private defence in civil society, as whether they have it at all, either in a state of society or in a state of nature.

* Grot. Lib. II. Cap. I. § V.

He is here explaining what sort of injuries, before they are committed, are, in his opinion, justifiable causes of war in general; not only of public war, which is the war of societies, but of private war likewise, which is the war of individuals. And since private war may begin, not only amongst individuals, who are in a state of society when civil jurisdiction happens to cease in fact, but amongst individuals who never were in a state of civil society, or under any civil jurisdiction; this question, whether the use of force is lawful to prevent a remote injury, if we extend the sense of the words as far as the point that Grotius had before him, requires, must mean not only whether such use of force is lawful amongst the members of the same society, when civil jurisdiction ceases, but whether it is lawful at all, even amongst individuals that are under no civil jurisdiction, or are not members of any civil society. We have just now assigned the reason, why such persons as are under the protection of the same civil society, are not at liberty to defend themselves, by their own force, against such remote injuries; not because they have no such liberty, where civil jurisdiction ceases, but because in respect of remote injuries, which in their own nature allow of time for an application to the magistrate, civil jurisdiction does not cease in fact. But * when we were explaining the right, that individuals in a state of nature have to defend themselves against injuries before they are committed, we showed in what manner this right may extend to such injuries as are at a distance.

† Where one part of a society is in a state of civil war against the other, or where the subjects are in a state of rebellion against their governors; individuals of the opposite parties, whatever they may be of right, are not in fact under the protection of the same society. Civil jurisdiction, therefore, in respect of such individuals as are of opposite parties, ceases in fact, not merely for an instant, but for an indefinite length of time; it ceases as long as the state of civil war or of rebellion continues; and in the meanwhile such individuals have the same right of private defence that they had in the liberty of nature.

It is a more material question, whether the natural right of private defence returns, where the civil magistrate refuses to take notice of the danger, that a man imagines himself to be in, and to obtain security for him against suffering the injury, that others, as he apprehends, are preparing to do him. When ‡ Grotius mentions this, as one instance in which civil jurisdiction ceases in fact, he must certainly suppose, that the man has met with this refusal not only from one civil magistrate, but from all that have any authority to interpose in his favour: for in most civil societies there is a subordination of magistrates; and if those of an inferior sort refuse to relieve the person aggrieved, he may apply to those of a superior sort, who have authority either to grant him relief themselves, or to compel the others to grant it. And there is plainly no ground for maintaining, that civil jurisdiction ceases upon account of his having met with a refusal from some of the magistrates, when there are others within the society, who might either defend him, or take care that he should be defended, if he had made his application to them. But suppose him to have met with a refusal from all that he can apply to; such a refusal as this, seems rather to be an act than a

* See Book I. Chap. XVI. § V. † Grot. Lib. I. Cap. III. § II. ‡ Grot. ibid.

failure of civil jurisdiction. Some injuries are so slight, that it is of no importance for him to obtain security against them. Suspicions of a future injury may be so uncertain, as to afford no ground for the society to interpose; or they may be so false, as to make it unjust to regard them; or they may be so malicious, as to deserve censure rather than redress. There may be these and many other reasons of the like sort, why his application to the public should be dismissed. When, therefore, the society, or the magistrate for the society, does dismiss it, this is to be considered as a determination of the society, that its interposition would be either unnecessary or improper. In this view of the matter, he can have no right of private defence, in consequence of such a refusal; unless we would suppose, what is confessedly false, that every man, after he is a member of civil society, has the same right to judge, whether the society has done him justice, that he has in a state of nature to judge whether an individual has done him justice.

Right of defence, where civil jurisdiction ceases of right.

VI. Civil jurisdiction, says our *author, ceases of right between persons who happen to be out at sea, or in an uninhabited island, or in any other place where no civil society is established. His opinion is, that persons in these circumstances have the full liberty of private defence: for as there is, by the supposition, no civil jurisdiction, as they are not under the protection of the same, or indeed of any civil society, there is nothing to restrain this liberty.

This opinion must, however, be understood with some restrictions: and we shall see more plainly what the necessary restrictions are, if we consider the person who is in danger of suffering the injury, and the others who are about to do it, either as members of no civil society, or of the same civil society, or of different civil societies.

If he, who is in danger of being injured, and the aggressor, are not members of any civil society, the case does not come within the present question. He has, indeed, a right of private defence; but the ground of this right is, not that civil jurisdiction ceases between them, but that they are still in a state of nature.

He and the aggressor may, when they are at home, be members of the same civil society; and if they are, civil jurisdiction will cease between them in fact only, and not of right, when they are abroad. The jurisdiction which a civil society has over the persons of its members, affects them immediately, whether they are within its territories or not. Both the parties, therefore, though they are out of the territories, are under the jurisdiction. As long as their claim to protection subsists, the jurisdiction of the society will subsist of right. And since, by the supposition of their being members of the same society, both of them have a right to its protection; civil jurisdiction can have ceased no otherwise between them, than as their accidental situation may have rendered it impossible for the person, who is in danger of suffering the injury, to apply for protection against the aggressor to the civil magistrate.

But if they are members of different civil societies, they are not of right under the protection of the same civil society; there is, therefore, no civil jurisdiction that can of right restrain the liberty of defence:

* Grot. Lib. I. Cap. III. § II.

the law of nature is the only restraint upon it; and he who apprehends himself to be in danger of suffering an injury, seems to be the only judge how far this law will justify him in making use of his own force to prevent or repel it.

The only ground for supposing the society, of which the person who defends himself is a member, to have a right of restraining him as to the occasion and manner of his defence, is, that they, against whom he defends himself, may under this pretence be injured by him; and they have a claim, as individuals in a state of nature, that this society should not make itself an accessory to the injury. * Amongst other ways by which the society may be an accessory to what he does, one is by protecting him against them after the injury is over. And since he, by the supposition, as a member of the society, has a claim to its protection, it does not appear, at first sight, how the society can, consistently with his claim, avoid being an accessory. The society may, by this means, be brought into great inconveniences; especially if they, who are thus injured, are members of another society, which will interpose in their quarrel, and call it to an account for what one of its members has done. The general good, therefore, seems to make it necessary, that every member of a society, merely as he is under its protection, should be subject likewise of right to its jurisdiction, without considering whether those against whom he defends himself, are under its protection or not; that so the society, as it might be led into inconveniences by his claim of protection, may have a right to restrain him from acting at discretion even against aliens. But this conclusion proceeds upon a mistaken notion of a man's claim to be protected by the society to which he belongs. He has only a claim to be protected in the enjoyment of his rights, and not a claim to be protected in whatever he does, whether it is right or wrong. The society, therefore, is not obliged to make itself an accessory, if, under the pretence of defending himself, he has done them an injury: it is at liberty, as soon as this appears, to deliver him up to those who have been injured by him, if he is not willing to make proper satisfaction.

Where civil jurisdiction ceases of right, we have supposed the persons concerned to be out at sea, or in an uninhabited island, or in some place where no civil society is established: because, if they are within the territories of any society, whether either of them are properly members of it or not, they have a temporary civil union with it, and are under its protection. The society would not allow them to stay within its territories, or even to come thither, unless they agreed to conform to its laws, whilst they are there. They, therefore, by staying there, or by coming thither, are understood to consent to these terms; and by so consenting, they make themselves temporary subjects. The society, in the meantime, by suffering them to be there, is understood to accept them in this character, and consequently to give them a temporary right to its protection.

The general consequence, which follows from hence, is, that after mankind are united into civil societies, the law of nature forbids private war in any instance; and particularly duelling, which is one instance of private war, even in one's own defence; except where an injury,

* See Book I. Chap. XVII. § VI.

which cannot be repaired, after it is over, is so near, that we cannot apply to the civil magistrate for the interposition of the society, which has both us and the aggressor under its protection; or where the aggressor is in a state of rebellion or of civil war against that part of the society which has us under its protection; or, lastly, where we and the aggressor are not within the territories of any civil society whatsoever. I call the obligation, which restrains us, an obligation of the law of nature; notwithstanding it arises from civil union. For civil union is an act of consent; and whatever obligation arises from our own consent is an obligation of the law of nature; whether that consent is such as may leave us still in a state of nature, or such as joins us to a civil society, or at least places us for a time under its protection.

Right to reparation, how subjected to civil jurisdiction.

VII. In a state of equality, after an injury is committed, they who have suffered any damage by it, are at liberty to make themselves amends, at their own discretion and by their own force: they are at liberty to take so much of the offender's goods, as is equal in value to what they have lost; and the law of nature will give them property in the goods so taken. But in a state of civil society, if both the offender and the sufferers are under the protection of the same society, their right of obtaining reparation is restrained, and becomes subject to civil jurisdiction. The sufferers, by having placed themselves under the protection of the same society, which is engaged to protect the offender, have consented, that as this society is to guard them against any causeless harm, which he might do them, so it shall guard him likewise against any causeless harm which they might do him. And from this consent of theirs, it acquires a right to stop them from acting for themselves as they please, wherever such a liberty might be hurtful to him. These, as we have seen already, are the principles from whence civil jurisdiction is derived, in respect of the right of private defence: and these are likewise the principles from whence it is derived, in respect of the right which individuals have in a state of equality, to obtain reparation for themselves. We may possibly pretend, that we have suffered some damage, when we have suffered none; or though some damage has been done, we may rate it too high; or though the offender is willing to make us amends, we may causelessly use force for obtaining it; or when he is unwilling, we may use more force, and may do him more harm than is necessary. But since the society has, in consequence of our consent, a right to take care that we do him no injury, under the notion of repairing our own damage, it has not only a right to restrain us from acting against him at all, upon this pretence, till it is satisfied both that reparation is due to us, and what that reparation is; but a right likewise to restrain us, after this point is settled, from using any force, but such as is under the conduct of the common understanding.

In the meantime, though a member of civil society is restrained in his right to obtain reparation, this right is not destroyed. He does not entirely lose his right to obtain reparation; he only loses his right to obtain it at his own discretion, and by his own force: he is not obliged to submit to damage without redress; but is obliged, if he seeks redress, to seek it by the use of the public force, which is under the direction of the common understanding. He has still the right to obtain reparation; and the society, when it interposes, either by itself or by the civil magistrate, to obtain reparation for him, interposes in his right, and not in its own.

Civil jurisdiction, in respect of reparation, cannot cease in fact, for the present instant only.

VIII. Though civil jurisdiction, in respect of the right of private defence, may cease in fact, for the present instant only, yet in respect of the right of obtaining reparation by private force, it cannot cease in this manner: if it ceases, so as to leave any person at liberty to act for himself, it must either cease in fact, for some indefinite length of time, or else it must cease of right. Where an injury is coming upon a man, it is possible that he may have no time to apply to the society for protection, but may be under the necessity either of defending himself or of not being defended at all. But after an injury is past, he cannot well be driven to these straits in regard to the obtaining of reparation for the damages that have been done by it. He can scarce want time to apply to the society for this purpose; because, though defence might be useless, if it did not come at the present instant, yet reparation may be obtained at one time as well as at another. When the injury is over, he has leisure enough to seek redress; and the assistance of the society, for obtaining reparation, will be as effectual at some future time, as it would be now.

*Grotius mentions one case, which is in part an exception to these principles. He supposes the offender to be removing out of the territories of that society, which is to protect the sufferers, and to be carrying his goods along with him. In these circumstances, if they do not stop either him or his goods, it will hereafter be impossible for the society to do him justice. Civil jurisdiction, therefore, will so far cease in fact, for the present instant only, as to leave them at liberty to stop either his person, or his goods, or both. But this does not come up to the right, which they had in a state of natural equality, of obtaining reparation by their own force and at their own discretion. The law of nature, in such a state of equality, would not only have allowed them to seize upon an equivalent out of his goods, but would have given them property in such equivalent. Whereas, in a state of civil society, the same law, in consequence of their own consent, will not allow them to act for themselves, when they can have recourse to the civil magistrate. Since, therefore, after they are in possession of the goods, they will have leisure enough for this purpose, however they may be at liberty to seize upon the goods, they are not at liberty to use them as their own, till they are adjudged to be their own by the civil magistrate: civil jurisdiction may so far cease, as to give them a right to take possession; but it will not so far cease as to give them a right to keep possession: they may seize upon the equivalent; but it is the civil magistrate that must give them property in it.

Civil jurisdiction, according to the opinion of †Grotius, ceases in fact for some continuance of time, when we are satisfied in our own mind of our right to reparation, but are morally certain, that we cannot recover reparation by the sentence of the magistrate; because we are not able to prove the injury or the damage in such a manner as the laws of the society require. But the contrary opinion seems to be the more probable. A right, which does not appear to the society, is in respect

* Grot. Lib. II. Cap. VII. § II.

† Grot. ibid.

of the society, no better than a right which does not exist. All the harm that we do to those who are under its protection, in support of such a right, must, in the judgment of the society, be so much causeless harm. They, therefore, by their civil union, have a right to be protected against this harm; and, consequently, we by our civil union with the same society have given up our right to do it.

What has been said already, concerning private defence, may easily be applied to reparation for damages, where civil jurisdiction ceases of right.

Right of punishing, how restrained by civil jurisdiction.

IX. If we ask how the right of punishing, which every individual had in a state of nature, comes to be restrained in a state of civil society, the usual answer is, that the several individuals have transferred this right from themselves to the civil magistrate. But this answer does not take the matter up high enough. The civil magistrate, in a civil society, is the executive body, which is appointed to act for the collective body of it, under the restraints of the law. And if the civil magistrate is appointed to act for the society, we must necessarily conceive the society to be in existence, before the appointment of such magistrate. The first social compact unites a number of independent individuals into one body, by binding them to act together for certain purposes. In such a perfect democracy as would arise from this compact, all the members are equal to one another: there is no particular executive body, consisting of one single person, or of a select number of persons, which has any authority to act for the rest. The question, therefore, is, how the right of punishing, which individuals had in a state of nature, comes to be restrained in such a society as this? And in this view, it will evidently be an unsatisfactory answer to say, that the several individuals have transferred their right of punishing, to the civil magistrate; because there is no such thing as a civil magistrate, to whom they could transfer it. If we think to correct this answer by saying, that they transfer their right of punishment from themselves to the society, such a correction will only serve to make it unintelligible. * Each individual who is a member of the society, would, in a state of nature, have had an equal right of punishing with the rest: for this right is not confined to that individual in particular, who has been injured by the crime, but extends alike to all mankind. The society, therefore, being nothing else but an aggregate body of individuals, who have each of them a natural right of punishing, a transfer of this right from themselves to the society, is nothing else but a transfer of it from themselves to themselves.

The restraint upon the right of individuals to punish a criminal separately, is produced by civil union, in the same manner with the restraint upon the rights of private defence, and of obtaining reparation by private force. If any person, who is under the protection of a civil society, is charged with having committed a crime, the society is obliged to take care that he is not injured, under the notion of punishing him. An individual, who undertakes to inflict the punishment by his own private force, and at his own private discretion, may possibly pretend that a crime has been committed, when nothing at all, or at least

* See Book I. Chap. XVIII. § VIII.

nothing criminal, has been done; or he may rate the guilt of a crime too high; or he may inflict a greater penalty than the guilt deserves. Upon any of these suppositions, the person, who is charged with a crime, and who, perhaps, has actually been guilty of one, would be injured by the punishment that is inflicted. The society, therefore, which has engaged by the social compact to protect him, is obliged to stop the punisher from proceeding, and to take the matter into its own hands. If the punisher is not under the protection of the same society with the offender; this society acts, in respect of the punisher, no otherwise, than any individual might have done in the liberty of nature: any individual, who thought that the offender was likely to be injured, was at liberty to interpose and to protect him against the injury. In respect of the punisher, all the difference between a society, with which he has no connexion, interposing in behalf of the offender, and an individual, in the liberty of nature, interposing for the same purpose, is, that the society is stronger than an individual, and will, therefore, be better able to take care that no injury shall be done. In respect of the offender, indeed, there is a farther difference; for, in the liberty of nature, he had no claim to be protected from injuries by any individual; but civil union gives him such a claim upon the society, which has taken him under its protection. But if this interposition of the society depends, in respect of the punisher, upon the same principles with the interposition of an individual in a state of nature; the restraint that arises from hence, upon his liberty of punishing separately, is a restraint rather in fact than of right: he is still at liberty to punish the offenders, if he could, and only gives up this liberty, because he cannot help it. But suppose the punisher to be under the protection of the same society with the offender; the restraint, in fact, upon his liberty of punishing separately, will then become a restraint upon it of right. By placing himself under the protection of this society, so as to acquire a claim to its protection, he must necessarily be understood to have given his consent, that the offender should be protected by it, as well as he: because the society, standing engaged to protect the offender, could not receive him under its protection upon any other terms. Now the protection of the offender consists in the interposition of the society to stop the punisher from acting separately, and to take the matter into its own hands: and since the punisher, by his civil union with the society, has consented to this; he has, by such consent, given up his liberty, or his right of punishing separately. What has been said of any one individual, whom we have here called the punisher, may be applied to every other individual, who is connected with the society by civil union. And thus, notwithstanding each of them, in a state of natural liberty, had a right of punishing a criminal separately, by their own private force, and at their own discretion; they cease, by their own consent, to have such a right, when they are united into a civil society, in respect of any criminal, who is a member of their body, or is under the protection of the same society with themselves.

From this account of the effect, which is produced by civil union upon the right of punishing, it appears, that there is no occasion to inquire, how the society acquires this right, when the individuals lose it. For, in fact, the right of punishing, which individuals had in a state of nature, is not lost, but restrained, by civil union. In the liberty of nature, each had a right of punishing separately: civil union only restrains them from punishing separately: and, consequently, they have still the same right of punishing, after they are thus united, that they had before; except, only, that they have agreed, if they exercise it at all, to exercise it together. And thus the right, which the society, consisting of a member of individuals, has to punish, appears, at last, to be nothing else but the joint right of all the individuals.

Difference between jurisdiction in matters of damage and of punishment.

X. Both the right of obtaining reparation, and the right of inflicting punishment, arise out of an injury, and are brought, in the same manner, under civil jurisdiction. But there is one material difference between these two rights, in a state of nature, which makes a difference, in a state of society, between the jurisdiction of the society in matters of reparation, and its jurisdiction in matters of punishment.

When an injury has been committed, in the liberty of nature, the only person who has a right to reparation, and to make use of force for obtaining it, is the person who has suffered damage by the injury. * Others, who choose to give him their assistance, are then only at liberty to give it, if he asks for it, or if they see that he wants it. As, on the one hand, he cannot compel them to assist him, so, on the other hand, if he waives his right, either expressly or tacitly; either by declaring openly, that he does not require any reparation, or by setting still and not endeavouring to obtain any, they have no right to take the quarrel upon themselves, of their own accord, and to enforce reparation for him. The reparation was due only to him: if, therefore, he gives it up, it is due to nobody else; so that the offender stands clear of all demands; and whatever they may take from him, under the notion of obtaining reparation for the sufferer, it will be taken from him unjustly. The consequence of this, in civil societies, is what we have just now hinted at: though he is restrained, by civil union, from obtaining reparation by his own force, and at his own discretion, yet the right to obtain it is still his: he is obliged, indeed, if he seeks it at all, to seek it by the public force, under the direction of the common understanding: but the society interposes with this force in his right, and not in its own.

When a crime has been committed, in the liberty of nature, the right of punishing the criminal is not confined to the person who has been hurt by the crime: every individual has the same right that he has, to correct or restrain such a bad disposition, as may be hurtful to any of them hereafter, if it is not corrected or restrained; that is, every individual has the same right that he has, to punish the criminal. The consequence of this is, that though in a state of civil society, each individual, who is a member of such society, is restrained by civil union, from punishing a criminal separately by his own force, and at his own discretion, yet each and all of them have still the right of punishing jointly, by the public force, and under the conduct of the common understanding. The society, therefore, when it inflicts punishment, inflicts it in the right of all the individuals that compose such society: or since the society is nothing else but the aggregate body of all these

* See Book I. Chap. XIX. § III.

individuals, we may say, that the society inflicts punishment in its own right, or, as it is more usually expressed, in the right of the public.

From hence it appears, why the same injury, when it is considered as doing damage, should be called a private offence, and when it is considered as a crime, should be called a public offence. It is called a private or a public offence in reference to the person who is offended by it, and has a right to take notice of it. When, therefore, it is considered as doing damage, it is called a private offence; because the reparation is due to some one or more private persons. But when it is considered as an evidence of a hurtful disposition, it is a public offence; because it gives the society, which is a public person, a right to punish the offender.

I have here called the jurisdiction, which a civil society has both in matters of private and of public wrong, by the general name of civil jurisdiction. * Though it is, I believe, more usual, to call only its jurisdiction in matters of private wrong, civil jurisdiction; and its jurisdiction, in matters of public wrong, criminal jurisdiction.

From hence, likewise, it appears, that after a man has been proved to have done any damage, and the public is satisfied both of the fact and of the reparation, which is due for it; there is no right in the society to remit such reparation; because it is due to the individual who has suffered the damage, and not to the society. But after it has been proved, in like manner, that a man has committed a crime, the society has a right to pardon him, or to remit the punishment: because the punishment is not due to any individual in particular, but to all of them equally; that is, to the society itself.

Right to punish, how vested in the civil magistrate.

XI. Now we have seen, how the right of individuals to punish separately, is restrained in a state of civil society, and by what means the right of punishing is vested in the collective body of the society; it will be no difficult matter to understand, how it comes into the hands of the civil magistrate. By the civil magistrate, is here meant the supreme executive body of the society; whether it consists of one or of more persons, acting under the checks and controls of the legislative. Indeed, we commonly take into our notion of the civil magistrate, not only the supreme executive body, but, likewise, all other persons who have any jurisdiction. However, as inferior magistrates have only a jurisdiction derived from the supreme executive body, it is not necessary to enlarge the definition of the civil magistrate, in order to include them in it. As the first social compact restrains the several members of a civil society from punishing a criminal separately, and vests the right of punishing in the society itself; that is, in all the members acting jointly; so when it is farther agreed to establish any particular executive body, or civil magistrate, the right of punishing, which was before vested in the whole society, collectively, is vested by this agreement in such executive body. A transfer here may be so explained as to be intelligible enough. For though the several individuals could not, in the first act of civil union, be understood in any sense, to transfer their natural right of punishing separately, to the civil magistrate, because the first act of civil union does not establish any civil magistrate; yet the society, after it is formed, or all the indivi-

* See page 275.

duals, after they are united into one collective body by the first social compact, may, if we like the expression, be said to transfer the social right of punishing collectively, to the executive body: only we should observe, that this transfer consists in nothing else, but in the society's having made a standing appointment of an executive body, to act for it with the common force in matters of punishment. In like manner, though the several individuals could not be understood, in any sense, to transfer the right of punishing from themselves to the society; because this would only be a transfer of it from themselves to themselves; yet we may say, that the society transfers the right which it has to punish collectively, to the civil magistrate; that is, to some part of the collective body: if we think that a standing appointment of this part to act for the whole can properly be called a transfer.

But it is to be observed, that an executive body, whether it consists of one person or of more, has not the full liberty or right of punishing which the collective body had, unless the legislative power is delegated to it, as well as the executive power. All punishment in a state of civil society is to be inflicted by the common force, under the direction of the common understanding. If the society, therefore, punishes in its collective body, it acts under no external restraints, but may punish or pardon according to its own discretion; by which I mean its own judgment of right and wrong: because the common understanding, as well as the common force, is in the keeping of the collective body. In like manner, if the same person, or the same select body of persons, to whom the executive power is committed, should be entrusted likewise with the legislative power; such an establishment would give this person, or this body of select persons, as absolute a power in matters of punishment, as the law of nature and the purposes of civil power can allow of. * But if thc executive body has only the executive power, which is all that the name of such body imports, it is under the restraints of the law, and can only punish under the directions of the legislative body: because the common understanding of the society speaks by its legislative body; whether that legislative is the whole collective body of the society, or some select part of it, to which the legislative power is committed. Nay, if the executive body has nothing else entrusted to it by the constitution, besides executive power, as it could not punish, so neither could it pardon at discretion: for the executive power in itself is not a discretionary power in any respect, but is either to act or not to act, as the common understanding speaking by the laws, directs it. When, therefore, the constitution of government allows the civil magistrate or executive body to have a discretionary power of pardoning, this is considered as something distinct from mere executive power, and is called prerogative.

But though the executive body acts under the restraints of the law, yet it is appointed, in matters of punishment, to act with the common force, instead of the society. In consequence of civil union, all the individuals act jointly; that is, the society acts with its public force, in matters of punishment, for the common security of all its members. But in consequence of the establishment of an executive body, this body acts with the public force for the same purpose. All crimes,

* See Book II. Chap. IV.

therefore, where such a body is established, may be considered as offences against the executive body in particular: because they are inconsistent with the common security, which this body is to guard and maintain with the public force of the society.

How far civil jurisdiction may cease, in respect of the right to punish.

XII. * Grotius seems to be of opinion, that civil jurisdiction cannot cease in fact, for the present instant, in matters of punishment. Mankind, in a state of society, are at liberty to defend themselves by their own private force against an injury, which is so near at hand as not to allow them time for applying to the civil magistrate to defend them. But though defence, at the present instant, may be necessary, there is not the same immediate necessity for punishing a criminal: punishment will answer the ends that are proposed by it, as well if it is inflicted some time hence, as if it was to be inflicted just now. There seems, therefore, in matters of punishment to be always leisure enough for applying to the civil magistrate. It may be said in reply, that, if the criminal is making his escape, there may possibly be no opportunity at all of punishing him, unless the present opportunity is made use of. When we have been robbed of our money or our goods, and the criminal is going away, so that we are in no danger of suffering any other harm at present, than what he has done already; if any thing can justify us in killing him with an arrow or a pistol, it must be either the purpose of obtaining reparation for what we have lost, or the purpose of punishing him, to prevent his doing the like mischief hereafter either to ourselves or to others. The mere taking away his life cannot come within the notion of reparation, any otherwise than as we may suppose it to be the only possible means of getting our money or our goods again, when he is going away with them. And it is most probable, if we were asked why we killed him, that, instead of taking notice of the reparation due to us for the damage which he had done, we should say, that we did it in order to take a dangerous man out of the way, and to prevent his doing any farther mischief. If this is the answer, which the common sense of mankind would suggest to them upon this occasion, it is plain, that, in the judgment of mankind, the death of the criminal, in these circumstances, is intended as a punishment: for the notion of punishment consists in making a person, who has shown a hurtful disposition by some harm already done, suffer such evil as will prevent his doing the like again.

But supposing it to be true, that, where civil jurisdiction thus ceases, the members of a civil society would be at liberty to punish one another separately, if they were under no other restraint but what arises from civil union, yet they may be still farther restrained by civil laws. And such laws would be reasonable upon account of the likelihood that this liberty might be abused: they might pretend, that they punished the criminal by their own private force, because they found it impossible to call in the civil magistrate, when perhaps no crime was committed which deserved punishment; or, at least, when they might have had the assistance of the civil magistrate, if they had chosen it.

We may observe by the way, that no person can inflict any punishment, less than death, by his own separate right, under the notion of a

* Grot. Lib. II. Cap. XX. § VIII, IX.

failure of civil jurisdiction, in fact, for the present instant. For if the punisher had the criminal so much in his power as to be able to choose what sort of punishment he would inflict, he certainly had an opportunity of applying to the civil magistrate, and consequently civil jurisdiction did not cease. But whoever ventures to punish a criminal with death, upon a supposition that civil jurisdiction does cease, ought to be well assured that the crime deserves death: for if it does not, however the laws of his country might acquit him of murder, he could not acquit himself of it in his own conscience.

Where civil jurisdiction ceases in fact for any length of time, as it does when the subjects are in a state of rebellion, those who are in such state, are not under the protection of the public: and though a man may be restrained by civil laws from punishing them for any crime which they commit, yet if we look no farther than the obligations arising immediately out of civil union, he would be at liberty to punish them.

Where civil jurisdiction fails of right, the natural liberty of punishing is governed by the same rules with the natural liberty of defence, or of obtaining reparation for damages. And as these rules have been already explained at large, it is needless to repeat them here.

Natural principles applicable to social punishment.

XIII. The reader will now perceive of what use it is to trace out, as we did in the former book, the natural principles of punishment amongst individuals in a state of equality; *to point out the ends which punishment has in view; and the reasons which justify it; to mention the rules that are to be observed in capital punishments; to determine the nature of those actions which are punishable; to explain the notion of guilt, and the manner of estimating it; to settle the proper measure of punishment; to show upon whom it may, and upon whom it may not be inflicted; and by what means, when it is inflicted upon the ancestor, it may affect the heir, notwithstanding the heir could not justly be punished for the crime of the ancestor. For though, when we were tracing out those principles, we applied them to mankind, considered as individuals in a state of equality; yet the principles themselves extend farther, and may be applied to mankind, considered as united into civil societies. The right which a society has to punish its members, whether it exercises this right by itself or by its civil magistrate, is nothing else but the joint right of all the individuals that make up the society. Whatever, therefore, are the principles by which the law of nature requires an individual to guide himself, when he punishes by his own private force, and at his own discretion; the common understanding of a civil society is to be guided by the like principles, when it punishes either by itself or by its civil magistrate.

Actions not punishable by individuals, may be punishable by magistrates.

XIV. We make a wrong application of the principles by which the law of nature requires individuals to guide themselves in matters of punishment, when we conclude that no actions are punishable by mankind, after they are united into a civil society, but those only which are punishable by individuals in the liberty of nature. In one sense, indeed, this rule will hold good. All actions which are punishable by a civil society, or by the civil magistrate of such society, must be of the

* See Book I. Chap. XVIII.

same sort with those which are punishable by individuals acting separately and independently; that is, *as none but unjust actions are to be punished in a state of nature, so none but unjust actions are to be punished in a state of civil society. But when the rule is thus expressed, we cannot infer from it, that the civil magistrate has no right to punish any other actions, besides those which independent individuals have a right to punish separately; unless it could first be shown, that no actions can be unjust in a state of society, besides those which are unjust in a state of nature. All actions which do harm, and by the harm which they do, are an evidence of a hurtful and dangerous disposition in the person who commits them, are crimes. The hurtful or dangerous disposition of the criminal is his †guilt, and makes it just to punish him; that is, to inflict some evil upon him, which may correct or restrain that disposition, in order to secure mankind against his doing the same or the like harm for the future. If, therefore, any actions which, in a state of nature, would have done no harm to mankind, become hurtful to them in a state of society; such actions, though they do not make it just for individuals, acting separately, to punish the doer of them, will make it just for a society, or for the civil magistrate to punish him.

Perhaps we may see the truth of this reasoning more clearly in the case of reparation, than we do in the case of punishment. The natural rule of reparation amongst separate individuals, is, that no reparation is due, where no damage has been done. And the rule amongst the members of a civil society is the same. But we cannot conclude from hence, that there is no reparation due amongst the members of a civil society, in any instance, but where it would have been due amongst separate individuals. ‡Mankind, in a state of civil society, acquire many strict or perfect rights which they had not in a state of nature: such actions, therefore, may do damage amongst the members of civil society, as would have done no damage amongst separate individuals. The natural rule is the same in both cases; but it is different in its application: in a state of society, as well as in a state of nature, no reparation is due, unless some damage has been done: but many actions may be attended with an obligation to make reparation in a state of society, which were not attended with such an obligation in a state of nature.

It may be farther said, that separate individuals cannot punish any thing besides natural injustice. But if we inquire what is meant by natural injustice, we shall find, that the words admit of three senses: in the first sense this principle is not true; in another sense, the reason why nothing else is punishable by mankind, when they are considered as separate individuals, does not extend to them, when considered as members of a civil society; and consequently this principle, though it is true, will be nothing to the purpose; and in a third sense of the same words, we may reduce whatever is punishable by the civil magistrate to the notion of natural injustice, though we contend at the same time, that the magistrate has a right to punish many actions which were not punishable, or which even could not exist in a state of nature.

Natural injustice, in its most proper and strict sense, signifies the doing harm to mankind by violating what are strictly and properly

* See Book I. Chap. XVIII. § IX. † Ibid. § X. ‡ See Book I. Chap. XVII. § III.

called *their natural rights; that is, such rights as belong to mankind originally by the gift of nature, without the intervention of any human act: their rights, for instance, to life, to liberty, to freedom from pain, &c. In this sense of the words—*natural injustice*—it is not true that nothing else is punishable by individuals in the liberty of nature. The law of nature forbids the violation of their adventitious rights, as well as of their natural rights; and allows them equally to secure the enjoyment of their rights of either sort, by punishing any person who, by having done harm already, in respect either of their strictly natural, or of their adventitious rights, has shown that he is disposed and is likely to do them harm again, if he is not corrected or restrained. Unless the right of punishing, as it subsists amongst individuals in a state of natural liberty, extended to the violation of their adventitious rights, it would not be lawful for separate individuals to punish theft; because theft is a violation of property, and the right of †property is of the adventitious, and not of the strictly natural sort.

But suppose we enlarge the meaning of natural injustice, and understand by it not merely the violation of what are strictly called natural rights, but the violation of any rights, whether original or adventitious; which are sometimes, in a larger sense, called natural rights, as belonging to mankind in a state of nature. In this sense it is true, that separate individuals cannot punish any thing besides natural injustice. But their right to punish even this, is founded merely in its being injustice, and not in its being precisely natural injustice. And consequently if any other sort of injustice, besides what is called natural, was possible amongst individuals in a state of nature, they would have the same right to punish this other sort; because this, likewise, though it was not natural injustice, would, however, be injustice. The reason, therefore, why they can only punish natural injustice, does not depend upon the nature of the right to punish, but upon the particular situation and circumstances of the punishers: they cannot punish any thing besides natural injustice; because, in their particular situation and circumstances, no other sort of injustice can exist. But if the reason which restrains their right of punishing, to natural injustice only, depends upon their situation and circumstances, and not upon the nature of the right itself; the principle here laid down, that individuals in a state of natural liberty can punish nothing else: besides, natural injustice will be little to the purpose, when it is alleged as an argument to prove, that the same individuals can have no right to punish any other sort of injustice, after they are united into a civil society. For, in civil society, their situation and circumstances are so altered, that another sort of injustice, besides what is here called natural, becomes possible. The cause, therefore, which in a state of nature restrained punishment to natural injustice, is then removed. It was before a restraint in fact and not of right; they could not punish any injustice, besides natural injustice; not because no other act of injustice is punishable upon the same grounds that natural injustice is, but because no other sort of injustice could exist. When, therefore, by the introduction of civil society, another sort of injustice becomes possible; the restraint that there was in fact, upon their right of punishing before, is taken off; and this other

* See Book I. Chap. II. § VIII. † See Book I. Chap. III. § II. VII.

sort of injustice becomes punishable upon the same principles of the law of nature, which gave them, in a state of equality, a right to punish natural injustice. This other sort of injustice may be called social injustice, which, as far as it can be distinguished from natural, consists in doing harm to mankind by violating any rights which belong to them in a state of civil society, and are different from the rights which belonged to them in a state of nature. Mankind in a state of nature, have a right to punish any person who has designedly and maliciously committed any injustice; because the law of nature, when they have suffered causeless harm from him already, and find from thence, that he is disposed to do them future harm, allows them to guard against such future harm, by correcting or restraining him. This principle of the law of nature extends to social injustice, and is not confined to natural injustice: because one sort of injustice does harm to mankind, as well as the other; and the law of nature no more forbids them to guard themselves against one sort of harm, than it forbids them to guard themselves against the other.

Natural injustice, in a third sense of the words, may mean the violation of any right which is under the protection of the law of nature; that is, any right of which the law of nature forbids the violation. In this sense individuals, in the liberty of nature, have certainly no right to punish any thing else, besides natural injustice: and we may grant, too, that a civil society or a civil magistrate has no right to punish any thing else. But it will be no consequence that the society, or the civil magistrate for the society, has not a right to punish many actions which were not punishable by separate and independent individuals. For the social rights of mankind are, in this sense of the words, as much natural rights as any that belonged to them originally by the gift of nature, or as any that belonged to them either originally or adventitiously in a state of nature. All their social rights are acquired consistently with the law of nature: they are acquired by consent either express or tacit, either direct or implied: and *all rights which are so acquired, are equally under the protection of the law of nature; because this law equally forbids the violation of any of them.

It is a crime for any man, who is a member of a civil society, to join with the enemy in time of war and to fight against that society. But if we confine the notion of natural injustice to the violation of such rights as belonged to mankind in a state of nature, this, though we call it a crime, cannot be an act of natural injustice; for it is so far from violating any such right, that, in a state of nature, the act itself would be impossible. No man can fight against the society of which he is a member, when he is not a member of any society at all. The social injustice of the act is what makes it criminal: the society, when he became a member of it, acquired, by his own consent, a right to his assistance towards securing and advancing the general good: and to join with the enemy in fighting against it is a violation of this right. In one sense, indeed, this is an act of natural injustice; and in such a sense as will make it punishable upon principles of the law of nature. Though it is not a violation of any right which belonged to mankind in a state of nature, yet it is a violation of such a right as was acquired agreeably to

* See Book I. Chap. II. § VIII.

the law of nature, and is under the protection of this law. What has here been said concerning one instance of treason, will be applicable to many other instances; the crimes, which are ranked under this head, consist in such acts, as were impossible, and, therefore, could not be punishable, in a state of nature. But he would, in the meantime, be thought to maintain a doctrine very unreasonable in itself, and very destructive to his country, who should contend, that treason is not punishable, in a state of society, because it is not a violation of any right, which subsists in a state of nature.

Where a man has wool produced by his own sheep; he would, in a state of nature, be at liberty to carry it to any place that he pleased; and to sell it to any persons that he pleased. This liberty is not restrained merely by the act of social union; he may be a member of a civil society, and yet be at liberty to carry his own wool to a foreign market, and to sell it there to foreigners. This is no act of natural injustice, in one sense of the words; because it is no violation of any right that belonged to mankind in a state of nature. And it is no act of social injustice, by any immediate effect of the social compact. When we consider the owner of the wool as a member of any civil society, the society has, indeed, a right, in consequence of the social compact, to hinder him from disposing of his wool in such a manner, as appears to the common understanding to be hurtful to the public. But whether the selling of it to foreigners will be hurtful to the public or not, in the judgment of the common understanding, appears only by the laws. He will, therefore, continue at liberty to sell it to whom he pleases; as long as the laws of his country are silent upon this head. But as soon as these laws have forbidden him to sell it to foreigners; such selling becomes an act of social injustice; and the society will, upon the principles of the law of nature, have a right to punish him for it. I say, upon the principles of the law of nature; because the law of nature leaves all the members of the society acting jointly; that is, it leaves the society itself, or the civil magistrate acting in its stead, at liberty to punish any person, who designedly does causeless harm; whether that harm affects mankind in such rights, as were the original gift of nature, or in such, as were acquired in a state of nature, or in such, as were acquired in a state of society agreeably to the law of nature.

Drunkenness, lewdness, prodigality, and idleness, do harm only to the vicious themselves, and no harm to others, when mankind are considered as separate and unconnected individuals. * They are, therefore, such crimes, as mankind are not at liberty to punish, in a state of nature. These vices may, and most probably will, lead men to some act of natural injustice; and when they do, though this act is punishable, yet still the vices themselves, as no natural injustice is included in the notion of them, are only the remote occasion of the punishment. But in a state of society it is otherwise. As the compact, which unites mankind into a civil society, binds all and each of the members on the one hand, to advance the general good, in such a manner as the common understanding shall prescribe, so it gives the society, on the other hand, a right to demand this of all and each of the members. When the laws, therefore, in view to the general good, have forbidden these

* See Book I. Chap. XVIII. § IX.

vices, they become matter of social injustice; and the society has a right, upon the principles of the law of nature, to punish those, who are guilty of them.

In like manner, offences against God, though they are * not objects of human punishment in a state of nature, may be punished by the civil magistrate, in a state of society. When we consider mankind as separate individuals, there is no natural injustice towards mankind included in these offences. But when the same offences appear to the common understanding of a civil society, either to dissolve the bands of civil union, or to obstruct the general good, by making men loose and profligate in their manners; the society has a right to forbid them: and when they are so forbidden, they become matter of social injustice, and are punishable by the civil magistrate. And, certainly, if such actions, as are in all respects indifferent amongst separate individuals, not only as they do no harm to mankind, but, likewise, as they are not forbidden at all by the law of nature, become punishable in a state of society, when the civil laws of the society have forbidden them, in view to the general good; there is no reason to imagine, that atheism, blasphemy, profaneness, and irreligion, are so far sanctified, by being in their own nature, offences against God, as to exempt them from civil penalties, when they are forbidden by the civil law with a like view to the general good.

† Grotius doubts, whether, in any instances, the want of benevolence is punishable by man. In a state of nature, it certainly is not punishable, for reasons, which are something different from those assigned by our author. These reasons have already been explained at large, in their proper ‡ place. And if we were disposed to allow any weight to our author's argument in favour of his own opinion, when mankind are considered as individuals; it has, certainly, no weight at all, when we consider them as united into a civil society. Those vices, he says, are not to be punished by men, whose opposite virtues cannot be produced by constraint, such as gratitude, liberality, compassion, and kindness. When he says, that liberality cannot be produced by constraint, I suppose him to mean, that force or fear, though they may make a man give his money away, cannot make him liberal; because liberality implies, that he is led to give it away by a disposition to do good. In the like sense, it may be said, that force or fear cannot make a man grateful; not because punishment, when it is either threatened or inflicted, cannot influence him to make suitable returns to his benefactors; but because no returns, which arise from constraint, and not from the good disposition of his own mind, can be called gratitude. The fear of punishment may, likewise, induce a man to assist those, who stand in need of his assistance: but Grotius would not call the good, which he does, for fear of being punished, if he was to do otherwise, by the name of kindness; because it does not arise from the benevolent disposition of his heart.

Now, supposing it, for the present to be true, that neither actual punishment, nor the fear of punishment, can produce those virtues; the only consequence is, that punishment, when it is either inflicted or threatened, in order to produce them, will be of no benefit to the per-

* See Book I. Chap. XVIII. § IX. † Grot. Lib. II. Cap. XX. § XX. ‡ Grot. ibid. § IX.

son, upon whom it is inflicted, or against whom it is threatened. What he has suffered already, or what he may be afraid of suffering hereafter, cannot produce these virtues in him, so as to make him a better man. But in the meantime, though such punishment should happen to be of no benefit to the vicious man himself, it may be of great benefit to others, by making him a more useful member of society, whether he will or not. Though it cannot produce the virtues themselves, it may produce the outward effect of them. Suppose, for instance, that punishment cannot make a man liberal, yet, certainly, it may force him to give what he can spare from his own expenses, to those who are in need; and it may force him, likewise, to spare more from his own expenses, than he otherwise would have spared. The naked may be clothed, and the hungry may be fed with his superfluities, not only when he is led to dispose of them for these purposes, by the good disposition of his heart, but when he is constrained thus to dispose of them by the fear of punishment. Suppose, that punishment cannot make a man grateful; it may, however, secure a return of what will be as beneficial to those who have done him favours, as if he had been led to make the return by his own virtue. Now the justice of punishment in those instances, where no one questions its consistency with the law of nature, does not depend upon the benefit which the criminal receives from it. * The primary end of it is to change his outward behaviour for the security of others: and this end is what makes it just to punish him; whether the punishment produces such a change by mending his inward disposition, or by making him afraid to offend again. If, therefore, the law of nature allows mankind to punish acts of injustice, notwithstanding such punishment, whilst it corrects the outward behaviour of the criminal, may fail of correcting his heart; the supposed impossibility of producing inward benevolence by punishment, can be no reason, why the law of nature should not allow mankind to punish acts of inhumanity, inclemency, or ingratitude.

But what has been hitherto supposed, is not universally true: we cannot grant, that the fear of punishment can never produce a benevolent disposition. Punishment, perhaps, may, in the first instance, seldom be attended with this effect: but it is not improbable, that what a man is constrained to do, in the first instance, through fear, may, in time, and by use, grow habitual to him. His bad disposition, when it has long been kept under by such constraint, may at length be corrected: and thus the punishment or the fear, which, at first, produced only the outward effects of benevolence, may, by degrees, produce the virtue itself. The common consent of mankind favours this opinion. Parents act upon it, when they discourage or correct their children for such instances of behaviour, as betray a want of gratitude, or liberality, or tenderness. They hope, by such discouragement or correction, not only to restrain the outward behaviour of their children, but to bring them, by degrees, to a better temper of mind.

However, neither the design of producing the outward effects of benevolence for the benefit of mankind, nor the design of amending the disposition of the vicious for their own benefit, will be sufficient to give individuals a right of punishing the vices, that are opposite to this vir-

* See Book I. Chap. XVIII. § III.

tue. For though the reason here alleged by our author, does not prove that they have no such right; it has been elsewhere proved by other reasons. We can have no right to make a man suffer for not doing what we have no right to demand of him; however reasonable it might be for us to expect it of him.

But what is matter only of imperfect right or reasonable expectation, amongst individuals, in the liberty of nature, may become matter of perfect right, in a state of civil society. A contract, even in the liberty of nature, will give us a right to a thing, which was not our own before: whoever withheld the thing from us, before it was made our own by some compact, might, perhaps, be chargeable with wanting kindness: but whoever takes it from us, or withholds it afterwards, is chargeable with injustice. This is the effect of compacts in general: and an effect of the same sort may be produced by the social compact in particular. All the members of the same civil society bind themselves by this compact, to do whatever the common understanding, speaking by the laws, shall direct them to do, in order to advance or secure the general good. And, consequently, whatever outward acts of benevolence the law prescribes, they become due of perfect right to the several individuals, who are the objects of those acts: not to do that good, which the law requires to be done, is to withhold what is no longer matter of favour, but of strict justice. When the want of natural benevolence, in any particular instance, is thus become social injustice by means of civil laws, which are founded in the social compact; that is, in our own consent; such want of benevolence, though it was not punishable by individuals in a state of nature, will, upon the principles of the law of nature, be punishable by the civil magistrate in a state of society

CHAPTER VI.

OF CIVIL LAWS.

I. *Difference between a civil law and a compact.*—II. *Civil constitutions established partly by law and partly by compact.*—III. *Internal and external obligation of civil law.*—IV. *A civil law obliges internally, when it is made and promulgated.*—V. *The sanctions of civil law produce its external obligation.*—VI. *Penal sanctions not essential to civil laws.*—VII. *Proper matter of civil laws.*—VIII. *Matter of natural right and wrong may be matter of civil law.*—IX. *Civil laws not confined to matters of natural right or wrong.*—X. *Rights of mankind may be changed by civil laws.*—XI. *Effect of civil laws on promises, contracts, and oaths.*—XII. *What obligation to perform a void promise, contract, or oath.*—XIII. *Effect of civil laws on the promises, contracts, or oaths of kings, who have legislative power.*—XIV. *Effect of civil laws on marriage.*—XV. *Civil laws are written or unwritten.*—XVI. *Unwritten laws, how established.*—XVII. *Unwritten law more difficult to be ascertained than written law.*—XVIII. *Unwritten laws, how repealed.*—XIX. *Written laws cannot be repealed by prescription.*—XX. *General division of civil laws.*—XXI. *In some constitutions the civil laws of succession to the crown cannot be fundamental laws.*—XXII. *Controverted succession may be settled by civil laws.*

Difference between a civil law and a compact.

I. WHEN we consider only the general notion of a law, there appears to be a plain difference between positive laws and compacts. * A compact is an act of two or more persons, which produces an obligation upon those who make themselves parties to it, by their own immediate or direct consent. † A law is an act of a superior, which obliges all who are under his authority, as far as they are concerned in the matter of the law, and as far as the legislator intended to oblige them; whether they immediately and directly consent to it or not.

But the superiority of a civil legislator; that is, the right which a civil legislator has to prescribe laws to the members of a civil society, arises from their own consent: and, consequently, whatever difference there may be between a positive law and a compact, when we consider only the general notion of a positive law, the difference between a civil law and a compact is less apparent: because the obligation ‡ of civil laws, as well as the obligation of compacts, arises from the consent of those who are obliged by them. The mark of distinction between them consists in the different sort of consent from which their obligation arises. No person is obliged by a compact, besides those who make themselves parties to it, by some immediate or direct act of consent. But all persons are obliged by the laws of a civil society, whether they make themselves parties to them by any immediate and direct consent or not; if they have only made themselves parties to them by a remote or indirect consent. When a society is formed for the sake of carrying

* See Book I. Chap. XIII. § I. † See Book I. Chap. I. § V.

‡ See Book II. Chap. III. § I. Book I. Chap. X. § III.

on some certain purpose, whether it is a civil society or a society of any other sort, the several *individuals who join themselves to it, either consent expressly, or by the act of so joining themselves to it, are understood tacitly to consent to the carrying on this purpose by such measures as the common understanding shall approve and prescribe. Now the purpose for which a civil society is formed, is the general security and the general interest of the whole and of its several parts. Every man, therefore, by consenting to make himself a member of a civil society, agrees immediately or directly, that these purposes shall be carried on, and that he will concur in carrying them on, by such measures as the common understanding of the society shall approve of and prescribe. Thus far he is engaged only in a compact, which obliges him by means of his own immediate or direct consent: and without such immediate or direct consent, he would be no party to it, nor be any ways concerned in its obligation. But by this compact he gives the society a legislative power over him; that is, he gives it a right to prescribe such rules for his conduct, as the common understanding of the society shall judge to be necessary or conducive to the general good. And consequently, by the same compact, he obliges himself to observe these rules, when they are so prescribed; whether at the time of prescribing them he immediately and directly consents to them, or disapproves them, and even protests against them. In the meantime, the obligation of these rules, which are nothing else but the civil laws of the society, is ultimately derived from his own consent. Though he does not immediately and directly consent to the laws at the time of making them, yet he remotely and indirectly consented to them by becoming a party to the social compact. If he had not consented to make himself a party to that compact, the society would have had no legislative power over him; and consequently he would not have been obliged to observe any laws that it might prescribe.

In some other instances the difference between that consent, which makes a law binding upon us, and that consent which makes us parties to a compact, lies nearer to view, and may perhaps be seen more clearly than in the complicated business of civil society. A number of individuals, suppose twenty, that have no particular connections with one another, have a design of engaging in some undertaking, which is to be carried on by their joint labour, and at their joint expense. When they meet to deliberate upon the proper measures which are to be pursued, each of them is at liberty to judge and to determine for himself concerning those measures: and though fifteen out of the twenty should agree in their judgment, yet no act of theirs would bind the other five. Nothing can bind all and each of them, but the immediate and direct consent of all and each. And such an act of consent is a compact. But suppose that these twenty individuals, before any particular measures were proposed, had formed themselves into a society for carrying on the undertaking which they have in view, and had entered into a general agreement to act jointly in carrying it on according to the common sense of the whole number, this agreement would likewise have been a compact; it would have obliged each of the individuals no otherwise, than as each of them had made himself a party to it by his own

* See Book II. Chap. I. § II. Grot. Proleg. XV.

immediate or direct consent. But the effect of such a compact will be, that when any measure is approved and prescribed by fifteen out of the twenty, the other five, though they dislike it and dissent from it, will be obliged to pursue it. Such measures, or such rules of acting, as are agreed upon by the majority, which speaks the common sense of the whole, are laws to the rest; they bind the rest, not as a compact does, upon account of their immediate and direct consent, but upon account of their remote and indirect consent, implied in a previous compact, by which they obliged themselves, in whatever relates to the common purpose, to observe such rules and to pursue such measures as the common understanding should approve and prescribe.

The case of a civil society, in a perfect democracy, is exactly the same with this: each individual, by becoming a member of the society, consents to carry on the purposes of a civil society jointly with the rest; that is, in such a manner and by such means as shall be approved and prescribed by the joint understanding or common sense of the society. This immediate or direct act of his own consent, is what gives the society a general legislative power over him, or a general right to lay down rules for his conduct, in order to secure and advance the common good. Whatever particular rules, therefore, are approved and prescribed by the majority, which speaks the common sense of the whole society, he is obliged to follow these rules, whether he happens to be in the majority or not. On the one hand, therefore, they are not compacts; because, by the supposition of his voting with the minority, he does not make himself a party to them by any immediate or direct act of his own consent. But then, on the other hand, they do not oblige him without his own consent; because he remotely or indirectly consented to them, by consenting originally to pursue the proper purposes of a civil society, jointly with the other members, under the conduct of the common understanding.

In such a perfect democracy, as we have here supposed, all the members of the society are equal to one another. It may, therefore, be asked, in what sense the civil laws of this society can be called the acts of a superior? But though in a perfect democracy no one individual is superior to any other individual, and much less to all the rest, yet the whole body considered jointly, is superior to any one of its members considered separately. The body of the society, when any individual has united himself to it, has a right to direct his actions for the general good, by the common understanding, and to compel him by the common force to observe its directions, if he is unwilling or refuses to observe them otherwise. Such a right as this, is all that we mean, when we say, that civil laws are the acts of a superior. And this superiority is as intelligible, when it belongs to a great number of individuals acting jointly; that is, to the collective body of a society, as when it belongs to a legislative body consisting only of a few, or perhaps only of one.

Civil constitutions established partly by law and partly by compact.

II. The mere act * of civil union, vests the civil legislative power only in the collective body of the society: no other laws will be binding upon each of the members in consequence of this single act, besides those

* See Book II. Chap. IV.

which are established by the whole or by the greater part of the whole. Wherever, therefore, any particular part of a civil society has an exclusive legislative power, this power must have been vested in such legislative body by some farther act of the society. And since no civil laws are binding upon the several individuals who are members of a civil society, but in consequence of their own consent, the act by which any legislative body, different from the collective body is established, must be an act of joint consent. *Sometimes we consider this act of joint consent as a law, and call it the law of the civil constitution. Sometimes we consider it as a compact, and say, that a king in monarchies, or the nobles in aristocracies, or the representatives of the people in democracies, which are administered by representatives, derive their power from compact. There is some reason for calling it by these different names; because, in respect of what passes between the collective body and the several members, it is a law; and in respect of what passes between the same collective body and the particular persons who are called to the office of civil legislation, and established into a legislative body, it is a compact.

When a civil society, in view to the general good, has agreed to introduce and establish any particular form of civil government, the several members are obliged to submit to this form; though some of them might, perhaps, be of opinion, that it is not a proper or a beneficial form, and might publicly declare, that they do not agree to it. There is no more reason in the nature of the thing, why this act of the society should not be binding upon all its members, without the immediate and direct consent of each, than there is why any other act of the society should not be binding upon all, without a like consent of each. The original compact of civil union gives the collective body a power to oblige each of its members to conform to whatever the common understanding approves and prescribes for the general good. If, therefore, it should appear to the common understanding, that a legislative body of this or of that particular form will be conducive to the general good, and the majority of the society should agree to establish such a legislative body, each of the members, even those who are in the minority, will be obliged to comply with such establishment. Thus far the constitution of civil government is established by a law. The legislative body, which is to be introduced, does not, indeed, make this law; for no act of this body, till it is established, can be binding either upon the society in general, or upon the several members of it in particular. The law, therefore, which introduces and establishes the form of the legislative body, must be the joint act of the collective body. And this act, when we consider it in respect of the several members, may rather be called a law than a compact; because it obliges even those who immediately and directly dissent from it, at the time of making it; and this obligation arises from that remote and indirect consent which they gave to the future acts of the society, by making themselves parties to the social compact. But this act of the collective body, though it binds the several members of the society as a law, can be binding upon the collective body itself only as a compact: nothing but the immediate or direct consent of the collective body of a civil society, can take from

* See Book II. Chap. IV.

such body the legislative power which it has by means of civil union, and lodge this power exclusively in some particular part.

Internal and external obligation of civil law.

III. When the right, which a civil society, or the legislative body of such society has to prescribe laws to the several members of it, is called a natural right or a right of the law of nature, it is necessary to observe in what sense we call it so.

No right of this sort belongs either to any one man, or to any number of men, by the gift of nature. All *mankind are placed by nature in a state of equality; and, consequently, whatever right any one man may have to prescribe laws to a number, or whatever right any number of men may have to prescribe laws to one, this right must be of the adventitious sort, and cannot, in the strictest sense of the words, be a natural right.

But we frequently enlarge the sense of the word, and mean by the natural rights of mankind, not only such rights as belonged to them by the gift of nature, but such adventitious rights likewise, as either did subsist, or might have subsisted in a state of nature. However, the right which a civil society has to prescribe laws to its members, cannot be a natural right in this enlarged sense of the words; because the notion of this legislative right limits it to a state of civil society.

There is still a third sense, in which the rights of mankind may be called natural rights, or rights of the law of nature: whatever rights are acquired by such means as are natural, or agreeable to the law of nature, are under the protection of this law, and may, therefore, be called natural rights, or rights of the law of nature, †because this law forbids the violation of them. The legislative power of a civil society, or of the legislative body of such a society, is a right of this sort. The society acquires it by the immediate and direct consent of the several individuals who make themselves members of such society; and the legislative body acquires it, as by the immediate and direct consent of the collective body of the society, so by the remote and indirect consent of the several members. ‡If, therefore, we trace the obligation of civil laws back to its highest source, we shall find that it is derived out of the law of nature. The immediate cause of the obligation of civil laws is the authority of the legislative body: this authority is vested in the legislative body, by a compact between such body and the collective body of the society: and this compact is binding upon the several members, in consequence of their having consented, and made themselves parties to the first social compact, which gave the society a right to bind all and each of them to whatever the common understanding should approve and prescribe for the security and advancement of the general good. But since obligations, arising from consent, are obligations of the law of nature, it follows, that the members of any civil society are obliged by the law of nature to obey the civil laws of it; because the obligation of these civil laws arises from their own consent.

The obligation of civil laws, as it is thus derived from the law of nature, rests upon the consciences of mankind, and is called the internal obligation of such laws. §Whatever is the foundation of moral

* See Book I. Chap. X. § III.
† See Book I. Chap. II. § VIII.
‡ Grot. Proleg. 15, 16.
§ See Book I. Chap. I. § VI.

obligation, in respect of any other parts of the law of nature, whether it is the will of God, who has made happiness the natural effect of our obedience, and misery of our disobedience, or the suggestions of a moral sense, or the fitness and relations of things, or all these principles taken together, there is the same foundation of our obligation to obey the laws of our country.

Civil laws, like the law of nature, from which they are derived, might fail of producing their effect; that is, they might fail of securing and advancing the good of the society in general, and of its several members in particular, if it was wholly left to men's own consciences whether they would observe these laws or not. But wherever the law of nature gives a right to demand that any thing should be done or be avoided, it likewise gives a right to support this demand by the use of force. Thus, in a state of natural liberty, as the law of nature forbids doing an injury, so it gives individuals a right to defend themselves by force against an injury, which they are likely to suffer, and to obtain reparation or to inflict punishment upon account of an injury which they have suffered. In like manner, where mankind are united into a civil society, as the law of nature forbids the violation of the civil laws of such society, so it gives the society a right to make use of force for the support of them. The only difference in this respect between a state of nature and a state of society is, that in a state of nature this force is in the hands of individuals, and may be used at their discretion; whereas, in a state of society, it is in the hands of the public or of the executive body, and can only be used under the direction of the common understanding.

If either through want of skill, or through want of attention, we see no reasons in point of conscience for obeying the laws of our country; or if through malice, or through selfishness, we allow no weight to those reasons, when we do see them, obedience may still be obtained by means of the common force. The apprehension that this force will interpose in support of the laws, and will either prevent us from being gainers, or will perhaps make us losers, by breaking them, is such a reason for obeying them, as lies plain and open to the most unskilful and inattentive, and will be likely, in point of prudence, to get the better of our malice, and to give a turn to our selfishness in favour of obedience. The obligation to obey the laws, which arises from this apprehension, that the public force will interpose in support of them, is called their external obligation.

A civil law obliges internally, when it is made and promulgated.

IV. The civil legislator makes or enacts a law, when he requires the subjects to do or to avoid this or that, which the law expresses. But the mere making of a law does not produce any internal obligation, or bind the subjects, in conscience, to observe it. No man is naturally obliged to obey a law, any farther than he knows, or might know, if he pleases, what the law is: the will of the legislator can be no rule to him, till he is acquainted with it, or has such an opportunity of being acquainted with it, that, if he is ignorant of it, his ignorance must be owing to his own neglect. Civil laws, therefore, before they can produce any internal obligation, must be promulgated or made known, as well as enacted.

V. What the legislator does farther, besides enacting and promulgating a law, in order to obtain obedience to it, is called establishing it upon some sanction. The external obligation of the law arises from its sanctions, which are nothing else but the directions that the legislative gives to the executive, concerning the purposes for which the public force is to be used, or concerning the manner of using it, against those who break the law.

The sanctions of civil law produce its external obligation.

From hence it appears, that the external as well as the internal obligation of civil laws arises from the legislator. For though the public force is in the hands of the executive body, and the laws more immediately produce their external effect by the use of this force, or by the apprehension of its being used, yet the executive body, in this instance, acts only in conformity with the sanctions which the legislative has established.

VI. The first intention of the civil legislator in establishing a law by any sanction, is to procure obedience to such law; to prevent the harm which the law forbids; or to obtain the good which the law commands. But his intention does not stop here: if he fails of procuring obedience to the law, in the first instance, his farther intention is to remedy the harm that has been done by breaking it; and to hinder them, who have broken it once, from doing the like again. These intentions of the legislator may be obtained by two sorts of sanctions: by such as provide that he, who breaks the law, shall be no gainer, or shall not obtain the purposes which he had in view by breaking it; and by such, likewise, as provide that he, who breaks the law, shall be a loser by breaking it. If the law says, that all devises of lands or tenements, by will, shall be void, (unless the will is subscribed by the testator in the presence of three witnesses, and is attested by those witnesses,) the sanction of such a law consists in making the will void: the testator cannot obtain the purpose which he had in view, by making such a will; and the testamentary heir has no temptation to put the testator upon making such a will, and no motive to claim under such an one, if it is made; because the law will prevent him from being any gainer by it. When the law forbids doing a damage of any sort, and commands that reparation shall be made if such damage is done, the sanction of the law, which consists only in the command to make reparation, does nothing more than hinder any person from being a gainer by breaking the law: and such a sanction provides for obtaining the first intention of the legislator; that is, it secures obedience to the law, only by making it not worth any person's while to break it. Now, if by a penal sanction we mean the appointment of a punishment, such sanctions as these cannot be called penal sanctions: here is no appointment of a punishment; the legislator does not aim at securing obedience by threatening to make them losers, who break the law, or to take any right from them which they enjoyed before, but only by providing, that they shall be no gainers, or that they shall obtain no right by breaking it. As sanctions of this sort do not, in the first instance, aim at securing obedience to the law by threatening punishment, so neither do they operate afterwards by inflicting punishment, in order to prevent those who have broken the law once, from breaking it again. They do not look forward to what may be

Penal sanctions not essential to civil law.

done hereafter, but only backward upon what has been done already: they do not endeavour to prevent or restrain him who has done wrong once, from doing the same or the like wrong at another time; they only endeavour, as far as may be, to undo the wrong which is past. If, indeed, we call every interposition of the public force, to support a law, by the name of punishment, then even those laws which only aim at undoing the wrong that is past, may be said to be established by penal sanctions: because when any person, who has broken the law, will hold out against it, and will keep possession of what he has unjustly gained by breaking it; the law, which forbids making such unjust gain, gives those who have suffered by the wrong which he has done, a right to the assistance of the public force, in order to compel him to do them that justice which he refuses to do otherwise. But, certainly, where the sanction of a law produces only such interpositions of the public force as this, it can with no more propriety be called a penal sanction, than what an individual in a state of nature does by his own private force for obtaining reparation of damages, can be called a punishment. When the law makes a will void, it will take care that what is devised in such will shall go to the heir in intestate succession. If the testamentary heir takes possession of the lands and tenements devised by the void will, and keeps possession till the other obtains a judicial sentence, (though what he has done is contrary to the law,) yet if he submits to the sentence, after it is given, the law is satisfied. When the sanction looks no farther than the wrong that he did, without regarding the bad disposition that led him to do such wrong, it only requires him to undo his own act, and inflicts no evil upon him for having done it. Or suppose, that he holds out after sentence, and that the public force interposes to compel him to quit possession, yet if it interposes for no other purpose, this is no punishment. The design of such interposition is only to make the act void in fact, which the law had made void of right; that is, to undo what has been done already, and not to make him suffer any harm, in order to prevent him from doing the like again.

What has here been shown to be the case in one instance, is in general the case of all laws, which consider only the damage, that a man has done by an injury, without considering the disposition of mind that led him to do it. These laws inflict no punishment, if he is willing to make reparation: and even if he is unwilling, though the public force interposes in support of the law; yet the design of this interposition is only to compel him to do what is just, and not to punish him for having done what is unjust.

Penal sanctions are properly acts of the civil law, by which it appoints, that he, who behaves otherwise, than such law directs, shall be a loser, shall be deprived of some right, which otherwise belonged to him, or shall suffer some evil, from which he had otherwise a right to be free. But since the rules which the civil legislator prescribes for the general good, not only oblige the consciences of the subjects, but may and do, in many instances, produce their external effect without such appointments; the consequence is, that penal sanctions are not essential to civil laws.

If we enlarge the notion of penal sanctions, and include in it any interposition of the public force, whether this force interposes to compel men to do what is right, or to make them suffer some evil for having done what is wrong; in this sense of the words, which seems, however, to be an improper one, civil laws must be allowed to depend upon penal sanctions for their external obligation. But still these sanctions are not so far essential to civil laws, as to make it impossible for any civil law to oblige without them: because the bare enacting and promulgating a law produces an internal obligation; though nothing, which can be called a penal sanction, should be added to the law. Unless, indeed, it should be said, after all, that the law of nature itself is supported by penal sanctions, and, consequently, that all civil laws, since their internal obligation is derived from the law of nature, must be ultimately supported by the same sanctions with the law of nature.

Proper matter of civil laws

VII. As the purposes, for which men unite themselves into civil societies, determine the nature and terms of the social compact; so the nature and terms of this compact, which is the foundation of civil legislative power, determine what are the proper objects of this power. Each individual is led by a view to his own security and benefit to associate with the rest; and they, by receiving him amongst them, as a member of the body politic, agree to aid him in pursuing this end. But since each and all of them have the same end in view; they cannot be supposed to receive him upon any other terms, but those of his consenting to join with them in maintaining their security and benefit. And, consequently, he, by the act of joining himself to them, must be understood to agree to these terms. Thus, the particular interest of each member is taken under the protection of the whole; so that the whole obliges itself to act for his security and benefit: but at the same time, a common interest of the whole is formed; and each member obliges himself to act jointly with the rest for this common interest. The claim of each member upon the society, is limited by the obligation that he lays himself under towards the society, and by the obligation that the society is under towards each of the other members. He can have no claim upon the society to act for his security and benefit, where it interferes with the common security and benefit of the whole; because he is obliged to act with the society for this common security and benefit: and whilst he lays himself under this obligation, he cannot be understood to acquire any claim which is inconsistent with it. He can, likewise, have no claim upon the society to act for his security and benefit, where it is inconsistent with the security and benefit of any of the other members: because the society is under the same obligation in respect of the others, that it is under in respect of him: and, consequently, it could not engage to advance his interest at the expense of theirs.

Upon the whole, therefore, a number of individuals, by joining in a social compact, oblige themselves to act together, for the purposes of obtaining the common good of all, and the particular good of each; as far as the particular good of any one is consistent with the common good of all, and with the particular good of others. But where a number of persons bind themselves to act jointly for any purposes, the common understanding of such society is their guide, in respect of what they are to do, and what they are to avoid, in order to obtain those purposes. A civil society, therefore, has a right, by its common understanding, thus to guide itself and its several members. And since the legislative power of such society consists in this right, it follows, that whatever is necessary or conducive to the common good of the society, or to the particular good of the several members, as far as the particular good of any one is consistent with the common good of all, and with the particular good of others, is the proper object of legislative power. Now, civil laws are nothing else but such rules as the legislative power of a civil society establishes for the direction of all and of each of its members. Whatever, therefore, is the proper object of civil legislative power, is likewise the proper matter of civil laws.

Matter of natural right and wrong, may be matter of civil law.

VIII. From hence it appears, that the matter of civil laws is not confined to such things as the law of nature has left indifferent, by neither commanding nor forbidding them. The law of nature commands whatever is necessary or conducive to the security and benefit of mankind, in general, and forbids the contrary. As far, therefore, as what is necessary or conducive to the security and benefit of mankind in general, is necessary or conducive likewise to the security and benefit of that particular part of mankind, which is united into the same civil society; and as far as what is inconsistent with the security and benefit of mankind in general, is inconsistent likewise with the security and benefit of that particular part of mankind, which is thus united; the civil legislator is employed about the proper objects of his legislative power, when he commands the former or forbids the latter. His laws, therefore, contain what is a proper matter of civil law, when they command such actions as the law of nature has commanded, or forbid such actions as the law of nature has forbidden.

Mankind are, indeed, obliged to do what the law of nature commands, and to avoid what this law forbids, without the aid of civil institutions. But we cannot conclude from hence, that it is needless, and much less that it is improper, for civil laws to command what is naturally a duty, or to forbid what is naturally a crime. For though the members of a civil society are obliged to observe the law of nature, whether its rules and precepts are transcribed into the civil law, and adopted by it or not; yet, till they are thus transcribed and adopted, the obligation to observe them rests only upon the conscience.

It may, perhaps, be asked, whether the law of nature has not an external, as well as an internal sanction in a state of nature; whether mankind have not a natural right, where any injury has been done by breaking this law, to make use of their private force to obtain reparation and to inflict punishment? And if such an external sanction takes place in a state of nature, it may be farther asked, whether the law of nature is not naturally supported in a state of civil society by the like sanction, without being made a part of the civil law of the society?

In answer to these questions we may observe, that this external sanction of private force, reaches in a state of nature no farther than * the duties of justice; and that the duties of imperfect obligation are supported only by the internal sanctions of the law of nature. The law of nature obliges mankind to promote the good of one another: but this obligation, in a state of nature, is of the internal sort: no man has a right to compel others, by force, to do any thing which is matter of favour; however reasonable it may be in him to expect the favour from

* See Book I. Chap. XVII. § III. Chap. XVIII. § IX.

them, and however wrong it may be in them not to do it. Nothing, therefore, in a state of civil society, besides the social compact, or some civil law which is founded in this compact, can bind the several members of such a society to do good either to one another, or even to their country, so as to make the doing good a matter of strict justice, which may be supported by the external sanction of force. But the obligation of the social compact is only a general one to advance the common good of all, or the particular good of each: it is left to the joint or common understanding; that is, to the civil legislator, to determine in what instances, and by what means this good is to be done. And, consequently, if civil laws are not necessary to enforce the law of nature in respect of any other duties, they are at least necessary to enforce it in respect of the duties of imperfect obligation.

This, however, is not the only reason why it is necessary for civil laws to establish the duties of the law of nature. Not only those natural duties, which, in a state of nature, have no external sanction, but those likewise, which, in a state of nature, are supported by the external sanction of private force, would, in a state of civil society, have no external sanction, without the aid of civil laws. For * social union restrains those who are members of the same civil society, from making use of any private force against one another: so that no external sanction can be left in respect of any duty whatsoever, besides what comes from the public force. But the public force is under the guidance of the common understanding; it cannot act of right either in matters of defence, or in matters of reparation, or in matters of punishment, any otherwise than as the common understanding directs it. No injury, therefore, can be guarded against, no reparation can be obtained, and no punishment can be inflicted, unless the injury, which is to be guarded against, or to be made amends for, or to be punished, is contrary to the civil laws: because the civil laws contain those directions of the public understanding, which the executive body is to follow in using the public force.

If punishment, in a state of civil society, can only be inflicted of right by the public force; and if the public can only of right inflict punishment as the laws direct it, the conclusion from hence will be, that no action can of right be punished in a state of civil society, unless the civil laws have forbidden it. This will explain what we frequently hear, that such or such acts are very malicious and very unjust; that they deserve punishment as much or more than some others, which the law does punish; and yet that these may be done with impunity. These acts, which are said to be so malicious or unjust as to deserve punishment, are such as would be punishable by private force, if every member of a civil society had the same liberty of acting for himself, that individuals had in a state of nature; or they would be punishable by the public force of the society, if the public force had no rule to guide it, besides the law of nature. But civil union has taken from the individuals the liberty of punishing by their own private force; and the public force of a civil society is under the direction of the civil law. If, therefore, the acts, how malicious or unjust soever they may appear to be, are such as have not been forbidden and made punishable by some

* See Book II. Chap. V. § II. VII. IX.

civil law, either written or unwritten, they cannot of right be punished by the members of a civil society, either acting separately as individuals, or acting jointly by the executive body.

It may, however, be proper to observe, by the way, that this civil impunity does not make such acts innocent: the law of nature has made them crimes, notwithstanding the civil law may have omitted to make them so, or to forbid them under any penal sanction. They, therefore, who are guilty of such acts, though they may escape human punishment, must stand condemned by the law of nature, and be liable to the natural sanctions by which the divine author of this law has thought fit to establish it.

Civil laws not confined to matters of natural right and wrong.

IX. Though civil laws may command such things as the law of nature has commanded, or forbid such things as this law has forbidden, yet civil legislators are not confined from commanding or forbidding any thing else. What is naturally right or wrong, is a proper matter of civil laws; but it is not the only proper matter of them. The social compact gives the society a right to command what is for the common good of the body, or for the particular good of its several members, and of forbidding the contrary. But the law of nature has left many acts indifferent, as doing neither good nor harm to mankind in general, which yet may be beneficial or hurtful to a particular body of men, united into a civil society. It is matter of indifference as to the good or harm of mankind in general, what sort of clothes I buy and wear; whether they are such as have been manufactured by those who live near me, and speak the same language that I do, or by others who live at a distance and speak a different language. It may, indeed, be most for the benefit of my neighbours, that I should trade with them and wear only such clothes as they deal in: but it will be of equal benefit to those who live in the Indies, that I should wear such clothes as they only can furnish me with. The law of nature, therefore, obliging me only to regard the benefit of mankind in general, leaves it indifferent to me whether I buy and wear such clothes as are manufactured in the Indies, or such as are manufactured in the place where I happen to live. But when they, who live near me, are united with me into the same civil society, if it appears to the public understanding to be for the benefit of such society, that no member of it should buy or wear such clothes as are manufactured in the Indies, the social compact has given the society a right to forbid this, or to make it criminal by a civil law, and then to punish me or any other member of the society for doing it. The law of nature, as it stood in a state of nature, has prescribed no particular form for the marriage contract, and has not enjoined that the parties should make it in any particular place. The form, therefore, of this contract is indifferent, provided it contains in substance all that is naturally essential to marriage; and the place, where the parties are when they make it, is likewise indifferent. But if it appears to the common understanding of a civil society to be for the general good, that all marriages should be solemnized under some particular form, and in some particular places, the civil legislator has a right to prescribe, by law, that all marriages shall be solemnized under such form, and in such places, and to punish those who shall solemnize any marriage otherwise.

Perhaps it may appear, at first sight, that whatever civil laws enjoin or forbid, with a view to obtaining good, or preventing harm to the body politic, or to its several members, is only matter of natural right or wrong. What in a state of nature was not matter of natural right or wrong, may seem to have been made so in a state of civil society by means of civil union. For the compact, by which men are united into a civil society, may be thought naturally to oblige them to do whatever is necessary or conducive to the general good of such society, and of its several members, and to avoid the contrary; whether the former is commanded, and the latter forbidden by any express civil laws or not. But this is not precisely true. The social compact obliges them, in point of justice, to do not whatever is for the common interest in their own private opinion, but only what they are directed to do for this purpose by the common understanding: in like manner it obliges them, in point of justice, to avoid not whatever may be hurtful to the common interest, in their own private opinion, but only what they are directed to avoid, with this view, by the common understanding. Until the civil laws, therefore, which are the dictates of the common understanding, have enjoined or forbidden what, in a state of nature, was indifferent, it continues to be so far indifferent, as to the members of a civil society, that it is no duty of strict justice to do or to avoid it. I would not be understood to mean, that a man is under no obligation of any sort to do what he thinks will be for the good of his country, or to avoid what he thinks will be hurtful to it, till the civil laws have enjoined the one or forbidden the other. I only say, that, till then, it is not a duty of strict justice, or that the social compact does not give the society a perfect right to demand this of him: because this compact does not oblige him to guide himself in obtaining the purposes of a civil society by his own judgment, but by the common judgment of the whole. This will appear to be the case, if we consider the difference between a strictly just member of a civil society, and a good patriot. The former is exactly punctual in complying with the laws of his country; whilst the latter, as far as he is able to judge, avoids every thing which may be hurtful to the public, and does every thing which may be beneficial to it, even in those instances where the laws are silent. The social compact itself is so far from binding a man in strict justice to hold this conduct, that the laws, which are founded in this compact, will frequently oblige him to do what, in his own opinion, may be hurtful to the society; and to avoid what, in his own opinion, might be beneficial to it. But if, whatever his own opinion may be, the civil laws are his proper guide, as to what is due to the society, of which he is a member, in consequence of the social compact, it follows, that what was indifferent in a state of nature, will be so far indifferent in a state of civil society; whilst it is neither enjoined nor forbidden by the civil laws, that the members of such society will be at liberty to do it, or to omit it, without being chargeable with acting contrary to their social compact.

Rights of mankind may be changed by civil laws.

X. The rights of mankind, as far as they consist in a full liberty of doing certain actions, or of possessing certain things, may be altered or restrained or given up by their own consent. Every compact produces this effect: it limits or restrains or takes away some right; that is, some instance of liberty, which the parties to it were possessed of, before they engaged in such compact. And we have *already had occasion to show, that the social compact, in particular, produces this effect upon such rights of mankind, as arise out of an injury: it restrains their liberty of defending themselves; of obtaining reparation for damages, and of inflicting punishment, by the use of their own private force, under the conduct of their own judgment. But this is not the only effect of this compact. As it alters or restrains some of the rights of mankind immediately or directly, so it subjects others of them to be altered or restrained by the legislative power of civil society: and thus, whatever alterations or restraints are produced in them afterwards by civil laws, which are acts of such legislative power, arise from this compact remotely or indirectly.

They who maintain that the liberty of individuals is universally unalienable, would do well to show how the obligation of civil laws is consistent with this principle; how individuals, who, in a state of nature, were at full liberty in any particular instance to act as they please, can be obliged, by the laws of their country, when they are members of a civil society, to act in this instance in one particular manner, or not to act at all, and yet have the same full liberty of acting as they pleased, that they had before, and would still have had, if they had not by compact united themselves to such society. For, certainly, if they have given the society a power to restrain their liberty of judging and of acting for themselves, their liberty must be alienated: as far as the society has a power to restrain them, they must have given up a part of their liberty.

This power of civil society, to alter or restrain the rights of mankind, is limited by its own nature. It extends no farther than the purposes of the social compact, by which it was produced: as the parties to this compact only bind themselves to act for the common good of the whole society and of its several parts, so the power, which is produced by this compact, can, in its own nature, extend only to such restraints or alterations of any of the rights of mankind, as in the judgment of the common understanding are necessary or conducive to those purposes. Civil legislative power, therefore, is not in the strict sense of the word an absolute power of restraining or altering the rights of the subjects: it is limited in its own nature to its proper objects; to those rights only, in which the common good of the society, or of its several parts, requires some restraint or alteration. So that, whenever we call the civil legislative power, either of society in general, or of a particular legislative body, within any society, an absolute legislative power, we can only mean, that it has no external check upon it in fact: for all civil legislative power is, in its own nature, under an internal check of right: it is a power of restraining or altering the rights of the subjects for the purposes of advancing or securing the general good, and not of restraining or altering them for any purpose whatsoever, and much less for no purpose at all. This internal check may possibly fail of guarding the rights of individuals against undue restraints or alterations: because, by the consent of such individuals, when they become members of a civil society, they left it to the common understanding of such society to determine what restraints or alterations of their rights might be

* See Book II. Chap. V.

necessary or conducive to the general good; and the society may possibly abuse this trust. The danger is still greater if the society has gone farther, and has established a particular legislative body: for this point is then left to be determined by the understanding of such legislative body. To prevent such abuse, it is necessary to provide some external checks upon the exercise of civil legislative power; more especially where it is not exercised by the whole collective body of the society, but by some particular part of it, which is called its legislative body. For, though it is possible that the whole collective body, if it could conveniently meet together, might, in the laws which it makes, exceed the limits of legislative power, and restrain or alter the rights of individuals, where the good of the whole, or of its several parts, required no such restraint or alteration; yet it is not very likely that this would happen: because, as each of the members will be ready to take care of his own particular interest, it is not likely that any of the rights of individuals should be altered or restrained by the act of all or of a majority, unless the restraint or alteration was necessary or conducive to the proper ends of a civil society. But where the legislative power is entrusted with a part of the society, if this legislative body has no checks upon it, besides the internal check of natural right, it might be led, by motives of private interest, or by caprice, or by partial regard, to alter or restrain the rights of some, or of all the subjects, without any view to the general benefit. It is the business of the politician, in order to guard against any such excess in the exercise of legislative power, to contrive some external checks upon the legislative body. I call them external checks, to distinguish them from the internal check arising from a sense of what is right; though, perhaps, some which are made use of for this purpose, as they arise from the nature of the legislative body, might themselves be called internal ones. When the legislative body consists of two, three, or more constituent parts, so that no law can be made without the joint act of all these parts, they may be a check upon one another. And this will be more likely to be the case, if they are so different from one another, that what might be for the private interest of one of them, would not be for the private interest of another of them; though what is for the common benefit of the whole society will, in some respect or other, be for the particular benefit of them all. This check will be the more effectual, if one or more of these constituent parts of the legislative body consists of a number of persons, each of which in his private capacity, is subject, in all respects, to the same laws with the rest of the people. For each member of such constituent part of the legislative body will be the more careful about unduly altering or restraining the rights of the other members of the society; since, in whatever manner, or in whatever degree, the rights of others are altered or restrained, his own rights will likewise be altered or restrained in the same manner, and in the same degree. If one of these constituent parts of the legislative body consists of temporary representatives of the people; that is, of persons who are chosen by the bulk of the society, and return again after a certain time to their private station, and to a level with the rest of the subjects, unless the society will choose them into the same office and trust again, this will be a farther check upon the legislative body, and will help to restrain it from any undue excess in the exercise of legislative power: because, the bulk of the society will have frequent opportunities of providing for its own interest, by displacing those who have been concerned in any such excess, and returning such a body of representatives, as may take care that the rights of individuals shall be no otherwise altered or restrained, than the ends of civil society require. Such checks as these, which the constitution of the civil government in any nation has provided for preventing any undue exercise of legislative power, are called constitutional checks. Perhaps many others, besides these, might possibly be contrived; but it is not our business here to inquire, either what others might be contrived, or how any checks of this sort operate to produce the end which is proposed by them. This is the province of politics, and not of natural law.

As the nature and ends of civil legislative power limit it in some instances, so the nature of the rights of mankind limit it in others. Some of the rights of mankind imply a duty, which is required of them by the law of nature, or the law of God. Every man has an unalienable right to do what these laws command, and to avoid what these laws forbid.

*But even such rights, as imply a duty, consist in a liberty, though not in a full liberty of acting. We are naturally at liberty to do what the law of nature or of God commands; not because we are at liberty to do the contrary, but because we are naturally free from all external force that might compel us to do the contrary. Thus, likewise, we are naturally at liberty to avoid what the law of nature or of God forbids; not because we are at liberty to do otherwise, but because nature has not subjected us to any external force that might compel us to do otherwise. The law of nature, or of God, has left some things indifferent, by neither commanding nor forbidding them: in such instances as these, our right of acting consists in a full liberty of doing them, or of not doing them, just as we please. The same laws have made some things duties, and others crimes; in these instances, we have not a full liberty, but are obliged to do the one, and not to do the other: so that, here our rights consist in a liberty on one side only; that is, in a liberty of obeying those laws, or in a freedom from all external force, that might compel us to disobey them.

Now, though our †rights are alienable, or may be parted with by our own consent, where they are absolute, or consist in a full liberty of acting as we please; yet they are unalienable, where they consist in a liberty, which is not full and absolute, in a liberty of acting only one way, or in a freedom from being liable to be compelled to act otherwise. The general rule concerning alienable and unalienable rights is, that those are alienable, which are not restrained or limited by any law; but that those, which are so restrained and limited, are unalienable. Where the laws of nature and of God, have left an action indifferent, by neither commanding nor forbidding it; our right to do or not to do that action is full and absolute; it is not restrained or limited either by the law of nature, or by the law of God; and, consequently, we may, consistently with these laws, alienate this right; that is, we may, by our own consent, give others a power to direct us to act either this way or that, for some reasonable purpose. But where the law of nature or

* See Book I. Chap. II. § III.

† See Book I. Chap. II. § III. IX.

the law of God has commanded an action and made it a duty, or has forbidden an action and made it a crime; in respect of such actions, our right or liberty of acting as we please, is not full and absolute; it is restrained and limited by the same law, which has commanded or forbidden the action; so that it consists only in a freedom from being compelled to disobey the law. We cannot, therefore, consistently with the law, alienate such rights; that is, we cannot part with our liberty, any farther than we have it: we may, by our own consent, give others a power to enforce the obligations of the law of nature or of God; but these laws, as they oblige us to act in one particular manner, have not left us at liberty to oblige ourselves by our own consent to act otherwise, or to give others, by such consent, a power of compelling us to act otherwise. But if mankind cannot, by consent or by compact, give others a power of binding them to do what the law of nature or of God has commanded, or to neglect what either of these laws has forbidden; the legislative power of civil society, which is derived from consent or compact, cannot imply a power of binding the members of such society to act contrary to these laws.

If I had not thought it necessary to apply here what has been already said, concerning the nature of the rights of mankind, and concerning the distinction of them into such as are alienable, and such as are unalienable; we might have come to this conclusion more readily. No man can oblige himself by his own consent to act one way, when he is already obliged to act the contrary way. But every man is originally obliged to do what the laws of nature or of God command, and to avoid what these laws forbid: so that notwithstanding individuals may bind themselves, by their own consent, to do or to avoid what God, by his natural or his revealed law, has neither commanded nor forbidden; they cannot so bind themselves to do what he has forbidden, or to neglect what he has commanded. And since the social compact itself, and civil laws, which derive their authority from this compact, are obligations arising from consent, either immediately and directly, or remotely and indirectly; the consequence is, that no man can be obliged, either by civil union or by civil laws, to act contrary to the natural or to the revealed law of God.

In applying this general principle to particular instances, we are apt, for want of attention, to make two mistakes. The first of these mistakes is, that since civil laws cannot oblige us to do what is contrary to the law of nature, or cannot so change the law of nature, as to make any action lawful, which this law has forbidden, we are apt to conclude, that whatever action is contrary to the law of nature, whilst the civil law is silent about it, must necessarily continue to be contrary to the law of nature, notwithstanding any appointment of the civil law in relation to it. But upon a closer inquiry into this matter, we shall find that the appointment of civil law, nay, that even the act of an individual, can make it naturally lawful to do or to omit what, without such appointment of the civil law, or such act of the individual, could not have been lawfully done or omitted.

The law of nature, in a state of equality, forbids me to force a man to work or labour for my benefit, who has not bound himself to me by his own consent for this purpose. But after he has so bound himself, such force is no longer contrary to the law of nature: not because the law of nature is changed by his consent; but because his circumstances and mine are changed by it. The law of nature still continues to forbid me to force any man to work or labour for my benefit, who has not bound himself to me by his own consent, thus to work or labour: but after he has so bound himself, this particular precept of the law of nature is no longer the measure of what is just and unjust between him and me. As long as his right to his liberty continues, my natural obligation not to force him to do what he has no mind to do, continues too: but when he has parted with this right by voluntarily making himself my servant; the natural obligation on my part ceases, and in consequence of his consenting to be my servant, I have acquired a right to force him to work for me, whether he is afterwards willing to work or not. It is contrary to the law of nature to take a man's goods from him; but after he has sold them to me, if he refuses to deliver them upon my paying him the purchase money, the law of nature does not forbid me to take them from him: not because the law of nature is changed; for what was forbidden by it before, is forbidden by it still; but because those goods, which were his own once, have ceased to be his own now: and thus the precept of the law of nature, which was, in respect of these goods, the measure of right and wrong between him and me, ceases to be the measure, in consequence of his having given up his property in the goods by his own consent. * When I owe money to a man, the law of nature commands me to pay it: but my creditor, without changing the law of nature, can set aside the obligation of this command as to himself, by releasing the debt without payment: for though the law of nature still commands me to pay what I owe; it ceases to command me to pay any thing to him, because by his release I cease to owe him any thing. In general, we may say, that no obligation of the law of nature can be set aside by the act of the party himself, who is under such obligation: but where the obligation corresponds to some alienable right of others, they, by relinquishing their right, can release him from the obligation. Neither do they, by their act, change the law of nature, when they set his obligation aside: they only change his circumstances and their own; and then the particular precept of the law of nature, which before was the measure of right and wrong between him and them, ceases to be so upon this change of circumstances.

From hence it will appear in what manner the civil law produces its effect; when such acts as were contrary to the law of nature before any appointment of civil law concerning them, become consistent with it, in consequence of such appointment. No person, by his own consent, either in the social compact or otherwise, could give the society, or the legislative body of the society, a power to dispense with his doing what the law of nature has obliged him to do, or to authorize his doing what the law of nature has obliged him not to do. But where his obligations correspond to such alienable rights of others, as are subjected by the social compact to the jurisdiction of the civil legislative power; the society has a power to restrain or to take away their rights, and by this means his obligation ceases. It is contrary to the law of nature to take a person's goods from him: but if the civil law has required the

* Grot. Lib. I. Cap. I. § X.

the subjects to pay some tax for the support of the society; the officers who are employed to collect this tax, if the civil law has authorized them, may, consistently with the law of nature, take from any subject, who refuses to pay his share, such goods as will sell for as much money as he ought to pay: not because the civil law can authorize them to take another man's property from him; but because the goods, which otherwise would have been his property, cease to be so by the appointment of the law. He has a right to his goods, indeed, and whilst this right subsists, it would be contrary to the law of nature to take them from him. But the law of nature does not forbid him to part with this right: and as far as it is necessary for him to contribute, with the other members of the society, to the support of the public, he has parted with this right, or however has subjected it to the jurisdiction of the public, by making himself a party in the social compact.

Since the civil law, when it thus releases a person from any of the duties of the law of nature, which he owes to other men, operates by an indirect act, that takes away such of their rights, as correspond to these duties; we may observe, by the way, that it cannot release him in the same manner from any of the duties which he owes by the law of nature either to himself or to God: because, in these duties, there are no corresponding rights, which are subject to the jurisdiction of civil society.

When we find it laid down as a general principle, that civil authority cannot establish any thing which is contrary to the laws of nature or of God; we are apt to fall into a second mistake, in applying this principle. We are apt to imagine, where the laws of nature or of God relate to persons, who are in particular circumstances, that it is not only impossible for any civil jurisdiction to dispense with their obligation, when they are in these circumstances, but that it is likewise impossible for any civil jurisdiction to make their obligation void by preventing them from bringing themselves into these circumstances: we are apt to imagine, that, where a duty of the law of nature or of God takes place upon the performance of some certain act, this act itself is not under the jurisdiction of civil society, and cannot be made void by the civil legislator.

The most remarkable instances of this sort are the obligations arising from promises, contracts, or oaths, and the obligations arising from marriage. These are points of some difficulty, and with the reader's leave we will examine them particularly.

Effect of civil laws on promises, contracts, and oaths.

XI. * No act of the civil law can excuse a man from performing a promise, or a contract, or an oath, by which he is bound: because where the obligation, arising from any of these acts subsists, the law of God, either as it is collected from natural reason, or as it is declared in his revealed word, requires performance. But the true state of the question, concerning the effect of civil laws, in relation to these acts, is, not whether the civil power can excuse performance, where there is an obligation upon a man arising from any of them; but whether the civil power cannot hinder the obligation from taking place. Though a man, when he is in such circumstances as to be bound by his promise, contract, or oath, cannot be

* Grot. Lib. II. Cap. XIII. § XX.

excused from performance by the civil law; yet it is no consequence, that the civil law cannot hinder him from being in those circumstances.

Now, the civil law can hinder or make void the obligation of a promise, contract, or oath, two ways; either by such an act, as affects the promiser, contracter, or juror immediately; or by such an act, as immediately affects those, to whom the promise, contract, or oath relates, and in the meantime affects him only remotely. And farther, where the act of the civil law affects him immediately, it may be either antecedent or subsequent to the promise, contract, or oath.

When the civil laws have antecedently forbidden the members of any society to promise, or agree, or swear, that they will do this or that, which the law expresses; no promise, or contract, or oath, which is contrary to such laws, can be binding upon them. Notwithstanding, where they are under an obligation by any of these acts, the law of nature and of God requires performance; yet this law requires no performance of what is contained in such promises, or contracts, or oaths, as the civil laws have forbidden; because the members of the society are, in these instances, incapable of obliging themselves. They, who are under the authority of another, have no liberty or moral power of binding themselves to do what this other forbids, or to neglect what he commands. As far, therefore, as the jurisdiction or authority of the civil legislator extends; the subjects are incapable of obliging themselves in opposition to his laws. They have, indeed, the natural power of repeating the words of such promises, or contracts, or oaths, as his laws have forbidden. And custom may lead us, or the want of another name may force us, to call the mere repeating of these words a promise, or a contract, or an oath. But they, from whom the civil laws have taken the liberty or moral power of acting for themselves, do nothing by repeating them: the words alone, without such liberty or moral power, produce no obligation.

This principle, upon which the civil laws make void such promises, or contracts, or oaths, as they have antecedently forbidden, may be placed in another light. An antecedent obligation will make void any subsequent obligation, which is contrary to it. But the civil law, which forbids the promise, or contract, or oath, and, consequently, the obligation of this law, is here supposed to be antecedent to the promise, or contract, or oath itself. The obligation, therefore, of the civil law, will make void the obligation of any of these subsequent acts. You may, perhaps, reply, that the obligation of performing our promises, or contracts, or oaths, arises from the law of nature and of God, and that this law is antecedent to all civil authority whatsoever. But this suggestion, though it is true, is nothing to the purpose. For though the general obligation of performing our promises, or contracts, or oaths, is antecedent to all civil authority; it will be no consequence, that the obligation of this particular promise, or contract, or oath, which the civil laws have forbidden, is likewise antecedent to all civil authority: unless you can show, that the law of nature or of God has required you to make this promise, or to engage in this contract, or to take this oath in particular. If you can find any covenant, which the law of God requires you to engage in; such, for instance, as you will probably understand the covenant of baptism to be; I will allow that no human authority can make void the obligation, that arises from such a covenant, by forbidding it. But where the law of nature, or of God, whilst it requires you in general to fulfil your promises, contracts or oaths, has left you at liberty as to any particular promise, contract or oath, whether you will engage in it or not; there the civil laws can take this liberty from you, if it appears to be inconsistent with the common good of the society: and then the obligation of the civil laws, being antecedent to your engaging in such promise, contract or oath, will make it void if you should engage in it. For, by the supposition of your being at liberty, by the law of nature or of God, to engage or not engage in this particular promise, contract or oath, this law had laid you under no obligation to engage in it; and, consequently, had laid you under no obligation to keep it, antecedently to any appointment of civil laws concerning it.

There is rather more difficulty in understanding how the act of the civil legislator can set the obligation of promises, contracts or oaths, aside by a subsequent act; that is, by forbidding performance after we have engaged in them, where no antecedent law had forbidden us to engage. * Grotius, in explaining this matter, lays it down as a general principle, that wherever an inferior enters into any obligation, such obligation must be a conditional one: an inferior, he says, has no power to bind himself without the consent of his superior: and upon this account every obligation of an inferior, if it does not express so much, must be understood to imply, that he consents to be obliged, provided his superior agrees to the obligation. But if our author, by making this a necessary condition in the promise, contract or oath of an inferior, means that no inferior can be obliged by any such act, unless his superior allows the obligation, either expressly, by confirming it, or tacitly, by not contradicting it, this principle is not universally true. This, indeed, is the situation of a slave: all his actions are subject to the authority of his master: no act, therefore, which he does, can be valid without the concurrence of his master. It is, likewise, the situation of children, who have not yet arrived at the use of their reason: all their actions, during this natural minority, are subject to the absolute control of their parents: they are, therefore, naturally incapable of binding themselves, unless their parents agree to the obligation, either expressly or tacitly. But where the superiority is in its own nature a limited one, and extends only to some actions of the inferior, no concurrence of the superior, either express or tacit, is necessary to make such acts of the inferior valid, as are not subject to his jurisdiction. The Mosaic law, indeed, gave the husband a power to make void any vow of the wife; or, rather, it placed the wife in such a state of subjection, that no vow of hers could be binding, if the husband declared that he disallowed it. But without such a positive law as this, many acts of a wife are naturally free from the jurisdiction of her husband, so that she is capable of binding herself without his concurrence. Now, civil subjection is in its own nature a limited one: the members of a civil society are subject to the legislative power of it: but the purposes of the social compact, from which this subjection arises, determine it to extend only to such things as are necessary or conducive to the common security or benefit of the whole, or of its several parts. In

* Grot. Lib. II. Cap. XIII. § XX.

all things, which have no relation to these purposes, the members of a civil society are free to act for themselves; and, consequently, have a moral power of binding themselves, without the concurrence of the civil legislator. If, therefore, the promise, contract or oath, is not contrary to some obligation of the social compact, there is no reason for supposing either that any concurrence of the civil legislator is necessary to make the act binding, or that any want of such concurrence would make it void. The civil legislator, however, though he cannot make the act void by a mere declaration of his not consenting to it, may produce this effect by forbidding performance. When we are under any antecedent obligation, we have no moral power of binding ourselves to do what is contrary to this obligation. The law, forbidding performance, is here, indeed, supposed to follow the act which it invalidates. But every member of a civil society is obliged, by the social compact, to obey all the laws of it, at what time soever those laws are made. And, consequently, as we are members of a civil society, all our acts must be done, though not under a condition of their being binding, if the civil legislator consents to them, yet under a condition of their being binding, if he does not forbid them; because we have no moral power, or are not at liberty to bind ourselves otherwise.

The reasons upon which this principle is founded, will appear more plainly, from observing what would be the consequence of supposing the contrary. If the civil legislator could not make void a promise, contract or oath, by means of a law which is subsequent to any of these acts, the subjects, or members of a civil society, would be able to exempt themselves from the obligation of all laws whatsoever, besides those which are now in being. They might, any of them, bind themselves to one another, by promise, or contract, or oath, never to obey any future law, which made any alteration in the present state of things. Or if they knew beforehand what particular law was likely to be made, they might thus bind themselves to one another not to obey this particular law. Or, in short, wherever they had a private benefit in view, however inconsistent such benefit might be with the good of the public, yet if it was not forbidden by any law now in being, they might in the same manner, bind themselves to one another never to give up this benefit, or never to obey any law which should restrain them in their pursuit of it. And then, upon supposition that the civil legislator cannot make void these acts by any subsequent law, the subjects who had entered into such engagements, would be discharged from the obligation of obeying all laws which are contrary to these engagements: because such laws can bind them no otherwise than by overruling the obligation of their promise, contract or oath. If, therefore, you can find any reasons to satisfy yourself that these laws would be binding upon them, the same reasons will serve to show you in general, that civil laws can overrule the obligation of promises, contracts or oaths, as well by a subsequent, as by an antecedent act. The reason upon which you would probably satisfy yourself in this case, is, that every member of a civil society has subjected himself by the social compact to the legislative power of such society; and, consequently, whilst he continues a member, he is not at liberty, or has not a moral power, to do any act with effect, which will exempt him from the authority of this power. But you may observe, that this reason will likewise prove, that the civil legislator can, by a subsequent act, set aside the obligation of promises, contracts or oaths in general: because, if any act of this sort was binding, when the civil law forbids performance, the person, whose act it is, would be thus far exempted from the authority of the legislative power.

You may, perhaps, find it difficult to reconcile this conclusion with a principle of natural law, which says, that no subsequent obligation can make void an antecedent one: for, since the law which forbids the performance, is, by the supposition, subsequent to the promise, contract or oath, you may from thence be induced to imagine, that the law cannot set aside the obligation of the antecedent act. Your mistake here is, that, because the law is subsequent to the promise, contract or oath, you suppose the obligation of the promiser, contractor or juror, to obey such law, to be likewise subsequent to these acts. Whereas, his obligation to obey the law is antecedent, not only to the making of the law, but likewise to the acts which are set aside by it. He could not, indeed, be specifically obliged to obey this law, before it was made, but he obliged himself, in general, to obey this and all other laws, whenever they should be made, by becoming a member of the society. For, the obligation of all civil laws is founded in the obligation of the social compact: and it is this obligation of the social compact which takes from him the liberty or moral power of obliging himself by any act which shall be contrary, not only to the laws that are already made, but to those likewise that shall be made hereafter. He bound himself by the social compact to obey the laws; and this obligation is antecedent to his promise, contract or oath. All that the subsequent law does, is to apply this general and antecedent obligation to some particular instance.

As the civil law may thus make void a promise, or a contract, or an oath, either by an antecedent or by a subsequent act, which affects the promiser, or contractor, or juror, immediately and directly; that is, either by forbidding him beforehand to engage in such promise, contract or oath, or by forbidding performance after he has engaged in it; so likewise the civil law may make a promise, or a contract, or an oath, void by an act which immediately and directly affects the persons to whom he promises, with whom he contracts, or for whose benefit he swears, whilst it affects him so as to discharge his obligation only remotely and indirectly. The manner in which the law operates to produce this effect, has been already explained: if we make a promise, or a contract, or if we take an oath, by which any person acquires a right, and the civil law takes from him the right so acquired, this act of the law affects him immediately and directly; but at the same time it will remotely and indirectly affect us, and discharge our obligation: because, where there is no right or claim on the one hand, there can be no obligation on the other.

What obligation to perform a void promise, contract or oath.

XII. Here, it may be asked, whether the civil law, when it makes void the promise, or contract, or oath of any person, discharges him from the natural obligation arising from such act, or only from the civil obligation; whether he is not obliged, in conscience, to performance, by the law of natural justice, notwithstanding he is not liable to be compelled to performance by the civil law? In answering this question, it may be proper to consider, whether his act was made void merely for his own benefit: if it was, and the law, whilst it offers him this benefit, does not compel him to accept it; he is then understood to be at liberty either to perform his promise, or contract, or oath, if he pleases, or to take the advantage which the law gives him. Where the civil law has fixed the age of discretion at twenty-one years, or at any other particular period of life, and makes void a contract of lending money to any person who is under this age, it takes from such minor the liberty or moral power of binding himself by this contract; so that, by making this contract, he has done nothing. He cannot, therefore, be under any natural obligation of strict justice to pay it. He might, perhaps, at the time of borrowing the money, be arrived at the use of reason: but till he is arrived at that point of life, where the civil law, to which he is subject, has fixed the age of discretion, this law deprives him of the liberty or moral power of obliging himself: and since this operation of the law is a natural one, he cannot, by any act of his own, lay himself under a natural obligation of strict justice: because he wants such liberty or moral power. But as this contract was made void for the benefit of the minor, he is at liberty, when he comes to the age of discretion, to refuse this benefit, and to pay the money, if he pleases. From hence arises an obligation in conscience; though, as we have seen already, it is no obligation of strict justice. For every man of integrity and honour, where he cannot receive a benefit himself, without making some other person lose what the person might reasonably expect, will think it his duty, though it is a duty of the imperfect sort, to part with such benefit.

But where the civil law, when it makes a promise, or a contract, or an oath void, designs to hinder the benefit of the person whose act is so made void, and by this means to prevent some harm to others; he is so far from being under any natural obligation, either perfect or imperfect, to perform what he had engaged to do, that performance of it is not a matter of indifference; he is not at liberty to perform it, and is guilty of injustice if he does perform it. To suppose the contrary, is to suppose that a member of civil society may be obliged, in conscience, to obtain a benefit for himself, to which, by the laws of his country, he has no right; or to do some harm to others, from which, by the same laws, they have a right to be free. If a number of men, who have conspired together to do what the civil law forbids, bind themselves to one another for this purpose by contract or by oath, and the same law, which forbids such conspiracy, makes this contract or oath void, they could be under no obligation, in conscience, to perform their engagement: because, performance does not consist in giving up a benefit of their own, which they are at liberty to waive, if they please; it consists in pursuing a benefit of their own, to which they have no right, and in obstructing a benefit of others, to which these others have a right.

The first occasion of the common mistakes in this matter, is an opinion, that where the civil law makes any act void, it leaves us at liberty to judge for ourselves, as if we were in a state of nature, whether the law of nature would, in the like circumstances, bind us to performance; and that, if we find it would, we are to look upon ourselves as obliged to performance by natural justice. Whereas, we should consider not what the law of nature would bind us to, in consequence of a promise, or contract, or oath, if we were in a state of nature; but what it binds us to, when we are members of a civil society, and under the jurisdiction of its laws; we should consider whether the law of nature requires performance, where the civil laws, which are founded in our own consent, have taken from us the liberty or moral power of binding ourselves. When a man, by some previous compact that falls within the notice of common observers, has parted with his right to bind himself by a second compact, which is contrary to the former; if he should repeat the words, or go through the forms of this second compact, we see plainly enough, that what he so does will stand for nothing, or will produce no natural obligation of justice. But this is the case of every member of a civil society, in respect of what is forbidden by the civil laws of it for the common or general good. These laws are founded in the original compact of social union, in which he made himself a party by becoming a member of the society. And though this is a remote compact, which does not fall within the notice of common observers, yet it is a compact, and will naturally operate just as any other compact would. If the civil laws, therefore, which are founded in this compact, have made a man's promise, or contract, or oath void, this act of the civil law as naturally takes from him his right of obliging himself to do what is contrary to the law, as if he had more immediately and directly given up his right by some private compact of the same tenor with the law itself. Where the civil law of a society has made void the promise, or contract, or oath of any person who is a member of this society, we cannot, consistently with these principles, suppose that he is as much obliged to performance by the law of nature, as if he had lived in a state of nature: because, in a state of nature he might have had a liberty, or moral power, of binding himself to do what is contained in such promise, contract, or oath; whereas, when he is a member of a civil society, the law of nature considers him as already bound by the social compact, to comply with the civil laws; and, consequently, as having no liberty, or moral power, of doing any act with effect, which those laws make void. You may say, therefore, if you please, that where the civil law has made his act void, he is to judge of his obligation by the law of nature. But still I contend, that he is not to judge of it by what the law of nature would dictate in the like case, if he was in a state of nature, but by what this law dictates in consequence of his having already obliged himself by the social compact to obey the civil laws of his country.

Another occasion of the common mistakes in this matter, arises from our not attending to the distinction already mentioned, between what the civil laws permit, where they make the act of any person void for his own benefit only, and what they require, where they make it void for the purpose of hindering a benefit of his own, which he had in view, and of securing others from some harm, which they might suffer by his pursuing this benefit. When we find, that the civil law, whilst it makes void the promise, or contract, or oath of any person, merely for his own benefit, permits him to perform what is contained in such promise, contract or oath, if he chooses to waive his benefit, and to perform voluntarily, though his act is void, what he might have been compelled to perform, if it had been valid; and especially when we find, that, in these circumstances, men of probity and honour esteem themselves to be bound in conscience to a voluntary performance; we first conclude, that this obligation, in conscience, must be a perfect obligation of natural justice; and then we form a more general conclusion, that what we are obliged to do in cases of this sort, we are likewise obliged to do in all cases of void acts; even in those, where our acts, instead of being made void with a design of securing our own benefit, are made void with a design of hindering it, and of securing to others such benefit as the law, which makes our act void, requires us not to deprive them of.

Effect of civil laws on the promises, &c. of kings who have legislative power.

XIII. * When Grotius proposes to inquire, whether kings can make void their own promises, or contracts, or oaths, in the same manner, as they can make void those of their subjects; he takes care to inform his readers, that he confines this question to kings, who are entrusted with legislative power. And, in fact, without such a limitation, here would be no question at all: because the acts of private persons are overruled or made void no otherwise, than by legislative power: and consequently, since they, who have not legislative power, cannot make void the acts of their subjects, they certainly cannot make void their own acts.

In regard to such civil laws, as immediately affect the subject, whose promise, or oath, or contract, is made void; they are either antecedent or subsequent to such promise, contract or oath. The first question, therefore, concerning kings, who have legislative power, is, whether, by any antecedent law, declaring that all obligations entered into in such circumstances, or for such purposes, as the law describes, shall be void, they can make void their own acts, as well as the acts of their subjects. Here Grotius distinguishes between such acts, as they do in their kingly capacity, by which he means their legislative capacity, and such as they do in their private capacity. Laws of their own making have no authority over them in their legislative capacity: because, if in this capacity they could not act freely, notwithstanding their own laws, they could not repeal those laws, after they have once made them. But since no promise, or contract, or oath of any person, can be made void any otherwise, than by the act of a superior, which takes from him his liberty, or moral power of obliging himself; the consequence is, that the law of a king having legislative power, since he is not his own superior, when we consider him in his legislative capacity, cannot make void any promise, contract, or oath, in which he engages in this capacity. Thus, for instance, whatever exception there may be to the contract of a subject, upon account of the civil minority of the party contracting; that is, upon account of his being of less age, than the law requires to make him capable of binding himself; yet there is not the same exception against a contract of a king, if he has legislative power, and makes this contract in his sovereign capacity, for the purposes of the state; notwithstanding he should be under the age, which the civil law has fixed as the limit of minority.

What has been here said proceeds upon a supposition, that no law has been prescribed by the society to their king, when he was called and appointed to his office, and was entrusted with legislative power. Any laws, which came originally from the legislative power of the

* Grot. Lib. II. Cap. XIV.

people, before they lodged the legislative power of the society in his hands, are binding upon him as compacts, to which, by accepting the crown under the limitations of these laws, he immediately and directly consented. Upon this account all promises, or contracts, or oaths of such king, if they are contrary to these laws, will be void. By this compact, he has given up his liberty or moral power of binding himself to do what these fundamental laws forbid: thus far, therefore, this compact may be considered as the act of a superior; because it is a standing check upon his power.

But though a king having legislative power is not his own superior, in respect of such acts, as he does in his legislative capacity, and, consequently, is not affected in these acts by his own laws; yet, in respect of any other acts of a private nature; that is, of any acts, which he does as a part of the community, he is bound by his own laws. Grotius considers this obligation of a king having legislative power, as an indirect one. Natural equity, or the nature of a civil society, requires, that all the parts of such society should conform themselves to whatever, in the judgment of the common understanding, is for the general good. When, therefore, the matter of any law, and the reason of it, is the same, whether it is applied to the king or to the subjects; such law, though it is of his own making, is binding upon himself: because, in respect of this law, he can only be considered as a part of the society; and it is as much for the general good, that he should comply with it, as that any of his subjects should comply with it. When he is considered in his legislative or sovereign capacity, he is superior to every part of the society: whatever laws, therefore, he prescribes to the society in general, they will affect all the members of it, to whom the matter or the reason of the law relates: and, consequently, he must be understood to design, that these laws should extend to all acts of his own, which are done by him as a part of the community; that is, to all acts of his own, where the matter and the reason of the law is the same, when applied to him, as when applied to any other part of the society. If the legislator, by any antecedent law of this sort, takes away from the other parts of the society, their power of obliging themselves by an act, which is contrary to such law; he is understood, by the same law, to take away his own power, or, at least, to renounce his own power, of obliging himself by a like act. Thus, though a king, with legislative power, would be obliged to pay any debts, which he contracted for the public use in his sovereign capacity, during his civil minority; yet his obligation to pay any debts which he contracted upon his own private account, would be void, in the same manner with the like obligation of any of his subjects; that is, there would be no obligation of strict justice, but only an imperfect obligation of honour or of benevolence. In like manner a civil law, which makes marriages void, upon account of some defect in the form of the contract, or of age in the parties, will make void the marriage of the king, though he had the sole legislative power; if he had not taken care expressly to except himself out of the law.

* Grotius observes, that if a king having legislative power, has only an usufructuary right in the crown; that is, if the people have, by a

* Grot. Lib. II. Cap. VI. § XI.

fundamental law of the constitution, reserved to themselves the right to dispose of the crown by a new election upon every vacancy, or have, by a like law, determined the future succession; he has, whilst in possession, no right to alienate, by promise or contract, or otherwise, any part of the patrimony of the crown. By the patrimony of the crown, he means such lands or such revenues, as are annexed to the crown by some act of the society, for the support of the government, or for the public purposes of the state. Such usufructuary kings have no other right in this patrimony, than they have in the crown, to which it is annexed. They have a right to the use and profits of it: but in the meantime the property of it is in the society. And since all alienations of a thing, which is not the property of the person who makes the alienation, are void; any alienation of this patrimony will be void, if it is made by the king alone, without the consent of the society, signified either by itself, or by its representatives.

Our author observes farther, that this general rule does not admit of an exception upon account of the small value of the thing, which is alienated. A man has no more right to alienate what is not his own, where the thing is of small value, than where it is of great value. The only difference arising from the value of the thing alienated, is, that where it is of small value, it is more reasonable to presume upon the consent of the people, from their silence, or their not opposing the alienation, than where it is of great value: because it is more likely, that the people are willing to part with the one, than with the other.

* But we are to distinguish between the patrimony of the crown, and the fruits or profits, which have accrued from that patrimony. For though the present possessor has no property in the patrimony itself; yet, since the use and profits are his, he will have property in such profits as have actually accrued. And thus, whilst the patrimony itself is not alienable without the consent of the society, such profits will be alienable by his own act. Thus the right to certain customs, duties, or tolls, may be a part of the patrimony: but the money, which has been already received from such customs, duties, or tolls, is the fruit or profit of it. The right to receive and obtain property in confiscated estates may be a part of the patrimony: but estates, which have been already confiscated, are amongst the profits. But whilst we say, that these profits are alienable; we should remember, that even in kingdoms, where the king has legislative power, such alienations may be prevented by fundamental laws; and in other kingdoms they may be prevented by laws, which are made by the legislative body.

† There is one contract, which Grotius says will be valid, notwithstanding the king has only an usufructuary right in the patrimony of the crown; though it is a contract, which seems to dispose of this patrimony. A mortgage of such patrimony, to raise money for the service of the state, will be so far binding, that the society will be obliged to redeem it. But then he rightly adds, that this contract produces such an effect only in those kingdoms, where the king alone has a constitutional right to tax the people for the public service. In such kingdoms, the society, as it is obliged to pay those taxes, which are laid upon it by the king, for the necessary purposes of government, will be obliged,

* Grot. Lib. II. Cap. VI. § XII.

† Grot. Ibid. § XIII.

likewise, to redeem the patrimony of the crown, when he has mortgaged it for these purposes: because such a redemption is, in effect, only the payment of such taxes. But this reason is plainly not applicable, where the king has no power to lay any taxes upon the subjects, besides what are proposed and consented to by themselves or their representatives. And, consequently, in such mixed constitutions of government, as he has no right to alienate the patrimony of the crown, so neither has he any right to mortgage it by his own act.

*Though a king, with legislative power, can, as we have seen, set aside the promises, contracts or oaths of his subjects, by a subsequent law forbidding performance; yet he cannot make his own acts void in the same manner: because this power, in respect of his subjects, arises from a principle which cannot be applied to himself. A subject, as far as the ends of entering into civil society extend, has no moral power of obliging himself, but under a condition, either express or tacit, that performance shall not be afterwards forbidden by the civil legislator. But this condition cannot be supposed to be contained in the promise, contract or oath of a king, having legislative power: because, he is not under the authority of any such legislator. His acts, therefore, when he has once engaged in them, if they were not invalid from the beginning, must stand good; as far as they are consistent with the law of nature, and the compact by which he holds his power. We have, indeed, distinguished above, between the private and the legislative, or sovereign capacity of such a king. But this distinction is of no use here: for the condition, which is the ground of the invalidity of promises, contracts or oaths, when they are once engaged in, consistently with the laws then in being, can be no otherwise made intelligible, than by supposing the promiser, contractor or juror, and the superior, who forbids performance, to be different persons: two different characters of one and the same person will not be sufficient to reconcile this condition with common sense. If we suppose the same person, acting in different characters, to have a power of undoing, in his legislative character, what he has done in his private character, his promise, contract or oath, with the tacit condition, in consequence of which it is supposed liable to be rendered invalid by some subsequent act of his own, will be to this effect:—I consent in my private capacity to be obliged, if I consent hereafter in my legislative capacity; which amounts only to saying, that I now consent to be obliged, if I consent hereafter.

But a civil legislator can release the members of the society from their promises, contracts or oaths, not only by a direct act, which affects them immediately, but likewise by an act, which in respect of them is an indirect one, as it immediately affects the persons to whom they are obliged, and affects them only remotely. This act of the legislator consists in taking away the claim, which arises from the promise, contract or oath. It may, therefore, be asked, whether a king, with legislative power, cannot release himself by a like indirect act from his own promises, contracts or oaths; that is, whether he cannot by a law of his own making, deprive the subjects of any claims which they have acquired by his consent. Grotius replies to this question, that a king, with legislative power, has no right, by virtue of such

* Grot. Lib. II. Cap. XIV. § III.

power, to deprive his subjects of their claims; whether they are claims upon himself, or upon one another; unless for the purpose of punishing those who have deserved it, or for some other purpose of public utility. And if, for any such purpose of public utility, he deprives any particular subjects of their claims, he is to take care that the society should contribute towards making them amends: because, by the social compact, the obligation of advancing the public utility rests equally upon all; and, consequently, the burden of advancing it cannot justly be thrown upon any one, or upon a few.. The master of a slave may, by the right of private despotism, deprive him of such claims as are contrary to his own benefit: because, the end of this right is the private benefit of the master. But a king, whose power is as absolute as the nature of civil power will admit it to be, has no such right: for though we speak of legislative power, when it is vested in one single person, as if it was absolute power, we only mean, that it is subject to no instituted or external restraints. It cannot be absolute, in the full sense of the word, so as to mean a power of doing whatever the person, in whom it is vested, has a mind to do: because it is in its own nature a limited power; it is only a power of governing a civil society; that is, of directing such a society and all its members, to what is for the general good, and of securing them in the enjoyment of all their rights, which are consistent with this general good. Whatever, therefore, a king, with legislative power, might be inclined to do; and whatever, with the help of executive power, joined to legislative, he might in fact be able to do, yet certainly, a power of directing a civil society and all its members to what is for the general good, and of securing them in the enjoyment of all their rights, which are consistent with this general good, can never give him a right to deprive them of any claims which they have acquired by his promises, contracts or oaths; unless where these claims are inconsistent with the ends of civil society.

Effect of civil laws on marriage.

XIV. The law of God, concerning marriage, whether we collect this law from the principles of right reason, or from his revealed word, has made this contract something different from others. It may, therefore, be proper to consider it separately, in order to determine how far the civil law can make it void, either for want of age in the parties, or for want of some particular ceremonies, either preceding or attending the contract itself. Most of the questions that arise upon this head, will be easily resolved, upon the same principles with these two, which follow: First, it is a question whether the civil law is consistent with the law of nature and of God, if it fixes the age of consent for marriage at twenty-one years, or at any other particular period of life; and enacts, that all marriages which are solemnized without consent of parents or guardians, where both or either of the parties are under this age, shall be nullities from the beginning, or shall be void to all intents and purposes whatsoever. And, secondly, it is a question, whether the civil law is consistent with the law of nature and of God, if it enacts, in like manner, that all marriages shall be nullities, or be void from the beginning, to all intents and purposes whatsoever; unless previous notice is given, that such marriages are intended to be solemnized, and unless they are solemnized in a church, or in some other particular place which the law appoints. The same principles that are to be made use of for resolving these two questions, will, if they are rightly understood, be equally applicable to all other questions of the like sort.

Our religious notion of marriage is contained in what Christ has declared concerning it. He has taught us, that when a man and a woman are bound to each other as husband and wife, they are to be deemed as inseparable, as if they were one flesh; that this was the original intention and appointment of God; and, consequently, that they who are thus joined together by his authority, cannot be put asunder by the authority of man. Our notions of marriage, as we collect them from God's natural law, are of much the same sort. This, then, being the law of God concerning marriage, we are to inquire, whether the civil law is inconsistent with it, when it enacts, that any marriages shall be void, to all intents and purposes whatsoever, for want of some circumstances which this law requires.

We have supposed the civil law to say, that all marriages shall be void, where both or either of the parties are under the age of twenty-one years, if they are solemnized without the consent of the parents or guardians of the party so under age. Now, a small alteration in the words of such a civil law, would make it speak the language of the law of nature. * All marriages are void by the law of nature, if they are solemnized without consent of parents; where both or either of the parties are too young to be capable of judging and choosing for themselves. Until we arrive at the full use of our reason, nature places us under the authority of our parents, if they are living; and either by their act, or by the act of the law, our guardians succeed into their place, if they are dead. In this period of life, as we have no understanding of our own to judge, and no will of our own to choose what is best for us to do, it is the duty of our parents to take care of us, and to contrive for our benefit: and this duty gives them a natural right to judge and to choose for us. A male or a female, though they are under the age of discretion, may, indeed, be able to speak such words, or to act over such ceremonies, as custom has made expressive of consent to a bargain of cohabitation for the purposes of marriage. But since they are then under the authority of their parents, they have no moral power of acting for themselves, or no liberty of giving consent without the concurrence of their parents. These words, therefore, and these ceremonies will stand for nothing; they will be attended with no moral effect; that is, they will produce no obligation. We may, if we please, give the name of marriage to what they have done; or, rather, to what they have attempted to do, by repeating such words, and by acting over such ceremonies. But if both the parties are too young to judge and to choose for themselves, it will be a void marriage: because neither of them are capable of binding themselves to the other, as husband or wife, by their own act. Or if only one of them is under such incapacity, this will be sufficient to make the marriage void: because, it is a well known rule in contracts, of the matrimonial as well as of any other sort, that there is no obligation upon either party, unless there is a mutual obligation upon both.

These are undoubted principles of the law of nature: and we no where find any positive law of God, which has changed or overruled

* See Book I. Chap. XV. § XIII.

them. He has no where enjoined, that, notwithstanding a male or a female are naturally incapable of binding themselves by any other contract, without the consent of their parents, whilst they are under the age of discretion, they shall be deemed capable of binding themselves by a matrimonial contract. His revealed law does, indeed, say, and his natural law speaks to the same purpose, that, when a man and a woman are become husband and wife, they are as inseparable as if they were only one flesh. But this law is nothing to the purpose in the question which is now before us. We are not inquiring whether a man and a woman can be separated from one another, consistently with the law of God, after they are become husband and wife; but whether there is any law of God which has empowered a male and a female, whilst they are under the age of discretion, to make themselves husband and wife, by their own act, without the concurrence of their parents. It is granted that the marriage contract is in its own nature perpetual and indissoluble; that they, who are joined together by the authority of God, cannot be put asunder by the authority of men. But it is not inconsistent with this notion of marriage to put a male and a female asunder, who come together under a natural incapacity of binding themselves to one another by a marriage contract: because it does not appear, that, in these circumstances, they are joined together by the authority of God. Though they make a bargain, or rather attempt to make a bargain, of cohabitation for the purposes of marriage, in any words, or according to any form whatsoever, we know, that God's natural law declares such bargain to be a nullity; and no positive law of God can be produced which says the contrary. Thus far, therefore, the civil law would agree with our natural notions of the marriage contract; and would not contradict our religious notions, if it was only to enact, that all marriages shall be void, which are solemnized without consent of parents, where both or either of the parties are under the age of discretion.

But we have supposed the civil law to enact, that all such marriages shall be void, where both or either of the parties are under the age of twenty-one years, or some other particular period of life, which the same law fixes as the age of discretion. The only point, which remains to be considered in this change of the question, is, whether twenty-one years of age can be fixed by the civil law as the age of discretion, consistently with the law of God: and this seems to be a point, which can scarce admit of any doubt. No law of God, either positive or natural, has fixed the precise age, at which all persons shall be deemed capable of acting for themselves, and be exempted from the authority of their parents. We are then capable of acting for ourselves, and are, consequently, then exempted from the authority of our parents, when we come to the full use of our reason. But since this may happen at different times of life to different persons, in different countries, or even in the same country, the civil legislator of any community is at liberty to fix that period of life, as the age of discretion, at which experience and observation have shown the judgment of those, who live in the same climate with himself, to be usually ripe.

Upon these principles, the civil laws of our own country have long determined twenty-one years to be the age of consent for other contracts; and the ecclesiastical canons have long considered all persons, till they are arrived at this age, as under the authority of their parents or guardians, in respect of the matrimonial contract. We may easily guess what principle our civil law proceeded upon, when it fixed the age of consent in matrimonial contracts lower than this, at twelve years for the woman, and at fourteen for the man. Perhaps these ages might have been well enough fixed, if marriage had been ordained for no other end, besides the production of children; or for no other end, besides what might have been obtained without any understanding or judgment in the parties concerned. But we are taught, that it was ordained, as well for the careful education, as for the production of children; as well for advancing the domestic happiness of the parties, as for satisfying their appetites in a regular manner, if they have not the gift of continence. And whatever other purpose of marriage a woman at twelve, or a man at fourteen years of age, may be supposed capable of answering; they are certainly not capable of answering these. The education of children, and the domestic comfort, which the husband and wife ought to have of each other, require more prudence than is commonly to be met with at these respective ages. There seems, indeed, to be a sort of contradiction in the civil law of any country, if it allows a male and a female to be capable of binding themselves by a contract, in which they undertake the duty of educating children, at a time of life, when it considers them, in other respects, as children themselves; if it allows them to dispose of their own persons for ever, at their own discretion, by a contract, upon which they stake their future ease and happiness, at a time of life, when it considers them as having too little discretion to be trusted with the disposal of five shillings, without advice and direction.

There can be no possible grounds for imagining, that either the nature of the marriage contract, or any positive law of God concerning this contract, has restrained the civil legislator from confining the civil advantages of marriage to those marriages only, which are solemnized in such places and according to such forms, as he prescribes for the general good. The husband's claim to the wife's personal estate, the wife's claim to dower, and some other claims of the like sort, are civil advantages of marriage, or advantages which the civil law annexes to this contract. Among these, we may likewise reckon the civil legitimacy of the children; that is, their claim to inherit or to transmit either honours or property in intestate succession. Such effects of marriage as these, were introduced at first, and are supported afterwards, only by civil laws, and not by any law of nature, or by any divine law of positive institution. And the same law, or rather the same legislative power, by which these claims were created, has an unquestionable right to regulate and to limit them. If, therefore, the civil law was only to say, that such marriages, as are solemnized without any previous notice, and such, likewise, as are not solemnized in a church, or some other particular place, which the law appoints, shall be void to all civil intents and purposes; there could be little reason to doubt of its consistency with the natural and revealed law of God.

But we have supposed the civil law to go farther, and to enact, that such marriages shall be void, not only as to all civil intents and purposes, but as to all intents and purposes whatsoever; by which we must understand the legislator to mean, that they shall give neither of the parties a right to the person of the other, nor be attended with any obligation on either side. Here the old question will return, whether a contract, which, in its own nature, is perpetual, can be dissolved by the civil law? whether they, who are joined together by God, can be put asunder by man? We cannot, indeed, deny the truth of the principle, upon which this question proceeds: but we may well maintain, that it is not applicable to the point in debate. The principle, upon which it proceeds, is plainly this:—When a male and a female are become husband and wife; the law of nature declares, that the contract which made them such, is perpetual; and the revealed law of God speaks the same language, and declares, that no human authority can put them asunder. The point in debate is:—Whether the civil law can take from a male and a female the power of binding themselves to each other as husband and wife, by a matrimonial contract, according to any form, or in any place, that they please. The question, therefore, arising out of this principle, as far as it is applicable to the point in debate, ought not to be:—Whether the civil law can dissolve a contract, which the law of nature has made perpetual; or whether they, who are joined together by God, can be put asunder by man? but;—Whether a male and a female can make any matrimonial contract at all, or bind themselves to each other as husband and wife; if they proceed in such a manner, as the civil law has forbidden, and declared not to be binding. For if, when they have proceeded in such a manner, there is no contract, and the two parties are not husband and wife; it does not appear, that they are joined together by God: and, consequently, as our natural and religious notions of marriage would allow them to be put asunder, so our common notions of decency will inform us, that they ought not to come together.

In the liberty of nature, if a single man and a single woman of full age were to make a bargain of cohabitation for the purposes of marriage, either in a church or in any other place, either in the words and according to the forms, which are prescribed in our book of common prayer, or in any other words, and according to any other forms of their own choosing, which sufficiently express their free and mutual consent; such a bargain would be a good and a valid marriage; the two parties would be bound to each other as husband and wife; and when they are so bound, the law of God, as we either collect it from reason, or read it in his revealed word, has made the obligation perpetual. But when the man and the woman are considered as members of a civil society; we should observe, that the act of joining themselves to such society, implies, that they agree to submit their rights or moral powers of acting at their own discretion, and amongst the rest, their right of marrying according to what form and in what place they please, to be regulated and limited by the common understanding of the society, either for the public good of the whole body, or for the general good of its several parts. For though the law of God has established the perpetuity of the marriage contract, and has, by this means, deprived the man and the woman of their liberty of parting from one another, after they are become husband and wife; yet it has not prescribed any particular place, or any particular form, for making this contract: so that the right of marrying in what place, and according to what form they please, as it consists in a full liberty, is alienable in its own nature, and is actually given up by the social compact, as far as the common understanding of the society shall find it to be necessary, or conducive to the general good, to restrain this liberty. Whenever, therefore, the laws of their country prescribe, that all marriages shall be solemnized in some particular place, and according to some particular form, and enact, that no marriage solemnized in any other place, or according to any other form, shall be binding; the effect of such laws will be, that the man and the woman will have no right, or no liberty, or no moral power, of consenting to a marriage contract any otherwise, than as the laws direct. If they make, or rather attempt to make, a bargain of cohabitation for the purposes of marriage, in any other place, or according to any other form; we may call this attempt a solemnization of marriage, for want of a better name for it: but in the meantime the bargain will not be binding upon either party; and what we call a marriage, will be a mere nullity, upon the principles of the law of nature. For it is a known principle of the law of nature, that no person can be bound by any act, where he has no right, or liberty, or moral power of binding himself; that no words or ceremonies, however custom may have made them expressive of consent, can produce any obligation, where the person, who makes use of these words or ceremonies, has not the liberty of consenting. A man and a woman may repeat such words, or go through such ceremonies, as are expressive of their consenting to a bargain of cohabitation for the purposes of marriage; but no obligation will arise from the words or ceremonies themselves; where the parties had no moral power of consenting. If they had an intention of binding themselves to each other as husband and wife; this, indeed, implies the consent of their minds: and, consequently, the words and ceremonies are in one respect not mere sounds and empty forms; because they are designed by the parties, who use them, to express this consent of mind. But if they had no liberty of consenting, then, in respect of any effect or obligation, which might be supposed to arise from this act, they will be mere sounds and empty forms; they may express the consent of the parties, but it is such a consent, as produces no obligation. For the marriage contract is thus far, like all other contracts: the natural power or intention of consenting does not make us capable of binding ourselves by this or by any other contract: we are no otherwise capable of binding ourselves, than by having a moral power; that is, a right or liberty of consenting. We allow, therefore, that, when a man and a woman are bound to each other as husband and wife, the law of God forbids us to put them asunder; we allow that, when a bargain of cohabitation, for the purposes of marriage, produces any obligation, the law of God makes this obligation perpetual. But in the meantime, we affirm the effect of such a civil law as we have been describing, to be, that, when a marriage is solemnized otherwise than the law requires, the parties are not bound to each other as husband and wife; the bargain, which they have made in words, is no bargain at all, and produces no obligation.

In short, when we are examining either these or any other questions, which relate to the power of the civil law, to annul a marriage once solemnized, we are apt to mislead ourselves by not taking the matter up high enough. By solemnizing a marriage, we only mean, that a man and a woman have repeated such words, or gone through such ceremonies, as custom or law has made expressive of a bargain of cohabitation for the purposes of marriage. When they have done this, we suppose them to be bound to each other as husband and wife, without inquiring, whether they were capable of so binding themselves or not. And then, upon this supposition, in which we take the very point in question for granted, we readily conclude, that they are joined together by God, and, consequently, that they cannot be put asunder by man. But instead of considering the effects of a good and a valid marriage, we should here consider, whether the marriage is a good and a valid one. If the male and the female are under the age of discretion, and are, therefore, subject to the authority of their parents; or if they are members of a civil society, and are, therefore, subject to the laws of their country; or, if upon any other account, they have no liberty, or no moral power of consenting; such words, or such ceremonies, as are expressive of consent, and in other circumstances would have produced a good and a valid marriage, will, in these circumstances, stand for nothing or have no meaning, and will produce no obligation. The male and the female, therefore, by repeating those words, and by going through those ceremonies, though this act, for want of a better name, is called solemnizing a marriage, will not have bound themselves to each other as husband and wife. But if they are not husband and wife, our natural or our religious notion of marriage is out of the question: if there is no contract at all, there cannot be any perpetual contract; if they are not joined together at all, they cannot be joined together by God; and, consequently, we can have no grounds for concluding, that they cannot be put asunder by man.

When a marriage is thus, to all intents and purposes whatsoever, made a nullity from the beginning, by the act of the civil law; there can be no obligation of natural justice upon the parties, to abide by the contract, and to cohabit as husband and wife. For if they have no right or moral power of consenting, they cannot lay themselves under any obligation of justice. And we have seen already that the civil law produces its effect, or makes the marriage a nullity, by taking from them their right or moral power of consenting. Indeed, where the civil law only makes a marriage ineffectual for obtaining certain civil purposes, upon account of its wanting some forms prescribed by such law, but allows the validity of it as to other purposes; the parties are obliged, in natural justice, to cohabit, and their bargain of cohabitation is naturally a good marriage: because, though, by a marriage contract, which wants those forms, they are incapable of obtaining the advantage annexed by the civil law to other marriages, in which those forms are observed; yet the same law, by allowing the validity of their marriage in other respects, leaves them at liberty to bind themselves to one another, as husband and wife. But where the civil law of any society enacts, that a marriage, for want of age in the parties, or of certain forms in the contract, shall be void to all intents and purposes whatsoever; it does not allow the validity of such marriage in any respect, but renders the parties, who contract otherwise than the law allows, incapable of so binding themselves to one another. And though this incapacity arises immediately from the civil law; yet since it arises ultimately from their own consent, as they are members of the society, it may properly be considered as an incapacity, by the law of nature.

Some contracts, which the civil law makes void, are understood to oblige in conscience, though not in strict justice; they produce an obligation to performance, though it is not a perfect obligation. But this obligation takes place only in such contracts as the civil law makes void for the benefit of one of the parties, and leaves him at liberty, if he pleases, to waive this benefit. It cannot, therefore, take place in void marriages: because the civil law makes them void in order to hinder the parties from obtaining any benefit by them, and by this means to secure some benefit to others, in particular to the parents of one or both the parties, who might be made unhappy by an improper marriage of their children. This circumstance alone is sufficient to distinguish the case of a marriage, which the civil law makes void, from the case of a debt which it makes void. But there is another very material circumstance, which puts a farther distinction between these two cases, and shows us, that, notwithstanding any obligation of the imperfect sort to pay a void debt, yet there is not the like obligation to cohabit upon a void marriage. What is contained in a contract of borrowing money might be performed by the borrower, though there was no contract at all. He might, if he pleased, give the lender the same sum of money, that he has borrowed, whether he had ever borrowed it or not. And, consequently, though the contract is a nullity, there is nothing vicious in the performance, merely for want of a contract. Whereas, what is contained in a marriage contract is unlawful, when there is no contract: for cohabitation without a marriage contract, is naturally vicious. Unless, therefore, we will maintain, that where a man and a woman are incapable of binding themselves to one another, as husband and wife, by a marriage contract, they are capable of binding themselves in conscience to do what is vicious, we must necessarily allow, that they can be under no obligation to cohabit, as if they were husband and wife, upon a marriage, which the civil law has made void to all intents and purposes whatsoever.

The law of God concerning marriage, produces its proper effect, not by making all persons, of any age or in any circumstances, capable of contracting a good and valid marriage, but by making all marriages perpetual or indissoluble, which have once been contracted by persons who are of such age and in such circumstances, as to have the liberty or right of binding themselves by a marriage contract.

Civil laws set aside other contracts two ways: either by enjoining beforehand, that they shall not be made so as to obtain any effect; or else, by enjoining afterwards, that they shall not be performed. No law of God, either natural or positive, has restrained the civil legislator from setting marriages aside in the former of these ways, by enjoining beforehand, that they shall not be solemnized with effect, or so as to bind the parties in any other manner than what the civil law prescribes. What the law of God enjoins is, that a marriage, which is solemnized in such a manner as to be once binding upon the parties, shall be of perpetual obligation. I do not say, that the law of God enjoins this merely concerning a marriage which is once solemnized. For solemnizing a marriage is an expression which is used in two senses. Sometimes when we say, that a marriage is solemnized between a man and a woman, we only mean, that they have repeated such words, or gone through such ceremonies as are expressive of a bargain of cohabitation for the purposes of marriage; whether any obligation arises from what they have done or not. Thus, if a man, whose wife is living and undivorced from him, should repeat such words and go through such ceremonies with a second woman, we should say, that a marriage had been solemnized between the man and this second woman; though in the meantime we know that no obligation of marriage arises from this act. But, sometimes, when we speak of solemnizing a marriage, we use this expression in a stricter sense; and mean solemnizing it with effect, so that the man and the woman, by what they have done, are become husband and wife. If we have been brought up from our infancy in a country, where the civil law has allowed almost all marriages to be binding, provided certain words and certain ceremonies have been made use of; it is no wonder, if we should be led to think, that what we have long found to be the same thing in fact, is likewise the same thing in right; that solemnizing a marriage in one of these senses, is solemnizing it in the other sense; that repeating these words and going through these ceremonies necessarily produces an obligation; and, consequently, that to set aside a marriage once solemnized, is the same thing as to set aside a marriage, which has been so solemnized as to be once binding. But by attending to this distinction, we may be enabled to see what effect the law of God, concerning marriage, does not produce, and what effect it does produce. This law does not make all marriages binding, which have once been solemnized; it only makes all marriages perpetual, which have been solemnized in such a manner as to be once binding. It does not make all words, that express a marriage contract, operate like a charm, and bind the conscience whenever they pass through the mouth; nor does it give those, who repeat such words, a liberty or moral power of consenting, in consequence of their being willing to be man and wife; that is, of their having a natural power of consenting; it only takes from mankind all right or authority to separate those, who being at liberty to consent; that is, who being under no restraint, either from the law of God or of man, which might take away their moral power of consenting, have bound themselves to each other as husband and wife, by a valid bargain of cohabitation for the purposes of marriage. The civil legislator, therefore, has the same authority to make marriages void from the beginning, that he has to make any other contract void, by some antecedent law, which takes from the parties their liberty of consenting, or renders them incapable of consenting with any effect.

The only difference between the marriage contract and other contracts is, that other contracts, though they are valid from the beginning, may be rescinded or made void afterwards by some subsequent civil law, which forbids performance: whereas, when a marriage is solemnized in such a manner as to be once binding, no subsequent civil law can rescind it afterwards, by forbidding performance, consistently with the natural and revealed law of God, which has made this contract perpetual. When civil laws rescind other contracts by a subsequent act of the legislator, forbidding performance, they produce this effect, consistently with the law of nature, by means of a condition, which is included in the obligation of every member of a civil society. This condition is, that he consents to be obliged by his contract, if the civil law does not forbid performance. The social compact, in which, as a member of the society, he is a party, makes such a condition natural: because, by this compact, he obliged himself to submit all his alienable rights to whatever restraints and regulations the common understanding should judge to be necessary for the general good. He cannot, therefore, whilst he is under this obligation; that is, whilst he continues in the society, lay himself under any other obligation, which does not include this as a necessary condition. If our right, in respect of the marriage contract, was a right of full liberty; if we were originally free to choose for ourselves, whether we would make this contract temporary and precarious, or perpetual and constant; this right amongst others of the same sort would be alienable; the social compact would subject it to the civil power; and as members of a civil society, we could only bind ourselves in marriage by a perpetual contract, upon condition that the civil law should not rescind it after it is made. But our right in respect of the marriage contract, is not a right of full liberty: the law of God has not left us free, when we bind ourselves by this contract, to make it either temporary and precarious, or perpetual and constant; we are at liberty, on the one hand, to bind ourselves by a perpetual contract, or not to bind ourselves at all; but if we choose to make ourselves parties in this contract, we are not at liberty on the other hand, but are obliged by the law of God to make it a perpetual one. We cannot, therefore, oblige ourselves to the contrary by the social compact; and, consequently, when we consent to a marriage contract, we cannot be understood to consent that it shall be perpetual, upon condition of its not being rescinded afterwards. This condition takes place only in respect of such rights to bind ourselves, as are subjected to the civil legislator by the social compact: whereas, the right to bind ourselves by a perpetual marriage contract, if we bind ourselves by any marriage contract at all, could not be thus subjected to the civil legislator, consistently with our obligation to obey the law of God.

Civil laws are written or unwritten.

XV. We commonly distinguish civil laws into written and unwritten: but we seldom form such precise notions of each as will keep up the distinction, and show us wherein the difference between them consists. Every rule of action which is enjoined by a civil legislator, and committed to writing, does not immediately become a written civil law. Such laws as are established by long and uninterrupted usage or custom, may certainly be committed to writing, as well as any other: but this does not change them from unwritten into written laws. Every precept of unwritten law may be expressed in words: and whatever can be expressed in words, may certainly be written down: and when any precept of unwritten law is thus written down, it will be as much a law, as it was before; and may be called a law in writing, if you please: but if you call it a written law, you will give it an improper name. We must, therefore, look for some other definition of a written law besides the common one; which only says, that it is a law committed to writing. No rule of action, though it is prescribed by a civil legislator, and is committed to writing, can be called a written civil law; unless the writing contains all that is essential to a civil law. Now, the essence of a civil law consists in its being a rule of action prescribed by the authority of a civil legislator. If, therefore, the writing only contains the rule which the civil legislator prescribed, but does not contain the evidence of its having been prescribed by his authority; that is, if such writing is not authenticated by him, it will not contain all that is essential to a civil law; and, consequently, it can only be called a law in writing, but will be no written law. But by defining a written law to be a rule of action, which is prescribed in writing by a civil legislator, or which is prescribed by the authority of a civil legislator, and is committed to writing by the same authority, we shall distinguish it from all those rules of action which are prescribed by the authority of a civil legislator, any otherwise than in writing; though they should afterwards be committed to writing by some one else, who has not the same authority.

When civil legislators are professedly employed in making laws, instead of trusting their acts to the precarious custody of unwritten tradition, they usually record what they have done in writing; that so the several members of the society, who are concerned in the laws of it, may know both where to find them and what they are. Unwritten laws, therefore, either were not made at first by a civil legislator, professedly employed in the business of legislation, but have arisen out of immemorial and uninterrupted usage and custom; or else, if they were made at first by a civil legislator, professedly employed in this business, the evidence of their having been so made is lost, and they have only the authority of the like usage and custom to support them.

Unwritten laws, how established.

XVI. Whatever usage has obtained in any civil society for time *immemorial, without being interrupted, may be presumed to be agreeable to the sense of such society, and to have obtained with its consent: because the usage must in so long a time have come to the knowledge of the public; and if the society had not consented to it, there must have been frequent opportunities either of interrupting it in fact, or of declaring a dislike of it in words. But whatever is consented to by a civil society, becomes a law of such society: and, consequently, any usage which has obtained for time immemorial, is established into a law by prescription. The particular consent of each member of the society is not necessary for the purpose of establishing any usage, or the rules arising out of any usage, into laws. For the general consent of the society binds each of its members: and any rules which arise out of such usage, as has continued for time immemorial, without being interrupted by any act of the public, become laws to all whom the society intended to include within those rules. Unwritten laws will establish themselves in the same manner; not only in a perfect democracy, where the legislative power is in the hands of the whole collective body of the society, but under such forms of government, likewise, as commit this power to some particular legislative body. The standing legislator of a civil society, if he does not consent to any usage, which generally obtains amongst the members of such society, might at any time interrupt or stop it, by forbidding it. If, therefore, it has continued long enough to be notorious, and is not interrupted by any act of his, he may be presumed to consent to it: and this concurrence of the legislator, thus collected, will be sufficient to give it the force of a law.

But though the consent of a civil society, or of its legislative body collected from long and uninterrupted usage, establishes such usage into a general law, yet a law so established admits of exceptions. It binds only those whom the society intended to bind by it: for no positive law

*See Book I. Chap. VIII. § I. V. VIII.

extends farther than the intention of the legislator: and, consequently, if any particular customs, different from the general usage, have obtained without interruption, for time immemorial, in respect of particular persons, or places, or things, these customs will be exceptions to the general law, and will themselves be the laws of those persons, places, or things, in respect of which they have so obtained. These particular customs, which are exceptions to the general law, are established by the same means, and upon the same authority with the law itself, by the consent of the society, or of its legislative body, collected from its not putting a stop to them, notwithstanding they have obtained for so long a time, that they must, in all probability, have fallen under public notice.

Unwritten law more difficult to be ascertained than written law.

XVII. There is a plain reason why it should be more difficult to find out what is prescribed by an unwritten law, than by a written one. The rules of unwritten law may, indeed, be committed to writing. But when they are, it will still be a question, whether such writing contains the law or not: because it will not appear, from the writing itself, that it is authenticated; or that the rules, which it contains, are prescribed by any legislator. The law is founded in usage or custom only: and, consequently, it can only be collected from usage or custom. In the meantime the members of a civil society are not left to their own observations to find out the unwritten laws of it. The records of what has been done, from time to time, in courts of judicature, are evidences of the unwritten law; not only as to the methods of proceeding in the court itself, but likewise as to those points which have come into question before it. If the methods of proceeding in the court itself are grounded upon unwritten law, the law which regulates its proceedings, having thus arisen out of its own practice, can appear only in its own records. The law, upon which any points of controversy have been determined by the court, will likewise appear in the same records: because they show what the usage and custom appeared to be upon the fullest information that the court could get. When * Grotius, therefore, teaches us to have recourse, not only to our own observations, but to the judgment of others, who have had more and better opportunities than we have had, of making observations upon such general usage or particular custom, as has established itself into a law, he points out the principle upon which the determinations of courts of judicature are to be received as the most authentic evidences of unwritten law. The principle is, that their determinations are authentic evidences of what the usage or custom appeared to be upon the exactest scrutiny.

Unwritten laws, how repealed.

XVIII. The unwritten laws of a civil society are sometimes repealed or altered by an express act of the legislative body of the society; that is, though they were established at first by usage or custom, they are sometimes repealed or altered afterwards by written laws. They may, likewise, be repealed or altered by long disuse or prescription: for, as the consent of the society, upon which they are established, is collected only from the presumptive evidence of usage or custom; so a long and uninterrupted disuse affords the same evidence, that the society has consented to repeal or alter them.

* Grot. Lib. I. Cap. I. § XIV.

Written laws cannot be repealed by prescription.

XIX. But if disuse repeals an unwritten law, only as it is a presumptive evidence that the society has consented to repeal such law, the consequence will be, that no written law can be repealed merely by disuse; *because no presumption can set aside a certainty: the record, in which the written law appears, is a certain evidence of its having been established by sufficient authority; whereas, disuse affords, at most, only a presumption of its having been repealed by the like authority.

Written laws are, indeed, sometimes said to be grown obsolete. But then, by their being obsolete, we are not to understand, that they have ceased to oblige, whenever it shall be found necessary to put them in execution. Sometimes a written law is said to be grown obsolete, when the circumstances of those, to whom it relates, are so changed, that the execution of the law would be of no use, notwithstanding it might be a beneficial law at the time of making it. This happens more particularly, where the legislator had not the special matter of the law principally in view; but designed either to guard against some particular evil which might, as he thought, probably be prevented, or to obtain some particular good, which might, as he thought, probably be advanced, by using such cautions, and by following such directions, as are prescribed by the special matter of the law. When the evil, therefore, which was in view, is no longer to be feared, or when the good, which was in view, is effectually obtained, the law becomes useless. Sometimes, though the execution of the law would be of the same advantage now, as when it was first made, we say, that it is become obsolete, if it has not for any considerable time been put in execution; so that, what it enjoins has been long neglected, or what it forbids has been long practised with impunity.

Where written laws are become obsolete in the former sense, it may, with some reason, be called a hardship, if it is nothing more than a hardship, to put them in execution. For, since all civil laws either have, or ought to have, the prevention of some evil, or the attainment of some good in view, it is scarce consistent with the nature of a civil law, to lay any restraint upon the members of a society, or to punish them for not complying with any restraint, where no evil will be prevented or no good be obtained by their compliance.

But where laws are become obsolete, in the latter sense, either by any neglect of those whose business it is to put them in execution, or by any other accident, if it can be called a hardship to put them in execution afterwards, the only ground for calling it so is a supposition, that, through such long disuse, many persons may be ignorant of what the law requires of them. This hardship is effectually prevented, if the civil magistrate, or executive body, gives public notice beforehand, that such a law will be put in execution: and though we usually say, that a notice of this sort revives an obsolete law, yet this revival is made without an act of legislative power: the law is then in being, and all the members of the society, that are concerned in it, are already bound to comply with it: the notice, which the civil magistrate gives, only informs them of what, through long disuse, they might possibly have forgotten.

* See Book I. Chap. VIII.

General division of civil laws.

XX. Civil laws may be divided into three sorts; they are either public, or private, or mixed. Public laws are such as have the civil power of the public for their object. These laws may again be divided into such as are fundamental, and such as are not fundamental. Such public laws are called fundamental, as prescribe the form, and establish the constitutional power of the legislative body of the society. Laws, which determine the form of the legislative body, and give one part of the society an exclusive right or power of legislation, cannot well be understood to have been derived, originally, from the legislative body itself. No part of the society has, originally, any exclusive right of legislation: this right or power, as it arises out of civil union, is vested in the whole collective body. And if no part has, originally, any right of this sort, it cannot acquire any such right, by any act of its own; unless the rest concur in this act, and by so concurring, make it the act of the whole.

Laws of this sort, are usually understood to bind the legislative body itself, and not to be alterable by its authority. And for this reason, when a legislative body, after it is established, declares any law of its own making, to be a fundamental law, or a law of the constitution, the meaning of this declaration is, that the legislative body looks upon itself to be bound by this law.

But there are many laws in every civil society, which are public, though they are not fundamental; many which relate to the civil power, though they are derived from the constitutional legislative body, and are at all times subject to its authority. All laws which regulate or restrain the executive body, either in the internal or external branch of its executive power, are of this sort. Those laws are public, but not fundamental ones, which determine the method of calling and appointing civil magistrates to their respective offices, which settle the extent and limits of their power, or which regulate the proceedings in courts of judicature; and those, likewise, which fix the manner of raising, and governing, and maintaining the military force.

Civil laws, which adjust the mutual rights and obligations of the members of a civil society, in respect of one another, may be called private laws: because they relate more particularly to private persons. Of this sort are all such laws, as regulate the right, that a man has over his own person, or to direct his own actions; all such, as either determine the manner of acquiring, or holding, or alienating private property, or regulate the several limitations, to which private property is subject; and all such, as prescribe the form, and settle the effect of promises, or contracts, or oaths, not only of those, by which private property, or a right in things may be acquired, but of those, likewise, by which one member of the society acquires a right over the person of another.

Those civil laws may be called mixed ones, which regulate and prescribe the mutual rights and obligations of the public or society, and of the several members or private persons, who are under its protection. Of this sort are all such laws, as guard the common welfare, by enforcing the duties, which we owe either to God or to ourselves; all such, as determine the right, which the public has over the persons of the subjects to demand their assistance, either in executing the laws within the society, or in defending it against its enemies from without;

all such, as prescribe what taxes, duties, or customs are to be paid by the subjects, by adjusting the demand of the public upon the private property of the individuals, for the support of the government, or for maintaining the common security, and advancing the common benefit; and all such, likewise, as regulate and ascertain the special obedience which the subjects owe to their established governors. To the same head, we may reduce all criminal or penal laws in general; because all crimes are offences of private persons against the public; and all punishment, in a state of civil society, is inflicted by the public, upon private persons.

In some constitutions the civil laws of succession to the crown, cannot be fundamental laws.

XXI. It may be a question, whether a civil law, which settles the succession to a kingdom, is a fundamental law or not. But unless this question is stated more precisely, it cannot well be understood: because, in some constitutions it may, and in others it cannot be a fundamental law. In order, therefore, to determine rightly upon this question, it will be necessary to distinguish between those kingdoms, in which the king alone is the legislative body, and those, in which he is only a part of such body, whilst the whole society, either by itself, or by its representatives, is the other part. And if the king alone is the constitutional legislative body, it will be necessary to distinguish farther between those kingdoms which are, and those which are not, patrimonial.

First, in a patrimonial kingdom, if the king is the sole legislative body, there is, by the supposition, no law at all, and, therefore, certainly, no fundamental law, which regulates the succession: because the law which settled the form of government, and the compact, made upon this law between the king and the people, are supposed to have given the king, who is in possession, a power of choosing and fixing his successor. If any thing, which relates to the succession, can be called fundamental, it is the obligation of the present possessor, to leave the kingdom to his successor in the same condition, in which he received it himself; that is, to leave it patrimonial, without entailing it any farther, than upon the next immediate successor, by any law of his own making. As he received it in this condition from the people, he has no constitutional power of altering their act, without their consent. And in fact, if he was to attempt to alter it, what he does would be prevented from producing any effect, unless he had the concurrence of the people: because, whatever he does without their concurrence, is done only by a law of his own making: and since he transmits his own legislative power to the next immediate successor, this successor will have the same right to alter this law, that he had to make it: the consequence of which will be, that the entail, which he introduces, cannot take place without the consent of such successor.

Secondly, if the law, which fixes the succession to the crown, can be looked upon as fundamental, it must be in those kingdoms, in which the king alone is the constitutional legislative body, and the crown is made hereditary by the same act of the people, which appointed their king to be their sole legislator. On the one hand, the king in possession, notwithstanding he is the sole legislative body, cannot change this law, without the consent of the people: because it was made, originally, by the legislative power of the society: and if it does not bind him as a law, yet it certainly binds him as a compact; because his immediate and direct consent to it, is implied in his acceptance of the crown, under the conditions, which the society has thus established. On the other hand, the people have, by the same compact, given up their legislative power to him, and, consequently, cannot, without his consent, repeal the law of the succession, which they have once established. The reader will do well to remember here, that we are now only considering the constitutional right of the people, and not any natural right, which they may have in cases of necessity, or where the constitution is broken.

However, without having recourse either to the equitable exception of necessity, or to a breach of the constitution, if the king in possession, and the body of the society concur in changing the law of the succession; there is no natural reason, why such a concurrent act should not be valid. For the notion of a fundamental law of any civil constitution does not consist in its being unalterable by any human power whatsoever, but in its being unalterable by the constitutional legislative body, where this body is only a part of the whole society. If there is any doubt, whether such a concurrent act can, of right, limit or alter the succession; this doubt must arise from a supposition, that the successors, before they come into possession, have acquired a right to succeed, which cannot, without their consent, be naturally taken from them. But it is evident, that if they, who would have succeeded, supposing the law had continued as it was, are yet unborn, they can have no right at all: and, consequently, no injury is done them, if the succession should, before they are born, be so limited or altered by the concurrent act of the king and the people, as to exclude them. The difficulty will be somewhat greater, if the successors are in being at the time, when this alteration is made. But there are two ways, in which we may explain this difficulty. In the first place, the supposed right of the successors is only an expectancy during the life of the present successor: this expectancy is supported by nothing but the law; it cannot become a right, in the proper sense of the word, till it is accepted: and as long as the present possessor lives, there can be no acceptance on the part of the successor. If, therefore, the law, which supported the expectancy, is changed, before the demise of the present possessor; this expectancy can never become a right at all. Or otherwise:—the successors must be considered either as parts of the legislative, or as parts of the collective body of the society. But during the life of the present possessor, the supposition here made, that he alone is the legislative body, excludes them from being considered as parts of this body. And if they are considered only as parts of the collective body, the general act of the society concludes them, whether they immediately and directly consent to such act or not.

Indeed, when we consider them only as parts of the collective body of the society, nothing but the general security or general benefit can justify a change of the succession: because the whole exercise of civil legislative power is to be directed by this end; whether that power is exercised to repeal an old law, or to make a new one; whether it is exercised by the constitutional legislative body, or by the collective body, or by both of them together. For since a civil society has no other power over its members, whether they are the successors to the kingdom, or others of inferior rank, besides what was originally designed for the general security, or general benefit; it has no right, either by making a new law, or by repealing an old one, to take away even the reasonable expectancy of advantage from any of its members, unless the general security, or general benefit requires that it should be taken away.

This account of what may be done in respect of the law of the succession to the crown, where the king alone is the legislative body, will show us, that this law is not a fundamental law of the constitution, but is liable to be changed by the legislative body, and may be changed by it, without breaking in upon the constitution; if the body of the society, either by itself, or by its representatives, is a part of such legislative. Where the constitution has given the sole legislative power to the king; he alone cannot change the succession, which was settled by a law derived from the original legislative power of the society: because this law is binding upon him by means of a compact between him and the people, which, as it established his right, established likewise the succession: and since he is only one of the parties to this compact, he cannot, by any act of his own, set the obligation of it aside. In like manner, the collective body of the society is only one of the parties to the same compact, which vested the legislative power in him: and, consequently, as it cannot, by any act of its own, make this compact void, so neither can it make any law which shall be binding, or repeal any which was binding: because, as long as this compact subsists, it has no legislative power. But neither of these reasons will hold in respect of a legislative body, of which the king is one part, and the body of the society, either by itself or by its representatives, is the other part. For, in such a mixed legislative as this, both the parties to the compact, which fixed the law of the succession, are always present: the king in possession is present on the one part; and the body of the society is present on the other part. If, indeed, the body of the society is itself distinguished into two parts; one of which consists of the select few called nobles, and the other of the bulk of the society, which is usually called the people; in all changes, that are made in the law of the succession to the crown, the concurrence of the nobles, when they are thus considered as a distinct part of the society, is as necessary as the concurrence of the rest of the people: because, the change, if it is duly made, must be made by the joint act of all who were parties in the compact, by which the succession was originally settled. No compact can be released, and no law can be altered, without the consent of all those who are parties to such compact, or without the concurrent act of all those by whose authority such law was established. The consent, therefore, of the king, in present possession, and of what is here called the people, either by themselves or by their representatives, will not be sufficient to produce a change in the succession, without the consent of the nobles; if they were distinct parties to the original settlement of it, and are not represented by the representatives of the people. But where the general body of the society is thus distinguished into the nobles and the people; if the constitutional legislative body consists of the king, who is in possession, and the nobles, and the representatives of the people, there are always present in such a legislative body, all the parties who could be concerned from the first in any settlement of the crown: and, consequently, such a legislative body will have a power to limit or to change the succession for the general security and benefit of the society.

Controverted succession may be settled by civil law.

XXII. * We may now understand what sort of kingdoms Grotius is speaking of, when he inquires, who can decide a controversy that arises in the life-time of a king, between two or more claimants to the succession. In those constitutions where the legislative body consists of the king and the whole body of the society, acting either by itself or by its representatives, this can be no question. For, since such a legislative body has a constitutional right of limiting the succession by a civil law, there can be no doubt of its having a like constitutional right of putting an end to a controversy of this sort by the same means.

The inquiry, therefore, relates to those constitutions only, where the king alone is the constitutional legislative body. Grotius tells his readers, in express words, that he had such a kingdom in his mind: and if he had not told them so, it might easily have been collected from the reason which he gives, why the people could not decide this controversy, and interpret the law of the succession authoritatively, so as finally to determine which of all the competitors has the best claim. The reason which he gives is, that the people have, by the constitution, entrusted all civil jurisdiction to their king. What he adds farther, would, if it was true, increase the difficulty. He supposes the civil jurisdiction to be given, not only to the king, but to his family likewise; so that the people, or the body of the society, whilst any of this family are in being, can have no jurisdiction at all, either by themselves alone, or jointly with the present possessor. But this supposition is not true: the several claimants, or any others of his family, have no civil jurisdiction in his life-time; they have only an expectancy of such a jurisdiction; and this expectancy will fail, if the law, which supports it, is altered before his death. However, the reason, which Grotius alleges, will conclude against the jurisdiction of the people to decide this controversy by themselves, or by their own authority, without this additional supposition: because, without considering the successors, the people have, by the civil constitution, vested the legislative power in the possessor of the crown for the time being.

As the people alone could not decide this controversy for want of legislative power, so neither could the king alone decide it: because, as Grotius observes, the right to the succession is not subject to the jurisdiction of the present possessor, unless in patrimonial kingdoms: in kingdoms, which are not patrimonial, if the king is the constitutional legislative body, the law of the succession comes originally from the people, and by compact between him and the people is made binding upon him.

But though the people alone cannot decide this controversy, for want of legislative power in general; and though the king alone cannot decide it, for want of legislative power in this particular instance, yet upon the principles which have just now been explained, the present possessor of the crown, and the body of the society together, have a right to decide it by a joint act. For all the parties to the original com-

* Grot. Lib. II. Cap. VII. § XXVII.

pact, by which the succession was settled at first, are included in the king and the body of the society: and, consequently, whatever they do, will be binding upon all.

CHAPTER VII.

OF INTERPRETATION.

I. *Interpretation, what.*—II. *Province of interpretation.*—III. *Three sorts of interpretation.*—IV. *Rules of literal interpretation.*—V. *Mixed interpretation, where to be used.*—VI. *Three topics of mixed interpretation.*—VII. *Words are to be construed agreeably to the subject matter.*—VIII. *Words are to be so construed as to produce a reasonable effect.*—IX. *Words of a law, or other writing, are to be construed by its circumstances.*—X. *Strict and large interpretation, what.*—XI. *Meaning of the writer how extended by rational interpretation.*—XII. *Meaning of the writer how restrained by rational interpretation.*—XIII. *Scarce any laws but what naturally admit of rational interpretation.*

Interpretation, what.

I. A *PROMISE, or a contract, or a will, gives us a right to whatever the promiser, the contractor, or the testator, designed or intended to make ours. But his design or intention, if it is considered merely as an act of his mind, cannot be known to any one besides himself. When, therefore, we speak of his design or intention as the measure of our claim, we must necessarily be understood to mean the design or intention, which he has made known or expressed by some outward mark: because a design or intention, which does not appear, can have no more effect, or can no more produce a claim, than a design or intention which does not exist.

In like manner, the obligations that are produced by the civil laws of our country, arise from the intention of the legislator; not merely as this intention is an act of the mind, but as it is declared or expressed by some outward sign or mark, which makes it known to us. For the intention of the legislator, whilst he keeps it to himself, produces no effect, and is of no more account than if he had no such intention. Where we have no knowledge, we can be under no obligation. We cannot, therefore, be obliged to comply with his will, where we do not know what his will is. And we can no otherwise know what his will is, than by means of some outward sign or mark, by which this will is expressed or declared.

From hence it appears, that the way to ascertain our claims, as they arise from promises, contracts or wills, and our obligations, as they arise from instituted laws, is to collect the meaning and intention of the promiser, contractor, testator, or lawmaker, from some outward signs or marks. The collecting of a man's intention from such signs or marks is called interpretation.

Province of interpretation.

II. †Words are the common signs that mankind make use of to declare their intention to one another: and

* Grot. Lib. II. Cap. XVI. § I.

† Grot. Ibid. § II. IV.

when the words of a man express his meaning plainly, distinctly and perfectly, we have no occasion to have recourse to any other means of interpretation. But sometimes a man's words are obscure; sometimes they are ambiguous; and sometimes they express his meaning so imperfectly, as either to fall short of his intention, and not express the whole of it, or else to exceed his intention, and express more than he designed. In any of these cases, we must have recourse to some other means of interpretation; that is, we must make use of some other signs or marks, besides the words of the speaker or the writer, in order to collect his meaning. These other signs or marks, are what Grotius ranks under the general head of probable conjectures. If we attend to this account of interpretation, to the end that it has in view, and to the means that it employs to come at this end, it will help us to distinguish interpretation from some other arts with which it is frequently confounded.

Both the end and the means of interpretation will distinguish it from criticism. The end which criticism aims at, is to find out what were the words of a writer; whether, for instance, the writing that is before us, is forged or genuine: whether any parts of it, or at least any material parts, have been foisted in, or omitted, or erased, or altered. The end which interpretation aims at, is to find out what was the intention of the writer; to clear up the meaning of his words, if they are obscure; to ascertain the sense of them, if they are ambiguous; to determine what his design was, where his words express it imperfectly. Without inquiring what means the critic makes use of, we may be sure that they cannot be the same with those that are made use of by the interpreter: for the interpreter's work does not begin till the critic's is ended. We must be in possession of the writer's genuine words, before we can either show from them what his intention was, or can have any grounds for calling in the assistance of conjectures to clear up their meaning, to ascertain their sense, or to determine that the intention of him, who used them, is in any respect different from what they express. It is one thing to determine whether a writing, that is before us, is the genuine will of the person whose will it is pretended to be; and another to determine what was the intention of the testator in that will. The former of these points must be settled, before the latter can properly come into question. We might, indeed, be able to clear up the meaning of the person who dictated that writing: but this would not determine the meaning of the testator with any certainty; if there was any doubt whether that writing was his genuine will or not; unless this doubt was first removed.

Sometimes we are at a loss to find out a writer's meaning, merely because we cannot read his writing: this obscurity may be occasioned by his using either a cypher, or abbreviations, or a hand, that we are unacquainted with. But the clearing up such obscurities as these, is not the proper object of interpretation. It is, indeed, the business of interpretation to find out the meaning or design of a writer. But then it supposes that we are in possession of his words. And where we cannot read his writing, the difficulty of making out his meaning arises from our want of knowing what his words are.

It is not very easy to determine exactly, where the provinces of the grammarian and the lexicographer end, and the province of the interpreter begins. But though these provinces run into one another at their confines, they are distinct enough at their remotest extremities. The boy who is learning the Hebrew language, by the help of his grammar and his lexicon, is certainly not employed in the same province with the divine, who settles the intent of the Levitical lawgiver. And yet the divine is frequently indebted to nothing else but his skill in the original language, for his discoveries of the meaning of the law. Interpretation certainly supposes us to have a competent knowledge of the language which the writer made use of, whose meaning we are to find out. Until we have acquired such a knowledge as this, we cannot say, whether his words are clear or obscure; whether they are ambiguous or precise. If we are able to read the characters in which he wrote; or if what he has written is read to us by any one else; the words will be only empty sounds, and cannot convey any meaning at all. We may, if we please, call our own ignorance of his language, an obscurity in his writing: but it is such an obscurity as is not to be cleared up by the topics of interpretation, but by the lexicon and the grammar. We do, indeed, call a man an interpreter who translates what is spoken or written in a language of which we are ignorant, into another language with which we are better acquainted. But such a man only supplies the place of a lexicon and a grammar: and if we would speak distinctly and properly, he is rather to be called a translator, than an interpreter. He gives us the words of the speaker or of the writer; and then, by means of the words, or of other conjectures, if such conjectures are necessary, we are to make out the speaker's or the writer's meaning. It seems to be an ignorance of the same sort, though in a less degree, which makes any writing obscure, where we have a competent knowledge of the language, but are not perfect masters of it. This happens sometimes even in our mother tongue, in which, if there are no other words not generally understood, there are at least many terms of art, which are a sort of language by themselves, and are not fully understood by the generality of the people, but by such only as have been employed in the trade or profession, or have studied the science, to which those terms belong. When a man's meaning, in what he speaks or writes, is obscure, because he uses such words as these, it can scarce be looked upon as the province of interpretation to explain it. The only way of clearing up the obscurity is to get a fuller knowledge of the language: this may be done by having recourse to those who understand the terms of art, or other words, that occasion the obscurity: but then, they to whom we thus have recourse, only instruct us in the language, and may be looked upon as translators: because the instruction which they give us, consists in nothing else but in substituting a word, that we do understand, into the place of another, that we do not understand. But since a technical, or other dictionary, would do all for us that they do; if we will call this by the name of interpretation, we may as well give the same name to what we do, when we learn a language of which we were totally ignorant before. In languages, of which we have a competent knowledge, but not so perfect a knowledge as we have of our mother tongue, this sort of obscurity is more frequent: and as we are rather indebted to nice observations of our own upon the language, than to a grammar or a lexicon, for the clearing up such obscurities, we look upon what we do, when we clear them up, as a sort of interpretation. But yet, since these observations chiefly consist in comparing the sense, in which the same words are used upon different occasions, all that they lead us to, seems to be nothing more than the common use of words in the language of the writer. We are constantly making the like observations upon our mother tongue, in our daily practice, without knowing that we do make them. And as study and attention fix them in our memories, when we make them upon other languages, so the frequency of them fixes them there, in the language of our own country.

There are, indeed, another sort of observations, which consist in etymological refinements. But these are as likely to mislead, as to assist us, in giving the proper sense to the words, either of our own or of any other language. All words have their meaning originally from nothing else but the common consent of those who use them. Their true signification, therefore, is to be determined by this common consent, which must be looked for, not in the etymology of the words, but in common use and custom. We may take pains, or may amuse ourselves, in finding out the roots of words, and in deriving them from these roots by rules of etymology. But when we have done all that we can do in this way, an ordinary man, who has no other verbal learning than what he has been furnished with by common discourse, in the language to which these words belong, will be more likely to give them their true sense, than we shall be with all our refinements. In dead languages, this sort of learning seems to have some use. We are forced to have recourse to its help, where we can get no better: we are forced to guess at the sense of a word, which is used but seldom, or perhaps only once, by the sense of the root from which that word is derived. But this can never be done with any appearance of reason, unless the root is used more frequently than the word itself: because, otherwise, the sense of the root will be as uncertain as the sense of the word. And even where the sense of the root is better ascertained, a few slight observations, either upon our own language, or upon any other that we are well acquainted with, will serve to show us, that derivative words have often a very different sense from what we should have imagined them to have, if, instead of attending to their common use, we had attended only to their etymology.

However, though the mere translator is certainly employed in a different province from that of interpretation, yet, since a more exact knowledge of language, than the grammar or lexicon can teach us, is frequently required to clear up the meaning of a speaker or a writer, where it is obscure, we may well consider this knowledge as having a share in the business of interpretation.

Three sorts of interpretation.

III. Interpretation, as we have already defined it, consists in finding out, or collecting, the intention of a speaker, or of a writer, either from his words, or from other conjectures, or from both. It may, therefore, be divided into three sorts, according to the different means that it makes use of for obtaining its end. These three sorts of interpretation are literal, rational and mixed. Where we collect the intention of the speaker or the writer from his words only, as they lie before us, this is literal interpretation. Where his words do not express his intention perfectly, but either exceed it or fall short of it, so that we are to collect it from probable or rational conjectures only, this is rational interpretation. And where his words, though they do express his intention, when they are rightly understood, are in themselves of doubtful meaning, and we are forced to have recourse to the like conjectures to find out in what sense he used them, this sort of interpretation is mixed; it is partly literal, and partly rational: we collect the intention of the speaker, or the writer, from his words, indeed, but not without the help of other conjectures.

Rules of literal interpretation.

IV. *If the words and the construction of a writing are clear and precise, we scarce call it interpretation to collect the intention of the writer from thence. But the definition of interpretation will best inform us whether it is to be called by this name or not. Interpretation consists in collecting the intention of a man from the outward signs that he makes use of to declare his intention: it must, therefore, certainly be one branch of interpretation to collect his intention from his clear and precise words, as they lie before us. The only reason that we can have to doubt whether this is to be called interpretation or not, is, that we commonly include something of art, or skill, or sagacity, in our notion of interpretation: and there does not seem to be any art, or skill, or sagacity, in finding out a man's meaning, where his words express it clearly and precisely. That this is the reason of our doubt, appears from our readiness to give the name of interpretation to our collecting the intention of a writer from his words only; when there is any obscurity arising either from unusual words, or from a perplexed construction, which cannot be removed without more skill in the language, that he writes in, than most people are masters of. But certainly, if this is to be called interpretation, we may as well give the same name to our collecting of his intention from his words only, when there is no such obscurity: because, though some art or skill is necessary to remove that obscurity, it is not properly the art or skill of an interpreter, but of a grammarian or a lexicographer. Sometimes, however, when the intention of a writer is to be collected from his plain words, we call it interpretation without any scruple. Suppose, that we had a will before us, which is to be interpreted, and that I was to contend for a rational interpretation of it: if you were of a different opinion from me, you would express this opinion by saying, that we ought to follow the literal interpretation. Now, as I, by contending for a rational interpretation, mean, that we are to collect the testator's intention from something else besides his words; you, by contending on the contrary, that we ought to follow a literal interpretation, must mean, that we ought to collect his intention from his words only. Thus, though we doubt whether literal interpretation, which consists in collecting a man's intention from his words only, is to be called interpretation, when we consider it alone; we have no such doubt, when we come to compare it with another sort of interpretation, which consists in collecting his intention from something else besides his words.

The principal rule to be observed in literal interpretation, is to follow that sense, in respect both of the words and of the construction, which is agreeable to common use, without attending to etymological fancies, or grammatical refinements. We have already seen the reason why we are to attend rather to common use, than to etymology, in de-

* Grot. Lib. II. Cap. XVI. § II, III.

termining the signification of words. And if the reader understands what I mean by grammatical refinements, he will readily see a reason why we are to attend to common use rather than to them. By grammatical refinements, then, I mean, such rules of construction as are not justified by the common usage of the language before us, and have nothing else to support them but some groundless conjecture, or some supposed analogy between this language and others. The rule, when it is thus explained, will be found not to differ from one which is more commonly laid down: we are usually directed, in interpreting writings, to follow the literal and grammatical sense; the literal sense, as to the words themselves, and the grammatical sense, as to the construction of them. In this rule, we are to understand, by the literal sense, such a plain sense of the words, as custom and usage has given them, and not such an etymological sense as fancy may have invented. And by the grammatical sense we are to understand that sense which arises from such a grammatical construction, as the like custom and usage will support, and not that refined sense, which depends upon a construction supported only by such rules of grammar, as, instead of being copied from common use, are intended to overrule its authority.

The Locrians, coming into the extreme parts of Calabria, found the Sicilians in possession of it. But the Sicilians, being alarmed at their unexpected arrival, made a league with them, in these words:—That the Locrians would preserve amity with them, and would allow them to enjoy that country in common with themselves, as long as they should tread upon this earth, and have these heads upon their shoulders. The Locrians, when they came to swear to this contract, had first put earth in their shoes, and had privately fastened upon their shoulders heads of garlic. And as soon as they had taken the oath, they threw the earth out of their shoes, and the heads of garlic from their shoulders; and upon the first opportunity, drove the Sicilians out of the country. In common use, the literal and grammatical sense of these expressions:—As long as we tread upon this earth, and as long as we wear these heads upon our shoulders—are equivalent to our saying—as long as we live. The Locrians might, indeed, call theirs a literal and grammatical sense. But it is such a literal and grammatical sense, as common usage knows nothing of. When Temures had articled with the garrison of Sebastia, that no blood should be shed, he ordered all the prisoners to be buried alive. He might say, that he kept to the letter and to the grammar of his articles; for though he took away the lives of the prisoners, he did not shed their blood. But, not to shed their blood—when the words are understood, according to such a literal and grammatical sense as common usage has given them, does not barely mean—not to kill them by letting out their blood; it means—not to kill them at all, in any manner whatsoever.

We may now, perhaps, be able to reconcile this seeming contradiction; that the literal and grammatical performance of a contract is not a due performance of it; and, yet, that every contract is to be understood according to the literal and grammatical sense of the words in which it is expressed. By the literal and grammatical sense, we sometimes mean such a sense, as the words will just bear; and sometimes we mean such a sense as common use has given them. All contracts ought to be understood according to this latter sense; and a performance of them, according to the former sense, is not a due performance.

Mixed interpretation, where to be used.

V. * Where the words of a contract, or of a will, or of a law, may be so strained as to admit of a sense which, though it does not hurt the grammar, and is not inconsistent with the letter, is such a sense as common usage will not justify, we can scarce call these words ambiguous. For words are then only to be looked upon as ambiguous, when they will admit of two or more senses, and either of these senses is equally agreeable to common usage. This is frequently the case: and when it is, instead of appealing to common usage, which is the sole principle of literal interpretation, we must have recourse to mixed interpretation, and must collect the intention of the speaker, or of the writer, partly from his words, and partly from other conjectures. When we have no reason to believe that his words express his meaning imperfectly; that is, that they express either more or less than he intended, we are to look for his intention within the literal and grammatical sense of his words: but, because his words will admit of two or more literal and grammatical senses, and common usage will not fix the precise sense in which he used them, we must have recourse to other conjectures to fix it.

The ambiguity of a writing, whether it is a law, or a will, or a contract, depends sometimes upon the doubtful sense of a single word; sometimes upon the doubtful construction of a sentence, and sometimes upon a comparison of one part of the same writing with another, or of the writing, which is before us, with some other writing which came from the same hand. If the law orders that a person shall do a certain act within the space of two, three, or more months, from such a particular time, the intention of the lawmaker is doubtful as to the time limited; and this doubt arises from the ambiguous sense of the single word month; which may mean either a calendar month, or a month consisting of twenty-eight days. Common use will not determine the sense for us: because, in common use, the same word is used in both these senses. I bequeath all my plate to my elder son, except one thousand ounces; which I bequeath to my younger son, and direct, that the elder shall, within a certain time after my decease, deliver to the younger one thousand ounces of my said plate, of such sort and such pieces as he pleases. The construction of the sentence will make it doubtful which of my two sons the word he, refers to; whether I intended to leave the choice of the sort and of the pieces, to the elder or to the younger. The Levitical law says:—† If brethren dwell together, and one of them die, and have no son, the wife of the dead shall not marry without, unto a stranger; her husband's brother shall go in unto her, and take her to him to wife. If we were to read only this clause of the law, we should have no doubt about the meaning of the word, son; but should naturally conclude, that it is used in its common acceptation for a male child; and, consequently, that, though the deceased brother had a daughter, the survivor is bound to marry the widow of the deceased. But, then, in the original language of the law, the word son is sometimes used generally to signify any child, either male or female: and we find, that where a man died without a male child, the

* Grot. Lib. II. Cap. XVI. § IV.

† Deut. XXV. 5.

*same law, in another part of it, substitutes his daughter into his place, and conveys the inheritance to her. From comparing these two parts of the law together, it becomes doubtful, whether the word son, in the former of them, is used, in its strictest sense, for a male child only, or in its general sense for any child of either sex. The common use of the word, will justify either acceptation: we must, therefore, have recourse to something else, besides the word, and the common use of it, to collect the intention of the lawmaker.

When †Puffendorf is to show how a clause in a law, which is precise and determinate in itself, becomes ambiguous, by comparing it with some other clause either in the same law, or in a different law, which came from the same legislator, he makes use of such instances, as belong to another head. One law, says he, enacts, that a statue shall be erected in the gymnasium, in honour of any person who kills a tyrant. Another law enacts, that no woman shall have a statue in the gymnasium. Now, it happens, that a woman kills a tyrant. Here, indeed, it will be a question, what is the intention of the lawmaker, when such a case happens. But the question does not arise from any ambiguity that there is in the words of either of these laws, when it is compared with the other. The words of each law are clear and precise; not only when the laws are considered separately, but likewise, when they are compared together. The doubt arises from the impossibility of complying with both the laws, in this particular case: and the question is, which of them we may neglect most consistently with the intention of the legislator. In this instance, we are not to collect his intention, as we do in ambiguous laws, from mixed interpretation, so as to act up to his words, but to give those words, which are doubtful in themselves, a precise and determinate sense by conjectures: we are left to collect his intention by rational interpretation, or from conjecture only: for, which ever of the two laws we comply with, it is impossible that we should, in any sense, act up to the letter, or keep within the words of the other. Another of his examples, is taken from a law which, by a particular accident, clashes with itself. The law says, that a woman, who has been ravished, shall have her choice, either to compel the man, by whom she was ravished, to marry her, or to have him put to death. The same man has ravished two women. One of them demands him in marriage; the other demands his life. We may have an use for this example hereafter; but this is certainly not the proper place for it. The case here supposed, does not make the words of the law ambiguous, but makes it impossible to comply with it in all its parts. The intention of the lawmaker is, indeed, doubtful. But this doubt does not arise from any ambiguity introduced into his words, by the accident here supposed. The doubt is, which part of the law he would have us comply with, when we cannot comply with both. And this doubt is not to be determined by settling the precise meaning of his words from conjecture. We here have recourse to conjecture for a very different purpose: for the purpose of finding out an intention, which is not expressed in his words, in any sense of them whatsoever. Grotius reduces all questions of this sort, to the head of ‡rational, and not of mixed

* Numb. XXVII. 8. † Book V. Chap. XII. § VI.

‡ Grot. Lib. II. Cap. XVI. § XXVII, XXVIII.

interpretation: he does not treat of them, when he is inquiring what conjectures are to be made use of to find out the intention of the lawmaker, where his words will admit of more senses than one; but when he is inquiring how we are to find out what his intention is in some particular case, which makes it impossible to act up to any intention, that the letter of the law expresses.

Three topics of mixed interpretation.

VI. In mixed interpretation, where the intention of the writer is expressed in his words, but the words are ambiguous, and will admit of more senses than one, so that we are forced to have recourse to rational conjectures, in order to determine in which of the several senses the words were used, *the topics, from whence our conjectures are drawn, are either the subject matter of the writing, or the effect that it will produce, according as we construe it in this or in that sense; or, lastly, some circumstances that are connected with it.

Words are to be construed agreeably to the subject matter.

VII. †When any words, or expressions in a writing, are of doubtful meaning, the first rule in mixed interpretation is to give them such a sense, as is agreeable to the subject matter of which the writer is treating. For we are sure on the one hand, that this subject matter was in his mind; and can, on the other hand, have no reason for thinking that he intended any thing which is different from it; and much less, that he intended any thing which is inconsistent with it. If a truce is agreed upon for thirty days, the word, day, must mean a natural day, consisting of twenty-four hours, and not an artificial day, or that space of time, during which the sun is above the horizon. This latter sense is inconsistent with the subject matter of the agreement. For a truce is a continued cessation of arms: and there can be no continued cessation of arms for thirty days, unless it is for thirty natural days: because, thirty artificial days are not a continued space of time, but are interrupted by as many nights. ‡When St. Peter had heard upon what occasion Cornelius had sent for him, he begins his discourse with saying, that God is no respecter of persons; but that in every nation, he that feareth him, and worketh righteousness, is accepted with him. We may understand St. Peter to mean either, that persons of all nations, whether they receive or reject christianity, if they only fear God and work righteousness, according to the principles of the light of nature, will be alike rewarded by him in a world to come; or else, that persons of all nations, as well as the Jews, provided they are ready to do the will of God, were alike designed by him to be admitted into the christian covenant. The subject matter, upon which the apostle was speaking, will determine us to give this latter sense to the doubtful expression of being accepted with God. The case before him was that of a religious Gentile, who had been called by God to the knowledge and belief of the gospel, and was desirous, if it might be, of being instructed in that knowledge, and of receiving that faith, at a time when the apostles, as well as the other christian converts, were of opinion, that this was the particular privilege of the Jewish nation. His intention, therefore, if we judge of it by the subject upon which he was speaking, must relate to such acceptance only, as consists in being admitted into the christian

* Grot. Lib. II. Cap. XVI. § V, VI, VII. † Ibid. § V. ‡ Acts X. 34, 35.

covenant. Whether God will reward those hereafter, who live according to the principles of the light of nature, though they reject the belief of the gospel, was a subject that did not then come before him. If, therefore, when he says, that, in all nations, they who fear God and work righteousness, are accepted with him, we suppose his intention to be, that whosoever lives according to the principles of the light of nature, though he rejects the gospel, shall be equally admitted to the future rewards of Heaven, with those who receive it, we give his words a groundless meaning; because we give them such a meaning as does not appear, from the subject matter, to have been in the mind of the speaker.

Words are to be so construed, as to produce a reasonable effect.

VIII. *The second rule, in mixed interpretation, is, to give all doubtful words or expressions, that sense which makes them produce some effect; this effect must, in general, be a reasonable one; and it must, likewise, be the same that the lawmaker, or the testator, or the contractor intended to produce.

First, all doubtful words or expressions, are to be taken in such a sense as will make them produce some effect; that is, they are so to be construed, as to give them some meaning: for to take them in any sense, that will make them produce no effect, is, in reality, to give them no meaning at all. The rule, therefore, of taking all doubtful words or expressions in such a sense as will make them produce some effect, amounts to the same thing as if we had said, that all words are to be construed in such a manner as will give them some meaning. Any other construction of them, instead of pointing out the intention of the writer or the speaker, supposes him to have used the word without any intention at all. If the testator, as we just now supposed, bequeaths all his plate to his eldest son, except one thousand ounces, which he bequeaths to his younger son, and directs that the elder shall, at a certain time, deliver to the younger one thousand ounces of the said plate, of such sort and such pieces as he pleases, this rule would determine the intention of the testator to have been, that his younger son should have the choice of the sort and the pieces. The ambiguous words, of such sort and such pieces as he pleases, would, in the contrary construction, be needless, and produce no effect. If the choice had been intended for the elder son, the testator would have had no occasion to add these words. For, by leaving all his plate to the elder, except one thousand ounces of it, which the elder, within a certain time, is to deliver to the younger, the sort and pieces to be delivered, would, of course, have been at the option of the elder; since the younger would, by the will, have had no claim but to a certain weight of plate. When, therefore, the testator goes on, and says, that it shall be of such sort and such pieces as he pleases; to give these words any meaning, or to make them produce any effect, which would not have been produced without them, it must have been the intention of the testator, to transfer the choice to the younger from the elder; to whom, of course, it would have belonged, if he had not added this clause.

Secondly, ambiguous words or expressions, are sometimes capable of two senses, and will produce some effect in either of the two. The

* Grot. Lib. II. Cap. XVI. § VI.

rule then goes farther, and says, that the effect must be a reasonable one. No other effect can be supposed to have been in the speaker's or writer's intention: because no man can be supposed to intend what is absurd or unreasonable. We meet with an example in Puffendorf, which belongs rather to this head, than to that under which he mentions it. Labeo having agreed, by a league with Antiochus, that the latter should give up half his fleet, cut every ship in two. The words would, perhaps, admit of this construction, and would certainly produce some effect, if they were thus construed. But it is such an effect, as can never be supposed to have been in the mind of Antiochus, when he agreed to these conditions; because it is an unreasonable and absurd one. If the words will admit of this meaning, yet it could not be his meaning: by agreeing to part with half his fleet, he cannot be supposed to have consented that the half, which he parts with, should be understood in such a sense as would, in effect, deprive him of the whole.

All civil laws, and all contracts, in general, are to be so construed, where the words are of doubtful meaning, as to make them produce no other effect, but what is consistent with reason, or with the law of nature. And where men live in a state of civil society, all doubtful words, in any of their contracts with one another, are to be construed in that sense which will produce an effect that is consistent with the civil laws of the society to which they belong. For, where nothing appears to the contrary, the presumption is, that they meant what they ought to mean; or that they designed nothing but what the law allows. Thus, if the civil law has fixed the interest of money at five pounds, for the loan of an hundred pounds, for one year, and the lender stipulates for the payment of fifty shillings, at the end of six months, we must here, by the word, month, understand calendar months. The word, indeed, would produce some effect, if we were to construe it to mean months of twenty-eight days, or four weeks; but this effect would be inconsistent with the law: because it would make the interest higher than according to the rate of five pounds for one year.

Thirdly, * Grotius ranks the reason of a law amongst those topics of mixed interpretation, which are drawn from its circumstances: but I should rather choose to rank it amongst those which are drawn from its effect. The reason, or final cause of a law, consists in the end which the legislator intended to obtain; or in the effect which he intended to produce by making the law. And when we argue, that any ambiguous words, which we meet with in a law, must be understood in one particular sense, rather than in any other, which they might possibly admit of, because this particular sense is agreeable to the reason of the law, our meaning is, that, in this sense of the words, the law will produce the effect which the legislator intended to produce by it.

The reasonableness of this topic of interpretation is evident. For, since the reason of a law consists in the end which the lawmaker intended to obtain, or in the effect which he intended to produce by it; and since he cannot be supposed to intend the end, without intending the means, if we give his words such a meaning as is agreeable to the reason of the law; or such a meaning as will make the law produce the effect which he intended to produce by it, we give them such a meaning as is agreeable to his intention.

* Grot. Lib. II. Cap. XVI. § VIII.

Our author cautions his readers not to confound the meaning of a law with the reason of it; but he does not explain either the one or the other distinctly enough to point out the mark of difference between them. The meaning of a law is the design of the lawmaker in respect of what he commands or forbids. The reason of a law is his design in respect of the end or purpose for which he commands or forbids it. If the words of a law, where it commands or forbids any action, will admit of more senses than one; this ambiguity renders the meaning of the law uncertain, or leaves it doubtful what action the lawmaker designed to command or to forbid. At the same time the reason of the law may be expressed in such clear and precise words, as to leave no doubt at all about the ultimate effect which the lawmaker designed to produce, or about the end which he designed to obtain, by what he has commanded or forbidden. The rule here is, that the meaning of the law is to be determined by the reason of it; or that the design of the lawmaker, in respect of what he commands or forbids by the law, is to be collected from the effect which he designed ultimately to produce by it.

A Levitical law, which has been already explained, will help to illustrate this rule. The law says:—Thou shalt not take a wife to her sister to vex her, to uncover her nakedness, besides the other in her life-time. Now, the idiom of the original language, has left the meaning of the law doubtful in respect of what is forbidden: it is not certain whether the lawmaker designed to forbid the marriage of a man with the sister of his first wife in particular, or whether he designed to forbid a marriage with any second wife at all, in the life-time of the first. But the reason of the law is expressed precisely enough to leave no room to doubt about it: whatever was here designed to be forbidden, the legislator, in forbidding it, designed to guard the domestic happiness of the first wife. Thou shalt not take a wife to her sister *to vex her*. If, therefore, we collect the meaning of the law from the reason of it; that is, if we give the doubtful words of prohibition such a sense, as will make the law produce the effect which the legislator designed to produce by it, we must construe it to be a general prohibition of marrying any second wife in the life-time of the first, and not a particular prohibition of marrying the sister of such first wife: because her domestic happiness would be as likely to be disturbed, if her husband, in her life-time, married any second wife, as if he married her own sister.

Some caution, however, is necessary to be observed in applying this topic of interpretation. Before we attempt to determine the meaning of ambiguous words or expressions in any writing, by arguing from the reason upon which the writer proceeded, or from the end which he had in view, we must take care to show, as evidently as we can, that we are in possession of his true reason. For if there is any doubt about this point, though the meaning which we give to his words may suit exactly with the reason which we suppose him to have had in view, our interpretation will be as doubtful in the conclusion, as it is in this first principle. The safest ground to stand upon, is what the writer himself affords us: when the legislator has plainly declared the reason of the law, in the body of it, we may argue from thence with certainty: but when we are left to collect it by some other means, the foundation of our argument will be only conjectural: and the justness of our interpretation of the law will depend upon the evidence by which our conjectures about the reason of it are supported.

Words of a law, or other writing, are to be construed by its circumstances.

IX. There are numberless * circumstances of laws, or contracts, or wills, which may help to ascertain the meaning of the writer, where he has made use of any ambiguous words or expressions. Grotius divides these circumstances into two sorts: into such as are connected with the writing in origin only, and such as are connected with it in place, as well as in origin. To these two sorts, we may add a third: for there are some circumstances which seem to be connected with a law, or a contract, or a will, rather in time, than either in origin or in place.

When the words of a law, or a contract, or a will, are capable of two or more different senses, so that the meaning of the writer is left doubtful, what has been spoken or written by the same lawmaker, or contractor, or testator, upon some other occasion, is a circumstance of the doubtful writing. But whenever we allege any thing as a circumstance of a doubtful writing, and argue from it to ascertain the meaning of the writer, it is necessary to show, that the writing, and what we so allege, have some connexion with one another. For nothing, which is wholly unconnected with such writing, can either be made use of to explain any ambiguous words in it, or with any propriety be called a circumstance of it. The origin of what has been spoken or written by the lawmaker, or contractor, or testator, upon some other occasion, makes it a circumstance of the law, or contract, or will in question; they had both the same origin, and are connected with one another by coming from the same person.

In doubtful matters, it is reasonable to presume, that the same person is always in the same mind, where nothing appears to the contrary; that whatever was his design at one time, the same is likewise his design at another time, where no sufficient reason can be produced to prove an alteration of it. If the words, therefore, of any writing will admit of two or more different senses, when they are considered separately, but must necessarily be understood in one of these senses, rather than the other, in order to make the writer's meaning agree with what he has spoken or written upon some other occasion; the reasonable presumption is, that this must be the sense in which he used them.

We frequently apply this rule of interpretation in reading the works of any author, either ancient or modern. If we meet with a passage which is of doubtful meaning, we usually make him, if we can, a commentator upon himself, by comparing this with some other passage in his writings. And whatever we find to have been his meaning, where he speaks plainly, we conclude to have been likewise his meaning where he speaks doubtfully.

The law of Moses says:—If thy brother be waxed poor, and fallen to decay with thee, then thou shalt help him, a stranger or a sojourner, that he may live with thee: thou shalt not give him thy money upon usury, nor lend him thy victuals upon increase. Here it is a question, whether the legislator meant that the Israelites should thus help a poor stranger, or that a stranger should thus help a poor Israelite. For the

* Grot. Lib. II. Cap. XVI. § VIII.

words, which are wanting to make the sentence complete, may be so supplied as to give it either of these senses. When I had occasion before to mention this law, I endeavoured to ascertain the meaning of it, by the help of another, which came from the same legislator. Unto a stranger thou mayest lend upon usury, but to thy brother thou shalt not lend upon usury. This second law puts a difference between an Israelite and a stranger, in respect of lending money to either of them, by allowing the Israelites to lend upon usury to strangers; whilst it forbids them to lend upon usury to their brethren. We must, therefore, understand the legislator to mean, in the former law, not that an Israelite should help a poor stranger, by lending him money without usury, but that a stranger, who was permitted to live amongst the Israelites, should thus help a poor Israelite: because, otherwise, the two laws would be inconsistent with one another; the legislator would, in one of them, expressly allow what, in the other, he expressly forbids.

When we explain a doubtful part of a law, or a contract, or a will, by the help of some other part of it, the clause which we make use of for this purpose, is a circumstance which is connected with the clause to be explained in place, as well as in origin: as they both came from the same hand, so they are both found together in the same writing.

Grotius might, perhaps, consider the reason of a law as a circumstance which is connected with the law in place and origin; because the enacting clauses of a law, and the reason upon which it proceeds, may both be contained in the same writing. But this is not always the case: a legislator sometimes only prescribes what is to be done or to be avoided, without mentioning any reason why he prescribes it. And certainly the reason of the law, when it is left to be collected by other means, and does not appear in the same writing with the law, cannot be considered as a circumstance which is connected with it in place. Nor can the reason of the law be properly considered as a circumstance which is connected with it in origin; whether such reason appears in the same writing with it or not. For the reason of the law arises from the nature of things, or from the particular situation of those who are to be directed by the law; whilst the law itself arises from the understanding and will of the legislator: it prescribes such a conduct as, in his judgment, is most likely to be for the benefit of those who are in that particular situation.

Contemporary practice is a circumstance which is connected with a law in time. It may, indeed, be said to be connected with the law, not only in time, but in place too: for it consists in what was usually done in the place where the law was made, at or near the time of making it. But this is not such a connexion in place as our author means, where he speaks of circumstances which are connected with a law in place, as well as in origin. He means, that a doubtful clause in a law, and some circumstance which will help to clear up the doubt, may be connected with one another by being contained in the same writing.

There are two sorts of contemporary practice; and either of them may be applied to the purpose of explaining any ambiguous words or expressions in a law. The first sort is the common practice which prevailed amongst the people at the time when the law was made. The second sort consists in what was done upon the law in the times immediately after the making of it. From the practice which prevailed amongst the people at the time when a law was made, we may, with some degree of probability, collect with what view it was made; what good the legislator designed to advance or to secure, and what harm he designed to prevent or to restrain. But this sort of contemporary practice, since this is the only use that can be made of it in interpreting laws, is only a remote topic of interpretation: it helps us in our conjectures about the reason of the law; and then, from the reason of the law, we ascertain the meaning of the legislator, in any ambiguous words or expressions that he has made use of. When I speak of what has been done upon a law, soon after it was made, I do not mean what has been done upon it by any court of judicature, which is an authorized interpreter of the civil laws of the society, where the law was made, but I mean the practice which it produced amongst the people; or what was done in consequence of it by those who were obliged, and might be supposed willing to comply with it. The practice of such a court of judicature; that is, its determination of any questions which have arisen upon the law, instead of being means which will help to interpret it, are themselves authentic interpretations of it. Thus far, indeed, the practice of such a court may be considered as a means of interpretation. Though the persons, who preside there in later times, may have the same authority to interpret a law that their predecessors had; yet what their predecessors have done, who were contemporaries with the legislator, will help to guide them in the use of this authority: because it will show them in what sense the law was understood by those who had the best opportunity of knowing the true sense, either by advising with the legislator himself, or, at least, by seeing the situation of things, which led him to make the law. In like manner, the effect which the law produced in the behaviour of those who were obliged by it, and who lived at the time of making it, will help us to form a judgment about the meaning of the legislator, where his words have left it doubtful: both because they had an opportunity either of finding out the reason of the law by their own observations, or of hearing it in their discourse with others; and because it is probable, that, if their practice had not been agreeable to the sense of the legislator, he would have taken care to correct it, by explaining his meaning more precisely.

A topic which is much the same with one sort of contemporary practice, may sometimes be applied to interpret wills or contracts: though, perhaps, when it is thus applied, it cannot properly be called by the same name. In the interpretations of wills, we usually consider the situation of the testator; what sort of persons he had about him; what their qualities, their conduct, or their characters were; what was his own temper and disposition; what views he had in general; and what views in relation to the persons, who were about him, in particular. By these means, we are enabled to form probable conjectures concerning the reason of any disposition of his goods, that he has made by his will: and then the reason of the disposition assists us in finding out the meaning of the words in which it is expressed. In like manner, where we are to interpret any ambiguous clause in a contract, we attend to the situation of the parties; to the inconveniences which that situation laid them under, and to the advantages which it held out to them; we consider their temper and character, and examine into every circumstance which might probably influence them.

We cannot apply the other sort of contemporary practice universally to the interpretation of wills or of contracts. Laws operate at a distance of time: those who live many years after the laws were made, are obliged to act upon them; and are, therefore, concerned to know their true meaning. But, in length of time, the meaning of a law may become doubtful, though it was clear and precise when it was first made. And since, by looking back into the contemporary practice; that is, into the practice which the law produced in the first instance, we may see in what sense it was then understood; a view of this practice will be a means of removing any doubts about the sense of it, which are owing only to our remoteness from its original establishment. But the obligation of wills or of contracts, is commonly a transient one; when they have been once duly acted upon, they have obtained the whole effect which the testator or the contractors had in view. If any doubts, therefore, arise about the meaning of a contract or a will, they commonly arise, in the first instance, when there is no practice, of past times, upon such contract or will, which might help to remove the doubts. But sometimes things are disposed of, by a will or a contract, for purposes that are of long continuance: of this sort are donations, in perpetuity, for charitable uses, or for other purposes of the like sort. At a remote distance of time from the original benefaction, doubts may arise upon the words of the will, or of the contract, by which such benefaction is settled; either concerning the persons who are to dispose of it, or concerning the persons who may claim it, or who are capable of holding it; or concerning the restrictions under which it is to be taken or holden. Here is an opportunity of having recourse to contemporary practice, in the same manner as we have recourse to this topic in the interpretation of laws. Though any practice, which began some time after the first settlement, will only show their opinion who began it; and though their opinion is no more to be relied upon than our own, yet a practice which began immediately with the benefaction, under the inspection of the benefactor himself, where the donation was made by contract in his lifetime, or under the inspection of his friends, who lived with him, where the donation was made either by will, or by a contract, which did not take place till after his death; such a practice as this may reasonably be supposed to have been agreeable to his meaning.

Strict and large interpretation, what.

X. The words—strict or large, when they are applied to interpretation, are not always used in the same sense; that is, we do not always mean the same thing, when we speak of strict or of large interpretation.

Sometimes common usage has given two senses to the same word, one of which is more confined, or includes fewer particulars; and this is called its strict sense; the other is more comprehensive, or includes more particulars; and this is called its large sense. Thus the word—warehouse—is sometimes used in a large sense, to signify any place where a dealer in any sort of goods or wares lays them up, till he wants to bring them out into a place of sale: and it is likewise used in a strict sense, to signify the very place of sale; and then is no otherwise distinguished from a shop, than as the former is a close, and the latter an open place of sale. When we meet with a word of this sort in a law, and are doubtful in which of the senses the legislator used it, we must have recourse to some other marks besides his words, to ascertain his meaning. Either of the senses is within the letter of the law: but because other marks must be used to ascertain the meaning of the legislator, besides his words, the interpretation is of the mixed sort. If we take the word in its more confined sense, we are said to interpret it strictly: if we take it in its more comprehensive sense, we are said to interpret it largely.

Thus far we keep within the letter, whether we interpret the law strictly or largely. But strict and large interpretation are frequently opposed to one another in a different sense. The words of a law may sometimes express the meaning of the legislator imperfectly; they may, in their common acceptation, include either more or less than was contained in his intention. And as we call it, on the one hand, strict interpretation, where we contend, that the letter is to be adhered to precisely; so, on the other hand, we call it large interpretation, where we contend, either that the words ought to be taken in such a sense, as common usage will not fully justify, or that the meaning of the legislator is something different from what his words in any usage would import. What is here called large interpretation, is the same that, in the general division, I have called rational interpretation. And what is here called strict interpretation, includes both literal and mixed interpretation: for even mixed interpretation is so far literal, that it keeps strictly to the letter, without giving the words any sense, which common usage has not given them; it only ascertains the sense, in which the writer used the words, when common usage has given them more senses than one. But, perhaps, it would be more proper, when literal and mixed interpretation are thus distinguished from rational, to call the former close, rather than strict interpretation, and to call the latter liberal or free, rather than large interpretation. The reason why these terms would be the more proper, will appear, if the reader considers the different sorts of rational interpretation. Where we make use of rational interpretation; sometimes we restrain the meaning of the writer, so as to take in less, and sometimes we extend or enlarge his meaning, so as to take in more than his words express. Now, if all rational interpretation, or all interpretation, which deviates from the letter, was to be called large interpretation, the consequence would be, that, when we come to divide rational interpretation into its two sorts, we must say, that as one sort of large interpretation extends or enlarges the writer's meaning beyond the letter, so the other sort restrains his meaning within the letter. And, certainly, a large interpretation, which restrains his meaning; if it is an intelligible expression, cannot be a very proper one. This impropriety will be avoided, if we call it close interpretation, when we keep close to the letter; and liberal or free interpretation, when we deviate from the letter, or do not confine ourselves to it. For then all rational interpretation will come under the notion of liberal or free interpretation: and there is nothing either unintelligible or improper in saying, that such interpretation, as is free, and does not confine itself to the precise letter, either restrains the meaning of the legislator within the letter, or enlarges and extends his meaning beyond the letter.

XI. * We have just now observed, that there are two sorts of purely rational interpretation: sometimes the meaning of the writer is extended, so as to take in more, and sometimes it is restrained, so as to take in less, than his words import in their common acceptation.

Meaning of the writer, how extended in rational interpretation.

In order to extend the meaning of a writer beyond the precise or common sense of his words, we may argue from the reason or motive upon which he proceeded, from the end which he had in view, or the purpose which he designed to obtain. When we thus argue from the reason of a law, or of a contract, or of a will, and would extend the writer's meaning to any case which is not included in his words; Grotius observes, that the case must be shown to come within the same reason, upon which the lawmaker, or the contractor, or the testator proceeded. If it only comes within a like reason, this will be no evidence that it is included in his meaning. There may be as much reason, why some other acts, which are not expressed in the words of a law, should be forbidden, as there is, why those acts should be forbidden, which are expressed in the words of it: but no argument can be drawn from hence, to prove that such other acts are within the meaning of the legislator. One reason may be like another, or one reason may be of equal weight with another: but notwithstanding their likeness or their equality of weight, though one of them was in the mind of the legislator, it will be no consequence, that the other must have been in his mind too. And certainly we can never argue, that his meaning ought to be extended beyond his words, upon a reason which does not appear to have been in his mind.

But every writing, and every clause in a writing, whether it is a law, or a contract, or a will, though it is not to be construed agreeably to the reason, upon which the writer might have proceeded, is certainly to be construed agreeably to the reason, upon which he did proceed. When we know what was the reason or final cause, which the writer had in view, what end he proposed, or what effect he designed to produce; and the meaning of the law, or contract, or will, if we were to adhere closely to the words of it, would not come up to this reason, or would not produce this effect; we may then conclude, that his words express his meaning imperfectly, and that his meaning is to be extended beyond his words, so as to come up to this reason, or so as to produce this effect. For it is much more probable, that the writer should fail in expressing his meaning, than that his meaning should fall short of the purposes which he designed to obtain.

Sempronius, who had said in his will,—I make Curius my heir, if the child, with which my wife is now big, should happen to die,—was mistaken in supposing his wife to be with child. And as no posthumous child is born, the heirs, in intestate succession, claim the estate: because Curius, according to the words of the will, could only claim, upon the event of such child's death. But though the words of the conditional cause include only this event of the child's death; yet the meaning of it may be extended so as to take in the other event of no such child's being born. For it is plain, upon the face of the will, that in the intention of the testator, Curius stands next to his own child:

* Grot. Lib. II. Cap. XVI. § XX.

and, consequently, that his reason for adding this condition was to make a provision for his own child, and not for any one else, in preference to Curius. If, therefore, we make this clause operate so as to exclude Curius, though there is no posthumous child to be provided for; we shall give it such an operation, as is not agreeable to the intention of the testator. His words, indeed, are—If my posthumous child dies. But if we interpret his will by the reason upon which he proceeded, his meaning is—If I have no posthumous child that lives.

If the law has prescribed a particular method of recovering possession, where the owner of any lands has been turned out of them by force; it may be a question, whether the same method is to be made use of, where a number of armed men have taken possession of his field in his absence, who, upon his attempting to come into it, bid him come in at his peril, and he withdraws without persisting in his attempt? The words of the law may be urged on one side; because he cannot be said to have been turned out of his lands, as he was not upon them. But the reason of the law is on the other side. The end or design of it is, not merely to place him upon his own lands, but to give him possession of them. If, therefore, where it speaks of his being turned out of his lands, we collect the meaning of it from this purpose; his being turned out of his lands, must mean, not merely his being put out of the lands themselves, but his being put out of the possession of them. And he is as much put out of possession, when he is hindered by force from coming upon them, as if he had been upon them, and had been driven off by force. What the law intends to restore him to, is what it supposes him to have been turned out of. But it intends, not merely to bring him into his lands again, but to bring him into the possession of them. When, therefore, it says,—if a man is turned out of his lands; it must be understood to mean,—if he is turned out of the possession of his lands.

* The Mosaic laws says, If a man shall open a pit, or if a man shall dig a pit, and not cover it, and an ox or an ass fall therein; the owner of the pit shall make it good, and give money unto the owner of them; and the dead beast shall be his. In our author's opinion, the reason of the law will extend it beyond the words, to any ditch, or to any tame animal. But this may well be doubted of: because the same reason does not extend to all ditches and to all tame animals. A ditch may be intended as a fence for a man's grounds: and the law cannot be supposed, either to require, that a ditch, when it is made for this purpose, should be covered, or to charge the owner of the grounds with the loss of any beast, which falls into such ditch, in attempting to come into a place, where it ought not to be. If the owners of sheep, in the country, where this law was made, were always used to have shepherds to take care of them; there is not the same reason, why the owner of a pit should be charged with the loss of a sheep, which falls into it, that there is, why he should be charged with the loss of any other tame animals, which usually stray without a keeper.

Meaning of the writer, how restrained in rational interpretation.

XII. † When we would restrain the meaning of a writer, and show, that it is less comprehensive than his words, or that some particular case, which is included in his words, is not within his meaning; we must argue,

* Exod. XXI. 28, &c.

† Grot. Lib. II. Cap. XVI. § XXII. XXIX.

either for an original, or for an accidental defect in his intention; either we must argue, that according to the state of things, which came within the notice of the lawmaker, or testator, or contractor, at the time of making the law, or the will, or the contract, he could not intend, originally, to include the case in question, however he may have so failed in his expression as to include it in his words; or else we must argue, that the case is an accidental one, which probably was not foreseen originally; and that, if the writer had foreseen it, if the present state of things had come within his notice, he would have limited his expression, and have particularly excepted the case in question.

In contending for an original defect in the meaning of the writer, the topics are the same with those, which we make use of in mixed interpretation; we argue from the effect, from the matter, or from the circumstances. Under the first of these topics may be comprehended what Grotius considers as a distinct topic, and calls the reason or ultimate design of the writer. For when we argue, that a particular case could not, originally, be included in the meaning of the law; either because some absurd consequence will follow from including it, or because some consequence will follow, which is inconsistent with the reason or end of the law; we plainly argue, in both instances, from the effect: in the former instance we contend, that the effect, which would be produced, by including the case in the meaning of the law, will be contrary to reason in general; and in the latter we contend, that it would be contrary to the reason of the legislator in particular. Our Saviour proves, from the reason of the law, that the fourth commandment, which prescribes the observance of the sabbath, admits of some exceptions, though the words of the law are general. When he reasons from the practice of the Jews themselves, who, upon that day, led their beasts to water; his argument may seem to conclude in favour only of works of necessity: but when he reasons from the end of the law, that the sabbath was made for man, and not man for the sabbath; the conclusion is more comprehensive, and takes in all works of pure charity.

The law says, that they, who in a storm forsake the ship, shall lose their right in the ship, and the lading; and that such ship and lading shall be the property of them who stay in it. A ship is quitted in a storm by all who were in it, except one sick man, who was not able to get out; and the ship, by accident, comes safe into port. The sick man claims the ship as his own, by the law, and the owners claim against him. Puffendorf makes use of this as an example of mixed interpretation, where the particular sense, in which words of more senses than one are used, is to be ascertained. But it seems rather to be an example of rational interpretation, where the writer's words express his meaning imperfectly, and the sense of them being too general, is to be restrained by the end which he had in view. Staying in the ship are words which, if we adhere to the letter, have only one sense; but this sense is very extensive, and would support the sick man's claim. The reason of the law, or the encouragement which the legislator designed to give those, who would expose their lives to save the ship, is what limits this extensive sense of the words, and shows the legislator to have meant, not any staying in the ship, as his words, unless we were thus to restrain them by the reason of the law, would import, but a voluntary staying there, for the purpose of contributing to save it.

Whatever case is not within the subject matter of what is spoken or written, is not within the meaning of the speaker or writer; though his words, if they were construed in their full extent, would include it: for nothing can be within his meaning, which was not in his mind; and the subject matter, upon which he spoke or wrote, is what his mind was employed about, at the time of speaking or writing. You sell me goods, and oblige yourself to defend me in the possession of them, under a certain penalty. If these goods are taken from me by force, and you refuse, upon my request, to defend me against such force, I have no claim to the penalty. By engaging to defend me in the possession of the goods, you could not mean to ensure my possession against such accidents as these. For though the words have this extensive sense, yet the subject matter of the agreement limits the sense of them. In a contract, which transfers your right in the goods to me, this right is the subject matter. Any loss of possession, therefore, in which this right never came into question, as it has no relation to the subject matter of the contract, could not, originally, be included within your meaning.

The circumstances, by which the meaning of a law is so restrained by rational interpretation, as to exclude cases, which are contained within the letter of it, are of the same sort with those, which are made use of to settle the sense of an ambiguous word in mixed interpretation: they are such as are connected with it, either in origin, or in place, or in time. Other laws, which were made by the same legislator, or some clauses in the same law, or the contemporary practice, by which is meant, either the practice which obtained, at the time of making the law, and which the law was designed to prevent, or the practice which followed, upon making it, among those who were under its authority, and were, in all appearance, disposed to comply with it; any, or all of these are circumstances, which will help to show, whether the meaning of the legislator was as extensive as his words; or whether any cases are to be excepted out of his meaning, which come within his words.

The arguments, which are drawn from these topics, sometimes conclude so strongly, that little can be said against them, with any appearance of reason. But sometimes they may be so urged, on both sides, as to leave room to doubt, on which side the truth lies. * Thus, where the law forbids or commands any thing in general words, and then goes on to enumerate the several particulars, which are included under such general words; if it omits any one particular, it may be a question, whether the meaning of the legislator extended to this particular or not. Now this enumeration of particulars being a circumstance, which is connected, in place, with the general words; as they are both found in the same law; we may urge, that it was designed to explain the general words, and to show how far the legislator intended to extend them, that, when he was enumerating the several particulars, if he had intended to take in any others, besides what he has expressed, he would have mentioned them, as well as these; and, consequently, that,

* Puffendorf, Book V. Chap. XII. § XIII. 5.

however extensive the general words of the law may be in themselves, the meaning of the legislator must be limited to these particulars, which are contained in such enumeration. On the contrary, we might argue from the effect, according to the rules of mixed interpretation; that, if any doubt concerning the legislator's meaning arises upon his words, we are to construe all his words in such a manner, as to give them some significancy, and to make them produce some effect. But if no particulars are to be included within his meaning, besides those, which are expressed in the enumeration, his general words would stand for nothing, and no effect would be produced by them. This argument will conclude most strongly, where the general words follow the enumeration. When the legislator begins his command or his prohibition with general words, and then goes on to enumerate particulars; there is some ground for surmising, that the enumeration of particulars is designed to be explanatory of the general words, and that his meaning stops, where he stops in his enumeration. But if he first mentions a number of particulars, which he commands or forbids, and then concludes with such general words, as will extend in their common acceptation to some other particulars not expressly mentioned; it seems to be a more reasonable supposition, that he apprehended it to be possible for him to have overlooked several particulars, which he intended to include within the law, and that he added these general words with a design to take in all such particulars, as he might have overlooked. And even where the general words stand first, though the enumeration of particulars, which follows them, must be allowed to be explanatory of such general words; yet there is no necessity for supposing, that the meaning of the legislator extends no farther than the particulars which he enumerates. He might design to explain, not the extent of the law, but the matter of it; to show, not what number of cases, but what sort of cases, was within his meaning. Now a few instances would be sufficient to explain the matter of his law, and to show what sort of cases come within the meaning of it. He might, therefore, leave his enumeration imperfect; not because his meaning stopped where he stopped in his enumeration; but because such an imperfect enumeration would answer the purpose, for which he designed it. * The law of Moses commanded, that three cities should be set apart in the midst of the land, that every slayer might flee thither. And this is the case of the slayer, which shall flee thither, that he may live: whoso killeth his neighbour ignorantly, whom he hated not in time past. Thus far it is plainly the intention of the lawmaker that every person who killed another in any manner, if there was no malice, should suffer no punishment, provided he took refuge in one of those cities of protection. But the law, after it has said this in general words, proceeds to mention a particular instance. As when a man goeth into the wood with his neighbour to hew wood; and his hand fetcheth a stroke with the axe to cut down the tree; and the head slippeth from the helve, and lighteth upon his neighbour, that he die; he shall flee unto one of these cities, and live. One can scarce imagine, that the legislator mentioned this particular case, with a design of limiting his meaning to this case only. He did, indeed, design, that it should be

* Deut. XIX. 3, 4, 5.

explanatory of his general words: but then he designed to explain by it, not the extent, but the matter of the law, to show what sort of cases, and not what number of cases, his meaning took in. But we should observe, in the meantime, that the force of this argument is greatly abated, where the law, instead of contenting itself with mentioning a few cases, mentions a great number. The more perfect the enumeration is, the more likelihood there is, that the legislator designed to limit his meaning to the particulars, which are enumerated. If he only designed to explain the matter of his law, or to point out the sort of cases, to which it belongs; a few particulars would be sufficient for this purpose. When, therefore, he enumerates many, it becomes likely, that he did not design to answer a purpose, which might have been answered with less trouble; but that he designed to mention all the particulars, to which the meaning of the law extends. What is thus urged in abatement, though it may have weight, where the enumeration of particulars follows the general words, will, for a reason, which has already been taken notice of, have little or no weight, where the general words follow the enumeration of particulars.

Many more examples of the like sort might be produced: but this, which we have been explaining, will be sufficient to show the reader, that the common topics of interpretation may frequently be alleged on both sides, with such an appearance of probability, as will make it difficult to come to any certain conclusion on either.

Sometimes a case is to be excepted out of the meaning of a writer, though no original defect of his intention can be shown. The state of things which fell under the notice of the legislator, at the time of making the law, may possibly afford no evidence that he did not intend, from the beginning, to include the case in question, within the obligation of the law; whether we were to argue from the effects, from the matter, or from the circumstances. We must, then, have recourse to the present state of things; and must endeavour to prove, that the law is more extensive than the legislator would have made it, if he had foreseen the accidents which have happened since it was made; that it was adapted to the state of things which he had before him; but that the present state of them in this particular instance is such, as makes it reasonable to believe, that, if he had been aware of it, he would have either expressly excepted the case in question out of the law, or would have otherwise provided for it.

The like method of reasoning may likewise be applied to wills and to contracts. Though the words of the will, or of the contract, may include the case in question; and though no original defect may appear in the intention of the testator or of the contractors, which might exempt this case from the general obligation produced by the will, or the contract; yet we may argue, that the reason why no such defect appears, is, because the testator or the contractor proceeded upon the state of things which was then before him; and that, if he had been aware of what might arise afterwards, if he had seen things in the same state in which, by accident, they are now placed, he would have added some clause in favour of the case now in question.

Great caution is necessary when we thus put ourselves into the place of the lawmaker, or testator, or contractor, and undertake to determine what they would do, if they were to declare their own meaning in a case upon which they have not already declared it. There will otherwise be some danger of our overruling their act and setting it aside, under the notion of declaring what they would choose to have done upon it. The proper qualifications for such an hazardous undertaking, are an exact knowledge of equity, and a firm resolution, as well as a sincere inclination of determining according to it. For, whatever grounds there may be to presume, that the lawmaker, or the testator, or the contractor, would be disposed to except any case, if it is equitable that such case should be excepted; yet we shall be unqualified to act upon this presumption, or to determine what cases are to be excepted upon this principle, unless we know what is equitable. Nor will our knowledge alone make us fit to judge about the mind or intention of others, where they have not declared or signified it in words, if we are either corrupt or timid: though we know what equity would dictate, we shall probably determine contrary to its dictates, if we are liable either to be biassed by interest or affection, or to be overawed by threatenings. By equity is here meant, a fair and honest correction of a law, or a will, or a contract, where it appears that the lawmaker, or the testator, or the parties in the contract, either would or ought to consent to such a correction, if they were to interpret their own act.

Under this head of interpretation, we argue, either that the accidental case in question ought, in reason, to be excepted, or else that it must of necessity be excepted out of the law, or the will, or the contract, though the writer has neither added, nor intimated any exception in favour of it.

When we argue, that an accidental case ought in reason to be excepted, the principal topic is the hardship which must be suffered, if it is not excepted. It is unjust to bring any evil upon a man, and unreasonable to deprive him of any benefit, where no good at all will be produced, or even where no such good will be produced, as is of equal importance with the evil that he suffers, or with the benefit that he loses. Since, therefore, the lawmaker, or the testator, or the parties contracting, may be presumed not to have intended, because they ought not to have intended, any thing which is unjust or unreasonable, we may conclude, that any case is to be excepted out of a law, or a will, or a contract, in which, if it was not excepted, a man must either suffer some great evil, or be deprived of some great benefit, either for no good purpose at all, or for a purpose which, though it may be a good one, is of less importance than the evil which he is to undergo.

Cicero mentions a case, arising upon a law of the Rhodians, as an example of such equitable interpretation. The law says, that any ship of force, which comes into any of their ports, shall be confiscated. A storm drives a ship of force into one of their ports, notwithstanding all the endeavours of the sailors to prevent it. The officers of the state claim the ship, as confiscated by the law. But, however such a claim may be supported by the letter, it cannot be supported by the equity of the law. The legislator may have made no express exception in favour of such a case; but it is to be presumed, that he never designed what was unjust or unreasonable; and, consequently, that he would have excepted it, if he had foreseen such a case, wherein a grievous hardship may be suffered for no purpose at all. And certainly no purpose can be answered by punishing those who have broken the law against their wills; because, where there is no disposition to offend, there is no future danger to be guarded against.

Grotius here excepts against a rule which Cicero has laid down, that such a promise is not to be performed, as brings more damage to the promiser than benefit to the person to whom the promise was made. For the promiser is not at liberty, or has no right, to judge concerning the benefit which would arise to the other party from his performance. Thus far, however, Cicero's rule may be admitted. Though the promiser is not at liberty to determine concerning the benefit which would arise to another from his performance, and, consequently, cannot release himself from his own obligation; yet, in civil society, where there is an authorized judge between them, such judge may proceed upon this rule, and may determine that the person, to whom the promise is made, ought in equity to release the promiser, if he finds that any unforeseen hardship would arise from performance; and particularly if it appears, that, by means of some accidental change, which has happened in the state of affairs, since the time of making the promise, performance will be attended with more harm on one side, than benefit on the other.

It may not only be reasonable, but necessary, to except an accidental case out of a law or a contract; though there does not appear to have been any original defect in the intention of the lawmaker, or of the parties contracting; that is, though they cannot be shown to have designed from the beginning to except that case. The general tenor of a law or a contract, may be consistent with the law of nature: and yet such cases may arise, accidentally, as will render it impossible to comply with the law, or to perform the contract, without transgressing the law of nature. It is necessary to except such cases as these, when they happen to arise; whether the legislator or the contractors originally excepted them or not. For the legislator, as he has no power to oblige others; and the contractors, as they have no power to oblige themselves to act inconsistently with the law of nature, certainly ought, and may therefore reasonably be presumed willing to except them. Grotius explains his meaning by the instance of a charge, which is a contract of the beneficial sort, and obliges the person, who receives any goods into his custody, to keep them safe, and to return them, either upon demand, or at the time agreed upon, to those from whom he received them. But if goods are thus left in charge with me, and before they are demanded by those who left them with me, it appears that they had stolen the goods, and the true owner demands them of me, the obligation of my contract, by this accident, becomes inconsistent with the obligation of the law of nature, which arises from the owner's property. And this exception, though it was not expressed in the contract, must be allowed of when the case happens: because I ought not, or, rather, had not power to bind myself to do what the law of nature has forbidden.

Where two civil laws, which come from the same legislator, relate to the same subject matter, and are contrary to one another, so that both of them cannot be complied with at any one time or place, or in any circumstances; the rule is, that the latter of these laws repeals the former. The legislator could not at one and the same time intend contrarieties. But when he established the second law, he intended that it should be complied with: and, consequently, he must then intend to overrule the other. In like manner, where two contracts, which are entered into at different times, are in all respects inconsistent with one another, so that the obligations of both these contracts cannot subsist together; the contractors are understood by the latter of them to release each other from the obligation of the former. As their joint will or consent, produced the obligation of the former contract, so they can, by a like joint act, destroy this effect, or set the obligation aside. But by entering into the second contract, they show that it is then their will to bind themselves to what is contained in this second contract; and, consequently, whatever obligation they might have laid themselves under by the first contract, it must then be their will to set this obligation aside, or to release one another from it. They cannot be supposed to will contrarieties; they cannot, therefore, intend to produce a second obligation, without intending at the same time to set aside the first, which, if it subsisted, would make the second impossible.

What is here affirmed concerning contracts, that a subsequent contract will make an antecedent one void, may be easily reconciled with what has been affirmed in another *place, concerning promises and obligatory acts in general, that any subsequent promise, which is contrary to one that was formerly made, cannot make the former void. For here we are speaking of what may be done by the joint act of all the parties in a contract; whereas, we were there speaking of what one of the parties in a promise or a contract might do by his own act. An obligation, which is produced by the joint will of two or more persons, cannot be destroyed by the single will of any one of them. If, therefore, two or more persons have bound themselves to one another by a contract, any other contract, which is made for a contrary purpose between any one of those persons and some one else, who was no party in the former, will be void. The former obligation still subsists, because his single act could not set it aside. And as long as it subsists, he has no moral power of binding himself to any thing, which is inconsistent with it. But if all, who were parties in the former contract, are likewise parties in the subsequent one, their joint act of binding themselves to one another by this subsequent contract, will make the former void. Though one of them, by his own will, cannot release himself, yet their joint consent is sufficient to release one another from the former obligation: and by this subsequent contract, in which they are all parties, they are understood to give such joint consent.

But there may be such an accidental situation of things, or such an unforeseen event may happen, as will render it impossible, in some particular case, to comply with two laws or two contracts, which, in their general tenor, are consistent with one another, and may well subsist together. One of these laws will not repeal the other; or one of these contracts will not make the other void in general: because, by the supposition, they are consistent with one another. But this particular case, which was not foreseen, and therefore was not provided against, must, when it arises, be of necessity excepted out of the obligation of one of the laws or one of the contracts; because they cannot both be complied with. The question here will be, which of the two laws, or of the two contracts, is to give way to the other? The case must necessarily be excepted out of the obligation of one of them: which of them,

* See Book I. Chap. XII. § IX.

therefore, will most reasonably, or most consistently with the intention of the lawmaker, or of the contractors, admit of the exception? Where two laws or two contracts are contrary to one another, in all respects, we say, that the latter makes the former void: because the lawmaker or the contractors could not intend the obligation of the latter, without intending at the same time to set the obligation of the former aside. But where they are, in general, consistent with one another from the beginning, and interfere only in some particular case, and by some unforeseen accident, the lawmaker or the contractors may well be understood to have intended, from the beginning, that both of them should be observed.

In determining which law or which contract is to be observed, where two laws or two contracts accidentally interfere, Grotius says, that the latter is to be observed in preference to the former. But then he proposes this as a rule which is only to be applied when all others fail; or when all other circumstances are equal; so that the point could not be settled without the help of this rule. The other rules which he lays down for this purpose, are these, which follow:—

First, a law, which only permits, must give way to a law which commands or forbids. For a permission is only a check upon the operation of that law which grants the permission, and not upon the operation of this other law, which happens to interfere with it.

Secondly, a law, which may be complied with at any time, must give way to a law, which, if it is not complied with now, cannot be complied with at all. When some of our Saviour's disciples were displeased with the woman, who had poured a box of precious ointment on his head, which, as they urged, might have been sold for much, and given to the poor, he defends her upon this principle. Jesus said, let her alone, why trouble ye her? she hath wrought a good work on me: for ye have the poor with you always, and whensoever ye will, ye may do them good; but me ye have not always. The reasonableness of this rule is evident. By holding the conduct which it recommends, we may satisfy both the laws; one of them now, and the other at some future opportunity, when they do not interfere. Whereas, by the contrary conduct, we can only satisfy one of them: if at present we act in compliance with that, which might have been complied with at any time, we lose the only opportunity of complying with the other.

Thirdly, Grotius deduces it as a consequence, from the rule last mentioned, that a negative law, or a law which forbids, is commonly to be observed in preference to an affirmative law; or to a law which commands, when they happen to interfere with one another. A negative law obliges, at all times, at the present as well as at any future opportunity: so that, if it is not complied with now, no future compliance will satisfy for the present violation of it. But an affirmative law is understood, then, only to oblige, when there is a convenient opportunity of doing what it commands: and certainly it is not a convenient opportunity, when we cannot do what this law commands, without doing what another law forbids. Our author has very rightly limited this rule, by speaking of it as a rule which commonly holds good. But Puffendorf unadvisedly delivers it in general terms, as if it was universally true, and admitted of no exception, or required no limitation. And yet when one law says, that no woman shall have her statue placed in the gymnasium; and another says, that whoever kills a tyrant, shall have a statue in the gymnasium, he determines, that if a woman had killed a tyrant, her statue should be placed there: notwithstanding this determination makes a negative law give way to an affirmative one. He judges in favour of the woman; because, by following that law, upon which she claims a statue, more benefit may arise to the public, than by following the other. The reason of one of these laws was, that the youth who were trained up to valour in the gymnasium, by seeing those who had freed their country from slavery, rewarded with the honour of a statue, might be incited to imitate their bravery. The reason of the other law was, that the virtues of women are not generally the object of their imitation, who are to be trained up to valour. And from hence he concludes, that, since a woman has outdone her sex, she the rather ought to have her statue put up in the gymnasium; because such valour in a woman would be a greater incitement to emulation in the men. I do not question the justness either of the rule upon which he proceeds, or of the determination which he deduces from it. My only reason for mentioning this determination here is, that it shows the rule, which is now before us, not to be so universally true as he seems to suppose it.

Fourthly, when two laws interfere, if they are equal in other respects, that which is more particular, takes place of that which is more general. The principal reason which supports this rule, seems to be, that the legislator, where he speaks particularly and exactly, appears to be more careful to guard against all exceptions which might arise accidentally, and may, therefore, be thought more unwilling to admit of any, than where he speaks in general, and at large.

Fifthly, a law, which is established upon a penalty, is to be observed in preference to a law, which has no penalty annexed; if they happen to interfere. This is not designed as a rule of prudence directing a person, when he is in doubt which of the two laws he should obey, to take the safer part, and to comply with the penal law, that he may avoid the penalty. For where two laws interfere, the question is, which of the two the legislator would choose to have him comply with; and when this question is rightly determined, the other law does not oblige him. From whence it follows, that if any reason could be given, why the legislator would choose to have him obey the other law, rather than the penal one; it would be as prudent to hold this conduct, as the contrary: because, upon this supposition, the penal law would not oblige him; and, consequently, by this conduct, as well as by the contrary, he might avoid the penalty. But the penalty, though it is not to be considered as a prudential reason, why the penal law should be obeyed, rather than the other, is a reason, why we should presume, that the legislator would rather choose to have this law obeyed: because, from his taking care to guard this law more strongly, we may conclude, that he thought it of more importance, than the other.

Sixthly, if both the laws are penal, the preference is to be given to that, which is established upon the higher penalty. We cannot well support this rule by the maxim, which is generally applied in doubtful cases, that of two evils, the least is to be chosen. In this maxim, by an evil, must be meant either a moral or a natural evil; that is, either an evil, which we are to do, or an evil, which we are to suffer. Now, if we understand the maxim in the former sense, which is the true one;

it will only amount to this; where we must do wrong either way, it is best to follow that course, in which we shall do the least wrong. But in this sense the maxim is so far from supporting the rule here laid down, that, where two laws interfere, and we are in doubt which is to be obeyed, it will afford us no help at all towards removing the doubt. For when we are in this situation, the very question is, whether we shall do the less evil by disobeying this, or by disobeying that law: and, consequently, to say here, that out of two evils, we should choose the least, cannot help to remove this doubt; because this maxim, since it contains nothing, but what is contained in the question, upon which we doubt, leaves the question just where it was. But if we take the maxim in the other sense, and consider it merely as a maxim of prudence, which directs us, where, out of two evils, we must suffer one, to follow that course, which will make us suffer the least, it is not applicable to the point which is now before us: because it supposes, that, whatever course we follow, we must suffer the penalty of one of the laws. Whereas, when two laws interfere, and it is impossible to obey both of them, if we choose rightly; that is, if we obey the law, which the legislator would, in such a case choose to have us obey, we shall avoid both the penalties. We comply with one of the laws, and, therefore, stand clear of the penalty, upon which it is established. And though we disobey the other, we cannot justly be punished for disobeying it; because, whilst we comply with that, it was impossible for us to comply with this. But the rule, which directs us, where two laws interfere, to give the preference to that, which is established upon the higher penalty, though it is not supported by the maxim, that out of two evils the least is to be chosen, may be supported by the same reason with the rule, which was last mentioned. The legislator has guarded that law the most carefully, which he has established upon the higher penalty: from whence we may presume, that he looked upon that as the law of the more importance, and, consequently, that he would choose to have us comply with that, if by any accident it becomes impossible for us to comply with both.

Seventhly, where two laws interfere, we should follow that, which is recommended by the most honest or the most beneficial reasons. The question, concerning the woman's claim to have her statue in the gymnasium, is determined in her favour by Puffendorf: because the law, which gives her this claim, is recommended by a more beneficial reason than the other law, which opposes her claim. Another question which has already been mentioned, where the same law, by accident, interferes with itself, may be determined, by comparing the honesty or justice of the reasons on both sides. Where two women had been ravished by the same man, and the law gave any woman, who had been thus injured, her option, that the man should either be put to death, or be compelled to marry her; one of them claimed to have him put to death, and the other claimed to have him in marriage. She, who claims to marry him, would lose her husband, if he was put to death: whereas, she, who claims to have him put to death, does not properly lose any thing by his marrying the other. The claim, therefore, of the former, seems to be recommended by a more honest and just reason, than the claim of the latter.

Scarce any laws but what will naturally admit of rational interpretation.

XIII. There are scarce any laws, but what will naturally admit of rational or liberal interpretation; that is, either of being so enlarged, as to take some cases into the meaning of the law, which are not contained in the letter, or of being so restrained as to exclude some cases out of the meaning, which are contained in the letter. For the intention of the legislator is the natural measure of the extent of the law, whether that intention is collected from his words alone, by literal interpretation, or from his words, and some other signs, by mixed interpretation, or from such other signs alone by rational interpretation. In like manner, wills and contracts naturally admit of being interpreted rationally, of being so enlarged, as to extend beyond the letter, or of being so restrained, as to fall short of it: because the intention of the testator, or of the parties contracting, as far as it is known, is the natural measure of the claim arising from these acts; whether that intention appears plainly in their words, or is ascertained by the help of some other signs, and of their words taken together, when their words leave it doubtful; or is collected from such other signs alone, when their words do not express it perfectly.

The design of the legislator, in some civil laws, or in some clauses of them, is, indeed, confined to his words: and where it is so confined, nothing can either be taken into the meaning of the law, or be left out of it by rational interpretation. The design of an explanatory law, is to explain, by words, the meaning of the legislator in some antecedent law, which was expressed ambiguously or imperfectly. An explanatory law, therefore, will not admit of rational interpretation: as the design of the law is confined to the words of it, we must look for the meaning of it in the words only. For the same reason, all definitions in a law are to be interpreted closely: they are neither to be enlarged to any thing more, nor to be restrained to any thing less, than the words express. The legislator designs, in such definition, to explain, by his words, the term, which he defines: whatever, therefore, is more than these words express, is not within the design of the legislator; and whatever is less, falls short of his design.

But either an explanatory law, which has reference to some antecedent law, or a definition in a law, which has reference to some term made use of in the same law, though they do not admit of rational or free interpretation, may possibly be ambiguous: and when they are, we must ascertain the meaning of the legislator by mixed interpretation. If the ambiguity in these laws arises, as it frequently does in other laws, from a word or a sentence, which will admit either of a more extensive, or of a more confined sense; we must have recourse to the topics of mixed interpretation, to determine in which of these two senses such word or such sentence was used by the legislator. For though explanatory laws are to be interpreted closely, and will not admit of any meaning, but what is contained and expressed in the words of them; yet no argument can be drawn from the nature of such laws, to prove, that, where the words themselves admit both of a strict and of a large sense, we must necessarily adhere to the former. We must, indeed, keep to the letter of the law: but there is no natural reason, why we must follow the narrowest and most confined sense, that the letter of the law is capable of.

Rational interpretation, both such as enlarges the meaning of the writer beyond his words, and such as restrains it to a less extent than what his words import, may be expressly precluded by some positive declaration of the writer himself. If the lawmaker, or the contractors, or the testator have directed that the law, or the contract, or the will, shall be construed according to the literal and grammatical sense of the words; this direction is a bar to all interpretation, which is purely rational: it shows, that the intention of the writer came fully up to his words, and went no farther; and, consequently, that whatever meaning we give to the writing, which either falls short of the words or goes beyond them, such meaning is not agreeable to his intention. But though a declaration of this sort precludes all interpretation, which is purely rational, and obliges us to interpret the writing strictly, or rather closely; that is, to adhere, in our interpretation of it, precisely to the words; yet, if the words themselves are ambiguous, if in their literal and grammatical construction they will admit of more senses than one, we may, notwithstanding such declaration, have recourse to mixed interpretation, and may argue from rational conjectures to determine, in which of these several senses the writer used them. For mixed interpretation is not inconsistent with the writer's declaration: because this sort of interpretation, whilst it proceeds upon rational conjectures, keeps to the literal and grammatical sense of the words. Now, amongst other causes of ambiguity, one is, that the words of a writing, in the common acceptation of them, are sometimes used in a more narrow, and sometimes in a more comprehensive sense. And since either of these senses may be called a literal and grammatical sense; because both of them are equally authorized by common usage; the consequence is, that, though the writer has required us, in our interpretation, to adhere to the literal and grammatical sense, there is no more reason, upon account of what he has said about this matter, to adhere rather to the narrow or strict sense, than to follow the comprehensive or large sense: notwithstanding his direction about following the literal and grammatical sense, we must make use of probable conjectures drawn from other topics, besides his words, to determine in which of the literal and grammatical senses he used the words, whether in their narrow and strict sense, or in their comprehensive and large sense. Thus, a declaration or direction of this sort, though it obliges us to interpret the writing strictly, in one sense of the word—strictly, does not oblige us to interpret it strictly in another sense of the same word: it obliges us to keep strictly to the words of the writing without deviating from them, either so as to leave any thing out of his meaning, which the words express, or so as to take any thing into his meaning, which they do not express. But it does not oblige us, whilst we keep strictly to the words, to follow the most narrow, or the strict sense of those words: it leaves us at liberty to follow either this sense, or the more comprehensive and large sense, according to what we find by rational conjectures to have been, most probably, his meaning.

If there are any other civil laws, in which we are not allowed to make use of rational interpretation, besides such as are merely explanatory; that is, if in the interpretation of any other laws, besides these, we are not allowed to take either more or less into the meaning of them than what the words express; this restraint arises, not from the nature of the laws themselves, but from some positive institution. And this positive institution may either be contained in the particular law, which will not admit of rational interpretation, as we have just now observed, that it is, where the legislator directs us to follow the literal and grammatical sense of the words; or else it may be introduced by a general law, which has been made concerning interpretation by the civil legislator of the society to which we belong. For the rules of interpretation are under the authority of the civil legislator, and are, therefore, to be applied in such a manner, and upon such occasions, as he shall prescribe, in view to the general benefit, either by a written law, or by usage and custom; the former of which is an express act, and the latter is a tacit act of his authority.

In like manner, where any words or sentences in a law or a contract, have two senses in common acceptation, one of which is more confined, and the other more comprehensive, there is not any particular sort of laws or contracts, which will naturally require such ambiguous words or sentences to be taken in the more confined sense; nor is there, on the contrary, any particular sort which will naturally require them to be taken in the more comprehensive sense. The intention of the legislator is the natural measure of the obligation arising from the law; and the intention of the parties contracting, is the natural measure of the claim arising from the contract. This intention is to be collected from the same topics of interpretation in laws and contracts of all sorts: unless the civil legislator of the society, in which the law is made, or to which the contractors belong, has expressly prescribed some particular rules of interpretation, or some particular method of applying the rules suggested by natural reason; or unless such particular rules, or such particular method of application have been introduced and established by long and uninterrupted usage, which has the same effect as if the civil legislator had expressly prescribed them.

CHAPTER VIII.

OF CIVIL SUBJECTION AND CIVIL LIBERTY.

I. *General notion of subjection.*—II. *Subjection private and public.*—III. *Different degrees and sorts of private subjection.*—IV. *Different degrees and sorts of public subjection.*—V. *Civil subjection of the parts and of the whole.*—VI. *What sort of subjection implied in the notion of a province.*—VII. *Civil liberty, what.*—VIII. *Civil liberty of the parts and of the whole.*—IX. *Slaves why incapable of being members of a civil society.*—X. *Where subjection ceases, right of resistance begins.*—XI. *Relation of governor and subject is a limited one.*—XII. *Resistance to the supreme power, how to be understood.*—XIII. *Right of resistance does not imply supreme civil power in the people.*—XIV. *Opinion of Grotius, explained.*—XV. *Civil judge not necessary to fix the point where right of resistance begins.*—XVI. *Treason and rebellion, how guarded against, notwithstanding right of resistance.*

General notion of subjection.

I. Every compact, in which a man consents to lay himself under an obligation of doing, or of avoiding what the law of nature had not otherwise obliged him to do or to avoid, is a diminution of his liberty. Before he had engaged in the compact, or had laid himself under the obligation, he was at liberty either to have done or to have avoided what is contained in the compact. But after he has consented to be thus obliged, he is no longer possessed of the same liberty: he cannot be obliged to do or to avoid what is contained in the compact, and at the same time be at liberty either to do it or to avoid it, as he pleases.

But every compact, which implies a diminution of liberty, does not imply likewise a state of subjection. The notion of subjection consists in the obligation of one or more persons to act at the discretion, or according to the judgment and will of others. When, therefore, the matter of an obligation, which arises from compact, is so precisely settled from the beginning as to leave nothing to the judgment or will of those to whom we are obliged, the obligation, though it diminishes our liberty, does not place us in a state of subjection. Such a compact gives them a claim upon us, without giving them any authority over us. Their claim is so limited from first to last, by our own act, and according to our own discretion and choice, as never to extend beyond such limitation. This claim, therefore, is all along rather the effect of the power, which we have over ourselves, than the effect of any power which they have over us. But when the compact is such from the beginning, as gives them a general demand upon us, and leaves the precise matter of the obligation to be in any respect determined by their discretion and choice, as far as it thus gives them a right to judge for us, and to prescribe to us, it gives them an authority over us, and places us in a state of subjection to this authority.

Subjection private and public.

II. Subjection is commonly divided into private and public. By private subjection, is meant subjection to the authority of private persons: and by public subjection, is meant subjection to the authority of public persons.

A civil society, though it consists of a great number of individuals, is considered as one artificial or collective person: because it is guided by one common understanding, which is its legislative power, and acts with one common force, which is its executive power. This artificial or collective body is called a public person. The subjection, therefore, which is due to a civil society, is public subjection. But the notion of a public person is not confined to the collective body of a civil society. Whether the legislative body of such a society consists of one natural person, as in monarchies, or is an artificial or collective person, consisting of many natural ones, as in aristocracies, and in mixed constitutions; this natural, or this collective person, has the keeping of the common or public understanding: and, in like manner, the executive body, whether it is the same with the legislative body, or different from it, acts with the common or public force. These bodies, therefore; that is, the constitutional governors of a civil society, are called public persons; and the subjection, which is due to them, is public subjection.

*Grotius divides subjection, as it is here divided, into private and public. But first, he distinguishes between association and subjection: and though he allows, that a right over persons may be derived as well from association as from subjection, yet this distinction implies that, in his opinion, the right which a society or collective body of men acquires over the persons of the several individuals who have associated or joined themselves into such a collective body, is different from subjection. †He then goes on to divide associations or societies, as he afterwards divides subjection, into private and public. Those he calls private associations, which are formed by a small number of private persons, who have agreed to act together for the purpose of carrying on some private design. Public associations are either such as produce a public person, or such as consist of public persons; that is, they are either formed by a large body of men, who have united themselves by compact into a state or civil society; or else they are formed by a number of states, which have agreed to act together in the prosecution of some common design. An association of the former sort produces a public person; and an association of the latter sort consists of public persons.

If the several persons, who have formed themselves into a society, either private or public, have proceeded no farther than to unite themselves by mutual consent into one body, under the obligation of jointly carrying on their common design, it must, indeed, be allowed, that the several members of such society will be equal to one another, when they are considered separately: such an agreement does not subject any one member to the authority of any other member; and much less does it subject all of them to the authority of any one, or of a few. But, in the meantime, it is plain, that, as far as the matter of the obligation, which the several members lay themselves under, is not precisely limited from the beginning, all associations produce subjection; not, indeed, a subjection of any one member to any other, but a subjection of any one to the collective body. For, as ‡we have elsewhere observed,

* Grot. Lib. I. Cap. V. § XXVI. VIII.

† Grot. Ibid. § XVII.

‡ See Book II. Chap. I. § II.

after our author, whatever measure is agreed upon in relation to the common purpose of the society, by a majority of the members, it will be binding upon all and each, not only upon those who make a part of the majority, but upon those likewise who disapprove the measure so agreed upon, or even protest against it. Grotius, whilst he distinguishes between the right over persons, which arises from association, and the right over persons which arises from subjection, seems to allow that such a subjection, as we have been speaking of, is produced by association: for, he observes, *that the body of a civil society, in particular, has a fuller right than any other society whatsoever, of binding its several members to act for the common benefit, in such a manner as the common understanding dictates. And certainly, if each member of a society, either private or public, has obliged himself by compact to be guided in pursuing the ends for which such society is formed, by a judgment and will which are not his own, this compact produces subjection; notwithstanding our author distinguishes its effect from subjection, and calls it association. Any particular member of a society may happen to concur with the majority; and if he does, he may appear, whilst he acts according to the judgment and will of such majority, to follow his own. But this concurrence, in regard to his obligation, is quite accidental: he would have been as much obliged to guide himself by the judgment and will of the majority, if he had dissented from the measure, which they agree upon, as he is when he happens to make a part of the majority, and to concur in what they establish.

Different degrees and sorts of private subjection.

III. †Private subjection admits of several different degrees, from a state of absolute or personal slavery to such limited obligations as can scarce be called subjection. A compact, by which we give any one person, or any number of persons, a general demand upon us to act for their benefit, or for the benefit of any one else, without fixing any limits at all to the matter of the obligation, produces perfect subjection or slavery. This sort of subjection, though it is sometimes called absolute subjection, is not absolute in the strictest sense of the word, so as to give the master a right to treat the slave in what manner he pleases, or to compel the slave to do any thing that he pleases: for we have already ‡seen, that the law of nature fixes some limitations to slavery, though the slave himself has not fixed any by the compact which produced his subjection. It is called a state of absolute subjection; because it is as absolute as the law of nature will allow it to be, or as the persons who place themselves in such a state can make it.

But all private subjection is not slavery. The compact, which produces it, may render it imperfect by limiting the matter of the obligation: and the subjection will be the less perfect, in proportion as less is left to the judgment and will of those, to whom we are subject. A labourer, who has bound himself to do only one particular sort of work, is in a state of private subjection: his master, by the compact, which is between them, has acquired a right to direct him in what relates to this work. But the subjection is imperfect: because his obligation to be directed by the judgment and will of his master is limited, not only by

* Grot. Lib. II. Cap. V. § XXIII. † Grot. Ibid. § XXVI.

‡ See Book I. Chap. XX. § V.

the general law of nature, as in the case of slavery, but likewise by the particular compact, from which it arose.

Private subjection may be divided into different sorts, as well as into different degrees. Where it has only the benefit of the superior in view; and all the benefit, which the inferior finds in it, is merely accidental; it is servile subjection. But where such conditions are annexed to it, as have the benefit of the inferior principally in view, either in whole or in part; that is, where the person, who is in subjection, is obliged, either in whole or in part, to act according to the judgment and will of another, for the same purpose, which he would naturally have pursued, if he had been free to judge and to choose for himself; this may be called liberal subjection. A child is in subjection to his parents, and a ward to his guardian: but this, though it is private subjection, is not of the servile sort; because the benefit of the child, or of the ward, is the end or purpose which it has in view. In these two instances, indeed, the right to direct does not arise from the consent of the person, who is in subjection: in the instance of a child and his parents, it arises out of the law of nature; and in the instance of a ward and his guardian, it arises either out of some act of a deceased parent, or out of the civil law, which places the child, during his minority, under the authority of his guardian. But where the civil law allows of adoption, and allows a child, before he is old enough to do any other valid act, to consent to adoption; the subjection of the child to the parents, who adopt him, arises from his own consent. In like manner, where the civil law allows an orphan to choose a guardian, before he is at a legal age to do any other valid act, the consent of the orphan places him in a state of subjection to his guardian. In both these cases, the subjection is of the private and of the liberal sort. It is private, because it is subjection to a private person: and it is liberal, because it has the benefit of the inferior in view. In private partnerships, each of the partners is in subjection to the collective body, as far as the matter of the partnership extends: but this subjection, as it has the common benefit for its end, in which benefit each has an interest, is liberal subjection.

Grotius considers subjection as imperfect, not only where the obligation, on one side, and the demand on the other side, are limited to some particular actions, and include a condition in favour of the person, who is in subjection; but, likewise, where the obligation and the demand, though they are under no limitation, in respect of the matter of them, are limited in respect of the time, during which they are to continue. He would, probably, have been of another opinion, if he had attended here to a principle, from which he argues * elsewhere. When he is proving, that civil power may be sovereign, notwithstanding it is temporary; he observes, that the nature of a thing is not changed merely by its duration, and in particular, that the nature of any moral power is to be judged of from the effects which are produced by it, whilst it lasts, and not from the time, during which it lasts. Indeed, the power of a master over his slave is not civil power; and the subjection of the slave is not civil subjection. But the principle, from which Grotius argues, is general: and if it is true, when applied to power and subjection of one

* Grot. Lib. I. Cap. III. § XI.

sort; it will be equally true, when applied to power and subjection of any other sort. Now, the effects of the master's power are the same, if the matter of the compact is the same; whether that power continues only for a determinate time, or for the whole life of the slave. If, therefore, the master has a power to direct all the actions of the slave without any limitation, except what arises from the general law of nature; the slave is as much in a state of absolute subjection, where this power continues only for a determinate time, for seven or fourteen years, as where it continues during the life of the slave. The condition of a temporary slave, if we only consider what it is, whilst the slavery lasts, is neither better nor worse, than the condition of a perpetual slave. Perhaps the prospect, which the former has, of recovering his liberty at a certain time, may make his present condition set easier upon him, than the present condition of the latter does, who has no such prospect before him. But the prospect of coming into a better condition, however it may encourage him to bear his present condition well, makes no essential difference in the nature of the condition itself. Though he may be cheered by the hopes of recovering his liberty hereafter; yet he is now, whilst his slavery lasts, as much in a state of perfect subjection, as the other is. It must, however, be allowed, that if we were to give our opinion upon the different conditions of the temporary and the perpetual slave, we should be apt to say, and should have some reason for saying, that the former is in a better condition than the latter. But the reader, I suppose, is aware, that when we make this judgment about the difference of their respective conditions, we consider something more than merely their present conditions: we take the whole of their respective lives, their future as well as their present circumstances, into the account, and reckon the condition of the one, to be better than the condition of the other, not because it is better just now, but because it is better upon the whole.

Different degrees and sorts of public subjection.

IV. All public subjection is not civil subjection: for in public, as well as in private subjection, there are different degrees and different sorts: and civil subjection is one particular sort and degree of public subjection.

Not only an individual or private person, but a nation, likewise, or state, which is a public person, may have slaves. Those, who are condemned to labour for the public in the mines, or in the gallies, or in any other work whatsoever, which the state thinks proper to employ them about, are in public subjection. But as the benefit of the superior is the only end, which this subjection has in view, it is of the servile sort; and as the matter of the obligation is not limited, it is absolute in degree. The supposition, that they, who are thus in subjection to the public, are condemned to slavery, implies, indeed, that their subjection does not arise from their own consent; but that it is the punishment of some crime, which they have committed: the instance, therefore, may seem not to belong to such subjection, as we are now speaking of, which is subjection, arising from consent. However, as it is possible for a man thus to subject himself to an individual or private person, by his own consent; so it is possible for him, in like manner, to subject himself, by a like consent, to a body politic, or public person.

Labourers, who let themselves out to the public, to do some particular sort of work, such as mending roads, or making fortifications, or building ships, and likewise, mercenary soldiers, are in a state of public subjection. Their subjection is imperfect in degree; because the matter of the obligation, on their side, and of the claim on the side of the public, is limited: but in the meantime, as the end of it is rather the benefit of the public than of themselves, it is of the servile sort. But it may be worth the while to observe, that, even in these instances, the subjection is looked upon to be less servile, or approaches nearer to liberal subjection, in proportion as the persons, who are in subjection, have a greater benefit from it. Thus the officers, the architects, and the master builders are in subjection to the public, as well as the common soldiers, and the under workmen: but the subjection of the former is more liberal, and of the latter more servile; only because the obligation, in which their respective subjection consists, has the benefit of the former more in view, and the benefit of the latter less in view.

Civil subjection is such public subjection arising from consent, as is limited in the matter of it to those actions or things, which relate to the general welfare and security of the whole civil society, or of its several parts. The individuals, who have consented to make themselves members of a civil society, are, in consequence of this consent, in a state of subjection: because they are obliged, by it, to act according to a judgment and will, which are not in their own keeping, but in the keeping of the public. This subjection, however, is neither absolute nor servile. For since the matter of the obligation is limited to what relates to the general welfare and security of the whole society, or of its several parts; this limitation makes the subjection imperfect. And since the members of the society have a common interest in the good of the whole body, and a particular interest in the protection, which they have a right to, as they are parts of the whole; this end or view of the obligation makes the subjection liberal.

Civil subjection of the parts, and of the whole.

V. It is very difficult to affix a precise sense to the words, civil subjection and civil liberty. For whatever sense we may endeavour to affix to them, any man who chooses to call it into question, may produce numberless instances, both from what he has heard and from what he has read upon these points, to prove, that the words are not always used in this sense: not because there is no sort of subjection, and no sort of liberty which may properly be called by these names; nor yet because the definitions, which we may endeavour to give of these words, do not fully express the nature of this sort of subjection, or this sort of liberty; but because the words are frequently used as words of course, both in common conversation and in many political writings; so that numberless instances are to be found, in which some person or other has used the words in speaking or in writing, without any determinate meaning, or perhaps without any meaning at all.

Indeed, the most accurate writers do not always use these words in one and the same sense. Thus, civil subjection means sometimes the subjection of the whole society, and sometimes the subjection of its several parts; that is, both the subjection of the collective body to its constitutional governors, and the subjection likewise of the several members, either to such constitutional governors or to the collective body, are usually called civil subjection. And if we would avoid being misled or perplexed, in what we read or hear upon these points, it will be necessary for us to distinguish these two senses of the same words from one another, and to observe in which of them the words are used.

The several members of a civil society are in a state of civil subjection, whatever form of government is established in the society. They are obliged by the social compact to follow the dictates of the public understanding in what relates to the general good; whether the constitution is popular, or aristocratical, or monarchical, or mixed. The seat of the civil power, indeed, is different, in these different forms of government: so that the subjection of the individuals is more immediately due to a different sort of public person. But wherever this power resides, the subjection, which is due to it from the individuals, is only civil subjection. For this is all that was due by the social compact to the collective body: and this collective body, in settling the constitution by a fundamental law, cannot give either to a king, or to a senate of nobles, or to any other civil governors whatsoever, a more extensive claim upon the several members, than such body originally acquired by their particular consent, either express or tacit, when they united themselves to it.

But though under all forms of government, the individuals who have made themselves members of a civil society, are of right, whatever they may be in fact, in a like state of civil subjection; yet in democracies, the collective body itself is not under any subjection: it governs itself freely, and is not bound by the act of any one or more persons. Whereas, in other forms of government, if they have no mixture of a democracy in their constitution, there is a subjection of the whole, as well as of the parts; a subjection of the collective body, as well as of its separate members. For the act of the constitutional governors is not only binding upon the several individuals who compose the collective body, but in consequence of the general consent, by which the constitution was established, it becomes binding upon this body itself.

From hence we may understand what sort of freedom it is, which puts the difference between free states and other states. The individuals in a free state, are not free from civil subjection any more than they are in any other state, which is governed by a king, or by a select body of nobles. But in a free state, the collective body of the whole society is free, or is not under any subjection: whereas, in absolute monarchies, or in absolute aristocracies, the collective body is in a state of subjection to its constitutional governors; because, as far as the power of these governors extends, their act is binding upon the collective body, as well as upon the several members. Whether common usage has given the title of free states, or not, to those nations in which the form of government is a mixed one, such nations have certainly the essence of a free state; notwithstanding a king may be a constituent part of the legislative body, and may be vested with the executive power; provided the collective body is not bound by any act of legislation, in which it does not immediately and directly concur, either by itself or by its representatives. The freedom of the collective body of a civil society is not necessarily connected with a mixed constitution: it is the particular nature of the mixture, upon which that freedom depends. If the legislative body consists of a single person, and of a select number of hereditary nobility; though the constitution will be a mixed one, yet the collective body of the civil society will be in subjection: because, in establishing the constitution, this collective body obliged itself, as far as the ends or purposes of social union extend, to follow a judgment and will, which is not in its own keeping, but in the keeping of that particular part which composes the legislative body. By adding to these two parts of such a mixed legislative a third, which consists of representatives chosen from time to time, by the general body of the society, this general body, which is usually called the people, does not, indeed, reserve to itself a full power of legislation, but it reserves such an independent power as prevents its subjection: though it has not a power of making laws by its own judgment and will, yet without its own judgment and will, signified by its representatives, no laws will be binding upon it.

A like independence, in such a form of government as we have been describing, is given to the single person or king, whom we have supposed to be a constitutional part of the legislative body: for though, by the supposition of his being only a part of such body, he has not, in matters of legislation, a power of binding either the general body of the society, or the particular members of it, by his own judgment and will, without the concurrence of the other parts of the legislative; yet neither he himself, nor any one else within the society, can be bound by any law to which he does not consent at the time of making it; except the fundamental laws of the constitution, to which he consented, either expressly when he accepted the crown, or tacitly by the act of accepting it. But when we say, that his consent is necessary to make a law binding either upon himself, or upon any one else within the society, we must be understood to include the consent of his predecessors, under the notion of his consent. For, as they acted by the same power which he is possessed of, the effect of their consent, in respect both of himself and of the subjects, is the same as if such consent had been his own immediate act. If, besides this civil independence, which is given to one single person within a society, by making him a constitutional and distinct part of the legislative body, we suppose the same person to be likewise invested with the supreme executive power; he may then very properly be considered as the supreme or sovereign head of the state. In this latter character only, as he is invested with the supreme executive power, all the members of the society would be accountable to him, or to standing judges, who act for him in matters of public wrong; and they must have recourse to him, or to the like judges, for redress in matters of private wrong. But if he was invested with no other power besides this; though he would be the supreme magistrate, he could not well be called the supreme head of the state: he would be supreme in reference to other magistrates, who hold an inferior executive power, derived out of his; but as the executive power, even in its highest degree, is subordinate to the legislative power; so he, if he was invested with no other power besides what is merely executive, would be subordinate to the legislative body. But by making him a constitutional and distinct part of the legislative, this subordination is so far taken off, and his executive power becomes so far independent or sovereign, that though he cannot exercise this power in all instances, according to his own judgment and will, yet as his consent is necessary in making the laws, which direct the exercise of it, he is not obliged to exercise it according to the judgment and will of any other persons, without the concurrence of his own.

What sort of subjection implied in the notion of a province.

VI. Where the general body of a society is in subjection, it is a material difference whether its civil governors have a claim to this subjection, as they are the ruling parts of this particular body; or whether they have the like claim, as they are the ruling parts of some other society. In the former case, the society, notwithstanding its subjection, continues to be a state; but in the latter case, it is a province of that other society or state, the ruling parts of which have a claim to its subjection.

The supposition, that a province is in subjection to the ruling parts of a state, implies that the state itself is in subjection. But we have here proceeded upon this supposition, only for the sake of showing, that, though the subjection is in all other respects of the same sort, the difference of external and internal subjection will make one society a province, and another a state. For, it is by no means essential to the notion of a province, that the state, of which it is a province, should be in subjection to any particular ruling parts. A society may be a province to a free state, as well as to a state which is not free. Though a free state is not in subjection to any particular ruling parts; yet if the general or collective body of some other society is in subjection to the general or collective body of such free state, this other society will be a province.

Civil liberty, what.

VII. By natural liberty, is sometimes meant the independent physical power, which individuals have of judging, choosing and acting for themselves. But when natural liberty is distinguished from civil liberty, the former means the moral liberty of mankind in a state of nature, and the latter means their moral liberty in a state of civil society. Now, the moral liberty of mankind in a state of nature, consists in a power of acting in what manner they think fit; as far as they are under no restraints from the law of nature, when they are considered as separate and independent individuals. And their civil liberty is sometimes defined to be the like power of acting in what manner they think fit, as far as they are under no restraints from civil laws. This definition of civil liberty is so contrived as to make it answer very well in the words of it, to the definition of natural liberty. But it is certainly liable to many objections, and does not fix the true point of difference between the two sorts of liberty.

All laws which are made by a civil legislator, are civil laws. Now, in perfectly monarchical constitutions, the monarch is the civil legislator. His laws, therefore, whatever may happen to be the matter of them, whether they tend to the general benefit of the society, or to his own particular interest, may be called civil laws. From hence it will follow, if civil liberty is as much liberty as is consistent with civil laws, that the subjects under all the oppression which the laws of a despotic monarch can bring upon them, will be in possession of their civil liberties, not only in right, but in fact. I am aware, however, that this objection may be obviated by looking back into the nature of the social compact: for as this compact limits civil power, or the power of a civil governor, so it limits, likewise, the matter of the laws, which he has authority to make, to such things as are necessary or conducive to the security and welfare of the whole society, or of its several parts.

No command, therefore, of the monarch, though he is the civil legislator, can properly be considered as a civil law, if it is inconsistent with the ends of social union and civil government. So that, notwithstanding civil liberty should be defined to be as much liberty as is consistent with civil laws, the subjects, who are oppressed by the unsocial commands of an absolute monarch, could not be in possession of their civil liberty: because they are under the restraint of such commands as are not civil laws. Without examining this answer, we will suppose it sufficient so far to obviate the objection, as to show, that the definition, when it is rightly explained and duly qualified, is a true one. But still this answer will not so far remove the objection, as to show, that the definition is a good one: for no definition can be a good one, which wants to be explained and qualified, before it will convey a precise notion of the term defined.

But we may object farther, that, if civil liberty consists in as much liberty as is consistent with civil laws, or in the power of mankind to act in what manner they please, where civil law does not restrain them, there can be no such thing as civil liberty in any society whatsoever. For the liberty of individuals is *restrained in many instances, particularly in such rights as arise out of an injury, by the mere act of civil union, without the aid of any civil law, and antecedently to the positive or express institution of any. In all societies, therefore, whatever the form of government, or the tenor of the civil laws may happen to be, the members are under some restraints, which do not come from civil laws.

Perhaps, by considering a consequence which will follow from this definition, we may be led to the true point of difference between natural and civil liberty. If civil liberty is as much liberty as is consistent with the restraints of civil laws, the consequence will be, that every new law, however beneficial it may be either to the whole body politic or to the several members, will be a diminution of civil liberty: because it produces a farther restraint, which the subjects were not under before the law was made. But as the private and servile subjection of a slave does not consist in his being restrained by the commands which his master has actually given him; so neither is there any reason to suppose, that the public and liberal subjection of a member of civil society consists in the restraints under which he is actually laid by the civil laws. A slave is in subjection, because he is liable to be restrained, not only by such commands as he has actually received from his master, but by such, likewise, as he may receive from him hereafter. And, in like manner, a member of any civil society is in subjection, because he is liable to be restrained, not only by such laws as the civil legislator has established already, but by such, likewise, as he may establish when some future occasion makes it necessary. The subjection of a slave is different, indeed, both in sort and in degree, from the subjection of a member of civil society. They differ in sort, because one of them is private and servile, and the other is public and liberal: and they differ in degree, because one extends to all a man's actions, and the other is limited to those actions only, which relate to the general security and welfare of the whole body politic, or of its several parts. But,

* See Book II. Chap. V.

however these two instances of subjection may differ in other respects, in this they agree, that both of them are subjection: the member of a civil society, as well as the slave, is under an obligation of acting according to a judgment and will, which are not in his own keeping. As far as this obligation extends; that is, as far as their respective subjection extends, neither of them is possessed of his natural liberty. The natural liberty of the slave is destroyed by his being obliged to follow the judgment and will of his master in all things: and the natural liberty of the member of a civil society is abridged by his being obliged to follow the judgment and will of the public in such things as relate to the common or general good. Thus we see, at last, that this obligation of a member of civil society, which is nothing else but the obligation of the social compact, is what puts the difference between natural and civil liberty. If, therefore, we define natural liberty to be as much liberty as is consistent with the obligation of the law of nature, we should define civil liberty to be as much liberty as is consistent with the obligation of the social compact.

Civil liberty of the parts, and of the whole.

VIII. In order to understand the several senses, in which civil liberty is spoken of, we must distinguish it, as we before distinguished civil subjection, into the civil liberty of the parts, and the civil liberty of the whole; that is, into the liberty of the several individuals, who have united together, and compose the collective body of the society, and the liberty of this collective body itself. The civil liberty of the several members of a society implies a freedom from all, except civil subjection: but the civil liberty of the whole body implies a freedom from all subjection whatsoever. After a number of individuals have united together and formed a civil society; though any one of them is equal to any other, when they are considered separately; yet each, by the social compact, is made subject to the joint authority of the whole or collective body. But in the meantime this whole or collective body is under no restraint, either from within or from without, except the restraints of the law of nature: the social compact does not give any particular part of such body a right or authority to direct or to bind the whole: and much less does it give such right or authority to any other society of the same sort, or to the ruling part of any other.

When the society has proceeded farther than the mere act of social union, and has established some other form of government, which is different from such a perfect democracy, as would result from this act alone; it will depend upon the nature of that form of government, which is so established, whether the civil liberty of the whole shall remain or not. An absolute monarchy puts an end to this kind of civil liberty. For where a single person in the collective body has a constitutional right of directing the whole, this collective body is in a state of subjection: because it is bound to act for the purposes of social union by a judgment and will, which are not in its own keeping. This, indeed, is, of right, only civil subjection. But though civil subjection is consistent with the civil liberty of the parts or several members; it is not consistent with the civil liberty of the whole or collective body. For civil liberty is as much liberty as is consistent with the obligation of the social compact: and this compact, whilst it placed the separate members of the society under civil subjection, left the joint or collective body free to judge and to choose for itself. An absolute aristocracy is likewise inconsistent with the civil liberty of the whole: because, though such a constitution puts the power of governing the society into the hands of more persons than one, yet it places the whole body in a state of subjection to a small number of men, who are only a particular part of that whole. A mixture of these two forms of government, in whatsoever manner the mixture is made, will be as inconsistent with the civil liberty of the whole, as either of them alone would have been: for under such a mixed government the collective body of the society will be in a state of subjection; that is, it will be under an obligation of acting according to a judgment and will, which are not in its own keeping, but in the keeping of a part. But in popular forms of government, and in such mixed forms, likewise, as are in part popular, the civil liberty of the whole remains: because the collective body is not bound to follow the dictates of any judgment or will, in which it does not concur, either by itself, or by its representatives.

In any of the other forms of government, as well as in the popular forms, the civil liberty of the parts, or several members of the society, remains of right. The subjection, which they owe to their constitutional governors, whether the government is in the hands of a king, or of a senate of hereditary nobility, is only civil subjection. No constitutional civil governors, whatever their titles or denominations may be, have any other right or moral power of restraining the several members, than the collective body of the whole society has in a perfect democracy: and this right is no other, than what is derived from social union; a right to direct them what they are to do, and what they are to avoid for the general good, and to enforce these directions, where it is necessary, by the use of the joint strength. You may, therefore, ask, perhaps, of what importance it is to individuals what form of government they live under; if an absolute monarchy, or an absolute aristocracy, whilst they take away the civil liberty of the whole collective body, leave the several members the same right to their civil liberty, that they would have had under a popular constitution? The answer to this question is obvious. There is a wide difference between the right of the individuals to their civil liberty, and their enjoyment of this liberty in fact. Under every form of government their civil liberty is the same in right; but there is not the same security under every form, that it will be so in fact. Though the members of a civil society are not slaves, in right, to an absolute monarch, who has all civil power in his hands, both legislative and executive; yet he is in such a situation, as gives him an opportunity, and arms him with strength enough to treat them in fact, as if they were his slaves. It is possible that a sovereign prince, who has as absolute authority, as the nature of civil power will admit of, may make the general good of his people the measure of his conduct. But it is possible, likewise, that he may hold the opposite conduct, and instead of regarding their interest, may compel them, as if they were his slaves, to advance a separate interest of his own; whether he places this separate interest in gratifying his ambition, or his avarice, or his vanity, or his love of pleasure. The several members of the society, when they are in such a situation, do not enjoy their civil liberty: but the nature of the constitution does not take it from them of right; the injustice of him, who administers the constitution, takes it from them in fact. Since, therefore, in the nature of the thing there is a possibility, and since from the general temper of mankind, there is some likelihood, that where all is left to the will of one man, the trust, which is reposed in him, will be abused; it is necessary, in order to secure the civil liberty of the several members in fact, to preserve and maintain the civil liberty of the collective body, by giving it so much weight and influence in the legislative, that nothing can be done there without its consent, or without the consent of its representatives.

We may now understand what is meant, when, upon a change of the civil constitution of government in any nation from popular or mixed, to aristocratical or monarchical, we say, that the nation has lost or has given up its civil liberty. What is thus more immediately lost or given up of right, is the civil liberty of the collective body, and not the civil liberty of the individuals. This body, whilst the form of government was popular, acted for itself, according to its own judgment and will: but upon such a change in the constitution, it is brought into civil subjection, and obliges itself, in pursuing the ends of a civil society, to act according to a judgment and will, which are in the keeping of the governing part; of one single person, if the new form of government is monarchical, or of a body consisting of a few hereditary nobility, if it is aristocratical. But whatever the collective body of the society gives up in this change of the constitution, the several members of it, when they are considered separately, have the same right to their civil liberty, that they had before. Whilst the popular form of government continued, each was obliged to pursue the ends of social union, according to a judgment and will, which were not in his own keeping; and each is obliged to no more than this under the new form: the only difference in right is, that in the popular form, this judgment and will were in the keeping of the collective body, or of its agents and representatives; whereas, in the monarchical or aristocratical form, they are in the keeping of the particular ruling part of that body. But though this, in respect of the separate members, is the only difference in right, there will, most probably, be another difference in fact: the civil liberty of the whole or collective body is the support and security of the civil liberty of the several parts or members. The loss, therefore, of the former in right, will commonly be attended with the loss of the other in fact.

Perhaps it may here be asked, how the several parts or members of a society, when they are considered separately, can possibly have a right to their civil liberty, where such a form of government has been established by consent, as is inconsistent with the civil liberty of the whole or collective body? because this collective body consists of all the members taken together; and it is not easy to conceive, that the several parts should retain a right to civil liberty, when the whole has lost it. This would, indeed, be impossible, if the same thing was meant by civil liberty, when we speak of the whole or collective body, and when we speak of the several parts or members of that body. But the civil liberty of the whole, consists in a freedom from all subjection whatsoever: whereas, the civil liberty of the parts consists in a freedom from all, except civil subjection. The collective body, therefore, when it is placed in a state even of civil subjection, is said to have lost its civil liberty. Now, this is all the subjection which such body owes in right to its civil governors. The subjection, therefore, of the whole; that is, the loss of the civil liberty of the whole, implies nothing more than the civil subjection of the several parts. But as long as the parts or several members, are only in a state of civil subjection, they have a right to their civil liberty; that is, they have a right to be free from all restraints, except those, which, being necessary or conducive to the general good, arise out of the social compact, or are derived from it.

In mixed forms of government, where the agents or representatives of the people make a distinct and constitutional part of the legislative body; it is commonly said, that the civil liberty of the people consists in their right of thus acting in the legislative by their representatives. But before we can judge either of the truth or of the propriety of what is thus said; it will be necessary to consider, what is here meant by the people: for the word—people—may either mean the collective body, consisting of all the members taken together, or it may mean the several members taken individually.

Now, the precise notion of civil liberty, when we speak of the whole people, considered as one collective body, consists in the freedom of this body from all subjection whatsoever, or in its right of not being obliged by any judgment and will, with which its own judgment and will do not concur. But this freedom of the collective body from all subjection implies, that it has a right of acting as a distinct and constitutional part of the legislative, or that nothing can be done by the legislative without its concurrence. For since the act of the legislative is binding upon the whole society; if the legislative could do any act without the concurrence of the general body of the people, this body would be in a state of subjection. From hence it appears, that, when we speak of the people as one general or collective body, we may very properly say, that the civil liberty of the people consists in the right of acting as a distinct part of the legislative: because the collective body, if it had not this right, would be in a state of civil subjection; and a state even of civil subjection is inconsistent with the civil liberty of such body.

But though the civil liberty of the collective body of the people necessarily implies a right of acting in the legislative, yet the particular manner of acting there by representatives is not essential to the general notion of civil liberty. The people, considered as one collective body, will not be obliged to follow any judgment and will, with which its own does not concur, whether it acts there by its individual parts, or by its representatives; that is, whether the concurrence of the several members taken individually, or of the majority of them, is necessary in making laws; or whether the concurrence of representatives, who are chosen and appointed from time to time by the collective body for this purpose, is sufficient. The constitution or established form of government in each nation, where the body of the people is possessed of its civil liberty, determines in which of these ways this body shall act in the legislative; whether it shall act by its several members, so that all the individuals shall have a right of voting in the legislative, or whether it shall act by its representatives, so that the right of voting there shall be confined to these representatives. If, therefore, by the constitution of any particular nation, the collective body of the people has only a right of acting in the legislative by its representatives; the constitutional liberty of the people may, in that nation, be said to consist in this right. For as the civil liberty of the collective body of the people in any nation implies, according to the general notion of it, a right of acting in the legislative in some manner or other; so in that particular nation, the constitution has settled the manner, and has determined this right of the collective body to be a right of acting there by its representatives. Thus we find, that the civil liberty of the people, when considered as one collective body, may properly enough be said to consist in their right of acting in the legislative; because such a right is necessarily implied in the freedom of this collective body from subjection: and we find, likewise, that their constitutional civil liberty, when they are thus considered as one collective body, may be properly said to consist in their right of acting in the legislative by representatives in those nations, where the constitution requires them to act in this particular manner, and does not allow them to act individually.

But if, by the people, we mean the several individuals, we cannot, with any propriety, say, that their civil liberty consists in their right of acting individually in the legislative, and much less that it consists in their right of acting there by their representatives. In a perfect democracy, if such a form of government was established in any civil society, each member of the society would have a right of acting individually in the legislative: no laws, indeed, would be established, or nothing would be done, upon the single authority of any one member: but the opinion or vote of any one would have as much weight and influence as the opinion and vote of any other. The civil equality of the several members consists in the right which any one of them has of thus acting in the legislative, with as much weight and influence as any other of them. But we cannot suppose the civil liberty of each to consist in the same right, without supposing some of the members in every civil society, even where a democracy is established, to have no civil liberty; unless the democracy is a perfect one. In all other democracies, only some of the members have a right of acting individually in the legislative; and many others of them are excluded from acting there at all. Either, therefore, in imperfect democracies, where the members of the society, who act in the legislative, act individually; those who are excluded from acting there, upon account of some defect in their age, their sex, or their fortune, have no civil liberty; or else, in perfect democracies, the civil liberty of the several individuals does not consist in their civil equality; that is, in the right which each of them has, of acting individually with an equal weight and influence in the legislative. The common mistake is, that we suppose the civil liberty of the individuals, like the civil liberty of the collective body, to mean a freedom from all subjection whatsoever. And since in a perfect democracy, where each member acts individually, with an equal weight and influence in the legislative, no one member, and no select number of members has any authority over the rest, we are apt to consider each as exempted from all subjection, and to place the essence of the civil liberty of individuals in such a civil equality. This principle, as we have seen already, will lead us to conclude, that many members of every civil society, even under a democratical form of government, can have no civil liberty; because, even in democracies, unless they are perfect ones, many of the members are so far from acting with as much weight and influence in the legislative as the rest, that they are excluded from acting there at all. But the civil liberty of the several members of a society, does not consist, as the civil liberty of the collective body does, in a freedom from all subjection whatsoever; it consists only in a freedom from all, except civil subjection. Unless, therefore, the members of a civil society, by ceasing to have a right of acting individually in the legislative, are in a state of any other besides civil subjection; they have not lost their civil liberty, by ceasing to have this right: and, consequently, the essence of their civil liberty cannot consist in this right.

We may show, in like manner, that, in those democracies, or in those mixed constitutions, where the collective body of the people acts in the legislative by representatives, though the civil liberty of such collective body may be said to consist in this right, yet the civil liberty of the individuals cannot be said to consist in it. There is, in fact, no democracy and no mixed constitution any where established, which allows every individual a right of voting in the choice of such representatives. Many are excluded from this right, not only upon account of their sex, or of their legal minority, but upon account likewise of the smallness of their property, or even upon account of the sort of property which they are possessed of, though it should in itself be ever so large. Shall we say, therefore, that those who are thus excluded from voting in the choice of representatives, have no civil liberty, and that those only have civil liberty who have a right of voting? This, I suppose, will scarce be said: and if it is not said, the consequence is obvious. If those individuals, who have no right of voting in the choice of the representatives of the people, either in a democracy or in a mixed form of government, have their civil liberty, the consequence is, that their civil liberty cannot consist in a right of acting by representatives in the legislative: for the agents or representatives of the people cannot naturally be considered as the agents or representatives of those individuals who have no right of voting in the choice of them.

It is, indeed, very intelligible, that, when the laws of a society have limited the right of voting, in the choice of the agents or representatives of the people, to those persons who have such qualifications as these laws describe, the agents or representatives so chosen, will have the same power of binding the several individuals, even those amongst the rest who had no vote in the choice of them, that the collective body, or the majority of such collective body, in a perfect democracy, has of binding its several members, even those amongst the rest, who do not concur with such majority. But, in the meantime, they are not properly the representatives of any individuals in particular, but of the collective body in general: and especially they are not the agents or representatives of those individuals who had no vote in the choice or appointment of them.

But though the civil liberty of individuals in any nation, where the collective body of the people acts in the legislative by representatives, does not consist in their right of thus acting, yet the right of the collective body thus to act, is of great importance to the civil liberty of the individuals: the essence of the civil liberty of individuals does not consist in this right; but this right is the support of their civil liberty. For the freedom of the collective body of the people, from all subjection whatsoever, is what maintains and supports the several individuals in their freedom from all, except civil subjection.

Slaves why incapable of being members of a civil society.

IX. It is essential to a civil society, that the several members of it should be persons of *free condition; so that no person, who is not of free condition, is capable of being a member of such a society. But the freedom here required, is not a freedom from all subjection, but only from absolute and servile subjection; that is, from slavery. A freedom from all subjection whatsoever, is so far from being necessary to qualify any person to be a member of a civil society, that the civil subjection which each member is under, either to the society in general, or to the ruling parts of it in particular, is the very reason why a slave is incapable of being a member. A slave is obliged to act for his master's benefit, in all things, according to the judgment and will of his master. He is, therefore, incapable of becoming a member of a civil society: because, whilst he is under this unlimited obligation to a private person, he is incapable, or has not the liberty, of obliging himself, as every member of a civil society is obliged to act for the general security and welfare of such society, according to the judgment and will of the public. If we were to suppose the several members of a civil society to be under no subjection to the civil government of it; that is, to be under no obligation of maintaining the general security, and of advancing the general interest of it, under the conduct of the public understanding, a slave would be as capable as any one else, of being a member of such a society.

Since slaves are not, and cannot be, members of a civil society, their situation is something singular, when they live within its territories, and their master is a member of it. As they have no will of their own, they cannot, by any express or tacit act, subject themselves to the laws of the society, either perpetually, as those persons do who become members of it; or for a time, as aliens do, who reside within its territories. And since they cannot subject themselves to the laws, for the benefit and security of others, they are, therefore, incapable of acquiring a right to the protection of the laws for their own benefit and security. But by means of their master, they are brought under the authority of the laws. They are considered as parts of their master; and are, therefore, subject to the laws, because he is subject to them. Or, to speak more plainly, the society would not suffer him to bring any person, and much less to bring any considerable number of persons, to live within its territories, unless he would agree to make them accountable to the laws, or to be accountable for them himself, at least as far as the general security requires: and his agreement for this purpose binds them; because their will is concluded by his. Upon his account, likewise, or by his means, they are placed under the protection of the society: for as he has a just right to be protected by the society, so he has a right, that his slaves, who are parts of him, should likewise be protected by it; that is, as far as he has an interest in their labour, they may be considered as his property, and will, therefore, be under the protection of the society, in the same manner with any other parts of his property.

* See Book I. Chap. I. § XI.

The principal question concerning the protection of slaves is, whether the society has authority to protect them against their master? * We have seen, that the power of the master is under some limitations, which necessarily arise out of the law of nature: and, consequently, by any such treatment of them, as exceeds these limitations, he does them an injury. The question then is, whether the society, of which he is a member, has authority to protect them against such injuries, or to punish him for having been guilty of them? The mere act of social union does not seem to give the society such an authority over the master for the benefit or security of his slaves. The society, in consequence of the master's act, by which he became a member of it, takes the slaves under its protection as a part of his property: but the authority thus acquired, is an authority to protect them for his benefit, and does not include an authority to protect them against him for their benefit. Civil laws, however, may do what the mere act of civil union had not done: if it appears to the common understanding, that the master's liberty of treating his slaves otherwise than the law of nature allows, will tend to make him a worse member of society, more imperious towards his inferiors, more assuming towards his equals, more insolent towards his superiors, and more cruel towards all; the civil legislator has a right to restrain him from these excesses, and to punish him if he is guilty of them.

Right of resistance begins where civil subjection ceases.

X. It is a question of some importance, and has been thought a question not easily to be determined, whether the members of a civil society have, upon any event or in any circumstances whatsoever, a right to resist the governors, or rather the persons, who are invested with the civil power of that society.

Without stopping here to inquire, whether some, if not most of the difficulties that we meet with in this question, have not arisen from the common manner of stating it, we will first consider the question itself, as it is here proposed, and then endeavour to clear up some of the principal difficulties relating to it, as well those which have arisen from the manner of stating it, as those which have arisen from some other cause.

The subjection, which is due from the members of a civil society; that is, from the people, to those persons, who are invested with the civil power of that society, or are appointed to govern it, may cease several ways. First, their subjection ceases, when the governors of the society abdicate or relinquish their power. Those persons, who were the governors of the society, cease to be the governors of it by abdication: whatever power or authority they might have before, they cease to have the same power or authority, after they have relinquished it. And if there is no power or authority on one side, no subjection is due on the other side.

Secondly, civil power or authority, in its highest degree, is limited by the laws of nature and of God: it does not give those, who are invested with it, a right of commanding what is inconsistent with these laws, or of compelling obedience to such commands. In respect, therefore, of what is inconsistent with these laws, civil subjection ceases. For where the civil governors have no right to command or to com-

* See Book I. Chap. XX. § V.

pel, the people are under no obligation to obey or to submit. A distinction, indeed, is sometimes made here between an active and a passive obedience, between an actual compliance of the people with any commands of the civil governors, which are contrary to the laws of nature and of God, and a passive submission to what these governors think fit to inflict upon them for not complying. But this distinction cannot be so applied, as to show, that where the people are not obliged, actively, to obey the command, they are obliged, passively, to submit to the evil, which is brought upon them for not obeying it. You may say, that the law of nature and of God, though it does not leave the people at liberty to do what it has forbidden, leaves them at liberty to suffer patiently what the civil governor thinks proper to make them suffer. But if this is all that you have to urge in support of the duty of passive obedience, where there is no obligation to an active one; this duty rests upon a very weak foundation. Though the people are at liberty to submit patiently, if they will; it will be no consequence, that they are obliged thus to submit: though no law of nature or of God has forbidden passive obedience; unless, perhaps, the law of self-preservation, upon which, however, I shall not insist; yet you cannot conclude from hence, that such obedience is a duty: to support this conclusion, you must produce some law of nature or of God, which enjoins it. In the meantime it seems to be self-evident, that, where the civil governors of a society have no right or authority to command, they have no right or authority to make use of force either to compel obedience, or to punish disobedience. But it is a known principle of natural law, that, where there is no right on one part, there is no obligation on the other part. The people, therefore, are not in subjection to any force, which is made use of by the civil governors for these purposes, or are not obliged passively to submit to such force.

Thirdly, according to the first and most simple notion of a civil society, the civil power is originally vested in the collective body of such society. Whenever, therefore, any civil governors are appointed, the degree and extent of their power will depend upon the constitutional laws: their authority can neither be more* nor less than these laws, or rather, than the people, by compact, in consequence of these laws, have entrusted them with. From hence it appears, that their power, if it is limited by the constitution, does not extend beyond these limitations: and where their power fails, the subjection of the people ceases.

Fourthly, though the governors of a society should be invested by the constitution with all civil power in the highest degree, and to the greatest extent, that the nature of civil power will admit of; yet this does not imply, that the people are in a state of perfect subjection. Civil power is, in its own nature, a limited power: as it arose at first from social union, so it is limited by the ends and purposes of such union: whether it is exercised, as it is in democracies, by the body of the people, or, as it is in monarchies, by one single person. But if the power of a monarch, when he is considered as a civil governor, is thus limited by the ends of social union; whatever obedience and submission the people may owe him, whilst he keeps within these limits; he has no power at all, and, consequently, the people owe him no subjection, where he goes beyond them.

* See Book II. Chap. VI. § II.

Having thus taken a short view of the several ways, in which the authority of the civil governors of a society fails, and the subjection of the people ceases, we may now return to the question which was before us. If you ask, whether the members of a civil society have a right to resist the civil governors of it by force? your question is too general to admit of a determinate answer. In some circumstances the people can have no such right; in other circumstances, they may have such a right. As far as the just authority of the civil governors, and the due subjection of the people extend; resistance, by force, is rebellion. Subjection consists in an obligation to obey: as far, therefore, as the people are in subjection, they can have no right to resist: because an obligation to obey, and a right to resist, are inconsistent with one another. But the power of civil governors is neither necessarily connected with their persons, nor infinite, whilst it is in their possession. It ceases by abdication; it is overruled by the laws of nature and of God; and it does not extend beyond the limits, which either the civil constitution or the ends of social union have set to it. The power, therefore, of the civil governors of any society fails of right; that is, they have no just authority; where they have abdicated what power they had; where they command what is contrary to the laws of nature and of God; where they usurp any branch of civil power, which the constitution of their country never gave them; or where they exercise a power, which is inconsistent with the ends of social union, and, consequently, which no civil constitution whatsoever could give them. Where their power thus fails in right, and they have no just authority, the subjection of the people ceases; that is, as far as of right they have no power, or no just authority, the people are not obliged to obey them; so that any force, which they make use of either to compel obedience, or to punish disobedience, is unjust force; the people may, perhaps, be at liberty to submit to it if they please; but because it is unjust force, the law of nature does not oblige them to submit to it. But this law, if it does not oblige the people to submit to such force, allows them to have recourse to the necessary means of relieving themselves from it, and of securing themselves against it, to the means of resistance by opposing force to force, if they cannot be relieved from it, and secured against it by any other means.

Relation of governor and subject is a limited one.

XI. In stating the question concerning resistance, I have chosen to call one of the parties the governors, or rather the persons, who are invested with the civil power of a society, and to call the other party the people or the members of that society; that I might avoid speaking of them in this question under the relation of governors and subjects. For though the two parties do stand in this relation to one another; yet the relation itself is a limited one; it is limited in the same manner with the civil power of the former, and with the subjection of the latter. As far as one of these parties has just authority, and the other of them owes subjection; so far they are governors and subjects: but where the authority of the former, and the subjection of the latter cease; that is, where the former have no right to command or to compel, and the latter are under no obligation to obey or to submit; there this relation ceases, and they are not to be considered as governors and subjects.

I have, indeed, for want of a better word, spoken of the former under the name of governors: and this word, in the common acceptation of it, has a relative meaning. But I have, at the same time, endeavoured to show the reader, that I would have him understand it here, rather in an absolute, than in a relative sense, by informing him, that, when I speak of governors, I mean those persons in a civil society, who are invested with the civil power of it.

The question, as we usually find it stated, is, whether subjects have a right to resist their civil and constitutional governors? When the two parties concerned in the question are thus spoken of under such names, as import the relation, which they bear to one another, and in consequence of which, one has a right to command, and the other is obliged to obey; we are first led by the terms of the question to imagine, that it regards them in this relation; that is, that it regards them in such cases as this relation extends to, and then to answer it in the negative: for where one of the parties has a right to command, and the other is obliged to obey; the latter can have no right to resist: because an obligation to obey is inconsistent with a right to resist. But since this question regards the two parties, when this relation ceases between them; that is, since it regards them in those cases only, to which the authority of the one, and the subjection of the other, does not extend; if we state it in such a manner, as not to mix this relation with the terms of it, the true answer will be more plainly seen, and more readily admitted.

But if any one chooses to state the question in the usual manner, and apprehends, that there may be some fallacy in stating it otherwise, there is no occasion to dispute this point with him. For let him state it as he will; the power, or authority, which the constitutional and civil governors of a society have over their subjects, ceases by abdication; and even whilst they are possessed of this power or authority, as they are only human, constitutional, and civil governors, it is limited by the natural and revealed laws of God, by the laws of the national constitution, and by the ends of civil union. He may, therefore, give them the name of governors, and he may, likewise, give the people the name of subjects, even beyond these limitations, if he thinks proper: but still the former can only be called governors, and the latter can only be called subjects in words; for beyond these limitations the relation of governors and subjects ceases in right.

Resistance to the supreme power, how to be understood.

XII. St. Paul uses the word, power, to signify a ruler, or a person invested with power, where he says, *" that rulers are not a terror to good works, but to evil; wilt thou then not be afraid of the power? Do that which is good, and thou shalt have praise of the same." He certainly here means the same thing by power and by ruler; since they who do good can no otherwise have praise of the power, than by having it of the ruler, who is invested with the power. The word is used in the same sense, when we ask, whether it is lawful to resist the supreme power? We intend, or should intend, to ask, whether the people, or members of a civil society have a right to make use of any forcible resistance, in opposition to such rulers or governors of the society, as are invested with supreme power?

* Rom. XIII. 3.

They, therefore, who deny, that the people have such a right of resistance, gain very little advantage to their side of the question, by changing the words of it from civil power to supreme power. For the power of civil governors, even in the highest degree of it, is only human power, and is only civil power. They may call it supreme power, with a design of setting it clear of any constitutional limitations: but if it has no other limitations, it will at least be limited by the laws of nature and of God, and by the ends and purposes of civil union.

Right of resistance does not imply supreme civil power in the people.

XIII. In this state of the question,—Whether the people have any right to resist the supreme power?—it is usually urged, in contradiction to such a right, that the people, if their power is inferior to the power of the civil governors, must be obliged to submission; and, consequently, can have no right of resistance. But it is absurd to say, that the power of the people is equal or superior to the power of the civil governors, when those governors are supposed to be invested with supreme power: because, in saying this, we suppose a power in the people which is equal or superior to the supreme.

Two ways have been thought of for avoiding this supposed absurdity. One of these ways is, by maintaining, that all civil constitutions whatsoever, are ultimately perfect democracies; or that every where, without exception, the supreme civil power is vested in the people, and not in the constitutional civil governors. The other way is, by maintaining, that, in all civil constitutions whatsoever, there is a mutual subjection of the civil governors and of the people; that the former have the supreme civil power when they govern well; but that the latter have it, when they govern ill.

But I cannot make use of either of these opinions, after what I have *said about them: if I have shown the falsehood of them, I cannot make use of them consistently with truth: and though I may have failed of doing this, yet I cannot make use of them consistently with myself. I must, therefore, endeavour to clear up this supposed absurdity, by some other means.

The right or liberty of resistance, which belongs to the people, is not properly a civil power, but a natural right: it is not an authority which civil union gives them; it is only what remains of natural liberty, exempted from the obligations of civil union. The constitutional civil governors are, by the supposition, invested with the supreme power. But this power, since it is only civil power, is limited in its own nature: it is limited by the ends and purposes of civil union. Beyond these limits, therefore, the natural rights, or natural liberties of the people still subsist; the civil governors have no power, and the people owe them no subjection. This right of the people may, perhaps, at first sight, appear to be a civil power; because it seems to arise out of the social compact, or at least to depend upon this compact. But it no otherwise depends upon the social compact, than as this compact does not extend to it. The social compact limits the civil power of the constitutional governors to the purposes of civil union: and this limitation is the foundation of the people's right to resist tyrannical power: not because it gives them any power, which nature had not given them,

* See Book II. Chap. IV. § XII.

but because it leaves them in possession of their natural liberty. They had naturally a right of resisting injuries by force. As far as the ends of civil union require this natural right to be given up or restrained, so far it is given up or restrained, either mediately or immediately, by civil union. But as far as these ends do not require this right to be given up, so far it still subsists in a state of civil society.

You will now, perhaps, see, that when you ask whether the people's right of forcibly resisting the tyranny of civil governors is superior, or inferior, or equal to the supreme power, with which we have supposed those governors to be invested, the question is an improper one. The right of the people, and the power of the governors differ from one another in sort; and, therefore, cannot be compared as to degree: neither of them can, with any propriety, be said to be superior, or inferior, or equal to the other. The supreme power of the governors is a civil power: the right which the people have to resist tyrannical oppression, is a natural right. The supreme power of the governors arose from civil union, and was vested in them by the law or compact, which formed the constitution: the right which the people have to resist tyrannical oppression, arose from nature, and subsists after civil union by means of the limits, which the ends of such union have fixed to all civil power.

If we were to maintain that the people's right of resistance is civil power, and were to suppose at the same time, that the constitutional governors have supreme civil power, we might easily be reduced either to the absurdity of supposing, that there is a civil power in the people, which is superior to the supreme, or else to the necessity of allowing, what we before denied, that in all constitutions of government the supreme civil power is vested in the people. But by looking into the origin of the people's right, to resist unsocial and tyrannical oppression, we find it to be a natural right, and not a civil power. All mankind, in a state of equality, had a natural right to resist injuries: and the right which they have in a state of society to resist unsocial and tyrannical oppression, is only so much of that natural right, as is not brought under civil subjection by the social compact. What we maintain, therefore, is, that the people have such a right of resistance as we have been speaking of; not because they have a civil power, which is either equal or superior to the supreme civil power of their constitutional governors; but because this supreme civil power, on the one part, and, consequently the civil subjection of the people on the other part, is limited by the ends and purposes of social union; so that beyond this limitation the natural right of resisting injuries still remains, even after mankind are united into civil societies, and have invested their constitutional governors with supreme civil power.

Opinion of Grotius explained.

XIV. The general question, says *Grotius, concerning resistance is, whether the members of a civil society have a right to resist either the supreme civil governors of it, or inferior magistrates, who act by the authority and under the commission of such governors? It is acknowledged, indeed, by all who have any sense of duty, that, if the supreme governors enjoin any thing which is contrary to the law of nature, or to the commands of God, we

* Grot. Lib. I. Cap. IV. § I.

ought not to obey them. But if they do us any injury, either because we thus refuse to obey them; or because, upon any other account it is their will and pleasure; is this injury rather to be submitted to, than resisted by force? I have rendered this latter sentence interrogatively; though from the present manner of pointing it in all the editions of our author's work, that I have seen, we may collect, that it is commonly supposed to contain rather a full declaration of his opinion, than a question, what the true opinion is. But whoever will be at the trouble of considering the construction of the sentence itself, and of comparing it with what goes before, and with what follows it, will find reason to think, that our author only designed here to state the question, and not to determine it.

But be this as it will, when he comes to declare his own opinion, he plainly favours the doctrine of non-resistance, though not without some restrictions. At the same time, he cautions his readers to observe, that many acts of the people, which go under the name of resistance against their civil governors, do not come within his notion of unlawful resistance. It may be proper for us to consider, in the first place, what particular instances of resistance he allows of, and upon what principles he allows of them: because some of these principles, when they are fully explained, will help us to correct his opinion upon the general question.

First, *if an absolute monarch, or any other civil governors, who have been invested with supreme power, abdicate, or otherwise plainly relinquish this power, Grotius allows that the people have then a right of resisting them by force: because, whatever power they may have been invested with, an abdication or dereliction of it, brings them back into the condition of private persons.

He extends the right of resistance, upon this principle, farther than the case of a voluntary dereliction. For though he had observed, that where the supreme civil governors are chargeable with some instances of negligent administration, these neglects cannot reasonably be construed as an evidence of their intention to relinquish their supreme power; yet where they become open and declared enemies of the society, such hostile conduct is, in his opinion, an evidence that they have no intention to govern it, and, consequently, is a dereliction or forfeiture of that power. For the protection of the society, or the security and advancement of its general good, is included in the notion of civil government. An intention, therefore, to govern, and an intention to destroy, are inconsistent with one another. Grotius has left his readers to conjecture what acts of hostile conduct he would allow to be an evidence, that the supreme governors of a civil society are become enemies to it. He seems to have had in his mind such a high degree of oppression, as consists in nothing less than an endeavour to extirpate the society: for he declares in general, that no king, who governs only one society, can be supposed capable of such hostile conduct, as he means, unless he is out of his senses; and that even where a king governs two societies, his attachment to one of them can no otherwise lead him to such conduct, than with a view of making room in the territories of the other, to bring colonies thither from his favourite society.

* Grot. Lib. I. Cap. IV. § I.

But whatever high degrees of tyranny Grotius might here have in his mind, if the principle, from whence he argues, will prove that civil governors forfeit their supreme power by endeavouring to extirpate the society; the same principle will likewise prove, that they forfeit this power by exercising such lower degrees of oppression, as necessarily destroy the welfare of it; though, perhaps, they may not destroy the existence of it. The welfare of a society, as well as the preservation of its being, is included in the purpose of civil government; no person, therefore, can at the same time have a will to govern the people, and a will to hold such a conduct, as is plainly inconsistent with their social welfare.

Grotius, as we shall see presently, maintains, in the general question concerning the right of resistance, that the people have no right to resist civil governors, who are in actual possession of supreme power. But in the meantime, as he was disposed to provide, in some measure, if not for the welfare, yet at least for the existence of civil society, he maintains, that civil governors, with whatever power the constitution may have originally invested them, forfeit that power, when they become enemies to the public. Upon this principle, the right of the people to resist a tyrant, who has been invested with supreme power, does not imply a right to resist a civil governor, who is in actual possession of supreme power: because such a right of resistance, as this, does not begin, till the civil governor, by a forfeiture of his supreme power, is reduced to the condition of a private person.

But we may observe, by the way, that the supposition of a forfeiture of supreme power, is not necessary to prevent this power and the right of resistance from interfering with one another. When civil governors degenerate into tyrants; whether they forfeit their supreme power, or continue in possession of it; to resist them in the exercise of a tyrannical power, and to resist the supreme civil power, is not the same thing. Supremacy of civil power does not imply, that they, who are possessed of it, have a right to do whatever they please. The notion of supremacy implies, indeed, that their power is under no constitutional restraints from without. But still it is only civil power, and is, therefore, under a natural limitation from within: it is limited, in its own nature, to the ends and purposes of civil union. The people, therefore, by resisting a civil governor, who is possessed of supreme power, in such acts as are contrary to the ends and purposes of civil union, do not resist the supreme power: for such acts, since they exceed the natural limitations of all civil power, even in the highest degree of it, are not acts of the supreme power.

When we speak of supreme civil power in the abstract, we may easily prove, that the members of a civil society have no right to resist it. The notion of supreme civil power implies a right to direct and to compel; and as far as there is such a right on one side, there can be no right to disobey or to resist on the other side. From hence it will follow, that civil governors, who are in possession of this power, cannot lawfully be resisted in the exercise of it. But it will be no consequence, that they cannot lawfully be resisted, when they exceed the natural limitations of supreme civil power, by exercising such an unsocial power, as is not included in the notion of it, and as they were never invested with. The double sense of the words—supreme power—has probably been the occasion of some mistakes in this question. Sometimes they signify this power in the abstract: and sometimes they signify a civil governor, who is invested with this power; that is, a supreme potentate. St. Paul, as we have observed, uses the words in this latter sense, when he commands christians to be subject to the higher or supreme powers. Now, since it is unlawful to resist the supreme power in one sense, we are apt to conclude, that it must, likewise, be unlawful to resist the supreme power in the other sense. But if, instead of speaking of civil governors under the abstract name of supreme powers, we would call them supreme potentates; we should find, that this conclusion is a mere fallacy, and has nothing to support it, besides the ambiguous sense of the words—supreme power.—However unlawful it may be to resist the supreme power, when this power is considered in the abstract, it will not follow from hence, that it must be equally unlawful to resist supreme potentates. The notion of supreme power, when we consider it in the abstract, includes its natural and due limitations: it is nothing else but the highest degree of civil power; that is, of a power to direct and to compel the several members of a civil society to act in such a manner, as the common benefit and general security requires: and since the several members have, by their civil union, agreed to form such a power, the same consent, by which they formed it, obliges them to pay obedience and submission to it. When this power is, by the constitution, lodged in the hands of certain persons; these persons become the supreme potentates of the society, and are usually called by the abstract name of supreme powers. As far as these supreme powers, or supreme potentates, exercise only the civil power, it is unlawful to resist them: for as the people are obliged to pay obedience and submission to the power, with which they are invested, it cannot be lawful to resist them in the exercise of this power. But supreme potentates have a natural strength in their hands, which may possibly be abused: though the supreme power is limited, in its own nature, to the purposes of civil union, it is possible, that they may be disposed to exercise this natural strength to contrary purposes. To resist them in this undue exercise of the natural strength, which is in their hands, can no otherwise be called resistance to the supreme power, than as these supreme potentates are, themselves, called by this abstract name. In the meantime, it is such a resistance, as cannot be shown to be unlawful. However the people may be obliged to obey them, and to submit to them, when they exercise the supreme civil power; it does not follow, that there is the like obligation, when they exercise any other power: and where there is no obligation to obey and to submit, the law of nature allows of resistance.

From hence we may understand what it is, that puts the difference between rebellion, and such resistance as is lawful. It is rebellion to resist the supreme governors, whilst they keep within the natural limitations of supreme power, and only command or enforce what is necessary or conducive to the general welfare and security. Whereas the resistance, which is lawful, is a resistance to these governors, when they abuse the natural strength, which the supreme power has put into their hands, to the unsocial purposes of tyranny and oppression.

From hence, likewise, we may understand what answer is to be made, when we are asked, whether it is lawful to resist the supreme power, if the commonwealth cannot otherwise be preserved? If by supreme power, is here meant supreme power in the abstract, the case, which the question supposes, is impossible. For supreme power, in this sense of the words, is a power, which operates only for the general benefit: and it is a contradiction to suppose, that the preservation of the commonwealth should ever require us to resist such a power as this. Or if supreme power means the supreme potentates, or supreme governors of a society; before we can answer the question here proposed, it will be necessary to inquire, whether it relates to them, when they exercise only the civil power, with which they are entrusted, or when they exercise an exorbitant power, which does not belong to them. In the former of these senses, instead of answering the question in the negative, we might observe, as we did before, that it supposes a case, which is impossible, or implies a contradiction. Civil power, in the highest degree that the nature of it will admit, is limited to the purpose of advancing or securing the general welfare: and such a power, whether we consider it as it is in its own nature, or as exercised by any particular persons, in whom the constitution has vested it, cannot be inconsistent with the preservation of the commonwealth. But in the latter sense, we may answer this question in the negative: for though the supreme potentates, or, as they are sometimes called, the supreme powers of a civil society, cannot lawfully be resisted, where they exercise only the social power, which was produced by civil union, and is vested in them by the constitution; yet where they exercise an exorbitant power, which is inconsistent with the preservation of the society, they may lawfully be resisted. The supreme civil power, of which they are possessed, gives them no right to exercise this exorbitant power: and where they have no right to act, there is no law of nature, which obliges the body of the society to submit to them.

But to return to our author. Barclay, * he says, is of opinion, that a king, notwithstanding he has been invested with supreme power, forfeits his power by alienating it; where the laws have either settled the succession to the crown, or have made the crown elective. Grotius is doubtful upon this head; and rather inclines to the contrary opinion. Where the tenure of the crown is of the usufructuary sort, he thinks, that the king, by alienating it, does nothing, and, consequently, that the alienation can produce no effect. The conclusion, which he leaves his readers to deduce from hence, is, that such an alienation, since it produces no effect, cannot produce a forfeiture. In support of this opinion, he alleges the Roman law concerning usufruct. But without inquiring what any positive law may determine in other cases of usufruct; let us inquire what the law of nature or reason, will lead us to determine in the case of an usufructuary kingdom. In respect of the person, to whom the king that is in possession, intends to transfer the supreme power, his act will produce no effect: the act is void in itself, and cannot make a valid transfer. But the question is, whether this act will produce no effect in respect of himself and of the people; whether, though it is void as a transfer, it may not be valid as a forfeiture? Some writers consider such an alienation as two distinct acts: it imports,

* Grot. Lib. I. Cap. IV. § X.

they say, an intention in the king to give up the kingdom for himself, as well as an intention to transfer it to another. And though they allow, that the latter of these acts is void, or produces no effect, because he has no power to transfer what he holds by usufruct; yet they contend, that the former act is valid, because he has a power of relinquishing what he so holds. This, however, is a groundless distinction: his act imports only an intention to give up his kingdom for the particular purpose of transferring it to a certain person; it does not import an intention of parting with it, either absolutely or for any other purpose. We may say with more reason, that he holds his kingdom by a compact between himself and the people, under a law, which, by the supposition, has either fixed the succession to the crown, or made it elective. This alienation, therefore, as it is inconsistent with this law, is a breach of the compact on his part; and this releases the people from it on their part.

But be this as it will, Grotius, even whilst he doubts whether such an act of an usufructuary king amounts to a forfeiture, and is rather inclined to think the contrary, maintains, that if the king attempts to make the transfer good in fact, by delivering up the kingdom, the people have a right to resist this attempt by force. Supremacy of civil power, and a supreme claim, or a claim of full property to this power, are different things. If any constitution, which has invested a king with supreme power, has at the same time made the crown elective, or settled the succession so as to make it unalterable without the consent of the people, he holds the supreme power, whilst he is in possession of it, only by an usufructuary tenure, and, consequently, has no right to alienate it. Nor can he give himself such a right by virtue of his supreme power: for the tenure, by which the supreme power is held, is not subject to the jurisdiction of this power: the law, which established it, came originally from the body of the society, and was made binding upon him by means of a compact, to which he consented, either expressly, when he accepted the crown, or tacitly, by accepting it under such a restriction as this law laid it under. But if he is thus bound by a compact with the people, not to alter the tenure of the crown, and make it patrimonial, when the constitution has made it usufructuary, the people have a right to oppose such an alteration, and to make use of force in opposing it, when they cannot prevent it by any other means.

As Grotius allows, in the first place, that the people have a right to resist such civil governors as have been invested with supreme power, when they have abdicated or forfeited this power; so he allows, secondly, that they have the like right, either where the constitution has laid the civil governors under any special limitations, besides what arise from the nature of civil power, or where it has reserved any special liberty to the people, besides what is included in the notion of civil subjection.

The example which we have been considering, seems, as Grotius explains it, to be of this latter sort: for, whilst he is inclined to think that an usufructuary king does not forfeit his crown by attempting to alienate it, he maintains, that the special tenure of the supreme power, which the constitution has settled in such a kingdom, will give the people a right to resist such an attempt of the king.

In one of the cases, where *he allows a right of resistance in the people, we cannot properly say, that there is a constitutional limitation upon the supreme power of the civil governors: because the case supposes the supreme power to be vested in the people, and the civil governors, who have the lead occasionally in public affairs, to be made accountable to the people by the constitution. The Spartan constitution was of this sort. It was a nominal kingdom, but a real democracy. The kings were, indeed, empowered to act for the state, but were made accountable to the people, or to officers who stood in the place of the people. Grotius observes, that wherever such a constitution has been settled from the first, or is settled afterwards by mutual agreement between the king and the people, there is a right in the people, not only to resist the king by force, but even to punish him, when he offends against the laws of the society, or acts inconsistently with the welfare of it. But what our author here calls resistance, is rather an exercise of constitutional power: the case supposes the supreme power to be vested in the people, and the power of the king to be made subordinate to theirs by the constitution.

In mixed forms of government, where the king has some parts of the supreme power, and the people have some other parts of it, †Grotius allows the people to have a right of resisting the king by force, if he invades those parts of the civil power which belong to them: because as far as the power extends, which is reserved to them by the constitution, the king has no authority, and the people are not in subjection. This right of the people to make war in defence of their constitutional power, may, perhaps, be questioned, if the civil power of making war is vested in the king. But Grotius replies, that the civil power of making war, which is here supposed to be vested in the king, relates only to foreign wars, and means nothing else but the ordinary right of directing the common force of the society against its enemies from without: it does not relate to such an extraordinary use of force, as may be necessary for maintaining the constitutional rights of the people against any attempts to invade them from within. The constitution, therefore, may have precluded the people from making war upon their own authority against the foreign enemies of the society: but as the same constitution has, by the supposition, reserved to the people a right to some parts of the supreme power, it must be understood to leave them at liberty to defend themselves by force, in the possession of this right, if they cannot secure it by any other means. To suppose that the people have a right, and yet that they are not at liberty to defend this right by such means as are necessary, is a contradiction; it is to suppose that they have a right, and that they have no right at the same time.

Grotius does not here consider the supremacy of the people, as the foundation of their right of resistance: he argues in favour of such a right from this general principle: that, as far as the power of the people extends, their civil governors have no authority over them, and they are not in subjection. In the next example, he argues still more plainly from the same principle; whilst he maintains, that the people may have a right of resistance, though they have no part of the supreme power.‡ He supposes a society to have established a despotic constitution, by

* Grot. Lib. I. Cap. IV. § VIII. † Grot. Ibid. § XIII. ‡ Grot. Ibid. § XIV.

giving the whole civil power, both legislative and executive, to the king, but at the same time to have expressly reserved a right of resistance to the people, upon some certain events. Reserves of this sort are, he says, a just foundation of resistance, when these events happen: because, though they do not imply that the people have retained any part of the supreme power, yet they imply that the people have retained some part of their natural liberty; and, as far as these reserves extend, have exempted themselves from subjection.

We may observe, that the principle upon which our author proceeds, in these two examples, to support the particular right of resisting unconstitutional usurpations of power, is the same that * we made use of above, to support a general right of resisting all unsocial and tyrannical oppression. Where the constitution has limited the power of civil governors by a division of the supreme power between them and the people; or where it has in part exempted the natural liberty of the people from subjection by any positive reserves, Grotius considers these constitutional limitations or reserves, as the foundation of a right of resistance; because the civil governors have no authority, and the people are not in subjection, beyond such limitations or reserves. Now, civil power, on the one hand, though it is under no positive or constitutional limitations, is limited in its own nature by the ends and purposes of civil union: and the notion of civil subjection, on the other hand, implies, that they, who owe no other subjection, retain as much of their natural liberty, as is consistent with the same ends and purposes; whether the constitution, under which they live, has made any positive reserves of it or not. So that beyond these natural limitations and reserves, the civil governors have no authority, and the people are not under subjection in any constitution, or in any form of civil government whatsoever. Thus the same principle which led our author to conclude, that the people may lawfully resist the civil governors of a society, where these governors exceed any constitutional limitations, which have been set to their power, or where the people have expressly made any constitutional reserves of a part of their liberty, may lead his readers to conclude farther, that the people have a general right of resistance, where the civil governors, even though they are invested with supreme power, exceed the natural limitations of all civil power; or where they break in upon that part of the natural liberty of the people, which is reserved to them of right, by the very notion of civil subjection, under every possible form of civil government.

But Grotius, whilst he furnishes his readers with this principle, does not follow it himself so far as it would have led him. For, in examining the general question, whether the members of a civil society have any right of resisting such civil governors as are invested with supreme power? he favours the negative part of it, and endeavours to support his opinion by arguing partly from the nature and ends of civil society, and partly from what he supposes to have been the doctrine of St. Paul and St. Peter. He allows, however, that the members of a civil society have such a right in cases of extreme necessity; except where they suffer for the religion of Christ; and there he thinks, that it is their duty to submit patiently, if they cannot save themselves by flight.

* See sect. XIII

What he urges *from the nature and ends of civil society, is of no great importance; and he does not seem to lay much stress upon it. "A civil society," he says, "as it is instituted for the purpose of securing the common tranquillity, has a general power of restraining and controlling its several members, as far as such a power is necessary for obtaining this purpose: and in particular it has a power, in view to the public peace and order, to restrain and overrule that promiscuous right of resisting injuries, which individuals were possessed of in a state of nature. As a civil society has this power, so we may be sure that it was the intention of mankind, when they formed themselves into such bodies, to make use of it: because, if this promiscuous right of resisting injuries is not restrained and overruled, civil society could not obtain its proper purpose of securing the public tranquillity. There might, indeed, be an assembly of men, though each of them continued to have this right; but it could only be a confused and unconnected assembly; it could not be a civil society." But the conclusion, which Grotius here endeavours to establish, will not determine the question which is now before us. Though we grant, that the promiscuous right of resisting injuries, which mankind were possessed of in a state of nature, is restrained and overruled in a state of society; yet it will not follow from hence, that their whole right of resisting injuries is thus restrained and overruled: they cease to have a promiscuous right of resisting injuries; but it is no consequence that they have no right of resistance at all. Our author, in order to support his own opinion, should have proved, not merely that the members of a civil society have not the same promiscuous right of resisting injuries, which they had in a state of nature, but that civil union destroys the whole right of resisting injuries; or, at least, the right of resisting such unsocial injuries, as are done to them by their civil governors: because, though they have not a promiscuous right of resisting all injuries whatsoever, they may possibly have a right of resisting the unsocial and tyrannical oppression of their civil governors. It must be allowed, that civil societies were instituted for the purpose of securing the common tranquillity. But this tranquillity does not consist in setting still and doing nothing; or in patiently submitting to injuries, without endeavouring to repel them for the present, or to guard against them for the future. If this was the notion of that tranquillity, which the institution of civil society has in view, we might easily prove, that all resistance of injuries whatsoever, is contrary to the nature of civil society. But the common tranquillity which civil union was intended to obtain, consists in the quiet and peaceable enjoyment of our rights; that is, it consists in a security against suffering injuries: and from this purpose of civil union we can only infer, that it restrains the promiscuous right of resistance, as far as is necessary to prevent mankind from doing injuries to one another; and not that it destroys their whole right of resistance, by obliging them to submit to injuries without seeking for redress. Where the members of a society injure one another, they are restrained from doing themselves justice by their own force and at their own discretion; because, under the notion of doing themselves justice, they might possibly injure others; and not because they are obliged to set still, whatever

* See sect. II.

they suffer: for civil society, though it does not allow the sufferers to redress themselves, makes a provision for redressing them by means of the public force, under the conduct of the public understanding. But where the governors of the society, who have the keeping of the public understanding, and act with the public force, injure the members of it by tyranny and lawless oppression, the social means of redress fail, and no other means are left besides resistance. It is true, indeed, that, in a society where the people have recourse to these means, there is no social peace and order. But it is equally true, that the social peace and order are not broken in upon by such resistance as is lawful: for resistance is then only lawful, when this peace and order have been already broken in upon by tyranny and oppression. Some sort of peace and subordination may, indeed, subsist in a civil society, notwithstanding the governors of it violate all the social rights of the people; provided the people will set still, and will quietly submit to the injuries which they suffer. But this is not social peace and order: for such peace and such order, as mankind intended to produce and to secure by civil union, are disturbed by tyranny and oppression. The right of resistance, therefore, as it does not take place till social peace and order are thus disturbed, cannot be the cause which disturbs them: it finds them disturbed already, and its proper end is to restore them for the present, and to secure them for the future.

Before we inquire what St. Paul has taught us upon this head, it will be proper to remind the reader, that the right, which is here contended for, does not imply, that all forcible resistance of the members of a civil society against the governors of it is lawful, or that the governors have no authority, and that the people owe no subjection. On the contrary, we maintain, that the governors of a civil society have authority to command and to compel, and that the people are obliged, of right, to obey and to submit, as far as the purposes of civil union extend. Though a right of resistance begins beyond these limits; because the civil power of the governors, and the civil subjection of the people end here; yet all resistance within these limits is contrary to the law of nature; that is, to the duty, which naturally arises from social union, and the appointment of civil governors. When St. Paul, therefore, *enjoins subjection, and forbids resistance, the question is, what sort of subjection he enjoins, and what sort of resistance he forbids? Whether he enjoins only such subjection, as is properly called civil subjection, and is limited by the ends, for which mankind formed themselves into civil societies, or such absolute subjection, as is implied in the notion of passive obedience? Whether he forbids all resistance whatsoever, even against such tyranny and oppression, as is destructive of the ends of social union; or such resistance only, as the law of nature has forbidden, a resistance to the governors of a civil society, where the nature and design of social union has given them authority to command and to compel, and has obliged the people to obey and to submit?

Many of the first converts to christianity imagined, that their religion had set them free from all subjection whatsoever; that it discharged them both from the subjection, which they formerly owed to the civil

* Rom. XIII.

magistrate, as they were members of society, and, likewise, from the subjection, which they owed to their masters, if they happened to be in a state of slavery, before they embraced it. If we read the apostolical epistles with any degree of attention, we shall see plainly, that this opinion generally prevailed at the time, when they were written, and that the writers of them took particular care to discourage and to disprove it. From the authority of St. Paul, when he commands "every soul to be subject to the higher powers," we may collect, that this opinion is false, but we can collect nothing farther. By giving this command, he determines, that the obligation of civil subjection extends to all mankind, to christians, as well as to other men: but he does not determine, either that the subjection, which is due to supreme civil governors, is absolute and unlimited in its own nature; or that it was the design of the gospel to make it so.

Perhaps the reason, upon which St. Paul supports the precept of subjection, may induce you to think, that the subjection which he enjoins, is absolute; though the words of the precept do not favour this opinion. The principle, upon which he enforces this duty, is, "that there is no power but of God, the powers, that be, are ordained of God:" you may, therefore imagine, that nothing less than absolute subjection can be due to a power, which is established by so high an authority. But though he informs his readers, that the authority of God is the ultimate cause of their obligation to be subject to supreme governors; it is your inference and not his, that this subjection must be absolute and unlimited. The power of supreme governors is established by the authority of God in the same manner, that any other power or right, which arises out of human compacts, or human laws, is established by the same authority. They are the ordinance of man in their immediate origin: because their power is immediately derived from those compacts and laws of mankind, by which they united themselves into civil societies, and established certain forms of civil government. But they are ultimately the ordinance of God: because the law of nature and of God, requires the observance of these compacts and laws, in the same manner that it requires the observance of all other obligatory acts of mankind, which are duly engaged in for beneficial purposes. You must understand St. Paul in this sense, when he calls civil governors the ordinance of God; or otherwise you will not easily reconcile him with St. Peter, who calls them the ordinance of man. Thus the reason, upon which he enforces the duty of civil subjection, will leave you to collect the measures of it from the nature and ends of civil union. The authority of God only confirms and establishes the power, which mankind have given to civil governors, and does not give them any extraordinary power beyond this. The extent, therefore, of their authority, and the subjection, which is due to them in consequence of it, must be determined by these human compacts and human laws, from which it is derived.

If you object, that the principle, which is here urged by the apostle, will answer no purpose, when it is thus explained; the objection is partly true and partly false. This principle will answer no purpose, when you allege it to prove the duty of passive obedience and unlimited subjection. But it will fully answer the purpose, for which he alleges it, and will clearly demonstrate the point, that he had undertaken to prove. We may learn, from his own words, what this point is. "Let every soul be subject to the higher powers." He undertakes to prove, not that the obligation of civil subjection extends to every act, which civil governors may possibly be led to do by an arbitrary pursuit of their own private interest, or by an undue indulgence of their passions and appetites, but that it extends to every soul, to christians, as well as to others. When he * elsewhere addresses himself to slaves, he commands them to "submit themselves to their masters in all things." But when he addresses himself here to members of civil societies, the extent which he gives to civil subjection, does not relate to the matter of it, but only to the persons concerned in it: he does not command them to be subject to the higher powers in all things, but only enjoins subjection as a duty, to which all persons are obliged. His plain design is to correct the mistaken notion, which then prevailed amongst the new converts, that the gospel had discharged them from civil subjection. And the principle, which he alleges, affords an unanswerable argument against this notion. As the gospel had not discharged them from the duty which they owed to God; they could have no reason to suppose, that it had discharged them from the duty of civil subjection: for civil governors are the ordinance of God: and, consequently, the duty of subjection to such governors is established by his authority.

Look farther into St. Paul's discourse, and you will find, that he represents civil authority, and the subjection which is due to it, as limited to the ends and purposes of social union. "Rulers, he says, are not a terror to good works, but to the evil. Wouldest thou then not be afraid of the power? do that, which is good; and thou shalt have praise of the same: for he is the minister of God to thee for good. But if thou dost that which is evil, be afraid: for he beareth not the sword in vain: for he is the minister of God, a revenger to execute wrath upon him that doeth evil." You see in what light St. Paul considers civil governors, whilst he enjoins the duty of subjection: the rulers, that he is speaking of, are such as no man, who does what is good, need be afraid of. You see, likewise, how far, and in what respects he considers civil governors as the ordinance of God: they are ministers of God for good to those who do well, and ministers of God for wrath, to those who do evil. If, therefore, we were to contend, that obedience and submission are not due to civil governors, when they are considered in this character; you might urge either the authority of St. Paul to overrule our opinion, or the principle, from which he argues, to confute it. But if you carry the notion of subjection farther, than he has carried it; neither his authority, nor the principles, from which he argues, will be of any use to you. He enjoins, that every soul should be subject to the higher powers: but whilst he enjoins this duty of subjection, he considers these powers as patrons of what is good, and as a terror to what is evil; that is, he considers them as pursuing the purposes of social welfare and social security. You cannot, therefore, allege his authority in favour of a like duty of subjection, when they counteract and defeat those purposes, and become patrons of what is evil, and a terror to what is good. The principle, from whence he argues in support of the subjection, that he enjoins, is, that civil governors are the ordinance of God: but

* Col. III. 22.

he informs his readers, at the same time, how far, and in what respects he considers these higher powers as the ordinance of God: they are ministers of God for the purposes of social security and social welfare, for the punishment of evil doers, and for the praise of them that do well. You cannot, therefore, infer from this principle, as he has explained and limited it, that there is the same obligation to subjection, where they counteract and defeat these purposes by making themselves, what man never designed them to be, and what God's ordinance never made them, the ministers of their own malice or revenge, of their own avarice or ambition, of their own lust or cruelty.

If St. Paul's notion of civil subjection does not favour your doctrine of unlimited submission and passive obedience, you will gain very little advantage to your cause by having recourse to what he says about resistance. "Whosoever, therefore, resisteth the power, resisteth the ordinance of God; and they that resist, shall receive to themselves damnation." The words, indeed, are general; and if you take them separately, they may seem to import, that all resistance to civil governors is unlawful; as well where they exceed the limits, which are set to their power by the purposes of social union, as where they act within these limits, and pursue these purposes. But if you observe the manner of expression, you will find, that the words now in question, contain a consequence which the apostle deduces from what he had been saying before. He had before enjoined the duty of subjection; and from this duty he here infers the unlawfulness of resistance. But we cannot suppose, when he thus infers the unlawfulness of resistance from the duty of subjection, that he designed to make the consequence more general than the premises, or that he meant any other sort of resistance, besides what is contrary to the duty of subjection, which he had before enjoined. Since, therefore, the duty of subjection, which he had before enjoined, is limited by the purposes of social union, his meaning, when he infers from this duty, that resistance is unlawful, must be restrained by the same limitations. You consider supreme governors as the ordinance of God, in whatever they do. If this principle of yours was true, the consequence would be, that to resist supreme governors, in any thing, would be to resist the ordinance of God. But St. Paul has shown us, in what sense and how far he considered them as the ordinance of God, by representing them as the ministers of God, only for the purposes of social welfare and social security. And the only consequence that will follow from the apostle's principle, is, that to resist them, where they act for these purposes, is to resist the ordinance of God.

There is, however, no reason to think, that the word, damnation, which our English translators have here made use of to express what St. Paul declares to be the event of such resistance as he forbids, ought to be softened into the milder word, condemnation; and to be explained, as if he only meant that they, who are guilty of such resistance, will be punished for it by the civil power, which they resist. Though unjust oppression and tyrannical cruelty may lawfully be resisted, yet there certainly is such a thing as criminal resistance or rebellion. This criminal resistance is what St. Paul is here speaking of: and since he declares it to be contrary to the law of God, we may reasonably believe that, when he speaks of damnation as the event of it, he means, that they, who are guilty of it, will incur such penalties of this law as the word damnation, in the usual sense of it, imports. It would, indeed, be unsuitable to the whole tenor of St. Paul's argument, to suppose that he only warns them of what they are likely to suffer from the sword of the civil magistrate. He set out with enjoining, that every soul should be subject to the higher powers; because these powers are established by the authority of God: and it would be a strange inference from hence, that, if we transgress this duty by rebellion, we shall suffer for it by the act of man. His general conclusion is, that "we must needs be subject, not only for wrath, but also for conscience sake:" and, though the external sanction of human punishment is a reason why we should "be subject for wrath," yet unless in what went before, he had taken notice of some other sanction, besides this, the principal part of his conclusion, "that we must be subject for conscience sake," would be unsupported.

When * Grotius alleges the authority of St. Peter in this question, he does not quote the apostle's words fairly. "Servants," says St. Peter, "be subject to your masters with all fear; not only to the good and gentle, but also to the froward: for this is thankworthy, if a man for conscience towards God endure grief, suffering wrongfully." This exhortation is plainly addressed to slaves: the measures of subjection, therefore, which are to be collected from it, relate only to servile and perfect subjection. But Grotius, in order to apply it to civil subjection, introduces it with the apostle's command of "honouring the king," which has no connexion with it, but is the close of what went before. St. Peter is so far from countenancing this application, that, on the contrary, when he addresses himself to the members of civil societies, he limits the authority of civil governors; and, consequently, the duty of civil subjection, to the purposes of social welfare and social security. In short, the doctrine of St. Peter and of St. Paul is the same in both cases. When they are speaking to slaves, the former says, "Servants, be subject to your masters, with all fear, whether they are gentle or froward;" and the latter says, "Servants, be subject to your own masters in all things." But when they are speaking to members of civil societies, the former says, "Submit yourselves to every ordinance of man, for the Lord's sake; whether it be to the king as supreme, or unto governors, as unto them, that are sent by him for the purpose of punishing evil doers, and for the benefit and encouragement of them that do well;" and the latter says, "Let every soul be subject to the higher powers; because they are the ministers of God, for the benefit and encouragement of those who do what is good, and for wrath to those who do what is evil."

But Grotius, though he favours the doctrine of passive obedience, in some instances, does not maintain this doctrine in its full extent and utmost rigour. Whilst he supposes the duty of non-resistance to be established by a general law of civil society, he allows, as we have seen already, that this law admits of exceptions, both where the constitution of civil government has given the people a part of the supreme power, and, likewise, where it has expressly reserved a right of resistance upon some certain events. The only point, therefore, in which the

* Grot. Lib. I. Cap. IV. § IV.

opinion here advanced differs from his, is, that, in his opinion, supreme civil power is unlimited in itself; and, consequently, they who are in possession of it, cannot of right be resisted, unless some express limitations have been set to their power, or some degree of liberty has been expressly reserved to the people by the constitution: whilst we, on the contrary, maintain, that even supreme civil power is limited in its own nature, by the ends and purposes of civil union, merely because it is only civil power; and that the subjection, which is due to this power, is limited in the same manner and for the same reason: so that they, who are possessed of this power, may of right be resisted by the people, when they exceed these limits and counteract these purposes; though no express limitations of their power, and no express reserves of the people's liberty, have been made by the constitutional form of civil government. * Grotius, indeed, so far agrees with us upon this point, as to allow, that the general law of non-resistance admits of a farther exception in cases of necessity; or that the people have a right in such cases to resist even supreme governors. But then he does not deduce this right, where he thus allows of it, from the nature of civil power or of civil subjection, but from an arbitrary reserve, which he supposes to have been tacitly made by mankind, when they united into civil societies; though they have afterwards made no express reserve, when the respective constitution of each society was settled. He argues, that the universality of his supposed social rule or law, which forbids resistance, is no reason against its admitting the equitable exception of necessity: because, even the laws of God, though they are expressed in the most general and comprehensive terms, admit of the like exception. Our Saviour allows of it in the instance of the sabbath, and mentions with approbation a similar allowance in the case of David, who was permitted by the high priest to eat the shew-bread. For, though God has an undoubted right to require that we should obey his laws, even at the expense of our lives; yet if he has not declared that he requires such a strict obedience to any particular law; and if, at the same time, the matter of the law does not appear to be of such high importance, as will lead us to think that he requires it; even his laws are understood to admit of an exception in favour of necessity, whether this exception is particularly mentioned or not. But if cases of necessity are thus excepted out of laws which are prescribed by the authority of God, there is more reason for presuming, that they are excepted out of laws which are prescribed only by the authority of man. Human laws may, indeed, require obedience, even at the hazard of our lives: of this sort are military laws, which require a soldier to maintain his post, to whatever danger it exposes him, and punish him with death if he deserts it. But we cannot, upon any slight grounds, suppose an human law to be thus rigid. It seems more probable, says our author, that mankind, in respect of one another, have no authority to overrule this exception of necessity; unless where an equal necessity on the other side requires that it should be overruled: because all human laws either are made, or ought to be made, with a proper regard to human weakness. What Grotius here calls the general law of civil society, is nothing else but the rule of action which arises out of social union.

* Grot. Lib. I. Cap. IV. § VII.

The extent of this law, therefore, must, as he argues, depend upon the will of those who associate themselves into civil communities. And if they were to be asked, whether they intend to bind themselves not to resist their civil governors, even though they must otherwise causelessly and unjustly suffer death, he thinks it unlikely that they would answer in the affirmative. In the meantime he doubts, whether it might not have been their intention to lay themselves under even this rigid obligation in all cases, where they could not resist such violence, without producing confusion in the state, and occasioning the destruction of many innocent persons.

Grotius was aware, that, as he thus rests the people's right of resistance, as far as he allows them to have any such right, upon the presumptive intention of mankind, when they form themselves into civil societies, the rigid defenders of passive obedience would have an opportunity of objecting that it is a divine, and not an human law, which obliges mankind rather to submit to death, than to repel the lawless violence of their civil superiors by force. He had, in some measure, obviated this objection before, if the foundation of it was true, by observing, that even the laws of God admit of exceptions in favour of extreme necessity. But he adds here, that the objection is raised upon a false foundation: for mankind were not brought together and united into civil societies by any express command of God, but came together of their own accord; and were induced thus to unite themselves, by a sense of their own inability, to guard themselves against violence, by their separate strength. Civil power, therefore, which is the result of this union, was instituted by an human act; and the obligation of civil subjection is the immediate effect of an human compact, and not of a divine law. In support of this opinion, about the origin of civil power, he alleges the authority of St. Peter, who calls it the ordinance of man; and then observes, as we have observed above, that, notwithstanding this ordinance of man, when it is once duly established, is confirmed by the divine law, and so becomes the ordinance of God; yet the authority of God, whilst it supports civil power, and enforces the duty of civil subjection, makes no alteration in either of them, but leaves the nature and the limits of them the same that the act of man, from which they immediately arose, had originally made them.

Grotius extends this exception of extreme necessity, as well to individuals, repelling a private injury, as to the body of a community repelling such injuries, as either immediately, or in their consequences, affect the public. Barclay, he says, who was a warm asserter of kingly power, allows, that the body of the people, or some very considerable part of this body, has a right to defend itself against the outrageous cruelty of its supreme governors, notwithstanding its general subjection to them. But for his own part, though he plainly understands, that, in proportion as what is to be preserved by an exemption from the obligation of a law, is of more value, the equity, which exempts it, is the stronger; yet he declares himself to be far from thinking, that even individuals, or, however, that a minority of the people, are to be condemned, if they defend themselves by force, under the favour of necessity; provided they do it in such a manner, as not to violate the regard which they owe to the general good of the society.

60

The character, under which he here speaks of Barclay, may, perhaps, lead the reader to imagine, that the question concerning the lawfulness of resistance, relates only to absolute monarchies. For this concession will have no particular weight, merely because it is made by a warm asserter of kingly power, unless the doctrine of passive obedience is peculiar to a monarchical form of government. But, in fact, the question concerning resistance, relates equally to all forms of government, except perfect democracies. In all other forms, there is one part of the society which governs, whilst the other part is governed: and the governing part is invested with the supreme power, either perpetually or for a time. If, therefore, in an absolute monarchy, where the king is invested with perpetual supreme power, the natural limitations of this power will give the people a right to resist him, when he is guilty of tyranny and unsocial oppression; the same limitations will, under any form of civil government, give that part of the society, which is in civil subjection, a like right to resist the tyranny and unsocial oppression of the governing part. And, on the contrary, if these limitations will not support a right of resistance in other constitutions, they will not support such a right against an absolute monarch.

There is another point still to be examined; which, though it does not belong to natural law, may be proper to be taken some notice of.* Our author is of opinion, that whatever right of resistance there may be in other instances, the gospel has made it unlawful for christians to defend themselves by force, where they are persecuted by their superiors, even to death, upon account of their religion.

One of the arguments which he makes use of to establish this opinion, has nothing else to support it, besides the silence of our Saviour. He says, that Christ, when he allows his disciples to fly from persecution, allows no more. But this direction, to avoid persecution by flying from it, cannot well be construed as a prohibition of all other means. And there is the less ground for construing it in this sense, because Christ gives such a reason for it, as shows, that it was not intended to be a general direction to all christians about what they may lawfully do to secure themselves against persecution, and much less to be a restrictive direction, which ties them down from doing any thing else. "When they persecute you in this city, flee ye into another: for verily I say unto you, ye shall not have gone over the cities of Israel, till the son of man be come." We may collect from the reason here given, that the direction relates only to them, who were at that particular time commissioned to preach the gospel to the cities of Israel; before the son of man came in power to cast off the Israelites from being the people of God, for rejecting the salvation which was offered to them. Christ intended to inform those whom he then sent, that the work upon which they were sent, did not require them to stay in any place where they should be persecuted. They were to preach the gospel in all the cities of Israel: and if, when they were persecuted in one city, they should flee to another, this would be no interruption of the work: because they had more places to preach in, than they could well go through in the time which was allotted them. There is nothing in any part of the instructions then given to the apostles, which has the ap-

* Grot. Lib. I. Cap. IV. § VII.

pearance of a design to restrain christians from making use of the same means to defend themselves against suffering injuries upon account of their religion, that the law of nature allows in other cases; except that they were commanded not to take a sword. And this restraint is so far from extending to all christians, that we find it to have been afterwards taken off from the apostles themselves in such a manner, as shows it to have related at first to the particular commission upon which they were sent. "When I sent you," says our Saviour, "without purse, and scrip, and shoes, lacked ye any thing?" And they said, nothing. "But now he that hath a purse, let him take it, and likewise his scrip: and he that hath no sword, let him sell his garment and buy one."

Christ, however, refused to be defended by force against the injuries which he suffered in his own person: and his patient enduring of persecution is alleged to prove, that christians, in general, ought to submit, with the like patience, to any injuries that they may suffer, upon account of their religion. When St. Peter had drawn his sword in the defence of his master, he was admonished to put it up again; because all they, that take the sword, shall perish with the sword. But no stress can be laid upon this admonition, as it contains rather a prudential caution, than a rule of duty. It is a matter of temporal interest, and not of conscience, to avoid perishing by the sword: the fear of such an evil may produce an external restraint; but it cannot, when it is taken alone, produce an internal obligation. The only circumstance in what passed upon this occasion, that seems to affect the present question, is our Saviour's ready submission to what he was about to suffer, and his express refusal of defence by force. But this circumstance will be found to be of no importance; if, instead of considering only the naked fact, we attend to the reason of his refusal. "Put up thy sword into its sheath. The cup, which my father hath given me, shall I not drink it? Thinkest thou, that I cannot now pray to my father, and he shall presently give me more than twelve legions of angels? But how then shall the scriptures be fulfilled, that thus it must be?" He argues against the lawfulness of defending him by force, not from the general nature of the religion, which he taught, but from the particular appointment of providence, which had made it his special duty to submit to the injuries, that were coming upon him. Our Saviour's submission, therefore, under the limitation, which arises from the reason of it, does not evince the necessity of a like submission, where there is not the same or a like reason. It will only teach us, that as far as the duty of our particular station or circumstances is attended with difficulties and hardships, whether they arise from the injustice of men, or from any other cause, we are obliged, as christians, to go through that duty patiently, and are not at liberty to decline it, or to endeavour, by force, to release ourselves from the outward necessity of performing it, upon account of those difficulties and hardships. Grotius falls in with the common notion, that St. Peter has extended this example to christians in all stations and all circumstances whatsoever, and makes use of this apostle's authority as his second argument to show, that however allowable it may be in cases of necessity to resist the supreme power in other instances; yet where we suffer for the religion of Christ, no necessity will justify resistance. For St. Peter having exhorted "servants to be subject to their masters, to the froward as well as to the gentle, and to take ill usage patiently, enforces his exhortation by observing, that they were hereunto called: because Christ also suffered for us, leaving us an example, that we should follow his steps; who, when he was reviled, did not revile again; when he suffered, he threatened not, but committed himself to him, that judgeth righteously." We must allow, that a general rule of behaviour arises out of this example, and such a rule, as all christians are obliged to follow. The rule is what was just now stated at large: whatever hardships the duty of our station brings upon us, we must bear them patiently; and must not desert our duty for the sake of avoiding them. Now absolute submission is the natural duty of slaves; and to such as these the apostle's exhortation is here addressed. The occasion, which led him to press the performance of this duty, will show us the great propriety of enforcing it by the example of Christ. We have already taken notice of a mistaken opinion, which then prevailed, that the gospel releases those, who embrace it, from all subjection whatsoever, and places them in a state of full liberty. St. Peter, therefore, in opposition to this opinion, first commands servants to be subject to their masters, and then informs them, that they mistook the design of christianity: for though slavery is a state of hardships, yet the religion which they had embraced, as they might learn from the example of its author, was not designed to release them from the duty of their station, upon account of any hardships, that attend the performance of it. I would be understood to mean, that this example of Christ can be applied only to slaves, and that no others are obliged to follow it. The general rule, which arises from it, is applicable to all persons in every station, where the duty of their station is attended with hardships. But before it can be applied, as Grotius applies it, to prove, that we are not at liberty, as we are christians, to resist the unsocial injuries which we suffer from our civil governors, upon account of our religion; absolute submission to all the unsocial injuries, which they can bring upon us, must be shown to be the duty of our station, as we are members of civil society. If such absolute submission is a duty, which naturally arises out of civil subjection, the example of Christ will show us, that his religion does not discharge us from it. But if our station does not naturally require it of us, the religion of Christ does not enjoin it; whether we suffer unjustly by the unsocial oppression of our civil governors, upon account of this religion, or upon any other account; and the example of Christ is out of the question.

Grotius, in support of the doctrine of passive obedience and non-resistance, when we are persecuted for the religion of Christ, urges, in the last place, that St. Peter exhorts us to rejoice, when we suffer as christians. But if this would prove any thing in the present question, it would prove too much. Grotius allows, that Christ has permitted us to save ourselves from persecution by flight: and yet, if the apostle's exhortation to rejoice, when we suffer as christians, would prove, that the members of a civil society have not the same right to resist the unsocial injuries which are done them upon account of their religion, that they have to resist the like injuries which are done them upon any other account, the same exhortation would prove, that they ought not to fly from persecution. For, if rejoicing in sufferings is inconsistent with endeavouring to repel them, it is equally inconsistent with endeavouring to avoid them. But mankind are forced, in fact, to submit to many evils, which, of right, they might repel or avoid, if it was in their power: and christians, like other men, are exposed to such evils as these, sometimes upon other accounts, and sometimes upon account of their religion. When we are in these circumstances, we have need of consolation: and the apostle gives us this consolation, if we are brought into them upon account of the religion of Christ, by assuring us, that such sufferings are matter of rejoicing; because they will be amply recompensed to us. If this is St. Peter's meaning, his exhortation to rejoice, if we suffer as christians, does not determine any thing about the right of repelling or of avoiding persecution: it is only an encouragement to us to bear persecution well, and not to despair under it, when we cannot secure ourselves against it.

Civil judge not necessary to fix the point where right of resistance begins.

XV. In the general question concerning the right of resistance, it is usually objected, that there is no common judge who is invested with authority to determine between the supreme governors and the people, where the right of resistance begins: and the want of such a judge is supposed to leave the people room to abuse this right: they may possibly pretend, that they are unjustly oppressed, and upon this pretence may causelessly and rebelliously take up arms against their governors; though they are laid under no other restraints, and no other compulsion is made use of, but what the general nature of civil society, or the particular circumstances of their own society require. But be this as it may, the possibility that a right may be abused, does not prove that no such right subsists. If we would conclude, on the one hand, that the people have no right of resistance, because this right is capable of being abused, we might, for the same reason, conclude, on the other hand, that supreme governors have no authority. Whatever authority these governors have in any civil society, it was given them for the common benefit of the society: and it is possible, that, under the colour of this authority, they may oppress the people, in order to promote their own separate benefit.

When they, who make this objection, have explained what they mean by an authorized judge, we shall be able to determine whether there is any such judge or not, and how far the nature of civil government, or of the right that we are speaking of, will admit of one. If they mean a civil judge, who is invested either by social union, or by constitutional appointment, with authority to declare, when the grievances of the people will justify resistance, there neither is, nor can be, any such judge. For, in the first place, the supposition, that the civil governors, from whom the grievances came, are invested with supreme power, makes the notion of such a judge a plain contradiction: because his office, as it would give him a civil power of controlling those governors, would imply, that he has a civil power superior to the supreme. And, secondly, the right itself cannot, in its own nature, be subject to the jurisdiction of a civil judge: because it is a natural, and not a civil right: it is so much of the natural right of repelling injuries by force, as is exempted from civil subjection.

To this question.—Who shall be judge, whether the supreme governors act contrary to their trust? *Mr. Locke replies, the people shall be judge. If he means, that the people have such a civil jurisdiction in this matter, as gives them, at least in the view of civil society, a right of resistance, whenever they determine for themselves, that they have such a right; it will be difficult to support the truth of this reply. The supposition of such a jurisdiction is attended with the absurdity already mentioned: it implies a civil jurisdiction in the people, which is superior to the supreme. Civil governors, who are invested with supreme power, are sometimes said to be accountable to God alone: and however exceptionable this rule may be, as it is commonly explained, we shall find it to have some truth in it, when it is explained as it ought to be. No persons whatsoever, either separately or collectively, have any civil jurisdiction over such governors; and, consequently, they are not accountable to any human superiors as to civil judges. But, in the mean time, they are not at liberty to do what they please, without any external control. Though they are not accountable to the people as to a civil superior; yet the people, as far as they are not in subjection, have a natural right to repel the unsocial violence of such governors. In the same sense, therefore, that supreme governors are accountable only to God, the people, however they may, in other instances, be accountable to their civil governors, are, in the exercise of the right of resistance, accountable only to God.

The people shall, indeed, be judge, when the supreme governors have acted contrary to their trust. But their right of judging is not founded in civil jurisdiction: it is such a right of judging, as all mankind were possessed of in a state of natural liberty. Mr. Locke compares the case of the people and of the supreme governors to the case of a private person, who appoints a trustee or deputy to act for his benefit, and asks, "Who shall be judge, whether his trustee or deputy acts well and according to the trust reposed in him, but he, who deputes him, and must, by having deputed him, have still a power to discard him, when he fails in his trust? If this be reasonable, in particular cases of private men, why should it be otherwise in that of the greatest moment, where the welfare of millions is concerned, and also, where the evil, if not prevented, is greater, and the redress very difficult, dear, and dangerous?" In order to see, whether this reasoning is applicable to the point in question, let us consider what that point is. The supreme governors of a civil society have a right to direct and to compel the people, as far as the purposes of a social union extend. It is an injury to these governors to resist them in the exercise of this right: and this injury is ranked amongst the worst of crimes, and is called rebellion. But where this right of the supreme governors ends, as it does where they exceed the limits of all civil power, the people have a right of resistance. The question then is, who shall judge, where the former right ends and the latter begins? Mr. Locke replies, that the people shall judge, in the same manner, and for the same reasons, that a private person, who has appointed a trustee or deputy to act for his benefit, is the judge, when his trustee or deputy has failed in the trust, and may discard him for having so failed. This, indeed, is certain, that where I have

* Locke's Works, V. II. p. 245.

appointed any person to act for me; and he, by this appointment, acquires no right of his own, but only stands obliged to me to act according to my pleasure and for my sole benefit; I may discard him, whenever I think fit; and since, by the supposition, he has no right in the trust or no interest in it, which is properly his own; I shall do him no injury, though I discard him without any reason. But it is possible, likewise, that my trustee or deputy, notwithstanding the appointment comes originally from me, may, in consequence of this appointment, acquire a right or interest of his own in the trust. Though this right should be so connected with the trust, as to be forfeited, when the trust is broken; yet he cannot justly be removed at my pleasure: it would be an injury to discard him, when he had not broken the trust: because it would deprive him of a right which is his own. Indeed he holds this right conditionally: he loses it, whenever he breaks his trust. But I should injure him, if I was to put him out of the trust before this event has happened. Upon this account, if he and I live in a state of civil society, the public will not suffer me to take the trust from him at my own discretion, but will judge by itself or its magistrates, whether he has so broken the trust, as to have forfeited the right which goes along with it. If we live in a state of nature, where no common judge is provided; then, indeed, I must judge for myself: but he, on the other hand, has the same liberty to judge for himself: and if he is persuaded, that the trust has been faithfully discharged, he is not obliged to give up his right upon my sentence. I am a judge indeed; but I am not an authorized judge: I may determine upon the matter, but I can only determine for myself, and have no authority to determine for him. I may, likewise, act upon my own judgment: if I am persuaded, that he has forfeited the trust, and with it, the interest which he had in it; I may endeavour to dispossess him by force: but he, on the other hand, may act upon his own judgment; and if he thinks, that he has not broken the trust, he may endeavour by force to defend himself in the possession of that right which he has in the trust. Now though we should consider a supreme civil governor as a trustee for the benefit of the people, yet the trust is plainly of this latter sort. He has an interest of his own in the trust, or acquires a right of his own by being invested with it. The people, therefore, are not at liberty to discard him at pleasure; as they would be, if he was a trustee for their sole benefit. Suppose him to incur a forfeiture whenever he breaks his trust; yet if the people deprive him of it under pretence, that he has broken it, when he has not, they injure him: because by depriving him of the trust, they deprive him of a right, which they gave him by appointing him to be their trustee. The question, therefore, is, who shall be judge between him and them, whether he has broken the trust? Civil society provides no authorized judge between these two parties. The people, indeed, shall judge: but they are not authorized judges: the supreme governor has the same right to judge, that they have, and is not bound to submit to their sentence. If they are persuaded, that he acts tyrannically; this persuasion may justify their resistance: but, in the mean time, if he is persuaded, that what he does is within the limits of civil power, this persuasion will equally justify him in supporting his own act. Both parties are naturally obliged to judge by the same rule: the arbitrary will of the supreme governor is not the measure of what he has a right to do; and the arbitrary will of the people is not the measure of their right of resistance. Whilst he acts within the natural limits of civil power, they have no right to resist him: and when he exceeds these limits, he has no right to direct or compel them. But each party has an equal right to judge whether he has kept within those limits, or has exceeded them: and, consequently, neither of them are authorized judges in the case. Whether the supreme governing body consists of a single person, as in monarchies, or of a number of persons, as in other forms of government; if we were to consider it as a trustee or deputy for the people, that holds the trust or deputation precariously, and has no right conferred upon it by being appointed to this office; the people would then be authorized judges of the behaviour of this supreme body: nothing, which they determined about its behaviour, could be wrong: they might remove it from its office for every fault, or for every suspicion, or even without any fault or any suspicion at all. But the governing part of a civil society, whilst it is a trustee for the general benefit, is not a precarious trustee, that has no right of its own, and holds at the will of the part, which is governed. Its power is limited indeed by the purposes of social union; so that the people are not in subjection to it, and may lawfully resist it, when it counteracts these purposes. But it has a right to this limited power, and cannot be justly deprived of it without cause, or be lawfully resisted in the exercise of it. Thus the nature of civil power does not give the people a full and absolute right to resist or to discard their supreme governors, whenever they please, or does not make them final judges by investing them with civil authority to determine, when resistance is lawful. Judges they are, but not civil or authorized judges. They judge in this case of their own right to resist, and of the right of the supreme governors to compel, in the same manner only, that individuals judge of each others right in a state of nature; where each party is at liberty to make use of his own force against others, for the support of what appears to him to be his own right: but those others are in the meantime as much at liberty to judge for themselves, as he is, and are likewise at liberty to make use of their force to oppose his demands, if force is necessary, and they are persuaded that the demands are unjust.

In short, when the question is, whether the supreme governors of a civil society have abused their trust by counteracting the ends of social union; the case is of such a sort, that no civil judge is or can be provided for it. But it does not follow from hence, that there is no judge at all: each of the parties are left to judge for themselves, as if they were still in a state of nature. Both parties are accountable to God, if they judge wrongly and act upon this judgment: but neither of them is bound to submit to the judgment of the other.

Treason and rebellion how guarded against, notwithstanding right of resistance.

XVI. It is a groundless suggestion, that a right of resistance in the people will occasion treason and rebellion; or that it will weaken the authority of civil government, and will render the office of those, who are invested with it, precarious and unsafe, even though they administer it with the nicest prudence and with all due regard to the common benefit. The right of resistance will indeed render the general notion of rebellion less extensive in its application to particular facts. All use of force against such persons, as are invested with supreme power, would come under the notion of rebellion, if the people had no right of this sort: whereas, if they have such a right, the use of force to repel tyrannical and unsocial oppression, when it cannot be removed by any other means, must have some other name given to it. So that, however true it may be, that in consequence of this right of resistance, supreme governors will be liable of right to some external checks, arising out of the law of nature, to which they would otherwise not be liable; yet it cannot properly be said to expose them to rebellion.

But the great stress of the present question is, not what name the use of force to repel unsocial and tyrannical oppression is to be called by, but what effect it will have upon the general security of those, who are appointed to govern a commonwealth, and upon the authority which is necessary to be kept up, in order to enable them to discharge their trust with benefit to the public. Now the security of civil governors depends partly upon the consciences of their subjects, and partly upon the natural strength and influence which they have in their hands. The ties of conscience procure them obedience and submission upon a principle of duty: and the strength and influence which goes along with their office, procure the like obedience and submission from such as would disregard their duty, if it was not enforced by compulsion. They will have this latter security to guard their persons, and to support their authority, whether the people have a right of resistance or not. And, in fact, there is more danger of their making an undue use of their strength and influence, to support themselves when they do wrong, than of their wanting a sufficient security against any attempts of faction, when they do right: it is more likely that they should have it in their power to compel the people to submit to unsocial oppression, than that they should be in danger of being hurt by rebellion, under the pretence of a right of resistance. But this strength and influence is not their only security: for as long as they pay a due regard to the common good, the principle of conscience will procure them social obedience and submission, and will support their authority: because a right of resisting lawless power can never be a foundation in conscience for using force against just authority. In short, upon whatever principles passive obedience and absolute subjection might be obtained, if the people had no right of resistance; upon the same principles social obedience and civil subjection may be obtained, though they have such a right. We cannot suppose supreme governors to have strength enough in their hands to enforce absolute subjection, and to secure them in the exercise of arbitrary power; without supposing them to have strength enough to enforce civil subjection, and to secure them in the exercise of social power. And if a sense of duty would operate effectually to prevent the people from resisting their governors at all, it will certainly operate as effectually to prevent them from resisting without a just cause.

CHAPTER IX.

OF THE LAW OF NATIONS.

I. *How far the law of nations is a positive law.*—II. *Nations are capable of an obligation by compact.*—III. *In what sense prescription is a right of the law of nations.*—IV. *No evidence of a positive law of nations to be collected from usage.*—V. *Law of nations may be found by reason, or by testimony.*—VI. *Effects of the right of territory.*—VII. *Questions about extent of territory, belong to the law of nations.*—VIII. *No right of territory in things that do not admit of property.*—IX. *Different sorts of war.*—X. *Solemn war, what; and why called just war.*—XI. *Justifying causes of war.*—XII. *A nation may be accountable for the act of one of its members.*—XIII. *Members of a nation accountable for injuries done by it.*—XIV. *One nation may lawfully assist another in war.*—XV. *What is lawful in war.*—XVI. *Property, how acquired in war.*—XVII. *What prevents prisoners of war from being slaves.*—XVIII. *Effects of a declaration of war.*—XIX. *Law of nations in respect of states that are neutral in a war.*—XX. *Privileges of ambassadors, how far natural.*—XXI. *Public compacts are either treaties or sponsions.*—XXII. *Compacts between nations at peace, or nations at war.*—XXIII. *Equal and unequal compacts of nations.*—XXIV. *Compacts of the same matter with the law of nature, or of different matter.*

How far the law of nations is a positive law.

I. In the general division of laws, *I have followed Grotius, and have reckoned the law of nations amongst the positive laws of human institution. But, though there is enough of positive institution in it to justify this division, yet there is reason to doubt whether it is such a positive law as he supposes it to be.

The law of nations, according to †his account of it, is a system, or collection of rules, which derives its authority from the positive consent of all, or of most nations. He first considers the several nations, or civil societies of the world, as so many collective persons, who are formed into one great society, including all mankind: and then he supposes the law of nations to be the dictate of the common understanding and will of this great body, in the same manner as the civil law of each distinct civil society is the dictate of the common understanding and will of these smaller bodies.

If we were only to object here, that, in the great society of all nations, there is no common superior invested with authority to prescribe laws, we should not take the matter up high enough. For, in a society of equals, where there is no common superior, who has authority over the whole, ‡the general body of the society, taken together, is superior to each of the members taken separately, and has authority to prescribe laws to each. But this authority, in a society of equals, arises from their social union; that is, from the compact by which they have

* See Book I. Chap. I. § XI. † Grot. Lib. I. Cap. I. § XIV. ‡ See Book II. Chap. VI. § I.

bound themselves to act for some common purpose, under the direction of the common understanding. And the want of such a voluntary union amongst the several nations of the world, is the reason why there is in this great society, no legislative power, or no authority to establish positive laws.

Some sort of union there is between all nations: they are all included in the collective idea of mankind, and are frequently spoken of under this general name. But this is not a social union: the several parts of this collective idea, whether we consider the great body of mankind as made up of individuals or of nations, are not connected, as the several parts of a civil society are, by compact amongst themselves: the connexion is merely notional, and is only made by the mind, for its own convenience.

Nature has, likewise, made such a connexion between all mankind, as obliges them to abstain from what is productive of harm to one another, and to do what is productive of mutual good. But this connexion, whilst it is the foundation of the law of nature, cannot, without the intervention of some social compact, be the foundation of any positive law. We find, that all mankind, when we consider them as individuals, are obliged, by their condition and circumstances, to do good, and to do no harm: but this obligation does not give them any power to prescribe laws to one another, till they have agreed to unite themselves into societies. In like manner, all nations, when we consider them as so many collective persons, are obliged to observe the same law of nature. But this obligation gives them no positive legislative power over one another: it does not give any one nation, or any number of nations, authority to bind the rest, either to do any thing which the law of nature has not enjoined, or to avoid any thing which this law has not forbidden.

But though, for want of a social union, and, consequently, of a legislative power, amongst the several nations of the world, there cannot be any such positive law of nations, as Grotius has imagined, yet the law of nations may be distinguished from the law of nature: and the foundation of this distinction is laid in general agreement and positive institution. A number of individuals, who have formed themselves by mutual compact into one body, under an obligation of acting by the direction of the common understanding, for some certain purposes, are bound to consider themselves, in respect of these purposes, as one moral person. But the rest of mankind, as they are not parties in this compact, are under no natural obligation to take notice of it, and are still at liberty to consider and to treat the society as a large company of unconnected and individual persons. Since, therefore, in the mutual intercourse of mankind, civil societies are universally considered, and treated by one another, as collective moral persons; and the several members of such societies are considered and treated, not merely as separate individuals, but as parts of these collective persons, this personality, which is thus given to civil societies, must be derived from some universal consent or agreement of all nations. We see something like this within a civil society, when some of its members have, by compact, associated themselves for a private purpose of their own. This compact obliges them to act together, and to consider themselves, in reference to this purpose, as one collective body, or one moral person. But the civil community to which they belong, considers them still as so many distinct individuals. For, however the civil law, in the case of partnerships, may support the particular claim, which the private compact that is between them, gives the several partners, either upon the common stock, or upon one another; yet it does not treat the associated body as one moral person. Such a body cannot receive a legacy, and cannot sue or be sued, in a corporate capacity: it has not this sort of personality in the view of the society, till it has been incorporated by some public act. In like manner, a civil community, within the great body of mankind, however the members of it may be connected amongst themselves by a social compact, is only a large company of unconnected individuals in respect of all others who are not parties to this compact; till mankind, by a general or public act, have agreed to consider it as a moral person.

This general act of consent is the foundation of the law of nations, as far as this law differs from the law of nature. The matter of both these laws is the same: the law of nations, as well as the law of nature, commands whatever is beneficial, and forbids whatever is hurtful to mankind in general. But whilst the matter of them is the same, the objects of them are different: the law of nature considers mankind as individual persons; the law of nations considers them as formed into collective persons. Thus the same law, which is called the law of nature, when it is applied to separate and unconnected individuals, is called the law of nations, when it is applied to the collective bodies of civil societies, considered as moral agents, or to the several members of civil societies considered, not as distinct agents, but as parts of these collective bodies.

Nations are capable of an obligation by compact.

II. The law of nature, in this application of it, is not the only measure of the obligations that nations may be under towards one another. When they are considered as moral agents, they become capable, as individuals are, of binding themselves to one another by particular compacts, or treaties, to do or to avoid what the law of nature has neither commanded nor forbidden. But these obligations, which thus differ in their matter from the law of nature, neither arise from a positive law of nations, nor produce such a law. They arise from immediate and direct consent, and extend no farther than to those nations, that, by their own act of immediate and direct consent, have made themselves parties to them.

In what sense prescription is a right of the law of nations.

III. In speaking of the right of prescription, * I had occasion to observe, that the natural foundation of it is only conjectural; and that the right itself would have been precarious and uncertain, if it had not been established by the general consent of mankind. But this right, notwithstanding it is thus established, will afford us no evidence, that there is a positive law of nations which is distinct from the law of nature applied to civil societies, as if they were moral agents. For the notion of such a law of nations not only supposes that it introduces and establishes rights which have no foundation, or no certain foundation in nature, but likewise that it regards mankind only as they are formed into civil societies. Whereas, the general consent, which establishes the right of prescription, though by ascertaining this right it produces an effect which the law of nature, without its assistance, would not have

* See Book I. Chap. VIII. § VII.

produced, regards mankind equally, whether we consider them as formed into civil societies, or as subsisting independently in a state of nature. And if the right of prescription would take place amongst individuals in a state of nature, we cannot, with any propriety, call the general consent, which establishes it, a positive law of nations: because the notion of a law of nations, which will subsist alike, whether any nations subsist or not, is unintelligible. The general consent, which establishes the right of prescription, is so far from being a positive law of nations, that it is no law at all. It is a positive act of all mankind: but this positive act is a compact, and not a law. All are bound by it; not because it is done by any legislative authority, but because all and each have either expressly or tacitly made themselves parties to it by their own immediate and direct concurrence. If this common act of mankind was a law, it could operate only in consequence of some sort of social union, by which they, who do not immediately and directly consent to it, are understood to consent to it remotely and indirectly. But the right of prescription, as it is established by general consent, takes place amongst independent individuals, who are in a state of nature, where there is no sort of social union; and, consequently, where no law can be made, and no common act can be done any otherwise than by compact.

The establishment of prescription is like the introduction of particular property. Nature did not appropriate any goods, either moveable or immoveable, to particular persons, by dividing the common stock, and assigning to each person his particular share. The claim of property was introduced by a positive act of general consent. But this act of consent is not a positive law of nations. For, since the right of property, which is the effect of it, takes place amongst unconnected and independent individuals, it can be no law. And, if it was a law, it could not be called a law of nations with any propriety; both because it does not presuppose mankind to be united into nations, and, likewise, because nations are not the peculiar objects of it.

A fixed and steady right of prescription, as it is thus established by a general compact of mankind, in a state of nature, is, in the first instance, an adventitious right of the law of nature. But after mankind have formed themselves into civil societies, and have agreed to consider these societies as moral agents, or collective persons, it then becomes a right, not only of the law of nature, but likewise of the law of nations: not because it was either established at first, or is supported now, by any positive law of nations: but because, amongst independent individuals, it is a right of the law of nature; and the law of nations is nothing else but the law of nature applied to the collective persons of civil societies, as if they, like individuals, were moral agents.

No evidence of a positive law of nations to be collected from usage.

IV. We may reasonably conclude, that there is no law of nations which is wholly positive, if such a law is no where to be found: for a law, that does not appear, is in effect, a law that does not exist. *Grotius allows, that a purely positive law of nations cannot be traced out, as the law of nature may, from principles of reason. It is not derived from the constitution of things and the circumstances of mankind, but from the will

* Grot. Lib. II. Cap. XVIII. § IV. Grot. Lib. I. Cap. I. § XIV.

and appointment of the legislators: and when we are to inquire what their will and appointment is, in respect of such things as are indifferent in themselves, this is a question of fact and not of reason. In civil laws, if they are written ones, authentic evidence of the will of the legislator is to be had: the law appears in the original record, and in such copies of this record, as are well attested. But such a law of nations, as Grotius contends for, is an unwritten one: there is no original record of it, and no copy of any such record. He, therefore, directs us, in searching for it, to have recourse to the same means that are made use of in searching for unwritten civil law, to usage or custom, to conjectures, and to the judgment and testimony of skilful persons.

Now, the usage in which unwritten civil laws appear, is mere usage, and consists in immemorial and uninterrupted practice. But if we look into the practice of nations, as it is related in history, it does not appear, in any instance, to have been constant and uniform; that is, no usage appears from whence we can collect what the positive law of nations is. Grotius was aware of this: and though he sets out with recommending history as a principal help for discovering the law of nations, yet he afterwards confesses, that this help, if we have no other, will be of little service: for, since it is the business of history to record all facts indiscriminately, we must necessarily find in it not only such practices of mankind as are right and proper, but such, likewise, as are wrong and contrary to law. When this help fails us, as it always will, he directs us to have recourse to conjectures. But if the practice of nations has been variable and contradictory, all conjectures will be nothing to the purpose: they can never make an usage out of a variable and contradictory practice; and usage is the only proper evidence of an unwritten law which is wholly positive. It will be as little to the purpose when we ask, where we may find this positive and unwritten law of nations, to tell us, that we may learn it from the judgment and testimony of skilful persons. This is no satisfactory answer to the question; it is only a change of the persons, about whom the question is asked. We ask, in the first instance, where we ourselves may find the law? and if we are only told, that we may learn it from the judgment and testimony of skilful persons, we may still go on to ask, where do they find it? Their skill cannot discover any usage of nations, where the practice, as history relates it, is variable and contradictory. Their judgment cannot lead them to the knowledge of the law; where the law is wholly positive, and cannot be deduced by the help of reason, from natural principles. And their testimony will prove nothing, where the law is an unwritten one, and, consequently, they can have no record of it before them.

Law of nations may be found by reason, or by testimony.

V. But if the law of nations, instead of being purely positive, is only the law of nature applied, in consequence of a positive agreement amongst mankind, to the collective bodies of civil societies as to moral agents, and to the several members of such societies, as to parts of these bodies; the dictates of this law may be found by the same means that we make use of in searching for the dictates of the general law of nature.

In laws which are purely positive, there is no arguing from reason to law. We may think, that many things ought, in reason, to be established by law, whilst the legislator has not established them in fact, and saw no reason why he should establish them: and, on the contrary, he may have established many things in fact, and for weighty reasons, where we are not aware of any reason at all. But the law of nations is positive only in the manner of applying it, and is natural as to its matter: it is the law of nature, applied by positive consent, to the artificial persons of civil societies: and, consequently, the dictates of it are only the dictates of right reason, and may be collected by arguing from the nature of things, and from the condition and circumstances of mankind, when they are considered as formed into such societies.

The history of what has passed, from time to time, amongst the several nations of the world, may, likewise, be of some use in this inquiry: not because any constant and uninterrupted practice in matters which are indifferent by the law of nature, is to be collected from thence; but because we shall there find what has been generally approved, and what has been generally condemned, in the variable and contradictory practice of nations. If the law of nations is founded upon natural principles, and is not merely a positive law, which has no other foundation besides the will of the legislators, the approved practice of mankind will help to inform us what its dictates are. There are two ways, says * Grotius, of investigating the law of nature: we find out this law either by arguing from the nature and circumstances of mankind, or by observing what has been generally approved by all nations, or, however, by all civilized nations. The former is the more certain of the two: but the latter will lead us, if not with the same certainty, yet with a high degree of probability, to the knowledge of this law. For such an universal approbation must arise from some universal principle: and this principle can be nothing else but the common sense or reason of mankind. Since, therefore, the general law of nature may be investigated in this manner, the same law, as it is applied particularly to nations as to moral agents, and is called the law of nations, may be investigated in the same manner.

From hence we may see what use is to be made of the judgment and testimony of skilful persons, in these inquiries. Their judgment will help to point out the law of nations: because, what is approved of by men of prudence, and honesty, and experience, is more likely to be conformable to the dictates of right reason, than what is approved of only by the vulgar, and unthinking, and dissolute. And their testimony will be of weight, as it will be an evidence not only of their own sentiments, but likewise of what they have found, upon diligent inquiry, to be the general sentiments of the civilized part of mankind.

It may be necessary here to caution the reader against imagining, that a law of nations, which is purely positive, might be established, if not by the constant and uninterrupted practice, yet by the approved practice of nations. For no practice which is indifferent in itself, and is neither commanded nor forbidden by the law of nature, can be approved, for any other reason, than because it is conformable to some positive law. The notion, therefore, of an approved practice of nations, where the law of nature is silent, must necessarily presuppose the existence of a purely positive law of nations: and approved practice, if it presupposes this law, cannot be the cause of it. If there is any such law,

* Grot. Lib. I. Cap. I. § XII.

it must have been introduced and established by mere usage, which consists in uniform and uninterrupted practice: but we have already observed, what our author confesses, that in the dealings and intercourse of nations with one another, as history relates it, no such usage is to be found.

As we have now seen what the law of nations is, and where this law is to be found; there will be no occasion to detain the reader with a particular examination of the several cases that may arise, in the intercourse of nations with one another. If he understands what the law of nature is, when it is applied to individual persons in a state of equality, he will seldom be at a loss to judge what it is, when he is to apply it to nations considered as collective persons in a like state of equality. But we may perhaps be misled in our judgment for want of observing, that in the intercourse of nations sometimes the civil law of each nation, and sometimes the general law of nature, which considers the several members of a civil society, not as parts of a collective person, but as so many individual persons, is the proper measure of what is right and what is wrong. It may therefore be necessary to consider such of the leading cases, as will help to point out the distinct provinces of these several laws.

Effects of the right of territory.

VI. A nation, *by settling upon any tract of land, which at the time of such settlement had no other owner, acquires, in respect of all other nations, an exclusive right of full or absolute property, not only in the land, but in the waters likewise, that are included within the land, such as rivers, pools, creeks, or bays. This absolute property of a nation, in what it has thus seized upon, is its right of territory.

When I say, that a nation's right of territory consists in the absolute ownership of the land, where it has settled, or of such waters as are an appendage to the land; I mean its right of territory, as far as other nations, or the members of other nations, are affected by this right. For in respect of its own members, its right of territory consists, not in an absolute, but in a paramount property. Occupancy in the gross, gave the nation from the first a right of absolute property in the land, where it settled. But a subsequent distribution and assignment, or a subsequent occupancy in parcels, gives the several members of the nation private property in their respective shares. This private property, which they acquire by the assignment of the public, or by their own particular occupancy, with the leave of the public, though it implies a right to use what is thus acquired, and to dispose of it, is not strictly a right of full property or absolute ownership. It is property; because it is an exclusive right, in respect of all other individuals, to use the land, and to dispose of it: but it is not full or absolute property in the strictest sense; because the public has a right to limit and to direct the use and disposal in such a manner as the common safety and welfare require. This right of the nation is a sort of property: it is an exclusive right in respect of all other persons whatsoever, whether individual or collective, to direct the use and the disposal of the land for the purposes of social union. And this sort of property, as it is thus distinguished from private ownership, is what our author calls paramount property.

* See Book I. Chap. III § XIII. Book II. Chap. V. § III.

But after the lands, which the nation has acquired, are thus distributed amongst the several members of it, and are held by them in private ownership, so that nothing besides paramount property remains to the public in respect of its own members; the nation, considered as one collective person, has still, in respect of all other nations, and of all other individuals, an exclusive right of full property in the whole tract of land: not only because what passes within the nation, the manner in which it parcels out the country where it settles amongst its own members, and the terms, upon which they hold their several shares, does not fall under the notice of foreigners; but, likewise, because when all the members of the society are considered as one collective person, the whole property of the land, as well what has been granted by the public to its several parts, as what remains in the public itself, is vested in this collective person.

In consequence of this exclusive right of property, which a nation has in its own territories, the law of nations is not the only measure of what is right or wrong in the intercourse of nations with one another. This right of territory extends the authority of civil law to all questions, which relate to the use or the private ownership of such moveable goods, as are within the territory of the nation, and of such immoveable goods as are confessedly a part of its territory; whether its own members only are concerned in these questions, or the collective bodies or the individual members of other nations. Thus every state has authority to determine, by positive laws, upon what occasions, for what purposes, and in what numbers, foreigners shall be allowed to come within its territories, to exclude them from trading there at all, or to regulate their trade, to leave them under their natural incapacity of inheriting immoveable goods, or to remove this incapacity, to prevent them from inheriting moveable goods, or to prescribe the conditions upon which they may inherit.

Civil laws, when they causelessly and unreasonably exclude foreigners either from coming into the territories at all, or from trading there, are inhospitable. But these inhospitable civil laws are no otherwise contrary to the law of nations, than as this law, like the general law of nature, enjoins the duties of humanity and benevolence. Every nation has, by the law of nations, as every individual has by the law of nature, a right to judge for itself, how far its intercourse, either of the commercial or of the friendly sort, is likely to be detrimental to itself. So that, to cut off either or both sorts of intercourse, will be no act of injustice; though it will be wrong, if it is done causelessly. A nation has a moral power to withhold its benevolence; and they, from whom it is withheld unreasonably, though they are not treated kindly, are not injured.

Inhospitality amongst nations is less usual now, than it was in early times. Indeed every nation might rather be said to use a prudent and necessary caution for its own security, than to be guilty of a breach of hospitality, by excluding foreigners from coming into its territories; when, upon account of the frequent practice of piracy and robbery, there was such a strong presumption, that all strangers came for these purposes, as made it no incivility to ask strangers, whether they were not freebooters, and to call them, in the common way of speaking of them, by the name of enemies. *Cicero gives a different turn to this kind of language. He remarks, that such a person, as should properly be called *perduellis*, or an enemy, was, in the early times of Rome, called *hostis*, which appears, from the twelve tables, to signify a stranger. This, he says, was a tenderness of expression: an enemy was called by the milder name of a stranger, with a design to abate the odiousness of the character. But †Grotius seems to have given a juster account of the matter, when he considers this rather as a harshness of expression towards strangers, than as a tenderness of expression towards enemies. An enemy, in the old language of Rome, was called a stranger, not because they, who used this language, intended to compliment their enemies with the tender name of strangers; but because, in those early ages, they considered every stranger as an enemy.

Though the civil laws of every nation are the proper measure of the right, which foreigners have to make use of its territories, for any purpose whatsoever; yet these laws, like all others, admit and require the equitable exception of necessity. If the civil laws have forbidden any particular foreigners to come within the territory, or to bring any particular goods into any of its ports, or to come into any of them with a ship of force, under a certain penalty; foreigners, who stray thither by land, or whose ships are driven into the ports by stress of weather, may, by the letter of the law, be subjected to the penalty, but the equitable rules of interpretation will exempt them from it.

In consequence of the property, which every nation has in its own territories, the rights of harmless profit amongst nations are of the same sort, and are under the same limitations, with the like rights amongst individuals in a state of nature. They are rights, which may be maintained in theory; but the nature of them renders them precarious in their exercise. This matter has been explained already in its ‡proper place. But we may add here, that though a passage for the goods of merchants or traders through the territories of a nation, either over the land, or upon the rivers, or upon such arms of the sea, as are appropriated, is commonly reckoned amongst the claims of harmless profit; yet it is consistent with the law of nations to demand some toll or other acknowledgment for such passage. Grotius allows, that all payments of this sort are just, as far as they have any relation to the safety of the goods, or other benefit of the trader. If a nation, upon account of such a passage, is at expense in keeping up a road by land, or in repairing locks and sluices for the convenience of navigation, or in maintaining light-houses upon the coasts, or in guarding the traders by an armed force against pirates or other robbers; so much may undoubtedly be required of foreigners in their passage, as will repay these or the like expenses. But the nature of all rights of harmless profit will lead us one step farther: for since bare passage through the territories of a nation, though it should occasion none of these expenses, cannot be claimed without the consent of the nation; if it is in any degree probable, that the nation, by granting such passage, will lose an advantage, which it might have made for itself; there is no injustice in demanding toll upon this consideration.

* De Offic. Lib. I. Cap. XII. † Grot. Lib. II. Cap. VII. § XIV. Cap. XV. § V.
‡ See Book I. Chap. V. § VIII. IX.

Questions about extent of territory belonging to the law of nations.

VII. Where a question arises between two nations about the extent of their respective territories; that is, about their respective right to this or that tract of land; the civil law of either nation cannot be the proper measure, by which the controversy is to be determined. The general property of a nation in its own territory, as it is an exclusive right to a certain tract of land, implies a right to prescribe to all others, whether they are nations or individuals, the conditions, upon which they shall be allowed to make use of this tract of land, or to take part of it in private ownership. By this accident the authority of the civil law of the nation is extended beyond its own members: and if foreigners want to use or to acquire in private property what belongs to the nation, they must submit to use, or to acquire it upon such terms as the nation will agree to. But when the question is about the right of territory itself, whether such a particular tract of land is included in the general property of the nation or not; the civil law of the nation has no authority in this question. The authority of the civil law can extend no farther than the nation's jurisdiction. But as it has no direct jurisdiction over the person of the other party in the dispute; that is, over the collective body of the other nation; so neither has it any indirect jurisdiction over this other party, by having a direct jurisdiction over the thing in question; because the question is, whether it has any such direct jurisdiction over the thing or not.

In a state of natural equality a controversy between two individual persons, about the extent of their respective property, must be decided by the law of nature. In like manner the law of nations is the rule for deciding a like controversy, where the contending parties are two nations, and the matter in question is the extent of their respective territories or general property. But since the law of nations is only the law of nature applied to the collective persons of civil societies, and these collective persons are, in respect of one another, in a state of natural equality; if we know what the law of nature would determine in any case between individuals, the law of nations will, in like circumstances, determine in the same manner between civil societies.

Express compacts, by which two nations have settled the bounds of their respective territories, are binding upon the nations, and will ascertain their respective claims. For want of such express compacts, recourse must be had to usage, which is a tacit compact. The mere cultivation, or other use of the land by the members of one of the nations, will prove occupancy: but if the land, which is thus seized, was at the time of seizing it, a part of the territory of the other nation; such cultivation does not prove property. All occupancy gives possession; but in order to produce property, either general or particular, it must be the occupancy of a thing, which, at the time of seizing it, had no owner. But if the land, which is in dispute, has been cultivated, or otherwise used exclusively, from time immemorial, by the members of one of the nations without any interruption at all, or without any but what has been withdrawn as wrongful; this is an evidence, either that this land was included in the occupancy, which the nation made at its first settlement, and so was a part of its original territory, or else that it was acquired afterwards by mutual agreement. A claim, likewise, may have been kept up, without any cultivation or use of the land, by including it from time to time, when the nation has made perambulations to ascertain the boundaries of its territories, or by setting up standing land-marks, or by notice to all persons, who have come thither for the purpose of settling upon it, to withdraw. But if the land has not been cultivated, or otherwise used exclusively, and no claim has been kept up by these means, or by others of the same sort; it is a part of the common stock of all mankind: so that either of the contending nations may appropriate it by occupancy; and the nation, which seizes it first, will have a right of territory in it.

*If a river, at the confines of the territories of two nations, changes its course, and any question arises between the nations, whether a change is made in the extent of their respective territories, so that their jurisdiction extends to the river, as it did before: this is to be determined in the same manner, and upon the same principles, as if a river, at the confines of the two estates of two individuals, who are in a state of nature, had changed its course, and a like controversy had arisen between these two private owners.

The principles, upon which Grotius argues in this question, are founded in the different sorts of limits, that are made use of to divide and set out lands. A parcel of land may be set out either by measure, or by such limits, as are apparent to sense: and these limits, which are apparent to sense, may either be artificial or natural. In the suburbs of the cities of the Levites, we have an instance of possessions, which were limited by measure. Moses commanded, that these suburbs should reach from the wall of the city a thousand cubits round about. The lands of private persons are sometimes distinguished by artificial limits, such as walls, or rails, or ditches, or hedges. Territories are likewise distinguished by limits of the same sort, such as pillars or mounds of earth. And either private estates or territories, may be set out by natural limits, such as mountains, brooks, or rivers. If these are the only ways, by which the lands of different owners can be bounded and separated; it is not worth the while to inquire, with some of the commentators upon Grotius, whether he has explained and applied the several technical terms made use of by those, who have professedly written about the boundaries of lands, in the same manner, and in the same precise sense, in which these writers explain and apply them.

If lands, whether they are in the general property of nations, or in the particular property of individuals, are set out by measure; no change is made in the boundaries, either of two private estates, or of two territories, though a river, which runs at the confines of them, should happen to change its course. Each party has a right to a certain quantity of land, estimated by measure: and this measure is the proper limit of each parties claim. The river is not the limit; it only happened, that this river ran at the limit, or where the respective measures ended. And, certainly, no change can be made in the extent either of private property, or of territory, by a change in what was not the limit of them.

In like manner, if the lands were set out and distinguished from one another by some artificial mark; though a river, which once washed this mark, should change its course, and run within it on one side,

* Grot. Lib. II. Cap. III. § XVI, XVII.

such a change does not enlarge the extent of private property or of territory on one side, or diminish it on the other: because the extent of such private property, or of such territory, cannot be changed upon account of a change, which is made in something, that was not designed to be the boundary of them: and here the artificial landmark, and not the river, was designed to be the boundary: it was merely accidental, that the river ever ran close to the landmark.

But in lands, which have no other limit besides a river, and were designed to have no other, Grotius distinguishes between a change made in the course of this river by imperceptible degrees, and a change made all at once. Whilst a change is making by imperceptible degrees, the river, at any one instant of time, is the same, as to sense, that it was in the next preceding, or will be in the next subsequent instant. In like manner, it will be considered all along as the same river; and, consequently, as the proper limit between the lands that are on each side of it. But as long as the river is the same, the private property, or the territories of the two parties on each side of it, will extend as far as the river, and no farther; though by this imperceptible change, the extent is enlarged on the one side, and diminished on the other. The change may at last become perceptible: but such a change does not make the river different; because it has all along been considered as the same. Whereas, if the river leaves its old channel all at once, and breaks out in a new one; such a change is perceived immediately; and the river is no longer reckoned the same, that it was before. For a river is not merely a stream of water coming from a spring, but such a stream running in a channel. The sameness, therefore, of the river, cannot be preserved, in the account of mankind, unless all the parts of this definition continue the same as to sense; that is, unless the channel, as well as the spring, continues the same. And however the old river might be the limit of property or of jurisdiction on each side; the new river is not the limit; unless the parties, who claim property or jurisdiction on each side, agree to make it so. In the meantime their claims will extend just as far as they did before this change; that is, to the old bed of the river.

In applying these principles, it will be necessary to know, whether the lands in question have any other boundary, or whether they were originally designed to be set out by the river, when the river changes its course by imperceptible degrees. For, in this case, the extent of private ownership, or of territory, will be changed, if the river was the proper boundary of the lands. Whereas, if they were set out by measure, or by artificial marks, such a change in the course of the river makes no change in the extent of private ownership, or of territory. The general rule here is, that if no evidence can be found of any other limit, we may reasonably presume, that the river was intended to be the limit: because it is most likely, where nothing appears to the contrary, that either individuals or nations would choose to have such a limit of their estates, or of their territories, as will be a natural fence to them, and may be had without any trouble.

No right of territory in things that do not admit of property.

VIII. After *Grotius had spoken of occupancy, as the means of acquiring either jurisdiction or property, he goes on to divide jurisdiction into two sorts: a jurisdiction over persons, and a jurisdiction over things. But his readers should observe, that occupancy is not the origin of both sorts of jurisdiction. No act of occupancy will produce a jurisdiction over persons: this can be produced no otherwise than †by generation, or by consent, or by a crime. The only jurisdiction, therefore, that is acquired by occupancy, is over things. And though Grotius has here occasionally mentioned both sorts of jurisdiction, we have no reason to suppose, that he considered occupancy as the means of acquiring both; not only because he elsewhere teaches us that a right over persons is to be acquired by other means; but because, when he here speaks of occupancy as the origin, not only of property, but likewise of jurisdiction, he seems to confine the jurisdiction, which arises from thence, to things only, by saying, that occupancy produces jurisdiction over such things as are not yet appropriated.

But, be this as it will, if occupancy is the origin of jurisdiction over things, the consequence will be, that no jurisdiction can be acquired over such things as are not capable of being appropriated. For the reason why some things do not, in the nature of them, admit of property, is, because they do not admit of occupancy: and where no occupancy can be made, no jurisdiction can be acquired. Thus rivers, or bays, or straits, which are capable of being appropriated by individuals, may, likewise, be part of the territories of a nation. But as no individual can acquire property in the main ocean, either in whole or in part, so the ocean cannot be within the jurisdiction, or belong to the territory of any nation.

Whilst ‡Grotius considers occupancy as the origin of jurisdiction, it is remarkable to find him contending, that, though the main ocean cannot, in whole or in part, be the property either of an individual or of a nation, yet it will admit of jurisdiction. His distinction between property and jurisdiction, if there was any real foundation for it, would not clear up this matter. For, whatever difference there may be between them, they have the same origin. And if the nature of the ocean excludes property, because it will not admit of occupancy, it will, for the same reason, exclude jurisdiction. But, in fact, there is no other real difference between property and jurisdiction, than that the former is either private ownership, which is vested in an individual, or the full ownership which a nation acquires by occupancy in the gross, and the latter is the paramount property which continues to be vested in a nation, after private ownership is granted to its several members. In common language, property in things signifies the private ownership of them; whilst the paramount property in them is expressed by the peculiar name of jurisdiction. But this is only a difference of words: both ownership and jurisdiction have the nature of property; for both of them consist in an exclusive right over things in some respect or other. §Grotius, in support of a distinction between property and jurisdiction, alleges, that the property of land may pass to an alien who

* Grot. Lib. II. Cap. III. § IV. † See Book I. Chap. X. § III. Chap. XI. § I.
‡ Grot. Lib. II. Cap. III. § III. Cap. II. § III. § Grot. Lib. II. Cap. III. § IV.

lives in a foreign country; but in the meantime the society, in the territories of which the land is, will retain its jurisdiction: and they must needs be different rights, which can thus be separated from one another. I shall not call the possibility of the fact, which is here supposed, into question: because, though an alien is *naturally incapable of inheriting land, he may be made capable by civil laws. I, likewise, allow, that, in the case which is here supposed, the property of the land would pass to the alien, and the jurisdiction would remain where it was before. From hence it will certainly follow, that jurisdiction is not the same right with what, in common language, is called property. But it will be no consequence that jurisdiction is not any sort of property. I do not suppose it to be the same sort of property with private ownership: if it is paramount property, it is such a right as can only be acquired by occupancy, either mediately or immediately; and as those things, which in their own nature, are incapable of being appropriated by occupancy, cannot admit of.

We may go one step farther. Whatever does not admit of full property, or absolute ownership, cannot be a part of the territory, or under the jurisdiction of a nation: because all jurisdiction, or right of territory, presupposes full property, or absolute ownership. The first acquisition that a nation makes, when it settles upon any tract of land, which was before in common to all mankind, is the ownership of the land. †Its jurisdiction, as far as it can be distinguished from ownership, is the paramount property in the land, or a right to direct the use and disposal of it for the general benefit and security of the nation, after the ownership has been granted by the public body to the several members. But this is not all. Whatever distinction there may be within a nation, between jurisdiction and ownership, there is no such distinction in respect of other nations. The jurisdiction of a civil society over its own territories is, in respect of its members, a paramount property to direct the use and disposal of such things as are parts of the territory, to the purposes of social union. But, in respect of other civil societies, jurisdiction, or right of territory, is a right of absolute ownership, or a full right to exclude them from having any thing at all to do with the territory.

There is another way in which a nation may acquire jurisdiction, or a right of territory, without acquiring the absolute ownership of the land, in the first instance, by occupancy in the gross. But this way, like the other, presupposes absolute ownership to have been acquired, though not by the nation as one body, yet by the several members of it, as independent individuals, before the right of territory could take place. If a number of individuals, whose lands are contiguous to one another, unite themselves into a civil society, this act of union, in the first instance, gives the society only a jurisdiction over their persons. But a paramount property, or jurisdiction, over their lands, is a necessary effect of this jurisdiction over their persons: because the public, by the act of social union, acquires a right to direct them, as in other particulars; so, likewise, in the use and disposal of their land, in such a manner, and by such rules, as the general welfare and security shall make necessary. The territories of nations were probably small at first,

* See Book I. Chap. VI. § VI.

† Grot. Lib. I. Cap. I. § VI.

and increased by degrees, till they arrived at the size of which we now find them. And in what way soever any nation made its first acquisition, the extent of its territories has, undoubtedly, in many instances, been increased, not only by seizing upon other land, which was near to the place of its first settlement, and had no owners, but, likewise, where the land had owners, by incorporating those owners into its body. But as far as the right, which the owners had in their lands, fell short of full or absolute property, so far the nation, which acquires jurisdiction over their persons, by their civil union with it, would fall short of acquiring a full right of territory, or full jurisdiction over their lands. When any civil society has received an alien as a member, by incorporating him into its body, the society, which, by thus receiving him, acquires jurisdiction over his person, will not acquire jurisdiction over any lands which belong to him in the territory of his native country. And the reason why one of these jurisdictions does not here follow the other, is, because his property in the land was not full and absolute: his native country had a right of territory, or a paramount property in it, by which his ownership was limited. * Grotius might, perhaps, have a view to this method of acquiring jurisdiction over land, in consequence of a jurisdiction acquired over the person of the owner, when he speaks of persons as the primary objects of jurisdiction, and of a territory as the secondary object of it. In the other method of acquiring jurisdiction over land, where a nation, after it is formed, settles upon a void tract of country, and by this act of settling upon it, which is an act of occupancy, acquires a right of territory or jurisdiction over it, the persons, of which the nation consists, may be called the first objects, and the territory may be called the second object of jurisdiction; because they succeeded to one another in this order of time. But since the jurisdiction over the territory does not, in this case, arise consequentially out of the jurisdiction over the persons, without the intervention of any other act, one of them cannot properly be called a primary, and the other a secondary jurisdiction. But whatever might here be our author's meaning, it is evident, that, where a jurisdiction over things arises consequentially out of a jurisdiction over persons, the things, over which such jurisdiction is acquired, must, at the time of acquiring it, be the property of those persons. And from hence it follows, that such things as are, in their own nature, incapable of being appropriated, cannot, in this way, be brought under the jurisdiction of a nation, or become a part of its territory.

† Grotius does not extend the jurisdiction, which he supposes that a nation may possibly have over the ocean, to the whole ocean, but only to some parts of it. This partial jurisdiction he explains to be a jurisdiction either in respect of persons, when a nation has a fleet, which is a maritime army, stationed in any part of the ocean, or in respect of territory, as far as a nation can from the shore command and restrain those who are upon that part of the ocean, which is next to the shore, as effectually as if they were upon the land. There can be no doubt about the jurisdiction of a nation over the persons which compose its fleet, when they are out at sea; whether they are sailing upon it, or are stationed in any particular part of it. But when they are thus sta-

* Grot. Lib. II. Cap. III. § XIII.

† Grot. Ibid.

tioned, this jurisdiction of the nation is merely a jurisdiction over their persons, and not over that part of the ocean, where those persons are. We may say, if we please, that the nation has jurisdiction in that part of the ocean; because the persons, over whom it has jurisdiction, are there. But we cannot say with any sort of propriety, that it has jurisdiction over the ocean itself: because, as the persons who are under its jurisdiction, have no property in the ocean merely by being upon it, the jurisdiction of the nation over the persons who are there, will give it no jurisdiction over the ocean. If a land army was passing through an uninhabited country, the nation to which the army belongs, would have jurisdiction in that country: because the persons, who are the objects of its jurisdiction, are in that place. But in the meantime, if the army acquired no property in the country, the nation would have no jurisdiction over the land, where the army happens to be; that is, the land itself, merely by the army's being there, would not become the object of the nation's jurisdiction. And a fleet, by being in any part of the ocean, where the persons who compose it, cannot acquire property, will no more make that part of the ocean the object of a nation's jurisdiction, than an uninhabited country is made the object of its jurisdiction, by the passage of a land army through the country, without acquiring any property there. An armed fleet, when it lies in any part of the ocean, may certainly repel any armed force, that attacks it; not because this part of the ocean is under the jurisdiction of the fleet, or of the nation, to which the fleet belongs; but because it is under no jurisdiction at all. A fleet of fishermen have likewise a right, when they are fishing in any part of the ocean, to drive all others from thence, that shall come to fish upon the same spot, where their nets are. But this right does not arise from any jurisdiction over the ocean, but from the community of it. The place is common to all mankind, to be used by all, as they have occasion; and those, who have first seized it to use it, have a right to use it first. This right, indeed, arises from seizure or occupancy: but we must distinguish between the occupancy of a common thing to use it, and such occupancy, as separates the thing from the common stock, and gives the occupant property in it.

A nation has jurisdiction in respect of territory, over so much of the ocean as is included within the land: so that all ships, and all persons who are in them, are under the jurisdiction of the nation, if they are in any of its ports, or in any bays, or other arms of the sea, which are appendages to the land. This jurisdiction extends itself likewise into the main ocean, as far as the low-water mark: for the shore itself, though this part of it is sometimes covered with water, reaches thus far. But all beyond this is out of the jurisdiction: the nation can have no right of territory in it; because, as it is in its own nature an uncertain and indeterminate thing, it will not admit of such occupancy as produces property; and those things which are incapable of being appropriated, do not admit of jurisdiction.

It is commonly said, that a more extensive jurisdiction will be of use to nations which border on the sea; that the sea is their bulwark; that in order to secure themselves against being attacked on this side, it is necessary for them to be lords of the sea, as far as they can extend their force from the shore by means of great guns, or other instruments of the like sort; and that it is reasonable the territory should extend so far because all armed ships, which come within that distance, are able to do them mischief, and are indeed within their bulwark. What is thus urged might have some weight, if foreigners, who come with armed ships, and are likely to do mischief to a nation, could be proceeded against only by the civil laws of the country. For its civil law takes place only within its territory: and, consequently, if as much of the ocean, as is here claimed, was not within the territory, an armed force must be near enough to do mischief from the sea; or if the territory reaches only to the low-water mark, it must even be landed, before the nation would have a right to repel it. But this is not the case: two nations in respect of one another are in a state of equality: and any danger, which one of them apprehends from the other, is to be guarded against or repelled, not by such means as the civil law will furnish, but by such as the law of nature, applied to the collective persons of civil societies, will allow of. Now, in a state of equality, where there is reason to believe, that an injury is intended, the law of nature will allow us to demand security, that we shall not suffer it of those who are otherwise likely to commit it; though the injury is a distant one: and where such security is refused, the same law will allow us to make use of force for obtaining it. Thus the law of nations will render the sea as effectual a bulwark to a nation which is washed by it on one side, or encompassed by it on all sides, though the territory of the nation ends at the shore, as the civil law would, if the territory extended from the shore to the utmost random of a great gun.

* If one nation has obliged itself to another, by particular compact, not to go into some particular part of the ocean with an armed ship, or not to come thither either for the purpose of fishing, or for such other purposes as are specified in the compact, the latter of these nations will have a right to hinder the former from doing what it has thus obliged itself not to do. But this right does not arise from any property in this particular part of the ocean, or from any jurisdiction over it, but from the good faith of compact. The effect of this compact may easily be distinguished from property or jurisdiction. Property or jurisdiction is a right of excluding all nations from the use of a thing: whereas, this compact produces such a right only against the single nation, which has made itself a party to it: this nation is not at liberty to go into that part of the ocean, into which it has bound itself not to come; but all other nations, that are not parties to the compact, are as much at liberty to go thither, as if no such compact had been made. It is possible, that a nation may, in much the same manner, acquire a sort of exclusive right of fishing in such parts of the ocean, as are near to its own coasts. For as one nation might bind itself by compact not to come thither for this purpose; so all nations, that are likely to come thither, might bind themselves in the same manner. A tacit compact might likewise produce a right of the same sort: those maritime nations, that are in the neighbourhood, may tacitly have consented to establish this right, by submitting, from time to time, to be excluded from fishing near to the coasts of the nation which acquires the right. But this consent does not give the nation, whose coasts they are, either property or jurisdiction in those parts of the ocean which are near to its coasts. This

* Grot. Lib. II. Cap. III. § XV.

usage binds only those who have made themselves parties to it by such submission or acquiescence: it does not bind remote nations, nor does it bind even neighbouring nations, that are lately become maritime ones: because, as neither of them have ever acquiesced in the usage, or submitted to be excluded from fishing in these particular places, they have never made themselves parties to the compact of exclusion.

Different sorts of war.

IX. We have * already explained the general notion of war, and have considered the nature of private war in particular. This is the only sort of war, that could happen in the liberty of nature. For though such a number of independent individuals might occasionally join together in the use of force, as would make an army equal to those, which nations commonly bring into the field; yet a war, which is carried on with an army of this sort, would not be a public one. Public war is distinguished from private, not by the number of forces, or the greatness of the army that is employed, but by the character of the persons, who are the contending parties in it. A war of private persons or individuals will be a private war, whatever the numbers may be that engage in it, and take part with one side or the other. † Public war is the war of public persons; that is, of civil societies: and, consequently, there can be no such war, where there is no civil union. But civil societies act, in their intercourse with one another, by their respective supreme executive bodies; whether it is the friendly intercourse of leagues and conventions, or the hostile intercourse of war. A war, therefore, will be a public one, though it is no otherwise the act of those civil societies, that are the contending parties in it, than as it is the act of their respective executive bodies.

All magistrates, indeed, are public persons: and from hence, a question may arise, whether every war, which begins from any magistrate whatsoever, is public war, or whether this name is confined to those wars only, that begin from supreme magistrates? ‡ Grotius treats this as a question about words, the use of which is arbitrary: we are at liberty to give the words, public war, either of these senses; provided we explain, beforehand, the sense in which we use them, and take care to use them steadily in this sense. But this answer will scarce satisfy the inquiry. For they, who make it, do not want to be informed, what sense they are at liberty to give these words; but in what sense they must use them, in order to speak the language of the law of nations.

To clear up this matter, we may observe, first, that since a magistrate in any civil society is no otherwise a public person, than as he is authorized to act for the society; no act that he does, without being authorized by the society to do it, is done by him as a public person, or can be called a public act. A war, therefore, though it begins from a person, who is a magistrate, will not be a public war, unless it begins from him as a magistrate; that is, unless he is authorized by the society to make war.

Secondly, in a civil society, there are commonly two sorts of inferior § magistrates invested with executive power: one sort is invested with the internal, and the other with the external branch of it: some

* See Book I. Chap. XIX. § I. II.

† Grot. Lib. I. Cap. III. § I.

‡ Grot. Ibid. § IV.

§ See Book II. Chap. III. § XI.

magistrates are commissioned by the society to act with the public civil force, to put the laws in execution at home; whilst others are commissioned to act with the public military force, to defend and maintain the rights of the society against its enemies from abroad. The civil law considers the former sort of magistrates as public persons: but in the view of the law of nations, as they have no concern with other nations, they have no public character, or are not public persons. A war, therefore, which begins only upon the authority of such magistrates as these, is not a public war in the language of the law of nations.

Thirdly, amongst those magistrates, who are appointed to act in the external branch of the executive power, some have only a subordinate authority: and as these do not act for the nation, at their own discretion, but are under the direction of the supreme executive body, their character, in respect of other nations, is not a public one. A war, therefore, which proceeds only from their authority, cannot be called a public one by the law of nations.

Upon the whole, whatever liberty we have to use words in what sense we please, the law of nations will call no war a public one, unless it proceeds on both parts, from those who are invested with supreme executive power in the external branch of this power: for in the view of this law no other magistrates have a public character in respect of war.

* Grotius extends the notion of public war to all war, which begins from any magistrate whatsoever: and to justify this extensive sense of the words, he maintains, that even inferior magistrates, since they are appointed for the defence and security of the people in their several districts, must, in consequence of their appointment, have a right to make war, where the defence and security of that part of the people, which is committed to their trust, requires it; unless they are laid under some positive restraint by civil law. He allows, however, that in fact, most, or rather all civil societies, have taken care, by some positive provision, to lay their inferior magistrates under such a restraint: because, as the safety of the whole society is hazarded in war, it was proper to confine the right of making war to the supreme executive body, which has the care of the whole. But the contrary opinion is more consistent with the nature and effects of social union. The appointment of an inferior magistrate, does not leave him at liberty to make war, till some positive civil law restrains him: on the contrary, such magistrates can have no right of making war, unless this right has been given them by some positive civil law. In consequence of social union, the exercise and direction of the common force belongs to the collective body of the society, and not to any particular part of this body: nothing but a positive appointment, made by this body itself, in settling the constitution, or by the legislative body, which, after the constitution is settled, acts for the collective body, can naturally authorize any particular part of the society, or any particular person in it; that is, any executive body, or any magistrate, to exercise and direct the common force. A magistrate, who is appointed to act in the internal or civil branch of the executive power, can only use this force at home, and is restrained, by the nature of his office, from using it any otherwise even

* Grot. Lib. I. Cap. III. § IV, V.

at home, than under the direction of the civil law. Such a magistrate, therefore, has no more right to make external war, than a private person. And the use, which he is authorized to make of the public force at home, to put the laws in execution, if it can be called public war at all, is only public war by the civil law, and not by the law of nations. In the external branch of executive power, the notion of an inferior magistrate, or subordinate commander, implies, that the society has appointed him to act, not at his own discretion, but under the direction of the supreme executive body. The nature, therefore, of his appointment, though he is a magistrate, gives him no right to begin an external war.

But though all magistrates of one sort, and all inferior magistrates of the other sort, are restrained by the nature of social union, and the terms of their respective appointments from making war; it may be asked, whether there are no cases, in which this restraint is taken off, and, consequently, in which a war, that is made upon the authority of any magistrate whatsoever, will be a public one? Grotius mentions two cases, which he supposes to be of this sort: first, when the ordinary officers of a magistrate are sufficient to restrain a few disobedient subjects without hazarding the safety of the whole society; or secondly, when some immediate danger arises, which will not allow him to have recourse to the supreme magistrate for his authority. In the first of these cases, our author proceeds upon the principles, with which he set out; that all magistrates are naturally at liberty to make war, if they are not restrained by some positive law; and that the design of such positive law is to prevent the safety of the whole society from being hazarded by a person, who is only entrusted with the care of a part: from whence he concludes, that where, without hazarding the safety of the whole, any inferior magistrates, by the help of their ordinary attendants, can repress a few rebellious subjects, the obligation of these restraining laws ceases, because the reason of them ceases. We must, certainly, allow, that, where a magistrate has any ordinary attendants assigned to him by the public, for the purpose of using the common force, he has authority to employ them for this purpose. But this authority extends no farther, than the nature and end of his appointment extends: if, in any instance, he uses even the force, with which he is entrusted, in any other manner, or for any other purpose, than is warranted by his appointment; this, as it is his own act, and not the act of the public, cannot be called public war. The restraint that he is under, does not arise from any positive act of the law, but from a negative act of it: he has no right to use the force that is in his hands, at his own discretion; not because any positive law has restrained him from doing any thing, which, as a magistrate, he might otherwise have done; but because, as a member of the society, he has no right to use the public force at all, without the concurrence of the society: and, consequently, though he is appointed to be a magistrate, he has no right to use it any farther than the law has empowered him. It is neither the equitable consideration, that he, who is entrusted only with the care of a part, ought not to hazard the safety of the whole, nor any positive law made upon this equitable consideration, that restrains an inferior magistrate from making war at his own discretion. The restraint arises, at first, from social union, and continues even after he is appointed to be a magistrate, as far as the law has not taken it off by the express terms of his commission, or by the nature of the magistracy, to which he is appointed. And if the law has not thus given him a discretionary power, however possible, or however likely it might be, that the force, which he could exert, by his ordinary attendants, would repel or stop an insurrection; yet he is not at liberty to exert this force as a magistrate, any otherwise than the law has commissioned him: because, beyond his commission, he has no more right, than a private person, to judge about this possibility, or this likelihood, and to act upon such judgment. In the second case, we agree with our author, that an inferior magistrate may use what force he has at hand, to repel such an immediate danger, as will not allow him time to have recourse to the supreme executive body. But this act of force is no more a public war upon account of his being a magistrate, than it would have been if the same private persons, who act with him, had acted without him. The force which he exerts for this purpose, if, in exerting it, he exceeds the commission under which he acts as a magistrate, is only private force. It is not his authority, but a failure of jurisdiction, upon account of the exigency of the case, that makes the force lawful.

After what has been said, it will be needless to inquire, whether an inferior magistrate, where he is not pressed by any such exigency, may make war, as he sees opportunity, upon a conjecture that the supreme executive body would authorize him, if he was to consult it. For an inferior magistrate has no right to act, with force, beyond his commission. If, therefore, the nature of his office, and the terms of his appointment, have given him no discretionary power, he has no right to act upon any conjecture, which he makes, about what he might probably be authorized to do, if he was to consult the supreme executive body.

All wars of a nation against its external enemies, are not public wars. To make a war a public one, both the contending parties must be public persons; that is, it must be a war of one nation against another; and, consequently, it must begin and be carried on by the authority of the supreme executive body on both sides. Where a nation makes war upon pirates, or other robbers, though these are external enemies, the war will be a mixed one: it is public on one side; because a nation, or public person, is one of the parties: but it is private on the other side; because the parties on this side are private persons, who act together occasionally, and are not united into a civil society. A band of robbers, or a company of pirates, may, in fact, be united to one another by compact; and may have stipulated with one another in this compact, to be directed by the common understanding, and to act by the common force, for their general benefit. But they are still, by the law of nature, only a number of unconnected individuals; and, consequently, in the view of the law of nations, they are not considered as one collective body, or public person. For the compact, by which they unite themselves, is void: because the matter of it is unlawful. The individuals, that form themselves into a civil society, are bound, by their social compact, to pursue and to maintain a common benefit: but this common benefit is such an one, as is intended to be consistent with the obligations which they are naturally under to the rest of mankind. Whereas, the common benefit, which a band of robbers, or a company of pirates propose to themselves, consists in doing harm to the rest of mankind.

When any of the members of a civil society make use of force to oppose the execution of the laws, or to support themselves in the violation of them, and the magistrates, who are entrusted with the internal executive power, exert the civil force to repel or to repress them, this is a contention by force, and may, therefore, be called war; though, in our common way of speaking, we do not usually give it this name. On one side it is a riot, or a tumult, or a sedition, or an unlawful resistance. But I do not know, that, in our language, there is any particular name for it on the other side. According to our author's notion of public war, this use of force, on the side of the magistrate, would be a public war, and the whole act of contention, if we take in both parts, would be a mixed war. But in the language of the law of nations, it is certainly neither public nor mixed. For this law relates only to the intercourse of a nation with the rest of mankind, and takes no notice of what passes within a nation, either between the several members of it, or between the body and any of the members. If the force, which is made use of for these unlawful purposes, by the members of the society, should be so great as to make it necessary for the civil magistrate to take the military force to his assistance, yet, as long as this force is under the direction of such a magistrate, the contention is still what it was before: it has no name on the part of the society, and is called a riot, or a tumult, or a sedition, or an unlawful resistance, on the part of the members.

When the seditious members are so strong, that the executive body is obliged to interpose, and to take the command and direction of the military force, this contention is called a rebellion on the part of the subjects; and may be called a civil war on the part of the society. A contention by force, is a mixed act of the same sort, and may, on each part, be called by the same names, where the subjects endeavour, by unjust force, to overturn the government, and the executive body, on behalf of the society, interposes with the military force to support it.

In monarchies, either absolute or limited, where the matter in dispute is the title to the crown, and this title has been left doubtful by the civil law, a contention by force is a civil war on both parts. But if the civil law has clearly determined the title, such a contention, by force, is a rebellion on the part that claims against the civil law, and a civil war only on the part that claims under it.

Where force is made use of by the members of a civil society, to resist such tyrannical oppression of the governors, as is subversive of the ends of social union, a war of this sort cannot properly be called rebellion; since this name imports a forcible opposition to lawful authority. And the presumption, that civil governors will always discharge their duty, has prevented mankind from giving it any name, which implies injustice on the side of the governors. Such a war, therefore, goes under the general name of a civil war.

If any one should ask, whether these internal wars of a civil society are public, or private, or mixed? we must certainly answer, that, in the language of the law of nations, they are neither. For, since this law takes no notice of what passes within a civil society, as far as what passes there has no reference to the rest of mankind, it has no occasion to mention wars of this sort; and, therefore, gives them no name: it does not so much as call them wars; and much less does it rank them under the heads of public, or private, or mixed. The reason why some writers have thought that these contentions, by force, within a society, are not to be called wars at all, may, perhaps, have been, that the law of nations does not call them so. But this reason is of no weight: for the law of nations does not call them wars; not because they are not wars, but because they are such acts as do not come within its view, and as it has, therefore, given no name to. They have certainly the nature of war; for they are contentions by force. Common usage, likewise, has given them this name, and calls them civil wars. And if, instead of attending to the precise language of the law of nations, we attend to the nature of the acts, we shall find, that civil wars may be either public, or mixed, or private. A civil war, upon a doubtful title to the crown, may be called a public one; because the heads of each party are respectively considered by their own people as public persons. Where the contention, by force, is a rebellion on the part of the people, and a civil war on the part of the government, this is a mixed war: one of the parties is under the conduct of a public person, and the other consists of private persons. And since the people cannot act upon a right of resistance, but only so far as they are not in subjection, and the governors have no jurisdiction, a civil war, which begins and is carried on upon this right, may be called a private one: because, where there is no subjection on one side, and no jurisdiction on the other, the persons concerned are, in respect of one another, private persons.

Solemn war, what; and why called just war.

X. Public war is divided into perfect and imperfect. The former sort is more usually called solemn, according to the law of nations, and the latter unsolemn war. Grotius defines perfect, or solemn war, to be such public war as is declared or proclaimed. Indeed, the very name of war, is so far appropriated, by common usage, to solemn war, that, when we speak of war, we are generally supposed to mean this sort; unless we add some term of distinction to show, that we mean some other sort, by calling it a private war, or a civil war, or a piratical war. Unsolemn, or imperfect wars between nations; that is, such wars as nations carry on against one another, without declaring or proclaiming them, though they are public wars, are seldom called wars at all: they are more usually known by the name of reprisals, or of acts of hostility.

Thus we find, that, to make a war a solemn one, according to the law of nations, *two things are required: first, it must be a public war; that is, the contending parties must be two nations, acting respectively under the direction and by the authority of their supreme executive body: and, secondly, it must be proclaimed, notified or declared. The use of the common force of a nation, by lawful authority, to quell insurrections, or to repress rebellions, though we find that there is sometimes a declaration of war, at least on the side of the rebels, is not a solemn war, according to the law of nations; because this law does not consider it as a public war: and reprisals, though they are contentions by force between two nations, and may, therefore, be called public wars,

* Grot. Lib. I. Cap. III. § IV.

are not solemn wars; because they are not preceded by any express and open declaration of war.

Perhaps another definition of solemn war may be found, which will help us in explaining the natural effects of proclaiming or declaring war. A solemn war is a war which appears evidently to be a national act on both sides; or to be the war of the whole collective body of one nation against the whole collective body of another. This definition includes all that is included in our author's definition. A war cannot be a national act on both sides, without being a public one: and it cannot appear evidently to be a national act without being proclaimed or declared.

When a solemn war is called, as it sometimes is called, a just war, according to the law of nations, *Grotius imagines, that this appellation is intended to denote, not that the law of nature, or of nations, allows only this sort of war, and forbids all other sorts, but that this sort produces,—*quosdam* juris *effectus*,—certain effects by the law of nations, which no other sort will produce. The effects, which he means, are impunity for what is done, and property in what is taken. We will inquire, presently, how far these effects are peculiar to solemn war; and, in the meantime, will examine our author's opinion about the reason for giving the name of just wars to wars of this sort. What he has advanced about the effects which the law of nations allows to solemn wars, and about the reason for calling them just wars, upon account of these effects, he explains by the two instances of marriages and wills. When the Roman law calls the matrimonial union of free persons a just marriage, this appellation, he says, is not intended to denote, that the matrimonial union of slaves, though this has not the same appellation given to it, is unjust or forbidden; but only that the former produces some effects, or some claims by this law, which the latter does not produce. In like manner, when a will, as it is distinguished from a codicil, is called a just will by the same law, we are not to understand from hence, that making a codicil is an unlawful act; but only that this law gives some effects to a will, which it does not give to a codicil.

But, perhaps, a just marriage and a just will might derive this appellation rather from their nature, than from their consequences. Some matrimonial unions seem to have been called just marriages, not upon account of the effects of law which they produced, but upon account of their legal perfection; that is, their exact conformity to the strictest or highest rules, which the law, relating to such unions, had prescribed: whilst other matrimonial unions, though the law, as it had not forbidden them, allowed of their validity, were not called just marriages; because they wanted this conformity to the highest rules of the law, and were, therefore, in the view of the law, imperfect in their kind. In like manner, one sort of disposition of a man's goods, upon the event of his death, seems to have been called a just will; whilst another sort was called a codicil, without the appellation of just; because the former was perfectly conformable to the strictest notion, that the law had of such a disposition, or was attended with all the qualities that the law required; whilst the latter, having no more requisites of law than were necessary to make it a valid act, fell short of legal perfection.

* Grot. Lib. I. Cap. III. § IV.

The Roman writers apply the word, just, to some wars, and distinguish them from other wars, to which they do not give the same appellation. But when the former are thus called just wars, this appellation is not designed to denote, that they produced any peculiar effects of law, but only that, in the manner of beginning them, they were exactly conformable to the rules of their fecial law, or law of arms. When they call this law the law of nations, we are not to understand from hence, that it was a positive law, established by the consent of all nations. It was in itself only a civil law of their own: they called it a law of nations; because the design of it was to direct them how they should behave towards other nations in the hostile intercourse of war; and not because all nations were obliged to observe it.

I do not deny, that such acts as are called just ones, upon account of their legal perfection, or their exact conformity with law, produce effects which other acts, that are less perfect in their kind, will not produce: I only deny, that these effects of the law are the reason why the acts are called just ones. And in denying this, I am supported by a very common use of the word, just. We frequently apply it, both to actions and to things, to denote that they are perfect in their kind. In this sense we speak of a just battle, a just army, and a just volume, to distinguish them from a skirmish, a small party, and a pamphlet. Since, therefore, actions are thus called just, to denote that they have a general perfection in their kind, it is reasonable to conclude, that, when they are called just in reference to any law, this appellation should be understood to denote, that they have a legal perfection in their kind.

For these reasons, I am inclined to think, that a solemn war is called a just one, according to the law of nations; because in the view of this law, it has some sort of legal perfection. But this perfection cannot consist in an internal conformity with the law: for, if it did, as this law is only the law of nature applied to the collective persons of civil societies, no wars could be called just, unless they were moved upon such reasons as the law of nature will justify: whereas, in the sense that we are now inquiring about, wars are called just, provided they are solemn, without any regard to their internal reasons. The legal perfection, therefore, upon account of which solemn wars are distinguished from other wars, by this appellation of just, is merely external. The reader may, probably, see by this time, what this external perfection is. As nations are the only proper objects of the law of nations, no contention by force, is properly called war, in the language of this law, unless nations are the contending parties; that is, unless it is a public war. But amongst the wars of nations, some are imperfectly public. If one nation seizes the goods of another nation by force, upon account of some damages which the former has suffered from the latter, such contentions, by force, are called reprisals. There may, likewise, be other acts of hostility between two nations, which do not properly come under the notion of reprisals: such as the besieging of each others towns, or the sinking of each others fleets, whilst the nations, in other respects, are at peace with one another. These are public wars; because nations are the contending parties. But as they are confined to some particular objects, they are of the imperfect sort, and do not come up to the highest notion of a public war; which consists in a war of the whole collective person of one nation, against the whole collective person of another nation. The design of a declaration of war, by which the war becomes a solemn one, is to bring it up to this highest notion of public war, or to make it perfectly public: and it is this legal perfection, from whence such wars have the appellation of just ones: by calling them just wars, we only mean, that they are perfect ones, according to the law of nations.

XI. The law of nations considers each civil society as a moral person, and all the several societies of the world as so many distinct persons, in a state of natural equality. Since, therefore, an injury is, by the law of nature, the only justifiable cause of war amongst individuals in a like state of equality; nothing but an injury will justify a war amongst civil societies by the law of nations. But *as amongst individuals, so likewise amongst civil societies, an injury will make the use of force just, either before or after it is done. Force may be made use of amongst nations, to guard against an injury before it is done; to stop it, when it is beginning; to obtain security, that it shall not proceed; or to repel it, when it is near at hand. After an injury has been done, it produces both a right to recover reparation for the damages, that have arisen from it, and a right likewise to inflict punishment, in order to prevent the nation, which has done harm now, from doing the like again.

Justifying causes of war.

By the law of nature, a future injury is not a just cause of private war, unless there is a plain design of doing it, and no other way of preventing it from being done. And this law, when it is applied to civil societies, and so becomes a law of nations, makes no farther allowance in favour of public war. †The growing power, therefore, of a nation, whilst it abstains from doing and from attempting to do injuries to its neighbours, is no justifiable cause for them to make war upon it, in order to stop the growth of its power, before it has acquired strength enough to give it an opportunity of injuring them. For it is only the apparent design of doing an injury, and not the power of doing one, that makes defence by force lawful. In deliberations about war, some regard may indeed be had to the probability, that a nation will grow too strong for us, if we do not take care to reduce it in time. But this can only be regarded as a prudential cause, and not as a justifiable cause of war. If other causes make a war just, this consideration will make it advisable: but this consideration alone is not sufficient to justify a war, if no injury has yet been done or attempted.

The law of nations being the same amongst civil societies with the law of nature amongst individuals; nothing but what is strictly or properly an injury, will justify a public war. From whence it follows, that where any nation makes war upon another only upon account of ‡some neglect or refusal of what is matter of favour, or of courtesy, or even of humanity, such a war is contrary to the law of nations. The false religion, likewise, of a nation, can be no otherwise a just cause of making war upon it, than as this religion has actually produced some real and proper injury, or some attempt to do such an injury.

Not only such injuries, as affect a nation immediately in its collective capacity, §but such, likewise, as are done to any of its members, are a justifiable cause of war. For these, by the law of nations, are parts of

* Grot. Lib. II. Cap. I. § II.

† Grot. Ibid. § XVII. Chap. XXII. § V.

‡ Grot. Lib. II. Cap. XXII. § XVI.

§ Grot. Lib. II. Cap. XXV. § I, II.

the collective person of a nation; and injuries, which are done to parts of this person, are done to the person himself. But when we speak of an injury which is done to one member or to a few members of a civil society, as a justifiable cause of war; it is necessary to distinguish between what is a just cause of war in respect of the nation itself, to which these members belong, and what is a just cause of war in respect of the nation that has done the injury. As a civil society is obliged, by the social compact, to guard the rights of its several members; so it is obliged likewise, by the same compact, to guard the common interest of the whole. Unless, therefore, the injury, which some of the members have suffered, affects, either in itself or in its consequences, the whole society, or such a part as bears a considerable proportion to the whole; however it might justify a war in respect of the nation which has done the injury, it would scarce justify the governors of the nation, to which those, who have suffered the injury, belong, in respect of the duty which they owe to their own society, if they should hazard the safety of the whole by a war, and sacrifice the lives of many, and the fortunes of most of their subjects, to redress such an injury. In the meantime, the duty which the society owes to its injured members, is not superseded. Though the society is not obliged to redress them by war, when this method of redress is inconsistent with the general interest; yet it is still obliged to secure their rights: and this obligation can be no otherwise discharged than by making them amends out of the public property for what they have lost.

Amongst the other ways, in which an injury is a just cause of war, we have mentioned the right of inflicting punishment, where an injury has been committed. And as *individuals have this right in a state of equality, the law of nations gives the same right to the collective persons of civil societies. Where an injury has been done, a nation, like an individual, has not only a right to a reparation of the damages, which it has sustained, but it has likewise a right, where there was any malicious design of doing harm, to take such measures with those who have done it, as may prevent them from doing the like again.

A nation may be accountable for the act of one of its members.

XII. The law of nations does not suppose that a civil society must necessarily be a principal or an accessory in every act which is done by any of its members. For this law, whilst it considers the several members as parts of the collective body, does not suppose each member to have no will of his own, or to be incapable of acting for himself, without the command or the consent of that body. But though a nation is not necessarily an accessory to every injury, which is done by any of its members, either to the general body, or to the particular members of other nations; yet it may make itself an accessory, either †by conniving at the injury, whilst it is committed, and neglecting to prevent it, or by protecting those who have done the injury, against the just demands of those who have suffered it. By means, therefore, of such connivance, or such protection, a society becomes accountable for the crimes or faults of its members.

Amongst individuals, the faults of servants may, in many instances, be charged upon their master; because they are under his authority,

* See Book I. Chap. XIX. § III.

† Grot. Lib. II. Cap. XXI. § I, II, III.

and it is his business to take care that they do not misbehave themselves. And, upon the same principles, the neglect of a nation, in not preventing the subjects of it from offending, will make the nation a party in their offence: for the nation, since they are under its jurisdiction, is obliged to take care that they do no harm to the rest of mankind. But such neglect does not make a nation accessory to the acts of subjects, that are in a state of rebellion, and have renounced their allegiance; or that are not within its territories: for, in these circumstances, the subjects, whatever they may be of right, are not under its jurisdiction in fact. The law of nature, as it respects civil societies, and is called the law of nations, is something different in this matter from the same law, as it respects individuals. Servants are commonly under the eye of their master, so that he has constant opportunities of knowing what they do: whereas, subjects are not so immediately under the eye of the society; that is, of the civil governors who act for it; and, consequently, many things, which are done by the subjects, may escape their knowledge. Now, the general rule of law is, that no person, either individual or collective, can, by means of any neglect in not preventing the fault of another, be an accessory to the fault, unless he was obliged to prevent it, and knew, likewise, that the fault was committed: for, however he might, upon other accounts, be under a general obligation to prevent it, yet, if he did not know of it, he could not in this particular instance, be under any such obligation; because no person's obligation extends beyond his knowledge. From hence it follows, that the same law of nature, which charges all the faults of slaves upon their master, will only charge such faults of subjects upon a nation, as were too frequent, or too notorious to escape the knowledge of the public.

After an injury has been committed, a nation, by protecting the offender against those who have a right to require reparation of damages, or to inflict punishment, in order to defeat their right, makes itself a party in the injury. Connivance, or neglect to prevent an injury, cannot make a nation a party to the injury, unless the offender is one of its own subjects; or, at least, was within its territories when the injury was done: because, in any other circumstances, he is not under the nation's jurisdiction. But by granting protection to an offender, it may become a party, not only in such injuries as are committed by its own proper subjects, or by foreigners, who, by being resident within its territories, make themselves temporary subjects, but in such, likewise, as are committed abroad, either by its own subjects, or by foreigners, who afterwards take refuge in its territories.

But the law of nations, by considering every civil society as a distinct and entire body, which is united into one collective person, by a social compact, for the purpose of securing and advancing its own welfare, allows every civil society to have an exclusive jurisdiction over its own members: for it could not be a distinct and entire body, if its members were subject to any other jurisdiction besides its own. Now, the notion of an exclusive jurisdiction, vested in each nation, implies, that it has a right to judge for itself how far its own members are to be punished, and whether they are to be punished at all, or to be pardoned. From whence it seems to follow, that a nation, by not punishing one of its members, or by not suffering any one else to punish him, only exercises such a jurisdiction as the law of nations allows. And the protection of a subject against punishment is, in this view of it, so far from making the nation a party in any injury which he has committed, that it discharges the subject himself from all obligations that arose from thence. But this difficulty, if it is one, arises merely from not attending to the nature of that exclusive jurisdiction which the law of nations allows to every civil society. For it is only a jurisdiction within the society itself; that is, a jurisdiction where none but itself and its own members are concerned; and, consequently, does not extend to such offences as we are now speaking of: to offences, which are committed by the members of one society, either against the body, or against the members of another. Neither the nature of social union, nor the consent of mankind to consider civil societies as distinct and entire collective persons, will give any nation an exclusive jurisdiction, where the offences are of this kind.

There is another difficulty in this matter, which is of more importance. Every nation has an exclusive property in its own territories. * No persons, therefore, who are not members of it, can lawfully come thither without its leave. And whatever right of harmless profit they might pretend, yet if the nation apprehends that it would be dangerous to itself to let them come thither, the law of nations does not oblige it to give them leave. If, therefore, any person is found within its territories, who has committed an offence against a foreign nation, or against the members of a foreign nation, what is to be done with him? The nation, in whose territories he is, cannot justly punish him, if what he has done, though it is a crime by the law of nature, or of nations, is not forbidden by its own civil law. It would be dangerous to the nation to admit foreigners to come into its territories, with an armed force, to punish him: and, consequently, as they cannot come thither without leave, so, in view to the safety, or, at least, to the peace of the society, it would be wrong to give them leave. And yet, if the nation screens him from punishment, it becomes a party in his crime, and gives those who are offended, a just cause of making war upon it. What remains, therefore, for the nation to do, is what the injured nation has a right to demand: he ought to be delivered up to those against whom the crime is committed, that they may punish him within their own territories. This is the right. But how far a nation, that has been injured in itself, or in its members, will choose, either to insist upon this right at first, by demanding the criminal, or to support it afterwards by force, if the demand should not be complied with, depends upon its own discretion. And if it is a general practice in Europe, as Grotius affirms that it is, to waive this right, unless where the crimes are very heinous, the practice has been taken up upon principles either of political prudence, or of tenderness towards the offenders: for, whatever may have been established amongst particular nations, by express compacts, there is no general law which obliges all nations in the world, or all nations in Europe, to hold this conduct.

We may observe, by the way, that when a nation thus delivers up one of its subjects, this is not inconsistent with the social rights of such subject: for by the social compact, he acquires only a right to be protected against suffering causeless harm, and not a right to be protected in doing causeless harm.

* Grot. Lib. II. Cap. XXI. § IV, V.

When a state delivers up an offending member to pacify an enemy, and the enemy, either having some other cause of war, or being resolved to make war at any rate, refuses to receive him; * Grotius inquires, whether he continues a member of the state, after this act, or whether it deprives him of his right of citizenship? Cicero maintains, that the right of citizenship continues; because such a delivering up of a member is a sort of donation, and can, therefore, produce no effect without acceptance. And, undoubtedly, if we keep to the strict notion of delivering up, there can be no such act on one part, if there is no acceptance on the other part: for the strict notion of delivery, implies acceptance: where there is no acceptance, there may be an attempt or endeavour to deliver, but there can be no actual delivery. But the question is, whether the act of the state, though it cannot be strictly and properly called delivery, is not of such a sort, as cuts off the right of citizenship? Grotius explains this act to be nothing more than a permission to the enemy to punish the offending member: and as the state, by such permission, does not give any right to the enemy over the offending member, but only removes the impediment, which its own right of territory had laid in the way of punishment; it cannot, by this act, be understood to deprive its own member of any right: for where no right is given on one side, no right can be taken away on the other side. But this is an imperfect description of the act of the state: this act does not consist merely in permitting the enemy to punish him, but in withdrawing protection. Scævola, as he is quoted by Grotius, explains it in this manner, and from hence, concludes, that the member loses his right of citizenship, or ceases to be a member, whether the enemy accepts him or not: because, where protection is justly withdrawn, there can be no right of citizenship. We may, however, reply, that the state withdraws its protection only for a certain purpose, and not absolutely; for the purpose of putting it into the enemies' power to punish the offending member, from whom protection is thus withdrawn. In all other respects, his right to protection, which is the foundation of citizenship, continues. And if this purpose does not take place, as it does not, where the enemy refuses to receive him; his right remains entire.

How far it would be † lawful for a state to deliver up one of its members, who has committed no crime, in order to preserve itself from being destroyed by a powerful enemy, depends upon the claims arising out of civil union, and not upon the law of nations. For we are not to inquire here, whether one nation can justify itself, in making such a demand upon another? but whether the nation, upon which the demand is made, can lawfully comply with it?

In speaking of the power of a society over a whole province, or any other considerable part of it, ‡ Grotius determines, that it has no right to alienate such parts, without their consent. For the right, which the society has over them, depends upon the original compact, by which they united themselves to it: and since the terms of this compact are, that they will pay allegiance to the society in return for protection; they cannot be understood to have given the society, by this act, a right

* Grot. Lib. II. Cap. XXI. § IV, V.

† Grot. Lib. II. Cap. XXV. § III.

‡ Grot. Lib. II. Cap. VI. § IV, V. VII.

to cut them off from it causelessly, and to put them under the jurisdiction of any other society: because, if the society has this right, the corresponding obligation of the parts must be, not only an obligation to be directed by the will of the society in return for protection, but even to obey the society, where their obedience would put them out of its protection. He determines, in like manner, that a part cannot transfer its allegiance to another society, without the consent of the society, of which it is a part. Necessity, however, would justify the part in thus transferring its allegiance: because the social compact, like all other compacts, admits of the equitable exception of necessity.

But here Grotius adds, that the part has, in this respect, a fuller right than the whole. Necessity, by superseding the obligation of the social compact, supersedes all civil jurisdiction. The part, therefore, in these circumstances, is under no other obligation towards the whole, than it would have been in a state of nature; where there is no such relation of part and whole, of subject and society, and, consequently, no obligation of one towards the other. But if this is the effect of necessity, if it reduces things to the state of nature, and so leaves no civil jurisdiction; the society can have no extraordinary authority over any part of it, grounded upon the plea of necessity, to cut such part off from the general body, and to place it under a new and foreign jurisdiction. Necessity, instead of giving the society such an extraordinary authority, puts an end even to its ordinary jurisdiction.

I agree with our author, that necessity does not give the society such an extraordinary authority. But he seems to be mistaken in supposing, that necessity gives the part a fuller or more extensive right in respect of the society, than it gives the society in respect of the part. For when a part of any society transfers its allegiance, this act, as far as it relates to this particular society, is only the withdrawing of allegiance. What follows this act, or what attends upon it, when the part, which so withdraws allegiance from one society, puts itself under the jurisdiction of another, has no relation to the former society. We do, indeed, call the whole act a transfer of allegiance: but what is done in such a transfer, relates to this society no otherwise, than as allegiance is withdrawn from it. Whether the part puts itself under another jurisdiction, by joining itself to some other nation, or whether it forms itself into a nation, and sets up a jurisdiction of its own; or whether the several individuals, that compose it, live independently afterwards in a state of nature; the society, to which the part belonged, is not concerned in any of these acts. If the part could, of right, withdraw its allegiance, any of these acts will be equally lawful. The question, therefore, about the right of any part of a society to transfer its allegiance to another society, when it cannot otherwise be preserved, amounts only to this, whether it has a right, in such circumstances, to withdraw its allegiance. And if necessity, by superseding the jurisdiction of the society, will give it this right; the part and the whole are in the same condition, or have an equal right, in respect of one another. For as necessity supersedes the obligation of the part to pay allegiance, so a like necessity will supersede the obligation of the whole to give protection. Grotius, therefore, is mistaken in his conclusion, for want of stating the question properly. He compares what the part does in transferring its allegiance, with what the whole does when it alienates the part. Whereas, when the part transfers its allegiance, this, in respect of the society, is only the withdrawing of allegiance, and ought, therefore, to be compared with what the whole does, when it withdraws protection. In this comparison, there is no difference between their respective rights: if necessity, by taking away the obligation of the social compact, allows the part to withdraw allegiance; a like necessity will, upon the same principle, allow the whole to withdraw protection.

This reasoning may, with very little alteration, be applied to a single member of a civil society, who, though he has committed no crime, is demanded by an enemy. Though no person has a right to leave the society, to which he belongs, unless the public either expressly or tacitly consents, that he should leave it; yet where the society is in such circumstances, that protection, which is the end of social union, cannot be had, this necessity will supersede the obligation of the social compact, and will allow him to provide for himself, by quitting the society. A like necessity, on the part of the society, where it cannot defend itself, if it undertakes the defence of some particular person, who is a member of it, will justify the withdrawing of protection. This conduct of the society will appear the more reasonable, if we observe, that it does no damage to the individual: for if the society could not defend itself, without deserting him, it certainly could not defend him, if it would.

But the notion of deserting a subject, differs from the notion of delivering him into the enemies' hands. A right only to desert him, leaves him at liberty to provide for his own safety as well as he can. Whereas, a right to deliver him up, implies an obligation on his part to submit to be delivered up, though he might be able to make his escape, and to secure himself; and a right in the society to seize him by force, and prevent him from escaping, till it has put him into the enemies' power.

The principle upon which Grotius sets out in examining this question, is, that the subject, whom the enemy has demanded, is obliged to deliver up himself: and from hence he deduces a right in the society to compel him, by force, to discharge this duty, if he refuses to discharge it of his own accord. It would, in effect, be to take the point in dispute for granted, if Grotius, when he argues from the obligation of the subject, to deliver up himself to establish the societies' right of delivering him up, by force, had considered this obligation as a matter of strict justice, which is due from the subject to the society. For, undoubtedly, the society has a right to compel the subject, by force, to do whatever, in strict justice, it can demand of him. So that, to lay it down as a first principle, that the subject is under a strict, or perfect obligation, to deliver up himself, is the same as if it had been taken for granted, or laid down as a first principle, that the society has a strict and perfect right to deliver the subject by force. But Grotius only supposes, that it is an obligation of the imperfect sort; a duty of humanity or benevolence on the part of the subject, to prefer the preservation of a multitude to his own safety. But if this is only an imperfect obligation, we might question, whether the subject can be compelled to discharge it: for, in general, where a duty is in its own nature of imperfect obligation, and there is no positive law which has so far changed the nature of it, as to make it a duty of strict justice, the law of nature gives no right to compel the performance of such a duty. To this our author replies, that amongst equals, there is, indeed, no right to compel any person to discharge a duty of imperfect obligation; but a superior can, of right, compel an inferior to the practice of any virtue whatsoever; and this right is necessarily included in the notion of superiority. The state, therefore, may lawfully deliver up the subject, by force, if he refuses to discharge the imperfect duty of delivering up himself. I shall not insist upon its being uncertain, whether, in such a distressed condition of a nation, as is here supposed, a powerful enemy, who makes this unreasonable demand, would be satisfied if it was complied with: for, though this uncertainty might be urged as a reason why the subject is not obliged, even imperfectly, to deliver up himself, because by such an act he might sacrifice his own safety without preserving the society, yet the terms of the question exclude the supposition of such an uncertainty; since the question is not what the society has a right to do, in order to try whether it cannot preserve itself, but what it has a right to do, when a compliance with the enemies' demand is the way, and the only way, to preserve itself. Nor shall I inquire how far the general law of benevolence would bind a man to give up his own life, for the sake of preserving a multitude; because this is an inquiry which is likely to introduce much declamation on both sides, and little precision on either. And it is the less necessary to enter into this inquiry, because if we suppose this first principle of our author to be true, it will not support his conclusion. Civil superiority is a right of prescribing to the members of a society such a conduct as is conducive to the general good, and of enforcing what is so prescribed. We must, therefore, allow, that where any duty, which is naturally of imperfect obligation, appears to the public wisdom to be conducive to this end, a civil society has an authority, derived from the social compact, to prescribe this duty by positive law: and when it is thus prescribed, it becomes a duty of strict justice, and the subjects may be compelled, by force, to discharge it. But though we are ready to allow this, I do not see how * Grotius can contend for it, or argue from it, consistently with himself: because his general opinion is, that no civil authority can make use of force to compel the practice of any duties that are of the imperfect sort, and particularly to compel the practice of benevolence. His consistency, however, is not the matter now in hand. If the principle itself is true, he may argue from it in this question, notwithstanding he elsewhere contradicts it, provided he argues from it rightly. But this is the point in which he fails. A civil society has authority to prescribe duties of imperfect obligation, and then to compel the subjects to observe them. But they must be first prescribed by positive laws, before such compulsion can, of right, be made use of: for, till positive laws have made them duties of perfect obligation, they continue to be, what they were naturally, duties of imperfect obligation, and cannot be exacted by force. If, therefore, our author's reason, upon which he endeavours to establish the right of a civil society to deliver up one of its innocent members to an enemy, that demands him, will establish this right at all, it can only be in those societies, if there are any such, which have prescribed, by positive laws, that any subject, who is thus demanded by an enemy, shall deliver himself up. You may say, that a command of the public,

* Grot. Lib. II. Cap. XX. § XX.

which is given at the very time, will stand in the place of a law, and that, if the society has a right to establish a positive law for this purpose, it has an equal right to give an occasional command for the same purpose. But this is a mistake: for, what is enjoined by law, relates equally to all the members of a civil society, so as to lay the same burden upon all in general: and it is merely accidental, if the law, when it comes to be put into execution, should affect only one member in particular: it had no view to him in particular, but was designed to affect all alike, whenever they shall happen to be in the same circumstances that he is. But the burden, that arises from an occasional command, is originally designed to be laid upon one only: and, without a fresh command, the like burden will not fall upon any others, even though their circumstances should happen to be the same with his. Now, each member is obliged, by the social compact, to join with the rest in supporting the state, and in advancing its welfare. But this compact does not bind any one member to pursue these ends alone; and, consequently, does not give the state any authority to prescribe, that any one member shall pursue these ends by such occasional commands as oblige him in particular, and produce no obligation upon the other members, even though they should come into the same circumstances. In military service, a soldier may, indeed, be ordered by his commanding officer to a post which he cannot defend, without the hazard, or rather without the probable loss of his life. This appears, at first sight, to be an occasional command of much the same sort with the command that we have been speaking of. But a little attention will show us the difference between them. All the members of a civil society, who have voluntarily engaged to perform military service, are subject to the military laws of it; which, however they may be distinguished by name, are part of the civil law. These members, therefore, are all of them obliged, as occasion requires, to hazard their lives in the same manner, by maintaining such posts as they are ordered to. And what the commanding officer does, by ordering any particular person to a post of certain danger, is only a particular application of this general law. Thus the occasional command, which is given to an innocent member of a civil society, to deliver himself up to an enemy, is not founded in any previous law, which would extend, in like circumstances, to all the other members, but is in the original design of it confined to him in particular. Whereas, what may be called occasional commands of superior military officers, are, in effect, only the occasional applications of such a general law, to one particular person, as, in its original design, extends to all who shall ever be in the same circumstances that he is in.

The topics that are commonly made use of in this question, are, on one side, that every person consents to become a member of a civil society, with a view to his own benefit; and, on the other side, that every member of a civil society is obliged to promote the benefit of the whole. But whilst I think, that a nation has no right to deliver up an innocent member to an enemy, and that the member demanded by the enemy is not obliged to deliver up himself, I do not think that the first of these topics will establish the truth of this opinion. For the private view, which a man has to his own interest, when he enters into a civil society, is not the proper measure of the societies' right over him, or of his duty towards it, after he is become a member. The social compact is a bargain between him and the society: and in this bargain, as in all others, the mutual rights and obligations, which are produced by it, are not determined by the particular view or purpose which led one of the parties to agree to it. These rights and obligations depend upon the mutual agreement of both the parties; and, consequently, cannot be settled, without considering the views of both. A member of any state might design to advance his own particular benefit by becoming a member: but the society no otherwise consents to this design, and no otherwise establishes it into a right on his part, or obliges itself to concur with him in it, than upon condition of his consenting to secure and advance the general good. Whatever extensive views, therefore, he might have of obtaining his own benefit, the extent of his right to pursue it, as he is a member of the society, and under the obligation of the social compact, will depend upon the limitation which arises from this compact, and respects the security and good of the whole. The other topic, however, which is commonly made use of, on the contrary side of this question, will not prove, that the state has a right to deliver up an innocent member to an enemy who demands him. He is obliged, as he is a member of the society, to promote the benefit of the whole. But this obligation is not absolute or unconditional. The benefit which he is obliged to promote, is a benefit in which he is to have a share in common with all the other members, and which they, according to the respective duties of their several stations, are obliged to assist in promoting, in common with him. And such an obligation, on his part, cannot give the society, which consists of all the other members, a right to compel him to advance or secure a benefit, in which he cannot possibly have any share, and towards the advancing and securing of which no member, besides himself, contributes any thing. But it is time to leave this digression, and return to the law of nations.

Members of a nation, are accountable for injuries done by it.

XIII. *The several members of a civil society are parties, by the law of nations, in any injury that the society does: for this law considers such a society as one collective person: and, consequently, an injury, which is the act of this collective person, must, in the view of this law, be the concurrent act of its several parts or members.

But in a perfect democracy, the act of the nation is the immediate and direct act only of the majority; whilst the minority of the members, who are overruled by the majority, dissent from it. And, in like manner, the act of a nation, under other forms of government, is the immediate and direct act of the supreme governors; whilst the subjects either know nothing of what is done, or contribute nothing towards it by their consent, or, perhaps, disapprove of it. How, therefore, can the law of nations be the same, as to the matter of it, with the law of nature: since the former law makes those parties in an injury, who have never immediately or directly consented to it, or whose consent was of no moment in producing it? What we have †elsewhere said about the obligation of civil laws, will help to explain this matter. No person is naturally obliged to do any thing, beyond what the law of nature prescribes, without his own consent. But, in a civil society, the several members are obliged by the civil laws of it; though these laws differ in the mat-

* Grot. Lib. II. Cap. XXI. § VII.

† See Book II. Chap. VI. § I.

ter of them, from the law of nature, and are established in a perfect democracy by the majority, without the direct or immediate consent, or, rather, against the immediate and direct declaration of the minority. For those members, who are in the minority, have, in the social compact, which made them parts of the society, consented to be concluded by the general act of the whole; which, if all and each of the members do not concur, is the act of the majority: and this remote, or indirect consent, will naturally make the act of the majority their own, without their immediate and direct concurrence. Under other forms of civil government, there is a farther act of consent, besides that which joined the several individuals into one civil society: this society, after it is formed, agrees to vest the supreme civil power in certain governors, or to give these governors authority to act for the whole. And what such governors do, in their respective departments, is, in consequence of this remote and indirect consent of the society, the act of the society itself, and of all the members of which it consists. These compacts may, in the first instance, be called private ones, in respect of the great body of mankind: they are made within the society itself; and others, who are not parts of the society, are neither obliged, nor have any right to take notice of them. But they become public, by the general consent of mankind to consider every civil society in the same light in which the several members of each society consider it, as one collective person; that is, under the direction of the constitutional governors, and that acts by these governors. This general consent is the foundation of the law of nations: and in consequence of such consent, what is done by any civil society, or by the constitutional governors of it, becomes, in the view of the law of nations, the joint act of the several members, even of those members, who have not directly or immediately concurred in the act: because, by the compact, which established the civil constitution, they have remotely or indirectly agreed to whatever is done by the constitutional governors.

But an injury lays the person, who commits it, under * two obligations. One of these obligations arises from the effects which the injury produces: it does damage to those, against whom it is committed; and from hence, the authors of it, and the accessories to it, are obliged to make reparation. The other obligation arises from the guilt of the person, who commits it; that is, from his disposition to do harm: this disposition lays him under an obligation to submit to punishment, and gives others a right to inflict it. Where an injury, therefore, is committed by a nation, the collective person of the nation is bound to make reparation for damages; and as far as it appears to have had any malicious design of doing harm, it is likewise liable to punishment. But it is necessary to inquire, whether all and each of the members of a civil society, are, by the law of nations, deemed parties to the injury, which the society does, in both these respects; so that the injured nation has a demand upon each of them, to make reparation for the damage that has been done, and may, likewise, inflict punishment upon them separately, for the guilt of the public.

We have † elsewhere shown, that every fault, though it is of the lowest sort, will produce an obligation to make reparation, and that

* Grot. Lib. II. Cap. I. § II.

† See Book I. Chap. XVII. § XIV.

those who are, in the lowest degree, accessories to an injury, are involved in this obligation. Thus far, therefore, the law of nations will be a natural law, if, in consequence of the general consent of mankind to consider nations as collective persons, it charges an injury, which has been done by the public, upon the several members of the society, who are parts of the collective person; whether they immediately and directly consented to it or not. There is, therefore, no occasion to have recourse, as * Grotius has, to any law of nations, which is positive as to the matter of it, in order to make the goods of the members of a society answerable for the damages that have been done by the society itself, or by the civil governors of it.

† But punishment is not just, where there is no guilt; nor can any act of consent make it just, by the law of nature, except such an act of consent, as is an evidence of a malicious temper, or of a disposition to do harm. Now, the consent, which makes all and each of the members of a civil society, parties in an injury that the society does, is only remote and indirect. All and each have consented immediately and directly, to be concluded by the act of the majority, or of the governing part. In this consent there is no guilt, or no evidence of a disposition to do harm: because a civil society is formed for such purposes, as are innocent, in respect of the great body of mankind. And whatever malice or disposition to do harm may be evidenced by any act of the majority, or of the governing part; the minority, or the subjects, consent to this act only remotely and indirectly. But a remote or indirect consent, which is inferred only from the social compact, cannot, consistently with the law of nature, be deemed an evidence of a disposition to do harm. The law of nations, therefore, which is nothing else but the law of nature applied to the collective persons of civil societies, will not allow the minority, or the subjects, to be punished separately, for what is done by the society, or by the civil governors, either against their immediate and direct consent, or at least, without it. All and each of the members are so far parties in an injury, which is committed by the society, as to be separately obliged to make reparation of damages: but those only, who are the authors of the injury, or have made themselves parties to it by their immediate and direct consent, can justly be punished for it separately. In the meantime, the law of nations, considering the whole society as one collective person, allows this collective person to be punished for such injuries, as argue any guilt, or are evidences of a disposition to do harm. And though the innocent members cannot justly be punished separately for the guilt of the public, yet, in the punishment of the public, they will be sufferers. Nothing can justly be taken from them, which they have a right to, as they are individuals: but when the society is deprived of what belonged to it as a society, the innocent members will share in the loss, in consequence of their accidental connexion with the society. ‡ Grotius has mentioned several ways in which a nation may be punished. First, he says, it may be punished by being dissolved, which puts an end to the existence of a nation, as death puts an end to the present existence of individuals. A second way of punishing a nation, is by reducing it to a province, which he compares with punishing an

* Grot. Lib. III. Cap. II. § II. † Grot. Lib. II. Cap. XXI. § VII. ‡ Grot. Ibid.

individual by servitude. Or thirdly, a nation may be punished by depriving it of its public goods, such as the walls of its towns, its naval stores, or ships of war, or arms, or treasure; and this sort of punishment he compares with the confiscation of the goods of an individual. The innocent members of the society will probably be in a worse situation than they were before, or will be losers, when the society is punished in any of these ways. But what they thus suffer from their accidental connexion with the society, is no more to be reckoned a punishment, than what one individual suffers by means of his accidental connexion with another individual, who has committed a crime, and is punished for it.

One nation may lawfully assist another in war.

XIV. * The law of nations allows civil societies, in the same manner as the law of nature allows individuals, to assist one another in war: and whatever makes a war just, in respect of the principal nation, will make it just, likewise, in respect of the assistant nations.

Where two nations are at war, the law of nations will not only allow a third nation to give its assistance to the party, which has a just cause of war, but may even enjoin this conduct as a matter of benevolence or humanity, if this party is too weak to do itself justice, and is in danger of being unjustly oppressed. But the duty of benevolence amongst nations, as well as amongst individuals, is of the imperfect sort, and admits of prudential considerations; provided these considerations are tempered with honesty and sincerity. As an individual is not obliged to undo himself, by his kindness towards others; so no nation is obliged to ruin its own affairs, by entering into a war in favour of another.

Express compacts will give one nation a perfect right to demand the assistance of another. But these compacts must be so construed as to make them consistent with the law of nature. A nation can no more bind itself by compact, than an individual could, to do what the law of nature forbids; such compacts are void, as far as the matter of them is unlawful: and, consequently, no compact of alliance will oblige any nation to assist another in war, if the war is unjust.

There is some room to doubt, whether unsocial and tyrannical injuries, which the subjects of one nation receive from their civil governors, will justify another nation in making war upon those governors: because, by the law of nations, every nation is one entire and distinct body, having an exclusive jurisdiction of its own, and no other nation can, of right, take notice of any thing which passes within it, and relates only to its own members. Upon this account I cannot agree with † Grotius, that a war undertaken by a foreign nation, in defence of the injured subjects, will be just, even though the subjects had, in those circumstances, no right to make war for themselves. If no foreign nation has any right to take notice of what passes between the subjects and the governors of another nation; the injuries, which the subjects suffer from the governors, can no otherwise justify a foreign nation in making war for the redress of those injuries, than as they are brought under its notice by a request from the subjects. And if the subjects have no right of resisting the governors, where they are thus injured,

* Grot. Lib. II. Cap. XXV. § IV, V, VI.

† Grot. Ibid. § VIII.

they can have no right to make this request; because they, who cannot lawfully make war by themselves, cannot lawfully employ another to make war for them. Grotius replies here, that where any person cannot lawfully do an act upon account of some impediment, which is merely personal, and does not arise out of the nature of the act itself; this act, if it will be beneficial to the person, who is so hindered from doing it, may lawfully be done by some other person, who is not under the same impediment. Thus a minor is hindered by the personal impediment of his nonage, from going to law for himself; but his guardian, who is not under the same impediment, may go to law for him. And in the case now before us, the impediment, which makes it unlawful, if it is unlawful, for subjects to make war in defence of themselves against the tyranny of their governors, is merely personal, and does not arise out of the nature of the act: for, in general, an injury is a justifiable cause of war; and it is nothing but the merely personal relation between the subjects and their governors, that can be supposed to render such a war unlawful to them. But the general principle, upon which our author here proceeds, cannot be applied to this question without a restriction. Where one person cannot do an act upon account of some impediment, which is merely personal; it is no otherwise lawful for another person, who is not restrained by the same impediment, to do this act for him, than upon a supposition, that this other person is not restrained by some other impediment. If the subjects in any nation could not lawfully resist the injuries of their governors, the impediment, which makes such resistance unlawful, would, indeed, be merely personal; and a foreign nation is not restrained from making war in their behalf by the same impediment. But there is another impediment in the way of this foreign nation: it is restrained, by the law of nations, from taking notice of any thing that passes in a society, which is distinct from it, and has a jurisdiction within itself. This impediment cannot be removed without the request of the injured subjects: and such a request could not lawfully be made, if the subjects had no right of resistance: for here their personal impediment takes place, and what they cannot lawfully do for themselves, they cannot authorize another to do for them. Thus the law of nations hinders the foreign nation from taking up arms for the injured subjects upon its own motion; and if the subjects have no right of resistance, there would be a personal impediment in their way, which would hinder them from calling it in to make war for them.

But upon supposition, that the injured subjects in any society have a right to resist the tyranny of the civil governors; as these subjects will have a right to make war for themselves, so they will, likewise, have a right to solicit and to procure all the assistance, that they can. And when a foreign nation is thus solicited to give them its assistance, the law of nations will not stand in its way. For this law regards civil societies only so far as they are collective bodies of men united by a social compact, and invested, by means of this compact, with civil jurisdiction. But the subjects have then only a right of resistance, when the social compact is broken, or in such cases, as civil jurisdiction does not reach. The law of nations, therefore, takes no notice of these cases: they only fall under the notice of the mere law of nature; and this law will not hinder any person from giving assistance to any other, who is injured.

What is lawful in war.

XV. We have *seen, that a solemn war is called a just one, according to the law of nations, because it comes up to the highest notion of war, in the view of the law of nature applied to civil societies as to moral persons, or is a perfectly public war; and not because it produces any effects of right by a positive law of nations. The peculiar effects, which † Grotius supposes to be confined to a solemn war, and to arise out of such a positive law, are impunity for what is done, and property in what is taken. If we would endeavour to justify all that nations do in war, and all the claims that they pretend to derive from it; we must, indeed, have recourse to a positive law of nations, which is not only different from the law of nature, but contrary to it. But instead of forming a law out of their practice, in order to justify the practice itself, it is more reasonable to inquire how far these two effects are produced by the only law of nations, that has any real foundation; that is, by the law of nature, as it is applied by positive consent to the collective persons of civil societies. And, perhaps, in the course of this inquiry, we shall find, that these effects, as far as they are consistent with reason, are not confined to solemn wars only.

The law of nature has not precisely determined, how far an individual is allowed to make use of force, either to defend himself against an injury, which is attempted; or to obtain reparation of damages, where he, who did the damages, refuses to make reparation; or to bring an offender to just punishment, where he holds out against it. What we can collect from this law, is only this general rule, that such use of force as ‡ is necessary for obtaining these ends, is not forbidden. If, instead of supposing one individual to be acting against another in the pursuit of these ends, we suppose a number of individuals to be occasionally combined on each side, the rule will still be the same: whatever one individual might lawfully do against another; a number of individuals, on one side, may lawfully do the same against a number of individuals on the other side. The difference between two such parties of individuals and two nations, depends upon the positive and general consent of mankind, to consider every nation as a collective person or moral agent. In a number of individuals, who occasionally combine together, no one is a party in any act, unless he consents to it, or joins in it immediately and directly: whereas, by the law of nations, each of the members of a nation is a party in the act of the supreme governors, without such immediate and direct consent. Upon this principle a whole nation, and each of its members, may lawfully be treated as enemies in a public war. But it does not follow from hence, that all the members may be lawfully treated alike: though we may lawfully kill some of them, it does not follow, that we may lawfully kill any of them without distinction. For the general rule, which is derived out of the law of nature, is still the same: no other use of force is lawful, besides what is § necessary. We have, therefore, no right to take away the lives of those parts or members of the adverse nation, that we can get into our power, without proceeding to this extreme use of force. The law of nature does not forbid the killing of those, who are actu-

* See § X.

† Grot. Lib. III. Cap. IV. § III. Cap. VI. § I.

‡ Grot. Lib. III. Cap. I. § II.

§ Grot. Lib. III. Cap. XI. § II.

ally in arms against us, and cannot be reduced into our power by any other means. But if an army, or any small parties of an army, come into the territories of the enemy, notwithstanding they are at liberty to treat the * inhabitants, who are not in arms, as enemies, yet they have not a general liberty to kill them. The plain reason, why they have not this general liberty, is, because the death of the inhabitants, who are not in arms, is not necessary for obtaining the just ends of war: and all harm, which exceeds what is necessary, is causeless harm. Even they, who are in arms, whether they are the standing armed force of the hostile nation, or any of the other members of it, who arm themselves occasionally, cannot lawfully be killed, if they quit their arms, and surrender their persons. It may be necessary, when they are thus in our power, to guard against any future opposition, that they might make to us, by taking their arms from them; or by compelling them to give security, that they will not bear arms against us for a certain time, or during the continuance of the present war; or by making them prisoners. But if their life can be spared, without defeating the just ends of war, we have no right to take it away. In the siege of a town, many of the inhabitants, who are not in arms, may happen to be killed. This is such a chance of war, as the law of nature will excuse. For if the act of besieging the town is lawful, the accidental consequences, which follow from taking the necessary steps to carry on this act effectually, are not chargeable upon the besiegers. The inhabitants, as they are members of the adverse nation, may be treated as enemies: and though the law of nature would forbid this harsher kind of hostile treatment, if there was an opportunity of obtaining our lawful purpose without it; yet where it was not principally designed, and was made necessary by accident, this law does not condemn it.

The exceptions to this rule of not killing those persons, who never were in arms at all, or who, though they have been in arms, have surrendered themselves, are very few. If they are considered as members of the nation, with which we are at war, nothing more is necessary in the first instance, than to get them into our power. The law of nature, therefore, will not allow us to go farther. But if they, whom we thus get into our power, have been guilty of any previous crime, for which they deserve death, this law does not forbid us to inflict this punishment, any more than if they and we were members of no society at all, but were still in the original state of nature.

† The obstinacy of holding out long in a siege is not one of these crimes: for a discharge of their duty towards their own nation, is not, in its own nature, a crime against the other. There might, perhaps, be some advantage in putting a garrison to the sword for holding out long: as such an example might be a means to deter others from giving the besiegers the same trouble. But neither this, nor any other motive of mere utility, will render it just to take away the lives of those, who are in our power, and have not deserved to lose them. Neither is retaliation a justifiable cause for killing prisoners of war: though our adversaries should have killed the prisoners whom they have taken from us, this will not justify us in killing the prisoners, whom we have taken from them. The law of nature allows of retaliation, only

* Grot. Lib. III Cap. XI. § IX, X. XII.

† Grot. Ibid. § XVI.

where they, who have done harm, are made to suffer as much harm as they have done. But to kill such prisoners of war as are in our power, because the nation, to which they belong, has treated our countrymen in this manner, would be to do harm to one person, because harm had been done by another. An injury, which is done by a nation, does, indeed, communicate itself to all the members of that nation; and such a communication of guilt is all that can be pleaded for the retaliation, of which we have been speaking. But *Grotius very truly replies here, that to punish captives or prisoners of war in this manner, would be to punish them in what is their own as individuals: whereas the national guilt can only be communicated to them, as they are members of the offending nation: and, consequently, the proper punishment of it should only be inflicted on them as they are members of the offending nation, and not as they are individuals. If retaliation is not a just cause for killing prisoners of war, much less will it be a just cause for killing hostages. Those persons, who are put into our hands as hostages, become pledges by their own voluntary act for the performance of something, which their nation has engaged to do. But by their own voluntary act, they can pledge only what is in their own power to dispose of. They may give up their liberty as a security for the fidelity of their nation: but their lives, though they are their own to keep, are not their own to dispose of, and, consequently, cannot be given in pledge.

The reason why the act of holding out long in a siege is no personal crime in them who hold out, has already been hinted at. This reason will conclude more strongly in favour of those, who have only borne arms, and have given us no more than the common opposition of war. The members of a civil society are obliged, in general, and those members, that have engaged themselves in the military service of it, are obliged, in particular, to take up arms, and to fight for it, at the command of the constitutional governors, in the defence and support of its rights, against its enemies from without. There is no crime in entering into the social compact, from whence the general obligation to bear arms for these purposes is derived. This compact, as it only binds the several members of the society to pursue the ends of civil union, is innocent in respect of the rest of mankind. And if there is no crime in this compact, which would bind all the members alike to discharge the duties of war, there can be no crime in a particular compact, by which some of the members undertake to discharge the same duties, instead of the rest. The consent, by which the subjects in general, or the soldiery in particular, lay themselves under these obligations, is the only act that can, by the law of nations, be looked upon as a personal act of the individuals who bear arms. In consequence of the general consent of mankind to consider nations as collective persons, whatsoever is done by the members of a nation, at the command of the public, or of the constitutional governors, who speak the sense of the public, is the act of the nation: and if the act is unjust, the guilt, in the view of the law of nations, is chargeable upon the nation, and not upon the individual members. I am now speaking, not of what will justify a man, who bears arms in war, to his own conscience, but of what will justify him to the nation, against which he fights, at the com-

* Grot. Lib. III. Cap XI. § XVI.

mand of the nation, to which he belongs. If the war is plainly and notoriously unjust, the obligation of the social compact, or of any other compact, will not justify him to his own conscience: because no compact whatsoever can bind him to do, or excuse him in doing, what the law of nature forbids. And if he was to fight as an independent individual, at his own choice, and upon his own motion; those, against whom he fights, might look upon the act of bearing arms against them in such a war as a personal crime. But when they, with all mankind, have agreed to consider the several members of a civil society only as parts of a collective person, that act under the direction of the common will of such collective person; however inexcusable a man, who fights against them, might be, in the view of his own conscience, or of the law of nature, which considers him as an individual, they cannot, consistently with this agreement; that is, they cannot, consistently with the law of nations, charge him with having been guilty of a personal crime, merely upon account of his having fought against them.

Thus far, therefore, I agree with Grotius, that some acts are lawful in war by the law of nations, which, by the law of nature, would be unlawful; and that this lawfulness consists only in impunity, or that it is only external in the view of mankind, and not internal in the view of conscience. But though I agree with him thus far, I differ from him in three particulars. First, this impunity does not arise from a law of nations, which is purely positive, but from the positive consent of mankind to apply the law of nature to civil societies, as if each society was a distinct moral person, made up of its several members. For though the law of nations does, in this instance, grant impunity, where the law of nature would not grant it; yet this difference arises only from the difference of the persons, to which the same law is applied. The law of nature applied to individual persons would make it a crime, not only in the view of conscience, but likewise in the view of mankind, to fight in an unjust war. But when mankind have agreed to keep individuals out of sight, as it were, and to apply this law only to collective persons; they cannot, consistently with this agreement, charge the parts of these collective persons with any separate guilt, for what is done under the direction of the common or collective will. Secondly, this impunity, for what is done in war, is confined to the acts of the separate members of civil societies, and does not extend to the corporate acts of the societies themselves. How far, what nations do collectively, obtains impunity by the law of nations, will appear hereafter. But we may observe here, that, if this law is nothing else but the law of nature applied to the collective persons of civil societies, no acts, which could not be done by individual persons, consistently with the law of nature, can be done by collective persons, consistently with the law of nations. Thirdly, Grotius confines the external lawfulness of what is done in a war, which is internally unjust, to solemn wars only: whereas, this external lawfulness, in respect of the members of a civil society, extends to public wars of the imperfect sort, to acts of reprisals, or to other acts of hostility. By giving the name of public war to reprisals, or other acts of hostility, which fall short of being solemn wars, I suppose the reprisals to be made, or the acts of hostility to be committed, by the authority of a nation, though it has not solemnly declared war. For if the members of the nation make reprisals, or commit acts of hostility, without being thus authorized, they are not under the protection of the law of nations: as they act separately, by their own will, so they are separately accountable to the nation against which they act.

* Prisoners of war are, indeed, sometimes killed; but this is no otherwise justifiable, than as it is made necessary either by themselves, if they make use of force against those who have taken them, or by others who make use of force in their behalf, and render it impossible to keep them. And as we may collect from the reason of the thing, so it likewise appears from common opinion, that nothing but the strongest necessity will justify such an act: for the civilized and thinking part of mankind will hardly be persuaded not to condemn it, till they see the absolute necessity of it.

The same general rule by which we are to guide ourselves in judging how far it is lawful to destroy the persons of our enemies in a public war, is the rule by which we must be guided in judging how far it is lawful to ravage or to waste their country. If this is necessary to be done, in order to bring about the just ends of war, it lawfully may be done; but not otherwise. Thus, if the progress of an enemy cannot otherwise be stopped, we may destroy the forage or other provisions that are in the way: or if towns or villages would afford them such posts as would give them a considerable advantage against us, and we cannot otherwise prevent them from gaining these posts, we may destroy such towns or villages. To waste a country, unless for some such necessary reasons as these, is causeless harm.

Under the notion of wasting or ravaging a country, I do not include plundering it: this may possibly not be causeless harm; because they, who plunder it, may acquire the goods which they take from the enemy: and if the law of nature will give them property in the goods which are so taken, the same principle upon which such property is acquired, will justify the act of taking them.

I shall not detain the reader here with a particular inquiry how far fraud is lawful in war. The general principles, upon which questions of this sort are to be determined, have been stated †already.

These rules, which are derived out of the law of nature, applied to the collective persons of civil societies, are represented by Grotius as temperaments, by which the law of nature qualifies and abates the rigour of a purely positive law of nations. He grants, that they are such rules as a nation must observe, if it regards what is intrinsically just; but contends, that there is a positive law of nations which allows a greater license, and gives an extrinsic justice to what is done in solemn wars, though these rules are exceeded. We have already seen, that there is no cause, or no legislative power, by which such a law could be produced or established; and may now inquire, whether the effects of such a law can be traced out in any extraordinary license, which is peculiar to solemn wars.

No evidence of such a law appears in the name of just war, which is usually given to wars of this sort, whether they are internally just or not. For the name of just war, as it is appropriated to solemn wars, without regarding the causes upon which they are moved, is not intended to denote any external justice, which a purely positive law of nations

* Grot. Lib. III. Cap. XII. § I.

† See Book I. Chap. XIV. § III, IV.

allows promiscuously to all such wars; it is only intended to denote that such wars are perfect in their kind, or come up to the highest notion of a war of nations.

In the practice of nations, that are at war with one another, all rules, which arise out of the law of nature, are, indeed, sometimes exceeded. The slaughter, which the army of a nation makes amongst its enemies, is not always confined to those who are in arms, or to those whose lives cannot be spared consistently with its own safety. Sometimes no quarter is given to such as surrender themselves, when it is not necessary to take away their lives. Sometimes prisoners of war are killed in cool blood, when there is no danger of their being rescued, or of their rising in arms against those who have taken them, and have them in their power. Sometimes, in what are called military executions, not only the inhabitants of an enemies' country, who are able to bear arms, though they never were in arms, are murdered; but the slaughter is extended to women and children. But though these and other enormities are practised in war, it is no consequence that there is any positive law of nations which makes them lawful.

One evidence which * Grotius produces of such a law is, that, however criminal these practices are by the law of nature, they meet with no punishment amongst nations; and that this general license of transgressing the law of nature, in war, extends to all solemn wars whatsoever; even to such as are internally unjust, in which the law of nature is so far from allowing outrageous or unnecessary force, that it does not allow the use of any force at all. The use of any force in an unjust war, and the use of outrageous and unnecessary force in any war, is criminal by the law of nature; and neutral states, or states who are not concerned in the war, might, if this law was the rule by which nations are guided in their conduct towards one another, punish the offending nation for such criminal uses of force. But since, in solemn wars, these criminal uses of force obtain impunity; that is, since neutral states do not interpose to punish a nation that is guilty of them, Grotius concludes, that such wars, however unjust they may be, either in their internal causes, or in the manner of carrying them on, have an external justice in the view of nations, which can only be given them by some purely positive law. The principal point to be considered here is, whether this is only an impunity in fact, or whether it is an impunity of right. Though neutral states do not, in fact, interpose to punish such uses of force in war as are internally criminal by the law of nature, it is no consequence, that they have no right to interpose. There is a prudential reason which will operate in this matter as universally as a law. Neutral states cannot punish the injustice of what has been done in war, without engaging themselves in a war with the state which they undertake to punish. And an impunity, which thus arises in fact, from the regard that every neutral state has to its own safety, is no evidence of a positive law, which has given an external rectitude to whatever is done in solemn war, and has established a right to such impunity.

Grotius, when he mentions this prudential reason, considers it, not as the immediate cause which restrains neutral states from punishing what has been done unjustly in a solemn war, but as a general motive,

* Grot. Lib. III. Cap. IV. § IV.

which induced all nations to lay themselves under such a restraint by a positive law. If the regard which neutral states have to their own safety, is the immediate cause of this restraint, it is only a restraint in fact; they are at liberty to judge for themselves, how far it is consistent with their own safety, or conducive to their own interest, to intermeddle in the quarrels of other states; and are farther at liberty to act upon this judgment, either to intermeddle or not, as they think proper. But if it is only a general motive which induced all nations to establish such a restraint by a positive law, they will then be under a restraint of right; and whatever their own interest may either allow of or recommend, they will be obliged to overlook whatever is done by other nations in a solemn war, whether it is internally just or not.

Whilst a war is depending, which either is naturally unjust in the causes of it, or is carried on by such outrageous and unnecessary acts of violence as are naturally unjust, there can be no doubt about the right of a neutral state to declare to the wrong doers, that it will join with the sufferers, or about its right to put this declaration in execution; unless the unjust war is put an end to, or the unjust means of carrying it on are corrected. The civil governors of a neutral society may, indeed, in one respect, be said to be restrained of right, by what I have here called a prudential reason. They are obliged, of right, not to hazard the safety of their own society in the quarrel of another. But this restraint arises naturally from social union, and from the trust which is committed to such governors, and not from any positive law of nations; it is an obligation which regards their own society only, and has no relation at all to any other civil society whatsoever.

I am aware, that the interposition of a neutral state, whilst a war subsists, to check what is done in it against the rules of natural justice, is capable of being considered rather as a defence of the sufferers, than as a punishment of the offenders. But it is not worth the while to debate, which of these two is the true nature and primary intention of such an interposition. For if we allow it to be only a defence of the sufferers, it will be an evidence that there is no positive law of nations, which gives an external justice to whatever is done in a solemn war. If there was any such law, nothing which a nation suffers in a solemn war, could be externally unjust in the view of other nations; and, consequently, no neutral state could, consistently with such a law, interpose to defend the sufferers. Since no person can lawfully be defended against what he suffers justly, it would be as contrary to the notion of this external justice, to defend those who suffer in a solemn war what is inconsistent with natural or internal justice, as to punish those, who, in such a war, do what is inconsistent with it.

After a war is ended by the consent of the parties who were concerned in it, there is some appearance of a law which restrains neutral states from taking notice of what has been unjustly done on either side whilst the war lasted. It would, in the common opinion of mankind, be thought no very justifiable reason, why one nation should make war upon another, that the latter had done something unjustly in some war with a third nation, which is now at an end, and in which the former, whilst it lasted, was no way interested. But there is no occasion to have recourse here to a positive law of nations. The law of nature favours peace; and will, therefore, readily presume, that no injustice has been done, or that all injustice which has been done, is made amends for, where the parties, who were concerned in a quarrel, have adjusted the matter that was in dispute between them, to their own satisfaction. Grotius mentions another reason, why neutral states have no right, after a war is over, to take notice of any natural injustice that has been done in it on either side. But it is a reason, which is founded in nature, and will operate as a law without the aid of positive institution. When the parties in a war are reconciled to one another, so that no complaint is made on either side, neutral states cannot have such evidence of what has been unjustly done in the war, as will warrant them to inflict punishment for what has been so done. The same hurt which would be causeless and unjust by the law of nature, if it was done even in war, designedly or out of choice, is allowed of by this law, if it was accidental or necessary. Without a fuller and clearer insight, therefore, than neutral nations can have into the causes and occasions of what has been done in a war, after the parties in it are agreed, they cannot determine whether it has criminally exceeded what the law of nature allows of, and is punishable or not.

But whether the impunity for what a nation does in war, is an impunity in right or only in fact, it does not seem, in the practice of mankind, to be peculiar to solemn wars. For it is as unusual for neutral states, which are not concerned in a quarrel between two nations, to punish either of them for what has been done, when the war, which they make upon one another, is imperfect, as when it is begun with the solemnity of a declaration.

The second evidence that Grotius produces, of a purely positive law of nations, is, that, in solemn wars, some practices are not allowable, which the law of nature does not forbid. The law of nature, where it allows us to take away the life of any person, prescribes, says * Grotius, no particular manner of killing him, but leaves it indifferent, whether we kill him by some open means, which he may be aware of, or by the secret means of poison or of assassination. But the law of nations, at least the law of more civilized nations, forbids the use of poison against an enemy in solemn war. An observation, which our author here makes, upon the permission of the use of poison in the law of nature, will help to explain this matter. It is generous to give any person, whose life we have a right to take away, an opportunity of defending himself: poisoning, therefore, which gives him no such opportunity, is a less generous way of killing him, than an open attack. However, if he has deserved death, the favour of giving him an opportunity of defending himself, is not due to him in strict justice. What Grotius here says about deserving death, wants to be explained. A criminal, who is by the civil law justly sentenced to die, is properly said to deserve death: and as the law of nature does not prescribe, so there is not, I presume, any natural principle of generosity which recommends one sort of death rather than another; except only that humanity suggests, and the law of nature requires, this punishment to be inflicted without any unnecessary torture. In like manner, an individual may, in a state of natural equality, have committed such a crime as to deserve death for it: and where he has thus deserved to die, they, who undertake to inflict

* Grot. Lib. III. Cap. IV. § XV, XVI.

the proper punishment upon him, may, consistently with strict justice and with generosity too, put him to death in any manner, provided they observe the same caution about not giving him unnecessary torture. But in a public war, the soldiers, against whom we fight, are not guilty of any capital crime in what they do, and deserve death no otherwise than as they stand in the way of the execution of our right, and cannot be put out of the way, or be brought into our power without it. And thus, notwithstanding it is indifferent by the law of nature, in what manner a person, who has deserved death, is killed; whether by poison or by open force, it does not follow, that they, who fight against us in public war, may lawfully be killed in any manner. In fighting upon the authority of their state, they commit no capital crime, and do not properly deserve death. Humanity, therefore, requires, that we should not put them to death at all, if we can obtain the lawful purposes of war without it; and generosity recommends it to us rather to run some hazard of our own lives, than to take away theirs unnecessarily. But by poisoning them, we put them to death at all events, whether it is necessary or not; that is, we take away their lives, without trying whether we cannot spare them, and yet put such a stop to their opposition, as to obtain the lawful purposes of war. From hence, likewise, we may understand, why the use of poisoned weapons should be more inconsistent with the law of nations, than the use of other weapons; not because there is any purely positive law of nations, which forbids the use of such weapons, but because it is forbidden by the natural law of humanity and generosity: for other weapons, though they may probably bring death, do not bring it so certainly as these, and leave even the wounded a chance of escaping with life.

In the business of assassinating the commanders of an army, or other leading persons of a nation, with which we are at war, we may distinguish with *Grotius between the persons who are employed in it, whether they are subjects of our own nation, or of the other. If they are our own subjects, the act cannot be defended upon his principle; which is, that we may lawfully kill an enemy wherever we find him; and that it makes no difference, as to the lawfulness of our act, whether it is done by many or by few; by a whole army, or by a single person. But the first part of this principle is not true: the only right that we have in public war, over the persons of our enemies, is to lay them under such restraints as are necessary to prevent them from opposing us: since, therefore, in order to prevent such opposition, it is not necessary to kill any, who are not in arms, because they are in our power, and we can restrain them by other means, the consequence is, that we have no right to kill an enemy, wherever we find him, unless he is in arms and resists us by force. Thus the lawfulness of assassination, in public war, will, at least, be confined to those who are in arms; and cannot be extended to any other persons of the adverse nation. In respect of those who are in arms, such as the general of an army, or some other principal commanders in it, though the persons whom we employ, are members of our own nation, all that can be said to defend assassination, in point of generosity, is, that such commanders either are, or ought to be, upon their guard against attempts of this sort; and when they are

* Grot. Lib. III. Cap. IV. § XVIII.

engaged in opposing force to our lawful demand, there can be no great want of generosity in taking away their lives by such means, as it is their particular duty to be aware of, and to guard against. But if we employ their own people, there is nothing to be said in excuse for the act: it is killing of them privately, in such a manner as they cannot be supposed to guard against; and may, in this respect, as to the want of humanity and generosity, be resembled to poisoning: and as the act is unjust in the persons who are employed, this injustice will be communicated to us, who make ourselves parties in it by employing them.

Property how acquired in war.

XVI. In a war, which is internally just, as a nation may take the persons, so, likewise, it may seize upon the goods of the enemies, either moveable or immoveable, as far as such seizure is a necessary means of bringing them to do what is right. But what is seized only for this purpose, does not become the property of the captors: the possession is just, till the purpose for which the goods were taken is answered; but as soon as the claims of the injured nation are satisfied, the justice of the possession is at an end.

There are, however, three ways by which a nation in a just war may acquire property in the goods which it takes from its enemies. First, a nation that has been injured, has a right to reparation of damages. Reparation is made according to the law of nature; not only by recovering the thing which we are unjustly deprived of, but, likewise, where the very thing cannot be had, by recovering an equivalent out of the goods of the person who has deprived us of it. And, by the law of nations, this right to obtain an equivalent, extends to the goods of all who are members of the nation, that has done the injury; not *because the goods of private subjects are, by any purely positive law, made pledges to all the world for the good behaviour of the nation, or of its constitutional governors; but because, by the positive consent of all mankind, the nation, though it consists of many individuals, is considered as one collective person; and, in consequence of this general consent, all the members of this collective body are deemed parties in any injury which the body does, as far as this injury produces a claim to reparation of damages in those against whom it is committed. †If a nation makes war to recover reparation of any damages that have been done to it, this claim to such goods as are taken in the war, takes place from the beginning of the war, to the extent of these damages. But if the enemy begins a war causelessly, and the nation which defends itself, has suffered no injury from the enemy before the war began, this claim does not take place from the beginning; because the nation can have no right to an equivalent, where it has sustained no damage. However, this claim, though it did not begin with the war, will arise in the progress of it: for the war itself is an injury; and, consequently, the nation, against which it is made, will have a right to reparation for all the damages which are done to it in the war.

Secondly, a nation has a right to be paid the expenses that it makes in a just war. These expenses are, indeed, so many additional damages: for whatever the nation is forced to expend in recovering its right, is a loss which is occasioned by the fault of the enemy who withholds that right. As the nation, therefore, acquires property in the goods

* Grot. Lib. III. Cap. II. § II.

† Ibid. Cap. XIII. § II, III.

which it takes from the enemy, to the amount of the original damages that occasion the war, and of the fresh damages that are done in the war, so, upon the same principle, it acquires property in what it takes as an equivalent for the current expenses that are made in carrying on the war.

Thirdly, a nation which has committed a crime, may be punished in the same manner with an individual, in the liberty of nature, by being deprived of its goods. But whilst the offending nation thus loses its goods, the nation that takes them, will acquire property in them no otherwise, than either by being the first occupants, or by receiving the goods as a ransom, by which the offending nation redeems itself from some other punishment. Grotius confines this way of acquiring property, in war, to such goods only as belong either to the collective body of the state, or to the criminal members of it. And this restriction is a very proper one: for though an injury, which is done by a nation, is communicated to all the members of it, as far as this injury produces an obligation to repair damages, yet the guilt of it, as it implies a disposition to do harm, is confined to the collective person of the nation, and to those particular members of it, who have made it their own act by their immediate and direct consent.

Grotius agrees, that these are the proper measures of what can be acquired, in war, by the law of nature. But *he contends, at the same time, that, in this instance, there are plain traces of a positive law of nations, which extend the right of war. For, in the approved practice of nations, or, at least, in such practice as is not condemned, whatever is taken in war is the property of the captors, though it is more than an equivalent for any damages that have been done, or any expenses that have been made; and this claim of property is not confined to such wars as are internally just, but is extended to all solemn wars whatsoever, whether they are internally just or not.

But here we are apt to mistake a right, which arises from the consent of a nation, whose goods we have taken in war, for a right, which a positive law of nations gives us to those goods, merely because we have taken them. Though we had no just claim to them from the first, yet, when we make peace with the nation, from which they were taken, if they, or an equivalent for them, should not be demanded, they become our own by the tacit consent of that nation, without the aid of any purely positive law of nations. The surest way of trying whether it is the claim of war, or the claim of a tacit consent in concluding a peace, which gives us property in all such goods as are taken in war, is to inquire what sort of a right we have to them, before peace is concluded. There is no law of nations, which forbids our enemies to continue a war, when no other cause of dispute remains, besides our detention of such goods, as we have taken in the war, beyond an equivalent for damages and expenses. As the law of nature will allow this to be a just cause of continuing a war, so there is no practice of nations, and no general opinion of mankind, that determines otherwise. But if any law of nations had given us property in such goods, the same law must necessarily condemn the adverse nation for continuing a war, merely because we would not give them up: for the design of such a war would

* Grot. Lib. III. Cap. VI. § II.

be to take from us what the law of nations had made our own. This opinion, that all goods which are taken in war, are not strictly our own by any law of nations, till peace is concluded; that is, till some consent, either express or tacit, has made them our own by the law of nature, seems to be the general opinion of mankind, in respect of immoveable goods: such as fortified towns, which have been taken; or provinces, which have been overrun in war. The captors are looked upon, whilst the war lasts, to be only in possession of them: and though this possession may help them to make a better bargain for themselves in a treaty of peace, than they could do otherwise; yet the property, which they have in things of this sort, is deemed to be precarious, till a treaty of peace has ascertained and established it. It is usual, in treaties of peace, to mention such immoveable goods particularly; and the captors, if they acquire property in them, acquire it by express consent. We may, therefore, reasonably conclude, that the property, which the captors have in all moveable goods, taken in war, is likewise acquired in the same manner. The only difference is, that immoveable goods are generally of the most importance, are in the hands of the public, and can readily be returned; whilst moveable goods are of less consequence, are in private hands, and, because they have either been consumed, or have not been kept together, cannot be returned so readily. For this reason, whilst the property, in the former, is adjusted by express consent, the property in the latter is left to pass from the original owners to the captors, by tacit consent.

The law of nature, which thus gives the captors property in what they have taken in a solemn war, either as an equivalent for damages and expenses, or by consent of parties, will likewise give them property by the same means, in what they have taken, in the less perfect kinds of public war; in reprisals, or in other acts of hostility, which do not come up to the notion of solemn war, for want of a declaration of war: the captors acquire a natural right, in an equivalent, for their damages and expenses: if they have a natural right to any thing more, it must be acquired either by the express or the tacit consent of the nation from which the goods are taken. And it will be difficult, either in the practice of nations, or in the general opinion of the thinking part of mankind, to find any positive law which will prevent the captors of goods, in these imperfect wars, from acquiring property in them by these means. It is not more usual for neutral nations to interpose, in order to compel the captors to restore what they have taken in imperfect wars, than it is for them to interpose for the same purpose, where the goods of one nation have been taken by another in a solemn war. The parties concerned, seldom meet with any obstructions, from without, in making the best bargain for themselves, that they can, in either sort of war: and, whatever we may hear said about a purely positive law of nations, they are left to guide themselves by no other law besides what obliges all nations, or, rather, the governors of all nations, in conscience; and that is the law of nature applied to the collective bodies of nations, as if they were moral agents. It will be nothing to the purpose to urge, that, whatever neutral nations may do, the nation, with which we are concerned, will enforce a positive law of nations; and if we have taken any thing from it in the way of reprisal, without declaring war, will not make peace with us again, till we have restored what was so taken, or an equivalent for it. For this, with very little variation, may be said of what is taken in a solemn war: the nation, from which we have taken it, if it has strength enough to support itself, will be no more willing to make peace with us, till we have returned the towns, or the ships, or the other goods, that we have taken from it in a solemn war, or an equivalent for them, than if we had taken the same towns, or ships, or other goods, in the way of reprisal, without declaring war.

In what I have here said about the captors of goods in war, I would be understood, under the name of captors, to mean the nation which takes them: for, whether the goods so taken, when property is acquired in them, are the particular property of the individuals who take them, or the general property of the nation of which these individuals are members, is a distinct question: and it belongs rather to the civil law than to the law of nations, to determine this question. Certainly no purely positive law of nations can naturally determine it: because, whatever other nations may have agreed upon amongst themselves, the laws which regulate the mutual rights of each particular nation, and its own members, must come from the nation itself. If in any particular nation, the claim to what is taken in war has not been adjusted by any written law, or by any custom, which is an unwritten law, or by any occasional grants, we may reasonably inquire, how it ought to be adjusted upon such principles as are founded in civil union. Since every member of a civil society acts in a public war as a part of the community, and not separately as an individual; that is, in the right or upon the authority of the whole, and not in his own right, or upon his own authority, the natural consequence is, that, whatever he acquires, it is acquired for the community, and not for himself. * Grotius makes a distinction in this matter between public acts of war, and private acts, to which the war gives occasion. He allows, that the acquisitions which are made by acts of the former sort, though they are made by means of private persons, are made for the public; because the private agents are here only the instruments of the public: so that, whatever is acquired by them, it will accrue to the public, in the same manner as what is acquired by those persons, whom any man employs to do work for him, accrues to him who employed them, and not to them who do the work: it is his own work, though he does it by others who are his agents; and, consequently, the fruits or profits of the work belong to him. But as soldiers may get possession of the goods of the enemy, whilst they are in battle, or whilst they are doing what the state has commanded them to do, so they, or other individual members of the state, may have opportunities of taking the goods of the enemy, where they are not acting under any immediate command of the state. When they are thus annoying the enemy, by the general right of war, it is our author's opinion, that the captures, which they make, are their own. But this distinction between what is done in the immediate service of the state, and what is done out of this service, by the general right of every member of the state to annoy the enemy, has no foundation in public war. For, as public wars begin from the authority of the state, so they are carried on by its authority: every member, therefore, of the

* Grot. Lib. III. Cap. VI. § VIII, IX, X, XI, XII.

state, who acts at all in such a war, acts as a part of the whole, and under the authority, or in the right of the public: he is an agent for the public, or acts in the service of the state, whether he has received any express command for what he does, or acts at his own discretion, as he sees opportunity: the only difference is, that in one case he acts by a particular commission, and in the other case by a general one.

Grotius allows, that the rule, which he draws from this distinction, admits of one exception. Whilst he contends, that what is taken in war by any members of a civil society, is the private property of the captors, if they were acting only by the general right of war, and not under any immediate command of the society, he confines this rule to moveable goods; because immoveable goods, such as provinces, or towns, or whatever other things adhere to the soil, and are parts of the territory, are not usually taken, and cannot usually be kept, without armies and garrisons. But if the rule itself was true, the reason, upon which he supports this exception, would not extend the exception universally to all immoveable goods, by what means soever such goods are taken. For though it may be more difficult for private persons to take and to keep provinces or towns, than to plunder some few of the inhabitants, and to seize their moveable goods: yet this is only a bar, in fact, and not a bar in right, to the claim of private captors, to what adheres to the soil, and is a part of the enemies' territory. Private persons will more seldom be able to take and to keep immoveable goods, upon account of this difficulty. But if, in fact, they have ever overcome this difficulty, and have been able to take and to keep them without an army or a garrison acting under the immediate and particular commission of the public, they will then have a right to these; if, in the like circumstances, they would have any right to moveable goods.

But there is a general reason, why all goods, which are taken in war, should accrue to the state, and not to the private captors; whether the captors act under a particular commission, or only under a general commission from the public; and whether the goods are moveable or immoveable. The goods so taken are not strictly appropriated either to the state, or to the private captors, whilst the war continues: the property in such goods is precarious, till a treaty of peace has established it. In the meantime, as the state is answerable for them to the enemy, it is natural, that this precarious property should be vested in the state; that is, that the state should have the custody of the goods. And as the effect of a treaty of peace is only to give the full property of the goods to those who had the custody of them before; the full property will, by this means, accrue, in the end, to the state itself.

I have here spoken of the property of all goods, which are taken in war, as ultimately transferred by consent in treaties of peace, without having any regard to what is taken for damages or for current expenses. As to expenses, whatever a private person, who is not immediately retained in the service of the public, lays out in a public war, whilst he is carrying on some particular design of his own, this is all expended voluntarily, and not through the fault of the enemy: so that this expense gives him no private claim upon the enemies' goods. The case of a claim to an equivalent for damages done is rather more intricate: because the damages, for which a compensation is due from the enemy, are sometimes such as have been done to the state, and sometimes such as have been done to some particular members of it. What is taken from the enemy to make reparation for damages done to the state in its corporate capacity, plainly belongs to the state itself, and not to the particular captors, who are members of the state. The only doubt is about what is taken, upon account of damages that have been done to private persons. And here it is plain, that unless the captors themselves are the persons, to whom these damages have been done, the purpose, for which the goods are taken, gives the private captors no claim to them. But if the captors themselves are the persons who have been injured, it will be necessary to consider, whether they make reprisals by their own authority without any commission either general or particular from the state, or whether they act under the general commission of solemn war, or under some particular commission of reprisal. Where they take the goods of another nation without having any commission from their own, this case is out of the present question: there is, by the supposition, no public war, or no war between the two nations; because, if there was, the captors would act, at least, by the general commission of war, though they had no particular commission of reprisal. If they thus make reprisals at their own discretion, the act is their own, and they are answerable for the justice of it. For though, by the social compact, they had a claim to be supported by the public, in obtaining reparation of such damages, as they have sustained from foreigners, yet if they will undertake, of their own accord, to obtain it for themselves, it is their business to see that what they do is no more than natural justice will warrant, and to support their own act, after they have done it. Since, therefore, they themselves are answerable for what they do, in thus taking the goods of foreigners, the goods which are so taken, are acquired for themselves; and the public, as it is not concerned in the act of taking them, can have no claim to them. Where the damages which the captors have sustained, is the cause of a solemn war, the state, by thus undertaking to recover reparation of their damages, makes itself answerable to them for what they have lost, as far as it recovers reparation. In the meantime, if they act only by the general commission of solemn war, and have no particular commission to make reprisals for themselves, they act no otherwise than as parts of the state: and notwithstanding the claim which they have upon the public, what they take belongs, in the first instance, to the public and not to them. But if they act under a particular commission from the state to make reprisals for themselves, whether the war is solemn or imperfectly public, they acquire property for themselves in the goods which they take; not because they are the persons, to whom reparation is to be made; for the same commission, if it had been given to any of the other subjects, would have produced the same effect; nor yet because they are the captors; for the goods, if they had taken them in a solemn war, without such a commission, would, in the first instance, have accrued to the public; but because the nation has conveyed to them its interest in what they take by the particular commission under which they act; by this commission the nation makes them its agents, but the nature of the commission is such as makes them the nation's agents for their own interest.

The army or the fleet of a nation is immediately employed by the public, and, consequently, what either of them takes, will naturally accrue to the nation. If it is otherwise in any nation; if the soldiers have in any nation a right to the plunder, or the seamen to the captures which they make; this right is derived, as we have already hinted, from an occasional grant, which the nation makes to them, or from a standing grant made either by the written civil law of the nation, or by custom, which is an unwritten civil law. But when a nation has expressly granted to its army, or to its fleet, property in what they take, whether the grant is made occasionally, or made by a written civil law; if the army or the fleet should take a town, or if the army should overrun and seize a province, they would have no claim, by this grant, to the jurisdiction or paramount property of such town or such province. For the word, property, is to be construed in such sense as is suitable to the condition of the persons, to whom it is granted. Subjects have usually no other sort of property besides what consists in private ownership. The notion, therefore, of property, when it is applied to them, does not include jurisdiction or paramount property. And, consequently, whatever other property the army or the fleet might claim by means of such a grant in the towns or the provinces, which they have taken; the jurisdiction or paramount property would, notwithstanding the grant, accrue to the nation. For a like reason, if such moveable goods, as the army or the fleet takes in war, have, by custom, been acquired for themselves, and not for the nation; such a custom will give them no claim to towns or provinces, which they take: because a customary claim to an inferior kind of property does not imply a claim to jurisdiction.

It is to be observed, that though, in treaties of peace, the property of such moveable goods, as have been taken from an enemy during the war, commonly passes by tacit consent from the enemy to the nation which takes them; yet this is not necessary. A nation, in an unjust war, has no claim to damages or to expenses, and, even in a just war, it may have taken more than its damages or expenses amount to. Whilst the war continues, the nation has, of right, nothing but the custody of the goods, which it has taken. If, therefore, it has granted the property of such goods to the private captors, and the enemy, when he comes to make peace, should insist upon restitution of what has been taken more than is due; it might be a question, whether the nation or the private captors are to make the restitution? In respect of the enemy, the obligation to make restitution rests upon the nation: because, in respect of him, the nation is the captor, and what has passed between the nation and its own members does not fall under his notice. But if the grant, made by the nation to the private captors, contained a reserve, that in case the enemy demands restitution of what they have gotten, they shall return it into the custody of the public; they are then obliged to return it, or an equivalent for it: because they have no fuller right to it, than they derive from the grant of the nation, and, consequently, hold it under all such reserves, as are contained in this grant. If there is no reserve of this sort, the nation, though it is obliged to make restitution, has no other demand upon the private captors than it has upon all its other members, to contribute towards this restitution. An absolute grant of property made by the nation will bar all other demands. For though it has granted absolute property, where it had itself only a precarious property, this is its own fault, and will not affect the claim of the proprietors. It would affect their claim, if they were responsible to the enemy: because, in respect of the enemy, the nation could not give them absolute property, where its own property was precarious. But as the nation is responsible to the enemy, and they are responsible only to the nation, the grant, which the nation has made, will hold good against itself, though such grant was made in its own wrong.

What prevents prisoners of war from being slaves.

XVII. Since all the members of a nation, against which a just war is made, are bound to repair the damages that gave occasion to the war, or that are done in it; and, likewise, to make satisfaction for the expenses of carrying it on, the law of nature will allow those, who are prisoners, to be made slaves by the nation which takes them; that so their labour, or the price for which they are sold, may discharge these demands. Thus the acquisition of prisoners of war; or, rather, of their personal labour, is made in the same manner, and is subject to the same rules with the acquisition of the goods of the enemy. Despotism, however, when it is thus acquired, cannot include a right in the masters or owners of such prisoners of war, as are made slaves, to dispose of their lives at pleasure. The captors have a right to every valuable consideration that the prisoners can make over to them, towards repairing the public damages, or returning the public expenses: but the death of the slave, whilst it is a loss to him, brings no profit to the nation that took him prisoner. And if the nation had no right to take away his life, no private owner, who claims under the nation, can have such a right. *Grotius here follows the common opinion, that, as the law of nations permits prisoners of war to be killed, so the same law has introduced a right of making them slaves, that the captors, in view to the benefit arising from the labour or the sale of their prisoners, might be engaged to spare their lives. In this account of the means by which prisoners of war become slaves, their slavery begins from the right which the captors have over their lives. The reader, therefore, may, perhaps, imagine, that the same right continues in their masters, after they become slaves. But we have already shown, that the principle, upon which Grotius here sets out, is not universally true. A nation has not, even in a just war, a general right to kill the prisoners that it takes. The only general right that it has over them, is the same that it has over all the members of the adverse society: those members, who are taken prisoners, are bound, as all the other members are, to repair the damages which it has sustained, and to return the expenses which it has made. Where it is inconsistent with the security of the captors to save the prisoners, they may lawfully kill them. But it is impossible, in the nature of the thing, that any question should arise, whether, if any prisoners have been reserved for slavery in such an exigency, the right, which the captors had over their lives, whilst they were prisoners, does not continue after they are made slaves? The case implies that the prisoners cannot be saved: for if they could be saved, the captors would have no right to kill them. We must either suppose, on the one hand, that the lives of the prisoners can be saved, consistently with the safety of the captors, and then the captors will have no right over their lives, from the first;

* Grot. Lib. III. Cap. VII. § V.

and, consequently, can have no such right, after they are reduced to a state of slavery; or else we must suppose that the prisoners cannot be saved, consistently with the safety of the captors; and then, though the captors have a right to take away their lives, this right cannot continue after such prisoners are become slaves; because they must all be destroyed, and, consequently, none will be left to make slaves of. The case will be the same, if we suppose that an army has taken so great a number of prisoners, that it cannot save them all consistently with its own safety; and that it, therefore, kills some, and saves as many as it can. We cannot ask, whether the nation, to which the army belongs, has a right over the lives of those who are killed, when they become slaves? because, as they are killed, they never can become slaves: and as to the rest, whose lives could be preserved, consistently with the safety of the army, neither the nation, nor its army, had, from the first, any right over their lives; and can, therefore, have no such right after they come into a state of slavery. If there are any particular prisoners who have committed such a personal crime against the nation, which takes them, as deserves death, though the general offence of the society, to which they belong, would give it no right to take away their lives, yet a crime of this sort may give it such a right. But if the nation, instead of killing these prisoners, makes slaves of them, whatever right over their lives it had before, by the act of making them slaves, it parts with this right: for, by this act, it consents to take their labour in exchange for their lives.

This is the general law concerning prisoners of war. In Europe, indeed, prisoners of war are not slaves. But their slavery is prevented by the law of each particular nation; and not by any law, which all the nations of Europe have agreed to establish amongst themselves, as the common rule of their conduct towards one another. The civil law of each particular nation, does not allow of slavery; unless, perhaps, where a subject of its own has committed a crime, for which this law condemns him to labour in the mines, or in the gallies, or in the foreign plantations. And if the civil law of any nation does not allow of slavery, prisoners of war, who are taken by that nation, cannot be made slaves. There are, however, even in Europe, some remains of the right which slavery produces over the persons of prisoners of war. They are exempted from the labour and drudgery of slaves; but the nation, which takes them, considers itself as having some right to their persons; and, accordingly, sells their liberty at the price of a ransom, or else barters them away in exchange for its own subjects, who have been taken prisoners in war by their nation. This right would continue even after peace is concluded between the two nations, if, in the treaty of peace, there was no express stipulation for a release of prisoners. But as no profit is to be had from their labour, and it would be expensive to keep them, there is always a prudential reason for releasing such of them, at least, as cannot pay their ransom, though no compact has been made about them.

Effect of a declaration of war.

VIII. After what has been said about public war, the effects of a declaration of war may be easily understood. One effect of it is merely nominal. Though every contention, by force, is war; and every contention of two nations, by force, upon the authority of their respective supreme governors, in external matters, is public war; yet, in the more common language, when we are speaking of the contentions of two nations, we call them reprisals, or acts of hostility; and do not give them the name of war, unless war has been declared. After war is declared, as we then call the contention of two nations, emphatically, war, so it is sometimes called solemn, and sometimes just war. But this title of just war is merely nominal; it imports, that a war, when it is declared, is perfectly public, and not that it has any peculiar sort of external justice, or that it produces any effects of right, by a purely positive law of nations, which other public wars will not produce, and much less that it is, of course, internally just.

The only real effect of a declaration of war is, that it makes the war a general one, or a war of one whole nation against another whole nation: whilst the imperfect sorts of war, such as reprisals, or acts of hostility, are partial, or are confined to particular persons, or things, or places. In a solemn war, all the members of one nation act against the other under a general commission; whereas, in public wars, which are not solemn, those members of one nation, who act against the other, act under particular commissions. I do not mean, that, when one nation has declared war against another, all the members of the former must necessarily be at liberty to act as they please against the latter. The nation, which has so declared war, has still authority over its own subjects, and may restrain them from acting against the other nation in any other manner than the public shall direct. So that, in consequence of such a restraint, none can act in the war, even though it has been declared, besides those who have particular orders or commissions for this purpose. But this restraint, and the legal necessity which follows from it, that they, who act, should have particular orders or commissions for what they do, arises not from the law of nations, or from the nature of the war, but from the civil authority of their own country. A declaration of war is, in its own nature, a general commission to all the members of the nation which has declared war, to act hostilely against all the members of the adverse nation. And all restraints that are laid upon this general commission, and make any particular orders or commissions necessary, come from positive and civil institution.

* Grotius distinguishes here between what is commanded by the law of nature, what is matter of civil institution, and what is required by the law of nations. The law of nature, he says, when it is applied to individuals in a state of nature, will allow us to make use of force against them, to punish them for any crimes which they have committed, or to recover our own goods, which they have unjustly taken from us, or to defend ourselves against any injury which they are attempting to do us, though we give them no notice beforehand that we will make use of such force. But before we can justly seize upon any of their goods, as an equivalent for what they have taken from us, the law of nature requires that we should make a demand of our own goods. For our primary right is a right to our own goods: the right to an equivalent is only a secondary one, and does not take place till the other is finally defeated. There is a farther reason against seizing upon the goods of a nation, or of some of the members of it, upon account of any damages which we have sustained from others of its members, till we

* Grot. Lib. III. Cap. III. § VI, VII.

have demanded of the nation to do us justice against its subjects. For, without a refusal to comply with such a demand, the law of nature will not make the nation a party in the offence of its members; and, consequently, will not justify us in making war upon it. But Grotius seems here to confound two things, which are widely different from one another. I allow, that the law of nature requires such a demand as this to be made, before it will justify a public war: but this is no evidence that it likewise requires a declaration of war: because, a declaration of war is not the same thing with a demand to have justice done us, which demand is made in order to avoid a war. These two acts may be done at one and the same time: as when we declare war, conditionally, unless our demands are satisfied: but still they are different acts. The declaration of war is void; that is, the war does not take place, notwithstanding the declaration, if the demand produces its proper effect, by obtaining reparation for the damages that we have sustained. Grotius allows here, that the law of nature does not require a declaration of war to be made, in order to prevent all appearance of deceit, or of clandestine management, and to give the adverse nation an opportunity of being upon its guard. This is not matter of strict right, however it may be matter of bravery, or of what goes under the notion of honour: as some nations have, upon the same principle, given notice to the enemy beforehand of the day and place of battle.

The formalities of declaring war belong to the civil law: each nation determines for itself by what officers, in what places, and with what ceremonies, a declaration of war shall be made.

Grotius derives the principal obligation to declare war, from a purely positive law of nations. This obligation, as he explains it, is derived from an external purpose, and not from any internal reason of natural justice. A war, he says, unless it is declared, does not give impunity to the parties concerned in it, and does not give one of the parties property in what it takes from the other. But if, by the parties concerned in the war, we mean the nations, neither the reason of the thing, nor the common practice of nations will give them any other impunity, or allow them any otherwise to obtain property in what is taken, where war has been declared, than in the less solemn kinds of public war, which are made without a previous declaration. Indeed, in solemn war, the individual members of a nation, which has declared war, are not punishable by the adverse nation for what they do: because the guilt of their actions is chargeable upon the nation which directs and authorizes them to act. But even this effect may be produced, though not in respect of all the members of the nation, yet in respect of some of them, without a declaration of war. For, in the less solemn kinds of war, what the members do, who act under the particular direction and authority of their nation, is, by the law of nations, no personal crime in them: they cannot, therefore, be punished, consistently with this law, for any act in which it considers them only as the instruments, and the nation as the agent.

Law of nations, in respect of states that are neutral in a war.

XIX. When two or more nations are at war with one another, the principal questions relating to neutral states; that is, to such states as are not parties in the war, are, * first, what these neutral states may do in re-

* Grot. Lib. III. Cap. XVII. § I. III.

spect of either of the nations, which are at war, without departing from their neutrality; and secondly, what conduct is allowable in the nations, which are at war, towards the neutral states.

The general rule, in the first of these questions is, that a neutral state is not at liberty to give any assistance to either of the states that are at war. This rule, when it is thus generally expressed, is not so to be understood, as if it was naturally unjust for a state, which is for some time neutral in a war, to join itself in the progress of the war to one of the contending parties. When we say, in general, that a neutral state is not at liberty to assist either party; we only mean, that it cannot assist either, consistently with its neutrality. But if we distinguish the notion of neutrality into general and particular; the rule, in a particular neutrality, will bear, or rather will require, a different construction. The neutrality of a nation is general, where it is not, in fact, a party in a war. The neutrality is particular, where the nation has bound itself by compact, to one or both the contending nations not to make itself a party. If the neutrality is only general; it is only inconsistent with such neutrality to give assistance to either of the contending nations; that is, the state, by giving its assistance to either of them, ceases to be a neutral state, and may be treated by the other of them as a party in the war. If the neutrality is particular, and a compact of neutrality has been made with both; it will then be a breach of compact, and consequently an injury against one of them, to give assistance to the other. Or if the compact is made with only one of them, the giving of such assistance to the other will be a breach of this compact: but to assist the nation, with which this compact is made, will only be a simple breach of neutrality in respect of the other.

The reason of this rule arises out of the nature of things, and shows it to be a rule of the law of nature, which may be applied alike either to individual persons, in a state of equality, or to the collective persons of civil societies. For the notion of neutrality in a war, whether the war is private or public, consists in avoiding to take part with either of the persons, who are engaged in it. But to give assistance to one of them, is to take part with that person, to whom such assistance is given, and, consequently, is inconsistent with the notion of neutrality.

The neutrality of a state abridges its liberty of trading with either of the contending nations, but does not wholly destroy this liberty. *Nothing is inconsistent with the notion of its neutrality, besides assisting one of them in the war. It may, therefore, supply either of them with all goods, as if they were at peace with one another, except such goods, as will help the party that is supplied with them, to carry on the war more effectually. Goods of this sort are called contraband. This word is sometimes used in another sense, and means all such goods, as a nation will not allow to be exported out of its territories, or to be imported into them. But this is not the sense in which it is commonly used in the question that is now before us. The notion of contraband goods is of some latitude: so that it is not easy precisely to determine what are, and what are not, of this sort. All warlike stores are undoubtedly contraband. But still the question returns, what are

* Grot. Lib. III. Cap. I. § V.

to be reckoned warlike stores? Grotius has removed some of the uncertainty in this question, by dividing goods into three sorts. Some goods have no use, except in war, such as arms and ammunition. Some are of no use at all in war, and serve merely for pleasure. And some are of use either for the purposes of war, or for other purposes; such as money, provisions, ships, and the materials for the building, fitting out, or repairing of ships. The first sort is plainly contraband: and the second sort is plainly not so. In the third sort, in order to determine whether they are contraband or not, we must consider the condition and circumstances of the war. Where a war is carried on by sea as well as by land, not only ships of war which are already built, but the materials for building or repairing of ships, will come under the notion of warlike stores. It may be said, indeed, that timber or cordage may be used for other purposes, besides the building or fitting out of ships, or that it may be used for the building and fitting out of other ships, which are not ships of war. But this will be of no great weight: for the same might be said of horses, or saddles, or many other things which are commonly reckoned amongst warlike stores: they are capable of being employed for other purposes; the uses of them are not necessarily confined to the purposes of war. But as arms or ammunition are warlike stores in their own nature, so timber, or cordage, as well as horses, or saddles, may, in all reason, be reckoned warlike stores; when from comparing the sorts or the quantities of them with the condition and circumstances of the war, it appears, if not to be impossible, yet, at least, to be in the highest degree unlikely, that they should be designed for any other purposes besides the purposes of war. Even common provisions for the support of life will come under the notion of warlike stores, when they are going to a place, which is besieged or blockaded. They are not, indeed, such weapons, as will annoy an enemy in war; but they are such stores as will help the nation, to which they are carried, to make its defence in war more effectually, than it could have done without them, when one of its towns is besieged or blockaded.

Sometimes, to remove all possibility of doubt about what goods are contraband, a nation that is at war, enumerates them particularly in treaties or compacts with neutral states: and such treaties leave the neutral states, with which they are made, at liberty to supply the enemy with all goods that are not enumerated in them. But these treaties do not operate as a law, and determine what shall, and what shall not be reckoned contraband amongst all nations whatsoever: they are, in this respect, like all other treaties, and are binding only between the nations that are parties to them.

*Grotius, himself, confesses, that he was forced to examine this question by the law of nature; because he could find no evidence of a purely positive law of nations. But the law of nature, when it is thus applied to the collective body of nations, though our author does not call it the law of nations, is what we have hitherto called by this name, and is the only law of nations that has any real foundation.

When contraband goods are carried to our enemy by a neutral state, which either did know, or might have known, that the assistance,

* Grot. Lib. III. Cap. I. § V.

which it thus gives to our enemy, will hinder the execution of our right; as this neutral state does us damage, it is obliged, in the opinion of *Grotius, to make us amends; and if such amends is refused, we may justly make reprisals upon it to the amount of the damage. But here he supposes the contraband goods to have been delivered, and some actual damage to have been done. For if the neutral state has not done any actual damage, but only designed to do it, he does not allow us a right of reprisal, or even a right to take the contraband goods to our own use, unless we take them upon the claim of necessity; that is, unless the exigency of affairs is such, that we cannot possibly do without them. All that he allows us to do, when we are not pressed by such a necessity as this, is to compel the neutral state to give us security, by hostages, or pledges, or some other means, that it will not attempt any thing of the like sort for the future. If, indeed, the neutral state not only does a simple injury, but appears plainly to have had a malicious design of hurting us, by confirming and assisting our enemy in an unjust war against us; this, says Grotius, is a criminal act; and as we may punish it for such an act, in some other way; so, likewise, we may punish it by deprivation of goods, and, particularly, by seizing the contraband goods, which it was carrying to the enemy. But there is a reason, which our author does not take notice of, why we may, consistently with the law of nature, seize upon the contraband goods of a neutral state, which it is carrying to the enemy, as if they were the goods of an enemy, without considering this act as a crime, for which we may punish those, who are guilty of it, by depriving them of their goods. If we meet with the contraband goods in their passage, and prevent the delivery of them to the enemy; there is, certainly, no actual damage done to us by the neutral state, from which they came: there is only a design of doing us damage. And this design, if it is considered separately from its circumstances, will give us only a right of guarding against it, or, perhaps, of taking some security against any future attempt of the same sort. But the first instance of such an attempt is a breach of neutrality: a neutral state, by sending contraband goods to our enemy, whether it delivers them or not, makes itself so far, at least, an accessory to the war, as it would have given assistance to our enemy, if we had not prevented it. We cannot, indeed, treat it as a principal in the war, where it does not assist the enemy with its whole force. But as far as it is an accessory to the war we may treat it as an enemy, and, consequently, may seize the contraband goods, as if they had belonged to an enemy. The injury, which the neutral state attempts, as it is not completed, produces no claim to reparation of damages: but the attempt itself makes the neutral state an accessory to the injuries which we have received from the enemy: and thus the neutral state, by communicating in the injustice of the enemy, gives us a right to demand reparation of damages, as far as it has communicated in this injustice.

Under the second question relating to neutral states, †Grotius takes no particular notice of any thing, which may be done against them by a nation, that is at war, except what it is compelled to do by absolute and unavoidable necessity. If it has any right at all to seize upon any

* Grot. Lib. III. Cap. I. § V.

† Grot. Lib. III. Cap. XVII. § I.

neutral towns, and to put garrisons into them to prevent them from falling into the enemies' hands, this right can arise from nothing but the extreme danger, which it would be in, if the enemy should get possession of them, and the plain evidence, that the enemy has a design to seize them, and would otherwise succeed in such a design. And even this right of necessity is subject to many restrictions. When we seize a town upon this pretence, we can only take the custody of it, and have no right to any jurisdiction over it: because, whatever the custody of the town may be, the jurisdiction over it cannot be necessary for our security. Whatever damages the nation, to which the town belongs, may suffer either upon account of our having the custody of it, or by our means, whilst it is in our hands, we are obliged to make reparation for them. And as soon as the necessity, with which we were pressed, is over, we are obliged to withdraw our garrison, and to give up the place into the hands of the nation, to which it belongs. But these are not the only restrictions of this right: there is another, which renders it so precarious in the exercise, as to be little better than no right at all. We cannot be justified, even by necessity, in seizing it, if the neutral state, to which it belongs, is pressed by an equal necessity. And since this state may reasonably apprehend itself to be in danger of being treated by the enemy as an accessory to our act of seizing the town, it has an equitable claim to judge of its own necessity: and, consequently, our claim of necessity can scarce take place consistently with justice, unless we have first obtained the consent of the state.

We have a right, in war, to take the goods of the enemy. But this right is restrained to such goods as are either in our own territory, or in the territory of the enemy, or in places which are not parts of the territory of any state. For if the goods of an enemy are in the territory of a neutral state; since we have no right to go thither in a hostile manner; they are under the protection of the state, and the law of nations will not allow us to take them. *In like manner we have no right to take them, if they are on board a ship, whilst the ship is in a neutral port; whether the ship itself is a neutral one, or belongs to the enemy; because the port is a part of the territory of the neutral state. When the goods of an enemy are on board the ship of an enemy, and the ship is in the main ocean, there can be no doubt about our right of taking both the goods and the ship: because they are then in a place which is not in the territory of any nation. But when the goods of an enemy are on board a neutral ship, and the ship is in the main ocean; though we have a right to take the goods, we have no right to take the ship, or to detain it any longer, than is necessary to obtain possession of the goods. For the ocean itself is no territory: and neutral ships, as they are moveable goods, are no parts of the neutral territory. As long as the ships continue in their own ports, the goods which are on board them, as well as the ships themselves, are within the neutral territory, and cannot be taken. But as soon as the ships come into the main ocean, the goods, which are on board them, are in no territory, and, consequently, are no more under the protection of the neutral state, than the same goods would be, if

* Grot. Lib. III. Cap. I. § V. Note.

they were passing through an uninhabited country, where no nation has jurisdiction, in neutral carriages, or on neutral horses. A neutral ship may, indeed, be called a neutral place: but when we call it so, the word, place, does not mean territory; it only means the thing, in which the goods are contained: and as this is a moveable thing, it is no part of the territory, and is no longer under the jurisdiction of the nation, than it continues within the territory. Though the goods of the enemy had been on board a ship belonging to the enemy, we might have said, in the same sense, that they were in a neutral place, if they had been locked up there in a neutral chest. But no one would imagine, that such a neutral place, as a chest, can be considered as a part of the territory of the neutral state, or that it could protect the goods; notwithstanding a neutral chest is as much a neutral place, as a neutral ship. The jurisdiction of a nation over things is confined to that tract of land, upon which it is settled, and to such waters as are appendages to that land. These immoveable things, which are called the territory of a nation, are the immediate objects of jurisdiction or paramount property. Moveable things are the proper objects of inferior property, or private ownership, and are no otherwise the objects of jurisdiction, than as they happen to be within the territory. Thus a ship, though it is a moveable thing, is under the jurisdiction of a nation, whilst it continues in one of its ports. But as soon as it is out at sea, only the private ownership or inferior property of the ship continues: it ceases to be under the nation's jurisdiction. The case will be the same, if, instead of supposing the ship to be the property of a private merchant, we suppose it to be the property of the nation. For though we cannot well call the property, which the nation has in such a ship, by the name of private ownership; yet when the ship comes into the main ocean, the jurisdiction or paramount property of the nation ceases; and the right that remains, is an inferior kind of property, which has the nature of private ownership. But if the jurisdiction, which a neutral state has over the ships of its members, or even over its own ships, ceases, when the ships are out at sea; the goods of an enemy that are on board such ships, cannot be under the protection of the nation in the same manner, as if the ships had been in one of its ports, or as if the goods had been on its land.

Notwithstanding a ship, when it is in the main ocean, is no part of the territory of a nation, and, consequently, is not subject to the jurisdiction, which the nation has over things; yet the men, who are in it, as they are members of the nation, are still subject to the jurisdiction, which it has immediately over the persons of its members. It is proper to take notice of this jurisdiction, though it is not material to the present question: because otherwise, when I say, that the jurisdiction of a nation over its own ships, or the ships of its members ceases, as soon as they are in the main ocean, the reader might have imagined, that I suppose the whole jurisdiction of the nation to cease its jurisdiction, as well over the persons, who are in the ships, as over the ships themselves. When the seamen are on land, or in port, the nation has an immediate jurisdiction over them, as they are members of it, and a mediate jurisdiction over them, as they are persons within its territory. But when they are out at sea, though in one of its own ships, only the former sort of jurisdiction remains, and the latter sort ceases.

In some nations, causes which arise at sea, and have no connexion with the land, whether they are civil or criminal, are cognizable by particular courts of marine or admiralty, which do not make use of the same forms that are used in other courts of the same nation, and do not proceed upon what is called the law of the land, or of the territory. It is plain, that, in the opinion of any nation, where such courts are established, a ship, when it is out at sea, is no part of its territory: for if it was, though there might be a distinction of courts, there could be no reason why the courts, which have cognizance of such causes as arise at sea, should decide according to any other law than what is the general law of the land, in all causes which are, in every respect, the same; except only, that they arise on the land, or are connected with it.

Though a neutral nation, when its ship is in the main ocean, has no such jurisdiction over the ship itself, as if it was a part of its territory, yet either the nation itself, or some of the members of the nation, which is the same thing in the view of the law of nations, will continue to have an inferior sort of property, or ownership in it. And this inferior property, or ownership, will render it unjust in us to take the ship, notwithstanding we may lawfully take any goods of the enemy which are on board.

But here a difficulty offers itself, which must not be overlooked. That inferior kind of property which we have called private ownership, to distinguish it from a jurisdiction over things, is an exclusive right: those persons who have such ownership in things, whether they are private or public persons, have a right to exclude all other persons from making use of these things. * By this means, the rights of others are frequently hindered from taking effect. Wild beasts, and birds, and fishes, are, till they are catched, in common to all mankind; and I have a right, with the rest of mankind, to catch them, and to make them my own by catching them. But I cannot hunt, or shoot, or fish, without using the soil or the water of another man. And as I have no right to use these without his consent, he may justly hinder me from doing any of these acts, as far as his right of property extends. Thus, therefore, by his private ownership, I am hindered from taking such things, as I should otherwise have a right to take, if they did not happen to be in such places as he has an exclusive right to. In like manner, though we have a general right to take the goods of an enemy, when they are out at sea, yet there is some reason to doubt, whether the effect of this right may not be hindered by the inferior property or ownership which a neutral nation has in the ship where the goods are. For it may be said, that, notwithstanding our general right to take the goods, the neutral nation considered merely as a private owner, has an exclusive right to its own ship; and, consequently, may hinder us from coming into the ship to take the goods. Those, who set up a purely positive law of nations, have nothing else to do here, in answer to this difficulty, but to prove the existence of such a law, and to show that this law has, in fact, determined otherwise. But if the law of nations is nothing else but the law of nature, applied to the collective persons of civil societies, instead of answering that the law of nations has determined otherwise, we must find out a natural reason why it should determine other-

* See Book I. Chap. V. § V.

wise. Where I have merely a right to acquire property in a thing, which is in common to all mankind, but cannot acquire property in it without the use of what is already the property of some other man, this man neither does me an injury, nor encourages or protects others, who have injured me, by excluding me from the use of what belongs to him. And thus, my right of acquiring things, which are in common, will, by his means, fail of producing its effect: whilst he, by whose means it so fails, will be chargeable with no crime, or no fault; because he has done nothing more than his property, in what I wanted to use, will justify him in doing. But where we have a right, in war, upon account of the damage which the enemy has done us, to take the goods of the enemy, and these goods are in a neutral ship; if the neutral state, though it has property in the ship, should make use of its right of property to protect the goods against us, this protection makes it an accessory to the injury which gave us a claim upon the enemy to obtain reparation of damages; and, consequently, is inconsistent with the notion of neutrality. But whilst this answer removes one difficulty, it brings on another. If a neutral nation makes itself an accessory to the damages that the enemy has done, by protecting such goods of the enemy, as we have a right to take for reparation, when these goods are out at sea in one of its ships; why might the same nation, without making itself an accessory to those damages, protect the same goods when the ship is in one of its ports, or when the goods are on land within its territory? A law of nations, which is natural as to the matter of it, and positive only as to the objects of it, will furnish us with an answer to this question. Every state has, by the law of nations, an exclusive jurisdiction over its own territory. As long, therefore, as a state keeps within its own territory, and exercises its jurisdiction there, we have, by this law, no right to take notice of what it does; unless, indeed, where, by protecting some person who has committed a crime in our territory, it infringes upon our jurisdiction. But when its ships are in the main ocean; as they are then in a place out of its territory, where, by the law of nations, it has no jurisdiction, this law will allow us to take notice of the protection which it gives to the goods of the enemy, and to consider it as an accessory to the damages done by the enemy, if it gives them protection.

The goods belonging to a neutral state, or to any of its members, cannot lawfully be taken, when they are on board the ship of an enemy. The neutral state has, indeed, no jurisdiction in the ocean where the ship is; but it has property in the goods: and as the law of nature will not allow us, so there is no purely positive law of nations that will warrant us to violate this right of property. In the meantime, the neutral goods will not secure the ship itself. For the ship is neither the property of the neutral state, nor within its jurisdiction.

Since the members of a nation, which is engaged in a war, whether they act under particular commissions, or under the general commission of public war, may take the goods of the enemy, but cannot lawfully take any goods or ships which are the property of a neutral state, unless the goods are contraband; who shall be the judge in these two questions; that is, who shall determine whether the goods or ships, which the members of such a nation have seized upon and gotten into their possession, are the property of the neutral state; and if they are its property, who shall determine whether they are contraband? Other neutral states, which have no interest in the goods or ships, might be unprejudiced judges: but the law of nations has not made them authentic judges. All nations are, in respect of one another, in a state of nature or of equality: no one nation has jurisdiction over the rest, and no number of nations has jurisdiction over any one. The same reason, which excludes all other nations from having jurisdiction in these questions, will exclude both the neutral nation, whose members claim property in the goods or the ships, and, likewise, the nation whose members have them in their possession, and claim them by the right of war. These two nations are, in respect of one another, in a state of equality; and neither of them has any authority over the other. The jurisdiction, which the neutral nation has over things, will not extend to the things in question: because they are not within its own territory. And its jurisdiction over the persons of its own members, will here give it no judicial authority: because, in these questions, its own members are the parties only on one side: the members of the other nation, are the parties on the other side; and the neutral state has no jurisdiction over their persons. In respect of these reasons, which exclude the jurisdiction of the neutral state, there is no material difference between that and the other, to which the captors belong. The things in question, will, indeed, be within the territory of the latter, if the captors have brought the ships into their own ports. But the controversy arose upon the main ocean, which is out of its territory: and, as it had no jurisdiction, in the first instance, the subsequent act of bringing the things into its territory, will not give it jurisdiction. If any subsequent act can give it jurisdiction, it must be a subsequent consent of the parties. The foreigners, who claim the goods or ships, may agree with the captors to have their respective claims decided by the state, to which the latter belong. And such an agreement will bind them to submit to the sentence of this state. But if the things were brought by force into the ports of the state, to which the captors belong, this act of force can produce no effects of right, till it appears whether the force is lawful or not; that is, till it appears whether the goods might lawfully be taken or not: and, consequently, this act can produce no jurisdiction in the state, to determine whether they might lawfully be taken. Until the force is determined to be lawful, it gives the state no jurisdiction, where it had none before. But the force cannot be determined to be lawful, till there is a definitive sentence, that the things which are in the possession of the captors, might lawfully be taken. The state, therefore, cannot have jurisdiction by means of this force, till the question, in which the jurisdiction that we are inquiring after, is wanted, has been determined.

In the usual practice of nations, the state, to which the captors belong, decides whether ships or goods, which are seized upon in war, are the property of a neutral state, or of an enemy; and whether the goods, if they are the property of a neutral state, are contraband or not. But since the law of nature does not give it any authority in these questions, which can properly be called jurisdiction, it will be necessary, if there is no purely positive law of nations, that has given it such jurisdiction, to inquire upon what natural reasons its right to decide about them is founded, and what sort of a right this is. The state, to which the captors belong, has a right to inspect into their behaviour; both because they are members of it, and because it is answerable to all other states for what they do in war; since what they do in war, is done either under its general, or under its special commission. The captors, therefore, are obliged, upon account of the jurisdiction which the state has over their persons, to bring such ships or goods, as they seize in the main ocean, into their own ports: and they cannot acquire property in them, till the state has determined whether they were lawfully taken or not. This right, which their own state has to determine this matter, is so far an exclusive one, that no other state can claim to judge of their behaviour, till it has been thoroughly examined into by their own: both because no other state has jurisdiction over their persons; and, likewise, because no other state is answerable for what they do. But the state, to which the captors belong, whilst it is thus examining into the behaviour of its own members, and deciding whether the ships or goods, which they have seized upon, are lawfully taken or not, is determining a controversy between its own members and the foreigners who claim the ships or the goods: and this controversy did not arise within its own territory, but in the main ocean. The right, therefore, which it exercises, is not civil jurisdiction; and the civil law, which is peculiar to its own territory, is not the law by which it ought to proceed. Neither the place, where the controversy arose, nor the parties, who are concerned in it, are subject to this law. The only law, by which this controversy can be determined, is the law of nature applied to the collective bodies of civil societies; that is, the law of nations. Unless, indeed, there have been any particular treaties made between the two states, to which the captors and the other claimants belong. They may have mutually bound themselves, by particular treaties, to depart from such rights as the law of nations would otherwise have supported: goods, which would naturally have been contraband, may, by express treaty, be made free; and, on the other hand, goods which would naturally have been free, may be made contraband: neutral goods, which are on board the ship of an enemy, may, by express treaty, be made lawful prize, though, by the law of nature, they would have been free: and the goods of an enemy, on board a neutral ship, may be made free, though, by the law of nature, they would have been lawful prize. Where such treaties have been made, they are a law to the two states, as far as they extend; and to all the members of them, in their intercourse with one another. The state, therefore, to which the captors belong, in determining what might, or what might not, be lawfully taken, is to judge by these particular treaties, and by the law of nations taken together.

This right of the state, to which the captors belong, to judge exclusively, is not a complete jurisdiction. The captors, who are its own members, are bound to submit to its sentence; though this sentence should happen to be erroneous: because it has a complete jurisdiction over their persons. But the other parties in the controversy, as they are members of another state, are only bound to submit to its sentence, as far as this sentence is agreeable to the law of nations, or to particular treaties: because it has no jurisdiction over them, in respect either of their persons, or of the things that are the subject of the controversy. If justice, therefore, is not done them, they may apply to their own state for a remedy; which may, consistently with the law of nations, give them a remedy, either by solemn war, or by reprisals. In order to determine when their right to apply to their own state begins, we must inquire when the exclusive right of the other state to judge in this controversy ends. As this exclusive right is nothing else but the right of the state, to which the captors belong, to examine into the conduct of its own members, before it becomes answerable for what they have done, such exclusive right cannot end, till their conduct has been thoroughly examined: natural equity will not allow, that the state should be answerable for their acts, till those acts are examined by all the ways, which the state has appointed for this purpose. Since, therefore, it is usual in maritime countries to establish, not only inferior courts of marine to judge what is, and what is not lawful prize, but likewise superior courts of review, to which the parties may appeal, if they think themselves aggrieved by the inferior courts; the subjects of a neutral state can have no right to apply to their own state for a remedy against an erroneous sentence of an inferior court, till they have appealed to the superior court, or to the several superior courts, if there are more courts of this sort than one, and till the sentence has been confirmed in all of them. For these courts are so many means appointed by the state, to which the captors belong, to examine into their conduct: and till their conduct has been examined by all these means, the state's exclusive right of judging continues. After the sentence of the inferior courts has been thus confirmed, the foreign claimants may apply to their own state for a remedy, if they think themselves aggrieved: but the law of nations will not entitle them to a remedy, unless they have been actually aggrieved. And even, if upon their own report, they appear, in the judgment of their own state, to have been actually aggrieved; yet this will not justify it in declaring war, or in making reprisals immediately. When the matter is carried thus far, the two states become the parties in the controversy. And since the law of nature, whether it is applied to individuals or to civil societies, abhors the use of force, till force becomes necessary; the supreme governors of the neutral state, before they proceed to solemn war or to reprisals, ought to apply to the supreme governors of the other state, both to satisfy themselves, that they have been rightly informed, and, likewise, to try, whether the controversy cannot be adjusted by more gentle methods.

Privileges of ambassadors, how far natural.

XX. *Though Grotius refers the privileges of ambassadors, to a purely positive law of nations; yet, after any person, who is sent from a foreign nation in the character of an ambassador, is received in that character by the nation, to which he is sent; the several privileges, that Grotius mentions, will arise out of the law of nature, applied to the collective persons of civil societies.

The law of nature does not give any one nation a strict right to demand, that any other nations shall receive ambassadors from it. This is no otherwise enjoined, than as a matter of mutual convenience, or at the most, of friendship or kindness. An intercourse of good offices is due to mankind in general, and particularly to all, who have not de-

* Grot. Lib. II. Cap. VIII. § I. III.

served to be treated as enemies. And this intercourse is kept up and carried on amongst nations by means of ambassadors; that is, of persons, who are sent from one nation to another to transact business between them. Sometimes they are thus sent to procure peace, where the two nations are at war, or to maintain peace, by adjusting such controversies as are arising between them, and might otherwise be occasions of war. Sometimes their business is to form an alliance between the nations for their mutual defence, or to establish other treaties, which tend to advance their mutual interest. It would be unkind and unfriendly, as well as imprudent, to refuse them admittance, when they come for such purposes as these. But since the rights arising out of those affirmative precepts of the law of nature, which relate to benevolence, are of the imperfect sort; if a nation should refuse to receive ambassadors, who are sent to it, this cannot properly be called an injury to the nation, which sends them. There may be such reasons against receiving them, as will vindicate it even from the charge of being unkind or unfriendly. *Grotius reduces these reasons to three general heads. First, there may be reasons arising from the nation, which sends them. A nation, which has broken friendship with us by acts of hostility, can have no pretence to charge us with being unkind or unfriendly, if we refuse to receive ambassadors from it; unless they come with proposals of amends. If it has been the practice of a nation to make use of its ambassadors to spirit up our people to rebellion, or to seduce away our manufacturers and artificers; the duty of benevolence does not require us to run the hazard of being treated in the same manner again. Secondly, sufficient reasons against receiving an ambassador may arise from the particular character or circumstances of the person, who is sent. If he is of a profligate character; if he has formerly behaved perfidiously towards us, or can justly be charged with having been guilty of any open affronts or insults towards our country in general, or towards the constitutional governors of it in particular; however unfriendly it might be not to receive any ambassador from the nation, to which he belongs, there can be no unfriendliness in not consenting to receive him in this capacity. Thirdly, the business, about which a nation is desirous of sending an ambassador, may be a reason, why he should not be received. For, certainly, if we know, beforehand, what instructions he is charged with, and what business he comes about, there is no more unkindness in refusing to treat about it at all, than in rejecting his proposals after they are made. Grotius informs his readers, that he is here speaking of such, as are called extraordinary ambassadors, who come charged with some particular negotiation: for as to ordinary ambassadors, that are sent from any nation to attend constantly upon the courts of another nation, not to carry on any particular purpose, but to manage its business generally in those courts, and to observe what passes there; the practice of the ancients, who knew of no such officers, has sufficiently shown us, that they are not necessary: and, consequently, there is no great occasion for being very scrupulous about refusing admittance to ambassadors of this sort.

†Our author's opinion about the personal privileges of ambassadors is, that whilst all other persons, who reside in the territory of any na-

* Grot. Lib. II. Cap. VIII. § I. III.

† Grot. Ibid. § IV.

tion, are subject, during the time of their residence there, to the laws of that territory, all nations have, by positive agreement, made an exception in favour of ambassadors; that as by one fiction of positive law, an ambassador is considered as the representative of the nation, which sends him, so, by another like fiction of the same law, he is considered as if he was out of the territory, though he is in it. But there is no occasion to have recourse here to any fictions of a purely positive law of nations. An ambassador, who is appointed by a nation to act for it, is made the representative of the nation, as far as his commission extends, by the same law, which would make any one individual in a state of equality, the representative of any other individual, who had appointed him to act in his stead. All that can be called positive in this whole matter, besides the appointment of an ambassador to be the agent of the nation, from which he comes, is the general consent of mankind to consider the collective body of every state as a moral person. For in consequence of this positive consent, every state will naturally be capable of appointing a proxy to act for it: and as the agent or proxy of an individual person, in the liberty of nature, is the representative of that individual by the law of nature; so the ambassador, proxy, or agent of a nation, is the representative of that nation by the same law of nature, when this law is applied by positive consent to the collective persons of civil societies. Such a law of nations as this, if we look no farther, will, indeed, subject every member of one nation, who resides in the territory of another, to the civil law of this territory, as long as he resides there. But if we attend to the act of the nation, which sends an ambassador, and to the act of the nation which receives him in this character, we shall find that there is a tacit compact between them, which produces an exception from this general rule in favour of ambassadors, without the aid of any purely positive law; in the same manner, as a compact between two individuals will, in respect of the contracting parties, produce such mutual rights and obligations, as would not have subsisted by the mere law of nature. When a nation sends an ambassador, the meaning of this act is, that it sends one of its own members into the territory of another nation to reside there as its own member, and to transact such business for it, as it wants to have done there. And the nation which consents to receive an ambassador, consents to receive him upon the same terms and in the same character, in which the other sends him. This act, therefore, of sending the ambassador on one part, and of receiving him on the other part, amounts to a tacit compact between the two nations, that he shall be considered in the territory of the nation, which receives him, as a member of the nation, which sends him. But if, whilst he resides in the territory of a foreign nation, he is considered as a member of his own; he must be exempted from the jurisdiction of that territory, in the same manner as he would be exempted from it, if he had been at home: because, if the nation, where he resides, claims any jurisdiction over him, it treats him as one of its own members, and not as a member of the nation, from which he comes.

The general consequence, from these principles, is, that an ambassador, when he commits any crime, cannot be punished for it by the nation, where he resides, when he commits it. This nation is bound to treat him, in all respects, as if he was resident in his own country

But if he had been resident there, it would have had no jurisdiction over him. He can, therefore, be proceeded against no otherwise than by a complaint to his own nation, which will make itself a party in his crime, if it refuses either to punish him by its own authority, or to deliver him up to be punished by the offended nation. By supporting the exemption of ambassadors from being punished by the nation where they reside, upon this principle of compact, we shall be excused from balancing the general utility, which might arise from inflicting punishment upon them according to the laws, and by the authority of this state, against the general utility which arises from such an exemption. It was necessary for Grotius to examine this question about utility; as he supposes the privileges of ambassadors to depend upon a purely positive law, established by the common consent of mankind. For where mankind are to give them privileges by positive agreement, one way of finding out what sort of privileges are given them, is to find out what sort of privileges will be most beneficial: because mankind are most likely to have agreed to give them such privileges, as will be attended with the most general benefit. But if their privileges arise out of the law of nature, applied to civil societies, in consequence of a tacit compact between the nation which sends them, and the nation which receives them, all doubt about the utility of these privileges is out of the question. For, though the law of nature is founded in the general utility of mankind, yet no considerations of any utility, which nations might obtain by making their compacts about ambassadors different from what they do make them, will outweigh the general utility which arises from strictly observing compacts, and keeping up to the terms of them, after they are made. When one nation sends an ambassador to another, the latter is at liberty to receive him upon what terms it pleases; and to model its compact, and restrain the ambassador's privileges in such a manner as it judges to be most advantageous. But then it will be necessary for the nation, to which he is sent, to express the particular restraints which it designs to lay upon his privileges, and for the other nation to agree to these restraints. For if he is sent generally by the one, as an ambassador, and is received by the other in this character, without any express reserves, the compact, which is between them, will produce such privileges as we have been describing: and the law of nature, upon account of the general utility of keeping compacts, will take from the nation, to which he is sent, the liberty of departing from the terms of the compact which it has made, upon account of any utility that might have accrued to it, if it had made a compact of different terms.

What *Grotius says here, about human laws, is equally true about human compacts: they admit of an equitable exception in favour of extreme necessity. But this exception will not affect the privilege which ambassadors derive, from compact, of not being punished by the state where they reside, for such crimes as they commit within its territory. For there is no absolute necessity, that a criminal should be punished at all: the law of nature does not enjoin, it only allows, the inflicting of punishment. And there is certainly still less necessity, that he should be punished by any particular person, or at any particular time, or in

* Grot. Lib. II. Cap. VIII. § IV.

any particular place. But if an ambassador should raise and head an insurrection, or should otherwise make use of open force, it is no breach of the law of nations to oppose him by force, even though he should happen to be killed in the quarrel. Grotius distinguishes here between what is done in the way of defence, and what is done in the way of punishment. Though the law of nations will not allow an ambassador's life to be taken away, as a punishment for a crime, after it is committed, yet this law, since it does not authorize him to do what he pleases, does not oblige the state to suffer him to make use of violence, without endeavouring to stop it. The foundation of this distinction will be evident, if we attend to the principles which we have been establishing. The law of nature, in consequence of our consent to receive any person in the character of an ambassador, does not exempt him from all civil jurisdiction: it only exempts him from the civil jurisdiction of our state, whilst it supposes him to be subject to the civil jurisdiction of his own. But where this jurisdiction ceases, the compact, by which his privileges are supported, ceases to bind us. This compact, like all others, becomes a nullity, when the matter of it fails. The matter of it is, that he shall be subject to the jurisdiction of his own state, and not to the jurisdiction of ours: and, consequently, the matter of it fails, where the jurisdiction of his own state ceases. This failure does not, indeed, bring him under our jurisdiction: the only effect of it is to leave us, in respect of him, in the liberty of nature; and to discharge us, at the same time, from the obligation that we have laid ourselves under, by compact, to consider him as under the jurisdiction of his own state. In these circumstances, therefore, we have the same right to act against him by force, that individuals have to act against one another in the liberty of nature. Now, the jurisdiction of his own state fails for a time, where he is attempting to injure us; and our danger is so immediate, as not to allow us time to have recourse to his own state to repress his violence: and, consequently, in these circumstances we have a right to make use of such natural means of defending ourselves against it, as his conduct makes necessary. But after an injury has been committed, there is no necessity that the punishment which he deserves, should be inflicted immediately. And since we have time enough before us to apply to the state from which he comes, there is, in respect of inflicting punishment upon him, no failure of the civil jurisdiction to which, by our compact, we have allowed him to be subject: and, consequently, we have no right to inflict punishment upon him ourselves.

*Since the privileges of ambassadors are immediately derived from the tacit consent of the nation which receives them in this character, it is plain, that they have no particular privileges in the territory of a state through which they are passing, either whilst they are going from home, or whilst they are returning thither; because they are not sent to this state as ambassadors, nor received by it in this character. If they meet with any ill usage there, the law of nations takes no other notice of it than if any other person, who is a member of a foreign state, had met with the same usage.

* Grot. Lib. II. Cap. VIII. § V.

*The attendants and the goods of ambassadors would be subject only to the jurisdiction of their own state, if they were at home: since, therefore, whilst they reside with us, they are considered as if they were at home, their attendants and their goods have the same privilege that they themselves have; that is, the privilege of not being subject to our jurisdiction.

But this privilege of the attendants of an ambassador, who is received by us, is not a privilege which is any otherwise annexed to their persons, than as they belong to him. As soon as they cease to belong to him, their privileges cease. It is, therefore, in his power to withdraw their privileges: because it is in his power to discharge them from his service, and from all connexion with him, whenever he pleases. But whilst they continue to be parts of his family, their offences, like his, are not punishable by our laws. The method of proceeding against them, is by applying to him to withdraw his protection. And if he refuses to withdraw it, he makes himself a party in their offence; and application is to be made to the state from which he comes, as if the offence had been his own.

When an ambassador has contracted any debts in the state where he resides, the civil law of that state cannot take his goods from him, and make them over to his creditors for the payment of such debts: because his goods, as they belong to him, are subject only to the jurisdiction of his own state. The method of recovering what he owes, is the same as if it had been a debt of any foreigner who is resident in his own country; that is, by an application to the state to which he belongs, and by making reprisals upon the state, if justice is denied.

It will be proper to observe, that, in the compact which produces the privileges of an ambassador, the nation, which receives him, is a party on one side, and he, in his own person, and the nation which sends him, are distinct parties on the other side: the nation, which receives him, tacitly agrees, by the act of receiving him, both with him and with the nation which sends him, to consider and to treat him as if he was at home. †From hence it follows, first, that though he, by misbehaving himself, breaks this compact, as far as he is a party in it, yet this does not discharge the nation, where he resides, from the obligation which it is under by the same compact to the nation from whence he comes. Secondly, it follows from hence, that, where we and any nation have, by mutual agreement, sent ambassadors to each other, if that nation should use our ambassador otherwise than the law of nations allows, yet we are not at liberty, by way of retaliation, to use their ambassador in the same manner. In such a mutual agreement, though their ill treatment of our ambassador is a breach of compact on their side, yet it will not release us from the obligation that we are under towards their ambassador, by the personal compact with him.

Public compacts are either treaties or sponsions.

XXI. The compacts of individuals, which are private compacts, have already been treated of at large. But it may be necessary to say something concerning public compacts, which are the compacts of nations. Our author's subject led him to apply the law of nations to compacts of this sort; particularly to such as have relation to war, in more instances than we

* Grot. Lib. II. Cap. VIII. § VIII, IX. † Ibid. § VII.

shall have occasion to go through. It will be sufficient for our purpose to explain the general principles of this law, and to show the reader, by applying them to a few instances, that there is no other difference in the rules of law, or in the rules of interpretation, when they are applied either to public or to private compacts, besides what arises from the difference between individual persons, who are the parties in private compacts, and collective persons, who are the parties in public ones.

* Public compacts are divided, in respect of the persons who make them, into treaties, conventions, or leagues, and sponsions or engagements.

Treaties, conventions, or leagues, as they are distinguished from sponsions, are made by those who are authorized by the constitution of a nation to act for it with other nations. But it is not necessary that these constitutional governors should act in their own person. What they do by their deputies, such as envoys, ambassadors, or plenipotentiaries, is their own act; and, consequently, in respect of the nation, it produces the same effect as if they had done it themselves. In public compacts, which sovereign princes, or other constitutional governors of a nation make by their deputies or agents, the law of nature is the same as in promises which individuals make by proxy: what the deputies do under the authority of their public commission, binds their principals; even though they exceed some private instructions which their principals had given them.

† Where the successors of a sovereign prince are chosen occasionally by the people upon every vacancy of the throne, or are appointed by the standing laws of the society, it is plain that the treaties of the predecessor do not bind them upon account of any immediate authority or power which he has over them. For since the right, which they have to the crown, is not derived from any act of his, but from the act of the state, he cannot have any immediate authority over them, either to limit this right, or to restrain them in the exercise of it. His treaties with foreign nations are made binding upon them by the intervention of the state. He is authorized, by the state, to act for it in consequence of the office, to which it has appointed him. His acts, therefore, will bind the state; because they are, in effect, its own acts. So that if, upon his demise, no successor was to be appointed, and a perfect democracy was to follow, the public, under this new form of government, would be obliged to fulfil his treaties. But since his treaties thus affect the state itself, the right of government, notwithstanding it is transmitted to his successors, not by his own act, but by the act of the state, cannot be transmitted free from the obligation of those treaties by which the state would have been bound if it had exercised this right itself, without transmitting it to any successor. But the power of sovereign princes, thus to bind their successors, by the intervention of the state, is not infinite. Besides the constitutional restraints which may be laid upon them by the established form of government, they are under a general restraint, arising from the ends of civil union. They are appointed by the state to act for the attainment of these ends; that is, for the security and advancement of the common welfare: and, consequently,

* Grot. Lib. II. Cap. XV. § III. XVI. See Book I. Chap. XII. § XVIII.

† Grot. Lib. II. Cap. XIV. § X, XI, XII.

as they are the agents of the state only for these purposes, no treaties of their making, if they are destructive of these purposes, will bind the state. We ought not, however, to conclude from hence, that the successor of any sovereign prince, who has made a treaty with a foreign power, is at liberty to break that treaty, when he finds that it would be for the interest of his nation to break it, upon pretence, that the nation could not be bound; and, consequently, that he cannot be bound by a compact, which hinders the advancement of the general good. For though a sovereign prince has no power to bind the state, and by the intervention of the state to bind his successor to any thing, which is inconsistent with the public good, yet Grotius very properly observes, that this rule is confined to what appears, in the first instance, to be likely to hinder the public interest, and does not extend to what seemed at first to be of general benefit, though by some unforeseen accident, it may become hurtful in the event. If there was a probable cause for making the treaty at first, it was binding from the beginning; and an accidental change of interests, which happens afterwards, will not destroy its obligation.

* Sponsions, or engagements, are compacts made by an inferior magistrate, or officer, on the behalf of the state, to which he belongs, without being authorized to act for it. Such compacts, since they are made without the authority of the state, do not bind it, unless it confirms them after they are made. But it is not necessary that this confirmation should be an express one. The state, to which the sponsors belong, tacitly binds itself to fulfil what they have engaged for on its behalf, by acting under the engagement, as if it understood itself to be obliged. But the notoriety of the engagement, and the mere silence of the state about it, will not amount to a tacit confirmation of it; as long as the nation or person, with whom the sponsors have treated, is in possession of no corporeal thing, and exercises no right, in consequence of its engagement. A thing, when it can be claimed by prescription, must have been, for some time, in the possession of the claimant: and then the true owner, by having knowingly neglected to reclaim it, is understood to have tacitly relinquished it. If the thing had been, all the time, in the possession of the true owner, there would be no occasion for him to make any express declarations that the thing is his, in order to keep up his property in it. In like manner, where a right is claimed by usage, the person, who claims it, must, for some time, have exercised it, and they, to whom this right belongs, must, knowingly, have neglected to stop him in the exercise of it. If he has never exercised it, their silence could be no mark of their intention to give it up to him: for they had neither occasion nor opportunity to speak about it. Now, a sponsion, whilst it proceeds no farther than a bare compact, does not give the person, with whom it is made, possession of any corporeal thing, and does not imply, that he exercises any right in consequence of it. The notoriety, therefore, of the sponsion, and the silence of the state about it, cannot give the person, with whom it is made, any claim upon the state by prescription or usage. The state, whatever it may know of the matter, has no occasion to speak about it, as long as nothing is obtained by it, or nothing is done in consequence

* Grot. Lib. II. Cap. XV. § XVI. Lib. III. Cap. XXII. § I, II, III.

of it. And, certainly, the silence of the state, or its neglect to declare, that it does not consent to the sponsion, whilst there is no occasion to say any thing, or to make any such declaration, is no evidence of its consent to the unauthorized act of some of its members. But if the sponsors, besides their bare compact, have given the person, with whom it was made, possession of some corporeal thing, which belongs to the state; or if that person, in consequence of this compact, exercises some right, which affects the state; then, indeed, the knowledge and silence of the state about what has been done, its neglect to reclaim the thing, or to stop the exercise of the right, is an evidence of its consent to the sponsion.

If the state, to which the sponsor belongs, neither expressly nor tacitly confirms what he has done, but, on the contrary, declares, that it will not make good his compact; we are next to inquire what the sponsor himself is obliged to. The compact, if we look no farther, binds him only to endeavour, to the utmost of his power, to prevail upon the state to make it good. He is bound to do this, because it is possible for him to do it: but as far as the state is concerned, he is bound to nothing more, because all beyond this is impossible. But if we look farther than the bare compact, we are then to consider, whether the nation or persons, with whom he treated, knew that he had no commission to act for his own state. If they knew this, he is still obliged only to endeavour to prevail with the state to make his act its own: whatever they may have granted to him, in consideration of the compact, which they have made with him, he is not obliged to return that advantage; unless they have particularly stipulated, that he should return it: because they granted it in consideration of a compact, for the performance of which they knew, that he could not be answerable: and it was their own fault, if they would grant it upon this consideration. But if he led them to suppose, that he had authority to act for the state, either by declaring so in express words, or by treating with them as if he had such authority, whilst they knew nothing to the contrary; this is a fraud: and the fraud will oblige him, though the compact does not, to make them amends for the advantages which they have lost, or for the damages which they have sustained by the compact. If his goods are not sufficient to make them amends, the obligation will extend to his person; not, indeed, to his life, for the loss of his life could be no amends to them, but to his labour, or to the sale of his labour.

* Compacts, which the chief commander of an army, or the governor of a town makes with the enemy, are valid, as far as the respective commissions of such officers usually extend: for so far they are understood to be empowered by the state to act for it. The chief commander of an army is authorized, by the nature of his commission, to exert, or to abate the hostile acts of his army in such a manner, as he finds to be most convenient. He is, therefore, authorized to grant a truce to a town that he is besieging, or to the army of an enemy, that he meets in the field. For a truce is only the abatement or suspension of hostile acts. But the obligation of this compact includes only himself, and the army, which is under his command; because his commission reaches no farther. If, therefore, during the truce, he and his army should be

* Grot. Lib. III. Cap. XXII. § VI. VIII.

called away to some other employment, and another commander, with another army, should be sent in his place; what he has done does not bind those, who succeed him: so that it will be no breach of faith in them, if they do not observe the truce, that he has agreed upon. But notwithstanding any compact, in which he agrees with the enemy to abate the hostile acts of his army, will bind him and the army; yet, if, in making that compact, he has abused his trust, to the advantage of the enemy, he is accountable to his own state for such abuse. The nature of his trust implies, that he has a power to enter into a compact of this sort; and this power is sufficient to render the compact valid. The obligation that he is under, not to abuse his trust, regards his own state only, and not the enemy; and, consequently, it cannot affect the validity of the compact, which he makes with the enemy.

*The commander of an army, though his office empowers him to grant a truce to the enemy, is not authorized, by the nature of his commission, either to make that truce general, or to make a peace. His power extends only to the army, which is under his command: a general truce, therefore, which is an entire cessation of hostilities between the two nations in all places whatsoever, and a peace, which puts an end, not only to all acts of war, but to the state of war between them, are not within the extent of his commission. If compacts, that produce a general truce, or a peace, bind the state, when they are made by the commander of an army; the obligation arises, not from the nature of his office, but from some special commission, which the state has given him for these purposes.

Things taken by an army in war, whether they are moveable or immoveable, are, in the first instance, taken for the state, to which the army belongs. †The commander of the army has, therefore, no right, after they are in his possession, to give them up to the enemy by compact: or if he has any such right, it is derived, not from the nature of his commission, but from some occasional or customary grant of the state. The rule about persons taken in war, is the same as the rule about things. So that the commander of an army has no other right to exchange prisoners with the enemy, than what comes from the special grant, or the custom of his country. But he is at liberty to treat with the enemy about such things or such persons, as are not yet in his possession: for the state has no claim upon these. He is, therefore, obliged to observe the articles, which he has agreed upon with a garrison, that capitulates, in respect either of the town, or the inhabitants, or the soldiery.

The governor of a town is the commander of the garrison; that is, of an army employed for the particular purpose of defending the town. The nature, therefore, of his trust implies, that his compacts about surrendering the town, will bind himself and the garrison. If he surrenders it, when he might have defended it, or upon worse terms, than he might have made, he is accountable to his own state for his misconduct; but the abuse of his power does not affect any compact which he makes, in consequence of that power.

‡When the governor of a town, and the garrison that is with him, in order to save their lives, agree with the besiegers, not to bear arms

* Grot. Lib. III. Cap. XXII. § VII.
† Grot. Lib. III. Cap. XXII. § IX.
‡ Grot. Lib. III. Cap. XXIII. § VII.

against them or their nation, either for a certain number of years, or for ever; some have thought this compact to be void, because it is contrary to the duty which they, who submit to this condition, owe to their country. But Grotius replies, that the duty which they owe to their country, does not affect this compact; since they were in the enemies' power, and could never have been able to have done their country either military or any other service, if they had not submitted to these terms.

Compacts between nations at peace, or nations at war.

XXII. Public compacts, in respect of the circumstances or condition of the nations, that are parties to them, are divided into such as are made by nations that are at peace, and such as are made by nations that are at war. Treaties of the former sort, sometimes relate to the terms or conditions of trade or commerce between the two nations; and then they are called tariffs: sometimes they relate to the assistance which one nation is to give to the other in war; and then, if no payments are to be made on either side, they are called alliances; or if one nation stipulates to pay for the assistance of the other, they are called treaties of subsidy. In short, any rights or obligations, which are consistent with the law of nature, may be produced; and any rights and obligations of the law of nature may be drawn out into view, or be ascertained by express treaties between nations that are at peace with one another.

Public compacts with an enemy, are either such as suppose the war to continue, or such as put an end to it. *Puffendorf has raised a groundless doubt about the obligation of compacts of the former sort. A state of war, he says, implies a liberty of taking all advantages that we can against our enemy. From whence he concludes, that it is a contradiction to suppose that a state of war continues, and yet that we are under any obligation of compact towards our enemy. For if, on the one hand, we are at liberty to take all advantages that we can against our enemy, we are at liberty to depart from our compact, whenever we can make any advantage by departing from it; so that our compact does not oblige us: and if, on the other hand, our compact obliges us to give up such advantages as we might gain by departing from it, the state of war does not continue; because a state of war implies a liberty of taking all advantages whatsoever against our enemy. This difficulty will be removed, if we distinguish between an absolute state of war, and a state of war under some limitations: an absolute state of war does, indeed, imply a liberty of taking all advantages that we can against our enemy. But we may give up this liberty, in part, by compact: and yet when we have done this, the state of war will still continue; not, indeed, in its full extent, but under such limitations as arise from this compact. For the effect of compacts which are made between nations that are at war, and which suppose the state of war to continue, is to abridge the liberty of war, without putting an end to it.

†A truce is a compact by which the persons, who are parties in it, bind themselves not to do any acts of war for a certain time, though the state of war continues. It differs, therefore, from a compact of peace, as it does not put an end to the state of war. The parties oblige themselves not to do any hostile act during the time that is agreed upon:

*See Book VIII. Chap. VII. § II.

† Grot. Lib. III. Cap. XXI. § I.

but when this time is expired, there is no occasion either for any new declaration of war, or for any new causes to justify going on with the war. The truce, whilst it lasted, restrained the state of war from producing its proper effects: but as soon as the truce expires, the state of war then exerts itself and produces these effects. Sometimes a truce is called a temporary peace: but when we call it so, we use the word, peace, only in opposition to acts of war, and not in opposition to a state of war.

One reason for inquiring, whether nations continue in a state of war during a truce, is, because there may be some treaties between them which are limited to times of peace; or some, on the other hand, which are limited to times of war; and then it may be a doubt, which of these treaties subsist during a truce? To this question, Grotius answers, that such compacts only as are limited to times of war, and not such as are limited to times of peace, will continue in force during a truce.

The chief questions relating to a truce, may be easily determined either by considering the nature of the compact itself, or by applying to it the common rules of interpretation.

* When a truce is, by agreement, to continue from some one certain day till another certain day, it may be a question, whether both these days are included in it, if the compact does not say, in express words, whether they are to be reckoned inclusively or exclusively. Grotius allows, that the day, which is fixed for the ending of the truce, is to be reckoned inclusively. This day is, indeed, the limit of the time: but the limits of natural things may be of two sorts; they may either be parts of the thing, as the skin, which is a part of the human body, is likewise the limit of the body; or else they may be different from the thing itself, and no part of it, as a river, which is the limit of a field, or of a meadow, is no part of the field or meadow. But it is most natural to reckon the limit of a thing as a part of the thing itself. He contends, however, that the day from which the truce is to begin, is not to be reckoned inclusively; because, the word, from, is disjunctive, and not copulative: this word, in its usual sense, separates the day which is first mentioned, from the rest, and does not join it to them. One would rather think, that this first day is the limit of the truce at one end, as the last day is the limit of it at the other end; and, consequently, that there is the same reason for reckoning the first day, that there is for reckoning the last day, as a part of the time which is included in the truce. Certainly, the common use of the word, from, is no objection against this way of reckoning: for when we say, from head to foot, the head as well as the foot, is included within the reckoning.

Truces, as we have already had occasion to observe, are either general or particular: if the parties agree to suspend all acts of war, in all places whatsoever, this is a general truce; if they agree to such a suspension in some one or some few places only, the truce is a particular one. † When a truce is agreed upon by the constitutional governors of the nations that are parties in the war, though it binds the whole nation on each side, no acts of war which are done by the members of either nation, will be a breach of the truce, unless those members knew that it had been agreed upon: because it can only oblige the whole

* Grot. Lib. III. Cap. XXI. § IV. † Grot. Ibid § V.

nation, when it is so promulgated, that the whole nation may know it. Such truces, as are granted by the chief commander of an army, are subject to the same rule. But in these truces, the rule has no great use; because they are commonly known immediately to all the persons who are concerned in them.

* Truces may either be absolute or conditional. A truce which is made without any conditions annexed to it, though it binds the parties not to do any hostile acts towards one another, leaves them at liberty to fortify their towns, to raise new armies, to build ships, or in any other respect to put themselves into a better posture of defence than they were in before. For, by agreeing merely not to do any hostile act, they cannot be understood to have bound themselves not to guard, as well as they can, against any future hostile acts which may be done against them. Conditional truces are broken, when one of the parties does any thing which is contrary to the conditions that have been agreed upon. And universally, a breach of truce, on one part, will justify the other part in beginning hostilities again before the time of the truce would have otherwise expired.

All truces, granted for a certain purpose, are confined to this purpose; and the party, which makes use of the cessation of hostilities, to do any thing that is not included within this purpose, and that is to the disadvantage of the other party, breaks the truce. For, as this purpose is the sole reason of the compact, the right, arising from the compact, can extend no farther than this purpose extends. Thus, when a truce is granted to a besieged town, for the purpose of burying the dead, it is a breach of compact to make use of the opportunity which such a truce may afford, to bring any new supplies of men or of provisions into the town: the besiegers, as they granted the garrison a cessation of arms only for the purpose of burying the dead, have a plain right, notwithstanding their compact, to hinder it, by force, from making any other advantage of this cessation.

† Passports, or letters of safe conduct, which are granted to enemies in time of war, are to be construed by the common rules of interpretation. The nature of a passport does not particularly require, that the words of it should always be understood in their most extensive sense; or that the meaning of it should always be extended beyond the common acceptation of the words, so as to make the favour, which it grants, as complete as possible: whether it is to be interpreted liberally or not, must be determined in the same manner, as if we had any other writing to construe. On the contrary, if there is any difference between the rules of interpreting passports, and of interpreting other compacts, there appears, at first sight, to be more reason for thinking that we ought, in interpreting passports, to adhere closely to the letter of them: because the circumstances of the parties concerned in them; that is, of those who grant them, and of those to whom they are granted, are such as afford no room to presume, that the former designed to bestow any extraordinary favour upon the latter. However, this is no general rule for the interpretation of passports: it is not necessary that they should always be interpreted closely; because, though we have no room to presume a design to bestow any extraordinary favour, we must allow those

* Grot. Lib. III. Cap. XXI. § VI. X. † Grot. Ibid. § XIV.

to whom a passport is granted, as much favour as they, who granted it, designed to bestow: and, consequently, we must collect the meaning of the writer, as we collect the meaning of other writers, from his words only, if they are clear and precise; or from his words and other signs together, if his words are obscure or ambiguous; or from other signs only, if there is sufficient reason to believe that his words do not express his meaning perfectly.

Cartels, which are compacts made between two nations that are at war, about the exchange or ransom of prisoners, are to be interpreted by the same rules.

There can be no doubt about the obligation of compacts, which put an end to war and restore peace: nor is there any appearance of reason for imagining, that these compacts are to be interpreted by any rules which are different from the common rules of interpretation. It may, however, be proper to observe, that, whilst * Grotius distinguishes between breaking a peace and giving a new occasion for war, the only real difference between them is, that, when a nation is said to break a peace, we mean, that it does an injury in respect of the rights which were acquired or ascertained by some compact of peace; whereas, it is more particularly said to give a new occasion for war, when it does an injury in respect of some other rights. But, notwithstanding this difference, breaking of a peace is, in effect, giving a new occasion for war: because the compact of peace, as it put an end to any former war, took away, at the same time, all former occasions of war.

Equal and unequal compacts of nations.

XXIII. †If we consider the terms or conditions of public compacts, we may divide them into equal and unequal.

The matter of equal compacts may either be the benefit of peace, or some other mutual benefit. All compacts are equal, where the inconveniences, which both parties stipulate to bear, or the benefits, which both parties stipulate to receive, are equal. Compacts for restoring peace are equal, if the parties bargain for a mutual restitution of prisoners, or of goods, which they have taken in the war, and for equal security, to be given on both sides, for preserving the peace. Other equal compacts, of mutual benefit, relate either to trade and commerce, or to mutual assistance in war, or to any other matter from whence benefit may arise to the contracting parties.

Public compacts are called unequal ones, when the inconveniences or the benefits, which they produce to the contracting parties, are unequal. Sometimes the weaker, or inferior party, is entitled, by the compact, to a greater benefit than the stronger or superior party; as when a stronger state engages to assist another, that is weaker, and stipulates either for a less assistance, or for none in return. Unequal compacts, which lay the greater burden upon the inferior party, are either such as diminish the sovereign power, which the inferior nation has over itself, or such as do not diminish this power. If the inferior nation binds itself not to make war without the consent of the superior, this condition diminishes its sovereign power: for the power of making war, by its own act, is a part of the sovereign power of a nation. Grotius goes on to divide the unequal burdens which may be laid by compact upon

* Grot. Lib. III. Cap. XX. §XVII.

† Grot. Lib. II. Cap. XV. § VI, VII.

the inferior nation, into such as are transient and such as are permanent. Amongst the former sort he reckons an obligation to pay the forces, that the superior party has employed against it in a war, or the dismantling of its towns, or the giving of hostages, or the yielding up of some part of its territory, or of its military stores, or of its ships of war: these are called transient burdens, because they soon end. But the burden will be a continued or permanent burden, if the inferior nation binds itself not to build forts in some particular places, within its own territory, not to go with ships of war, or with any other ships, into some particular parts of the ocean, or not to keep up more than a certain number of ships: these, and many other burdens of the like sort, though they are of indefinite continuance, do not make the inferior state dependent upon the superior for the exercise of its sovereign power. *A farther burden of this sort is an obligation of the inferior party to pay a proper respect to the superior, and to acknowledge its superiority. This, however, does not imply a loss or a diminution of sovereign power; provided all the superiority, which it is obliged to acknowledge, is a superiority only of rank or dignity, and not of power: for one state may be acknowledged superior to the other in rank or dignity, whilst the latter still continues to govern itself independently of the former.

Compacts of the same matter with law of nature, or of different matter.

XXIV. †Grotius observes, that some public compacts are of the same tenor with the law of nature, or contain nothing but what is matter of natural right; whilst others are of a different tenor, and produce such rights as the law of nature would otherwise not have given us. Compacts of the former sort are more particularly useful, where the law of nature admits of some latitude, and the precise rights which arise out of it, depend upon the circumstances that we happen to be in. Express treaties, though in these instances they contain nothing but what is matter of natural right, serve to ascertain such rights as might otherwise have been controverted. Thus it is matter of natural right, that a neutral state shall not convey any contraband goods to our enemy. But what are, and what are not, to be reckoned contraband goods, depends upon such circumstances as may leave some room for cavil, if the several sorts of goods, that are to be reckoned contraband, have not been specified in some express treaty.

This observation of Grotius will furnish us with another, that may be of some use in judging about the law of nature or of nations, from what nations have stipulated with one another in express treaties. Though most nations should, at some time or other, have made treaties, in which they have stipulated the same thing; yet we cannot conclude from hence, that what they have thus stipulated is a right of the law of nature or of nations; because the matter of express treaties is not always matter of natural right. On the contrary, we cannot conclude, that what has been thus stipulated, is not prescribed by the law of nations; because express treaties sometimes contain what would have been matter of natural right, though no such treaties had ever been made. We may explain this observation by the instance which we just now mentioned. If, in enumerating the several sorts of contraband goods

* Grot. Lib. I. Cap. II. § XXI.

† Ibid. Lib. II. Cap. XV. § I.

any particular sort of goods has been omitted, in ever so many express treaties, this is no evidence that it is not contraband by the law of nations: because, though a neutral state would naturally have had no right, in time of war, to carry this sort of goods to our enemy, yet we might give it such a right by express treaty; and any other nations that have ever made any treaties, about the like goods, may have done the same thing. On the contrary, if, in any express treaties, we find, that some particular sort of goods has been excepted as not contraband, this exception is no evidence that they are contraband by the law of nature: because express treaties are sometimes of the same tenor with the law of nature; so that the exception may possibly have guarded against nothing, but what the law of nature or of nations, when rightly understood, would have guarded against without it.

CHAPTER X.

OF THE CHANGES THAT ARE MADE IN STATES, AND IN THEIR CIVIL CONSTITUTIONS.

I. *Three ways in which civil constitutions are liable to be changed.*—II. *Usage may change a civil constitution.*—III. *Civil constitutions may be changed by express consent*—IV. *Unjust force does not change a civil constitution in right.*—V. *Constitutions may be changed upon failure of supreme governors.*—VI. *Abdication may occasion a change in civil constitutions.*—VII. *Patrimonial kingdoms are not naturally divisible.*—VIII. *Rules of simply hereditary succession.*—IX. *Lineally hereditary succession, what.*—X. *Effect of abdication in lineally hereditary succession.*—XI. *Change of constitution upon breach of compact.*—XII. *Sameness of a civil society, what it consists in.*—XIII. *Several ways in which a state may cease.*—XIV. *Change of constitution does not change a state.*—XV. *Some sorts of changes in a state, do not destroy it.*—XVI. *Variable qualities of a state*—XVII. *Conquest in an unjust war produces no effects of right.*—XVIII. *What effects may be occasioned by conquest in a just war.*

Three ways in which civil constitutions are liable to be changed.

I. *THE civil constitutions of all states are established by a compact between the governing part of the state and the body of the people: and as long as the obligation of this compact continues, neither of the parties in it can, of right, change the constitution; because the law of nature requires both of them to observe their compact. But this obligation may cease three ways. First, though it cannot be made void by the separate act of either party, yet they may release one another by mutual consent. Secondly, if, at any time, there is no governing part in being, the obligation will be void; because there can be no compact, or no obligation of a compact, where there is only one party. Thirdly, a wilful and notorious violation of the compact, on the side of the governors,

* See Book II. Chap. IV. § IV. Chap. VI. § II.

will discharge the people from their obligation. Upon any of these events, the people; that is, the body of the society, will be at liberty, as they were originally, to establish any form of government that they please.

Usage may change a civil constitution.

II. Civil constitutions are ultimately founded in a law, which proceeded from the collective body of the state, before the legislative power was vested in any particular part of it. But we may argue about them as if they were wholly founded in compact: because a compact between the governing part of the society and the people is the immediate cause, which establishes this law so as to make it binding upon both of them; and whatever alters the terms or conditions of that compact, will likewise alter the tenor of the law, that is established by it.

* Both the law and the compact, that we are speaking of, are commonly unwritten ones: and usage or continued practice is the only evidence of the tenor of either of them. Whatever constitution, therefore, might appear, from former usage to have been established in any civil society; a different or a contrary usage, after it obtains, will afford the same evidence, that the governors and the people have mutually agreed to change the constitution, by releasing one another from the terms or conditions, to which they had obliged themselves, by their former compact, and by entering into a new one, in which the terms or conditions are different. Thus an absolute monarchy may become a limited one, or a limited monarchy may become an absolute one, by usage; that is, by the tacit consent of the king and the people.

Civil constitutions may be changed by express consent.

III. † If the constitutional governors and the people, release one another by express consent, from the obligation of the compact, by which the old form of government was established; the body of the society will then be at liberty to establish a new one. Or if, without any such antecedent release, the constitutional governors and the people, expressly agree to establish a new form of government; this agreement will be a tacit release of both parties from their respective obligation of adhering to the old one: because they cannot intend to bind themselves by a second compact, without intending, at the same time, to set aside the obligation of the first, which, if it still subsisted, would make the obligation of the second impossible.

The legislative body of a state is only one of the parties in the compact, by which the constitution of the state is established: and, consequently, the acts of this body, though they bind the whole society in other things, will not be sufficient to change the constitution, without the immediate and direct consent of the people. In limited monarchies, where the people act in the legislative by their representatives, if we do not attend to this rule, we may be apt to imagine, that as the consent of the representatives, is in no other instances the consent of the people, so their consent, in concurrence with the rest of the legislative body, would be sufficient to change the constitution from a limited to an absolute monarchy. But these representatives are a part of the legislative body; and the joint consent of this whole body, though they are included in it, is only the consent of one party in the compact, by

* Grot. Lib. II. Cap. XI.

† See Book I. Chap. XII. § IX.

which the constitution was established. When a constitution is dissolved by a notorious and wilful violation of compact on the part of the civil governors, or by the abdication or other failure of these governors; the people may choose representatives to act for them, in restoring the old constitution, or in settling a new one: and what these agents, who are chosen and appointed for this purpose, shall do on the behalf of the people, will bind their principals. But agents, who are chosen and appointed by the people to exercise their constitutional share of the legislative power, act under the constitutional compact, and, consequently, are not authorized by such an appointment, to change the terms of this compact.

But what the legislative body of a state does with a design to change the constitution, either in a mixed form of government, or in any other form, though it does not, in right, produce the change, which was designed, may be the occasion of producing it. If the people acquiesce in what the old legislative has done, and submit, without being compelled, by force, to act under the new one, as if they approved of it; this acquiescence and submission is an evidence of their consent.

Unjust force does not change a constitution in right.

IV. *Unjust force, whether it comes from the civil governors, or from the people, can only change a constitution in fact, and not in right; till the power, which has been seized by either party, contrary to the constitutional compact, has been given up by the express and free consent of the other. Usage alone is not sufficient to establish a constitution, which has been thus introduced: †for usage or prescription will give the possessor no claim either to corporeal, or to incorporeal things, where the first possession is dishonest. And the subsequent consent of the injured party, even though it is express, will do nothing, if any unjust force is made use of to obtain it.

Constitutions may be changed upon failure of supreme governors.

V. When there are no supreme governors in being, the constitution of government ceases, because the people are then the only remaining party in the compact, by which it was established. Such a failure of supreme governors is possible in almost any of the forms of government, but it is most likely to happen in those, which are monarchical, either in whole or in part. A monarchy is, indeed, so far from being a firm and lasting constitution in itself, that it will fail, upon the death of the first monarch, ‡if such positive provisions are not made for continuing it, as do not arise out of its own nature.

The law, by making a kingdom hereditary, will preserve the constitution, upon the event of the possessor's death: for as the ancestor was a party to the constitutional compact, and supported the obligation of it, as long as he lived; so, immediately upon his death, the law brings the heir into his place, and makes this heir a party in it. But the constitution may possibly fail, notwithstanding this provision has been made for the continuance of it. If the family, upon which the law entails the kingly power, is wholly extinct, or if no such heirs are left in it as the law describes; the people will then be at liberty, either to choose a new monarch, or to introduce a new form of government.

* See Book I. Chap. XII. § XVI. † See Book I. Chap. VIII. § IV.
‡ See Book II. Chap. IV. § V. VIII.

Abdication may occasion a change in civil constitutions.

VI. When the constitutional governors of a state have abdicated or relinquished their power; there will be no such governors in being: the people, therefore, will be released from the obligation of the compact, which supported the constitution, and will have a right to alter it, if they think proper.

* Constitutions, that are monarchical, either in the whole or in part, will cease, upon the abdication of the present possessor of the kingdom, notwithstanding the law has provided for the continuance of them, by making the kingdom hereditary: for, by abdicating for himself, he abdicates likewise for his children or other heirs, and cuts them off from the succession. The whole effect of a civil law, which establishes inheritance, consists in transmitting to the children or other heirs, what the ancestor possesses at the time of his death. If he, therefore, in his life-time, has abdicated or relinquished his right, the law will produce no effect at his death; there will be nothing left for them to claim, under the law, and nothing left for the law to transmit to them.

If we should be asked here, whether a civil law, by making a kingdom hereditary; that is, by appointing an heir to the person, who possesses it at present, will not bring this heir into the right of his ancestor, immediately upon the abdication of the ancestor? the terms of the question will supply us with a proper answer to it. A man may have a successor at any time, but he cannot have an heir, till he is dead: for an heir is a person, who succeeds into the right of another, not upon any event whatsoever, but only upon the event of this other's death. If the law, therefore, has done nothing more than make the kingdom hereditary, by appointing a succession of heirs, it only provides, that no vacancy of the throne shall happen by the death of the present possessor: a vacancy that is made by his abdication, does not come within the view of the law, and no provision is made by it for filling up such a vacancy.

Since an abdication thus dissolves a monarchical constitution, the people are at liberty, upon this event, either to introduce a different form of government, or to restore the monarchy, either in its former extent, or under new limitations. And in whatever shape they restore it, they may grant the kingly power to a new family; or they may pass over the person, who would have been the heir to it, if no abdication had happened, and may grant it to others, who stood more remote than he, in the former succession; or, lastly, they may call him to the throne by express grant, or may suffer him to take possession of it without interruption. But whether he obtains it by grant or by sufferance, his right is derived from the immediate consent of the people, and not from the operation of the civil law, which had established an hereditary succession, before the abdication of his ancestor.

Hitherto, we have argued in this question from our author's principles. But hereditary succession may be either simple or lineal: and Grotius confines these principles to the former sort. He maintains, that a law, which establishes lineal inheritance, will produce a different effect from a law, which establishes simple inheritance; that where lineal inheritance is established, the abdication of the ancestor will not

* Grot. Lib. II. Cap. VII. § XXVI.

affect the heirs, though where simple inheritance is established, it will cut them off from the succession. To clear up this matter, it will be necessary for us to take a view of what Grotius says, concerning the several rules of succession to kingdoms.

Patrimonial kingdoms are not naturally divisible.

VII. * Our author's first rule about the succession to patrimonial kingdoms is, that they are divisible inheritances, that as the present possessor of such a kingdom is empowered to appoint his own heir, so he is not obliged to transmit the kingdom entire, to any one person, but is at liberty to divide it into as many parts as he pleases, and to appoint as many successors, as there are parts, with sovereign power over each part. We will inquire presently, whether the state could not give him this power by an express act? or whether the acquiescence or tacit consent of parties will not confirm such a division after it is made, though he had originally no power to make it? The point, that we are to consider now, is, whether a patrimonial kingdom is, in its own nature, a divisible inheritance? The nature of civil society and of civil power, will lead us to think differently from Grotius upon this point. All the parts of a state are united into one body by the social compact, and must remain united as long as no alteration is made in this compact. But a civil governor cannot change this compact; because he is obliged, by the nature of his office, to act under it; and, consequently, he cannot divide the state or separate the parts of it from one another. The civil power, with which he is invested, gives him a right to govern the state; but it only gives him a right to govern it as a state; that is, as a body of men, who are united by compact, for the purposes of securing their rights, and of advancing their general benefit.

† The tenure, by which this power is held, will not alter the nature of it. If states are indivisible things in themselves, the power of governing them, though it should be patrimonial, will not extend to a power of dividing them. The notion of a patrimonial kingdom implies, that the possessor of the kingly power is at liberty to dispose of it, to whom he pleases. But this liberty cannot extend farther, than the nature of the thing, which is to be disposed of, will allow. Where kingly power is the thing to be disposed of, the possessor, though he holds it as a matter of patrimony, can dispose of it only as kingly power; that is, as the power of governing a collective body of men, all the parts of which are united to one another by the social compact.

‡ Grotius allows, that kingdoms, which are made hereditary in intestate succession by any act of the people, are indivisible things: because it may be presumed, that the people, when they made such a settlement, intended what is most for the common benefit: and the security of the whole will be better provided for, if the state continues entire, than if it was to be divided upon every descent of the civil power into a number of lesser states. But this reason may be applied as well to patrimonial kingdoms, as to kingdoms which are hereditary in intestate succession. Grotius, indeed, speaks of patrimonial kingdoms, as if the right of governing them was acquired and transmitted independently of the people's consent. But by whatever means the

* Grot. Lib. II. Cap. VII. § XII.

† Grot. Lib. I. Cap. III. § XI.

‡ Grot. Lib. II. Cap. VII. § XIV.

kingly power might be acquired, we have shown, in another * place, that the consent of the people is as necessary to make it patrimonial, as to make it hereditary in intestate succession. If, therefere, we may presume, that a state is an indivisible thing, where the civil power is made hereditary by the consent of the people; there is the same presumption, that it is an indivisible thing, where this power is patrimonial; because it could not be made patrimonial without the like consent of the people. Or, if we should suppose, with our author, that the consent of the people has nothing to do, either in acquiring or in transmitting the civil power in patrimonial kingdoms; yet still the security and common interest of all the parts of a civil society, as it is the end of social union, must, likewise, be the end of all civil government: because, when a society is formed for any particular purpose, it is impossible, that the power of governing this society after it is formed, should not have the same purpose in view. Since, therefore, our author allows, that the security and common interest of all the parts of a state, will require, that it should be indivisible; the consequence is, that the civil government of it, cannot, in its own nature, be transmitted in such a manner as to divide the state: though the people have not made it indivisible by any other act, the mere act of social union is sufficient to make it so.

When I say, that a patrimonial kingdom is indivisible in its own nature, I do not mean, that no act whatsoever can divide it. The social compact makes a state one indivisible thing in its own nature; and it must continue one thing, as long as this compact subsists, without being altered. Now the civil power of governing a state is ultimately founded in this compact: for if there was no such compact, there could be no state; and, consequently, there could be no civil power. But since the nature of civil power thus presupposes the obligation of the social compact; the person, who is in possession of this power, though he holds it patrimonially, is not authorized by it, to alter the terms of this compact. The people, however, as they are the parties to this compact, may release the obligation, and alter the terms of it, by their consent: not, indeed, without the consent of the person, who is invested with the sovereign power; because he has an interest, that the state should not be divided, and this interest cannot, of right, be taken from him, unless he agrees to give it up. But there is nothing, which will hinder the state from being divided by the joint consent of him and the people. A state is naturally one thing, as long as the compact, which united the members, or parts of it, into one body, continues the same in all points; it cannot naturally be divided, till this compact is altered. And though this compact may, in part, be released by the joint consent of the sovereign governor, and of the people; yet since it cannot be so released by the single act of the sovereign governor; a kingdom, though it should be patrimonial, cannot be disposed of as a divisible inheritance, by the possessor of it.

Thus, whilst Grotius maintains, that a patrimonial kingdom is, in itself, a divisible inheritance, and cannot be made indivisible, without some positive act of the society; the nature and ends of social union, and of civil government, will rather lead us to conclude, on the con-

* See Book II. Chap. IV. § XIV.

trary, that all states, whether the civil power in them is held patrimonially or otherwise, are indivisible in themselves, and cannot be made divisible without some positive act, in which the people concur to make them so.

Though the possessor of a patrimonial kingdom, if such a tenure of civil power had been any where established, would have a right to appoint his successor by will, or by any other act of his own; yet if he had neglected to appoint a successor, it may reasonably be questioned, whether the kingly power would descend in intestate succession, unless the civil law had made the kingdom hereditary upon failure of such an appointment. For a patrimonial right in the sovereign power, which is an incorporeal thing, is, in this respect, like the property of an individual in corporeal things: * the proprietor of a thing has a right to dispose of it by will; but if he has made no will, neither his children nor any one else, can claim it in intestate succession without the aid of positive law. Upon these principles, the death of a patrimonial king would put an end to the succession, and the sovereign power would return to the body of the society from whence it originally came, if he had appointed no heir, and the civil law had not appointed one for him.

If we suppose, what our author takes for granted, that, in a patrimonial monarchy, the tenure, by which the sovereign power is held, will make it descend as an intestate inheritance without the aid of any positive law, when the last possessor has not appointed an heir; the next question will be, to whom this power will descend? Let us suppose that it will descend to his children; and then the question will be, in what order his children are to inherit? All of them have equal claims: but they cannot all inherit at once. The state cannot be divided amongst them, so that each of them may have kingly power over a separate part: because a state is, in its own nature, one indivisible thing. And they cannot inherit this power jointly; because the constitution is monarchical, by the supposition; and such a joint inheritance of the sovereign power would change it into an aristocracy. Therefore, to satisfy their equal claims, they must take one after another. This is the rule in all indivisible things, whether they are corporeal or incorporeal. Thus the several fellows of a college in our universities, have an equal right to the common emoluments of their places or fellowships. The rents and other profits arising from the estate of the college, are divisible emoluments, and each of the fellows may receive his respective share of them at the same time, in such proportion as the statutes or customs of the college direct. But the right of succeeding to an ecclesiastical benefice, which is in the patronage of the college, is an indivisible emolument: they have all an equal right to succeed to it, when it happens to be vacant, but only one of them can succeed at one and the same time. Therefore, to satisfy this right, they must succeed to it one after another, in that order which has been established by the local statutes, or by the customs of the college, or by the particular appointment of the donor.

Our author's rule in patrimonial kingdoms, when they become hereditary by accident, is, that each child of the last possessor, whether it is a male or a female, is to succeed according to the order of birth. † In

* See Book I. Chap. VII. § IV. † Grot. Lib. II. Cap. VII. § XVII.

kingdoms, which are not patrimonial, but are made hereditary in intestate succession, by the act of the people, he proposes a rule, which is something different from this, and gives a preference to the males before the females, though the males should happen to be younger than the females. He does not inform his readers why he makes this difference: but the reason, by which he supports the latter rule, will help us to conjecture upon what reason he founds the former. In kingdoms, which are made hereditary by the act of the people, he says, that the males will be preferred, in the succession, before the females; because the former are more fit for the business of war and of civil government. But if a view to the security and common interest of the society is what gives a preference to the males before the females, in kingdoms which are made hereditary by the act of the people, we may reasonably conclude, that he gives no such preference in patrimonial kingdoms which become hereditary by accident, because he supposes, that, in the succession to kingdoms of this sort, no regard is to be had to the security and common interest of the society, that nothing is to be considered besides the benefit of the reigning family; and, consequently, that the order, which is to be followed in the succession, is the order which nature has marked out in this family by priority of birth. But if this was the reason why he made a difference between the rules of succession in these two sorts of kingdoms, it will not be sufficient to support this difference. For, since the security and common interest of the state is the end of social union, it must, likewise, be the end of civil government: and, consequently, wherever civil law has given no express directions about the order of succession to the civil power, the succession is to be directed by this principle, as well in patrimonial kingdoms, which become hereditary in intestate succession, by accident, as in kingdoms which are made hereditary by the free consent of the people.

Rules of simply hereditary succession.

VIII. It will be needless to inquire what the order of succession is, where the law has exactly pointed it out. But if the law has done nothing more than make the kingly power hereditary in intestate succession, by transmitting it to the heirs of the last possessor of it, without allowing him to dispose of it by will, or by any other act of his own, we are then to inquire what will be the natural operation of such a law.

Hereditary succession, as we have before observed, is either simple or lineal. * Grotius, indeed, does not give the name of hereditary succession to the latter sort. But we shall find, presently, that lineal succession is hereditary in its own nature, and differs from simple succession only in respect of the order in which the heirs are placed.

The succession is simply hereditary, if, upon the death of the last possessor of the kingly power, those persons who are nearest to him in blood, stand first in the order of succession, and all, who are equally near to him in blood, have an equal right to succeed him.

† Our author's first rule about kingdoms, which are made simply hereditary in intestate succession, by the free consent of the people, is, that such kingdoms are indivisible. But this rule, as we have already proved, is not peculiar to kingdoms of this sort: it extends to patrimonial kingdoms, whether they are disposed of by any act of the last pos-

* Grot. Lib. II. Cap. VII. § XXII. † Ibid. § XIV.

sessor, before his death, or become hereditary in intestate succession for want of such a disposition.

.* Secondly, where the civil law calls the head of any family to the succession, and makes the kingly power hereditary in his family, no persons come within the view of this law, besides such as are descended from him. His collateral relations, by affinity or by blood, cannot claim to succeed to what was given to him for his personal qualities, and to his family after him, either as a reward of his merit, or upon the prospect that the like personal qualities would be cultivated in that family. Therefore, if his direct descendants fail, the power with which he was invested, reverts to the body of the society, notwithstanding there should be some collateral branches left, that descended originally from the same stock with him.

† Thirdly, his descendants, if they are not born in such marriage as the laws of the country have established, cannot claim to succeed him by the aid of the law. A perpetual contract of cohabitation in any other form, though it might be a valid marriage by the law of nature, is not sufficient to give them such a claim: both because they will be liable to contempt upon their mother's account, if she was not thought a fit person to be received as the wife of their father, according to the matrimonial laws of the country; and, likewise, because the state, which has fixed the succession, has a right to as great a degree of certainty, as the nature of the thing will allow of, that the person, who succeeds to the crown, is not spurious; and this degree of certainty cannot be had in the view of the civil law, unless the marriage of the parents is conformable to this law. ‡ Puffendorf observes farther, that, in order to take away all suspicion of a supposititious birth, it is the custom, in some countries, for the queens to be delivered in an open chamber, before a large assembly of the nobility, or other principal persons of both sexes.

Fourthly, § amongst those who are equally near in blood to the last possessor of the kingly power, the males are to be preferred to the females. The reason of this rule has been mentioned before: in this case, as in all others which are not provided for by the express directions of the law, regard is to be had to the common interest of the society in interpreting such laws as relate to the civil government, and in determining their operation: and the presumption is, that the males are generally better qualified than the females, not only to defend the society in times of war, but, likewise, to contrive for its benefit in times of peace.

Under this fourth rule, Grotius has occasion to mention substitution, which is an act of the civil law that brings the child into the place of his deceased parent. We shall find, presently, that substitution is of two sorts. But the sort which takes place in simply hereditary succession, only makes the child, by fiction of law, as near in blood to the grandfather or other ancestor, as the deceased parent would have been, if he had been living; that is, it places the child in the same degree of proximity to such ancestor, that the deceased parent stood in before his death. Thus suppose, that the last possessor of a kingdom had any

* Grot. Lib. II. Cap. VII. § XV.
† Ibid. § XVI.
‡ See Book VII. Chap. VII. § XII.
§ Grot. Ibid. § XVII.

number of sons and daughters; that one of these sons died before him, and that the son who died, left a child, which will, in course, be the grandchild of the last possessor: then, if the civil law has established substitution, this grandchild will stand in the same degree of proximity to the grandfather, by the act of the law, that his parent stood in by nature. From hence it follows, that, in determining the operation of a civil law, which establishes simply hereditary succession, we are to consider whether the laws of the country have introduced substitution or not. If substitution is not allowed of, the surviving children of the last professor of the kingly power, are nearer to him, in blood, than the grandchild; so that they will stand before the grandchild in the succession, and amongst them the males will stand first. But if the law has introduced substitution, the grandchild and the children will be in the same degree of proximity; and, consequently, as the kingly power can descend only to one of them, if the grandchild should be a male, and the children females, it would descend to the grandchild, and not to one of the children.

Fifthly, *in simply hereditary succession, amongst the male descendants, who are in the same degree of proximity, either by nature or by substitution, or if there are no males, then amongst the females, the eldest will stand first in the succession: because, where other circustances are equal, that person, who has the advantage of age, is presumed to be of more perfect judgment than the rest, and, upon this account, to be more fit for the business of government: or if all of them are too young to be fit for this important business just now; yet the person, who has the advantage of age, will be sooner fit for it than the rest.

It is possible, that one persen may have the advantage of age, whilst another has the advantage of sex; that is, one of the female descendants may be older than any of the males: the question then would be, which of these two ought to stand first in the order of succession; whether the preference is to be given to the female on account of her age, or to the male on account of his sex? Grotius replies, that the advantage of sex is perpetual; whereas, the advantage of age is only temporary. Though the male claimant should not happen to be, at present, as mature in judgment as the female, yet he will be as mature after some time: whereas, the female can never obtain that advantage, in respect of the business of government, which the male derives from his sex. Since, therefore, a perpetual advantage is to be preferred to a temporary one, our author determines the question in favour of the younger male.

Lineally hereditary succession, what.

IX. The substitution that we have been speaking of, is of the imperfect sort; it only brings the child into the same degree of proximity with the deceased parent, in respect of the parent's father, who is the child's grandfather; and then leaves such child, as to the order of succession, in the same place which its own sex, or its own age, gives it. But perfect substitution goes farther, and brings the child, in all respects, into the place of its deceased parent: the law, by this sort of substitution, looks upon the child not only to be as near to its grandfather, as its deceased parent was, but, likewise, puts it into the same place that its parent was in, as to the order of succession.

* Grot. Lib. II. Cap. VII. § VIII.

Hereditary succession, which would be simple if the civil law of the country only allowed of imperfect substitution, will become lineal by means of perfect substitution. Where sovereignty is transmitted according to the order of simple inheritance, the eldest son of the person, who was in possession of it, will succeed to it upon the death of his father, if he survives his father. But if he dies before his father, and his children are brought into his place only by imperfect substitution, though the law will look upon them to be as near to their grandfather as their father was, it will not bring them fully into his place, or will not give them the same rank, in the order of succession, that he had: their uncles and aunts, who are the children of their grandfather by blood, will have the same legal right to succeed to their grandfather upon his death that they have, who are considered as his children by legal substitution; and amongst the equal claimants, the eldest male, whether it is a younger son, or a grandson by the eldest son, will stand first in the order of succession. But perfect substitution brings the children of the eldest son fully into their father's place upon his death; it makes them, in all respects, the perfect representatives of their father, and, consequently, gives them the same rank, in the order of succession, that he had. It produces the same effect, in respect of his grandchildren, or other remoter descendants; that is, in respect of the whole branch or line, which is derived from him. As he, therefore, if he was alive, would stand before his younger brothers, so his whole line, his children, and grandchildren, and other remoter descendants, whether they are males or females, will stand before those brothers and all their descendants. In this eldest line the males, upon every descent, will be preferred to the females, who are in the same degree, or same part of the line; and amongst the males, the eldest will be preferred to the rest, as they are in simple succession: for the only difference between simple and lineal succession is what arises from the difference between imperfect and perfect substitution: and when we have allowed for this difference, both sorts of succession are governed by the same rules. Thus, by means of perfect substitution, and of a constant preference given to the eldest son, where there is any son, the inheritance will, upon every descent, be transmitted in the line which is derived from the eldest son, as long as there are any descendants in this line, without passing to the younger sons, or to any of their descendants. If it should happen, that, in any part of this line, there are no male heirs, the inheritance will not pass from thence into any other line, in which there are male heirs, but the females, being brought by substitution into the place of their male ancestor, will inherit, and amongst these the eldest will stand first, as in simple succession; and then the inheritance will be transmitted to the eldest male line, which is derived from her; or if she has no male issue, then to the eldest female line. When no issue, either male or female, is left in the eldest line, the inheritance passes into the next line: but in determining which is the next line, we are to go no farther than to a line, which is derived from the same immediate ancestor with the last possessor, if there is any such line: for, since perfect substitution brings all the descendants of this ancestor fully into his place, the several lines, which are derived from him, will stand in the succession, as he did; that is, before all his collateral relations, and before all the lines which are derived from them.

Perhaps the following diagram may help to clear up this whole matter:—

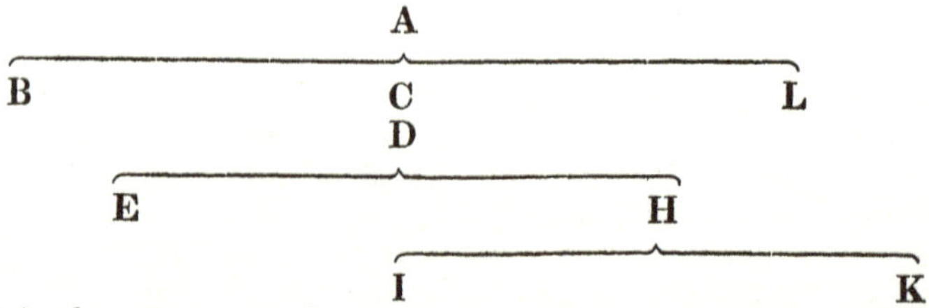

First, if A, the possessor of sovereign or other civil power, has three children, B, C, L, or any other number, of which B, the eldest child, is a daughter, and the two other children, C and L, are sons; all these children are, by birth, in the same degree of proximity to A, or are equally near to him. And upon his death, if they all survive him, and the law has made the power, which he possessed, hereditary, this power will be transmitted by the law to C, the eldest male, either in simple, or in lineal succession.

Secondly, suppose C to die before A, and to leave a son D; then, if the law has not established substitution, of any sort, B and L will be one degree nearer to A than D is; and, upon the death of A, B and L will stand before D in the succession; and, of these two, L, upon account of his sex, will stand first. This is hereditary succession without substitution.

Thirdly, if the law has established substitution, it brings the grandchild, D, into the place of its deceased parent C. But if the substitution is only of the imperfect sort, the law only brings D into the place of C, in respect of proximity to the ancestor A, and not in respect of the order of succession. Thus, B, D and L, being in the same degree of proximity, B and L, by birth, and D, by imperfect substitution, the eldest male amongst them, or the eldest female, if there is no male, will stand first in the order of succession, upon the death of A. So that, if B is a female, and D and L are both males, the advantage of sex will place both D and L before B, whether she is older or younger than they; and it will depend upon the comparative ages of D and L, which of these two shall stand first. If D is a male, and both B and L are females, D will stand first, by the advantage of his sex, of whatever age he is. If there is no male L, and B and D are both females, then the comparative ages of these females will determine their respective places in the order of succession. For though D, by the supposition, is a grandchild of A, by an eldest son, C, yet imperfect substitution, which brings D into the place of C, only in respect of proximity to A, does not give the grandchild, D, that place which its father had in the order of succession, but leaves D in the place or rank which its own sex and age will give it, when compared with the sex and age of B and L, who are as near to A, by birth, as D is by substitution. This is the form of hereditary succession, with substitution of the imperfect sort.

Fourthly, if the laws of the country establish perfect substitution, the order of hereditary succession will then be lineal. D, the grandchild of A, by the eldest son, C, will, upon the death of C, be brought, by perfect substitution, into the place of C, in all respects: the law, by considering D as the perfect representative of C, brings D not only into the same degree of proximity to A, in which C stood, but, likewise, into the same place in the order of succession. Therefore, upon the death of A, the inheritance will, by this perfect substitution, be transmitted to the grandchild, D, in preference to either B or L, as it would have been transmitted to C, if C had been alive; notwithstanding D should be a female, and either B or L should be a male; or notwithstanding D should be a younger male than either B or L. For perfect substitution, when it has brought the grandchild, D, into the same degree of proximity to A, in which the deceased parent, C, stood, does not leave D to take that place in the order of succession, which its own sex, or its own age, would give it in this degree of proximity, but gives it, in all respects, the place of its parent C. By the same sort of substitution, all the descendants of C; that is, the whole branch of the family, or the whole line, which is derived from C, will be brought up into the place of C, in the same manner with D: and, consequently, all the descendants, in this line, will stand before B and L, in the order of succession, and before all their descendants. The inheritance, upon every descent, will be transmitted in the same order. The eldest son will stand before all the other children of the same family, if he is alive, as he would in simple succession; and his children, if he is dead, will, in lineal succession, be brought by perfect substitution into his place, and the inheritance will be transmitted to them, as it would have been to him; and the eldest male, or, if there is no male, the eldest female amongst them, will stand first. E and H, the immediate descendants of D, are in the same degree, or same part of the eldest male line, which is derived from C; that is, they are children of the same parent in this eldest male line; and amongst these, the eldest male will stand first, as in simple succession. If, therefore, E, the eldest child, is a daughter, and H, the younger child, is a son, the inheritance will be transmitted to H, and to the line which is derived from him. But if H, the son, was to die without issue, the inheritance would be transmitted to E, the daughter. Or if E and H are both daughters, then the inheritance will be transmitted to E, who is the elder. Upon either of the events last mentioned, or upon others of the like sort, where there is a failure of male issue in the eldest male line, the inheritance will not pass from thence into any younger male line derived from L, though there should be male issue in this younger line: for E and H, and all other children, if there are any other in this part of the line, derived from C and D, are brought, by perfect substitution, into the place of D; and though, amongst these children, the eldest male, if there are any males, stands first, yet the females are only postponed till there are no males, they are not excluded from the succession. If E and H are both males, or if they are both females, so that E, who is the eldest of them, stands first in the succession, then, upon the death of E, without issue, the eldest line, derived from D, will be extinct, and the inheritance will pass into the next line. But in determining which is the next line, we are to go back, not to any remote ancestor, A, but only to the next immediate ancestor from whom the line, that is extinct, and some other line, that is not extinct, were derived. If, therefore, the line E, which is supposed to be exhausted, and some other line, H, which is not exhausted, but has the heirs, I and K, in it, were both derived from some immediate ancestor, D, the inheritance will pass into the line H, and not into any other line, B or L, which was derived from some remoter ancestor, A. For all the descendants of the immediate ancestor, D, are brought, by perfect substitution, into his place in the order of succession; and, consequently, as he stood before any of his collateral relations, B or L, so his descendant, H, will stand before them, and before any of their descendants.

In any country, where the law has made the succession to kingly power hereditary, *Grotius informs his readers by what means they may be enabled to judge, whether this succession is of the simple or of the lineal sort. If the written law of the country has expressly declared what sort of hereditary succession it designed to establish, there can be no room to doubt about this matter. Or if the written law has only established hereditary succession, and has not declared of which sort it shall be, we must be guided by the unwritten law of custom or usage. It can scarce be supposed, in any state, where a monarchy, either absolute or limited, and an hereditary succession to the kingly power have been long established by law, that there has been no custom or usage relative to the descent of kingly power, which will determine whether it is to descend in simple or in lineal succession. But if such a case should happen, we are then to consider what sort of succession obtains in other indivisible inheritances. Where the titles of honour, which are incorporeal things, are indivisible inheritances, and where land, when it descends in intestate succession, is an indivisible inheritance, if the law, which makes them hereditary, transmits them according to the order of lineal succession, this is an evidence, that the law, whenever it speaks of hereditary succession, means lineal, and not simple succession. Grotius adds, that if a child of an eldest son, has the same rank or precedence in all public assemblies, upon the death of its father, that the father would have had if he had been alive, this shows us, that the child is brought, by perfect substitution, into the place of his father, and, consequently, that the legal succession is of the lineal sort.

†Lineal succession may be either cognatic or agnatic. The English reader should here be told, that all the kindred of a man, or all who are derived from the same stock with himself, whether by a male or by a female line, are included in the general meaning of the Latin word *cognati:* whereas, those only who are derived from the same stock, by a male line, are included in the word *agnati*. From hence, he will understand, that the lineal succession, which we have been describing, is cognatic; as it calls all the descendants, in the eldest line, to the inheritance, whether they are males or females; though it postpones the females, and calls the males to the inheritance before them, in the same part of this line. But all females, and all who are derived from females, are excluded from the inheritance in agnatic lineal succession. Therefore, in cognatic succession, the inheritance will not pass out of the eldest line into the next, as long as any issue, whether male or female, remains in the eldest. But in agnatic succession, it will pass out of the eldest line into the next, when all the males, who are derived from males, are exhausted in the eldest, though there should be females or males, derived from females, still remaining in it.

* Grot. Lib. II. Cap. VII. § XXII.

† Grot. Ibid. § XXIII.

The operation of civil law, where it establishes lineal succession, is explained by *Grotius in a different manner. He agrees with us in maintaining, that, in simple succession, the law gives the immediate heir only an expectancy of succeeding to the kingdom; and that this expectancy never amounts to a perfect right, till the death of his ancestor brings him into actual possession. But then he contends, that, in lineal succession, the immediate heir of a kingdom, though he cannot have possession of it in fact, till the death of his ancestor, has possession of it in law, as soon as he is born; that the law first changes his expectancy into a perfect right of succeeding to the kingdom, and then, considering this perfect right as if it was in possession, transmits it, upon his death, from him to his descendants, not only if he survives his ancestor, and so comes into possession in fact; but, likewise, if he happens to die before his ancestor, and so never has possession, in fact, at all. We shall be able to judge, whether the law operates in this manner, if we examine some of the effects which are produced by it. Let us suppose the possessor of a kingdom to have two or more daughters; the eldest of them, if there was no son born before her, is, at the time of her birth, the expectant heir, where the law has established cognatic lineal succession: and if no son is born afterwards, she will succeed her father in the kingdom. Shall we say here, that this eldest daughter has possession of the kingdom, in law, from the hour of her birth? that the law changes her expectancy into a perfect right, and will transmit this right to her issue, whenever she dies? If we say this, the consequence will be, that notwithstanding there should be a son born after her, yet this eldest daughter will take the inheritance before him: for the same law, which had improved her expectancy into a perfect right of succession, before he was born, cannot defeat this right afterwards, by calling him to the inheritance instead of her. And thus a female would be placed before a male, of the same degree, by such an operation of law as Grotius describes. Or shall we say, on the contrary, that the law does not improve her expectancy into a right, because it is only an eventual expectancy, and may be defeated by the birth of a son? If we take this part of the alternative, the consequence will be, that she never can have a perfect right at all, as long as her father lives; because so long the birth of a son is a possible event. Let us, therefore, suppose farther, that this eldest daughter dies before her father, and leaves issue, and that her father dies afterwards without having a son; then, in the usual course of cognatic lineal succession, one of her children will succeed her father in the kingdom, in preference to her sisters, and to all their descendants. But the law certainly does not produce this effect, by giving her a perfect right to the succession, and by transmitting this right to her children upon her death: for it was granted, from the beginning, that the law gave her no such right, and, consequently, it must be granted, likewise, that no such right could be transmitted from her to them.

But the common rules of simple succession, with the help of perfect substitution, will explain this whole matter. Though all the daughters are expectant heirs of their father, yet only one of them can inherit the kingdom; because it is an indivisible thing: and the advantage of age

*Grot. Lib. II. Cap. VII. § XXII.

will give the preference to the eldest. The law, therefore, by making the kingdom hereditary, will transmit it to her upon the death of her father, if he dies possessed of it, and has no son, and she survives him. Or if she dies before him, and leaves issue, perfect substitution will bring this issue up into her place, and will enable it to take the inheritance, as she would have taken it; that is, before any of her sisters. Or, lastly, if there should be a son born after her, this son will be an expectant heir amongst his sisters, and the advantage of his sex will place him before them all, and before all their descendants, in the order of succession.

We may try whether our author's principle would produce the proper effects of lineal succession in another example. When the possessor of a kingdom, where lineal succession is established, has a brother; this brother will have an expectancy of succeeding him in the kingdom, as long as he has no children. But the law cannot, from the first, improve this expectancy into a perfect right of succession: because if it did, the brother would stand in the order of succession before any children of the king, that might be born afterwards. Upon our author's principles, this consequence, as inconsistent as it is with the order in which the heirs are placed in lineal succession, cannot be avoided, without affirming that the expectancy of the brother is not improved by the law into a right of succession, till it appears that the possessor of the kingdom will have no children. And this answer, whilst it removes one difficulty, will bring on another. It cannot appear, with any certainty, whether he will have children or not, till he is dead; so that, in the mean time, his brother cannot have a perfect right of succession. From hence it will follow, that, if he should have no children, the law, which makes the kingdom hereditary in lineal succession, cannot operate in such a manner as Grotius imagines. For, upon this event, the brother will be the heir in lineal succession; and yet he never has a perfect right of succession, or a possession of the kingdom in law, till the law transmits the inheritance to him, upon the death of the last possessor, and gives him possession in fact. This example may be varied a little, by supposing, that the brother has issue, and that the possessor of the kingdom survives him, but dies without issue. The inheritance will then descend, in lineal succession, to the issue of the brother. But we should be at a loss to explain this descent upon our author's principles. We cannot say, that the brother, before his death, had a perfect right of succession, and that the law transmits this right to his children, as if it had actually taken effect, or as if he had been in possession of the kingdom; because the consequence of this would be, what has been mentioned already, that the brother, in virtue of this perfect right, would have stood first in the order of succession, whether the last possessor had issue or not. Nor can we say, consistently with our author's principles, that the law will call the issue of the brother to the inheritance, if the last possessor dies without issue, though it had given the brother no perfect right of succession, and could, therefore, transmit no perfect right from him to his issue: because our author imagines, that the proper operation of a law, which establishes lineally hereditary succession, consists in giving the expectant heir such a right, whilst he lives, and in transmitting it to his issue when he dies.

This case may be explained, as the other was, by the common rules of simple succession, with the help of perfect substitution. If the possessor of a kingdom dies without issue, his brother will be called to the inheritance, according to the common rules of simple succession; though, till this event happened, he had only an expectancy, and no perfect right of succession, or no possession of the kingdom in law. His children are, upon his decease, brought into his place by perfect substitution, where the succession is lineal; the inheritance, therefore, will descend to the eldest male amongst them, as it would have descended to him, if he had been alive. And thus, upon the death of the present possessor of the kingdom, without issue, the law will give the inheritance to this eldest male, though it had before given him only an expectancy of succeeding, and had not improved this expectancy into a perfect right of succession.

Effect of abdication in lineal succession.

X. We may now return to the question, which made it necessary for us to take this view of the operation of civil law in succession to kingdoms.

When * Grotius contends, that the abdication of the ancestor will not affect the heir, where the law has established lineal succession, the reader should observe, that he does not suppose a divine hereditary right, which cannot be defeated by any human act whatsoever, to be inherent in the heir. A right of this sort is inconsistent with his whole opinion about the origin of civil society, and the nature of civil government. He argues, therefore, only from a right, which he supposes to be vested in the heir, by the operation of civil law, where this law has established lineal succession; and contends, that this is such a right, as the abdication of the ancestor will not defeat. In kingdoms of simply hereditary succession, he grants that the abdication of the ancestor will cut the heir off from the succession; because, where the ancestor has relinquished his interest in the kingdom, or his legal right of civil government, in his life-time, he cannot transmit that interest or right to his heir. But in lineal succession, he maintains, that the heir has a perfect right of succession given to him by the law, as soon as he is born; and, consequently, that the abdication of the ancestor cannot affect this right, which he thus derives from the law. But we have just now shown, that the heir, in lineal succession, has no other sort of right than the heir in simple succession; that, as the heir in simple succession has only a legal expectancy, during the life of the ancestor, so, in lineal succession, he has only the like expectancy: for these two sorts of succession do not differ from one another in respect of the right which the law gives to the heir, but in respect of the substitution, which the law establishes. Where the law has made the kingdom hereditary, if it admits of no substitution at all, or only of imperfect substitution, the succession will be simple: but if it admits of perfect substitution, the succession will be lineal. Since, therefore, upon the abdication of the ancestor, the sovereignty, or the regal power will not devolve upon the heir in simple succession, during the life of his ancestor, the consequence is, that, upon the like event, it will not devolve upon the heir in lineal succession. And thus, in either case, a vacancy will be made in the throne, and the people will be at liberty to change the constitu-

* Grot. Lib. II. Cap. VII. § XXVI.

tion. Upon the abdication of the ancestor, perfect substitution will not operate so as to bring the heir immediately into his place, and fill the vacancy before his death. For perfect substitution is, in this respect, like imperfect substitution; it brings the heir into the place of the ancestor only upon the death of the ancestor, and not before.

When a kingdom is resigned with the consent of the people, the heir may succeed to it immediately, whether the kingdom is simply or lineally hereditary. But this effect is brought about, not by the operation of any former law, that may have made the kingdom hereditary, but by the positive consent of the society, obtained upon this occasion, and for this purpose. In an absolute monarchy, the immediate consent of the collective body of the society is necessary thus to bring the heir into the place of his ancestor, upon a resignation. But in limited monarchies, where the body of the society acts in the legislative, by representatives or otherwise, the consent of the legislative body will be sufficient: for, in such forms of government, this is a change only of the civil law, that regulates the succession, and not of a fundamental law of the constitution.

Change of constitution upon breach of compact.

XI. In those states, where the constitution has divided the supreme power between the king and the people, * Grotius allows, that the people have a right to resist the king, by force, when he invades their part of this power; and then he goes on to observe, that, in a civil war, which is thus occasioned, the king may lose his part of the supreme power by the right of war; and, consequently, that the constitution may be thus changed. The right of war, which he here speaks of, certainly cannot be such a right as he elsewhere supposes to have been introduced by a purely positive law of nations. For if there is any such law, the rights, which are derived from it, can only take place where nations are the parties in the war: a law of nations, whether it is purely positive or not, relates only to nations in their intercourse with one another, and produces no rights or obligations amongst the parts or members of the same nation. † Indeed, his whole opinion, about a purely positive law of nations, and a right of war arising out of it, is without foundation. War, of all sorts, is governed by the law of nature only; whether it is a solemn one between different nations, or a civil one between different parts of the same nation. No right, therefore, either to corporeal or to incorporeal things, can be acquired by taking them in war, unless it is acquired by the aid of the law of nature. But since war is only the use of force, the mere taking of a thing in war can give us no right to it; because, by the law of nature, no effects of right are produced by mere force. If the thing, which we take, was our own before, and we were unjustly kept out of the possession of it, our right to the thing may be maintained, and the possession of it may be recovered by war: but if we had no such antecedent right, arising from some other cause, the mere right of war is no right at all. The consequence of this is, that, in showing how a limited monarch, who has invaded that part of the sovereign power, which the constitution has reserved to the people, may, in a civil war, be deprived of the other part, which the same constitution had granted to him, we must look farther than a mere right of war, and must inquire,

* Grot. Lib. I. Cap. IV. § XIII.

† See Book II. Chap. IX. § I. III.

whether the people, in these circumstances, have not an antecedent right to take it from him. Now, that part of the sovereign power, which the monarch has, was granted to him, at first, by the compact which settled the constitution, and is holden by him afterwards, under the same compact. As long, therefore, as the obligation of the constitutional compact continues, he has a right to this part of the sovereign power; and the people have no right to take it from him, either by war, or by any other means, without his consent. But by wilfully and notoriously invading the other part, he breaks the constitutional compact. And this compact is so far like all other compacts, that a violation of it, on his side, will leave the people at liberty to choose, whether they will abide by it or not. A compact, when it is violated by one of the parties, is usually said to be void; but if we speak accurately, we should rather say, that it may be made void at the discretion of the other party. Perhaps, in the instance which is now before us, those, who dislike monarchical governments, of all sorts, may think, that the people will suffer no inconvenience from a failure in the obligation of a compact, by which they had granted any part of the sovereign power away from themselves, and had vested it in a king. But it is not worth the while to debate this point with them in the present question: because, whatever general rule the law of nature has established, in other compacts, the same rule will be applicable to this. And, certainly, it would, in general, be a hardship upon one of the parties in a compact, if the obligation of it was to be necessarily void, whenever the other party breaks the conditions of it: for, by this means, if the latter did not choose to comply with any of the claims which the compact has given to the former, he would have nothing else to do but to break the compact, and then these claims would cease. This, as it is inconsistent with natural equity, is inconsistent, likewise, with natural reason: not only because the party, who breaks a compact, might, in many instances, gain a benefit by his own injustice, if his breach of it would make it void; but, likewise, because the obligation of a compact, though it arises from the joint will of two parties, might be thus destroyed by the sole will of one of them. However, it is sufficient for our present purpose, that, when the compact by which the people have given their civil governor a part of the sovereign power, is broken on his side, the obligation of it is voidable, or may be set aside, at the discretion of the people. For it will follow, from hence, that, as they are at liberty to continue the same constitution, and to leave him in possession of his former power, if they can stop his usurpations either by force or otherwise, so they are at liberty, if they think proper, to release themselves from the obligation of their former compact, and to make such alterations either in the constitution, or in the persons who are to administer it, as they shall judge to be convenient: they may restore the old form of government, and may call a different succession of persons, either of the same family, or of another, to the throne; or they may change the constitution, in part, by setting new limitations to the power of their future kings, whether they continue the old succession, or introduce a new one; or, lastly, they may change the constitution entirely, by establishing a new form of civil government. The people, in making these changes, may possibly meet with such opposition, as will occasion a civil war, and as cannot be surmounted without conquest. This is all that war and conquest have to do in the matter; they may be necessary to do that, in fact, which the people had otherwise a right to do. Any of these changes, therefore, if they can be made peaceably, will be made as effectually, in right, as if war had made way for them, and conquest had established them. Though Grotius here speaks only of mixed forms of government, these principles are equally applicable to despotic forms. We cannot, indeed, say, that the people, in absolute monarchies, have any constitutional part of the sovereign power. But in all forms of civil government, they have a right to be free from all unsocial subjection: so that tyranny, or unsocial oppression, though it cannot, in an absolute monarchy, be called an invasion of the people's part of the sovereign power, will be an invasion of a natural right, which is reserved to them in the constitutional compact. Thus tyranny, or unsocial oppression, even in despotic forms of government, will be a breach of this compact, and will discharge the people from the obligation of it, if they think proper to be discharged.

When the people, in a mixed form of government, causelessly and unjustly invade that part of the sovereign power, which they have granted and confirmed to their monarch by the constitutional compact, this act of the people cannot, of right, diminish his power, unless he consents that it should be diminished: because the people cannot, by their own act, discharge themselves from the obligation of the compact, that they have made with him. But, in the meantime, this act of the people, however injurious it may be, will not increase his power, or will not give him a right to any more power than the constitution had given him: for, since the whole sovereign power was originally vested in the collective body of the society, which I here call the people, he cannot, of right, claim any greater part of it than the people have granted to him, by compact, in forming the constitution. There is a remarkable difference between the effect of the same wrong, when it is done by the monarch, and when it is done by the people. Upon any failure in the obligation of the constitutional compact, by which a part of the sovereign power was granted to him, this part will revert to the people: because it belonged to them originally, and is holden by him under this compact. When he violates this compact, on his side, it is voidable at the discretion of the people: and if they choose to make it void, his power reverts to them. On the other hand, when the people violate it, on their side, it is voidable at his discretion: if he chooses to abide by it, he has no right to any other power than he derives from it: and if he chooses to make it void, instead of gaining a greater part of the sovereign power, he will lose what he had, and it will, as in the other case, revert to the people. Thus the people may claim to change the constitution, when he invades their part of the sovereign power; whereas, he can only claim to continue the constitution, though the people should causelessly and wrongfully invade his part. This is the whole of his right, and no event whatsoever can give him a more extensive right, without the consent of the people. If the struggles between him and them should end in a civil war, and victory should declare itself on his side, yet conquest will not, of right, increase his power, however strongly we may put the case in his favour, by supposing the breach of the constitution to have begun from the people, and the whole blame of the war to rest upon them; for the use of force, though it should be superior to the force which is opposed to it, only serves to support a right which might otherwise have been hindered from taking effect; it does not produce a right, where there was none before.

Sameness of a state, in what it consists.

XII. A number of men, though they happen to live near one another, to meet frequently, and to work or to travel together, will be only a herd, or company of detached and independent individuals, till they have bound themselves to one another, by compact, to act jointly, under the direction of their common understanding, for the preservation of their rights, and the advancement of their general interest. The existence of a state begins from the social compact: though the persons, out of which it is formed, might exist before they entered into such a compact; it is this compact that forms them into a civil society. From hence we may easily discover, what it is that makes any one state different from all others; and what it is that makes any one state, at different times, the same with itself. Any one state is different from all others; because it had a different beginning of existence; that is, because it began from a different compact. And any one state will, at all times, be the same with itself; because it had the same beginning of existence; that is, because it began from the same compact.

*A state, in respect of its members, is a fluctuating body; some of them are constantly falling off from it by death; and others are as constantly joining themselves to it: so that, in a course of years, all the members of it will be changed. But if this change is made gradually, the society will remain the same: because the social compact is the same all the time; notwithstanding such a change is made in the persons who are the parties to it. In a gradual change, though some of the members fall off from the society, yet the same compact subsists amongst those that remain; and the new members, who join themselves to it, become parties in this compact. As others fall off, the same compact is still kept up in the same manner, and will continue to be kept up, though all the old members will, in a course of years, be gone, and the society will consist wholly of new ones. Any subsequent changes, that are made in these new members, will affect the society no otherwise than the former changes affected it. The persons, who are parties in the social compact, will be different; but the society will continue the same: because these different persons are successively joined to it by the same compact. A society, therefore, may be a perpetual body, notwithstanding all the parts of it are mortal. It will continue as long as the same social compact is kept up; and this compact may be kept up for ever, by a constant succession of new members.

Several ways in which a state may cease.

XIII. This is the only sense in which a society can be called a perpetual body. We may call it a perpetual body, because it may, and not because it must, continue for ever. For though the same compact may be kept up for ever by a constant succession of new members, yet there are several ways in which it may possibly cease; and whenever it ceases, the society perishes.

†First, if all the members of a state are washed away by the sea, or swallowed up in an earthquake, or put to the sword at once, the society will be destroyed. Where the members drop off gradually, and new

* Grot. Lib. II. IX. III.

† Ibid. § IV, V, VI.

ones join themselves to the state, before all the old ones are gone, the same social compact is kept up by a succession of different persons. But where they all die at once, this compact must necessarily cease; because there is no succession of persons to keep it up. If the land, upon which the society was settled, is left, as it will be, where all the members are put to the sword, another company of men, who are united as they were, into a civil society, may succeed into their place, by settling upon the same tract of land. But this new company of men will be a different society; they only succeed into the possessions of the old inhabitants, and not into the same social compact by which they were united. This compact ended with them, and it is a different compact that unites the new inhabitants.

Secondly, a state will cease, if all the members of it are brought into perfect servitude. The social compact is destroyed by the slavery of the parties in it: because the obligations of slavery are inconsistent with the obligation of this compact. The members of a civil society are obliged to act under the direction of the public understanding, for the security of their rights, and for the advancement of the general interest. But when the same persons, who were members of such a society, become slaves, they are obliged to act, in all things, as their master shall direct them to act, for his benefit. This latter obligation, therefore, sets the former aside, by rendering it impossible.

Thirdly, a state will cease, if the members of it are so dispersed that they can neither be directed by a common understanding, nor act jointly with a common force, for the purposes of civil union. If they are dispersed, by means of some external violence, the social compact ceases; because the matter of it is impossible. But if they have dispersed themselves, by mutual consent, this compact is dissolved.

Fourthly, a state will cease, if it is subjected, as a province, to another state. The social compact had originally collected all the parts of it into one body, and obliged them to act for the purposes of civil union, under the conduct of their own common understanding. This compact, therefore, ceases when the society becomes a province: because it then becomes an inferior or subordinate part of another society; and though it is not obliged to pursue any other purposes, yet it is obliged to pursue these under the conduct of a foreign understanding.

The rights, which belong to a civil society, fail or are lost, when the society ceases to exist. And, upon the same event, the members of it lose their rights. But this is to be understood of those rights only, which belonged to them as members of the society, and not of those which belonged to them as individuals. The right, which each of them had to his life, to his liberty, to his lands, or to his moveable goods, and other rights of the same sort, are not directly affected by the destruction of the society of which they were members, however they may happen to be remotely affected. In one case, indeed, the members of a society, which is destroyed, lose their personal liberty: but this loss, instead of being produced by the destruction of the society, is the cause why the society perishes.

The same effect, that is produced by the destruction of a society in the rights of the whole collective body and of its several members, will be produced, likewise, in their respective obligations. Thus the debts of a society are cancelled when the society perishes; and though the members, whilst the society subsisted, were jointly bound to contribute towards the payment of the public debts, this obligation will cease when the society subsists no longer. But the destruction of the society, does not cancel any debts which the members of it had contracted, as individuals, upon their own private account.

Change of constitution does not change a state.

XIV. A civil society continues the same, notwithstanding any changes that are made in its civil constitution. * When a monarchy is established in a free state, or when, on the contrary, a popular form of government is introduced, instead of a monarchy, it is the constitutional compact that is changed, and not the social compact.

In the language of the schools, the essence of a state consists in its form. An union of men, of free condition, by compact, for such purposes, as we have already had frequent occasion to mention, is the form of a state. This union is certainly essential to a state; for there can be no state, where no such union subsists, and wherever such union does subsist, it produces a state. Now, a change of the civil constitution of a state, is a change of form in the state. And this is sometimes urged to prove, that a change of the civil constitution of a state must be a change of the state itself: because a change of form is a change of essence. But the answer is obvious. A change of civil constitution is a change of the form of government in a state, and not a change of the essential form of the state itself. The several members of the state, notwithstanding the form of government is changed, still continue to be bound by compact, as they were before, jointly to pursue the purposes of civil union, and are still parties in the compact, by which the state was originally produced.

From hence it follows, that a state neither loses any of its rights, nor is discharged from any of its obligations, by a change in the form of its civil government.

Some sorts of changes in a state do not destroy it.

XV. † When two states unite themselves into one, by mutual agreement, so that the several parts or members of each are admitted alike to the same, or to similar privileges, neither of them becomes a province to the other, and neither of them is destroyed by this union. The members of each continue to be joined to one another by social compact, as they were from the first, and their original compact is only changed in part, it is not made void. The only change that is made, consists in enlarging the terms of this compact on each side, so that the members of each state mutually receive the members of the other into the same body with themselves.

Since both states thus continue in this united body, and neither of them ceases to exist, the rights and the obligations of both will remain, and will become the rights and obligations of the united body; that is, whatever rights belonged to each state separately, before they were united, will afterwards be the rights of the collective state; and the same obligations, that each state was under separately before, the collective state will be under afterwards.

‡ In monarchies, whether they are absolute or limited, two states may accidentally have the same head. But this unity of head does not join

* Grot. Lib. II. IX. III. § VIII.

† Grot. Lib. II. Cap. IX. § IX.

‡ Grot. Lib. I. Cap. III. § VII.

the two states into one. Each state was originally formed by a different compact; and as long as no alteration is made in these compacts, either in whole or in part, the two states will continue to be two distinct bodies. They are not made one, merely by being in subjection to the same person: for he is called to govern each of them as a distinct state from the other; and the appointment of him to govern them as two distinct states, cannot make them one. Neither has he, by means of this appointment, an authority to unite them without their direct consent: for he is appointed, by each, to govern it as a distinct body; and such an appointment cannot imply a power of joining it to the other.

* Whilst the same person thus governs two states, one of them, as Grotius says, is not a province to the other, if he is called to govern each by two different appointments; whether these appointments are made by distinct elections, or by the distinct laws of succession, that are established in each. But if, by being appointed to govern one, he has an immediate right to govern the other, without the aid of any distinct election, or any distinct civil law of the latter, then the latter is a province to the former.

† Though a number of states should have formed themselves into a system or aggregate body, in order to carry on and secure some particular purpose, it does not follow, that they are united into one state. This union reaches no farther than the particular purpose for which it was formed: and the several states, after they are thus united, will continue to be as distinct from one another, in all other respects, as they were bfore. Such an union does, indeed, diminish the independency of each state: because, as far as the purposes of it extend, each state is no longer at liberty to choose and to act for itself, without the concurrence of the others. But this diminution of independency, since it affects all of them equally, will not reduce any of them to the condition of provinces.

‡ When a state, by the general consent of the whole body, divides itself into two or more states, it does not cease. All the members of it, before this division was made, were united by a social compact into one body; and after it is made, all the members of each part continue to be united by the same compact. The division only changes this compact in part, and does not put an end to it. Before the state was divided, the compact was so general, as to comprehend the individual members of all the parts: but in making the division, all the members of each part agree to make it less general, and to include only themselves in it.

But if the social compact, by which the whole state was once united, is only changed in part, and is not entirely destroyed, when the state is thus divided, the rights and obligations of the whole state will remain. If these rights and obligations have not been distributed amongst the several parts by special agreement, the rights must be enjoyed, and the obligations must be fulfilled by all the parts in common.

Variable qualities of a state.

XVI. Some qualities, which we usually speak of as if they belonged to a state, are derived to it from the qualities of its individual members, and are said to belong to the state, only because many of its members are endued with them. § Such

* Grot. Lib. II. Cap. IX. § VIII.
† Grot. Lib. I. Cap. III. § VII.
‡ Grot. Lib. II. Cap. IX. § X.
§ Grot. Ibid. Cap. XXI. § VIII.

qualities as these are variable; they may either be lost or acquired, though the state remains the same.

The integrity or the valour of a state are qualities of this sort: the state loses its integrity, when the members of it become perfidious; and loses its valour, when they become cowardly and effeminate. But by means of a continued succession of members, united in the same social compact, the state itself, when it is perfidious and effeminate, is the same that it was before, whilst it was faithful and valiant.

The same thing happens in other societies, that are continued by a succession of different parts, as well as in civil societies: though the societies continue to be the same, the qualities which they derive from the qualities of their members, may be changed. The same society, which is a learned one now, may hereafter be an illiterate one: the learning of the society is only the learning of its members; it will, therefore, lose this quality, whenever it is filled with illiterate members. Mankind are, indeed, very ready to claim a share in the credit of their predecessors: and for this reason, in speaking of any society, of which we are members, we are apt to take in the whole compass of its existence, and to call it a learned or a valiant society; if its members, in any former period of time, have been possessed of these good qualities; though few or none of them should be possessed of the same qualities now. But where the change has been made the other way, we seldom deceive ourselves in the same manner. When the society, to which we belong, is become learned or valiant, we look no farther back than the present times in speaking of it, and are apt to complain, if any one should so far impute the bad qualities of our predecessors to us, as to call it an illiterate, or an effeminate and cowardly society, only because it was such in the time of some of our predecessors.

We may reckon guilt amongst the other variable qualities of a state. A disposition to do harm belongs, primarily, to the individual members, and is no otherwise a quality of the body, than as the body derives this quality from its members. From hence it follows, that a state cannot justly be punished now, for any crime that it committed in some remote period of time. Where there is no guilt, the law of nature does not allow any punishment to be inflicted. No punishment, therefore, can justly be inflicted upon a state, after none of the members of it, that committed the crime, are left; because, in respect of that crime, the guilt of the state ceases, as soon as these members are gone.

But the obligation of a state to make reparation for the damage that it has done, will continue, till reparation is made; though none of the persons, who were concerned in doing the damage, remain in it. Guilt, as it is a personal quality, ceases with the persons of the criminals, and does not descend to their successors. But the obligation to repair damage, affects the goods of those, who have done the damage, and consequently, descends to their successors along with the goods.

Conquest in an unjust war, produces no effects of right.

XVII. Nations, which are conquered in war, by a foreign enemy, are sometimes reduced to provinces, or if they continue to be distinct societies, they are sometimes compelled to receive such a form of civil government, or such civil governors, as the conqueror thinks fit to impose upon them. These are the effects, which conquest in war produces in fact, whether the war is just or not. But some of the plainest principles of the law of nature will serve to show us, that conquest, in an unjust war, produces no effects in right. Conquest is only the suppressing of a force, which is used against us, by the use of a superior force on our side. But all unjust war is only the use of unjust force: and the law of nature gives no effects of right to unjust force, though it should happen to be superior to the force which is opposed to it.

We might, perhaps, find reason to determine otherwise upon this question, if there was any purely positive law of nations, by which all public wars, or however all solemn wars were rendered externally just, as to their effects, and by which the captors might claim whatever they can get into their possession in such wars, whether they are internally just or not. But we have * already proved, that there is no such law. And, certainly, the effects, which conquest, even in an unjust war, sometimes produces, in fact, may be accounted for, without supposing, that all nations have ever established such a law by general consent. The desire of power, or of profit, leads the conqueror to get whatever he can into his possession, and to keep whatever he has gotten. The vanquished nation submits to his will, because it is not able to make an effectual resistance. And if neutral states do not find, that their interest is concerned to stop the growing power of the conqueror, they are not likely to hazard their own safety, and the lives of their members, by engaging in the quarrel of the vanquished nation, and assisting it to repel, or to throw off his unjust usurpation. Thus the ambition or the avarice of one party, the weakness of another, and the caution of a third, will explain the events of conquest, without supposing, that any purely positive law of nations has given the conqueror a right to dominion, has obliged the vanquished state to submit to him, and has restrained all other states from affording it relief.

What effects may be occasioned by conquest in a just war.

XVIII. The same principles may be applied to conquest universally; even though it is obtained in a just war. We cannot say, that a conqueror can have no right of civil dominion; merely because he comes in by force at first, and continues to hold his power by force afterwards. † If he has such a right arising from some other cause, the law of nature will allow him to make use of force to support it, when any opposite force would otherwise hinder it from taking place, in fact, and will not vacate the right, merely because it is thus supported. But we certainly may say, that no such right can arise out of mere conquest. Though the law of nature allows either states or individuals to bring their rights into execution by force, when they cannot be brought into execution by any other means; yet this law does not produce any right out of mere force, though it happens to be superior to the force which is opposed to it.

But where a war is just, on the part of the conqueror, he has a right to require reparation of damages; and he has a farther right to punish the nation, that did the injury, which occasioned the war, if this injury proceeded from any public malice or hurtful disposition. And though mere conquest could give him no right of civil dominion over the vanquished nation, yet it may still be a question, whether such a right

* See Cap. IX. § I. IV

† Ibid § XI.

will not arise out of his right, to obtain reparation, and to inflict punishment.

There is but little use to be made of some of the principal topics, from which Mr. Locke argues in this question. * He contends, that those members of a state, who do not actually concur in the wrong which is done by the governors of it, are neither liable to punishment, nor obliged to make reparation of damages; but that the punishment and the reparation ought, of right, to be confined to the governors, and to their direct and immediate assistants or abettors. As far as the members of a society are to be punished individually, we must necessarily grant, that this opinion is true. † But in respect of any punishment, which is inflicted upon the body of the state, and affects the individual members no otherwise, than as they are parts of this body, and especially, in respect of the obligation to repair damages, the law of nations looks upon all the members of it as accessories to the acts of their constitutional governors, and as abettors of their injustice.

Mr. ‡ Locke contends farther, "that even those members of a state, who have directly concurred in the wrongs done by the civil governors of it, cannot forfeit the full property of their lands or other goods, either in the way of punishment, or in the way of reparation of damages: because nature, which willeth as much as may be the preservation of children, has given their children a right to their land or other goods." But the law of nature, as we have seen in another § place, knows nothing of any such indefeasible right in children to inherit the lands or other goods of their parents. Or even if we were to suppose, that the law of nature has established a right of inheritance, yet, as long as the parent lives, the children can have only an expectancy of succeeding to his goods, whether those goods are moveable or immoveable: because a right of inheritance is only a right of the heir to take such goods, as the ancestor leaves behind him at his death. Since the parent, therefore, will leave no goods behind him, if he has been justly disseized of them in his life-time, the child's right of inheritance will fail; that is, it will have no right to inherit any thing. Thus, the child's right of inheritance can never be urged to prove that the parent cannot justly be disseized of his goods, because we must first prove, that the parent cannot be so disseized, before we can establish the child's right of inheritance.

But as no use can be made of these principles, so we have no occasion to use them, in showing, that a conqueror's demand to have his damages repaired, will not be sufficient to give him civil dominion over the vanquished state without the consent of the people. The damages must be unusually great, if the vanquished state is not able to satisfy the conqueror's just demands in money, or in moveable goods, or in both together. And if it is able to make him reparation by such payments as these, he has no farther claim to any property in the lands of its members, and much less to any right over their persons.

Mr. ‖ Locke, indeed, maintains, not only that the damages of an unjust war, will seldom be high enough to give the conqueror any demand upon the land of the vanquished people, but that it is impossible

* Verse II. page 226. † See Book II. Chap. IX. § XIII. ‡ Verse II. page 226.
§ See Book I. Chap. VII. § IV. ‖ Verse II. page 228.

for his just demands to amount to the value of all their land. The calculation has something very extraordinary in it, which makes it deserve the reader's notice. This writer sets the whole amount of the damage, that can possibly have been sustained by the conquering nation, at five years' product of its land. For a war seldom continues longer than five years, and if it should have continued longer, we cannot suppose the enemy to have destroyed the whole product of the land every year. But there are two general articles left out of this account in the first instance. A just war is sometimes made to obtain reparation of damages, that have been done by the enemy before the war began: and these damages are to be repaired, as well as the damages, which the same enemy does by destroying the yearly product of the conqueror's lands, during the course of the war. And from whatever other just cause the war might begin on the part of the conqueror, he has a right to reparation, not only for the damages which he suffers, but, likewise, for the expenses that he makes in it. Besides these two general articles, Mr. Locke has omitted numberless particular articles in this account, which are included in the damages that are frequently done in war. When Athens was destroyed by the Persians, Rome by the Gauls, or Corinth by the Romans, the loss of five years' product of the lands of the inhabitants, would have borne a very small proportion to the loss which these states had sustained. Small states consist of little more than one capital city; and the damage that is done to the state by demolishing this one city, is almost irreparable. And when we are calculating the possible damages of a public war, in order to see what effects of right these damages may produce, we are to consider not merely what is likely to happen to such large societies, as mankind are commonly united into at present, but what might possibly happen either in these, or in such small states as subsisted formerly, and as may subsist again. * Mr. Locke estimates the loss of money, or other treasure of the like sort, at nothing; for the value of them, he says, is fantastical and imaginary; nature has put no value upon them, and, consequently, they are of no account by nature's standard. It must be confessed here, on the one hand, that the value of money is imaginary; and yet it would be contrary to the common sense of mankind, to affirm, on the other hand, that the law of nature would not charge us with doing any damage to a nation, if we should rob its mint or its treasury, because the value of money is imaginary. All the value that any thing can have, must be imaginary, when the thing itself is in its own nature of little or no real use. The value, therefore, of money, considered merely as metal, is imaginary; because little or no real use can be made of this metal. But if we would determine whether it is to be reckoned of any value, when estimated by nature's standard, we must consider, not only whether it has any real use in itself, but likewise whether it has any real use at all. For the law of nature, as it relates to mankind, sets a value upon whatever is of real use to the owner; whether its uses are derived from the nature of the thing itself, or from the labour of mankind, or from their general consent, or from any other accident. A transparent stone, or a mass of yellow metal, are not fitted, by nature, to answer any beneficial purposes: thus far,

* Vol. II. page 228.

therefore, they are worth nothing in nature's account. If the owner should be led, by his own fancy, to value either of them at the rate of twenty oxen, or of eighty quarters of wheat, this would be only an imaginary value; and the law of nature would take no notice of it, as long as this fancy was peculiar to himself, and no one else was led by the like fancy to rate them at the same value with him, or at any value at all: if he keeps the stone, or the metal, they will be of no use to him; and if he is disposed to part with them, no body will give him any thing for them, that will afford him any real benefit. But if mankind, in general, have the same fancy that he has, and are led by it to rate the stone, or the metal, as high as he rates them, the value of them, though it is still imaginary in its origin, becomes real in the application of them to the purposes of human life, by this accident of its being general. The jewel, or the gold, if he keeps them, will do nothing towards answering the calls of nature; but if he is disposed to part with them, the value which mankind have agreed to set upon them, will enable him, at any time, to procure a dwelling, food, clothing, physic, and whatever else he wants, in exchange for them. Besides the loss of money, or other treasure of the like sort, a nation may suffer much more damage in war, than the destruction of the bare product of its lands, for as many years as the war continues. Goods, that have been manufactured, are of much more value than the simple materials out of which they were made. If the enemy has destroyed woollen or linen cloth, we should not estimate the damages done, according to nature's standard; if we were to set them no higher than the original value of the wool or the flax, that was used in making the cloth. For nature, in these and in other instances, sets a price upon the labour of the manufacturer: and the value of his labour is, in most instances, vastly greater than the value of the original materials, as they came out of the hands of nature. Wool, indeed, is the immediate product of the live stock of the landholders, and not of the land itself. But Mr. Locke has omitted this whole article of live stock in his account: for certainly the damage that is done, in war, to the oxen, horses, sheep, or other animals belonging to the members of a state, is not included in the damage that is done to the yearly product of their land. Amongst other goods, that are of more value than the materials out of which they are made, we may reckon ships of all sorts, and naval stores, household furniture, instruments of husbandry, and the tools, and other necessary utensils of manufacturers and artificers. When timber, that was growing, is destroyed in war, the damage that is done, does not come under the notion of a loss of the yearly product of the land: timber is, indeed, the product of land, but not the yearly product of it: a war of one year may waste the product of twenty or of forty years in timber. The plundering of a city, even though the buildings are not destroyed, will occasion a farther damage to the state, than the mere loss of goods: the labour of its manufacturers will be stopped; and more than five years' time may be necessary to bring them together again, and to supply them with materials and instruments for working. Add to all these, the immediate damage that is done to a state, by putting a stop to its foreign trade, and the consequent damage that it will suffer, if the trade, in which it was engaged, should, in the meantime, take a different course, and the state should wholly lose it. After Mr. Locke has thus set the damages of war too low, he goes on to set the value of land as much too high. He rates the value of land at an hundred times the value of one years' product: and, consequently, if one years' product is worth three rents of the land, the land itself must be worth three hundred years' purchase. Nay, what is still more extraordinary, this is the value that he sets upon the reversion of land: for he does not apply this calculation to show that the present possessors of the land cannot be disseized of it for damages done; but that the posterity of the wrong doers cannot be hindered from re-entering upon it at the death of their parents.

Though it is very unlikely that a nation, which is victorious in the end of a war, should have suffered all these damages, in the course of it; yet certainly there is a possibility of its suffering so many of them, as may make the demand of reparation fall very little short of the value of the enemies' land. But suppose the value of the damages to be equal to the value of the land of the conquered people; yet the conqueror's demand would give him no immediate right to civil dominion. The state, that he has subdued, is at liberty to transfer its land to other purchasers; and if it can raise money enough by this means to pay for the damages that it has done, the demand of the conqueror is at an end. Or if he should seize upon the land for the reparation of damages done, the conquered people are not obliged to stay upon it, and to submit themselves to his will: they may either continue united, and seek a new habitation, or they may disperse by mutual consent, and become members of any other societies that are willing to receive them. The distress of a state, that has done any great damages, and is compelled by conquest to repair them, may make it more eligible for the people to receive the conqueror for their civil governor, than to try any other expedients; even though the demand of the conqueror, for these damages, should not amount to the value of their lands. * Such a consent of the people, though they are driven to it by distress, would be binding upon them: for it is not a consent that is extorted by unjust force: the conqueror was doing only what he had a right to do; and a consent, which follows from the use of force, if the force was just, is binding. Thus conquest, in a just war, may be the remote occasion of acquiring civil dominion; but the immediate cause of it is the consent of the people.

If we carry the conqueror's just demand of reparation farther than this, and suppose, what is next to impossible, that it amounts not only to the value of the land, but likewise to the value of the personal service of the several members of the state, such a demand might give him private despotism over the individuals: but this right of the conqueror, instead of producing civil dominion, would put an end to the state: the several members of it will thus become a family of slaves, but the collective body will not be a civil society. To change this family of slaves into a state, the conqueror must manumise them, and they must consent both to form themselves into a civil society, and, likewise, to accept of the terms which he offers them, when they are thus united, of allowing him to have civil power over them, in return for the personal liberty which he grants them.

* See Book I. Chap. VI. § XVI.

The punishment of a state, like the punishment of an individual, consists in inflicting some evil upon it, in order either to correct a disposition of doing harm, which has appeared from the harm that it has already done, or to prevent the same disposition from breaking out again in doing the like harm. Amongst the several ways of punishing a state, * Grotius, as we have already hinted, mentions the dissolution of it. And there seems to be no room to doubt, but that a society of men, who were united for better purposes, may possibly have shown, by their conduct, that, as long as they continue to act with a joint force, other states can have no effectual security against the harm which they are likely to suffer from the evil disposition of the individuals who compose that society. If such a case as this should ever happen, we cannot reasonably doubt about the natural right of mankind, in general, and of the neighbouring states, in particular, who have been more immediately injured, to dissolve the union, from which they have suffered harm already, and are likely, if it continues, to suffer more. Or, rather, the social compact will be dissolved in right, when the state is thus become a band of robbers: and we cannot reasonably question, whether the law of nature will allow other states to dissolve a compact, in fact, which the same law has before dissolved in right. By such a punishment as this, the conqueror, instead of acquiring civil dominion over the state, puts an end to the existence of it. But if the individuals, who were the members of the state, before it was dissolved, continue to live near one another, they will have the same opportunity of acting together, after the dissolution of the state, that they had before. There is, therefore, no way of dissolving a state, effectually, without inflicting some punishment upon the individual members. † But no punishment can justly be inflicted upon each of the members, individually, without distinction, unless all and each have actually assisted, or have directly and immediately concurred in the general crime of the society: the consent, which they have remotely and indirectly given to the acts of the public in the social compact, though it obliges all and each of them to repair the damages that the society does, will only make the whole body collectively, and not the several members individually, liable to punishment. The guilty members may, however, be deprived of their lands; ‡ and though the general property of these lands, if the society subsisted, would be vested in the society, when the individual proprietors thus lose them, so that the conqueror could not justly seize them, and make them his own by occupancy, yet this general claim of the society to all the lands of its territory, that have no private owners, ceases when the society is dissolved: the conquering nation, therefore, may acquire property, by occupancy in the lands, of which the guilty members are thus deprived, and may grant these lands to new inhabitants, to colonies of husbandmen, manufacturers, and artificers, or to the army, which it employed in making the conquest. But no sovereign power over the state, that was dissolved, or over the innocent members of it, is acquired by this means. Though the remaining inhabitants of the conquered country should incorporate into a civil society, with the new colony, this union is made by consent; and neither the leader of the

* Grot. Lib. II. Cap. XXI. § VII. See Chap. IX. § XIII.

† See Chap. IX. § XIII.

‡ See Book II. Chap. III. § XIV.

conquering army, nor any one else, can acquire civil power over this new society, without a farther act of consent.

*Grotius says, indeed, that a vanquished nation, which has deserved such a punishment, may be made a province to the nation that has subdued it. But our author should have shown, how a nation can, consistently with the nature of a civil society, be reduced to the condition of a province without its own consent. The weak condition that it has brought itself into by supporting an unjust war; the distresses that arise from being compelled to make reparation of damages to the conqueror, and from being farther compelled, in the way of punishment, to dismantle its towns, or to give up its public treasure, or its arms, or its ships of war, may induce the people to consent to become a province of the conquering nation: but without their consent the conqueror has no right to make the vanquished state a province; because he has no right to compel the people to abide by their social compact, and to continue united in one body. It will, indeed, be a bad alternative, when the people must choose either to become a province, or to dissolve their state by mutual consent. But as they will always be at liberty to choose the latter part of the alternative, the conqueror can never acquire any right over them, as a collective body of men, without their own consent.

†Upon the whole, though private despotism may arise immediately out of damage done, or out of punishment inflicted without the consent of the individual who is brought into a state of slavery; yet civil despotism, or sovereign power over a state, cannot be produced by the same causes, without the consent of the collective body of the state. For the several parts, or members of a state, are kept together only by a compact, in which none besides themselves are parties. And since a right to obtain reparation, where a state has done damage, or to inflict punishment, where it has committed a crime, does not make the person who has this right, whether it is an individual person, or the collective person of another state, a party in that compact; his right to obtain reparation, or to inflict punishment, cannot produce a right to insist that this compact shall be observed, and that the members of such an artificial body shall continue to be united. They are at liberty, notwithstanding his right, to release one another from their social compact by mutual consent: and when they have so released one another, the notion of civil despotism becomes unintelligible; because the state will then have ceased to exist.

* See Lib. II. Cap. XXI. § VII. See Cap. IX. § XIII. † See Book I. Chap. XX. § IV.

THE END.

www.ingramcontent.com/pod-product-compliance
Lightning Source LLC
LaVergne TN
LVHW102012210926
848483LV00011B/276

* 9 7 8 1 5 8 4 7 7 4 5 7 0 *